THE ELEMENT ENCYCLOPEDIA OF 20,000 DREAMS

THE ELEMENT ENCYCLOPEDIA

OF 20,000 DREAMS

the ultimate A–Z
to interpret the secrets
of your dreams

Theresa Cheung

HarperCollins*Publishers*
77–85 Fulham Palace Road,
Hammersmith, London W6 8JB
www.harpercollins.co.uk

First published by HarperCollins*Publishers* 2006

10 9 8 7 6 5 4 3 2 1

© Theresa Cheung, 2006

Theresa Cheung asserts the moral right to be
identified as the author of this work

A catalogue record of this book is
available from the British Library

ISBN 978-0-00-792268-0

Printed in China

CONTENTS

ACKNOWLEDGMENTS

This project could not have been completed without the help of some wonderful people.

Thank you to Katy Carrington for her vision and encouragement; to Mark Boland for his brilliant editing; and to Simon Gerratt, Kathy Dyke, Colin Hall, Charmian Parkin and Kay Carroll for making sure everything came together in one piece and on time.

I am also grateful to the hundreds of people who have talked to me about their dreams over the years as I gathered material for this book, and the insight this has given me.

Last, but by no means least, special thanks to Ray, Robert and Ruth for their love, support and patience as I went into self-imposed exile to complete this project.

PREFACE

'What if you slept, and what if in your sleep you dreamed, and what if in your dream you went to heaven and there plucked a strange and beautiful flower, and what if when you awoke you had the flower in your hand? Ah, what then?'

Samuel Taylor Coleridge

A dream can sometimes feel incredibly real – as if the sensations experienced are actually happening – but then as we wake up to everyday reality we cannot make sense of anything and wonder what it all meant.

Most dream analysts believe that dreams are not meaningless but littered with messages from our unconscious. They are inner communications that, if heeded, have the potential to set us on the road to a richer, more fulfilling path in waking life. Sadly, many of us forget our dreams upon waking and this is a great loss. According to the Talmud: 'A dream which is not interpreted is like a letter which is not read.'

If we are to remember, understand and work with the messages from our unconscious minds, we first need to learn how to interpret them. *The Element Encyclopedia of 20,000 Dreams* is an illuminating and comprehensive exploration of the symbols that appear in our dreamscape, and a rich source of information to help you unlock the messages, possibilities, richness and wisdom of your dream world. Use it to find out the fascinating things your dreams are trying to tell you!

HOW TO USE THIS BOOK

The *Element Encyclopedia of 20,000 Dreams* is arranged in three parts: the Introduction, the main section covering the Dreams themselves, and the Dream Directory.

The *Introduction* discusses the hows, whats and whys of sleep and dreams, the complexities of dream interpretation and what you need to know about unlocking the meaning of your dreams.

The Dreams is the main section of the book. Dream messages can be difficult to decipher until you have learned their secret language; this section will give you the key to your unconscious mind's wealth. The entries are arranged in sixty thematic chapters, beginning with ACCIDENTS, ACTION AND ADVENTURES and finishing with WEATHER, and cover approximately 20,000 different dreams. Each chapter begins with a short introduction that talks about the kind of dreams covered in the section. The dream entries that follow are arranged in thematic order and you'll also find cross references to relevant dream entries

elsewhere in the book. Some chapters also contain an 'A to Z' of relevant dream objects and situations. You can dip into this massive resource to gain insight into a specific dream you may have had; for example, if you dreamt about a horse you can look for it in the chapter devoted to the theme of animals. Here you will be able to read about specific horse dreams, but at the same time you can cast your eye on entries covering similar or related animal topics which may throw light on your particular dream.

For ease of reference you may prefer to first turn to part three of the book: *The Dream Directory.* This lists every dream entry in the book in alphabetical order, so it is simple to look up specific dreams; it also functions as a cross-reference to other relevant entries.

INTRODUCTION

'I dream, therefore I exist.'

J. August Strindberg

Dreams. They tantalize us with their mystery. What are they? Why do we have them? Where do they come from? What do they mean? Are they a preview of things to come or glimpses of the past? Are they a vital link to our inner world; a gift from our intuition? Can dreams lead us to important insights in our waking life, and help us decide which action to take and which path to follow?

The Hows, Whys and Whats of Sleep and Dreams

'Sleep is the balm for hurt minds, nature's great second course.' William Shakespeare

Sleep is absolutely crucial for our physical, mental and emotional health and well-being. It is during sleep that we abandon conscious control of our physical body and the unconscious mind is allowed to roam free, giving rise to dreams.

Although we now know a lot more about dreams, their real purpose isn't yet fully understood. It wasn't until we approached the middle of the twentieth century, with the first electronic monitoring of the brain, that we began to get a clearer idea of the nocturnal adventures of the mind. For centuries it was thought that the purpose of sleep was to rest the body and the mind, but this reasoning was disproved when it was shown that both the body and mind are active during sleep. If sleep doesn't rest the body or mind, then what is it for?

Sleep researchers may not yet have discovered the exact reason for sleep or dreams but they have discovered some fascinating things. For example, it seems that when we are asleep our brains are a bit like computers that are offline. This means they are not idle but are filing and updating the day's activities. They take stock of your body and release a growth hormone to repair damaged tissues and stimulate growth, while the immune system gets to work on attacking any viral or bacterial infections that may be present. Some experts believe the brain also jettisons trivial information during sleep to prevent it becoming overburdened with unimportant information, but this explanation is perhaps too simplistic, as no memory can be totally eradicated.

The advent of space travel gave scientists the opportunity to prove that resting the body was not the main function of sleep. What they found instead was that prolonged periods of isolation decreased the need for sleep. In other words, the fewer stimuli received from people or external contacts during the day, the less sleep was required. It seems we have a sleep control center at the base of our brain linked with activity during wakefulness. When that gets overloaded we get tired, but if there have not been enough stimuli from the outside world, the sleep mechanism isn't triggered. It seems, therefore, that boredom and lack of stimuli may account for many cases of insomnia. (Paradoxically, overstimulation also produces insomnia.)

The Four Stages of Sleep

'Yet it is in our idleness, in our dreams, that the submerged truth sometimes comes to the top.' Virginia Woolf

Perhaps the best way to understand sleep and dreams is to understand the brain. At the very start of the twentieth century it was found that the brain gave off electrical impulses, and by the 1920s scientists could measure brain waves. To obtain these readings, electrodes were attached to various parts of the head, the impulses being transformed onto electroencephalograms (EECs) on computer screens.

It seems that once you settle down to bed, your brain and body undergo radical changes from their waking state. The difference between being asleep and being awake is loss of conscious awareness, and once you start to doze, dream researchers believe you progress through four stages of sleep. These form the basis of a cycle that repeats up to four or five times every eight hours of sleep.

During the first stage, your body and mind become relaxed. Heart and breathing rate slow down, blood pressure lowers, body temperature drops slightly and eyes roll from side to side. You are neither fully conscious, nor fully unconscious, and could easily awake if disturbed. This stage of gradually falling asleep is also called the hypnagogic state (the hypnopompic state is a similar state when you are just waking up) and you may experience hallucinations that float before your eyes.

In stage two, breathing and heart rate become even slower, eyes continue to roll and you become more and more unaware of the noises of the outside world. It isn't until the third stage of sleep, however, that you are sleeping soundly and it would be difficult to wake you. Finally, you enter a deep sleep state known as non-rapid eye movement (NREM) when your brain is released from the demands of the conscious mind. It will now be quite hard to wake you and, although you may sleepwalk or have night terrors, you will rarely be able to remember them. This slow-wave sleep cycle lasts about ninety minutes. At the end of stage four, you move back through stages three and two and one, at which point you enter a phase called rapid eye movement, or REM, sleep.

REM Sleep

REM sleep is recognized by tiny twitches of facial muscles and slight movements of the hands. Blood pressure rises, breathing and heartbeat become faster, eyes dart rapidly around the eyelids under closed eyelids as if looking at a moving object and, if you are a man, you may have an erection. Researchers have discovered that when sleepers are awakened during REM sleep they typically say they have been dreaming. (You may also feel temporarily paralyzed if awakened during this stage, as if something malevolent is pressing down on you; this phenomenon can explain the supposed succubus, incubus and alien abduction experiences.)

Most of the dreams you remember occur during the REM stage when the brain is fully active. After about ten minutes of REM you enter stages two, three and four again, and keep moving backwards and forwards through the sleep cycle. As the cycle continues, however, the REM phase gets longer and longer with the longest phase being around thirty to forty-five minutes. Of all your dreams during all the stages of REM and NREM (it has recently been discovered that we can dream then too), the final REM stages are the ones you are most likely to remember.

How much sleep do we need?

We spend approximately one third of our life asleep. This means that by the time we reach the age of ninety we have been asleep approximately thirty years. The exact amount of sleep each person needs depends on many factors, including age and activity levels during the day. Babies sleep for about fourteen hours a day, whilst teenagers need about nine hours on average. For most adults occupied physically and mentally during the day, eight hours a night appears to be the average amount of sleep needed, although some people may need as few as five, or as many as ten hours, of sleep each day. Older people tend to need around six hours sleep a night.

Because sleeping and dreaming are so crucial, your brain may sometimes demand the sleep it needs so that you don't get into mental or physical overload. That's why you may sometimes drop off for no apparent reason when you're traveling by car or train, or watching TV.

Research on sleep-deprived animals shows that sleep is necessary for survival. For example, whilst rats normally live for two to three years, those deprived of REM sleep survive only about five weeks on average, and rats deprived of all sleep stages live only about three weeks. Other studies have shown that subjects repeatedly awoken during REM – which means they were deprived of dreams – become anxious, bad tempered and irritable. This suggests that sleep is vital for physical rest and repair, and REM sleep, when we are most likely to dream, is essential for our emotional well-being. Therefore, although we still aren't sure about the whys, whats and hows of sleep and dreams, it's possible to conclude that the reason we sleep is to dream.

A Brief History of Dream Interpretation

'Now Allah has created the dream not only as a means of guidance and instruction, I refer to the dream, but he has made it a window on the World of the Unseen.'
Mohammed, the Prophet

Ancient art and literature are crowded with references to dreams. For thousands of years dreams have been credited with supernatural or prophetic significance by the majority of the world's spiritual traditions. The Bible, for instance, makes it clear that dreams are divine messages and this explanation for dreams was shared by the ancient Egyptians, Greeks and Romans, all of whom also believed that dreams had healing powers.

Certain cultures, such as the Australian Aborigines and many African and Native American tribes, have always believed dreaming to be a way in which an individual can enter into the collective spirit memory. To this day, dream pooling plays an important role in those societies where tribal members gather together for the purpose of interpreting dreams. Another view is held by the Inuit of Hudson Bay in Canada, who believe that when a person falls asleep and dreams, their soul goes wandering.

The Egyptians are thought to have been the first to develop a system of contrary dream interpretation; a positive dream, for example, predicts misfortune and a nightmare predicts an improvement in waking fortunes. They produced the earliest known dream dictionary, written approximately 4,000 years ago. Now called the Chester Beatty Papyrus, it came from Thebes in Egypt and is kept in the British Museum.

It was the ancient Greeks, however, who first proposed the theory that dreams were not from some external, divine source but internal communications, or the divine spark within. Plato (427–347 BC) suggested that dreams were expressions of a person's hidden desires, whilst his pupil Aristotle (384–322 BC) speculated that dreams shared similar themes and were not divine oracles but coincidences. It was the 'father of medicine' Hippocrates (460–377 BC) who proposed that dream symbols reflect the state of the dreamer's body – for example, fire denoted indigestion – and should be regarded as valuable diagnostic tools.

The first fully-fledged dream researcher to focus on dream symbols and dream themes was a Roman living in Greek Asia Minor called Artemidorus (AD 138–180), who wrote a book about dream interpretation that is still in print. As far as Artemidorus was concerned, dream

The Element Encyclopedia of 20,000 Dreams

symbols had certain meanings but the most important aspect of dream interpretation was the symbols' personal significance to the dreamer, along with the dreamer's personal circumstances.

In much of Europe, even though the early Christians respected dreams for their spiritual significance, the repressive control of the Roman Catholic Church put a stop to any attempts at dream interpretation. By the fifteenth century, dreams were regarded as no longer significant or important. Even a century or so later, Shakespeare called them 'children of the idle brain'. This school of thought persisted into the eighteenth century, when dreams were still thought to be meaningless.

In the early nineteenth century, when the restrictive influence of the Church began to wane and members of the German Romantic movement – in their quest for spontaneous expression – rediscovered the potential of dreams, a revival of interest in dream interpretation began to trickle into the mainstream with the publication of popular dream dictionaries such as Raphael's *Royal Book of Dreams* (1830). The stage was now set for Freud and Jung; two men who continue to have the greatest impact on the way we interpret dreams today.

The Freud and Jung Revolution

'Dreams are often most profound when they seem the most crazy.' Sigmund Freud

Austrian psychoanalyst Sigmund Freud (1858–1939) opened the door to the scientific study of dreams with his book, *The Interpretation of Dreams* (1900). In a relatively prudish age, he caused general outrage with his controversial theory that dreams are wish-fulfillment fantasies that have their origins in our infantile urges, in particular our sexual desires.

Freud believed that the human mind is made up of the id, the primitive or unconscious mind; the ego, the conscious mind which regulates the id's antisocial instincts with a self-defense mechanism, and the superego, which is the consciousness that in turn supervises and modifies the ego. According to Freud, the id is controlled by the pleasure principle (the urge to gratify its needs) and the instinct that the ego finds hardest to manage is the sexual drive first awakened in childhood. The id comes to prominence in dreams, when it expresses in symbolic language the urges repressed when we are awake. Symbols are used, because if these drives were expressed literally, the ego would be shocked into waking up. To successfully interpret a dream the symbols need to be uncovered and their true meaning discovered. The way that Freud suggested doing this was a technique called 'free association' or spontaneously expressing the responses that immediately spring to mind when certain words relating to the dream are put forward. The aim is to limit interference from the ego to discover the dreamer's unconscious instincts.

Swiss analytical psychologist Carl Gustav Jung (1875–1965), although an initial supporter of Freud's ideas, could never fully agree with them. He felt there was far more to dreams than hidden sexual frustration and put forward the theory of the 'collective unconscious': a storehouse of inherited patterns of experiences and instincts common to humans and expressed in dreams in universal symbols, which he called 'archetypes'. According to Jungian theory, the psyche is made up of the personal unconscious and the collective unconscious, and when a symbol appears in a dream, it is important to decide whether it relates to us personally or is an archetype. The way Jung suggested we do this is by a technique called 'direct association', i.e. concentrating *only* on the dream symbol when you think about the qualities associated with it.

Jung speculated that the unconscious mind projected dream symbols in an attempt to bring the conscious and unconscious mind into a state of balance he called 'individuation'. According to his theory, the only way the unconscious mind can express itself fully is in dreams, so it will flood our dreams with symbolic messages that reflect our current progress in waking life. These messages can bring comfort and guidance, or bring repressed urges to the fore, but their aim is the same – to lead to our fulfillment. However, before we can benefit from such intuitive wisdom, we first of all need to understand the language of symbols.

Other Important Dream Theorists

Austrian psychologist Alfred Adler (1870–1937) suggested that dreams are all about wish-fulfillment because they allow the dreamer to have skills and powers denied to him or her in waking life. According to Adler, 'the purpose of dreams must be in the feelings they arouse.'

Gestalt psychologist Fritz Perls (1893–1970) believed that dreams project hidden aspects of our personalities and the best way to interpret them is to use a non-interpretative interviewing technique. In other words, you ask your dream character or object what they are trying to say. Then you try to adopt the dream's mindset and answer the questions.

Australian dream expert Gayle Delaney suggests using an interviewing technique that addresses questions such as 'how did the dream make you feel?' or 'how can you connect your dream with your waking life?'

Some dream theorists believe dreams deal with problems we can't solve in waking life and offer solutions. Looking at them in the light of waking day, and believing them to be full of insight, we may sometimes come up with new ideas or insights while studying and interpreting them.

Thanks to the work of Jung and Freud and other influential dream theorists, dream interpretation is now accessible to everyone. It's as popular today as it has ever been, with people from all walks of life using dreams as unique and personal sources of guidance and inspiration, or as tools for change, growth and personal development. As we've seen, there are many approaches to the study and interpretation of dreams and you'll find a fusion of all of these in this book.

Famous dreams

Through the centuries, the dreaming mind has been credited with being the source of ideas, insights, revelations and guidance, some of which have changed the course of history. Here are just a few well-known examples:

Julius Caesar's decision to cross the Rubicon is attributed to a dream in which he saw himself in bed with his mother (Mother Rome, the seers told him). His assassination was foretold in his wife's Calpurnia's dream. 'She held him in her arms, bleeding and stabbed.' Another Caesar, Caesar Augustus, is said to have walked the streets as a beggar because of instructions he received in a dream.

St Francis of Assisi founded the Franciscan Order because of a dream in which Jesus Christ spoke from the cross, telling him to 'go set my house in order'.

Dante relates that the whole story of *The Divine Comedy* was revealed to him in a dream on Good Friday in 1300. When he died in 1321, part of the manuscript was lost. His son Jocojso found the manuscript after a dream in which his father showed him where to look.

Genghis Khan is reported to have received his battle plans from his dreams. He is also reported to have been told in a dream that he was a chosen one.

Samuel Taylor Coleridge's famous poem, 'Kubla Khan', was written upon awakening from an opium-affected dream.

Robert Louis Stephenson believed that his best stories came from his dreams. He reported that the theme for Dr Jekyll and Mr Hyde was derived from a dream. He also reported other breakthroughs in his writing that came from his dreams. He suffered as a child from nightmares and learned to control his dreams to change the nightmares. He said he used his dreams to revise plays and stories while asleep.

Abraham Lincoln dreamt, days before his assassination, of great cries coming from the East Wing of the White House. When he investigated, he was told by soldiers on guard that they weeping for the president who had been assassinated. Days later, his body was held in state in the East Wing so people could pay their last respects.

Friedrich August Kekulé von Stradonitz was a chemist working on the chemical structure of benzene. He reported that he got fed up with his data, which made no sense interpreted as a 'long string' molecule. He was dozing in his comfy chair when he was startled by the image of a snake biting its own tail. He woke and worked out the mathematics of the benzene molecule as a ring rather than a long string.

Guiseppe Tartini (Italian violinist and composer) composed one of his greatest works, 'The Devil's Trill', as a result of a dream he had in 1713. In the dream, he handed his violin to the devil himself, who began to 'play with consummate skill a sonata of such exquisite beauty as surpassed the boldest flights of my imagination. I felt enraptured, transported, enchanted; my breath was taken away, and I awoke. Seizing my violin I tried to retain the sounds I had heard. But it was in vain. The piece I then composed … was the best I ever wrote, but how far below the one I heard in my dream!'

Elias Howe, the inventor of the sewing machine, wrote that he got the core idea, the breakthrough concept, from a dream. It was a nightmare. He had been captured by cannibals. They were preparing to cook him and they were dancing around the fire waving their spears. Howe noticed at the head of each spear there was a small hole through the shaft, and the up and down motion of the spears and the hole remained with him when he woke. The idea of passing the thread through the needle close to the point, not at the other end, was a major innovation in making mechanical sewing possible.

Niels Bohr reported that he developed the model of the atom based on a dream of sitting on the sun with all the planets hissing around on tiny cords.

Paul McCartney heard a haunting melody in one of his dreams, confirmed that none of the Beatles had heard it before, and wrote it down. It became the tune for the famous song, 'Yesterday'.

Dream Types

'I can never decide whether my dreams are a result of my thoughts, or my thoughts the result of my dreams. It is very queer. But my dreams make conclusions for me. They decide things finally. I dream a decision.'
D. H. Lawrence

Just as there are different types of music – classical, rock, jazz – there are different kinds of dreams. Although different types of dream can blend and merge, modern dream researchers tend to break dream types into the following categories:

AMPLIFYING DREAMS

These can exaggerate certain situations or life attitudes in order to point them out sharply for the dreamer. For example, someone who is very shy may dream that they have become invisible.

ANTICIPATING DREAMS

These are dreams that may alert us to possible outcomes in situations in our waking life; for example, passing or failing an exam.

CATHARTIC DREAMS

Such dreams evoke extremely emotional reactions, when the unconscious is urging us to relieve pent-up feelings we may feel unable to express in waking life. For example, you may find yourself bursting into tears on a packed commuter train in your dreams, or you might punch your irritating neighbor or tell your boss exactly what you think of him or her.

Daydreaming

There is a big difference between daydreaming and dreams when you are sleeping, even though the physical state we enter when we daydream has much in common with the relaxed state we assume during sleep. However, when you are daydreaming, you are not actually asleep. When you are asleep, your defense mechanisms are down and you are psychologically more vulnerable. In other words, we shed the masks we wear in public. Therefore what is expressed in night dreaming is probably a better representation of whom we are, not just our waking hopes and fears. Feelings and thoughts we might be unwilling to acknowledge in waking life often surface boldly in dreams. Night dreams also speak to us in the powerful language of symbols, whereas the language of daydreams tends to be more tangible, reflecting events that have a clearer reality to them.

CONTRARY OR COMPENSATORY DREAMS

In these types of dreams, the unconscious places the dreaming self in a totally different situation to the one we find ourselves in waking life. For example, if your day has been filled with unhappiness and stress due to the death of a loved one or the end of a relationship, you may dream of yourself spending a carefree, happy day by the seaside. Your unconscious may also give you personality traits that you haven't expressed in waking life. For example, if you hate being the center of attention you may dream about being a celebrity. Such dreams are thought to provide necessary balance and may also be suggesting to you that you try incorporating some of the characteristics that your dream underlined in your waking life.

DAILY PROCESSING DREAMS

Also known as factual dreams, daily processing dreams are dreams in which you go over and over things that happened during the day, especially those that were repetitive or forced you to concentrate for long periods; dreaming about a long journey or a tough work assignment, for example. These kinds of dreams don't tend to be laden with meaning, and most dream theorists think of them as bits and pieces of information your brain is processing.

DREAMS OF CHILDHOOD

Dreaming about your childhood may reflect a childhood dynamic which hasn't been worked out yet and requires a resolution.

False awakening

It is thought that many reported sightings of ghosts are caused by false awakening, which occurs when you are actually asleep but are convinced in your dream state that you are awake. This is the kind of vivid dream in which you wake up convinced that what happened in your dream really happened.

Incubated dreams

This is when you set your conscious mind on experiencing a particular kind of dream. For example, you may incubate a dream of a loved one by concentrating on visualizing your loved one's face before you sleep, or you may ask for a dream to answer your problems immediately before going to sleep. The theory is that your unconscious responds to the suggestion.

Inspirational dreams

Many great works of art, music, literature have allegedly been inspired by dreams, when the unconscious brings a creative idea to the fore. For example, English poet and artist William Blake said that his work was inspired by the visions in his dreams. One night in 1816, Mary Shelley, her husband and a group of friends were challenged to write a ghost story. That night Mary Shelley dreamed of a creature that would later become the monster created by Dr Frankenstein in her yet-to-be-written novel.

Lucid dreams

These occur when you become aware that you are dreaming when you are dreaming. It takes time and practice to stop yourself waking up, but it is possible to learn how to become a lucid dreamer and control the course of your dreams.

Mutual dreams

When two people dream the same dream. Such dreams can be spontaneous or incubated, when two people who are close decide on a dream location together and imagine themselves meeting up before going to sleep.

Nightmares

Dreams that terrify us or cause distress in some way by waking us up before the situation has resolved. Nightmares occur during REM sleep and typically arise when a person is feeling anxious or helpless in waking life. Once the dreamer has recognized what is triggering this kind of dream, and worked through any unresolved fears and anxieties, nightmares tend to cease.

Night terrors

These are similar to nightmares, but because they occur in deep sleep (stage four) we rarely remember what terrified us, although we may be left with a lingering feeling of unexplained dread.

Out-of-body experiences

Also known as astral travel or projection, out-of-body experiences are thought to occur at times of physical and emotional trauma. Researchers tend to dismiss the idea but those that experience such dreams say that their mind, consciousness or spirit leaves their body and travels through time and space.

PAST-LIFE DREAMS

If you dream of being in a historical setting some believe this is evidence of past-life recall, although most dream theorists dismiss the existence of past-life or far-memory dreams, or genetic dreams when you assume the identity of an ancestor.

PHYSIOLOGICAL DREAMS

These dreams reflect the state of your body, so, for example, if you have an upset stomach, you may dream that you are being violently sick. These dreams may highlight the progress of serious physical conditions or in some cases predict the onset of them.

PRECOGNITIVE DREAMS

Most dream researchers dismiss these dreams but precognitive dreams are thought to predict real-life events of which the dreamer has no conscious awareness. These dreams tend to happen to people with psychic abilities. They are extremely rare but there have been many instances when people claim to have dreamt of things before they happened. For example, many people reported dreaming about 9/11 before it occurred. Other people tell of cancelling trains or flights because of a foreboding dream. There are also reports of people who dreamt the winning numbers of the lottery.

PROBLEM-SOLVING DREAMS

These occur when you have gone to bed mulling over a problem and found the answer in your dreams. This could be because your unconscious has already solved the dream and sleeping on it gives your unconscious a chance to express itself. Many famous inventions were allegedly prompted by a dream. For example, Scottish engineer and inventor of the steam engine James Watt (1736–1819) dreamed of molten metal falling from the sky in the shape of balls. This dream gave him the idea for drop cooling and ball-bearings. The model of the atom, the M9 analogue computer, the isolation of insulin in the treatment of diabetes, and, as we have seen, the sewing machine, were also ideas that sprung from inspiration in dreams.

PSYCHOLOGICAL DREAMS

These are dreams that bring things we would rather not think about to our attention. They make us face an aspect of ourselves or our life that might be hindering our progress. They are often about our fears, anxieties, resentment, guilt and insecurities. For example, if you dream of yourself running around and around on the wheel of a cage unable to stop, this could suggest that in your waking life you are taking on too much and not giving yourself enough time to relax.

RECURRING DREAMS

Dreams that reoccur typically happen when the dreamer is worried about a situation that isn't resolving itself in waking life. When the trigger in waking life is dealt with the dreams usually end. Recurring dreams can also occur when a person is suffering from some kind of phobia or trauma that has been repressed or not resolved. If this is the case the unconscious is urging the dreamer to consciously receive and acknowledge the issue and deal with it.

SEXUAL DREAMS

In dreams, sex can reflect the archetypal pattern which underlies the waking sex life or may represent a hoped-for reunion with another part of ourselves into a whole.

TELEPATHIC DREAMS

This is the kind of dream when someone you know appears in your dream in acute distress and you later learn that that person was experiencing a real-life crisis at the time, such as extreme unhappiness, an accident or even death. It is thought that telepathic dreams are a meeting of minds between two people who are close to each other emotionally.

VIGILANT DREAMS

These are processing dreams that involve your senses. For example, if your mobile rings or a picture falls to the ground while you are asleep, the sound may be incorporated into your dream but appear as something else, such as a police siren or a broken window. The smell of flowers in your room may also become a garden scene in your dreams.

WISH-FULLFILLMENT DREAMS

These are the kind of dreams in which we quite literally live the dream; we might win the lottery, date a celebrity, ooze charisma or simply go on a long holiday. In these kinds of dreams our unconscious is trying to compensate for disappointment or dissatisfaction with our current circumstances in waking life.

Walking and talking in your sleep

Sleepwalking or moving is an attempt to put a dream into action. Most likely you have grown out of the habit, if you ever had it, but if an occasion arises which is very stressful, we may, like Lady Macbeth, re-enact the nightmare in this way. Talking in your sleep is similar in cause to sleep movement. It is an attempt to carry a dream on verbally. You are more likely to walk or talk or move in your sleep when you are under mental pressure. Most of the time this is totally harmless but some sleepwalkers and talkers can put themselves in real danger. Precautions should therefore be taken. Make sure windows are closed and, if stairs are a hazard, doors locked. If you're really worried about your sleepwalking, seek advice from your doctor and if someone you know is sleepwalking don't try to wake them – just guide them quietly and gently back to bed.

Interpreting Your Dreams

'If the dream is a translation of waking life, waking life is also a translation of the dream.' René Magritte

If you have ever wondered why dreams often appear so difficult to make sense of, it is because the information they contain is presented in a different language; the language of symbols: of people alive or dead, known and unknown, animals both domestic and wild, landscapes and buildings familiar and strange, or any number of symbolic objects such as shapes, colors, signs, numbers, jewelry, food, clothing and so on.

These images are your own thoughts, feelings and ideas turned into a series of pictures like ordinary scenes in your daily life. For example, if you feel overwhelmed you may have a dream you are swimming but finding it hard to keep your head above water. If you feel confused you may have a dream when you are wondering about lost in a dark forest. The number of symbols and images that your mind can translate into dream pictures is practically endless.

Words just can't convey the countless powerful feelings that symbols do. These symbols are often chosen from something that has caught our attention in waking life, triggering a memory, conflict or concern that resonates both in the present and in the past.

One tried-and-tested way to uncover the meaning of your dream images is by direct association. You simply go with the first thing that pops into your head when a trigger image from your dream is given. If you don't immediately get an associative thought, try working through all your feelings about that image. For example, if you saw a caterpillar in a dream. Do you like caterpillars or do you find them a bit creepy? Try to discover what the image means to you right now, for the meanings of your symbols will change over time.

The more you work with your dreams, the more familiar you will become with your personal images. You'll probably find that you dream the most about the things that you are familiar with every day: your family, your colleagues, your friends and your pet. Each time you dream about these familiar things they will have personal significance to you alone.

The great majority of dreams are not to be taken literally and you need to do a bit of detective work to get to the real message. Just because you dream that a friend is dying does not mean that he or she will die, but rather that they are going through a period of enormous change. In fact, interpreting dreams literally can be harmful. As pointed out earlier, you have your own set of unique dream images and symbols. If you love dogs, what a dog means to you and what a dog means to someone who can't stand dogs will be very different. Always bear in mind that your dream symbols and images are unique to you.

Although the images and symbols in your dreams do need to be interpreted, their purpose isn't to mystify you. They are simply trying to get their message across in the best way that they can. If you do find yourself getting tense, confused or frustrated when trying to interpret a dream, let it go. Dream interpretation is best approached with an open mind and in a relaxed state.

You don't need to interpret every single dream you have. In the same way that some movies are more compelling and thought-provoking than others, some dreams, like those when you do fantastic things like flying into space or surfing in Hawaii, are simply to be enjoyed. You don't always have to dig deep for meaning. It's good to be aware that a dream might contain a message of importance, but don't get obsessed with finding meanings for every single detail – just interpret what you can. Dreams, like life, are full of big and little stuff. Don't sweat the 'small stuff'.

Capturing Your Dreams: How to Recall and Record

'Dreams are illustrations ... from the book your soul is writing about you.' Marsha Norman

We all dream several dreams a night and it's been suggested that we each have 100,000 dreams over the course of our lives. So you might be wondering why you can't remember a single one. Medications, alcohol, too little sleep and anxiety about the content of our dreams can all block dream recall.

We're most likely to remember the dreams closest to awakening, but with a little effort you can boost your dream recall. In fact the more attention you pay to your dreams, by thinking about them, writing them down, working with them, the more likely you are to remember them. Keeping a note pad and a pen beside your bed and recording your dreams immediately on waking is one of the best ways to help your dream recall.

Some dreams fade quickly from memory, so it is crucial you capture them as soon as you can. Immediately on waking, write down your dream or dreams – even if this is in the middle of the night; don't brush your teeth first or leave it until your alarm clock goes off. If you do that, you'll probably forget all about it and will lose a valuable dream. If you record your dreams in words, you create permanent reminders that you can use to help you figure out what they are trying to tell you.

Later in the day, transfer the information to a dream diary, specifically set aside for your dreams. In this diary include: the date of your dream, any people involved, the moods and feelings expressed, prominent colors, numbers, or shapes, the problems and conflicts encountered, prominent symbols or stories, information about the dream landscape, whether it was past, present or future and, finally, how the dream ended.

With practice, you will soon get the hang of remembering and writing down your dreams. Use this encyclopedia to help you unlock the meaning of your dream themes and symbols, but never forget that the best book you will ever read about dreams is the one you write yourself: your dream journal.

Programing your mind for dream recall

Some dreams are so vivid you can't forget them but many are so fleeting they can vanish without a trace. One way to make sure you remember them is to talk to yourself in a positive way. Before going to sleep tell yourself that you will remember your dreams on waking. Try this visualization technique.

When you feel sleepy, turn off the lights and settle down in your favorite sleeping position. In a relaxed way, think about your dreams. Breathe in for a count of five, and out for a count of ten. Repeat this, and then breathe normally. Now imagine you have just woken in the morning and, as you slowly move back into consciousness, you reach for your pen and write down your dream. Bring your attention to the present again, and feel comfortable, warm and sleepy. Tell yourself that in the morning you will remember your dreams.

Dream Maker

'The dream was always running ahead of me. To catch up, to live for a moment in unison with it, that was the miracle.'
Anaïs Nin

Some dream experts believe it is possible to take charge of your dreams and turn them into creative and helpful experiences that can help solve problems in your waking life. To do this you have to get your waking mind to work more fully with your dreaming mind; you need to think about what problem or issue you want your dream to resolve. This is a process called dream incubation.

STEP-BY-STEP GUIDE TO DREAM INCUBATION

Step 1: Decide what you want to dream about, what you want your dream to resolve or help you with and what question you want answered.

Step 2: Write down your question or desired dream on a piece of paper as if you were chatting to a friend — because that's what your dream self is. Be as specific as you can, but don't ask about silly or trivial matters, such as should I go to this or that party.

Step 3: Read this over and over again during the day and keep it in your mind during the day and again as you get ready for bed.

Top tips for perfect sleep and dreaming

1. Before you go to bed, lessen tension with a relaxing massage or warm bath, some gentle stretching exercises or a short walk. Avoid taking a shower as this will invigorate you.

2. Ensure you leave at least two hours between sleep and your last meal. Food and the process of digestion can encourage strange dream images. If you want a snack, make it light: a biscuit and a glass of milk.

3. Avoid alcohol, caffeine and cigarettes if you want to have a restful, untroubled sleep. Caffeine is a stimulant, and alcohol and cigarettes will inhibit REM sleep when dreaming occurs.

4. Make sure your bed is comfortable, your bedroom well aired and neither too hot, nor too cold. A temperature of 65°F (18°C) is about right. Keep the room dark, as light is a cue for waking, and block out any unwanted sound.

5. The calmer and more relaxed you are the better. Cleanse and calm your mind with some reading, meditation or listen to some relaxing music. If any worrying thoughts refuse to leave, jot them down in a note pad beside your bedside and consider the matter closed until morning. If you want to sleep and dream well – don't take your worries to bed.

Step 4: Once in bed read over the question again and ask your dreaming self to bring you the answer during sleep. Put the paper under your pillow or near your bed.

Step 5: Tell yourself before you go to sleep that you will have the dream you want and trust yourself to dream the dream that you ask for.

Step 6: Tell yourself you will remember your dream. Be prepared to write down the dream when you wake up and be open to whatever comes to you.

Step 7: Leave your dream intention to incubate. What you are doing here is programing your dreaming self – giving it a particular task to focus on.

Step 8: Stop thinking about your intention to dream. Let it go. Relax and calm your mind before you sleep and don't stress about whether or not you are going to have a dream.

Step 9: Be willing to experiment and try again if necessary.

You may not want to ask your dreaming self a question and may simply want a happy, harmonious dream. If this is the case think of a place or person you'd like to dream about – perhaps a holiday or loved one – write down a simple description and ask your dreaming self in the same way to give you a happy, inspiring dream.

Dream Magic

'One of the most adventurous things left us is to go to bed. For no one can lay a hand on our dreams.' E. V. Lucas

Whether you decide to practice dream incubation or not, remember that any dream you have has the potential to take you to a world of mystery and wonder that can keep you spellbound for days trying to understand it. The dream interpretations that follow will help you unravel some of the mystery, but never forget that *you* are the dreamer and *you* do the dreaming and that in understanding your dreams, you can reach a better understanding of yourself.

Use the explanations offered in the pages that follow for the interpretation of your dream symbols, and combine them with your own circumstances to work out an understanding of the likely significance of your dreams. In this way, your innermost feelings, hopes and fears can be highlighted, hopefully resolving issues in your waking life and enriching it by revealing your hidden strengths and creativity.

Dreams offer you an incredible opportunity to connect your outer and inner worlds to illuminate your waking life. So, try to take the time to enjoy the excitement, mystery, wonder and magic each and every dream brings. Dare yourself to discover and believe in your creativity and your dreams – wherever they may lead you.

THE DREAMS

ACCIDENTS, ACTION
AND ADVENTURES

When you dream that you are the Lara Croft and Indiana Jones of your own adventures, it can be action packed and thrilling; but when you dream that you are in a car or plane crash, the dream can feel rather different.

The traditional interpretation of dreams involving accidents of any kind is that we are receiving some kind of warning to be on our guard against possible danger or hidden aggression, either our own or others'. From a psychologist's point of view, such dreams may highlight anxieties to do with safety or fear of taking responsibility. Spiritual interpretations of such dreams suggest the need for some kind of intervention from an authoritative source.

According to Freud, accidents in dreams, like slips of the tongue in waking life, are not accidents but dream events with a meaning that can help us to unravel the often incomprehensible maneuvers of our unconscious mind. For Jung, accident dreams, as well as offering insights into our unconscious thought processes, can provide a reaction to a traumatic experience or the fear of it. For example, if you were in a car accident or are anxious about having one, you may dream of being involved in one. People who suffered great trauma, such as rape victims or war veterans, may have nightmares that are exactly like, or very similar to, actual life events.

The most commonly accepted theory is that accident dreams show how your unconscious has noticed things that you may not have noticed in waking life. They are both a reminder and a possible warning. You may, for example, dream of a teenager being knocked down on a busy street outside a petrol station, only to read a few weeks later that a teenager has been seriously injured in just this way. The most likely explanation is that you have unconsciously noticed how dangerous the crossing was, having read somewhere about the growing number of teenagers killed on the roads due to the use of mobile telephones, and without realizing it, you have observed that an accident was highly likely. These kinds of subtle clues and subliminal suggestions are around us every day.

Adventure dreams can be a reflection of your waking life, which may have become more adventurous recently, but it could also suggest the need to experiment, physically, emotionally and spiritually.

The Jungian archetype of the hero, starting out on his adventure and battling adversity in order to learn, mature and grow, dominates the interpretation of adventure-themed dreams. Adventure dreams urge the dreamer to take on new challenges or seek out aspects of themselves or talents that remain hidden in waking life. They point the way towards a new understanding, and the discovery of inner strength and creativity that can empower the dreamer.

Finally, activities or actions within dreams are often concerned with hidden motivations and agendas, and, interpreted within the context of your mood and emotions within the dream, are particularly important. The psychological meaning is that action needs to transfer from dreams to waking life in order for progress to be made. Symbolically the action can give an indication of the dreamer's spiritual progress.

Typically, activities in dreams are associated with moving forward or making progress in waking life. They reflect how well you are doing in your quest to achieve your ambitions. Do you need to move on? Take another route? Speed up or slow down? That's why it is particularly helpful to take note of the details in your dream. What was the goal you were running, walking, climbing or swimming towards? Did you feel exhausted or were you in peak form? Were you competing against anyone? Did you reach your destination or achieve your goal? Did you feel satisfied or disappointed? The answers to these questions will help you assess your progress and identify any obstacles or attitudes that may be holding you back.

Accident Situations

ACCIDENT TO THE DREAMER

If you dream that you **have an accident yourself**, you should take note of the details, especially if it was caused by something you use every day, such as a **bicycle, a car or a lawn mower**, and check that it is in good working order before you use it the next day. On the other hand, an accident dream could also be warning you of potential danger or loss of control if you continue a particular course of action. For example, you may dream that you are **hit by a car** as you run across the road to talk to a married colleague you've been thinking of having an affair with. An obvious interpretation of this dream is that the accident signifies pent-up guilt for something you have thought, said or done, and that you are sub-consciously punishing yourself over it. You could also be harboring deep anxiety over being found out. Dreams of car accidents might be urging you to slow down before you hit disaster, or telling you that you are 'driving' yourself too hard. You need to rethink, or re-plan, your course of actions and set yourself on a better path. Your accident dream may also represent your straightforward fears of being involved in an actual, physical accident. You may just be nervous about getting behind the wheel, or going on a train, boat or plane trip.

Whatever happened in your dreams, notice how you emerge. Did you manage to rescue something or someone? If you did,

The Element Encyclopedia of 20,000 Dreams

Dreams that foretell accidents

A number of well-recorded dreams have appeared to foretell accidents and some researchers believe that accidents in dreams are a warning. Research, however, does not support the idea that dreams predict impending disaster. *See also* DISASTERS.

The story of the SS *Titanic* is well known. On 14 April 1912, the *Titanic* struck an iceberg and sunk in the North Atlantic, carrying with her more than 1500 lives. The lack of sufficient lifeboats has often been blamed as the leading cause of fatalities; experts will tell you, however, that there were hundreds of causes leading to the accident, including everything from faulty construction of watertight compartments to a failure to pay attention to numerous warnings of icebergs in the area. What is important here, however, is the huge number of accident dreams that foretold this disaster.

Immediately after the *Titanic* sank in the North Atlantic, there were at least two dozen reports of people who cancelled their trip because of **precognitive dreams they had about the sinking**. No one knows how many had the same warning and ignored it, going to a death they could have avoided. There is one businessman that had the same precognitive dream of the *Titanic* sinking three times and chose to ignore the warning. He still intended to make the trip, until a sudden turn in business forced him to cancel.

this could suggest someone who needs your help or protection. It could also suggest an aspect of yourself that is worth saving. Were you hurt, or did you come out of it unscathed? If you weren't injured, this could suggest that you have the strength to overcome what fate throws at you, but if you were wounded, you need to take better care of yourself and 'toughen up'.

ACCIDENT IN THE HOME

Dreaming of **accidents in the home** means tension may be building up in your home life, although it occasionally means you have unconsciously noticed something that might cause a domestic accident. Therefore check whatever it is that caused the accident; if you **dream of falling down stairs**, is the stair carpet loose? A dream that focuses on your home may also be saying something about your personality and approach to life. It may be that in order to progress with your life you need to make changes, and these changes may involve destroying what you have built up for some time.

ACCIDENT TO LOVED ONES

To dream that a **loved one dies in an accident** indicates that something in your own self is no longer functional, and is 'dead'. It is also symbolic of your own relationship with that person. Perhaps you need to let go of this relationship, or let go of a particular phase in that relationship and move towards the next. For example, the first throes of passion may have ebbed away, but you can replace them with love, stability and commitment.

ACCIDENT AT SEA

To dream of an **accident at sea** suggests potential problems with those who are close to you, or some kind of disappointment in love. If **water overwhelms you**, you are likely to feel overwhelmed by emotions. If this is the case, you need to assess how best to manage your feelings and put them into context. If you are **trying to save other people in a shipwreck**, you need to think about what these people represent to you. For instance, if you are **trying to save a baby**, perhaps that represents an element in your waking life, such as unconditional love, or wonder and excitement, that you need to develop in your waking life to help you cope with your emotional response.

ACCIDENT TO SOMEONE ELSE

This could be hidden aggression towards that particular person or an aspect of yourself that person represents that you recognize in yourself. It could also suggest anxiety about the welfare of the person in your dream.

CAR CRASH

A **dream of a car crash** represents tensions about your efforts to 'get somewhere' or achieve your goals. You could be driving yourself too hard, or perhaps you are too eager to get ahead. If your **car suddenly spins out of control** and crashes into pedestrians, your unconscious may be alerting you to the need to have your steering and brakes checked. Alternatively, your unconscious may have been commenting anxiously on the way you are living your life. Are you in danger of losing control, coming to the end of the road, or have you set yourself on a collision course because of your life in the fast lane? If so, pay attention to who you hit in the dream and who was affected by the accident. For men, **driving cars** tends to relate to sex, so it could be some kind of warning. Perhaps you are being careless or casual in protecting yourself.

PLANE CRASH

Dreams of **plane crashes** are typically provoked by worries about over-extending yourself, such as a project or business collapsing, or not being able to pay bills. It is likely that you may be afraid of failing in some other way, especially if you are about to take an exam or test, or have set yourself an unrealistic task or objective. Have you been flying too high? *See also* DISASTERS.

TRAIN CRASH

A dream of a **train crash** could suggest the need for extreme caution concerning financial matters. It could also indicate an exaggerated sense of self-worth as a stumbling block in the dreamer's path.

The Element Encyclopedia of 20,000 Dreams

Minor accidents

Accidents from above

To **see something hanging above you about to fall** implies possible danger. If **it falls and misses you**, perhaps you have had a narrow escape from some misfortune, or your unconscious is warning you to be alert to potential danger.

Breaking things

To dream that you **break something**, like a window or a chair, indicates that changes lie ahead and that you want to change the direction in which your life is heading. Alternatively, it suggests that you need to take things more slowly. If you **drop or smash things** in your dreams, this indicates that you are letting go of – or need to let go of – some project, relationship, person or idea. Be sure to analyze the significance of what is being dropped or smashed. Another explanation for dreams of breaking things is that you are express-ing some dismay or regret at how you let something slip through fingers.

Burning

To **set something on fire by accident** suggests intense emotions and/or passionate sexual feelings. Alternatively, it may suggest that you need to take time off for yourself and relax, or that your unconscious is alerting you to the need for a smoke alarm.

Cut

To dream that you **have a cut** suggests that you are being let down or being undervalued. If the **cuts are on your legs**, then it symbolizes an imbalance and an inability to stand up for yourself. To dream that you are **cutting or harming yourself** in some way, either accidentally or on purpose, indicates that you are experiencing some over-whelming turmoil or problems in your waking life. You are trying to disconnect yourself from the discomfort or pain you are experiencing.

Farting or burping in public

To dream that you accidentally **fart or burp in public**, suggests that you are being passive-aggressive. You need to express your feelings in a more direct manner.

Slipping, tripping and stumbling

To dream that you **slip** or that you make a **slip of the tongue** suggests that you are doing things you do not really want to do, or saying things you do not really mean. If you **stumble but do not fall**, it may suggest that you will meet obsta-cles but will be able to surmount them. If you fall, obstacles may lie in your path in waking life and you need to find a way to work round them. **Trying in vain to climb a slippery slope** suggests you may have taken on more than you can cope with, and are in danger of backslid-ing under the pressure. It could also be a warning against being a control freak; you cannot control everything and everyone, and need to show more regard for the views of others. To dream that you **trip up** or **stumble** indicates that something is out of control in your waking life and you need to deal with it. Things are not going as smoothly as you want, as you are faced with minor obstacles. It could also indicate social awkwardness; perhaps you are worried you might get off on the wrong foot. Does your self esteem need a boost, or are you simply not looking where you are going?

Adventure Scenarios

BEING CHASED

The way we respond to anxiety and pressure in real life is typically manifested as a chase dream. Often in these dream scenarios, you are being **pursued by some attacker** who wants to hurt or possibly kill you. You may be **running away, hiding, or trying to outwit your pursuer**. Chase dreams may represent your way of coping with fears, stress or various situations in your waking life. Instead of confronting the situation, you are running away and avoiding it. Ask yourself, who is the one chasing you, and you may gain some understanding and insight on the source of your fears. The dream could also indicate that you are refusing to acknowledge a certain viewpoint or idea. On the other hand, the pursuer or attacker who is chasing you in your dream may represent a part of yourself. Your own feelings of anger, jealousy, fear, and possibly love, can assume the appearance of a threatening figure. You may be projecting these feelings onto the unknown chaser and your dream is calling your attention to your own self-destructive actions. A more direct analysis of chase dreams is that they reflect the simple fear of being attacked. Media hype and overexposure play on this fear and magnify our level of risk.

ESCAPING DANGER

If you wake up **before being caught, eaten or beaten**, you need to ask yourself what you need to wake up to. What are you missing or avoiding in waking life? Things won't get better until you face up to them? Dreams about **breaking free from jail, cages, ropes or shackles** may point to a desire for release from a situation, such as a job that is causing stress. The elation surrounding dreams of leaving jail may suggest feelings about a new opportunity in our life. However, if no joy accompanies the liberation, this could suggest anxiety about the challenges that lie ahead. Breaking out of jail on the other hand testifies to a determination to create your own chances and give free reign to talents that have too long been repressed. Alternatively, if you have been depressed recently, break-out dreams could suggest the need to seek serious help, as the dream may signify a yearning for the ultimate release – death. If, on the other hand, you are **rescued** in your dreams, or **help rescue someone**, this can express the need to liberate creative energies or some aspect of yourself that isn't being developed in waking life.

Falling

Falling, and the accompanying sense of vertigo, is, along with flying, one of the most often reported dream topics. Falling dreams typically occur during the first stage of sleep. Dreams in this stage are often accompanied by muscle spasms of the arms, legs, and the whole body. Sometimes when we have these falling dreams, we feel our whole body jerk or twitch, which provokes us to awaken.

Typically, the act of falling in dreams suggests loss of control and anxiety in the sleeper's waking life. The anxiety could be related to work, or it could be related to sexual inhibition or low self-esteem. Such may be the fear of the fall that you could awake with a jolt. If this occurs, it is important to remember the circumstances of the fall in your dream, as this will help you understand its hidden message. According to Freudian theory, dreams of falling indicate that you are contemplating giving into a sexual urge or impulse. You may be lacking indiscretion. According to biblical interpretations, dreams about falling have a negative overtone and suggest that man is acting and walking according to his own way of thinking, and not that of the Lord.

Flying

Dreams of **flying** are very common and vary from dreamer to dream. Most typically dreamers don't go on long, high flights; instead they hover about a hundred or so yards from the ground. The most simple explanation of these kind of dreams was put forward by English physician Havelock Ellis in his book *The World of Dreams*, in which he suggests that it is our breathing whilst asleep that suggests the idea of flying (and falling) to the unconscious mind. Freud suggested that dreams of flying were nothing else but the desire for sexual freedom, and the idea that dreams of flying are associated with sex is shared by some other dream researchers. However, as with all dreams, there can be many interpretations.

Flying dreams and the ability to control your flight can be representative of your own personal sense of power. If you are **flying with ease, and enjoying the scene and landscape below**, then it suggests that you are on top of a situation. You have risen above something. It may also mean that you have gained a different perspective on things. **Having difficulties staying in flight** indicates a lack of power in controlling your own circumstances. You may be struggling to stay aloft, and stay on course. Things like birds, trees or telephone poles may further obstruct your flight. These obstructions represent a particular obstacle or person standing in your way in your waking life. You need to identify who, or what, is preventing you from moving forward. If you are **feeling fear when you are flying** or **feel that you are flying too high**, then it suggests that you are afraid of challenges and of success. Are you trying to

Varieties of flying dream

Another way of interpreting **flying dreams** is that they symbolize your strong mind and will. You feel invincible and nobody can tell you what you cannot do and accomplish. Undoubtedly these dreams leave you with a great sense of freedom.

Flying high

Liberation from something that troubles you. Nevertheless, **flying high** has its perils. The ancient Greek myth of Icarus warns against flying too high. Your dream may show that you are being overambitious.

Flying low

Native Americans, Tibetan Buddhists and others claim that all people have a light body that can leave the physical body during sleep. The light body can travel great distances and communicate with angels. To dream of flying may indicate the need or desire to develop the mystical side of your nature. Alternatively, it could be a warning to keep your feet firmly on the ground.

Hovering

If you are **hovering or floating in the sky** and looking down on earth this may represent feelings of optimism and success – the world is at your feet. However, as floating is impossible the dream may also be a warning against pride and over ambition and the possibility of coming down to earth with a bump.

Parachute

If a **parachute opens as you fall**, this may express your relief following a dangerous event, such as a car accident that you survived. Alternatively, it could suggest the need to bail out of a difficult situation, as a parachute offers a safe way to fall rather than a means to fly.

Shot at

If you are **shot at or hit by something when flying**, you need to be on your guard against people who might want to restrain your advancement into the higher spheres.

Sun

If you **see the sun while flying**, this could suggest that your worries will melt away.

Terrain below

If you are **flying over muddy or broken places**, this could be a warning to be on your guard against potential enemies or misfortune.

Wing color

If you are **flying with white wings**, this dream could represent the expansion of your awareness and the unfolding of your higher self. If your wings are black this could indicate the need for change in your waking life. *See also* COLORS.

rise above something in waking life? Are you developing an idea? Are you flying in the face of fortune? Flying into a rage? Flying off the handle? Flying high?

Jail

Prisons can often stand for a set of beliefs that limit the dreamer's personal development or progress. The dream may help us escape this limitations by forcing us to confront them and examine what triggered them. A similar symbol of psychological entrapment, a **cage**, may also represent some kind of frustration with our life. There may be feelings of inferiority or a desire to break free from social convention.

Lock and key

According to Freudian analysis, a **lock** is commonly interpreted as a symbol of the female sexual organ with the **key** representing the phallus. A dream of **unlocking a box of treasure** may indicate sex as liberating. If, however, **the box won't open** this indicates sexual frustration or dissatisfaction with the sexual side of a relationship.

Kidnapped and taken hostage

If **kidnapping** features in your dream, this may suggest the desire to dominate or be dominated by another person. If you are the victim but don't feel afraid, this could lend a sexual connotation to your dream. If you are **held hostage** in a dream, this could indicate that you feel someone has a hold on you, or that you are subject to some influence that prevents you from doing what you need to do. Hostage-takers often make demands for money, personal recognition

and so on. Is there someone in your waking life who is placing unnecessary demands upon you, or making you feel guilty? In some hostage dreams, as in real life, a rapport develops between the victim and the hostage-taker; if this is the case, it could indicate a love-hate relationship in your waking life. Finally, might this kind of dream not also suggest that you are held hostage, not by a person, but by your fears? *See also* CHANGE AND CONFLICT; NEGATIVE EMOTIONS.

Courage

Courage in dreams involves turning to face your enemy or someone who threatens you, standing up for yourself or someone vulnerable or outwitting those who might want to harm you. How do your dreams display your courage? If you **run in fear** your dreams are urging you to discover your inner strength. If you **stand up for yourself** your dreams are telling you about something you need to recognize about yourself in your daily life. The feeling of courage in dreams can play a special role in empowering you in daily life. With or without lucid dreaming techniques the more courage you start to show in your dreams the more courage you are likely to display in your waking life.

PURSUIT

To dream that you are **in pursuit of someone or something**, suggests that you are being denied your power and influence. You may need to re-evaluate your strengths and concentrate your efforts on something more worthwhile. It is important to identify what exactly you are pursuing, but bear in mind that it may not be a person, or an animal, but an idea.

Activities A to Z

CLIMBING

Dreams of **climbing stairs, hills or mountains** reflect on your ambitions and your ability to face up to challenges in daily life. Were you climbing with ease or difficulty? *See also* AMBITION AND SUCCESS.

CRAWLING

To dream that you are **crawling on your hands and knees or stomach** suggests some kind of humiliation in waking life.

DANCING

A dream of **dancing** suggests an enjoyment of life and a go-with-the-flow attitude. This dream may contain elements of wish-fulfillment, but there is the underlying theme of years of hard work and dedication. Such a dream may be encouraging you to have more discipline or, alternatively, to have the

courage to take up artistic skills. *See also* ARTS AND CRAFTS.

DIGGING

If you were **digging or excavating** in your dream you may need to resolve some deep-rooted emotional problems, with or without the help of a counselor.

EXERCISING

Do you need to exercise more in waking life? If you dream of **exercising with weights**, perhaps you need to lose some weight? Alternatively, your unconscious may be urging you to exercise your mind or your common sense in a particular situation. If you dream that you are **jogging**, you appear to have your responsibilities under control but you may also feel dissatisfied or bored with certain aspects of your life, especially if you dream you are on a **treadmill**. If you are **jumping or leaping** in your dream, this suggests ambition and a desire to move forward with your life, or progress in your career.

If you are **kicked, or kick someone** else in your dream, perhaps there is something in your waking life that you disagree with or disapprove of. To dream that you are **hopping** could suggest childish or immature behavior on your part. Alternatively, it may indicate your tendency to jump from task to task, or not being able to stay in one place. If you are **stretching** in a dream, your unconscious may be reminding you to work on your flexibility, not just in your body, but in your approach to life. To dream that you are **skipping** suggests you need to be more light-hearted and friendly in waking life. Alternatively, the dream may

Cleaning

Washing in dreams is a fairly common theme, and almost always relates to something that is troubling or worrying the dreamer in waking life. The **harder the hands or body are scrubbed**, the greater the need for the unconscious to be free of guilt or some kind of burden. The same applies to **washing stains in clothes**.

If you are **taking a shower or bath** in your dream, this could indicate a problem that overshadows you in waking life. If you are **washing your hair**, this is connected to your emotions, and if you are washing your genitals, there may be some kind of sexual adventure in waking life that you are ashamed of. You could also be worried about sexually transmitted diseases. If you are **cleaning your home**, this could suggest that you want to get more organized in your waking life, but before you can do that you need to dispose of dirt or dust; this may refer to ways of thinking or responding that are clouding your judgments in waking life. If you were **watching a washing machine** in your dream, this is a reference to your daily routine and the boredom you feel. If you are **trapped in the washing machine**, you feel stifled by your daily routine; it will therefore be important to make changes in daily life as soon as possible.

indicate that you have skipped something important. *See also* LEISURE.

PUSHING

To dream that you are **pushing something** suggests energy and drive to succeed in life. Consider also how you, or someone you know in waking life, may be a 'pushover'. To dream that you are **being pushed** signifies that you are under some sort of pressure, or feel coerced into doing something. Alternatively, it implies that you feel you don't have enough time to complete a task perfectly.

RIDING A HORSE

A dream of **riding a horse** may be associated with your sex life, and how fulfilled or inhibited you are. If you are **enjoying the ride**, it could indicate a rewarding love affair, or the desire for one. On the other hand, if you are **afraid of falling**, you may feel inhibited sexually, or be unable to commit to your partner. The same meaning is applied to dreams of **riding a motor cycle or a bicycle**. If you were riding another animal, think about what that animal represents in waking life.

Standing/Sitting

To dream that you are **standing** suggests that you are asserting yourself and feeling proud of your achievements. To dream that you are **sitting** indicates indecision and not knowing what to do with your life. It could also suggest laziness.

Skating

Dreams of **skating** suggest that the dreamer is enjoying his or her life. If you are **performing like a professional skater** (and aren't one), this could suggest that you are about to take off in some way in your waking life. If, however, your **skates are out of control**, this could suggest that in your quest for enjoyment you are acting recklessly. On the other hand, this dream could be telling you to get your skates on and put more pace and activity into a particular project or relationship.

Swimming

Water in a dream almost always indicates emotions. To dream that you are **swimming** suggests that you are exploring aspects of your unconscious mind and emotions. This is a common dream for people going through therapy or counseling, as it suggests the need for emotional support. To dream that you are **swimming underwater** suggests that you are completely submerged in your own emotions and need to deal with emotional difficulties. If you dream of **diving**, perhaps this indicates your desire to throw yourself into a relationship or project. The erotic sensation of water passing over the body led Freud to equate swimming with sexual intercourse. If you feel relaxed and happy, this foretells a long and happy relationship with your partner, but if you are **struggling against the tide**, the relationship may be in trouble.

Throwing and catching

If you **throw or catch** something in a dream, you need to pay attention to what it is you are throwing and catching. Are you throwing something away, or catching something you need, or something you don't want?

Weaving/Knitting/ Crochet/Sewing

Are you bogged down with routine in your waking life? Dreams of **weaving, knitting, crochet and sewing** could suggest that you need to broaden your horizons, as these tasks all require attention to detail and constant repetition. If you are **joining together pieces of fabric, or creating an exciting design**, this could, however, indicate that you are bringing together certain aspects of your waking life. If you **make mistakes with your craftwork, drop a stitch or break your thread,** perhaps you have recently been tactless in your daily life or had a quarrel with someone. Were you successful in patching up your differences? *See also* ARTS AND CRAFTS.

Walking/Running/Cycling

In general, activities such as **walking, running and cycling** are self-sufficient, pro-active and personal modes of progression, owing their movement entirely to will and physical effort. A possible Gestalt interpretation would be to regard dreams of walking, running or cycling as projections of the dreamer's developing independence and autonomy. Your competence within your dream activity depicts your emotional stage. If you are agile, this suggests you are coping well. If movements flow, you feel in harmony with your emotions and your sexuality. If, however, you get stuck, feel stiff and cannot move easily, this could indicate that your personal development is held back by anxieties and fears. To dream you are walking is probably a comment on the pace of your waking life, and how well you are coping with all your responsibilities. If you are **walking confidently**, it could indicate that you are in control and taking things in your stride. Consider your destination. Do you know what it is?

To dream that you are **walking at night** signifies discontent. If you are **limping**, this refers to a lack of balance in some area in your life. Perhaps you feel that you are giving more than you are getting back at work, or in a particular relationship. To dream that you are **marching** suggests teamwork, or the need to involve yourself more with other people in order to achieve results. If you were **running or racing** and keeping up with the others, this is a positive sign, but if you were **falling behind or trying and failing to win a race**, you need to rethink your schedule in daily life to relieve some of the pressures on you.

When specific activities appear in a dream, you might also need to consider whether or not you are filling your waking hours with productive and positive activities. It may be that changes need to be made. For example, if you dream of running, this could simply indicate your need to exercise more. Alternatively, it could suggest that you are exercising too much, and need to get balance back into your life.

See also AMBITION AND SUCCESS; LEISURE.

AMBITION AND SUCCESS

We all have ambitions and strive to achieve our ideals of success in waking life. These ambitions often surface in our dreams in symbolic disguise.

According to Adler, dreams are an expression of our ambitious desire for power and success, a way of overcompensating for shortcomings in our waking life. For example, if a person is unable to stand up to their boss, they may safely lash out in anger at him or her in a dream. Thus dreams offer some sort of satisfaction that is socially acceptable.

Although some dreams can be interpreted as wish-fulfillment, most modern dream researchers believe that dreams have another purpose, to periodically present us with reports on our progress to date. Sometimes these updates are purely expressions of wish-fulfillment, and therefore easy to interpret: for example, those fantastic dreams in which you win the lottery, or audition successfully for the lead role in a Hollywood blockbuster. Sometimes, though, dreams are harder to interpret because the dreaming mind speaks in the confusing language of symbols. Understanding such dreams is, however, important because they often contain pertinent observations and warnings – not yet registered by the conscious mind – that can help us achieve our goals in waking life.

Ambition Scenarios

CLIMBING

Freud considered dreams of climbing to represent a longing for sexual fulfillment. Other dream researchers believe climbing dreams suggest moving steadily towards your goals. What you climb signifies the scale of the task you have set yourself, whilst reaching the top signifies the height of your aspirations. Did you reach the top, or have you lost sight of your target?

One step at a time

Climbing a hill

This indicates a harder, and perhaps longer, challenge that you anticipated. Did you experience an uphill struggle in your dreams? If you did, how did you tackle it? Did you **see the top of the hill,** or did you **keep your head down,** suggesting that you may have lost sight of your goals. Were you **climbing the hill with anyone**? Did they help or hinder you?

Climbing a ladder

This could signify a corporate or social ladder, with each rung indicating promotion or another step towards social elevation. Alternatively, the ladder could be interpreted as a phallic symbol representing the so-called masculine qualities of power, drive and ambition that you need to adopt if you want to get to the top. The dream oracles say that to **climb a ladder to the last rung** means you will succeed in business.

Climbing a mountain

This represents the ultimate challenge of endurance, skill, strength and stamina. Were you equal to the task? Did you tackle it bravely, or with feelings of dread and anxiety?

Climbing stairs

You have great ambition, but are you climbing with confidence or with fear? Your unconscious may be reminding you not to become egotistical and climb too high, as other people despise arrogance and may try to knock you down. A meteoric rise to fame is not as easily sustained as a gradual and well-planned move to prominence. Be cautious, and take one step at a time.

Climbing over walls

If you dream that in front of you there is a **wall you need to climb over** to get to where you want to be, this suggests obstacles you may encounter in life that you need to overcome before you attain success.

On top of the world

If you **got to the top**, did you feel on top of the world? If you did, your dream mind is motivating you to re-enact that same feeling of success, achievement and liberation in your waking life. What did you see below you? Did you see people and places that you have distanced yourself from in waking life? If you **didn't get to the top**, did you retrace your steps? If you did reach the summit, your dream mind may be urging you to reconsider your goals.

Struggling uphill

In this kind of dream you are **climbing or driving up a steep incline**. Progress is slow, and it seems to take more than you or your engine can handle. You may even wonder why you took this particular route. From a psychological point of view, the uphill struggle represents a challenge you are dealing with right now that feels like it is too much. You hadn't expected it to be so tough. The over-worked junior doctor, the programer who must create complicated software within a week, the busy mum of newborn twins – all may have this dream. The steepness of the incline is an indication of how difficult the challenge feels to you.

The only way to reach the top is to pace yourself, so perhaps this dream is suggesting that you take better care of yourself and get plenty of rest. To put this advice into practice will improve your odds of success, and taking things one step at a time will make the process seem less overwhelming.

JUMPING

The act of **jumping up** in a dream can suggest trying to better ourselves. **Jumping down** can signify going down into the unconscious and those parts of ourselves we have yet to discover. **Jumping on the spot** is similar to dancing and signi-fies joy. If you made **a perfect jump**, this could suggest that you have made or are about to make a quantum leap in the form of an important decision. If your **jump misses the mark**, however, you may have made the wrong choice or are about to make it.

RACING

If you dreamed of **racing against rivals or the clock** to achieve personal, national or Olympic records, your dream probably relates to your career, as work is often called the 'rat race'. The **clock** represents the pressure you feel you are under and the level of attainment you hope to achieve. The other people in the race represent competition or threats to your chances of winning the prize money, admiration or status. If you **fly ahead of the competition**, you may feel as if you are ahead in waking life, but if you are **just keeping pace**, this could suggest that you are coping but could easily fall behind. If you're **struggling to keep up**, you may not be making the grade in real life. If you know who your dream rivals are, their position in the race will tell you how you think you compare with them. If you aren't working, **racing dreams** could suggest a long, hard struggle for success in love and life. If you **win the race**, this signifies that your poten-tial will be recognized; but an overzealous will to win may reveal a needy desire for others to acknowledge that potential. On the other hand, if you **lose the race**, espe-cially if you get pipped at the post, this signifies the frustration of understanding the limits of your potential. It can also suggest that lack of confidence is thwarting your progress.

RUNNING

To dream that you are running is consid-ered a positive sign, as it suggests speed, energy and direction. If you are **running forwards**, this indicates confidence or taking responsibility. To be **running backwards or away from something** signifies fear, or an inability to achieve your goals. A spiritual interpretation of running dreams could suggest that you are trying to do something too quickly. To dream that you **want to run but cannot** suggests that your ambitions are harder to accomplish than you thought.

Running events

Hurdles: In your dreams **hurdles** represent the obstacles that hinder your progress. Did they knock you over, or did you knock them over? Did you navigate your way successfully over them without touching them?

Marathon: If your race was a **marathon**, this indicates that work or life has become an exhausting slog. If you **win the marathon**, this suggests you have the confidence to achieve your aims, but if you **fail to finish**, this suggests that insecurities in waking life are holding you back.

Relay race: In the **relay race** of your life, were you successful at passing the baton or did you fumble things and ruin your team's chances?

Desperate for Success Scenarios

CHEATING

Are you **cheating** in your dreams in order to pass an exam or test? If you dreamed of running, did you **take a shortcut in the race**? What happened? Were you caught, or did you get the gold star? How you feel about all this is important. Often dreams in which **we win by cheating** are similar to gray areas in waking life. They are actions that express a lack of self-confidence. Why do you think you couldn't win the prize without cheating? Why do you feel inadequate? Why are you afraid to lose?

In your dreams, winning by cheating may leave you with an empty feeling. If you **get caught cheating** in your dream, this can leave you feeling anxious as well, and these feelings are your unconscious reminding you that you don't feel worthy of the prize. Sometimes, though, cheating dreams can be positive, indicating that you're beginning to see yourself as a potential winner, but are not yet ready to recognize this inside yourself. The best way to make sense of these sorts of dream is to think about how you feel, and what situation in waking life they may be referring to.

DODGING

If you are **dodging flying objects or balls** in your dream, this could be an image of your ability to go out of your way to achieve

The audience

Who is the **audience** in your dreams when you receive or don't receive recognition? Who is there to see you succeed or fail? How does their presence make you feel? Scared? Supported? Distracted? Proud? Are they cheering you on? Or are they holding you back?

Typically the people we choose to watch and comment on our progress dreamland are those **authority figures** who exist in both our waking land and our memories. **Parents and family members** tend to be the most persistent authority figures in dreams about success and recognition. It is up to you to work out how much their values and dreams guide and nourish you, and to what extent they keep you from the finishing line. How often does your **boss or a work colleague or an old teacher or friend from school** appear in your dreams? Chances are when they do, your dreams are about proving yourself, and either failing or succeeding?

Is your **partner** there cheering you on, or is he or she absent? Which **friends** are there to watch your moment of glory in your dreams? If it is someone who hasn't been in your life for years, what does he or she stand for? We all have authority figures in our dreams and in our lives. They are necessary because they each represent something important. They can guide us, warn us, and give us the feeling that we are supported. On the other hand, they can also undermine us, hold us back when we need to be moving forward, or drive us harder towards impossible to reach goals. *See also* ARCHETYPES.

your goals. That is, until you have the confidence in waking life to follow your dreams.

FAME

Dreams of **being famous or basking in the glory of fame** usually reflect a need to be recognized and respected by those around you, but they could also be messages from your unconscious to have more self-belief, and to recognize and give yourself credit for your own abilities. In waking life, you may be a little shy, but your dreams have shown you that within you is the ability to achieve great things, if you have the courage to stand out from the crowd. Alternatively, such dreams could warn people in high positions that it is impossible to be at the top for any length of time and when the moment comes he or she needs to accept that fact with love and understanding. The dream may also imply that the dreamer must remember what modesty is and what things were like before they acquired their present status. **Dreams of other people becoming famous** suggest that the dreamer may soon receive help from friends who will offer it unstintingly.

The Element Encyclopedia of 20,000 Dreams

RECOGNITION

We all need a pat on the back now and again for work well done. It's normal to want validation for your efforts. If you are having dreams where you are **hoping for and getting a gold star, or a grade A, an honor in front of your peers, recognition at work or reward from someone you want to impress,** such dreams are subconscious messages that you're feeling a bit underappreciated, neglected or unsure of how your efforts are being received. Sometimes this sort of dream can be a gentle reminder that a loved one has lost that loving feeling, and once we realize that, we can address the problem directly. If you **receive the recognition in your dream gracefully**, this suggests that you are ready to accept the positive aspects of yourself, but if you **feel uncomfortable or someone else steals the limelight**, then you need to work on your self-esteem.

TREASURE

Dreams of **finding treasure or valuable objects or ordinary objects with magical properties** have numerous variations, but the one constant theme is the discovery of something precious and magical. The psychological interpretation of such a dream urges you to seek out what is magical in your life, perhaps in the ordinary things you've been taking for granted.

TRIUMPH

Dreams are often the perfect forum for experimenting with courageous impulses. Triumphant or courageous dreams when you **succeed in a task, pass a difficult test or win when you thought you would lose** can bring a great sense of elation. If you have such a dream it could be because you undervalue your abilities. Is it a wish-fulfillment dream to compensate for failures and inhibitions in waking life? Or is it a motivating dream that encourages you to become more confident about succeeding in waking life by rehearsing your success in dreamland?

TRYING HARD

In dreams where you are **given a challenge or task and have to work on it for endless hours**, do you curse or do you give up? The **number of times you attempt to succeed** could suggest how important you feel the struggle is that it represents in waking life.

WEALTH

If you dreamed of **winning the lottery** or acquiring **money, jewels or other valuable assets**, such dreams are purely wish-fulfillment, especially if you are experiencing financial troubles. It could also suggest that you feel you deserve a pay rise. **Symbols of riches, such as precious jewels or cash** don't always represent money, however. For example, **gold** may not suggest the metal but a heart of gold and a **casket of treasure** could indicate the people in your life that you treasure. Free association could help you discover what such symbols really mean to you. Do you really believe that money can buy happiness? Thinking about such questions can help you decipher the secret message your unconscious is sending you, and cast a new light on what really matters to you. *See also* SHOPPING AND MONEY.

Personal Achievements A to Z

Symbols of personal recognition – such as **being awarded the highest honor**, or **stepping on stage to rapturous applause** – feature in dreams as reflections of your aspirations. The images you see within your dream reflect your ambitions and the ways in which you hope to reach your goals. Depending upon the details, feelings and other images conjured up, your dreams may be urging you to raise your ambitions, or telling you that your goals are unrealistic.

ADVERTISEMENTS

The purpose of **advertisements** is to sell something, and a dream in which you **see an advertisement or create one** may be reminding you about some ambition or target. What the advertisement was displaying is important. If it was clear and convincing, you are keeping your focus in waking life, but if it was confusing, you have not kept your ambitions clear. *See also* LEISURE AND ENTERTAINMENT.

ANGLING

If you dream of **fishing or angling**, what are you fishing or angling for in waking life? Is the dream telling you to take extreme care and to have plenty of patience if you are to achieve your ambition.

AUCTION

If an **auction** figures in your dreams, what was the identity of the object you, or others, were bidding for? Was it a position at work? Was it for a lifestyle change? Was your bid too low or too high, or did you pay more than the object was worth? If so, should you re-evaluate your ambitions in waking life?

BRIDGE

Crossing a bridge indicates an ability to move forward and achieve the success you long for. It is a dream action which represents your underlying strength to cope with life's journey, especially in the face of difficult challenges, such as divorce, redundancy or moving home.

DECORATION/MEDAL

To be decorated or to see others decorated for some heroic action suggests that you, or someone else, deserves recognition for some action but has not received it in waking life.

FAWN

To dream that **people fawn on you**, or satisfy your every whim, could suggest your desire for more attention in waking life, but it could also be a warning against enemies in the guise of interested friends. Dreams of **people imitating you** could have a similar interpretation.

FLYING BIRD

This represents aspirations, desires and the feeling that your spirit is soaring. Its association with the element of air – itself associated with aspirations and ideals – means a **flying bird** might have also become a symbol of high-flying ambition and the quest for enlightenment. *See also* BIRDS.

GIFTS

Could the **gift** represent a creative talent or skill you aren't expressing in waking life? If you were given a **gift of an expensive box of oil paints**, for example, could this be encouraging you to make use of your artistic talent?

All wrapped up

Giving and receiving gifts in dreams indicates a need to give and take within a relationship, perhaps to share with others what we have and to create an environment that allows for give and take. Sharing is a fundamental human need, so if you are giving in a dream, this suggests your internal relationship with yourself, the environment or others. **Giving a present** usually suggests a need to express love or consideration for another person, whereas **receiving it** suggests your need for the love and consideration of another person. **Receiving a shower of gifts** suggests that you are held in high esteem.

A dream of **unexpected gifts** can have several meanings. The gift can point to the need for you to recognize your own worth. If you are the giver, the dream may be warning you to be more open and direct with other people, so that you are not caught off guard. An **inappropriate gift** of something you do not like, or have no use for, may indicate that someone's attentions in waking life are not welcome. If you receive an **unpleasant gift in a beautiful gift box**, this image may reveal your intuition that someone's apparently good intentions may disguise selfish motives. Finally, the image of an **empty gift box** may suggest that in waking life, things are not as attractive as they seem. Perhaps you have to face the reality of a relationship ending, or need to lower your expectations in some way.

A **gift of chocolates** may hark back to your childhood and infantile oral pleasures. According to Freudian theory, chocolates are a dream image of excrement, representing an anal fixation that may indicate a tendency to be overly formal or uptight. Beware of overanalysing here though, since dreams about chocolate sometime suggest a longing for love, affection and … chocolate.

The highest honor

If you are bestowed with the **highest honor** in your dream, such as the Nobel peace prize or a bravery award, this could suggest a desire for your qualities and actions to be recognized by the appropriate person or authority in waking life. Dreaming of **winning a particular prize**, such as the Booker prize for literature, could be encouraging you to develop your interest in writing and those ideas for a novel that you have never put down on paper. Perhaps you have an unknown potential to be a best-selling author and your unconscious mind is urging you to have a go. The same applies to dreams when you create a **beautiful painting or sculpture**. Your unconscious is indicating that you should explore your artistic potential.

Receiving a diploma

If you dream of **stepping onto stage to receive a degree, diploma or award**, this is pure wish-fulfillment. In your dreams, you have the recognition, the qualification, the status, the applause and the sense of achievement you long for in waking life. Although this kind of dream does not predict that your wish will be fulfilled in waking life, it is an indication that you feel you deserve the recognition. Self-belief is a powerful tool in waking life and a key ingredient for success.

Sky

A dream of **observing the night sky** may be a hint that you intend to reach as high as you can in your particular field.

Sporting prowess

If you are an athlete and dreamed that you **scored the winning goal, a perfect 10 or hit a vital home run** in a professional game, such dreams are pure wish-fulfillment. If, however, you have little or no sporting ability, it is likely that your unconscious mind is rewarding you for something you have done in waking life for which you haven't been recognized. For example, your son or daughter may have recently gained entry to university and your dream is congratulating you on the part you played in helping them achieve their success. *See also* LEISURE AND ENTERTAINMENT.

Star/Planet

A dream of **one bright star and your desire to capture it** may refer to someone you desire to capture in waking life. A dream of **mapping the sky or stars** could refer to a number of ambitions you have in waking life – from which you should probably choose one. Dreams of **specific planets** may also be significant. *See also* SPACE AND SCIENCE.

Trophies, medals and other prizes

These are all symbols of success and achievement, and if you dream of **receiving trophies and other prizes**, the chances are you are yearning to be recognized and praised for your efforts in waking life. Again the type of prize will give you an idea of the area of endeavor in which you feel you should be rewarded. For example, to be **honored with the Nobel peace prize** could refer to your peace-making skills

Crowns and Tiaras

Badge

Badges in dreams draw your attention to your right to be part of a team or group of people. It could also mean that you are being singled out for special recognition. The spiritual interpretation is that you need to be accepted, not just as yourself, but as part of a greater whole.

Coat of arms

To see a coat of arms in your dream represents your familial roots and identity.

Crowns

To dream of a **crown** is to acknowledge your own success and to recognize your ability to forge ahead in life. You may also be about to receive some sort of honor or award. If you dreamt that a **crown or laurel wreath was placed on your head** or a **garland of flowers was placed around your neck**, this could suggest that you crave to be acknowledged as head and shoulders above the rest in your waking life. As well as wish-fulfillment, such dreams can also be literal. Perhaps you have recently been promoted at work or been given new authority over a number of people.

Cup

Receiving a cup is less about wish-fulfillment than about the symbolism of the chalice, indicating a receptive state that encourages intuitive development and a go-with-the-flow approach to life.

It may be encouraging you to be more open to the feminine side of your nature, and to give and receive in equal measure. A common dream among men is the **presentation of the football cup**, suggesting they feel as if they should be declared the 'first among men'.

Diadem/Tiara

The **diadem or tiara** in a dream suggests mental or intellectual abilities that are not being acknowledged in waking life. It could also signify a desire for the magical and unknown.

Flowers

If you were **presented with a bouquet of flowers** in your dream, you need to notice who or what gave you the flowers, what kind of flowers they were, and what color they were, as all these messages are significant. The giver may be someone who you already know who holds you in high regard, but if it is someone you don't know so well, your unconscious may be alerting you to their secret admiration. It is also possible that your unconscious is compensating for lack of recognition from other people and expressing your desire for them to be more demonstrative. If the **flowers are dying or have wilted** this could suggest that the giver's admiration is wilting, or that your expectations are disappointed. If the **dreamer discards the flowers** this signifies bad relations between the dreamer and someone close to him or her, or the people around him or her, both at work and in the family.

Medal

A **medal** is a reward for bravery or good work, so when it appears in a dream it is recognition of your own abilities and achievements in life. If you **give the medal to someone else**, then you are honoring a part of yourself represented by that person.

Prizes

Dreams of prizes can denote a feeling of well-being, but they can also indicate financial worries. **Gaining a prize** can also be associated with winning a loved one's sexual favors, especially if the **prize is accompanied by a bunch of flowers**. Prizes can also warn against unwarranted expectations. Jung cites as a universal dream type the Greek myth of Bellerophon, who received the winged horse Pegasus from the goddess Athene, and then presumptuously tried to fly to the heavens – the god Zeus sent a gadfly to sting the horse, and Bellerophon fell crashing to earth.

Shield

A **shield** is a symbol of preservation and protection. It can appear in dreams as a symbol of protection, or as a barrier between you and the rest of the world. Are you erecting the shield, or is it being erected by someone else?

Trophy

Recognition in your dreams that you have done something you should be proud of and have overcome your fears.

when a feud was about to erupt at work, but no one thanked you for your efforts.

WINNING

If you dream of **winning**, whether it is a prize, competition or contest, this illustrates your feelings of confidence. It may be a reassurance from your subconscious that you have what it takes to be a success in waking life. On the other hand, dream oracles suggest that this kind of dream can sometimes mean the opposite. If you **dream of winning a lottery ticket**, this indicates a new-found sense of optimism in your waking life. If you **see numbers on a lottery ticket**, consider buying a lottery ticket and use the numbers you saw in the dream. **Losing or drawing the lottery** in the dream, is a warning that you might be surrounded by false friends or that your hopes are unrealistic. *See also* NUMBERS.

The Element Encyclopedia of 20,000 Dreams

ANIMALS

Animals in dreams represent primitive drives and desires, such as fear, lust and anger that can only be really understood on an instinctual level.

Thus, to dream of a certain animal could suggest an aspect of your personality that is instinctual, hidden or striving for recognition. It could also represent a part of yourself you find hard to control. And because we often assign characteristics or personality traits to animals, dream animals may also symbolize gut feelings we have about others. An attacking lion, for example, may depict how we see someone who is being aggressive toward us.

Animal dreams rouse special interest because they contain images that are familiar to us, but at the same time we recognize something that is unfamiliar and obscure. Traditionally, the characteristics of the dream animal are applied to the world of humans, often seeing the animal as a harbinger of misfortune or good luck; for example, a wolf is often thought to predict thieves or misfortune. According to Freud animals in dreams are not predictive of future events but a classic expression of repressed or unexpressed sexual and aggressive tendencies. Jung, however, argued that animals in dreams should be

analyzed individually, depending on the character they portray in the dream and the association the dreamer has to them.

Jung believed that animals are sublime and, in fact, represent the 'divine' side of the human psyche. He suggested that animals live much more in contact with a 'secret' order in nature itself and – far more than human beings – live in close contact with 'absolute knowledge' of the unconscious. In contrast to humankind, the animal is the living being that follows its own inner laws beyond good and evil – and is, in this sense, superior and a source of inspiration and guidance.

Although animals are one of the most common dream symbols, dreams that feature them can be complex and hard to interpret. Perhaps the simplest way is to first think about how you feel about the specific animal in your waking life. You may, for example, adore cats and think of them as lovely creatures because you have a much-loved pet cat, or you may associate cats with feeling unwell because you are allergic to them. Thinking about how that animal makes you feel within the context of your dream should help you recognize if that feeling is struggling to the fore, or is already expressing itself in daily life.

If, on the other hand, you have no feelings in particular about the animal in your dream, you need to think about the quality you typically associate with it; for example, a fox with cunning and stealth, an elephant with strength and mystery, or a dog with unconditional loyalty and love. Because animals are thought to represent unedited feelings and drives, it's possible that your unconscious used the symbol of the fox in your dream to alert you to your own or someone else's cunning. Thinking about that aspect of yourself – again within the context of your dream – should tell you whether you need to nurture and develop it, tame it or be on your guard against it in someone else.

If you still feel puzzled, it may be that the hidden meaning lies in archetypal, traditional, legendary, mythical or magical associations. Dream animals may also embody a pun. For example, if you dream of a badger, are you feeling badgered or aggravated in some way? If you dream of a zebra, could this refer to your black and white view point?

Dream animals, no matter how problematic, offer us an opportunity to contact and explore both the parts of ourselves that we have shut away and the parts that we have yet to discover. In general, researchers believe that animal dreams mean that the subconscious has woken up and has come to life.

Our dreams will be selective and personal in the choice of animal used to portray our life situation, but as you interpret never forget that animal symbols in dreams typically represent a fundamental push toward life and living it with passion. *See also* BIRDS; REPTILES, FISH AND AMPHIBIANS; PETS.

Animal Situations

AGRICULTURAL ANIMALS

Neither pets nor wild creatures, **agricultural animals** often represent personal traits that you may have tamed to a certain extent, although there is always the risk that they will escape conscious control and run wild. It's important to reflect on the context of the dream involving a working or farmyard animal as it may reflect how you feel about the burdens and responsibilities of your daily life

ANIMALS IN PAIN

To dream that you are **rescuing, caring for or saving the life of an animal**, suggests that you are successfully acknowledging certain emotions and characteristics represented by the animal. A **wounded animal** can mean a pain you need to come to terms with that has caused an instinctive reaction, such as reactive anger or terrible fear. To find yourself in the **waiting room of an animal hospital** suggests a desire to avoid a responsibility or commitment you have in your waking life. To see **lab animals** in your dream, suggests that an aspect of yourself is being repressed. Alternatively, it suggests that you need to experiment with your fears, choices, and beliefs. Try not to limit yourself.

ANIMALS IN WATER

Dreams about **animals in water** are symbols of our emotions. Water is a symbol of emotion because water, like emotion, constantly moves and flows. How the animal moves within the water reveals our emotional mood. For instance if the water is calm and beautiful then it shows our emotions are good.

ANIMALS WITH THEIR YOUNG OR BABY ANIMALS

Maternal and paternal instinct; your basic childhood need for love and protection or your own experience of being parented. A **baby animal** can refer to yourself when young and vulnerable; feelings or memories concerning your childhood; desire for babies; vulnerability; fundamental survival instincts such as crying out for protection and comfort and the need for dependence and bonding. If the **young animal is injured or dying**, this could suggest problems with maturing or dealing with adult life.

CAUGHT OR CAGED ANIMALS

To see **wild animals caged** suggests that you are in control of your instincts. If you are in the cage with them, it could suggest a need to break free from constraints. If you dream of **an animal tangled in barbed wire or in a trap**, this could suggest an unhappy relationship with yourself or someone else. If the **animal seems calm**, it suggests inner strength during adversity but if the **animal panics**, unhappy memories or unhealthy habits are limiting your potential for development and growth.

CHANGING INTO AN ANIMAL

Also known as zoomorphism, to dream that you are **changing into the form of an animal** indicates that you are becoming less civilized and restrained, and becoming more free and instinctive. You may be expressing your new-found freedom and independence. Alternatively, taking the form of an animal can also suggest repressed urges that need to be understood and managed. Consider also the qualities of the animal that you turn into and what happens to you in the dream. According to Jung the end of the dream is particularly significant. Favorable resolutions direct us to the most constructive ways of solving problems, whilst unfavorable dream resolutions contain a warning of negative changes. Dreaming of **animal skin** could mean you may have found or need to acquire the traits, power and wisdom of the animal concerned.

DOMESTIC ANIMALS

Domestic animals symbolize fundamental urges and drives in ourselves which we have learnt to meet and direct with reasonable success. They still have to be cared for though or they may rebel against what we ask of them. **Buying and selling an animal** may indicate the need for the dreamer to be aware of possible tensions with the people close to him. If the dreamer is selling an animal, this could indicate delays and frustrations; the need for inner calmness to help the dreamer through until he or sees the light at the end of the tunnel. *See also* PETS.

KILLING OR EATING AN ANIMAL

Attempting to **kill the animal** within (our lower brain functions) can cause tension, depression and illness; giving in entirely is no answer either as our higher brain functions need expression also. One of the challenges of maturing and growing is to meet and relate to our 'animal instincts', and if possible find ways to express them positively. To dream of **eating an animal** suggests that you need to draw upon your own inner wisdom and energy, but it can also suggest a desire for sensual pleasure.

NEGLECT OF ANIMALS

A common dream symbol that typically represents neglect of some aspect of your inner nature. For example, you may have been **given an animal to look after**, usually somebody else's pet, while they were away on holiday and then completely forgot about the animal, only to discover it later starving, injured or even dead. This dream is reminding you that you have a responsibility to yourself and to see that your own sexual, nutritional and bodily needs are met.

PARTS OF ANIMALS

These have the same interpretation as parts of the human body (see BODY). If a **four-legged animal** has a leg or legs missing, it suggests a personality that is not fully rounded. If you dream of a **tail**, this could signify a need for balance and adjustment in tough circumstances. It can also indicate sexual arousal or the penis. If **claws** figure prominently in the dream, this could suggest spitefulness; desire to hurt; hidden aggression; clinging, or 'getting one's claws in someone'.

WATCHED, ATTACKED OR CHASED BY AN ANIMAL

Hiding from or being trapped by animals can suggest you are feeling controlled or threatened by your urges or the emotions or feelings of others. If the **animal is watching you**, your unconscious is reminding you not to forget or neglect the instincts that it represents. If the **animal is attacking you**, this could indicate that you are in the grip of a rage that you fear you may unleash. Your dream is urging you express or deal with your anger in a controlled way. If an **animal is chasing you** in a dream, this may suggest that in real life you are in flight from some area of your personality that wants to be expressed. If you are **trying to find refuge from animals** – either by building a defense or running away – this indicates a struggle with instincts that threaten your safety in waking life. In some cases dreams of **being threatened or attacked by animals** may be telling you that you are repressing your instincts – perhaps being too civilized – and you should try and loosen up more. Being **bitten by an animal** could indicate aggression from someone close to you or that our own aggressive instincts are not under control. Any threat from a **sinister animal** suggests fears and doubts you may have about your ability to manage your emotions. *See also* SURREALISM AND FANTASY.

The Element Encyclopedia of 20,000 Dreams

Animal noises

If you hear **animals making sounds** in your dream, you need to consider what these sounds mean to you in waking life and then to make a symbolic link. For example, if you hear an **animal barking, wailing or whining for attention**, these sounds could be calling your attention to the qualities that that particular animal represents to you. If you hear **ominous growling, roaring or cackling**, it could reflect pent-up anger either within yourself or another person. If you hear **braying**, it could indicate a need to overcome basic animal instincts. If you hear **bleating**, you may be taking on new cares and responsibilities that could be positive or negative depending on your attitude towards them. *See also* SENSES.

WILD ANIMAL

The symbol of a deep-rooted instinct or the beast within you. Freud suggested that dreams of **wild animals** represented our most sensual passions, and sometimes the 'evil instincts' that lie deep within our unconscious. The more wild and dangerous the beast, the greater the danger that suppressed aspect of yourself will break free from the control of your conscious mind and force you to confront and deal with it in waking life. If you dream of a **herd of wild animals**, this could suggest you are meeting, or need to meet, aspects of yourself you have not yet learnt to direct or usefully integrate. **Taming or harnessing a wild animal** indicates a need to control your instincts and if possible make them productive and useful.

Do animals dream?

It seems that they do, although we can't know for sure. All we can measure is whether or not they have REM (rapid eye movement) sleep, which is more or less associated with dreams. All mammals have REM sleep, and that increases the likelihood that they do dream.

Because REM sleep is recognizable in mammals and birds, but not in snakes and other reptiles, scientists think that most warm-blooded animals dream. Studies have monitored the sleep of goats, sheep, cats, dogs, rats, mice, monkeys and apes, and all had dream periods and symptoms; all except the spiny anteater, which seems to be a dream-free mammal.

Watch a sleeping dog or cat sometime, and you can tell if it is dreaming of running after something. Its eyes twitch, sometimes it moves its paws – something could be happening in its dreams.

Wise or talking animals

To dream of **wise animals** suggests important information from your intuition or inner wisdom. This intuitive wisdom is within every one of us and the result of thousands of years of life experience. Many cultures all over the world represent great wisdom and holiness as animals or animal-headed beings. To dream that **animals can talk** represents a wisdom inside yourself that is innocent and simple. It could also represent your potential to be all that you can be.

Animals A to Z

More than anything else, dream animals represent powerful instinctive reactions to situations, for example, fight or flight, the urge to find a mate and protect our young, the desire to have standing and recognition within a group, and so on. When instincts need to be understood, expressed or controlled in some way animals can often appear in our dreams to symbolize them. By understanding animals in dreams and the qualities they represent, we can approach life in a more instinctive, simple and natural way.

Bear in mind though that there is a huge difference in meaning between wild animals and domesticated animals in dreams. In general, domesticated animals or pets, such as a dog or rabbit, represent those urges we have more control over and are therefore less threatening to our conscious desire to be in charge. The wild animals we dream of are more threatening to our ego, but they are also more powerful, because if we can develop a working relationship with them they offer incredible potential for growth.

Ape/Monkey

To dream of **apes, monkeys, gorillas or baboons** suggests a link with the impulsive, imprudent, inquisitive side of ourselves, such as the self-centred grabbing of food, or sexual gratification without concern for the needs of the other person. It can also suggest the ability to mimic or copy, as well the childish, foolish and infantile side of the dreamer's character that delights in mischief-making.

On the other hand, to dream of apes or monkeys, especially if they are **white haired**, can link in with the dreamer's own unconscious wisdom: the wonderful experience of existing, of being alive with all the powers of a living creature such as strength, passion, awe and wonder in meeting life and the stars. Does your dream monkey reveal a wider side of you? The three mystic monkeys cover their eyes, ears and mouth showing that they 'see no evil, hear no evil, and speak no evil'. Do you need to keep your own counsel?

■ *Idioms: make a monkey of; monkey business; monkey with; monkey tricks; monkey's uncle; monkey on your back.*

Badger

Define what you associate with the **badger**. For most of us, the play on words will feature strongly as a dream about badgers can often refer to badgering people, or feeling badgered and needing to get away from the influence of other people.

BAT

Bats can see in the dark suggesting thoughts or influences that emerge from our intuition or inner wisdom.

BEAR

Often represents the mother figure in dreams and depending on the dream, this image can be caring or uncaring, or possessive and all devouring. If the **bear is recognized as male**, then it could refer to an overbearing person, or perhaps the father figure in a person's life.

The bear is largely a solitary animal that prefers to live and survive alone. This, and its human way of standing, may be major reasons for bears appearing in dreams. We can therefore link the bear with feelings about living alone or surviving by one's own strength. Because of the bear's ability to hibernate, it can also represent our ability to recreate ourselves after a period of rest and reflection.

Bears in dreams may also link to feelings we have about becoming independent, or meeting strength and independence in someone else, or even wild rage as 'the bear with a sore head'. If the latter is the case, it could suggest your relationship with someone who is touchy or grouchy or powerfully possessive in a smothering relationship. It could also indicate the danger of sudden unpredictable reactions.

■ *Idioms: look out also for possible plays on words, such as bare facts; bearing with something or someone; bearing ones soul; bearing in mind; a bearer of tidings; come to bear; overbearing; getting one's bearings; bear fruit; bear-hug. If there is a hint of money in the dream, this might refer to a 'bear market'. Does your dream bear mean that you need to take on the power of the bear? Can you 'bear' up – keep your spirits raised – or do you need to enlist help to do so?*

BEAST

Many dreams feature **beasts or animals that are of no particular characteristic or type**. In some cases the **beast is terrifying** and we awake with a feeling of dread. Such creatures are usually an expression of memories, or instincts and drives, which have been repressed or avoided in our waking lives for one reason or another. *See also* SURREALISM AND FANTASY.

BEAVER

Beavers are typically associated with industriousness and independence, although the word does also have sexual connotations with the female sexual organs. If a dam is being built, this could suggest holding back feelings or the need to conserve energy. In Native American tradition the beaver is considered holy and **if a beaver should speak to you** in a dream, this may be an expression of your inner wisdom trying to make itself heard.

BOAR

Boars are symbols of the magical spirits that protect the woods. If they appear in dreams, they can suggest protection from danger and hardship in waking life.

BULL

When **bulls** appear in dreams they might refer to powerful instinctual responses that can sweep us along or cause problems if we try to deny them. Such instinctual urges may be to do with lust and desire, anger at people invading our space, paternal or maternal love and protectiveness, or simply an aggressive bullish trait within ourselves or someone else. It can also suggest personal traits to do with being earthy, basic or sexual in our approach as well as strength, obstinacy and power. If the **bull is aggressive**, this shows the frustration that can arise from basic drives being thwarted. For example, a person may have a high libido and feel frustrated with a partner who does not care for sex as much. If the **bull is wounded or killed**, this suggests a killing of natural urges or drives for sex and procreation. If the **bull is sacrificed**, this can suggest generosity and self giving. The **ridden bull** indicates harmony between instinct and decision making.

In many cultures or myths around the bull there is the theme of the Hero confronting and overcoming the bull; for instance Theseus and the Minotaur. **Victory over the bull** therefore represents the human struggle and victory over instinctual or reactive forces influencing consciousness. From this victory a new life or consciousness can be born.

■ *Idioms: like a bull in a china shop; red flag to a bull; take the bull by the horns; bull at the gate; scoring a bull's eye. For example, if your dream is of someone acting like a bull in a china shop, knocking everything over, it could be a warning to slow down and take more care. If you dream of hitting the bull's eye, it means you stand every chance of achieving your goals. If you are a bully in your dreams, perhaps you are trying to impose your will on others. If you are being bullied, you need to stand up to someone.*

CAMEL

Suggests the dreamer's ability, or the ability of someone the dreamer knows, to face adversity – especially over the dry and barren aspects of life. It may also link with inner strength, endurance, patience and plodding perseverance. Occasionally the **camel's hump** may suggest pregnancy or the desire for children.

CAT

Jung saw **cats** in dreams as representing the hidden or secretive side of a person's nature. Cats often feature in dreams of women to represent the urge to care for someone or in some cases a desire for sex and the need to reproduce. In men's dreams, a **cat or group of cats** may refer to a woman or group of women, or to the intuitive side of men's nature, perhaps warning him of hidden dangers; cattiness, jealousy in a relationship. On the other hand it can also suggest independence, stealth and fertility. An **alley cat** indicates promiscuity. In some dreams, a **black cat**, depending on

The Element Encyclopedia of 20,000 Dreams

Big cats

Stealth, ferocity, power, strength, cunning and the will to survive are suggested by wild cats in dreams.

Jaguar

Assertiveness and fierce anger.

Leopard

The **leopard's spots** – which can be seen as eyes – represent watchfulness or the need for it. As with all the big cats, leopards in dreams suggest anger, speed, courage, passion and, in some cases, cruelty.

Lion/Lioness

Generally a positive symbol that suggests physical strength and success in waking life. It can also suggest self-assertion or the need for it to be expressed in waking life because of the **lion's roar**. If, however, the **lion is small or injured or in a vulnerable situation,** this could suggest that the dreamer feels he or she is in a dangerous place, but also that these difficulties can be overcome with strength and daring. If a **lion is chasing you**, this is most likely due to a struggle with natural feelings of anger or aggression.

■ *Idioms: lion's den; lion's share; head in the lion's mouth*

Lynx

Shares the same qualities as all the big cats, with an emphasis on the vigilance and the keenness of the lynx.

Panther

A Christian symbol, representing power to protect against evil. It also suggests anger and fierceness.

Tiger

Similar to the lion in many ways but with the emphasis on uncertainty and unpredictability. For example, tigers in dreams may suggest the possibility of plans changing unexpectedly. It can also warn against trusting a new acquaintance. The tiger can also represent sexuality but, depending upon how it is presented in the dream, a sexuality of uncertain elements – for example, will I be attacked or ignored.

■ *Idioms: fight like a tiger; paper tiger.*

what the dreamer associates with it, may indicate good or bad luck or fear in general. If the dream suggests cats are to be feared, this can indicate fear of the female in oneself, fear of females or a particular 'catty' female, or difficulty in meeting feelings and intuition. If you are allergic to cats and dream of one, it might signify a negative and threatening reaction to a situation or relationship. If **cats speak in your dreams**, this suggests sexuality, femininity and an ability to express it.

▪ *Idioms: copycat; bell the cat; cat and mouse; cat's whiskers; cat out of the bag; cat and dog life; cat on hot bricks; something the cat brought in; a cat's paw; cat amongst the pigeons; while the cat's away.* See also PETS.

CATERPILLAR

Often this represents male sexuality, or sexual intercourse, but it can also suggest untrustworthy acquaintances. If **moving to chrysalis stage**, this suggests you may be moving towards making very profound life changes. If **already a chrysalis**, a new aspect of yourself is forming and is ready to emerge. **Caterpillars** may also indicate a desire to withdraw from social activity.

CHAMELEON

The dreamer is recognizing in themselves the ability to change and adapt to circumstances.

COLD-BLOODED ANIMALS OR REPTILES

The unfeeling, cold, almost inhuman element in some human instincts is often suggested by **cold-blooded animals or reptiles**. *See also* REPTILES, FISH AND AMPHIBIANS.

COMPOSITE OR DEFORMED ANIMALS

To dream of **animals mixed up with each other**, for example, half animal-half man, could suggest confusion in finding the best approach to a situation in waking life. Perhaps the qualities of the animals in the dream need to be assimilated and integrated? The dream could also suggest that the dreamer is recognizing his or her potential for development.

COW

Similar to the bull in many ways but suggesting the female aspect of a person's nature, in particular a willingness to put the needs of others before one's own. **Cows** can symbolize motherliness, receptiveness, nurturing and the feminine energy that can lead or direct the masculine energy in oneself. They may also indicate being taken advantage of by someone in some way.

DEER/REINDEER/ANTELOPE

The gentle side of oneself that can be hurt or wounded easily by cynicism and aggression or criticism. Generally, a **deer** symbolizes vulnerability and, in some cases, lovesickness. In a man's dream, the deer may depict a young woman the man is in pursuit of. If the dreamer is **pursuing a deer**, this indicates success in overcoming fears. If the dreamer sees himself **killing a deer**, this is a warning dream to indicate the possibility of someone hurting them in waking life through no fault of their own. To dream of a **stag** suggests male sexual drive and virility, courage, and both life and healing energies. The stag may also represent a man or father figure that the dreamer admires in some way and the dream expresses the dreamer's desire to become more like the admired person. Finally, a **deer or reindeer herd** have a strict hierarchical structure and the dream could suggest that the dreamer needs to recognize his or her own place in the world. Is it time for you to branch out from this place in the world and make new connections? Are you in the process of renewal or do you need to be?

Dinosaur

The **dinosaur** indicates the most primitive, unsocialized, basic urges of human nature such as fear, reproduction, and survival. Such instincts are still alive within us and need to be integrated otherwise they remain in a primitive form, perhaps in conflict with our personality. To dream of dinosaurs could also indicate some aspect of our personality or approach to life that is outdated and no longer needed for survival.

Dog

The **dog** depicts natural urges that are well integrated, but still have the tendency to revert back to the spontaneous or 'wild' state quite easily. For instance, our anger might usually be well under control but, if

someone teases us, we might unexpectedly erupt with uncontrollable anger. Like the cat, the dog can also represent affection or caring. A **black dog** suggests depression or fear of death.

- *Idioms: die like a dog; dirty dog; dog eared; dog eat dog; dog in the manger; gay dog; go to the dogs; let sleeping dogs lie.* See also PETS.

Dolphin

Sea-dwelling mammals much loved by man. However, despite their fondness for human companionship and joyous sense of fun, **dolphins** in dreams can foretell anxious times ahead; this is especially the case if a dolphin is seen leaping out of the water. *See also* REPTILES, FISH AND AMPHIBIANS.

Donkey/Ass

In the Bible, the **ass** carries Christ and is often thought to represent humbleness and humility but it can suggest the stubbornness arising perhaps out of long-entrenched habits and automatic behavior. Generally the **donkey** represents the plodding, long-suffering body and its basic needs, and a dream in which the dreamer is riding on a donkey hints at progress, even if it is slow. Do you feel impatient with your progress or overburdened? Are you refusing to give way on an important issue? Don't forget about Eeyore, of Winnie the Pooh fame. Eeyore is a depressed and sluggish donkey. Are you feeling that way?

A dream that features a **donkey braying** implies that the dreamer is on a liberating journey from some kind of family or health trauma. A dream in which the **donkey is**

tied up attests to the dreamer's fierce will power that can 'move mountains' if directed towards a positive goal. If the **ass or donkey is being ridden by or pulling someone else**, you may be feeling you are doing all the hard work in a relationship, or working like a beast of burden.

ELEPHANT

To dream of an **elephant** is to recognize the qualities of patience, long memory, strength, wisdom and loyalty. It's a particularly good sign if you are riding it. If other people are **riding the elephant**, it could suggest help from a friend or a close strong friendship. To **feed an elephant** suggests meetings with people in key positions. If you run from a **herd of stampeding elephants**, this could suggest being afraid of your own strength or inner power. If a **rogue elephant stampedes**, it could represent a chaotic element in yourself that threatens to wreak havoc in the waking world if it isn't controlled. The question is, can we meet this enormous strength and energy in ourselves and learn to direct it positively? The **elephant's trunk** is sometimes said to be a sexual symbol indicating the ability to satisfy needs.

■ *Idioms: white elephant; pink elephants; rogue elephant; memory like an elephant. Is there a memory you are holding onto that you need to get rid of? Do you need elephantine strength for a task?*

ELK/MOOSE

Suggests the wild drives or emotions that can carry us along, or trample us.

FERRET/ERMINE

Suggestive of inquisitiveness – the ability to ferret or find out things – as well of selfish actions that can injure another person's feelings. (The **ermine** was traditionally linked with virgin saints and thus purity.)

FOX

A **fox** symbolizes shrewdness in dealing with life's challenges, but also a tricky person or relationship, or false or deceptive rumors. It also suggests unpredictable behavior and a refusal to conform. If the dreamer **chases a fox** in a dream, it suggests that he or she is too detached from reality and is in danger of floating in a sea of untruths. Do you need to be as 'wily as a fox' at present? Does your dream fox need protection from the hunt and if so, what can this be linked to in your daily life?

FROG

Symbolic of the deeply unconscious psychobiological processes which can transform us from a tadpole/sperm into an air-breathing **frog**. In dreams, frogs suggest an extra, deeper element to ourselves and if we can integrate it, our life will become richer. The frog has also been associated with the power of resurrection and renewal by meeting that which we find difficult or repulsive in life and ourselves. The **frog into the prince story** suggests this power to transform the dark, unformed side of oneself, the toad or beast, into something which is fully aware and radiant.

The Element Encyclopedia of 20,000 Dreams

Game animals

Game animals – notably the deer, rabbit and hare – offer encouragement, and dreamers should view their presence optimistically. The rabbit's renowned ability to breed offers the promise of fertility in women and virility in men. Hares are closely associated with the moon goddess and they suggest an ability to see the magical in everything. Deer are also viewed as animals of the spirit. Due to the branching nature of their antlers, stags have been linked with the 'tree of life', and are thought to impart intuitive wisdom to those who dream of them.

GOAT

Traditionally a symbol of virility, and so if a **goat** appears in a woman's dream, it can be linked to a lover she desires, or to fertility and procreative power. Similarly, if a goat appears in a man's dream, it attests to the amount of importance he ascribes to his virility and, in context with the rest of the dream, should be interpreted in this way. It can also suggest the ability to 'climb' and survive difficulties, personally or socially. Occasionally it is connected with natural drives which, if they become repressed, are associated with the devil. If the **goat is attacking**, this may indicate somebody butting into your life or some form of conflict.

■ *Idioms: separating the sheep from the goats; get my goat; an old goat (an aging man still lusting after women).*

HARE

In past cultures, the **hare** was often given great respect. It stood for intuition, rejuvenation and resurrection, and thus of the immortal nature of humans. Because of the **hare's habit of bounding up suddenly from hiding places**, to dream of a hare suggests sudden, powerful intuition. If the **hare appears as a supernatural figure giving advice or as a sacrificial animal**, it indicates the ability to draw on hidden potential and make great changes in life. On the other hand dreams about hares and rabbits can also symbolize timidity and inhibition as far as sex is concerned. Having said that, if the **hare is running or in flight** it could suggest that great changes are about to take place, and a positive change in status, environment and finance are on the cards. If a person dreams he is **eating a hare**, this can suggest that he or she is envious of someone's good fortune or that someone is envious of them.

There is a legend that a hare breeder has only to tell a hare to kill itself and it will do so, thus showing its capacity for self-sacrifice. Are you making sacrifices at the moment? Are you thinking clearly or doing yourself an injustice?

HEDGEHOG/PORCUPINE

If a **hedgehog or porcupine** appears in a dream, it might indicate that the dreamer, or someone they know, is very prickly, easily offended or irritated by the remarks or actions of other people. It might also represent a vulnerable part of oneself that is quick to withdraw, but can react by lashing out and hurting others.

HIPPOPOTAMUS

A dream about a **hippopotamus** suggests the dreamer is suffering from feelings of inferiority. He or she is not satisfied about him or herself, both physically and mentally. These feelings do not always have a basis in reality but represent how the dreamer views him or herself. The hippopotamus is considered to be clumsy, ungainly and overweight, and the dreamer may also feel this way about themselves. Whether true or not in waking life, this inner feeling of being a loser will hold the dreamer back and prevent him or her succeeding in life. The dream implies that the image the dreamer has of themselves is a figment of their imagination. If they could only shake it off and see themselves in a less critical light, they would feel much better about themselves and be able to attract success into their life. Dreams about hippos can also represent concerns about fertility and childbirth as the female hippopotamus represents the Egyptian Great Mother, Amenti, the goddess of childbirth.

HORSE

Studies show that the animals that most often appear in dreams are **horses,** along with cats and dogs, and women seem to dream of horses more often than men do; indeed, Artimedorus of Daldis (2nd century AD) lists horses amongst the most common dreams of women. Some dream interpreters suggest that horses represent male sexuality.

According to Freud, horses symbolize the sexual drive. Jung noted that horse dreams could often be indicative of health conditions. Horses, like dogs, represent urges and passions in ourselves that we have learned to harness or direct, and in general they represent positive things that are about to happen in a dreamer's waking life. Horses suggest the sort of enthusiasm or feelings of well-being that can carry us through the day and through life. Having said that much depends on the context of the dream; for instance, if the dreamer **falls off the horse**, this may suggest relating badly to urges and passions and the resulting tension this creates. If the **horse is wild**, this suggests undirected energy, such as sexual desires which override personal or interpersonal needs.

■ *Idioms: back the wrong horse; from the horse's mouth; don't look a gift horse in the mouth; horse sense; you can lead a horse to water; wild horses; workhorse; horsing about; getting on your high horse; eat like a horse; back the wrong horse; beating a dead horse. For 'equestrian issues' and dreams concerning working or domesticated horses,* see also *PETS.*

HYENA

The appearance of a **hyena** in a dream suggests taking advantage of someone, or being taken advantage of. A dream about an **attack by a hyena** may foretell an attempt to ruin the dreamer's reputation.

Jackal

Similar to 'dog', but a wilder version. The **jackal** is a cunning scavenger and as a result is sometimes associated with death. It can also see in the dark and the ancient Egyptians believed the jackal to be a pathfinder in the underworld – i.e. the unconscious – leading the dead to the other world or enlightenment. Be aware too of the 'Jackal and Hyde' phenomenon that exists inside all of us.

Kangaroo

A dream about a **hopping kangaroo** suggests a problematic relationship, or the potential for problems, if one person spends too much time with other people or refuses to commit. It could also indicate problems with concentration and focus in waking life.

Lamb

The childlike, vulnerable, dependent, innocent, pure part of a person that Christlike has the power to defeat evil. A dream about **slaughtering lambs** will suggest success at the expense of peace of mind. If **wolves or dogs are tearing lambs apart**, it means innocent people are suffering at the hands of unscrupulous others. A dream about **carrying lambs** means that the dreamer is carrying the burdens of the people he or she loves happily. If **lambskins** appear in a dream, this suggests that the dreamer or other people have been deprived of joy and comfort.

Mole

Associated with solitude, seclusion and the avoidance of human company, the **mole** can represent the attitude of a recluse. It might also indicate problems festering beneath the surface, as in molehills.

Mouse

Suggestive of the mousy, shy or timid part of the self, dreaming of **mice** could also suggest small but important developments or subtle changes that can gnaw away at our self-esteem. Dreaming that you are a mouse could mean you feel dull, undistinguished and lacking in confidence in waking life. The sexual organ which goes in and out of a hole is another association. If a person sees a **mousetrap or a mouse caught in a trap**, it could mean they need to watch out for people who gossip or take advantage of them.

Otter

Ancient cultures saw the otter as a pure, holy creature and to see an **otter** in a dream suggests an ability to adapt to circumstances without 'drowning' and to clearly see what is really going on under the surface of everyday life.

Ox

Very similar to 'bull', with the possible exception that **oxen** are often castrated, so dreams in which they feature could suggest frustration. Can you recognize the strength of the ox within yourself? Are you engaged in a task that demands great commitment?

Pig/Wild boar

Pigs are symbolic of a life governed by untamed physical needs and passions; they can also suggest impossible ventures, or inappropriate behavior and neglect of the spiritual side of life. By contrast, amongst the peoples of the East, a dream about a pig is interpreted as a good dream that attests to prosperity.

■ *Idioms: pig in a poke; happy as a pig in shit; make a pig of oneself; pig in the middle; pigs might fly; pig headed; piggy bank (is your dream linked to savings?).*

Rabbit

The **rabbit** breeds easily, so in dreams it is often linked to sexuality. It is also associated with the soft, vulnerable part of ourselves that can be easily hurt or hounded. If the dreamer is **hunting wild rabbits**, this could suggest that they are being criticized, attacked, 'hunted down' or hounded. *See also* PETS.

Ram

Representing masculine sexual energy, the **ram** can also indicate a refusal to conform or be part of a group, together with an unconscious desire to lead rather than follow.

■ *Idioms: battering ram; ramming one's point home; like a ram among sheep.*

Rat

The **rat** is a symbol of fears and anxieties, or is the diseased or devious part of a dreamer or his or her situation. It can also represent something which is repulsive in some way. The dreamer may be experiencing disloyalty from a friend or colleague. Other associations are of dirt and squalor, or of time gnawing away at our life and the unacceptable parts of oneself. By contrast, dreaming about a **pet rat** suggests the opposite: vulnerability and the responsibility for caring.

■ *Idioms: rat on someone; rat race; smell a rat; feeling ratty; cornered rat; rats leave a sinking ship.*

Seal

Dreaming of a **seal** suggests the dreamer is at one with the life they have chosen to lead. If the seal is wounded, injured or hunted, the opposite might be suggested.

Sheep/lamb

Sheep in dreams represent the aspects of oneself that conforms to social pressures, such as feeling part of a crowd or being herded by others. Dreaming of **sheep** can also suggest aspects of ourselves that are the same as other human beings or working hard to accomplish a goal. If the dreamer is **caring for sheep**, this may indicate a desire to grow spiritually.

■ *Idioms: make sheep's eye at someone; follow like a sheep; being sheepish.*

SNAKE

See REPTILES, FISH AND AMPHIBIANS.

SQUIRREL

The **squirrel** represents the hoarding aspect of the personality.

TOAD

To dream of a **toad** suggests that the dreamer needs to become aware, and come to terms with, what is ugly in life, or in his or her behavior. However, the ugliness does have within it the power of transformation and growth into something beautiful.

UNICORN

A symbol of purity and a return to innocence; can also suggest the control of the ego, and selfishness. *See also* SURREALISM AND FANTASY

VERMIN

Dreams involving any sort of **vermin** suggest that you need to contemplate, or take into consideration, something that is unwanted or that has invaded your space.

WEASEL

The **weasel** highlights the devious and more dubious side of our personalities.

WHALE

The **whale** is a mammal that lives beneath the waters and it suggests the power of rebirth, our ability to reinvent our approach to life, or circumstances in life which are holding us back. *See also* REPTILES, FISH AND AMPHIBIANS.

WOLF

Dreaming of a **wolf** suggests that the dreamer may be feeling threatened by other people, or may be vulnerable in some situation. The wolf, as suggested by fairy stories like Red Riding Hood, also represents the female fear of powerful male sexuality, and yet might also figure in female sexual fantasies. Wolves are also symbols of repressed sexuality and anger.

- *Idioms: wolf at the door; wolf in sheep's clothing; cry wolf; throw to the wolves; a wolf (a man who lusts after women and pursues them like a predator).*

ZEBRA

In dreams, the **zebra** has much the same significance as the 'horse', but with the additional meaning of balancing the black and white aspects of the personality into a powerful whole.

ARCHETYPES

'Collective unconscious' is the term Carl Jung used to describe the part of the unconscious that everyone has access to, a sort of psychic storehouse for all humankind.

The contents of this storehouse are called 'archetypes': patterns and symbols that can be found within the unconscious of everyone. These archetypes represent the broad human memory within each of us. They appear as mythical images that occur in every culture throughout recorded history – the images appearing in the dreams of our ancestors are those that speak to us today.

According to Jung, dreams are attempts to guide the waking self. He thought that the purpose of life – and for him, dreams play an important role in it – is to understand and integrate all parts of ourselves; dreams are simply one aspect of the self trying to communicate with the conscious part. Dreams don't disguise the unconscious, they reveal it, through archetypes.

Sigmund Freud disagreed with Jung, as he believed that dreams were disguised attempts to hide, not reveal, true feelings from the waking mind. Freud did, however, recognize a concept of 'archaic remnants', inherited – rather than learned – beliefs, through which basic emotions and responses are represented. For example,

the mother figure is a universal symbol of nurturing and protection.

Today, most dream researchers believe that we are more likely to see archetypal figures in our dreams at transition points in our lives than at other, more stable times. Change generally brings about anxiety and self-reflection. Going from education to the workforce, singlehood to marriage, or childless to parent are some typical archetypal transitions. Many of these archetypes are very familiar to us already, because they can be found in myths, legends, fairy tales, books and movies: the wicked stepmother, the authoritative father and the vulnerable maiden. We are as familiar with the superhero in films like *Spiderman* or *Batman*, as we are with the character of the dastardly joker or villain. All these characters are archetypes, and enduring representations of basic human qualities, instincts and experiences.

The first step in analysing an archetype, as with any symbol, is through personal reference. For example, a dream about monsters may refer to our inner fears, but it

Jungian constructs

The Persona

In your dreams are you wearing a **disguise or mask**? Are you a **regal persona** or did you become a **superhero**? Are you using **cosmetics or wearing a wig**? Are you **worried about your appearance** in some way? Are you **naked**? Are your **clothes torn and ragged**? If so, this kind of dream concerns your persona or personas, as we all have more than one.

The persona represents your public image, the part of yourself that is presented externally by what you say, wear and look like. The word is obviously related to the words 'person' and 'personality', and comes from the Latin word for mask. So the persona is the mask you put on before you show yourself to the outside world.

Your persona's wardrobe of masks comprises the various faces you use to present yourself to different audiences in waking life – for example, your family, friends, colleagues and strangers. We wear these masks to help us relate better to different groups of people, but these masks are not the real you. Depending on the context of your dream and how you felt, your unconscious may be warning you that one of your personas is in conflict with your true self, or that you need to adopt a different persona to achieve your goals.

The persona is rarely personified in a dream. It is usually a dream theme, rather than a dream figure: for example, the persona can be said to be present in a dream in which your **clothes are stained**, or you are **naked or inappropriately dressed**. At its best, the persona is just the 'good impression' you wish to present as you fill the roles society requires of you. But, of course, it can also be the 'false impression' you use to manipulate people's opinions and behaviors. And, at its worst, it can be mistaken, even by yourself, for your own true nature; sometimes we believe we really are what we pretend to be!

The Anima and the Animus

A part of our persona is the role of male or female we must play. For most people, that gender role is determined by their physical sex. But Jung, like Freud and Adler and others, felt that we are all really bisexual in nature. When we begin our lives in the womb, we have undifferentiated sex organs that only gradually become male or female, under the influence of hormones. Likewise, when we begin our social lives as infants, we are neither male nor female in the social sense until society molds us into men or women.

In all societies, the expectations placed on men and women differ, but in our society today, we have many remnants of traditional expectations. Women are still expected to be homemakers and nurturers; men are still expected to be strong breadwinners.

But Jung felt these expectations meant that we had developed only half of our potential.

The anima is the unconscious female aspect present in the collective unconscious of men, and the animus is the unconscious male aspect present in the collective unconscious of women. The function of the anima/animus is to help the dreamer establish a good working relationship with his or her male/female counterpart. This is an important step in the development of the personality.

The anima or animus is the archetype through which you communicate with the collective unconscious generally, and it is important to get into touch with it. It is also the archetype that some researchers believe guides our choice of partner. We are, as suggested by an ancient Greek myth popularized by Plato in the *Symposium*, always looking for our other half – the half that the Gods took from us – in members of the opposite sex. When we fall in love at first sight, then we have found someone that 'fills' our anima or animus archetype particularly well!

If someone of the opposite sex played a leading role in your dreams or aroused feelings of deep yearning, attraction and fascination, then your dreaming self has witnessed the appearance of the anima/animus, the opposite of your conscious personality. This is why if you are an indecisive, shy man your animus may take the form of a party-loving woman who is resolute – or if you are a cautious, rational female your anima may take the form of a spontaneous, passionate man. The anima/animus may be either positive or negative and both can be symbolized by people you know or don't know in waking life, as well as mythical, symbolic, and legendary characters, or by objects that somehow represent the masculine or feminine to you. Typically, the anima is personified as a single figure image; for example, a young girl, a witch, or an earth mother. It is likely to be associated with deep emotionality and the force of life itself. The animus may be a plurality of figures, for example a band of robbers or a council passing judgment, although it is also often personified as a wise old man. It is likely to be presented as logical, rationalistic, and judgmental.

By introducing the anima/animus, your unconscious is urging you to seek balance and compensate for those attitudes or behaviors that dominate your thinking and being in waking life. Heeding the promptings of your anima/animus can help you become a more content and rounded personality, and perhaps strengthen your relationships with the opposite sex

The self

The most important archetype of all is the self – the higher, more spiritual aspect of the personality. In dreams it can appear in many forms; most typically as a **child or baby**, suggesting vulnerability, freshness, spontaneity and potential. It can also be symbolized by the **circle, the cross, and the mandala figures** that Jung was fond of painting.

(See SYMBOLS.) To a woman, the self may also be presented as a **wise old woman, priestess, fairy godmother, biological mother, queen or princess**. To a man, the self may manifest as a **king, priest, wise old man, guru, prophet or philosopher**.

The shadow

Did you dream of someone, perhaps a **stranger, or someone you know who behaved in a repulsive, hateful or shocking way** and your instinctual response was one of loathing? If so, you may have encountered your shadow. In waking life, your consciousness represses your shadow, but in dreams it can come to the fore. A useful indicator of your shadow is the quality you despise most in other people, such as boastfulness or cowardice. When your shadow appears, it may be telling you to embrace that part of yourself you find hard to accept, so that you can enhance your creativity.

The shadow is the unacceptable or unknown aspect of ourselves. It derives from our pre-human, animal past, when our concerns were limited to survival and reproduction, and when we weren't self-conscious.

Symbols of the shadow include the **snake, the dragon, monsters, and demons**. It can appear in many different dream disguises: **a foreigner, gypsy, tramp, prostitute, murderer, thief, stranger, alcoholic, drug addict, rapist, burglar, crippled, deformed, blind, a servant or someone following you**. It often **guards the entrance to a cave or a pool of water**, which is the collective unconscious.

The shadow is not always represented as an enemy in dreams. It often contains values that are needed by consciousness and only becomes hostile when ignored or misunderstood. Although it suggests the 'dark side' of the ego, the shadow is actually amoral – neither good nor bad, just like animals. An animal is capable of tender care for its young and vicious killing for food, but it doesn't choose to do either. It just does what it does. It is 'innocent'. But from our human perspective, the animal world looks rather brutal, inhuman, so the shadow becomes the part of ourselves that we can't quite admit to.

may also be a carry-over from the horror film you watched the same night. The next step is to take into consideration the other images in the dream, as well as the feelings and general atmosphere.

When archetypes appear in your dreams you will rarely feel indifferent to them and your instinctive response is crucial to the interpretation. Do they make you feel angry, inspired, sad, protective, frustrated or liberated? Never forget that such images spring from the deepest levels of the unconscious, and it is up to you to discover why they have been conjured up.

Jung contributed to our understanding of dream archetypes with constructs of his own, which some dream researchers find helpful in interpreting dreams. Although Jung believed that there is no fixed number of archetypes which we can simply list and memorize, he did believe that most archetypes are aspects of the following constructs: the persona, the anima and the animus, the ego, and the shadow. As you interpret your dreams you might want to consider these constructs along with the other archetypal images suggested in the pages of this book.

Archetypes A to Z

The archetypes listed here are just a few of the many ancient patterns that exist in human consciousness and manifest as symbolic figures, played by yourself or someone else, in your dreams. See also SYMBOLS.

ADDICT

[DREAM IMAGES: CONSPICUOUS CONSUMER; GLUTTON; WORKAHOLIC ETC.]

Besides the usual suspects – drugs, alcohol, food and sex – one can be addicted to work, sports, television, exercise, computer games, spiritual practice, negative attitudes, thrill seeking and many other activities. When this archetype appears in dreams, it suggests the need to confront some kind of addiction and restore balance in your life. From a symbolic perspective, the shadow aspect of the **addict** represents a struggle with will power and the absence of self-control.

ADVOCATE

[DREAM IMAGES: ATTORNEY; DEFENDER; ENVIRONMENTALIST; LEGISLATOR; LOBBYIST ETC.]

The **advocate** embodies social justice and a sense of devotion to championing the rights of others in the public arena. The shadow advocate manifests in commitment to false or negative causes, or in committing to causes for personal gain. If this figure appears in your dreams, you should ask yourself how much of your life is dedicated to the welfare of others, and a willingness to take action on their behalf.

ALCHEMIST

[DREAM IMAGES: INVENTOR; MAGICIAN; SCIENTIST; WIZARD ETC.]

The **alchemist, wizard and magician** are capable of transforming the ordinary into the extraordinary. Whereas a wizard is associated with magical powers, the magician tends to be seen more as an entertainer.

The Element Encyclopedia of 20,000 Dreams

The alchemist tries to turn base metals into gold, but in its highest manifestation, alchemy seeks complete spiritual transformation. The **scientist and inventor** are associated with advances and developments in human history. The shadow sides of these archetypes are found in the misuse of the power and knowledge to transform people's lives. This archetype may appear in your dreams if your work or living situation demands that you be especially inventive. On the other hand, it could suggest that you, or someone you know, may be using skills and knowledge for unethical purposes.

ANDROGYNOUS BEING

[DREAM IMAGES: HALF MAN-HALF WOMAN; HERMAPHRODITE; TRANSVESTITE]

The symbol of a person who has attained the perfect balance of male and female characteristics, an **androgynous being** represents the union of opposites, an important idea in Jung's theory. In dreams, this archetype is not so much referring to your sexual nature, but more to the union of your inner and outer world. Your interpretation will depend on how this dream image made you feel; were you relaxed and natural, or did you feel repulsed or confused? The latter suggests disharmony, whilst the former suggests harmony.

ANGEL

[DREAM IMAGES: FAIRY GODMOTHER/GODFATHER]

Angels are typically represented as winged beings who intervene at times of great need, or for the purpose of delivering a message of guidance or instruction from God to human beings. Therefore in dreams, angels represent your higher self-image and offer guidance from within, but they can also represent an evil being of similar powers: the fallen angle who has been led astray, or is leading other people astray. Bear in mind, too, that the dream may refer to someone in your life who is an angel because of the loving and nurturing qualities of character that they embody. One may also play the role of a **fairy godmother or godfather** by helping someone.

ARTIST

[DREAM IMAGES: ARTISAN; CRAFTSPERSON; SCULPTOR; WEAVER ETC.]

In dreams, the **artist** archetype suggests the need for self-expression. The shadow artist indicates an eccentric nature and the madness that often accompanies genius. In evaluating your relationship to this archetype, recognize that the need to inspire others in some way – for example through teaching, writing, listening and encouraging – is as much an expression of the artist archetype as actually holding a brush in your hand. *See also* ARTS AND CRAFTS.

ATHLETE

[DREAM IMAGES: FITNESS INSTRUCTOR; OLYMPIAN; SPORTSPERSON ETC.]

This archetype represents the ultimate expression of the strength of the human spirit as represented in the power and magnificence of the human body. **Athlete** dreams should not be interpreted in terms of whether your body is perfect in form and function, but whether you have the willpower and strength of spirit to achieve your goals. The shadow aspect of athletes may manifest in dreams about **cheating**, suggesting a lack of honor in yourself or someone you know. *See also* LEISURE.

AVENGER

[DREAM IMAGES: AVENGING ANGEL; MESSIAH; SAVIOR]

This archetype suggests a need to balance the scales of justice in your waking life. Dreams about **bringing war criminals to trial, or legally pursuing corporations that harm society, or saving the world from impending disaster** are examples of the **avenger** archetype in action. The shadow side of the avenger manifests in dreams with acts of violence and a burning desire to get even at all costs as their themes.

BEGGAR

[DREAM IMAGES: HOMELESS PERSON; INDIGENT ETC.]

Homeless and penniless, the **beggar** is associated with dependence on the kindness of others, living on the streets, starvation and disease. It is easy to believe that when this archetype appears in your dreams, the interpretation should be a negative one, but this isn't always the case. People don't just beg for money; they can also beg for attention, love, authority, success and material objects. Learning about the nature of generosity, compassion and humility, and understanding what it is you really need, are fundamental to interpreting this dream image.

BULLY

[DREAM IMAGES: COWARD; DEMANDING BOSS/TEACHER; GANG OF INTIMIDATING THUGS; SCHOOL BULLY ETC.]

The archetype of the **bully** manifests the core truth that the spirit is always stronger than the body, and your relationship to this archetype should be evaluated within a framework far more expansive than evaluating whether you bully people or are being bullied. Consider whether in waking life you are giving up on things and people too easily. Conventional wisdom holds that underneath a bully is a coward trying to keep others from discovering his or her true identity. If the theme of **cowardice or intimidation by a boss, teacher or gang of thugs** appears in your dreams, perhaps your unconscious is urging you to stand up to being bullied by your own inner fears.

CHILD

[DREAM IMAGES: CHILD OF NATURE; DIVINE; MAGICAL/INNOCENT; ORPHAN; WOUNDED]

The **child of nature** archetype inspires deep, intimate bonding with natural forces. Although the nature child is loving and giving, it can also have an inner toughness and ability to survive – the resilience of Nature herself. Nature children can develop advanced skills of communicating with animals, and in dreams reflecting this archetype, an **animal often comes to the rescue of its child companion**. Such dreams can reflect a compassionate, nature-loving aspect of our character, or the need to stop abusing the environment (understood in its widest sense) and reconnect with nature.

The **magical child** embodies qualities of wisdom and courage in the face of

The Element Encyclopedia of 20,000 Dreams

difficult circumstances. In dreams, it suggests the power of imagination and the belief that everything is possible. If, however, the **magic is not put to positive use**, the dream image is a negative one, and indicates lack of energy and action in waking life.

The **orphan child** is the major character in most well-known children's stories, including 'Bambi', 'Cinderella', 'Hansel and Gretel', 'The Little Mermaid', 'Little Orphan Annie', 'The Matchstick Girl', 'Snow White' and many more. The pattern in these stories is often reflected in the dreams of people who feel from birth as if they are not a part of their family or community, or who fear surviving alone in this world.

The **wounded child** archetype in dreams holds the memories of the abuse, neglect and other traumas that may have been endured during childhood. From a spiritual perspective, a wounded childhood cracks open the learning path of forgiveness. The shadow aspect may manifest as an abiding sense of self-pity, a tendency to blame your parents for your current short-comings and to resist moving on through forgiveness.

Whilst dreams about **children that never grow old** reveal a determination to remain eternally young in body, mind, and spirit, they can also suggest an inability to grow up and embrace the responsible life of an adult. Peter Pan is the most obvious example of this archetype – he resists ending a cycle of life in which he is free to live outside the boundaries of conventional adulthood. For women, this archetype may manifest as extreme dependency on those who take charge of their physical security. A consistent inability to be relied on, and

the inability to accept the aging process, are also markers of this archetype.

Carl Jung claimed that the dream symbol of a child is a metaphor for the forgotten things in childhood. For example, your dream may be telling you that you have forgotten how to play, or that you should take a more innocent, carefree attitude. The symbol of the child also represents possibilities and paves the way for future changes in the personality. In addition, it can also represent the part of you that needs security and reassurance. *See also* BIRTH AND CHILDHOOD.

CLOWN

[DREAM IMAGES: COURT JESTER; FOOL; TRICKSTER]

If a **clown** appears in your dreams, ask yourself if you need to bring humor into a situation or carry truth into closed circles or closed minds. Did a **clown or trickster try to undermine you** in your dream? Did someone you know play a trick on you? Playing pranks is associated with the clown or trickster, who delights in challenging the status quo and rebelling. Although confusing, this attention-seeker is worthy of your attention, as it represents the part of yourself that wants to challenge you out of your complacency. If you listen to the message, the clown can transform your waking life into a more carefree, spontaneous and happy one.

DAMSEL

[DREAM IMAGES: PRINCESS; YOUNG GIRL ETC.]

The **damsel in distress** may be the oldest female archetype in all of popular literature and the movies. She is beautiful, vulnerable and in need of rescuing. If this image appears in your dreams, it may suggest your intense desire to be rescued or protected by a loved one; it may also suggest the need to go it alone. When disappointed, a damsel must go through a process of empowerment and learn to take care of herself in the world.

DESTROYER

[DREAM IMAGES: ATTILA; MAD SCIENTIST; SERIAL KILLER; SPOILER]

The impulse to destroy and rebuild is archetypal. We are bound to that cycle so that new life can begin. Dreams which have **destruction as a theme, or where you or someone else are destroying things or people** often refer to releasing emotions or behavior that are destroying us. It can also represent an aspect of yourself that destroys relationships or promotes attitudes and opinions that destroy others' dreams or potential.

DETECTIVE

[DREAM IMAGES: DOUBLE AGENT; PRIVATE INVESTIGATOR; SHERLOCK HOLMES; SLEUTH; SNOOP; SPY ETC.]

Positive characteristics of the **detective** include the ability to seek out knowledge and information that supports solving crimes and protecting the public. The shadow side of these archetypes can manifest as **voyeurism, falsifying information, or selling out to the highest bidder**. If the detective archetype appears in your dreams, it could be encouraging you to become more inquisitive. On the other hand, it could be questioning your motives for seeking out information.

DON JUAN

[DREAM IMAGES: CASANOVA, GIGOLO, SEDUCER, SEX ADDICT]

Although associated with sensuality and sophistication, this archetype represents a man preying on others for the sake of conquest alone. Like the Femme Fatale, if the **Don Juan** archetype appears in dreams, it can make us aware of falling into sex-role clichés, and misusing the power of romantic attraction and pursuit.

ENGINEER

[DREAM IMAGES: ARCHITECT; BUILDER; SCHEMER]

The characteristics of the **engineer** reflect the grounded, orderly, strategic qualities of mind that convert creative energy into a practical expression. This archetype also manifests as a talent for designing solutions to common dilemmas. Are these talents ones you are expressing or need to develop? The shadow engineer manifests as a master manipulator, **designing and engineering situations to one's own advantage**, regardless of the needs or desires of others.

EXORCIST

[DREAM IMAGE: SHAMAN]

Shamans and exorcists conduct rituals for the release of negative spirits, and if this archetype appears in a dream, it suggests a form of possession by destructive or antisocial impulses in oneself or others, and the need to confront it.

Father

[DREAM IMAGES: PATRIARCH; PROGENITOR]

This dream archetype represents the guiding wisdom that comes from within. A true **father** guides and shields those under his care, sacrificing his own desires when that's appropriate. The shadow father emerges when that caring guidance and protection turns into dictatorial control or abuse of authority. *See also* FAMILY.

Gambler

The **gambler** is a risk-taker who plays the odds. In dreams of winning lotteries and gambling at casino tables it can suggest following hunches, and believing in your intuition, even in the face of universal doubt. To assess whether you are a gambler, review your ability to follow your intuition and what others might consider risky inner guidance. Ask yourself how many of your decisions are based on gut instinct, rather than facts and figures. Alternatively, gambling dreams may refer to the way you are focused on looking for lucky breaks, rather than doing the hard work needed to succeed.

God

The God archetype, whether represented as deity or a worldly power in dreams, represents the ultimate in male dominance. On the positive side, a God can be benevolent and compassionate, willing to use his powers to help others out of love for humanity. The shadow God easily becomes a dictator or despot, oppressing others with those same powers, or using his physical attractiveness to get what he wants without ever returning the affection he elicits. Such dreams suggest that you have a life-long sense of great power. Are you using this power selfishly or selflessly?

Goddess

The oldest religious tradition on earth may well be **Goddess** worship, which some archaeologists trace back further than 30,000 years. It was certainly natural to worship the archetype of woman as the source of all life, especially in the age before male warriors replaced Her with their combative sky gods. The Goddess archetype in dreams can be inspiring as it embodies wisdom, guidance, physical grace, athletic prowess and sensuality. If a particular goddess appears in your dream, study the specific qualities of that goddess and evaluate how much of your sense of self is reflected in one of those patterns. For example, Venus/Aphrodite: love and fertility; Diana/Artemis: nature and hunting; Minerva/Athena: strength, clear thinking; Ceres/Demeter: motherhood; Juno/Hera: queenship and partnership; Proserpina/Persephone: mysticism and mediumship; Sophia: wisdom

Gossip

The **gossip** archetype is associated with rumor-spreading, backbiting, and passing along information that is exaggerated, harmful, and intended to disempower. If a gossip or gossiping figures in your dreams, the archetype is connected to lessons of truth, integrity, and honoring the trust another has placed in you.

Guide

[DREAM IMAGES: CRONE; EVANGELIST; GURU; SAGE; SPIRITUAL MASTER; WISE WOMAN]

You do not have to be a professional preacher or guru to have this archetype, as we can all learn to lead others spiritually through developing our own intuitive spiritual awareness and passing on whatever we have learned with genuine humility. If a **guide or spiritual master** appears in your dreams, your unconscious is urging you to pass your wisdom onto others. Alternatively it can warn against controlling others rather than guiding them.

Healer

[DREAM IMAGES: ANALYST; CAREGIVER; COUNSELOR; NURSE; THERAPIST; WOUNDED HEALER; INTUITIVE HEALER]

The **healer** archetype in dreams is encouraging you to guide and support others in some way. Alternatively, it could be urging you to heal and transform your pain into a sense of direction and purpose. The shadow of the healer manifests through a desire to take advantage of those who need your help.

Hedonist

[DREAM IMAGE: BON VIVANT, CHEF, GOURMET]

This archetype has an 'appetite' for the pleasurable aspects of life, from good food and wine to sexuality and sensuality, and when it appears as a theme in your dreams, it could simply be urging you to enjoy yourself more. As scientific research has shown, pleasure can improve our health and extend our lives, and needs to be part of a balanced life. The shadow **hedonist** may manifest as pursuing pleasure without regard for other people or one's own good health.

Hero/Heroine

The **hero** is a classic figure in ancient Greek and Roman literature, often portrayed as one who must confront an increasingly difficult path of obstacles in order to mature into adulthood. Today this archetype still holds a dominant position in the social mind, and can appear in dreams as a superhero or heroine, or similar icon of male and female power. Such dreams suggest that you have within you the courage and determination to face the challenges that lie ahead.

Judge

[DREAM IMAGES: ARBITRATOR; CRITIC; EXAMINER; MEDIATOR]

One need not be an **attorney, judge, or critic** by profession to identify with this archetype; it can appear in your dreams if you are, or need to be, a natural mediator or are involved in interventions between people. It can also appear if your unconscious requires you to learn justice and compassion. The shadow judge manifests as consistently destructive criticism, judging without compassion or with a hidden agenda. Legal manipulation, misuse of legal authority, and threatening others through an association with the law are other expressions of the shadow.

The Element Encyclopedia of 20,000 Dreams

King

[DREAM IMAGES: CHIEF; EMPEROR; LEADER; RULER]

The **king** is an archetype that represents the height of temporal male power and authority. He represents the father figure in your life, or the dominant ruling power – the part of you that is in control. Both benevolence and cruelty in their extreme expressions are associated with this archetype. Whether your kingdom is a corporation, community, family or your own life, such dreams suggest the need to rule compassionately.

Knight

Loyalty and self-sacrifice are the **knight**'s great virtues, along with a natural ability to get things done. The black knight donning dark armor and riding a black horse represents the shadow characteristics of this archetype, especially the absence of honor and chivalry, or loyalty to a questionable cause. In its negative aspect, the knight can fall into a pattern of saving others but ignoring his own needs. Such dreams may be urging you to find a balance between self-sacrifice and self-neglect.

Lover

This archetype appears not only in the dreams of those who are romantically inclined, but also in anyone who exhibits great passion and devotion. One can be a **lover** of art, music, gardening, dog, cats, nature, or needlepoint. Such dreams are related to a sense of affection and appreciation of someone or something, and the need to find or express that passion. The shadow lover figure in dreams of a lover who doesn't turn up or lets us down in some way suggests an obsessive passion that has a destructive effect on your physical or mental health and self-esteem. *See also* RELATIONSHIPS; SEX.

Mentor

[DREAM IMAGES: JEDI; MASTER; TUTOR]

Mentors do more than just teach; they pass on wisdom and refine their students' character. In dreams, they represent aspects of yourself you can trust, or people you can rely on. In its shadow aspect, however, the mentor can take on an overbearing attitude that is more about imposing control than imparting wisdom. They can appear, for example, in dreams about people who undermine you or refuse to help you for no good reason.

Midas/Miser

Midas turned everything he touched into gold, including, tragically, his beloved daughter. The archetype is associated with entrepreneurial or creative ability, and appears in dreams where wealth and luxury figures strongly. That Midas was a king symbolically implies that the Midas figure has the power to generate wealth for an entire kingdom, yet is interested only in his personal aggrandizement. Greed is his downfall. For that reason, lessons of generosity are a large part of the characteristics of this archetype. The shadow Midas or miser creates wealth by hording money and emotions at the expense of others, and refusing to share them.

Monk/Nun

If a **monk or nun** appears in your dreams, the positive aspects of this archetype are fairly obvious: spiritual intensity, devotion, dedication, persistence, and perhaps wisdom. Are these qualities you need to develop within yourself? The monk archetype can also suggest the ability to be single-minded, assiduous, devoted to a spiritual path or to any great achievement that requires intense focus. On the shadow side, the role of a religious recluse could be seen as being removed from the real world, overly pious, even privileged in the sense of not having to be concerned about earning a living, or raising a family.

Monster

Your innermost fears or negative attitudes that are seen as larger than you can handle. *See also* NIGHTMARES; SURREALISM AND FANTASY

Mother

[DREAM IMAGES: MATRIARCH, MOTHER NATURE]

The **mother** archetype appears in many forms – mother, princess and witch – and is symbolized by the primordial mother, or 'earth mother', of mythology, by Eve and Mary in Western traditions, and by less personal symbols, such as the church, the nation, a forest or the ocean. According to Jung, someone whose own mother failed to satisfy the demands of the archetype may well be one that spends his or her life seeking comfort in the church, or in identification with 'the motherland', or in meditating upon the figure of Mary, or in a life at sea. In dreams, mother figures suggest nurturing aspects of ourselves and others, or the need for greater compassion and self-lessness; they can, however, also suggest the shadow side, which is overprotection, abandonment, cruelty and abuse. Bear in mind that the qualities that are associated with this archetype can be expressed in other than biological ways, such as giving birth to books or ideas, or nurturing others. *See also* FAMILY.

Networker

[DREAM IMAGES: COMMUNICATOR; COURIER; HERALD; JOURNALIST; MESSENGER]

Although networking seems like a very modern skill tied to career advancement in the media age, it is actually quite ancient. Networking would also have been an integral part of any military alliance as well as all social and clan confederations in prehistory. If a **messenger or journalist** appears in your dreams, this suggests that you have the skills to bring information – or power – and inspiration to others. The question is will you use these skills for the good of the group, or for personal gain?

Pioneer

[DREAM IMAGES: EXPLORER; PILGRIM; SETTLER]

The **pioneer** discovers and explores new lands, whether that territory is external or internal. The passion to explore the South Pole is as much a pioneering endeavor as the passion to explore medicine or spiritual practice. Even initiating new fashions, art, music, or literature may qualify as expressions of this archetype. The core ingredient is innovation – doing and creating what has not been done before. In dreams, this archetype suggests a need to step on fresh and undiscovered territory in at least one realm. The shadow pioneer manifests as restlessness and a compulsive need to abandon one's past and move on.

POET

The **poet** combines lyricism with sharp insight, finding the essence of beauty and truth not only in the great epic affairs of humanity, but also in everyday acts and objects. Great poetry extols momentous events and great deeds, and also expresses wonder at the hidden joys and sorrows that most of us might overlook. If you dream you are a poet, or a poet figures in your dream, this suggests the need and the ability to discover beauty in the people and things around you, and to express it in a way that helps others, too, see that beauty. The shadow poet turns his gift for lyricism to negative or destructive effect, as in songs or poems written in support of military aggression or genocide. *See also* ARTS AND CRAFTS.

PRIEST

[DREAM IMAGES: EVANGELIST; MINISTER; RABBI; VICAR]

A **priest** may represent traditional religion with its spiritual rules and regulations. Are you making moral judgments? Alternatively, the priest could represent your own spiritual wisdom. The shadow side of this archetype manifests in lapses of personal morality.

PRINCE

The true **prince** is a ruler-in-training who is in service to the people over whom he will rule, whether that is a literal kingdom or a figurative or spiritual one. The shadow prince can manifest as a young man with great feelings of entitlement, or an heir apparent who uses his position solely for self-aggrandizement. Are you dedicated to service, or do you feel that the world owes you a living?

PROSTITUTE

This archetype activates the aspects of the unconscious that are related to seduction and control. Prostitution should also be understood as the selling of your talents, ideas, and any other expression of the self – or the selling-out of them. This archetype is universal, and in dreams it relates to the need to birth and refine self-esteem and self-respect.

QUEEN/EMPRESS

Freud believed that the king and **queen** represent the dreamer's parents, whilst a prince or princess represents the dreamer. The queen is a symbol of power and authority in all women. She may also stand for the unconscious, intuition, nature and the instincts. Jung saw royal figures as representations of the animus and anima – the male and female principle – and the queen personifies the feminine forces within the psyche, the unconscious feeling for life. The shadow queen can slip into aggressive and destructive patterns of behavior, particularly when she perceives that her authority or capacity to maintain control over the court is being challenged. The ice queen rules with a cold indifference to the genuine needs of others – whether material or emotional. The queen bee is a mixed image – the astonishing ability to power the entire hive without leaving her 'chamber,' yet at the cost of enslaving the rest of her community.

REBEL

[DREAM IMAGES: ANARCHIST; NONCONFORMIST; PIRATE; POLITICAL PROTESTER; REVOLUTIONARY]

The **rebel** in a support group can be a powerful aid in helping the group break out of old tribal patterns. In dreams, it can also help you see past tired preconceptions in your field of professional or creative endeavor. The rebel can also lead you to reject spiritual systems that do not serve your inner need for direct union with the divine and to seek out more appropriate paths. The shadow rebel, conversely, may compel you to rebel out of peer pressure, or for the sake of fashion, and so become mired in another manifestation of conformity.

SEEKER

[DREAM IMAGE: NOMAD; VAGABOND; WANDERER]

This dream archetype refers to the search for wisdom and truth wherever it can be found. The shadow side of the archetype is the 'lost soul', someone on an aimless journey, without direction, ungrounded, disconnected from goals and others.

SERVANT

[DREAM IMAGES: INDENTURED SERVANT; SLAVE]

To dream that you are a slave suggests that you are not taking charge of your own life. Have you become so consumed by the needs of those around you that you have lost all focus on the value of your own life?

STUDENT

[DREAM IMAGES: APPRENTICE; DEVOTEE; DISCIPLE; FOLLOWER; PUPIL]

The **student** archetype suggests an open mind and the ability to absorb new information as an essential part of one's well-being. The shadow student usually manifests in learning all the tools of the wrong trade or misusing the knowledge learned. The shadow can also show up as the eternal student who never embarks on the sea of life in earnest, but manages to find ever new reasons to continue being schooled without ever putting that knowledge to the test. *See also* SCHOOL AND WORK.

TEACHER

Teaching is the art of communicating knowledge, experience, skill, and wisdom to another. Teaching, or offering instruction of any kind, can manifest through parental guidance, business apprenticeship, or by inspired instruction in ethics or kindness. If this archetype appears in your dreams, it can suggest that others seek you out for the richness of your experience or that you need to seek out someone or something to teach you the ropes. The shadow teacher manifests as a desire to manipulate or abuse those you are instructing, and to

The feminine and masculine principles

The feminine principle is embodied in the archetype of the great mother: the complete woman within whom the primary qualities of femininity manifest in harmony. Whether you are a man or a woman, take note of the female figures in your dreams – be they a person, animal, quality or object – as they carry a message from your unconscious. If the **selfless, loving mother** figure appears in your dream, ask yourself if you need to develop motherly qualities within yourself. If the **dark side of motherhood** appears – dominating, criticizing and devouring – ask yourself if you or someone you know has a damaging, suppressing effect on you or someone else. If the **romantic, innocent princess figure** appears in your dreams ask yourself if you need to rediscover your optimism. If the **seductress** appears, ask yourself if you are being warned against selfishness and immaturity. If you dream of a **wise woman or a witch**, ask yourself if you are working with integrity or if you are alienating others with your selfishness.

The masculine principle is typically represented as the **wise old man or father** and suggests so-called masculine qualities of strength, authority and virility. If any of the masculine archetypes appear in your dream ask yourself if it is highlighting an aspect of yourself that you need to take a closer look at. If a **father figure** appears in your dreams he may simply be a role model of authority with compassion but if the ogre appears he may represent a threat of some kind to your authority. A dream that features a **young, idealistic prince** may be encouraging you to recapture some of your youthful optimism, while dreaming of a **wastrel** may be a warning that it is time to act with maturity and take on responsibility. If a **warrior** appears in your dreams, this could suggest the need to take decisive action in waking life, be it to promote your aims or to make a decision. If you dream of the **high priest** or his counterpart, the **black magician**, you need to question your motives or those of the person you feel they might represent: are they altruistic and wise, or selfish and misdirected? *See also* FAMILY; PEOPLE.

be more concerned with recognition than with imparting knowledge.

THIEF

[DREAM IMAGES: BURGLAR; CON ARTIST; PICKPOCKET; ROBIN HOOD; SWINDLER]

Symbolically, theft can take many forms, including plagiarism, stealing ideas and even affection. If the figure of a **thief** appears in your dreams or you become a thief, it suggests that you may be taking what is not yours because you lack the ability to provide for yourself; you therefore need to learn self-respect. This archetype prods you to learn to generate power from within.

VAMPIRE

See SEX.

VICTIM

When we become a **victim** in our dreams, it can be a tremendous aid in letting us know when we are in danger of letting ourselves be victimized, often through passivity, but also through rash or inappropriate actions. It can also help us to see our own tendency to victimize others for personal gain. In its shadow aspect, the victim shows us that we may like to play the victim at times because of the positive feedback we get in the form of sympathy or pity. Our goal is always to learn how to recognize these inappropriate attitudes in ourselves or others, and to act accordingly.

WARRIOR

[DREAM IMAGES: AMAZON; CRIME FIGHTER; GUNSLINGER; MERCENARY; SOLDIER OF FORTUNE; SAMURAI; SOLDIER]

The **warrior** archetype represents loyalty, physical strength and the ability to protect, defend, and fight for one's rights. To be unbreakable and to fight to the death is a large part of the warrior archetype, which is also associated with the passage from boyhood to manhood. Such dreams appeal to our fantasies of independence, and the power to defend ourselves and right wrongs. The shadow warrior distorts or abandons ethical principles and decency in the name of victory at any cost. The warrior archetype is just as connected to the female psyche as to the male. In today's society, the warrior woman or Amazon archetype has emerged in its glory once again through women who liberate and protect others, especially women and children who need vocal and financial representation. The concept of the spiritual warrior directs us to use the classic warrior virtues of heroism, stoicism, and self-sacrifice for conquering the ego and gaining control of our inner lives.

The Element Encyclopedia of 20,000 Dreams

ARTS AND CRAFTS

Dreams of the creativity of artistic endeavor are as common as action and adventure dreams. Whether you dream of composing a symphony, painting a masterpiece, writing a best-selling novel, singing in an opera or designing a scrapbook, such dreams with yourself in the artist's role represent the creative or intuitive side of your nature.

You may feel a need in waking life to express yourself in some way, to be more creative or to enjoy public recognition. If you are meeting an artist in your dreams, this suggests that you are becoming aware of an aspect of yourself that is creative. If, however, you are watching another artist at work, this suggests that you are recognizing artistic or creative ability in yourself but remain passive about it.

Dreaming of creating something will be less significant if you are a naturally creative person than if you are not. If you have never been artistic or worked with crafts, dreaming that you are a potter making a pot – or an author completing a novel – may carry the implication that you should do so, or at least be more imaginative and creative in your waking life. *See also* LEISURE; MEDIA AND TECHNOLOGY.

Arts Situations

In general, dreams about the **performing arts**, i.e. **dancing, singing and acting**, suggest that you are concerned with your personality and how you appear to others.

ACTING

This can suggest a desire for public attention but it can also suggest not expressing your real self – acting a role. If you dreamed that you were **acting on stage**, how did the audience react to your performance? We all role-play during our waking life, projecting a persona that may not be entirely who we are, in order to make ourselves more appealing to others; so it is possible that your unconscious was commenting on how your performance was perceived. The part you were playing and the scene you were acting could be particularly relevant to situations in your waking life. Were you a tremendous success on stage and did you receive a standing ovation? If you did, your unconscious may be telling you that the image you are presenting is convincing to others. If, however, **your act was not well received**, this might suggest that the image you are projecting is unconvincing to others and unhelpful to you.

If you dreamed that you were **unwilling to step into the spotlight**, this could suggest that your unconscious is mirroring your reluctance to be someone you are not in waking life, or it could simply suggest that you dislike being the center of attention. If you **forgot your lines** or needed the assistance of a **prompter**, you could be suffering from a lack of confidence in waking life, perhaps because you feel unprepared in some way. You may also be relying on someone else in waking life to guide you towards success. If an **actor or actress dies or is dead** in your dream, this could suggest that a particular role you have been playing in life has outlived its usefulness and relevance. On the other hand, dreams about acting may simply be reminding you that life is not a dress rehearsal and that you only have one chance to make a success of it.

■ *Idioms: act a part; act on impulse or information; acting up; caught in the act; get in on the act.*

ARTIST

To dream that you are an **artist painting a picture** is a reference to the creative and intuitive side of your character. The dream alerts you to talents that you may not know

you have. It urges you to recognize the artist within, that aspect of yourself that is in contact with the irrational, creative side of your unconscious.

AUDIENCE

To dream that you are **in front of an audience** suggests that people you know in waking life are paying close attention to your actions. It could also refer to your fear of having your private thoughts and feelings discovered or revealed. If you are part of the **audience**, you need to pay attention to the **plot of the play**. Symbolically, the stage is a representation of your own life play. By observing and being objective about the action being played out, you can gain a new perspective on your life.

AUDITION

If you are **attending an audition** in your dream, this could refer to feelings of insecurity about expressing yourself in waking life. You may also feel as if you are being put to the test in some way, or that you are in a vulnerable situation. The **response of the audience** will reveal how you feel others perceive you.

BOOKS

To dream of **books** can symbolize knowledge, wisdom, intelligence, the search for knowledge and the ability to learn from the opinions of other people. If you are **surrounded by books** in your dreams, this might suggest that you are more concerned with theory than practice. Depending on the kinds of books that figure in your dream, they can also suggest the world of

The Element Encyclopedia of 20,000 Dreams

Circus

Circus dreams represent the instinctive, passionate, creative sides of our nature. How well are these instincts performing? Have they been brought under control? If you're enjoying the performance, this suggests that you are expressing your creativity. If you dislike or are bored by the performance, your dream mirrors a sense of frustration in your daily life. If you are **performing in the circus** it might be a sign that you need a more fulfilling job where you can show off your talents. If an **animal escapes** or you feel unhappy about the animals being involved in the performance, this could indicate a change of direction in your life or a love interest outside marriage. The circus **audience** in your dream is also significant because it suggests how your efforts are being received in waking life. Finally, don't forget that circus dreams may simply be an observation that your waking life resembles a chaotic circus and has become thoroughly disorganized.

If your unconscious portrayed you as a **juggler** in your dream, was it referring to the many commitments you have to juggle or manage in your waking life? Did you drop any of your dream balls or did you keep them in the air? If you were **walking a tightrope** or **performing acrobatics** in dreamland, this may suggest that you feel you are treading a fine line to maintain balance in a tricky situation in waking life. If you were **dressed as a clown, sporting a huge smile painted on your face,** do you feel under pressure to present a cheerful front to others during your waking hours, when you actually feel the opposite? If **someone you know was transformed into a clown,** they may be the ones feeling under pressure to 'perform' in waking life. Also consider if your dream clown was a manifestation of the archetypal **trickster/clown** whose jokes have a serious meaning.

imagination and escape. Are you surrounded by literary novels, racy best-sellers or fascinating biographies? If the **books are very old**, this suggests learning and inherited wisdom. If the books are **account books**, this indicates a need to take care of financial matters.

Sacred books, such as the Koran or the Bible, signify a search for hidden or sacred knowledge. Dreaming of a sacred book can also represent a need to know you are heading in the right direction. To dream of an **encyclopedia** suggests a hunger for knowledge and new experience, as an encyclopedia represents collective human wisdom. On the other hand, it can also suggest information overload and a need to find focus. To dream you are **searching in a**

dictionary suggests a need to find answers to a particular problem or situation in your life. It can also suggest an over-reliance on the opinions of others. If you look up **a particular word** in your dream, this can be very significant (*see* LETTERS AND COMMUNICATION; SOUNDS). Finally, a poem is the ultimate form of self-expression, so if **you are a poet, or a poet figures in your dream, or you are reading poetry**, your unconscious is urging you to find a creative outlet in waking life.

DANCE

In dreams, **dancing and skating** (*see* ACCIDENTS, ACTION AND ADVENTURES) usually express a sense of happiness and celebration, or a freedom of movement and emotion. Perhaps you are feeling pleased about a particular project or relationship. You may also be feeling a sense of freedom from restraint. Other things may also be expressed by dance. For example, if you **danced with another person**, the intimacy could suggest sexual intercourse. If a **man and a woman dance together**, it could suggest a union of the masculine and feminine aspects of your personality. If, however, the dance was awkward, this suggests a lack of harmony. **Animals dancing** can suggest a feeling of harmony with your unconscious drives and sexuality. **Skeletons and dark things dancing** suggest meeting what you fear in your waking life.

DRAWING

This could simply mean that you have latent artistic talents that should be given expression. But it can have other meanings.

Are you overdrawn at the bank? Are you drawing on inner resources? What you draw is very significant, as it can reveal the issues and problems you are trying to resolve in waking life. An ancient tradition says that if a **woman dreams she is drawing with a pencil and then rubs it out**, her lover will be unfaithful.

MAKE-UP/GREASEPAINT

Actors use **make-up** to help convince their audience that they are not themselves, but someone else. In waking life, are you – for good or bad reasons – involved in some kind of deception?

MUSEUM

In dreams, **museums** typically suggest old-fashioned ideas or ways of thinking. They can also represent places where we store cherished memories; the living past within us that we can learn from, but also need to move away from in order to progress.

MUSIC

Many of the world's greatest composers claimed that they heard their greatest works whilst dreaming, or immediately after waking. Mystics talk of the **music** of the spheres, the ethereal music that symbolizes the harmony of the universe. In dreams, music represents harmony and the creative potential. Your dream music can also express the emotions you are currently feeling in waking life. Is the tone happy, sad, angry or threatening? If the music you hear is **discordant**, it may suggest that your creative potential isn't being expressed. *See also* SOUNDS.

Dancing in the dark

Ballet

If **ballet or ballet dancing** appears in your dream, or if you are performing ballet, this suggests a search of poise and balance in your waking life. The ballet dancer symbolizes music and the inner aspect of feeling. You may be aware of the creative side of yourself and feel the need for controlled movement to express it. Dreams of ballet may be wish-fulfillment if becoming a professional dancer was, or is, your dream; alternatively, they may refer to losing or keeping your balance in some waking situation. They may also be encouraging you to persevere with artistic skills, or they may be a general comment on your attitude to work that demands discipline.

Ballroom dancing

Who was your partner? If the two of you were **dancing together as one**, this could suggest your longing to get closer to the person you were dancing with. If you **didn't know the identity of the person with whom you were dancing**, it could suggest longing for a relationship or greater intimacy in the relationship you already have.

Disco dancing

If you were **dancing alone**, this could be a simple expression of joyful feelings in waking life. If you were **dancing with a group of people**, this could suggest good team spirit in waking life. A dream about a **discotheque** is a sign that the dreamer may be feeling excited but confused about a new relationship or project

Line dancing

Were you **dancing in line** with people you know in a country music scene? If so your unconscious may be reflecting on your tendency to conform or else your habit of stepping out of line or of failing to conform to the behavior your loved ones expect. Were you dancing in line or were you out of step?

Other kinds of dancing

Dreams that feature movement could indicate that you need to move on take another route, or speed up your progress in some way. Dancing a **jig or waltz** can suggest simple, innocent pleasures. **Jumping or leaping** in a dream can suggest ambition or the desire to improve your status. If you were at an **exercise class**, perhaps in waking life you should take more exercise?

Musical harmonies

Clarinet/Flute/Recorder

Wind instruments express extremes of emotion and excitement. Because of their shape, wind instruments are sometimes associated with masculine virility, but can also represent anxiety. The **flute** expresses the sound of the spirit and, as such, it can be a symbol of both joy and sorrow. A **musical pipe** suggests connection with the rhythm of life.

Cymbal

Associated with rhythm and sound, the appearance of **cymbals** in a dream suggests the need for a basic sense of harmony. The cymbals consist of two halves and represent the reconciliation of passion with practicality. There can also be a link with sex as, along with the **drum** and **tambourine**, they are used to induce an ecstatic state.

Drum

The basic rhythm of life needed to stay healthy and happy. The importance of being more in touch with your natural urges. If you are **playing the drum**, this suggests that you are responsible for the rhythm of your life.

Gong

If you **hear the sound of a gong** in your dreams, this suggests the end of a phase in your life and the beginning of another. If you are **striking the gong**, this suggests a need to find strength in waking life or to wake up to the reality of a particular situation. See also SOUNDS.

Guitar

If you are **playing the guitar** in your dream, this can suggest your need to be more creative in daily life. If you **hear guitar music**, it can indicate a need for caution or the possibility of a new romance.

Harp

The **harp** is the symbol of music and indicates the correct vibration we need to create harmony in our lives. To **harp on** about something is a term used to describing keeping on about something in waking life, and dream harps may well be urging us to be persistent in some activity.

Horn

A **musical or hunting horn** in a dream suggests some kind of summoning or warning in waking life.

Organ

In dreams, an **organ** can often represent the dreamer's feelings about religion, but recall that in some circles, organ is a slang term for penis. The **organist** as an image in a dream is the part of us that knows how to bring the parts we play into harmony. It represents the discipline and determination we need to manifest in daily life in order to make ourselves heard.

Piano

In dreams, **pianos, piano players and piano playing** are symbols of your own creativity. To be a great piano player you need to learn and practice, and the same applies to using your creativity. Pay attention to the piece you are playing. Is it one you have composed, or is it by someone else? Often in life we need to be creative with someone else's work. Is it time for you to create something of your own?

Tambourine

If you are **playing the tambourine in a group**, this suggests your ability to participate effectively in life. If you are **playing alone**, you have some control over the basic rhythm of your life.

Trumpet

In a dream of a **trumpet**, it suggests the need to be ready for action. It may be alerting you to some danger you might be facing. Angels are often depicted blowing trumpets, and it could also suggest the call to reach your potential and find the best within yourself.

Violin

If you are **playing a violin** well in your dream, or **hear violin music**, this could suggest that you are expressing your creativity with skill. If you **aren't playing well**, or the music sounds discordant, this could suggest the opposite. Violins can also represent sexual intercourse or even masturbation. Be aware of the term, 'get the violins out', as your dream may be suggesting that you are trying to get unnecessary sympathy. It could also relate to 'fiddle' as another word for violin. Are you 'fiddling about' and doing nothing constructive? Are you playing 'second fiddle' and feeling second best in waking life?

MUSICAL INSTRUMENTS

To see **musical instruments** in your dream suggests an anticipation of fun and pleasure in your waking life, but if the **instruments are broken**, this denotes the interruption of pleasure.

ORCHESTRA

If an **orchestra or musical concert** figures in your dreams, it refers to those aspects of your personality that must work together with one another in order for you to function properly. Such dreams suggest ways for you to bring all these aspects of yourself together to create a balanced whole. If you **orchestrate something**, this means you make it happen and this dream may also be urging you to take action in your waking life. If you find yourself **conducting an orchestra**, this means that you need to take control, but are you creating sweet music or disharmony? If you are a **member of an orchestra**, you are a vital part of a greater task. Are you in or out of tune? This could refer to your waking life, in which you might be blending in harmoniously with friends and colleagues, or conflicting with them.

OPERA/SINGING

If you are **watching an opera** in your dream, this suggests that you need to observe the drama taking part around you in waking life. If you are **taking part in an opera, but not singing**, this suggests that you need to inject more drama into your waking life. If you are **singing in the opera**, you are beginning to express your emotions more fully in everyday situations.

If you **hear singing** in your dream, this suggests that you are, or need to be, in touch with your emotions and creativity. Singing is a way of raising your vibration to a higher level, emotionally and spiritually. If you are **singing**, this is a pure expression of joy and love of life. If you are **singing alone**, you have learned to enjoy your own company. If you are **singing in a choir**, you are able to express yourself well in a group.

PAINTING

To be **looking at paintings or painting** in a dream suggests that you are paying attention to new ideas, and making changes in the way you think and feel. It may also refer to the need to take note of the details of a certain situation in your life. Painting has a lot to do with self-expression, and what you are painting and the colors you are using are important. If you are **painting a miniature**, perhaps you need to concentrate on small details. If you are **painting a nature scene,** perhaps you need to spend more time in the fresh air. If you are **painting larger pictures**, perhaps you need to see the larger picture. The actual image that you are painting in your dream may symbolize the way that you are visualizing your current situation in your waking life. If you are painting as in **decorating**, this could suggest making changes in the way you feel about yourself. It could also represent changes in your appearance or lifestyle. *See also* COLORS; PLACES.

PHOTOGRAPHS

Photos in dreams represent some aspect of yourself that you need to be looking at, perhaps your younger self, or a part of yourself that you have grown out of but need to understand. If you are **developing photos**, this suggests discovering hidden talents or abilities. If you are **looking at family photos or an album**, this refers to an appreciation of past influences in your life. If the **photo is of yourself**, this suggests you need to take an objective look at yourself, especially if you are given the photo in your dream. You need to stand back and see clearly. If the **photo is of someone you know**, perhaps you need to look at that person's qualities and make use of those qualities yourself. If the **photos in your dreams come to life**, this indicates your continuing involvement in what the picture depicts, or that the past as a whole is still influencing you.

If you are **taking a photograph**, this suggests that you need to remember or take notice of something. If you are **using a camera** in your dreams, this might suggest that you need to remember what is important in your life and perhaps take more notice of certain situations or people. You may have noticed something out of the 'corner of your eye', but not yet have processed it into waking consciousness. If you are **being filmed or having your picture taken**, you need to take a careful look at your thoughts and responses to certain situations.

PICTURES

Pictures in dreams often represent situations in our lives, or a view we may have about something. The subject matter will suggest what we should be looking at in our lives. The condition of the picture will be significant, as will the colors (*see* COLORS). If a **drawing fails to appear, a video**

refuses to focus or a photo refuses to develop properly**, there may be something wrong with your own vision of an important part of your life. Are you seeing things clearly?

PLAY/PANTOMIME

Typically, **plays** in dreams are images of yourself and your life projected by your unconscious. They represent an aspect of your past or your character that you are repressing in waking life or, depending on the play, particular moods or feelings. Alternatively, such dreams can suggest a desire to escape from the pressures of everyday life. If the play is a **tragedy**, is the routine and repetition of your life restricting your creativity? If the play is a **comedy**, do you need to lighten up a little in waking life? If what you are watching is a **pantomime**, has the time come to stop fooling about and get serious about something or someone in waking life?

STAGE

To be **on stage** in your dream suggests a desire to become more visible. If the **stage is open air**, this suggests communication with a large audience, not just a selected few. If the **stage is moving**, this indicates your desire to keep moving, even when acting a role. Carl Jung once wrote, 'The whole dream-work is essentially subjective, and a dream is a theatre in which the dreamer is himself the scene, the player, the prompter, the producer, the author, the public, and the critic.' In other words, dreams are themselves like a theatre in which your problems, hopes and fears are acted out by characters generated by your imagination. To dream of a **theatre** is therefore like a dream within a dream. If you dream of watching or acting a **play, pantomime or circus**, consider what aspects of your personality each character represents. Do these characters raise the curtain on some of your most poignant questions and experiences in life? This dream is showing you your life, the way you behave and the way you present yourself to others from a new perspective. The scenes being played out are typically ones that are being played out at present; they are experimenting or exploring an idea, relationship or situation. For example, if you watched **members of your family or a group of friends performing a play**, your unconscious may be telling you that in waking life they may be deceiving you in some way or not revealing their true feelings. If the **stage was empty**, your unconscious may be referring to the lack of creativity in your waking life and the need for more color, variety and stimulation. A curious superstition claims that if you dream you **cut new teeth**, it is a sign that you will hear of the birth of a child who will do great things in theatre.

■ *Idioms: set the stage for; stage fright; stage-manage; act a part; act on; catch somebody in the act; get in on the act; get one's act together; act one's age; play a role.*

VENTRILOQUIST

To see a **ventriloquist** in your dream symbolizes some sort of deception in your waking life that is affecting you in a negative way. If **you are the ventriloquist**, there is a part of yourself that you are not revealing in waking life.

WRITING

If **writing** figures in dreams, this is an attempt to communicate information when spoken words are inadequate. Your dream may be reflecting your true thoughts and feelings. If you are **writing down names and addresses** in your dream, this may be a reminder to remember your friends and take note of your enemies. It also suggests a need to reflect on something, or sort out your ideas and decisions. Perhaps the instrument with which you are writing is significant. For example, to write with a **pencil or chalk** would suggest the information is less permanent than were you to write with a **pen or fountain pen**, and a **typewriter or word processor** would suggest that the information is connected to business, rather than personal, issues. **Writing a novel** or writing in general can also suggest a desire to leave your mark on the world in some way. If the **writing is by someone you know**, this refers to their influence over your life and thought processes in waking life. If you are **writing to someone you know**, he or she may represent the nature of the issues you are trying to express. If you dream of **someone else writing**, this can show an aspect of yourself that is seeking to express itself.

The Element Encyclopedia of 20,000 Dreams

Crafts and Creativity Scenarios

HANDICRAFT

In dreams, doing any **handicraft**, from **embroidery to pottery**, suggests that we have situations in hand, but also that we need to take responsibility for our actions. Pay particular attention both to what is being made and to how well it is being made, as it will reflect a situation in your waking life.

KNITTING

If you were **knitting or doing crochet**, the symbols may be indicative of some waking situation. For example, if you **dropped a stitch** in the dream, have you been tactless in waking life? If there was a **break in your yarn**, have you argued with someone? **Wool** has from the earliest of times represented warmth and protection, and if you are **knitting with wool or see wool** in your dreams, it can suggest gentleness or motherly qualities within yourself. Be aware, too, of the phrase 'pulling the wool over someone's eyes'. There might be things that you don't know about or don't wish to see at the present time.

MAKING A SCRAPBOOK

If you are **making a scrapbook** in your dreams, or looking through one, this is about making memories. Are you taking the time to treasure the uniqueness of each new day in your waking life?

NEEDLEWORK

If you are **sewing** in your dreams, your dream may be suggesting that your waking life has been taken over by boredom and routine. This is because sewing requires constant attention to detail and much of the work is repetitive. Your dream may be urging you to broaden your horizons. If you are **sewing pieces of fabric together** in your dream, this may suggest that you are bringing aspects of your life together.

PLANTING A SEED

A dream of a **seed or a pip** may suggest the germ of an idea that will grow into something important, if you find the determination and patience to follow it through. A dream about **spreading manure** carries the same implication, suggesting that an idea or notion needs feeding and nurturing. *See also* NATURE AND THE SEASONS.

POTTERY

If you are a creative person, a dream about **making a pot** may refer to another aspect of your life that is just as important as your creative work. If you are not creative, such a dream may suggest the need to find ways to express your creativity in waking life. Try to recall every detail of what you are making. To **see, or work with, clay** in your dream represents the ability to change or shape your mind. Alternatively, it indicates your need to set some goals and plans for yourself. You have some growing-up to do and need to plan for the future. According

Mending

To dream that you are **mending a garment** symbolizes your attempts to fix a problem or situation in waking life. In your dream, are your attempts successful or are you frustrated by lack of resources?

Buttons

Buttons hold things together and are used to open and close garments. In your waking life, are you opening or closing yourself to others?

Needle

In dreams, **needles** signify the power to heal through penetration. In other words, some concept or knowledge has to be introduced from outside. This may feel uncomfortable at first but it will eventually make us feel better. Depending on whether or not **you are using the needle or it is being used on you**, the ability to have penetrative insights can come from within or without. From a Freudian perspective, the needle can also suggest masculine sexuality.

Pins

If you dream that you are **pricked by a pin**, this signifies a difficult situation or relationship. You may be feeling anxious or feeling the need to hold together a particular relationship. Consider the pun of someone who may be a 'prick'. Alternatively, to **see pins** in your dream may suggest you are feeling stifled or trapped, as indicated by the phrase 'being pinned down'. If a **pincushion** appears in your dream, this can indicate stinging or hurtful comments in waking life. You may be feeling manipulated or attacked in waking life, or perhaps you are being hurtful to someone else. For particular materials used in mending, for example, cotton, linen, silk, *see also* CLOTHES AND IMAGE.

Scissors

In dreams, these can suggest cutting remarks or decisiveness and taking control. They can also suggest separation or independence – as in cutting the umbilical cord – or the need to get rid of someone or something out of your life that isn't working anymore. The type of scissors may be important for the dreamer. **Surgical scissors**, for instance, could suggest the need to be more precise. **Kitchen scissors** might suggest a need to be more practical. If the **scissors are blunt**, this suggests you may be creating problems through speaking bluntly. If you are **sharpening scissors**, this suggests the need to be more tactful. If you dream of a **hairdresser using scissors**, this could refer to your fear of losing authority and status. In folklore, **clean scissors** suggest that you have nothing to fear from your enemies. If the **scissors are rusty or broken** however, this is a less favorable.

Tape/thimble/thread

Tapes are used to measure things in waking life. In your dreams they can suggest a need to measure and evaluate the potential of a current project you are involved in. To use a **thimble** in your dream suggests that you need to be thinking of the welfare of others. Ancient dream oracles say that **losing a thimble** is a sign of misfortune but **receiving or buying a thimble** signifies new friendships. To see **thread** in your dream suggests that you need to strengthen commitments and relationships in waking life. Ancient dream oracles say that to see **broken threads** in your dream signifies unreliable friends.

to Freudian interpretation, clay symbolizes feces. But to see a **clay pot** in your dream signifies devotion, healing, virtue or purity.

SCULPTOR

If you are a **sculptor** in your dreams, you are working on finding yourself and are overcoming obstacles by getting to the core of things. If a **sculpture** appears in your dreams, you may find it hard to accept things as they are really are. You may also be overly concerned about projecting a positive image. A **statue, bust or obelisk** often suggests the desire to put someone or something on a pedestal. If you are doing this, you increase the feelings of remoteness and unattainability of that person or thing in waking life. If a **statue comes alive** in your dreams, you may revive a long-lost interest or rebuild a friendship. Ancient dream oracles indicate that dreaming of **being a statue** is a sign that your fortunes will change for the better.

WEAVING

Weaving is taken to symbolize life itself and the way in which we run our lives. Most cultures contain images in which our fate is being woven in a pattern. Although at the mercy of chance, we are supposed to be in control of that pattern.

BAD DEEDS

Any violence or negative action in your dreams is typically a reflection of your own inner feelings.

According to Jung, negative actions in dreams symbolize the shadow or dark side of your nature. The shadow is everything that you are repressing or denying, the hidden side of yourself that you refuse to recognize. By conjuring up such images in your dream, your unconscious is urging you to bring these hidden feelings into the light of day so that they have less hold over you, otherwise you are in danger of projecting this 'other self' onto other people.

Dreams about violence, crime and other actions may not only reveal your inner feelings about yourself, they may also reveal your feelings about the situation around you or in some cases, your feelings about other people in your life. The type of negative action highlighted in the dream will be worthy of your attention if you are to fully understand yourself and your situation. Although disturbing, and unfortunately more common than positive actions in dreams, dreams in which the action focuses on bad or negative feelings, words and actions are seldom predictive, so you don't need to worry that the horrifying events will be repeated in your waking life.

Recurring dreams of committing rape are a different concern, suggesting violent urges that are in danger of spilling over into your waking life. If this is the case, professional therapy and counseling is strongly recommended. *See also* ACCIDENTS, ACTION AND ADVENTURES; NEGATIVE EMOTIONS; NIGHTMARES.

Crime

DECEPTION

If you find yourself **lying or cheating** in your dream, or **overhear someone else doing so**, this indicates that you are feeling guilty about not being honest in waking life or that someone is cheating or being dishonest with you. If you have **recurring dreams in which cheating or lying** feature, your dreaming mind is suggesting that you are living a lie in waking life and that you need to be true to yourself. Dreams of **stealing, cheating, forgery, fraud and blackmail** send the same message. If you are an **accessory or witness to a crime** in your dream but **didn't commit it**, this suggest your feelings of guilt about colluding with something or ignoring something you knew to be wrong. If, however, a **crime or deception was committed against you** in your dream, ask yourself whether someone is committing a wrong against you.

PUNISHMENT

You may have had a dream in which you **committed a crime and found yourself being punished for your actions**. You may have woken from such a dream feeling extremely relieved that you have not committed a crime or been punished, but lingering feelings of anxiety may stay with you. Try to identify your feelings about such a dream as they will help with the interpretation. Did you feel guilty or angry that an injustice had been done to you? If you can discover how you feel about the punishment, this may hold the key to the interpretation. If you **felt guilty**, perhaps there is something in your waking life that you feel is wrong or is destroying your peace of mind. If you are actually **caught in the act in your dream and find yourself awaiting or being sentenced to punishment of some kind**, this is a clear message of disapproval from your dreaming mind and a warning that if you don't change your ways, you will be in danger of being found out in waking life. Try to identify who punished you in your dream. If it was **someone you know**, you may be feeling remorseful towards them in waking life, but if it was **someone you do not know**, you

may be feeling guilty about breaking a law or rule in waking life or showing disrespect for authority.

If a **lynch mob attacked you**, have you committed a crime against society in general by not paying your taxes or dropping litter? If you dreamed of being **accused of a crime you did not commit and nobody believed your protestations of innocence**, do you feel you are being treated unfairly in your waking life? When the **punishment was pronounced** in your dream, did you feel that is was out of proportion to the wrongdoing. If you felt the **punishment was far too severe**, this suggests that you are feeling extremely guilty about someone thing you have done in waking life. If you were **whipped** in your dream, do you feel as if life has dealt you some harsh blows?

If you were **arrested** in your dream, this suggests the need for some kind of restraint in your waking life, or a fear of authority in general. If a **crime scene or forensic team** appears in your dream, your dreaming mind is encouraging you to understand your motives. If you were **chained, imprisoned or sentenced to death** in your dream, *see* NEGATIVE EMOTIONS. If your dream features the ultimate crime of **murder**, *see* NIGHTMARES.

STEALING

Dreams of **stealing, pickpocketing, burglary, robbery, theft, petty crime or taking what is not yours** generally suggest that you feel envious of another person in some way and want to have what they have. The key to the dream's interpretation is to identify who you are thieving FROM and what you are trying to take. If you are blackmailing someone in your dream or they are trying to blackmail you, this indicates emotional blackmail that you may be using to try and force someone to do as you want, or emotional blackmail used on you by someone else to get from you what they want.

Violence

ACCIDENTS

Dreams of accidents and catastrophes are examples of violent, negative actions with destructive consequences that warn you of the need to take urgent remedial action in an area of your life that is about to collapse into chaos. *See also* ACCIDENTS, ACTIVITIES AND ADVENTURES.

AMBUSH

Dreams in which you ambush or abduct someone reflect your desperation in waking life to ward off potential humiliation. If the person you are ambushing is someone you know, you also need to consider if you are secretly envious of this person in waking life. If this is the case, your unconscious may have been expressing your desire to capture or kidnap the qualities you admire and make them your own. Alternatively, you may have a hidden desire to control that person. If, however, you were ambushed, abducted or kidnapped in your dream, this suggests that someone or something in your waking life is trying to take control of you. Your

dream expresses your surprise and uncertainty about losing control.

ATTACK

Dreams in which your anger turns into violence and you start attacking someone usually suggest hidden hostility towards someone or something in your waking life. If you do find yourself punching, kicking or fighting with someone in your dream, try to think about what triggered the violent attack. It is possible that your dreaming mind conjured up the image of an attack as a safety valve through which you can release your frustration. Another interpretation suggests that dreams in which you inflict violence on someone or something may be prompted by a sense of helplessness or resentment in waking life. Perhaps there is someone whose authority you find powerless to resist? If this is the case, your dream may be compensatory by allowing you to exact revenge against the person or object of your resentment. It is also possible that your unconscious was encouraging you to stand up for yourself.

Alternatively, dreams which feature violence can symbolize your hidden desire for power and control in waking life. When interpreting this dream, try to identify whether the target of the violence represented an aspect of yourself, particularly if the victim was a stranger. Or could your unconscious have conjured an archetypal image of the stranger to bear the brunt of your anger?

RAPE

A dream of **rape** can be incredibly disturbing and you are unlikely to want to dwell on it, but it might be worth your while to ask yourself why your dreaming mind would put you through such an ordeal. If you have been a victim of sexual violence, then your dream may have been trying to resolve your feelings about the trauma. If this isn't the case, however, your dream may have been warning you about a predatory person in your life or warning you about someone in your life who is forcing you to do something against your will.

Whether you are **raped by a person of the same or the opposite sex** in your dream, the images reinforce your feelings of powerlessness and shame at having to bend to (non-sexual) demands in waking life. Your dreaming mind may have sent you this shocking image to encourage you to assert yourself and fight back. If you are **raping someone else** in your dream, this expresses your desire to humiliate or put someone in their place in waking life. If you **witnessed someone else being raped** in your dream but could not or would not prevent it, the message is again one of powerlessness and your feelings of frustration at being unable to right a wrong in waking life, or protect someone who is vulnerable. *See also* NIGHTMARES; SEX.

SHOUTING

Arguments and shouting in dreams, as in waking life, suggest that you are feeling in conflict or have opposing views on something or someone. Alternatively, they may be simply a release for negative feelings about someone or something that you are unable to express in waking life; in other words, your dream is allowing you to vent your frustration. The dream may also refer back to anxiety you experienced as a child when your parents were fighting and you felt powerless to stop them.

VICTIM

If **violence or negative actions are directed against you** in your dream, you may be punishing yourself in some way or feel guilty about something. Alternatively, you may be feeling vulnerable. If you **knew your attacker**, you may be unconsciously aware of a real threat that they pose to you in waking life. Another interpretation suggests that if others are behaving violently towards you in your dream, you need to take care not to upset others in waking life.

If your dream portrayed you **in front of a firing squad**, this is a symbol of your feelings of victimization in waking life. If your **attacker was female**, this may represent the archetypal terrible mother or huntress archetype, whilst a **terrible male attacker** may have represented the archetypal villain or ogre. In either case, try to identify who or what it is in your waking life that makes you feel so consciously or unconsciously afraid. If your dream **attacker was an animal**, the most likely interpretation is that the animal represents a problem within yourself rather than an external threat. The type of animal attacking you and your personal associations with it will be significant. Your unconscious often employs animals to symbolize aspects of your 'animal' or instinctual nature, so it is possible that you have neglected a basic human

The shadow

According to Jung, the shadow is the repressed or unacceptable part of your own personality, so if a **shadow or shadowy figure** appears in your dream, this represents an aspect of yourself that you are rejecting. The image may also suggest feelings of being overshadowed, put in the shade or feeling inferior in waking life. The shadow may also express a fear of the unknown, or of negative impulses.

A shadow can be a sign of coming events or a shadow cast from the future, because you often see a person's shadow before you see them. Bear in mind that the shadow or hidden part of your personality can express itself in many different guises in your dreams, although there is usually an air of disrepute, danger or negativity about the image.

■ *Idioms: afraid of your own shadow; shades of; shadow of your former self.*

urge or instinct that the attack is an attempt to have recognized.

If a dream attack leaves you **feeling battered and bruised from the array of blow and kicks that rained down upon you**, it is possible that your unconscious is trying to kick-start you into action. Is there something you need to do or have you been lazy recently? If your **injuries are serious**, however, this suggests deep emotional hurt. Try to identify who attacked you or stabbed you in the back, as this could help you with your interpretation. Try to recall also if any **weapons** were used, as weapons often have phallic or sexual associations. If **blood is pouring out of your wounds**, perhaps you are feeling drained of energy and vitality, or someone is sapping your strength.

Superstitions

Bad luck superstitions have been around for centuries and vary from culture to culture. Here are some of the most common in Western culture and their appearance in your dream may, depending on the context and mood of the dream, be a sign of misfortune or of the need to be cautious and consider all your options before moving ahead

Friday the thirteenth: The Scandinavians believed that the number thirteen was unlucky due to the twelve mythological demigods being joined by a thirteenth, an evil one, who brought misfortune upon humans. It was also said that Christ was crucified on Friday and the number of guests at the party of the Last Supper was thirteen, with the thirteenth guest being Judas, the traitor.

Walking under a ladder: A leaning ladder forms a triangle with the wall and ground. Triangles represent the Holy Trinity, and violating the Trinity by breaking it (walking through it) would put you in league with the Devil himself.

Black cats: Although sometimes thought to be a symbol of good luck (in ancient Egypt, the Goddess Bast was a black, female cat), during the Middle ages cats were thought to be demons in disguise and should thus be destroyed.

Spilling salt: Salt used to be an expensive commodity used mainly for medicinal purposes. For this reason, spillage was to be avoided at all costs. The idea that it is unlucky to do so probably stems from the belief that Judas spilt salt during the Last Supper.

Other superstitions associated with bad luck and misfortune include: **A bat flying into the house. An owl hooting 3 times. 3 butterflies together. Looking at the new moon over your left shoulder. A 5-leaved clover. Breaking a glass whilst proposing a toast. Putting a shirt on inside out. Red and white flowers together. Hearing a rooster crow at night. Cutting your nails on a Friday. Putting a hat on a bed. Getting out of bed left foot first. Violets blooming out of season. A picture falling. Breaking a mirror. Singing before breakfast. Opening an umbrella indoors. Giving away a wedding present. Stepping on cracks in the sidewalk. An itch inside your nose. Crossed knives. Seeing an owl during daylight. Spilling pepper. Killing a sparrow. Black birds. Dropping a wedding ring. Breaking a plate, especially if it has not already been cracked. Mending a garment whilst wearing it. Signing contracts in the months of April, July or November. Spilling ink. Breaking a bottle. Fastening a button into the wrong buttonhole. A candle falling over.**
Stepping on board a ship with your left foot. Tripping over when you leave your house.

Negative symbols in dreams

Dream symbols can have both positive and negative associations, but some dream symbols do tend to have more negative associations than positive and these include:

Acid: This suggests a corrosive, negative influence in your life. **Adder**: There may be a situation in which another person cannot be trusted. **Atom bomb**: Fear that someone else might destroy your happiness. **Avalanche**: A destructive force in your life. **Bad**: If you feel bad in your dream, this suggests that something is off balance in your waking life and that your environment is not positive for you. **Barbed wire**: Hurtful remarks are preventing you moving forward. **Bed wetting**: Anxieties over lack of control in your life. **Behind**: To be behind someone in your dream suggests that you feel inferior to them. **Bite**: Being bitten or biting someone is a symbol of aggression or hostility. **Boar**: Lust and gluttony. **Brutality**: The darker, more animalistic side of your nature. **Burglar**: Violation of personal space. **Chain**: Restriction. **Choke**: Inability to express yourself. **Crooked line**: Insincerity. **Devil**: Personification of the evil side of yourself. **Dirty**: Not at ease with your body, or lack of trust in someone or something. **Drowning**: Feeling overwhelmed. **Earthquake**: Emotional upheaval. **Empty and failure**: Lack of energy and enthusiasm. **Falling**: Lack of confidence. **Gall**: Feelings of bitterness. **Hole**: A difficult or tricky situation;

can also suggest emptiness. **Hood**: Deceit. **Ice**: Frozen emotions. **Immobility**: Feeling stuck. **Leak**: Losing energy. **Leper**: Feeling inferior or unworthy. **Maggots**: Impurities that can eat away at you; fears of death and illness. **Mantis**: Something devious within your life. **Marsh**: Feeling held back or bogged down. **Mist**: Emotional confusion. **Noose**: Fear of being trapped. **Obscenity**: lower aspects of the self. **Parasites**: Someone is attempting to live off your energy. **Poverty**: Feeling deprived of the ability to satisfy your basic needs. **Pus**: Something which is festering and has gone bad in your life. **Sadism**: Desire to cause harm to yourself or others. **Scar**: Old hurts that have not been dealt with. **Sick**: Bad feelings you need to get rid of. **Tar**: Emotions have become contaminated. **Torture**: Trying to come to terms with a great hurt. **Traitor**: An aspect of yourself that is letting you down. **Trespassing**: Intruding on someone else's personal space; lack of healthy boundaries. **Unemployment**: Not making the best use of your talents. **Vampire**: Fear of the unknown and negative energy. **War**: Conflict. **Winter**: Time in your life which is unfruitful. **Wound**: Hurt feelings or emotions. **X**: An error or something of which you need to take notice. **Yawn**: Boredom, but also a warning against aggression or abuse.

BIRDS

W**hat sets birds apart is their ability to fly and escape the boundaries and limitations of earth.**

For this reason, they are a universal symbol of transformation and the progress towards wholeness and harmony. Their association with the element of air – itself associated with aspirations and ideals – means they have also become a symbol of high-flying ambition and the quest for enlightenment. In Greek mythology, birds are often messengers of the gods, so in psychological terms they show that the unconscious is offering you wisdom and insight. Birds can take a bird's-eye view of the world and are therefore associated with the ability to take an objective overview of a situation.

Birds can also symbolize relationships with other people. For example, thieving birds, such as magpies, may suggest a threat to a relationship and the possibility of an affair; territorial birds, such as blackbirds, might suggest jealousy. Baby birds of all species can symbolize relationships with children or dependents. Freud believed that birds were sexual symbols that represent the penis, whereas Jung believed that birds in dreams were messengers from the unconscious, offering insight and wisdom.

Some people call women 'birds', and birds in dreams can sometimes denote the feminine principle or the anima in a man's dream.

Birds in dreams therefore represent freedom, transformation, insight, objectivity, relationships, intuition and the ability to see the bigger picture. If you see a bird alight, appear or take flight in your dream, ask yourself if you are wishing you could escape from pressures and responsibilities. Do you want to be free from a situation and alight at pastures new? Do you want freedom from a particular relationship or an outstanding debt? Or is it an attitude or situation you want to rise above? Do you long to travel or take flight? Alternatively was your unconscious referring to a 'flight of fancy', something you were hoping and wishing for in waking life? Or do you need to see the bigger picture and leave the details behind? And finally, because your unconscious conjures up bird images to reflect certain attitudes or situations in life, you also need to consider the symbolism associated with the following bird situations and different types of birds. At all times, the condition or health of the bird is important. If the bird is suffering in any way, this will suggest a certain degree of frustration. If the bird is flying or is in good condition, feelings of freedom and liberation may be indicated.

For centuries it was considered a good omen to dream of birds, but bear in mind that there are also many negative superstitions about birds. Here are some well-known ones that might influence your dream interpretation and your feelings towards a particular bird, or birds in general: albatross, sign of bad luck; black crow, sign of misfortune; buzzard, beware of gossip; cock, if it crows good news; dove, peace; eagle, success in business; goose, improvement in fortune; hawk, a bright future; magpie, a change of plan; owl, disappointment; stork, family problems; and turkey, bad luck, unless you are eating or killing it.

Bird Types and Situations

BIRD COLOR

The colors, as well as the general interpretation for birds, are significant here. For example, **black birds** represent one's shadow side and **white birds** one's open, expressive and free side, whilst **golden-winged birds** represent ambition. A **display of plumage** represents the way you see yourself. Is the plumage a gorgeous display of vibrant color, or a disappointing shade of shabby brown? *See also* COLORS.

BIRD EGG

Often a symbol of money in dreams, as in 'nest egg'. The condition that the egg is in will say a lot about your current financial situation, or your dreams of financial success. A **clutch of eggs** can also express your wish to have a large family, or represent the dawning of a new, exciting idea. If the **eggs are smashed**, have your dreams and hopes been smashed in some way? If you dream of **hatching birds**, this may suggest the birth of new ideas, projects and relationships, whilst if **baby birds** appear in your dreams, they are usually symbols of childhood and new beginnings.

BIRD'S NEST

A symbol of independence, refuge, home and security, which might indicate that you need something to fall back on. Alternatively, it may signify a prosperous endeavor, new opportunities, or an imminent fortune. **Making a nest** suggests homebuilding and the accumulation of material possessions, as in 'feather the nest', or partnership with someone else and the parental urge. If you dream of **birds leaving the nest**, it might suggest that you are taking on new responsibilities in waking life or are the parent of a child who is about to leave home. Similarly **an empty nest** can suggest your own sense of loneliness. Has your brood flown away to make their own way in the world?

BIRD SONG

If you hear bird song in a dream, the same interpretation as for **birds** in general applies. Pay attention to the sound. Is it

The Element Encyclopedia of 20,000 Dreams

sweet, happy, anxious, excited or alarming? All these impressions will help you with the interpretation.

CAGED BIRD

This can indicate restraint or entrapment or feeling stuck in a job, lifestyle or relationship. Is your freedom somehow restricted in waking life? Are your inhibitions stopping you expressing your personality? Is your job humdrum? Is your partner possessive? If you opened the door in your dream and **let the bird out** to fly away with joy in your heart, this is almost certainly a message from your unconscious to take steps in waking life to release yourself from restrictions and or inhibitions. If the **bird wouldn't or couldn't fly away**, are you putting limitations on yourself? If the **bird's wings were clipped**, is someone deliberately holding you back? **Freeing a bird from its cage** relates to expressing your emotions. If the bird in the cage is a **pet bird**, this often suggests happy memories. *See also* PETS.

Feathers

Your interpretation of feathers will be influenced by whether or not you are allergic to feathers but there are some common associations with features. If you are allergic to feathers, they may have a negative interpretation, but in general, feathers represent the beauty of the bird from which they came. If you know the bird from which the feather came, see the BIRDS A TO Z on page 84, and follow that interpretation. If you don't know the species, the general interpretation for **birds** applies. The color, or colors, of the feather are also significant. (See COLORS.) Feathers can also represent flight to aspects of yourself, and because of their connection with wind and air can suggest a connection to the more spiritual side of yourself.

If a **feather drops on you** from above in a dream, this is a message from your unconscious but what is that message? Features are light and so do you need to lighten up and take a more relaxed and softer approach to life? A **white feather** suggests cowardice. A **black feather** relates to the unconscious and your ability to explore it. **Feathers on a ceremonial headdress** suggest achievement (having a 'feather in your cap'). Features may also suggest disagreements of some kind; has someone ruffled your feathers? Alternatively are you taking a feather-brained or frivolous approach to some aspect of your life? Or do you need to feel comforted in some way? Feathers are often stuffed in pillows and are therefore associated with warmth and comfort.

FLYING BIRD

Represent a sunny outlook in life, rising above everything, a sense of freedom, independence and liberation, as if a weight has been lifted off your shoulders. **Flying birds** can also suggest aspirations and desires, and if the bird is flying high, an expansion of your viewpoint. Another interpretation is that flying birds represent sex, a similar form of release and uplift.

FLOCK OF BIRDS

A group of birds can often symbolize yourself and the people in your life. Are the birds flying in the same direction? If they are, this can suggest harmony; if they are not, confusion may be indicated. Are the birds huddled together? If they are, do you prefer to surround yourself with people similar to you, as in 'birds of a feather?' A flock of birds can also represent your need to be part of a group that you identify with and admire; but is the flock celebrating or stifling your individuality? If the birds are in a tree, the branches of the tree may represent your family life, and the leaves and birds your thoughts. If the birds are fighting, this suggests disagreements about viewpoints, or differing opinions, in waking life. If a bird is attacking you, it may represent an attack on your ideas and opinions, such as being criticized by a parent; another interpretation is it symbolizes a fear of others, or of going beyond your boundaries.

LARGE BIRD

A **large bird** represents the power of the unconscious to uplift or terrify, and can also suggest a threat or a parent.

WOUNDED OR DEAD BIRD

If **dead birds** appear in your dreams, they might represent a threat to your freedom, depression or the loss of purpose and meaning. In your waking life, an ideal or hope may have died, or your creativity has been stifled. **Wounded, molting or songless birds** can also represent problems that are constantly on your mind.

Birds A to Z

BLACKBIRD

Ancient dream oracles suggest that to see a **blackbird** in your dream is a bad omen, bringing about misfortune for you in the coming weeks. It is a good sign, however, if the **blackbird is flying**. Modern dream researchers suggest that anxiety is expressed by the presence of black birds, or a blackbird in particular, in dreams. If the **blackbird is attacking someone or something** in the dream, it is a comment on how you may be relating to your emotions in waking life.

BLUE JAY

If a **blue jay** appears in your dream, it could be calling your attention to something or someone you are neglecting in waking life. Alternatively, it can also suggest the need for humility, as you may be arrogant and over-confident.

The Element Encyclopedia of 20,000 Dreams

BUZZARD

An almost universal symbol of death and decay. It could represent an ugly or rotten part of yourself or your life.

CANARY

If the **canary is healthy**, it represents your own happiness. The opposite also holds true – if the **canary is hurt or injured** in any way, your own pain or injury is being mirrored.

CARDINAL

If a **cardinal** appears in your dream, it represents a sense of vitality and happiness. You feel as if you could accomplish anything.

CHICKADEE

Is there something or someone unique in your waking life that you need to pay more attention to? Small miracles happen every day in the most ordinary of activities. Perhaps your children are reaching milestones of development? Is your garden blossoming? Have you noticed how much your family and/or partner is supporting you?

CHICKEN

To see **chickens** in your dream can symbolize cowardice and stupidity, or chatter and gossip. Listen closely to what people may be saying about you or what you are saying about others. Alternatively, chickens can also show that there is potential for growth but this may only come about with the support of others. A **group of chickens** can also suggest that something you have done in waking life is about to rebound on you: as in chickens come home to roost.

The **cock** suggests male sexual characteristics and so the need to be more assertive. It is also the symbol of the new day and of keeping watch. Less positively, it might suggest that you are being overbearing and trying to rule the roost. The **hen** suggests being totally immersed in the concerns of motherhood. If a **hen crows** in your dream, this is taken to represent maternal domination. A **group of hens** may symbolize gossip and calamity. It may also suggest being 'hen-pecked' or that you feel being picked on, like chicken feed. **Chicks** represent babies or very young children in your life, or your feelings about your own childhood. They can also point to vulnerability. Are you counting your chickens before they have hatched?

CORMORANT

Symbol of introspection or inner wisdom. Are intellectual theories and ideas, or your studies in waking life, helping you to understand yourself better?

CRANE

Symbol of maternal love and of acts of kindness performed by yourself or others. Can also suggest the ability to cope with difficult situations and/or emotions in waking life.

CROW

To see a **crow** in your dream represents darker aspects of your character that need to be managed. Traditionally, crows are symbols of approaching death or bad news but they can also represent wisdom and or deviousness.

CUCKOO

Interpreting the presence of the **cuckoo** in your dream is difficult, as it can be a symbol of unrequited love or deviousness, whilst also being the herald of spring and an indicator of change from old to new. Do you need to change your direction or alter your approach in how you approach some situation? Alternatively, there may be someone in your life whose presence is unwelcome or annoying.

DOVE

The peaceful, calm side of a man's nature can often appear in a man's dreams as the **dove**. To see doves in your dream suggests peace, harmony, and innocence, or the longing for these in your waking life. The dove is furthermore a symbol of the Holy Spirit in Christianity, so if this resonates with you, your unconscious could be urging you to seek fulfillment. In particular, to see **white doves** in your dream symbolizes loyalty and friendship. It may also represent a message from the unconscious to become aware of your potential, and let go of thoughts of hate and revenge. A **pair of turtle-doves billing and cooing at each other** in your dream may suggest that you are longing to find a gentle, loving person with whom to settle down. **Doves that are building a nest** symbolize a joyous home life and obedient children.

DUCK

To see a **duck** in your dream can suggest childish behavior. If flying, it can represent freedom from superficiality; if swimming, it can represent the unconscious. Ducks can walk, swim and fly and may therefore represent your flexibility and ability to adapt to various situations. They may also warn against being superficial in the process, especially if you see a **white duck**. When interpreting the meaning of birds in dreams, it's always helpful to mull over any meanings that are attached to their names. For example, if you dreamed of an **albatross**, do you feel as if a burden has been placed around your neck? If a **duck waddled in**, are you trying to duck out of a situation, instead of confronting it head on? Or is criticism like water off a duck's back to you? Perhaps have you taken to a new hobby enthusiastically like a duck to water? Alternatively, the dream may indicate that you are setting yourself up or being set up in some way, as associated by the phrase 'sitting duck'.

EAGLE

As a bird of prey, **eagles** in dreams suggest precision, perceptiveness and far-sightedness. They also suggest dominance and supremacy. If **you are the eagle** in your dream, or associate yourself with it, this represents your wish to dominate. If you feel threatened, someone may be trying to dominate you. Eagles symbolize nobility, pride, fierceness, freedom, courage, and powerful intellectual ability. Eagles also

The Element Encyclopedia of 20,000 Dreams

indicate persistence, and the desire to realize your highest ambitions and greatest desires. If the **eagle is chained or has its wings clipped**, this suggests that you may be feeling trapped in a desperate situation where you feel you can't express yourself. To discover what is holding you back, consider what the eagle is chained to. To see a **nest of young eagles** in your dream signifies social advancement. If you **kill an eagle**, this suggests your ruthless determination to succeed: nothing is going to stand in your way even it if means upsetting people around you. If **someone else kills the eagle**, then your power may be taken away from you. If you **eat an eagle** in your dream, this shows that your strong and powerful character will lead you to success.

FALCON

As a bird of prey, the **falcon** has similar symbolism to the eagle and hawk. It is a symbol of freedom and hope over those who feel they may be restricted, but also suggests that your success may make others jealous. If you are **hunting a falcon**, you may be too aggressive in waking life and this aggression could cost you dear.

FLAMINGO

If a **flamingo** appears in your dreams, you may be experiencing or longing for new experiences or situations. You may also be in danger of worrying about how you appear to others too much.

FOWL

Symbol of potential worry, or of disagreements with friends in waking life.

GOOSE

A symbol of conformity, but also a sign that you are well grounded and practical. **Geese** are thought to represent loving relationships and, like the swan, can represent the possibilities of new beginnings. A **flock of geese** could be a warning against some kind of misfortune or silliness. Are you trying to kill the goose that laid the golden egg? **Wild geese** can represent the soul, the wanderlust and longing for freedom within all of us.

GULL

To see **gulls** in your dream represents the relationship between your emotions and your logic. If the **gulls are soaring**, you have a clear perspective on things but if the **gulls are wounded or dead**, this suggestions confusion and struggles between what your heart and your mind are telling you.

HAWK

As a bird of prey, with all the aggressive intentions associated with this class of birds, could your unconscious be urging you to watch someone like a **hawk**?

HUMMINGBIRD

To see **hummingbirds** in your dream can suggest concern with the details of your life, or the need to show that concern. Alternatively, it indicates your inability to commit to a relationship or project.

IBIS

Often associated with the stork, the **ibis** can be a symbol of determination and ambition.

JAYBIRD

Symbol of enjoyment and contentment. If the **jaybird** is dead or wounded, however, this suggests domestic troubles.

KINGFISHER

A symbol of dignity and calm.

LARK

Symbolic of a desire to transcend the mundane and fly high, if **larks fall during flight**, this suggests that your success will be bittersweet. To hear **larks singing** in your dream foretells of success in business, or happiness in a new situation. If the **lark is dead, wounded or injured** this denotes sadness and gloom. If you **kill a lark** in your dream, this suggests a loss of innocence.

LOON

Symbol of unconscious wisdom and your ability to search deep within for answers. To dream of a **loon** may also be a metaphor for someone who is 'loony', or crazy.

MAGPIE

Because of the belief that **magpies** are thieves, dreaming of one may suggest that someone is trying to take something away for you. Alternatively, it can be a sign of good news.

MOCKINGBIRD

Symbol of independence that can easily cross over into cockiness. You may be taking credit for the work of others, or getting what you want at all costs.

NIGHTINGALE

To see **silent nightingales** in your dream signifies disagreements among friends that can be easily resolved if communication is resumed. If the **nightingales are singing**, this suggests harmonious relationships or the desire for them.

OSTRICH

The **ostrich** famously sticks its head in the sand, so are you attempting to run away from responsibility? Are you not facing reality and living in a world of your own? You may be in denial, or unwilling to accept a situation.

OWL

Owls have the ability to see in the dark, and therefore represent your intuition or ability to really see what is going on around you and within yourself. The owl is also a wise advisor, but because of its association with darkness, it can also suggest fear or danger. In Jewish lore, it is unlucky to dream of an owl, but lucky to dream of any other bird. In some ancient traditions, the owl is connected to death. Death in this sense may also represent a symbolic death, such as an important transition in life or the end (death) of one phase and the beginning of a new one.

*Idioms: wisdom of the owl; night owl. To hear the **hoot of an owl** denotes disappointments, and forewarns that death creeps closely in the wake of joy and health. To see a **dead owl** signifies a narrow escape from a difficult situation or illness.*

PARAKEET

If a **parakeet** appears in your dream, it might suggest that your unconscious mind is trying to send you a message. The details of the dream should help you discover what that message is.

PARROT

To see a **parrot** in your dream represents gossip, repeating what others have said or copying the actions of others. It may also mean that you, or someone else, are being repetitive.

PARTRIDGE

A sign of independence and your leadership skills. On the other hand it can also suggest some kind of deception is occurring.

PEACOCK

To see a **peacock** in your dream is a sign of pride and vanity. In some traditions, however, it is a sign of the soul and because the peacock can shed its feathers and grow new beautiful ones, for Christians it is a symbol of resurrection or new life. As a male bird displaying its feathers, the peacock is a symbol of male sexuality and may be a warning against arrogance over your success. It also indicates a surge of new understanding from the plain and unadorned bird to the beauty of the fully-plumed bird.

PELICAN

To see a **pelican** in your dream represents devotion, sacrifice and compassion for others.

PENGUIN

Penguins are symbols of adaptability, but they can also represent stupidity or coldness in a relationship. They could be a sign that your problems are not as serious as you may think and that you need to keep your cool and remain level-headed.

PHEASANT

Depending on the circumstances of the dream and the condition of the **pheasant**, a symbol of prosperity and good fortune in your waking life.

PHOENIX

The **phoenix** is a universal symbol of rebirth, new life and immortality; of the power in oneself to transform from the depths of darkness or depression into new awareness.

PIGEON

To see a **pigeon** in your dream represents gossip or news. You may also be expressing a desire to return home.

Quail

To see a **quail** in your dream is a symbol of courage and good fortune. On the other hand it can also represent deviousness. To see a **live quail** is a sign of good luck. To see a **dead quail** symbolizes bad luck, especially in gambling. To **shoot a quail** in your dream suggests disagreements with your best friend. To **eat quail** in your dream warms against extravagant spending.

Raven

To see a **raven** in your dream can be suggestive of betrayal, disharmony, misfortune and dishonesty, but if the **raven is talking**, it can indicate insight. The meaning is complex, as it can symbolize both evil and wisdom.

Roadrunner

To see a **roadrunner** in your dream represents intellectual prowess, but might suggest that you are running from idea to idea. Do you feel the need to stop and consider your next plan of action?

Robin

Symbol of new beginnings and growth. It may also be a pun on someone whose name is **Robin**.

Rooster

Are you, or someone you know, being arrogant and over-confident with little regard for the feelings of others? If you **hear a rooster** in your dream, this suggests bragging. If **roosters are fighting** in your dream, this indicates rivalry and disagreements.

Seagull

Symbol of freedom and ambition.

Sparrow

Symbol of hard work, business and discipline.

Stork

Symbol of birth and babyhood, or new life and new beginnings.

Swallow

Symbol of hope and new beginnings.

Swan

The **swan** is often regarded as a divine bird. In a dream it suggests grace, beauty and dignity, especially if the **swan appears swimming in a pond**. In mythology, it represents the soul and its connection with the side of your nature that may be hidden. It may also be linked with endings or death ('swan song') as well as purity and innocence. On the other hand do you sometimes wish you could 'swan around' in your waking world?

Turkey

Have you been foolish or irresponsible in some way? Or have you not been thinking clearly? Alternatively, the turkey is associated with Thanksgiving, and therefore suggests family and a time of togetherness.

The Element Encyclopedia of 20,000 Dreams

If you are **hunting turkeys** in your dream, this suggests that you are trying to succeed through dishonest means. If the **turkey is flying**, you may soon rise from obscurity into a position of prominence. If you see **sick or dead turkeys**, your pride may have been injured in some way.

VULTURE

The **vulture** is a scavenger and feeds on the spoils of others. Are people around you taking advantage of you or are you concerned about the well-being of dependents? Alternatively, a vulture in your dreams can suggest that past experiences can give valuable insights into a current situation or problem. Do you need to 'pick off the bones' of a failed relationship or project, so that you can learn from your disappointment and move forward with your life?

WOODPECKER

The **woodpecker** symbolizes industry and diligence, and so to dream of one may suggest that there is something in your waking life that you have overlooked and need reminding about. In mythology, the woodpecker is the guardian of both kings and trees, and it is thought to have magical powers; therefore in dreams they may indicate that you have hidden powers and potential that need to be developed.

YELLOWBIRD

Symbol of good fortune when it concerns work or money, but not such a good sign for affairs of the heart.

BIRTH AND CHILDHOOD

Whilst pregnant women often dream about giving birth in anticipation of the upcoming event, dreams of giving birth typically have very little connection with the biological process of reproduction and more to do with a sense of being reborn, of fresh beginnings, of ideas coming to fruition or a period of personal growth. This sense is mirrored in everyday language: 'giving birth to a new idea', which refers to a project, not a baby.

For Jung, dreams about giving birth were important because he believed they represented a stage in the process of what he called 'individuation', the growth of the human psyche to maturation and wholeness. Birth therefore represents the start of an important new stage in your life and psychological development. We tend to dream of birth at the beginning of a new life stage, way of life, attitude, ability or project. We also have such dreams when we need to let go of the past and come to terms with the new. Birth is symbolic of new beginnings: beginning college, starting or ending a relationship, launching a new career and moving house are all associated with birth themes in dreams. Although women from their teen years onwards tend to have birth dreams more than men, it can happen to anyone at anytime. There may often be something strange or unusual

about the birth of the child. These details are important as they can symbolize what part of your life is changing and how others will receive this new development.

Jung also claimed that the symbol of the child, as with the symbol of birth, represents new beginnings and possibilities, and paves the way for future changes in your personality. A common theme in mythology is the 'divine child' or mystical hero or savior; for instance, the baby Jesus who saves the world from damnation. The divine child is the symbol of the true self, both vulnerable and pure, but also capable of great transforming power. In your dream, it may represent your true self urging you to explore new possibilities and reach your full potential. Therefore dreaming of a baby or child who could be yourself, one of your own children, a child you know or an unknown child, gives access to your own inner child. We all have parts of ourselves which are childlike, curious and vulnerable, and when we are able to get in touch with these parts we are reminded of our true potential for wholeness.

Although dreams of birth and childhood may appear to be simply nostalgic memories, most dream researchers believe that they have a strong bearing on your current circumstances in waking life. For example, your dream may be telling you that you have forgotten how to play or that you should take a fresher, more innocent approach to life. They may also be manifestations of an unconscious desire to escape from the responsibilities and problems of waking life. In addition, they may represent a part of you that needs reassurance and comfort, or a part of you that needs to care, to love and to begin anew. As such they can represent important psychological, spiritual and physical needs.

Birth and Baby Scenarios

PREGNANCY

If you dream that you are **pregnant, or hoping to be**, this is an example of wish-fulfillment. It may also indicate a fear of getting pregnant or anxieties about pregnancy and giving birth. Pay attention to your reaction to pregnancy dreams. Were you overjoyed, horrified, terrified? If you were **terrified**, it could be that you are worried you may have got pregnant by accident and your unconscious is urging

you to be more careful in waking life. **Men who dream of being pregnant** may also be giving unconscious expression to their apprehension about becoming a new father. If you are a woman, a dream about **being close to birth** may again be wish-fulfillment. Many expectant mothers claim to have had dreams about their **unborn baby** as it develops in this womb, and this could be an unconscious method of bonding. On the other hand, your unconscious may be presenting you with an unborn baby scenario to give you the opportunity to experience or role-play how you might feel if you were in that situation.

There is, however, an entirely different interpretation for pregnancy dreams that is especially pertinent if you are not pregnant, or hoping to be, or if you are a man. **Pregnancy dreams if you are not pregnant** suggest a yearning for unconditional love and acceptance. They can also indicate a period of necessary waiting before the completion of a project. A new area of your personality or potential is developing or 'hatching'; the seeds of a new concept are sprouting. If you are currently mulling over a new project or idea, pay attention to the details in your dream as they can reflect your feelings of confidence or anxiety about how well your idea is developing. Were you plagued with **morning sickness** or did you **sail through your pregnancy** without a setback?

If you felt sick and uncomfortable in your dream, this may reflect your waking anxieties, whereas if you glowed through your pregnancy, this may reflect your growing confidence. If you dream that **someone else is pregnant**, this can suggest an aspect of yourself that is ready to develop new skills. If a **woman dreams**

about a man being pregnant, this suggests her desire for a man to take more responsibility in waking life. If a **man dreams he is pregnant**, this suggests the discovery of new talents or potential within.

ABORTION/MISCARRIAGE/ STILL BIRTH

Dreams about **abortion, miscarriages and still birth** are likely to leave you feeling traumatized on waking, whether you are pregnant or not. And if you were expecting a baby such a dream is likely to be a nightmare. If this is the case, your dream was simply playing out your natural feelings of anxiety. However, most dreams about abortion, miscarriage and still birth aren't to be interpreted literally, as they refer to a concept you may have been mulling over, or an idea that is not realizing its potential or is not supported by your confidence or desire. There may be a need to reject a feeling, emotion, belief or concept which could be problematic in waking life. Decisions need to be taken which will help you get rid of what is no longer wanted in waking life.

How did you feel about the abortion in your dream? If you were **distressed**, perhaps someone or something is trying to prevent you from succeeding. If you were **relieved**, your unconscious may be urging you to change direction or change your mind. Perhaps the concept is too demanding or the idea is flawed in some way. On the other hand, the dream may also have referred to something or someone about which you feel guilty. Dreams that focus on miscarriage may have the same interpretation but they may also refer to a miscarriage

of justice, especially if you felt anger in your dream. Is someone in waking life taking the credit you deserve? Still birth dreams are in some ways more devastating and sad than dreams about miscarriage, as the baby has been brought to full term with the only element missing being the spark of life. In dreams, a **still born baby** may represent a talent you have allowed to die, or a relationship that has died due to neglect.

Birth control

To **see or use contraceptives** in your dream suggests that you are not allowing your creativity to express itself and that you are holding back some aspect of yourself. Alternatively, it signifies your anxieties about pregnancy or sexually transmitted diseases. In waking life, birth control is used to prevent a pregnancy and the details of the dream should indicate what it is in waking life you are trying to prevent. This could be pregnancy, but it could also refer to the suppression of creativity, maternal and paternal feelings, anxiety about sexual activity, and feelings or attitudes regarding responsibility.

GIVING BIRTH

If you are a woman and you dream of **giving birth**, the first question to ask yourself is do you actually want to get pregnant? If you do, your dream may be an example of wish-fulfillment. The purpose of your unconscious was probably to fulfill your fervent desire for all to go well. There have also been recorded instances of women and men dreaming about the birth of a baby before they even knew they were expecting; somehow the dream was a response to the presence of an actual fetus, not yet detected by doctors and pregnancy tests. If you are pregnant and you dream that **labor and delivery was difficult**, it probably reflects anxieties about the impending birth. The same applies to dreams about giving **birth to an animal**; they are simply mirroring your concerns and anxieties. If you are a prospective father, your dream may also be depicting your hopes and fears for the welfare of your unborn child.

If you are not pregnant, birth dreams can indicate a desire for children but are more likely to represent something else in waking life. The birth of a child signals a new beginning and the emergence of new life; in dreams the meaning is much the same: a new way of life, a new attitude, a new discovery, a new project and so on. If you **hear about a birth, or watch or witness a birth** in your dream, this also suggests the beginning of a new and fruitful cycle in your life. Birth dreams therefore are an expression of big changes that have been occurring for a long period of time. Did the **dream delivery go well or was it difficult**? Again, the answer may indicate the likely ease of turning your hopes into reality. If this doesn't apply, then dream births may symbolize your brain child, perhaps an idea or a project you are longing to complete successfully.

Alternatively, did your dream focus on one aspect of birth – the **umbilical cord**, for example? If the **cord was wrapped**

Birth dreams during pregnancy

Pregnancy is one of the most life-changing, and physically and emotionally demanding challenges a woman can face in her lifetime. Research shows that the dreams of pregnant women can comment on the physical, psychological and emotional issues she has to deal with. The most common dream themes at this time concern **animals and water**. In the early stages of the pregnancy, these dreams may be gentle and calming, but towards the end of the pregnancy they can be traumatic or even become nightmares. Such alarming dreams are considered a normal reaction to the anxiety every woman unconsciously feels about her unborn baby and about giving birth.

It is also very common for pregnant women to dream about having the baby and these dreams are again often bizarre and disturbing; for example, dreaming about a **baby that is born dead, malformed or with a monster's head**. It has been suggested that such anxiety dreams serve a purpose: they release a lot of unconscious tension and fear, allowing the mother to be more relaxed at birth.

around the baby's neck, this may indicate that your ideas are being strangled or in danger of being strangled. If the **cord was neatly severed**, this can indicate that your ideas have been cut free and are now independent of you. If there were **problems cutting the cord**, this could be a symbol of a grown-up family that is beginning to leave home. Or it may be that you yourself are finding it hard to fly the family nest and branch out on your own. If you are **not able to see your baby after a difficult labor**, this can indicate that you are laboring in vain in waking life and aren't being rewarded by the sight of your mental offspring.

BABY

If a **baby is born or appears in your dream**, were you the proud parent? If you were, this suggests a budding talent or creative potential that is just emerging. If you **give birth to two or more babies**, this may symbolize groups of ideas or personal talents. On the other hand, it could also suggest that you need to lavish extra care and attention on your 'brainchild' if it is to be a success; if the dream baby is **premature**, this message is stressed further.

If you are **looking after someone else's baby** in your dream, it could indicate that in waking life you feel as if you have been left 'holding the baby' in some way. Did you **enjoy holding the baby or feel panicked** by the responsibility? If you **felt anxious**, maybe you are worried about the responsibility that has been placed upon your shoulders in waking life. Pay attention to the behavior of the baby. If the **baby is happy**, this suggests that you are fulfilling the needs of your brainchild, but if the **baby is**

distressed, this suggests that your idea, project or talent isn't being developed or cared for.

If you **lost or injured a baby** in your dream, this can suggest a loss of confidence on your part and an inability to put in the hard work required to see a project to completion. If you are the parent of a young baby and you have this kind of dream, it could indicate that you are finding it hard to cope with the demands and responsibilities of caring for a baby in waking life. Your unconscious could also be highlighting your sense of guilt about not being a perfect enough parent and your desperate need for time to yourself.

If, however, procreation in waking life is not at the forefront of your conscious mind, dream babies may be an expression of an unconscious counterpart trying to acquaint you with the baby, or your own inner child, within. This is an aspect of yourself that is dependent on others for financial or emotional support, or the part of you that longs to be reborn and relive your life again. Or perhaps this 'baby' is a part of the personality or aspect that has not been 'born' or expressed before. If your dream baby is **born with an adult body and a baby head**, this suggests an approach to life that is still immature. If your dream baby is **born with a baby body and an adult head**, it suggests adult intellect but emotional and sexual immaturity. If the baby is **beautiful, gifted or remarkable** in some way, this represents the emergence of personal insight and previously unconscious elements of yourself.

A **baby boy** in your dream suggests the birth of a new phase of self-expression and new activities and achievements, whereas a **baby girl** suggests new aspects of feeling

The Element Encyclopedia of 20,000 Dreams

and relationships with others. If the **baby is crying**, this indicates that your fundamental needs for love, support, comfort and happiness are not being met. Is there something distressing you at a feeling level that you are not acknowledging? If you **drop a baby** in your dreams, this suggests carelessness in dealing with your basic needs, especially as it concerns connection with others. It can also refer to a mistake or missed opportunity, or a feeling that someone has dropped or lost interest in you. If the **baby is smiling**, this suggests a deep level of comfort, security and satisfaction.

HOLE/TUNNEL

Some dream researchers believe that birth dreams lead us back to life in the womb and the traumas associated with our own experience of birth. The psychoanalyst Nandor Fodor has written extensively about the subject of birth dreams, and gives the example of a woman who was born with the umbilical cord wrapped around her neck and who, in adult life, frequently dreamt of **being strangled**. She also gives an example of a person who received a head injury during birth, and in adult life frequently dreamt of **being scalped**. For example, dream attempts to **escape from a tunnel, especially if small and dark**, may refer either to memories of birth or to strategies you need to develop to reach inner resources. **Seeing or going into a hole** in your dreams may refer to a place, such as the womb, into which you might fall to feel protected.

FOSTERING AND ADOPTION

Dreams of **fostering and adoption** suggest a new approach to life, or taking on the responsibility of someone, or something, that needs your care and help to grow. If you fostered or adopted a baby in your dream, did you welcome the child into your home with love and gratitude? If you are thinking about adopting or fostering, your dream could reflect your feelings about this, but if this isn't in your plans, the dream may be showing you how satisfying it can be to offer love and guidance to someone who needs your care. Do you need to find an outlet for your urge to love and nurture selflessly in waking life? This doesn't have to be a child, but perhaps a partner, a pet, a friend, a project or a charity. If you dreamed of **fostering or adopting someone you know in waking life**, perhaps you long to lavish attention on that particular person.

BAPTISM AND NAMING CEREMONY

To dream of **being baptized** suggests a new influence is entering your life. You are leaving old attitudes behind and opening yourself up to new possibilities. Is there an idea or a concept that is about to be presented to an appreciative audience? Or perhaps your unconscious is urging you to transform your mindset radically and make positive changes to your lifestyle? If **godparents** appeared in your dream, were they people you knew? If they were, perhaps your unconscious is suggesting that they are the ones you should turn to for help. If you didn't know who they were, you should seek out the necessary help and support.

Baby extras

Breast-feeding

To dream that you are breast-feeding symbolizes tenderness, love, nurturing and motherly love. It indicates your unconscious connection with the nurturing principle. To **see someone nursing or dream that you are nursing** suggests that you are nurturing, or need to nurture, aspects of yourself.

Cradle and cot

To **see a cradle** in your dream represents a new project or a fresh start. As a precognitive dream it may represent pregnancy, and in a man's dream it can represent the need to be protected and cared for. Your dream may be telling you to regain some control and independence in your life. An **empty cradle** suggests fear about not having children, or fears about the responsibility of becoming, or being, a mother. If you are **rocking the cradle**, this may be a reference to your power: think of the saying 'the hand that rocks the cradle'.

Dummy/feeding-bottle/ nappy/pacifier/rattle

If you are pregnant, any baby-related items that appear in dreamland may be reflections of your current preoccupation with all things baby. If you are not pregnant or thinking about starting a family, baby-related items in dreams link in with the birth theme of new beginnings and possibilities. They can also represent your desire to be supported, loved and protected. If you dream of a **baby sitter or nanny**, this may be a warning or a comment on your own security and ability to handle things by yourself.

Nursery

A nursery full of babies suggests that starting a family may be high on your agenda, but it can also mean that you may be thinking about keeping a pet, or nurturing a group of people or a project. If the **nursery is badly run,** this is a reflection of your anxiety about leaving your children or a sick family member under other people's supervision. If the nursery school in your dream is **full of very young children**, this suggests that your ambitions will take you far, but if the **nursery is empty or deserted**, your plans may be unrealistic and you should review them before proceeding further. If you dreamed of being **back at kindergarten**, or some other environment strongly associated with the early years of learning, it may be that your unconscious is transporting you back to that time in order to remind you of a valuable lesion that you learned, or failed to learn, there. For example, did your kindergarten teacher encourage you to join in with the activities, and have you been aloof in waking life recently? On the other hand if you dreamed that you were **playing around with your friends and driving the teacher to distraction and received a bad report** as a result, could this be a pattern that is being echoed in waking life? By reminding you of the relationship between cause and effect, your unconscious may be urging you to stop using immature strategies to gain popularity or impress others, and start applying yourself instead. *See also* SCHOOL AND WORK.

If **you are baptizing someone**, this means you are ready to pass on your knowledge to others. There is also a possibility that you may be having religious beliefs imposed on you if you have this dream. Baptism is symbolic of many things: rebirth, regeneration and renewal and the common theme for all these is the sense of optimism surrounding them. If you are a Christian, baptism is associated with a washing away of original sin and the start of a new life as a Christian; your dream may have been denoting your wish to be reborn or – depending on who is being baptized or christened – your desire for someone else to undergo a transformation of some kind. On the other hand, your unconscious may also be recalling a baptism you witnessed in waking life.

Childhood Scenarios

ABANDONED BY PARENT/CARER

You may have a dream in which you are a child again and are being **left at school, in a shop, in the street or park by your mother and running after her, perhaps not being able to reach her or not being heard**. To be abandoned by a parent or carer in a dream – or to be separated from them so you feel lost and vulnerable – may represent a sense of not being wanted when you were young. This may not actually have been the case, but you may feel that way. Alternatively, such a dream might also suggest that you are searching in waking life for the emotional freedom to be yourself and to be independent. On another level it may be pointing to your need to find guidance or help from others; many people have dreams of childhood abandonment after the death of a loved one. If you are **trying to attract your parents' attention but they cannot hear you**, such a dream may be saying that you feel neglected emotionally and you need to express your feelings and be understood by others.

Boy/Girl

If the child in your dream is a **boy**, you know the dream is commenting on your feelings about the boy but referring these things to yourself. For example, if the **boy is disruptive**, it may depict your own desire to cause disruption of some kind in waking life. It may also indicate a male child in waking life who is giving you cause for concern. If you **do not recognize the boy**, it suggests that you need to be a little more adventurous and bring excitement to your life. In a man's dream, an **unknown boy** can represent new potential and the part of himself he needs to 'father' in order to grow and mature. In a woman's dream, an unknown boy can suggest your developing ability to express your feelings in actions.

If the child in your dream is a **girl**, this may be a symbol of your spontaneous, vulnerable side trying to emerge, regardless of whether you are male or female. In a man's dream, it can refer to feelings about a daughter, or emotions and sexual feelings towards the opposite sex in general. In a woman's dream, the girl can represent a sister or a daughter, but can also represent aspects of the dreamer portrayed by the girl. According to ancient dream oracles, **threatening a girl or boy** in a dream is an ominous sign that indicates you should take extra care of your health in the weeks ahead.

CHILD

A dream about a **child** (under the age of thirteen or so) may be a dream about yourself. If you are having a wonderful time **playing and dressing up**, the dream may be encouraging you to have more fun in your adult life. A dream about a child **refusing to share or being inconsiderate** may be a comment on your own weaknesses. Has your recent behavior or approach to life been a little childish? If **you are the child** in the dream, this can suggest a need to shed some of your current responsibilities in real life or express your real self.

If you are **caring for a child or infant**, and not really wanting to, perhaps someone in waking life is being demanding and requiring too much attention. If you **want to have a child and dream of one**, you may become a parent in the not-so-distant future. If you **lose a child**, whether your own or an unknown child, you may be anxious that you have taken on responsibilities you cannot handle. If the child is **one of your children**, look up son and daughter. If your dream did not evoke specific memories of your own childhood or an **unknown child** appeared, your unconscious may have summoned up an archetype in the staring role – that of the inner child. Whether your inner child was portrayed by you or by another character in the dream, he or she represents the part of you that, Peter Pan-like, has never grown up, or a part of you that you have banished from your waking life, but longs to be rediscovered. Your unconscious may therefore be highlighting your own immature behavior, or else your longing to recapture childhood innocence. Once again, the clue lies in the child's behavior.

If the child in the dream is **bullying another child**, this could be related to how you are cruelly treating someone in real life. If, however, **you are the victim** in the dream, do you feel vulnerable, abused and powerless in waking life? If the child in the dream is **happily playing with their toys**, do you long to return to the optimistic, childhood state of mind before the realities of life closed in avenues of opportunity? Do you long to return to a time when anything seemed possible? Try to remember the child's behavior – was he or she **friendly or unfriendly, smiling or throwing a tantrum** and consider whether the dream is commenting on your own current life and behavior. Do you have a tendency to fly into a childish rage when you don't get your way in waking life?

The Element Encyclopedia of 20,000 Dreams

CHILDREN

Children in a dream are symbols of joy and warmth, or of your desire for joy and warmth in waking life. If **children are giving flowers, fruits or sweets**, this suggests unexpected success or happiness. If, however, the **children are quarrelling**, this indicates domestic problems. Children in dreams can also represent feelings about your childhood, or current feelings of dependency or vulnerability. What is happening to the child in the dream will help you determine the interpretation.

If the children in your dream are **boys**, they symbolize high energy levels and new beginnings. If the **boys are playing**, this suggests the resolution of domestic or financial problems. If, however, the **boys are quarrelling**, this dream may be a warning to listen to the advice of people around you, especially if they are older than you. Perhaps you have been acting rashly. If one or more of the **boys are injured**, it is a serious warning to take a sober look at how you run your day-to-day life.

If the children in your dreams are **girls you know** and they are smiling, friendly or affectionate, this suggests that your general attitude of honesty will be much appreciated by those around you. If you **don't know the girls**, this can suggest the beginnings of a new relationship. If **the girls are untidy, disruptive, crying, angry or abusive**, this could be a warning to show more understanding to your partner and those around you to avoid arguments and unnecessary misunderstandings.

EXAMINATION

Fear of failure can often originate in childhood and stem from fears of abandonment, so dreaming you are a **child sitting for an examination or revising for a test and worrying that you won't pass** may express a fear of failure. Dreams of being **late, unprepared or failing an examination** show that you feel unprepared for the challenge life is currently throwing at you. Examinations are stressful and they can highlight your shortcomings. Your dream is urging you to stop fearing failure, to emphasize what is right and not what is wrong, and to give yourself permission to succeed.

Childhood Dreams

The following dreams are typical of childhood and mirror the stresses, experiences and questions associated with this stage in life. It is possible, however, to have one of these dreams at any stage in your life. *See also* STAGES OF LIFE.

BECOMING A SUPERHERO

In this dream, a child may find themselves **faced with an evil force or power** and, as in the breathing underwater dream, just when the situation becomes desperate or hopeless, they find that they **transform into a superhero with extraordinary powers**. As a superhero, they destroy their enemies and resolve the conflict. Not surprisingly, this dream is more common with boys than girls, perhaps because from an early age boys are influenced by superhero role models, such as Spiderman or Power Rangers. The dream may also continue into adulthood.

The child who has this kind of dream tends to be coping with some kind of problem or obstacle; for example, financial hardship, or family tensions and conflicts, and the dream may reflect these tensions. The child may feel that they are trapped by the situation and are helpless to do anything about it; the dream refers to their desire to make problems disappear magically. But this kind of dream may point to more than a wish for magical powers, as it also shows the dreamer that within them these magical and unique powers are just waiting to be discovered.

BREATHING UNDER WATER

In this nightmare with a happy ending, a child may dream that they are **drowning and unable to reach the surface to breathe**. Then, incredibly, just as they realize they are going to drown, they continue breathing and **can breathe underwater** in their dream. Like the dreams of flying, this dream is also about discovering abilities during times of crisis or when thrown into a particular situation. The water theme suggests a sense of being overwhelmed and vulnerable to the situations that surround us. It shows that a sense of panic is not only natural but necessary to discover the ability to breathe (survive) in a new environment (underwater).

This kind of dream tends to be outgrown by the time one reaches the age to leave home, but it can and does re-emerge if you are thrown into difficult, new or challenging situations in adult life. It should be seen as a reminder of your ability to survive tough circumstances, even when you feel out of your depth. The dream can also arise among adults who find themselves not only in a difficult new situation, but in a situation that does not allow them to express their own concerns.

Childhood dreams

Research has shown that sensitive or gifted children tend to be more prone to dreams and nightmares. Dreams in childhood often mirror the stress and confusion that is associated with the early years of our lives. Frightening dreams or nightmares are common to children up to the age of around eight. If you are a concerned parent, simply talking about the dream with your child can help dissipate the tension around them. Avoid the instinct to tell the child that it was just a dream and that dreams aren't real, as this may discourage your child from confiding in you, or simply frustrate them because you don't take it seriously. You may also have a child who dreams with their eyes open for a few seconds after the dream is over and they are awake. In general, such experiences are not signs of a disorder, but if you are concerned, talk to your doctor or a pediatrician.

The Element Encyclopedia of 20,000 Dreams

FLYING

Dreams about **flying** are common to late childhood and early adolescence. The dreams vary: some dream of **jumping or falling from a great height**, others **run and jump into flight**, whereas others **jump from a great height and discover that they can fly**. Dream researchers believe that dreams about flight can reflect the drive within each of us to be free to express, explore and experience life, so it makes sense that we dream most often about flying during a stage in life when we are becoming aware of abilities that will take us places later in life.

MONSTERS

Monster dreams in childhood reflect dramatically frightening things that have disturbed a child, in particular how frightening it can be for a child when the people they love and trust behave in an angry or scary way. This may be, for example, when a loving mother loses her temper or a caring dad disciplines his child. According to some psychologists, children dream of monsters because they are unwilling to believe anything bad about the people they are dependent on. If you are a parent and feel that you are reflected in monster dreams, try to encourage your child to share these dreams with you. Bear in mind that, in some instances, the monster may reflect someone else in your child's life: a sibling, an uncle or aunt, or even a neighbor. This is particularly so among school-age children who have to meet the expectation of peers and teachers.

PERFECT MONSTERS

This dream is common to the middle childhood and preteen years. In the dream there is a **repetitive task that needs to be performed usually at the command of monsters**. The task is usually something gruesome or sinister, like **digging graves or sorting body parts**. The dreamer is horrified by the task but numbed by the repletion and tedium, and in the dream more likely to be upset about the workload than the actual nature of the task. This dream often reflects the stress of young children who feel they must achieve and meet standards imposed upon them. The unconscious is reminding them that the casualties of a task-orientated approach to life may be other desires, interests and feelings. Although many dreams during this stage of life reflect the joy of achievement and the desire for recognition, this dream represents the tension associated with high achievement.

SINISTER TOYS

Another very common childhood dream is of a **toy or other harmless object, such as a book or pencil, that suddenly becomes menacing**. Again such dreams can reflect tensions about situations the child find threatening or disturbing. If your child has such dreams, you may want to consider if a normal aspect of your life, for example, a camping trip or relatives visiting, is making a child feel uncertain.

SOMETHING IN THE BEDROOM

One of the most common dreams of early childhood is that there is something scary in the bedroom: a **monster in the wardrobe or aliens in the corner of the room**. A child may feel as if something or someone is coming to get them. These kinds of dreams tend to reoccur and it is easy to assume that something is upsetting the child in waking life; it is worth noting, however, that these dreams are amongst the most common in childhood, as a child reaches out to discover the world with all its excitement – and sometimes dangerous possibilities. If there is tension in the home or a lot of uncertainty and inconsistency, this can trigger stressful dreams for a child. **Scary monsters** tend to represent people, whereas **bugs or slimy things** may represent situations. You may have to be patient and gentle, and create a feeling of stability as your child learns to adjust to changes in the world around them.

WILD ANIMAL ATTACK

When children begin school they often dream of **wild animals attacking**, such as lions, bulls, alligators and bears. Wild animals tend to reflect a person or situation that is upsetting the child. For example, a child may be worried about parents who are constantly fighting, and this fear can be symbolized as a bear fight. Or a child may be frightened by a strict head teacher, who subsequently appears in their dreams as a mean lion.

Childhood Revisited Scenarios

It is during childhood that we learn many of the fundamental rules and responsibilities of life. It is also the time when we develop our personalities and become increasingly socialized. It makes sense, therefore, that dreams of **revisiting a place or a scenario from your own childhood** often focus on lessons that you learned, or failed to learn, and these lessons may be relevant to your current situation. If you dreamed of a **particularly happy childhood memory** – for example, you are seven years old and your dad brings home your first bike, or you are five years old sitting happily on your mum's lap sucking your thumb – the dream could either be pointing to your nostalgia for a time when life was full of fun, or it could be more concerned with your present feelings of insecurity. The dream is reminding you of a time when life was simple, and in so doing, it compensates you for your current feelings of confusion. If you are facing a difficult decision, it could also have been highlighting your need to put yourself forward and take a risk by focusing on your new bike – something you wanted but also feared, as you weren't wholly confident riding it yet.

Consider, too, whether your unconscious has cast archetypal figures in the role of your mother and father. Relation-figures in dreams of childhood can often represent archetypes rather than actual family members. Alternatively, if your

unhappy childhood returns to haunt you in dreams (which may reoccur), your unconscious may be forcing you to relive those miserable times in an attempt to make you confront the source of your distress and deal with it, now that you have an adult understanding of the situation. Your unconscious is trying to help you come to terms with what happened to you, so you can put it behind you.

Activities and environments associated with childhood

Dreams about **activities and environments associated with childhood** can be either motivating or discouraging, depending on the details of your dream and how you felt. For example, if you had a happy time playing with your dolls or a toy train set, your dream may simply be reminding you of the simple pleasure of letting your guard down from time to time to do nothing useful but play and relax. These kinds of dreams are particularly common if you have been extremely busy recently and haven't had time to have fun. If, however, you were bored by the toy or activity in your dream, your unconscious may be urging you to put away childish things that don't really give you stimulation and satisfaction, and to spend your time more productively.

Toys in dreams not only reflect your desire for more play, or urge you to grow up in some way, they can also suggest nostalgia for childhood that has been lost. **Dolls** are especially important because they so resemble the human form, and because children endow them with emotions and characters. Your dreaming mind may therefore use a doll to symbolize something or someone in your life. For example, if you **stick needles or pins in the doll, or mistreat it** in any way, this can represent negative feelings towards a particular person. Many doll dreams use the doll as a target for violence and, if this is the case, it could also refer to how the dreamer felt as a child when smacked emotionally or physically – like a helpless child. Dolls can also represent emotions that the dreamer would like to discharge on someone else, or the feeling of wanting to be a precious doll to someone. It may also express some undeveloped part of the dreamer's personality and the need to relearn some childhood lessons we may have forgotten.

If you dreamed that you were in a **playground surrounded by other children**, were you enjoying yourself or did you feel left out? If you felt exhilarated, your unconscious may once again be signaling your need to have more fun in waking life, but if you felt aloof or alone from the other children, it could suggest that you prefer to play no part in the immature behaviour currently displayed by a group of people in your waking life. *See also* references to toys and games in LEISURE.

BODY

Typically, dreams about the body, or parts of the body, occur for four reasons.

The first is that in waking life, your body and/or body image has taken center stage. For example, if you had a manicure yesterday or cut yourself shaving, your unconscious may simply be recalling that. The second reason is that dreams about your body, or body parts, can signal ailments before you consciously recognize what is wrong with you; sometimes even before there are any physical signs. This isn't to say every nightmare suggests serious illness, but if you do have a dream about any part of the body that is injured or painful, especially if it is a reoccurring one, it might be worth booking an appointment for a check-up.

The third reason is that some dreams about the human body are simple reflections of the dreamer's feeling about their own body or appearance. These dreams can be significant markers of the dreamer's self-esteem regarding their physical appearance. If in the dream the body appears beautiful and healthy, then the dreamer may be feeling good about themselves. However, an unattractive or unhealthy body could point to signs of insecurity, or body image problems.

The fourth reason is that in dreams, the body often represents the ego, the self or the lifestyle of the dreamer. That is why broken bones or injuries can symbolize emotional pain, or losing parts of yourself. When you lose or give up parts of yourself in order to fit in with or please others, psychologists call this 'fragmentation'. We all do this to a certain extent in our lives, but when we do it too much or for the wrong reasons, the unconscious may send out warning signals. The dreaming mind may then express its concern in body image dreams, not only about your health and happiness, but about your ability to cope when your true nature is profoundly censored.

For instance, if you dream of missing a hand or foot, or having an organ or other body part removed, this can be a sign that a portion of your potential is being lost as a result of a path you have chosen in waking life. A common dream is one where you lose teeth; this is a great example of your dreaming mind issuing you with a warning. It is asking you just how far you are willing to compromise, and reminding you that what you are losing may be irreplaceable.

If body images appear in your dreams, it can help to think of body-related expressions you may use to describe feelings; for example, 'I lost my head,' 'feels like I'm losing my right arm,' 'I don't have a leg to stand on,' or 'can you stomach it?' When we say these things, we are not being literal. We haven't lost a leg or an arm, we are expressing an emotional response and our unconscious uses images to express the emotions these phrases convey; typically, a sense of loss of direction, helplessness or confusion. Such dreams often begin to make sense when you view the body images as parts of yourself, and connect their meanings to your emotional responses. *See also* SICKNESS AND HEALTH.

Body Images Scenarios

ANESTHETIZED, COLD OR DEAD BODY

The image of an **anesthetized body** can represent a deadening of feeling, or a loss of passion and creativity in waking life. The same meaning applies to **coldness of the body**, with the implication of emotional coldness, lack of enthusiasm or distancing oneself from others. If the coldness is in the **lower part of the body**, this suggests sexual coldness and again, lack of passion. **Coldness in the chest** (heart) suggests lack of feelings or feeling cold towards someone. **Cold feet** indicate a fear of doing something or indecision. The image of a **dead body** in a dream depicts feelings and

potential to which we have not given expression in daily life.

APPEARANCE

How your body appears in a dream can offer vital clues when it comes to interpretation. In many cases, the interpretation is fairly obvious: if you are **smiling** you feel confident, if you are **frowning** you feel annoyed. Are you confident and tidy in your dream, or are you tired and unhappy? All these factors represent the state of your mind, and perhaps your health, at the time of the dream. If your **body disappears** in a dream and you **become invisible or you aren't aware of your body**, this clearly suggests that you are feeling ignored, isolated and perhaps lonely. If you **leave your body** in a dream, this indicates a need to get away from cares and responsibilities. If you **grow tall** in your dream, your unconscious may be mirroring waking feelings of satisfaction with yourself; but if you were horrified to **shrink small**, it may be that you feel insignificant and looked down upon, or that you long to shrink away from a problematic situation. To dream that you are **becoming fat** is to recognize that you need to widen the scope of your activities in some way. It can also indicate fear of taking on too much responsibility.

DISEASED, DISMEMBERED, INJURED AND DEFORMED BODY

If the **body is diseased** in a dream, this suggests a sickness of attitude or it could simply indicate extreme emotional and physical fatigue. A **dismembered body** indicates emotional and mental distress; perhaps you are tearing yourself apart over something or someone, or your life is falling apart. **Half a body** dream images suggest a lack of balance in your life between your outer and inner life. If the **top half of your body is missing**, this indicates lack of reasoning and emotional intelligence. If the **bottom half is missing**, this relates to loss, or denial of instincts and sexuality. If the **body is injured or you see injuries**, this suggests emotional scars or hurts, or repressed anger. If the **body is cut open**, this indicates a vital change within yourself or the release of emotional tension. In times past, such dreams were interpreted as the release of 'evil spirits', hence the association of a sometimes painful release of tension.

Loss of limbs in a body usually indicates a sense of inadequacy, sometimes connected with the limb that is lost. For example, **loss of legs** could suggest an inability to stand up for yourself or someone dependent on you. **Loss of an arm** could indicate an inability to influence other people, or to give and receive. If your **body is burnt** in the dream, this suggests an emotional scar, and if the **burn is painful**, this suggests that you are relating to this hurt in an unhelpful, self-destructive way. If, however, the **burning isn't painful**, it has a more positive interpretation: feelings of potential and new beginnings.

Marks on the body in a dream suggest things you carry with you in life, or experiences that have marked you. If your body is **crawling with maggots**, this indicates the need to cleanse your body of toxins, infection or resentment. A **murdered body** in a dream represents aspects of your life that you find hard to deal with, such as anger towards a family member. Sometimes such anger may be a way of avoiding the real

issues involved and, if this is the case, the dream murder may show how you feel about being 'murdered' by lack of love or trust. If you are **pulling things out of your body** in your dream, this suggests growing self-knowledge; you are becoming aware of thoughts and emotions of which you were previously unaware. *See also* SICKNESS AND HEALTH.

Ugliness

Dreaming that you are **ugly** may indicate anxiety about what others think of you. The central question when it comes to interpretation is whether you believe yourself to be ugly, or whether others are imposing this view on you. Perhaps your feeling of physical inadequacy is due to a change in your waking life, such as being pregnant.

Other changes that may influence your body image include a shift in physical or moral behavior, such as smoking, drinking, using drugs, becoming sexually active, or participating in sexual experiences you once considered taboo. This dream is worth serious consideration as how we feel about our bodies is often a significant part of how we feel about ourselves overall as a person. If you are having recurring dreams of personal ugliness, then counseling for self-esteem or eating disorders may be worth considering.

The Element Encyclopedia of 20,000 Dreams

Toilet and elimination themes

Elimination in dreams can symbolize release and self-expression. When we **urinate or eliminate**, we are ridding ourselves of bodily waste and when these actions occur in dreams your unconscious is referring to the removal of emotional waste, such as unhappy memories. So, if you dream of rushing to the bathroom, what are you trying to flush out of your system in the real world? Or do you wish you could purge yourself of destructive, negative emotions such as jealousy or envy? Is there something you need to let go of in your waking life? Did you find it hard to let go in your dream or did everything go smoothly. The answer will help you see how emotionally blocked or constipated you are.

Perhaps you were **searching frantically for a toilet** in your dream, but couldn't find one. If this is the case, you need to find the catalyst for emotional release. Dreams about being clogged-up, or about a lack of toilets, are not so much about emotional baggage as about a lack of proper outlets for your own creativity and self-expression. They can also suggest that you are the kind of person who takes on the problems of other people, leaving no room for your own. Dreams about frustrating attempts to find a toilet could also suggest that you have over-committed yourself in waking life, and that there is no opportunity for you to express your own feelings and talents. On the other hand, you may also feel that you have been taken advantage of or dumped on by someone in waking life? Finally, such dreams may also be due simply to a physical need to pee in the night.

Other elimination dreams include **using a toilet in a strange place, in front of people or in the middle of a conversation**. In such dreams, the elimination represents the expression of an opinion or insight unsuitable for public consumption, or not appropriate to the situation. It could also reveal concern that you might have been too impulsive in the way you have expressed yourself, and your dreaming mind is urging you to bear in mind the possible impact of your words. If you **can't find a private toilet** in your dream, perhaps you are living or working in a crowded environment and your dreaming mind is compensating for a lack of privacy and personal space in your waking life. If you dream of a **bathroom and a toilet**, this may suggest your need to clean up your sexual attitudes or attitude to others and yourself.

If you **put anything down a toilet** in your dream, take careful note of what it is, as it will symbolize what your dreaming mind considers to be the least important or unpleasant aspect of yourself or your experience. **Urine** suggests letting go of strained feelings or the release of sexual feelings. **Feces** indicate letting go of parts of yourself that you need to let go of. It can also indicate new beginnings, as excrement makes great fertilizer. **Evacuation of the bowel** usually highlights a need to be free of responsibility, or sometimes the need to be uninhibited. If you are **eliminating over someone** in your dream, this can indicate a repressed desire to belittle that person or feel superior.

Playing with excrement can represent money, so playing with it in a dream may suggest anxiety about money and fear of responsibility. If the **excrement is transformed into an** **animal**, this suggests that the dreamer is coming to terms with the fact that he or she is responsible for managing their own instincts. If you are **vomiting** in your dream, this indicates a discharging of unpleasant feelings, or experiencing something unpleasant. Finally, if you realize you are **sweating** in a dream, you are alerted to the amount of energy you may be expending handling your own emotions and fears in waking life.

LEFT AND RIGHT SIDE OF THE BODY

Typically, the left side of the body represents feelings, intuition and the irrational, whilst the right side suggests the rational and logical. The left side is also associated with maternal influence, and the right with paternal.

External Body Parts A to Z

In dreams, body parts can be interpreted in the following way*:

* or dreams of **internal organs, fluids and other bodily functions,** *see under* SICKNESS AND HEALTH.

ABDOMEN/STOMACH/BELLY

When dreams focus on your **abdomen, belly or stomach**, they are referring to repressed feeling and emotions. The stomach is often seen as the center of emotions. This symbol may also have purely physiological origins if you have been experiencing constipation or indigestion. From a psychological point of view, seeing your abdomen in your dream may imply something in your real life that you 'cannot stomach' or have difficulties accepting, something you want to get out of your system. If your **abdomen is exposed**, this signifies trust and vulnerability, and in women it may indicate a desire for motherhood. If you are **injured or shot in the stomach**, this is about emotional hurt. Traditional folklore says that dreaming of your abdomen can foretell infidelity. A **shriveled abdomen** warns of lies, a **swollen abdomen** promises success. To see your **navel** in your dream represents your being and self. The dream may suggest that

The Element Encyclopedia of 20,000 Dreams

you need to find your center and middle ground.

ANUS

This suggests repressed emotion or an aspect of childish behavior, as the child's first experience of control is when they gain control over bodily functions. Consider also if you or someone in your life is anal retentive and perhaps need to loosen up a bit. To see **buttocks** in your dream represents your instincts and urges. It can also indicate feelings of insecurity, especially if the **buttocks are misshaped**. If you see your **pelvis** in a dream, you may be dealing with issues of creativity and self-expression.

■ *Idioms: pain in the ass; talking out of your ass; an asshole; head up the ass; all tits and asshole (i.e. unable to reason)*

ARM/ARMPIT/ELBOW

To see your **arms** in your dream highlights your ability to reach out to others. Alternatively, it may represent the struggles and challenges in your life, loss of confidence and not being able to reach out or create. Consider also the pun, 'arm yourself', which implies that you need to protect yourself, or be more aggressive and take a firmer stance on things. So if arms appear in your dream, are you defending yourself, fighting or being held, or showing passionate commitment?

To dream that your **arm has been injured or your arms are tied up** signifies your inability to care for yourself, or your helplessness in reaching out to others. The **right arm** signifies your outgoing nature and is associated with masculine energy, while your **left arm** signifies your supportive or nurturing nature, and is associated with feminine qualities. **Losing either arm** may suggest that you are failing to recognize its respective characteristics. To dream that you **rip someone else's arms out**, indicates that you are extremely upset with something that this person has done or represents, but you have not been able to fully express your anger.

If you **see, notice or smell someone's armpit** in your dream, this represents the characteristics and personality that you choose to display to the public. To **smell your armpit** in your dream indicates that you are hoping for some kind of acceptance in waking life. If you **see your elbow** in your dream, perhaps you need more personal space in waking life?

■ *Idioms: give one's right arm; arm twisting; at arm's length; with open arms; one hand tied behind the back; babe in arms; strong-armed tactics.*

BACK

To dream of your **back** represents parts of yourself hidden from view, secrets that you are keeping from other people or aspects of your personality you would prefer not to think about. Your dream could be pointing to some aspect of your life that is behind you, or a situation that is over. Maybe your dream contains some other play on words: is someone getting your back up? Do you feel the need for a pat on the back? Do you need to watch your back? Is somebody on your back or trying to dominate you? Are you engaged in a back-breaking task? Is your back against the wall? Do you wish someone would get off your back? Have you been stabbed or scratched in the back? Traditionally, **seeing a back** in your dream forewarns that you should not lend money to anyone. In particular, lending money to friends will cause a rift in your relationship. If a **person turns their back on you**, this may suggest that you may be deeply hurt in waking life or that other people may not be ready to share their thoughts with you.

■ *Idioms: backbreaking; back to the wall; pat on the back; stab in the back; turn one's back on; scratch my back; get off my back; rod up one's back.*

BREAST

Usually, to be aware of **breasts** in a dream indicates your connection with the mother figure, and your need to be nursed and cared for. Does a part of you long to again be an infant without responsibilities? Alternatively, breasts represent sexual arousal and raw energy. **Seeing naked breasts** can also denote a feeling of exposure and invasion of privacy. In particular, for a woman, the dream may indicate anxieties about becoming a woman/mother. If a **chest** appears in a dream, this indicates a sense of social confidence or good feelings about yourself. Alternatively, it represents feelings of being overwhelmed and being dangerously confronted by something. Consider also if the dream is telling you that there is something that you need to 'get off your chest'. If **nipples** appear in your dream, this signifies dependency. If you **squeeze pus out of your nipples** you may be feeling inadequate sexually.

EAR

If you see **ears** in your dream, this suggests that you could be more responsive or receptive to guidance and assistance from others. Alternatively, it signifies your immaturity and lack of experience. Such dreams may be about the need for the dreamer to listen to their own true feelings and make a connection with their unconscious self. Dream ears may also reveal a concern on the part of the dreamer that someone close to them is not being totally straightforward. If you have **more than two ears** in your dream, you may be feeling valued and respected. The **size of ears** in a dream can have important interpretative associations. **Small ears** could suggest that someone is not telling you the whole truth, whereas **large ears** can suggest the help and support of a colleague or friend. **Ears being pulled** in a dream can represent disagreements in waking life. If there has been a dispute, perhaps the time is right to move forward with a sensible solution. If you are **cleaning wax out of your ears**, perhaps you are not listening, or refusing to listen, to the opinions of others. Are you turning a deaf ear?

EYE/EYEBROW/EYELASH

Any dream connected with the **eyes** is associated with observation and judgment. It suggests wisdom, enlightenment and the dreamer's attitude to, and understanding of, the world. These windows of the soul can give vital clues to the state of your true health and well-being. Are the eyes bright? If they are, this suggests awareness. Are the eyes happy, sad, angry, kind? What **color** are the eyes? All this can tell you a lot about

The Element Encyclopedia of 20,000 Dreams

your way of looking at things. **Darker eyes** are linked to emotional and romantic relationships, whereas **pale eyes** are seen as connectors to the more social side of one's world.

If the dream eye is **wide open**, this can refer to innocence or the excitement caused by a new undertaking. **Narrow eyes** on the other hand may be a symbol of deceit or cheating. Dreams about eyes may also be a pun on 'I' or the self. If you dream that **your eyes have turned inside your head** and you can now see the inside of your head, then it symbolizes insight and something of which you need to be aware. This dream may literally be telling you to look inside yourself, and trust your own intuition and instincts. To dream that you **have something in your eye** could represent your critical view and how you tend to see faults in others.

To dream that you have **one eye** indicates your refusal to accept another viewpoint. To dream that you have a **third eye** symbolizes inner vision and insight. You need to start looking within yourself. To dream that your **eyes are closed** suggests your refusal to see the truth about something or the avoidance of intimacy. You may be expressing feelings of hurt, pain or sympathy. To dream that you have **crossed eyes** denotes that you may be getting your facts mixed up. **Loss of eyesight** suggests loss of clarity, and, depending on which eye is lost, can be the loss of logic (right eye) or intuition (left eye) If **eyesight is regained**, this suggests a return to clarity or clear-sightedness. **Lack of eye contact** suggests avoidance of intimacy.

To notice **eyebrows** in your dream represents expressions of disbelief, surprise or doubt. Eyebrows are also thought to reflect dignity and honor, and could indicate the fact that you are about to be recognized or appreciated by some unexpected source. If **hair is being shed from the eyebrows**, you may be worried about how others view your status. **Eyelashes** are thought to represent secrets or secretive pursuits.

Idioms: you must be blind; I saw it with my own eyes; all eyes; eye opener; evil eye; sheep eyes; one in the eye; turn a blind eye; easy on the eyes; keep your eyes open.

FACE

If you dream of your own **face**, it may represent the persona you present to the world and not your real self; this is particularly so if you are **putting on make-up**. A dream face therefore refers to how you would like to be seen. If a **beautiful face** appears, this may be connected to feelings of pride and satisfaction. If the **dream face is unknown**, this suggests a possible change in the dreamer's waking life. If a **dream face is being washed or cleaned**, this can have links to guilt or sin, as the act of cleaning indicates a desire for a fresh start. If the **faces are familiar**, it could be a portent of future social gatherings. To dream that your **face is flawed or pimply** represents erupting emotions. You may have suffered an attack on your reputation in waking life. If you are **blushing**, this suggests embarrassment and feelings you do not want to reveal to others. An elderly face may simply be a projection of life in the future. However, **aged faces** also carry symbolic ties to the notions of wisdom and longevity.

If you are **hiding your face**, you may be ashamed of something or be feeling low in confidence. If your **forehead is fine and smooth** in your dreams, this suggests good judgment and intellectual ability. To see a **wrinkled forehead**, however, suggests worries and burdens. If you see your **cheeks** in your dream, this symbolizes commitment, intimacy and closeness. To see **rosy-colored cheeks** in your dream signifies enthusiasm and energy. Bear in mind the significance of puns too; are you facing up to your problems, or do you need to deal with someone or something face to face? Ancient dream oracles say that to **see your face in a mirror** in a dream means that a secret will be discovered.

■ *Idioms: face the facts; face the music; face value; flat on one's face; face-lift; long face; blue in the face; poker-face; two faced.*

Feet/Toes

If you see your own **feet** in your dream, your unconscious may be advising you to keep your feet firmly on the ground, as feet symbolize your foundation, stability and sense of understanding. Such a dream signifies your need to be more practical and sensible. Alternatively, it represents mobility, independence and freedom. Perhaps you are reconsidering the direction of your life and your dream is advising you to move forward one step at a time. **Slow-walking or lazy feet** may reveal uncertainty, whereas **feet marching powerfully** link to feelings of confidence and purpose. Thereafter, the strength and determination of your dream feet may indicate how you are approaching a certain task.

For a Christian, dreaming of **washing feet** is a sign of forgiveness, but it can also mean that you are keeping a safe distance from a current problem and will return to it when you feel better able to tackle it. In India, to dream of the feet may symbolize divine qualities in the dreamer, since the feet are considered the holiest part of the body. Consider also the pun of putting your foot in your mouth or putting your foot in it. If you are **walking barefoot** in your dream, you have your feet firmly placed on the ground in waking life. **Loss of a foot or feet** in a dream indicates feelings of help-lessness in waking life. To see **toes** in your dream represents the minor details of life and how you deal with them. If your **toenails are growing** in your dream, this symbolizes an extension of your under-standing in a particular matter. If your **toe is hurt**, perhaps you are feeling anxious about moving forward with someone. If someone is **kissing your toe**, they may be trying to reassure you in waking life.

Finger/Thumb

According to Freud, **fingers and thumbs** are prime examples of phallic symbols. They can, however, also represent physical and mental dexterity or quickness, as well as their opposite: clumsiness and ignorance, as expressed in the saying 'being all thumbs'. In some cases, fingers may be expressive of your feelings, and many of the idioms involving fingers —the finger of scorn, the accusing finger, the finger of suspicion — suggest problems with self-image and trust. If a **finger is pointing at you** in your dream, you could feel guilty about something you have done. Alternatively, the dream could be pointing you in a new direction.

The Element Encyclopedia of 20,000 Dreams

Fingers can also denote partnership, especially if the **wedding finger** is highlighted. If your **fingers are injured or cut off**, perhaps you feel anxious about your ability to accomplish some demanding task or perform in some waking situation. Consider what aspect of yourself the dream is pointing out. If the dream focuses on your **finger-nails**, this suggests that you enjoy being surrounded by grace, beauty, glamor and art. If your **finger-nails are dirty**, you may be disappointing your family in some way. If your **finger-nails break**, you may be trying to avoid some situation or trying to get out of a responsibility. Dreaming of a **thumb** suggests awareness of how powerful you are, depending on whether the **thumb is pointing upwards** (positive) or **downwards** (negative). The latter was used as a death signal by the ancient Romans in gladiatorial games. According to ancient dream oracles, an **extra finger** suggests that you will receive an inheritance.

■ *Idioms: at your fingertips; snap your fingers; itchy fingers; fingers crossed; get one's finger out; beckoning finger; fingering things; put your finger on.*

GENITALS

If you dream of your **genitals**, this most likely represents your feelings and attitudes towards sex, and towards your femininity or masculinity. To see an **exceptionally large or small penis** suggests doubts and anxieties about your sexual drive and libido. For a man, a penis represents not just sex, but the whole drive of life, and his self-expression and capability in the world. In a woman's dream, the penis represents desire for a partner as well as a relationship to so-called male characteristics, such as ambition and aggression. If the **penis is bleeding**, this suggests emotional hurts that are inhibiting libido and self-expression. **Testicles** in a dream depict the male sexual drive, so loss of testicles, or small testicles in a man's dream, could suggest anxiety about sexual performance with a woman. In a woman's dream, testicles could indicate her feelings about sex with a man or what she is doing to the man in herself.

Dreams of a **vagina** are more to do with self-image. In a woman's dream, a vagina represents her receptivity, her nurturing feelings, her desire for a mate and the sense of connection with other women. In a man's dream, it highlights his need to thrust forward both physically and mentally. If the **vagina is bleeding**, this suggests fears about sexuality and femininity. *See also* SEX.

HAIR/BEARD

In dreams, **hair** is a symbol of strength and virility. If the **hair is in a good condition**, the dreamer may be feeling vital or strong, but if **hair is in a bad condition**, this can reveal feelings of low self-esteem or a lack of strength. If you are **combing hair**, this suggests your attempts to untangle a particular problem or attitude you have in waking life. If your **hair is being cut**, perhaps you are trying to create order, or sort out your responsibilities. Traditionally, a haircut represents success or an achievement in a new project, but if you are unhappy with the haircut it can also indicate a loss of strength and worries about your self-image. Another interpretation is that cutting hair suggests conformity, as long hair was a symbol of rebellion in the 1960s. If you are **cutting someone else's hair**, this may be a warning to be on your guard in relation to anyone around you who is acting negatively towards you.

Hair blowing in the wind or flowing free suggests you need to feel free and express your feelings in an uninhibited way. **Brushing hair** indicates clarity of thought. **Changing your hairstyle or washing your hair** suggests a change in attitudes or a change of mind; you may want to 'let your hair down'. If **hair is disheveled**, this suggests mental confusion. A **plait or a ponytail** suggests discipline and self-restraint, and also links in with childhood. If the **hair is overly perfumed**, this can be linked to your vanity. If you applied the perfume yourself, then perhaps you are acting in an arrogant way about something in your life. A **wig** signifies a false attitude or persona. If you are **bald** in your dream, this can highlight your intelligence, but it can also highlight anxiety about growing older. Alternatively, it could suggest a loss of self-esteem or, according to Freud, a fear of castration. Dreams about hair loss can also represent worries about getting older.

If a **beard** appears in your dream, this suggests feelings about manhood, or so-called masculine qualities within yourself. If the **beard is cut off**, it suggests uncertainty, whilst a **long, thick beard** suggests the opposite. **Hairs on the chest or other parts of the body** can also indicate male characteristics or expressions of sexuality.

■ *Idioms: keep your hair on; make your hair curl; hair-raising; didn't turn a hair; put hairs on your chest; let your hair down; tear your hair out; split hairs.*

HAND

Hands can signify power and creativity. You use them to express yourself and as extensions of your personality. Consider the nature of the gesture of your hands in your dreams because it signifies what sentiments your dream is trying to express. If the **hands are dirty**, perhaps you are behaving in an inappropriate manner and you need to think about cleaning up your act. A **fist** can suggest anger or passion, **folded hands** can suggest acceptance, **joined hands** affection, and **upheld hands** justice or a blessing. **Clasped hands** indicate friendship, a **hand on the breast** submission, and, if the **hands are placed together,** this suggests vulnerability. If **hands are covering the eyes**, this represents shame or disgust, whilst **hands bound or tied up** suggest feelings of restriction. If you **place your hand on someone else** in a dream, this can suggest a pledge of service and **wringing your hands** suggests grief. If **hands are raised to the head**, this can indicate the need for greater care and thought. A **handshake** suggests contacting an aspect of yourself or the growth of a new friendship.

Generally, **left hands** symbolize feminine, receptive qualities, whilst **right hands** symbolize so-called masculine, active attributes. Sometimes in dreams the **left hand** can suggest cheating. If you **hold a different object in each** hand in your dream, this indicates some kind of conflict between your beliefs and your actions in waking life. To dream that your **hands are injured** denotes an attack on your ego. **Large hands** signify enormous powers of self-expression. To dream that your **hands are hairy** denotes that you will play a part in falsely incriminating someone. To see

blood on your hands signifies that you are experiencing some sort of guilt. To dream that you are **washing your hands** represents a worrisome issue that you need to work through. If you dream about the palm of your hand you may be thinking about your future (see PALMISTRY). Thankfully you have free-will, so positive actions taken now can determine your future.

■ *Idioms: second hand; in the hands of; bite the hand that feeds; hands are tied; soil one's hands; hand to hand; hand to mouth; hands off; hands on; helping hand; hard hand; open handed; lend a hand; upper hand.*

HEAD

To see a **head** in your dream signifies wisdom, intellect and logic; it may also represent your accomplishments. That the head stands for the themes of decision making, intellect and thought is fairly obvious, given the huge number of idioms for head and face; if we think of an idiom such as 'to lose one's head' or 'to lose face', it is fairly clear what dreams of **headless or faceless bodies** might mean. Dreams may also use the image of a head to show that you are in two minds about something, or in the process of changing your mind. For example, if you **change your head** in your dream, this indicates a change of attitude, being uncertain about something, or even being two-faced.

■ *Idioms: in over your head; swollen or big head; head in the sand; egghead; square head; off the top of my head; hold your head up high; head over heels; get it through your head; heads up.*

LEG

To see your **legs** in your dream suggests that you have gained enough confidence to stand up for yourself. If your **legs are weak**, then you may be feeling emotionally vulnerable. If you see the **legs of someone else** in your dream, this may indicate your admiration for them. Perhaps you need to adopt some of the attitudes of this person. If your legs are **wounded or crippled**, this signifies an inability to stand up for yourself. Perhaps you are lacking courage and refuse to make a stand. If **one leg is shorter than another** in your dream, this suggests some kind of imbalance in your life. You are placing too much emphasis on one thing and ignoring other important aspects of your life. If you have **three legs** in your dream, then perhaps you have taken on too many responsibilities. According to ancient dream lore, if you have a **wooden leg** in your dream, you will have many new worries. Bear in mind leg-related idioms such as: legless, didn't have a leg to stand on, can't stand up for myself, ball and chain on my legs.

To see **thighs** in your dream indicates strength and endurance, and it refers to your ability to make things happen. To dream of your **knees** indicates feelings of inadequacy and vulnerability. You may have taken on more than you can handle. To see your **calves** in your dream suggests movement and versatility, and your ability to jump from situation to situation. It can also suggest that you are involved with someone who is needy and over-dependent. To dream about your **ankles** indicates that you are seeking support and direction in your life. Ask yourself where you want to be headed. Bear in mind the phrase '**Achilles** heel'; could dream of heels be referring to your vulnerability or a particular weakness?

Mouth/Jaw/Lips/Tongue

The **mouth** represents the devouring, demanding aspects of yourself; it can also signify your need to communicate about something that is upsetting you. If the **mouth is open**, this may represent your receptive side, as in mouth-watering. On the other hand, perhaps too much has been said and it is time to close your mouth – in other words shut up. A dream of your **mouth being buttoned or sewed up** can again suggest regret over what has been said or done. If you dream that you are **chewing**, it might suggest that you are mulling over, or considering, something. If you are **pulling something out of your mouth**, perhaps you need to clear the air by expressing your feelings, or do you have a nasty taste in the mouth?

To see your own **tongue** in your dream signifies self-expression. Have you said too much or do you need to say more? If you **rip someone's tongue out** in a dream, this means that you are extremely upset by what someone has said in waking life but have been unable to express your anger. To dream of your own **jaw** in your dream represents your stubbornness, determination and forcefulness. If your **jaws are tight**, this could suggest unexpressed anger and other powerful feelings that you are holding back. If **lips** appear in your dream, this is associated with sensuality, sex, love and romance, as well as communication, as in 'read my lips'.

Neck/Shoulder

To see your own or another person's **neck** in your dream signifies your need to control your feelings and keep them in check. Consider the familiar phrase, 'don't stick your neck out', which serves as a warning against a situation. If your **neck is injured**, this can indicate a separation between heart and mind. If your **neck is thick**, perhaps you have been quick-tempered recently. Consider also the following idioms: breaking one's neck, up to one's neck, stick one's neck out, dead from the neck up/down. **Shoulders** in a dream suggest strength, responsibility and burdens. Do you feel that you have much responsibility to bear in waking life? On the other hand, shoulders can also represent support and your ability to soothe others, as in the phrase 'a shoulder to cry on'. To see your **throat** in your dream symbolizes the ability to express yourself and communicate your thoughts and ideas. If your **throat is sore**, perhaps you are having problems expressing yourself. Alternatively, you may need to swallow your pride. If a **graceful, long neck** appears in your dream, this suggests good fortune in waking life.

Nose

The **nose** in dreams represents curiosity and intuition. To dream that **hair is growing on your nose** signifies extraordinary undertakings needing a strong will and character to be carried through. To dream of a **bleeding nose** is prophetic of disaster and danger. Consider also the following idioms: have a nose for, nose out of joint, rub one's nose in, up one's nose.

Skin

Your **skin** is your shield against the outside world and your dream may be referring to the way you present yourself to others. A **skin rash** may be a pun, suggesting that you are making rash decisions or it may highlight concerns about your appearance. Are you thick skinned and reluctant to express your feelings?

■ *Idioms: under one's skin, a thick skin, skin alive.*

Teeth

Dreaming about **teeth falling out** represents feelings of insecurity or inadequacy, and such dreams often occur at transition times in a person's life. This is because losing your milk teeth is associated with the loss of childhood innocence. The dream could also highlight anxieties about getting older. According to Jung, if a **tooth is being pulled out** in a woman's dream, this represents giving birth and in general it has associations with some kind of painful experience or loss that will lead to a new beginning. **Animal teeth** represent aggression and **false teeth** concern about self-image.

If you are **toothless or see someone without teeth**, this suggests loss of effectiveness or feelings about aging. Don't, however, neglect the possibility that the dream may have been triggered by toothache or a recent trip to the dentist. If **teeth are rotten or decayed** in your dream, perhaps you have said something you regret. **Spitting out lots of teeth** indicates something you need to spit out or admit in waking life. If you are **brushing your teeth** in your dream, this may suggest you are experiencing a hard struggle in waking life; it could also, of course, echo your dentist's plea to take better care of your teeth. If **something is lodged between your teeth**, this suggests that a problem which seemed impossible in waking life may be easily resolved.

If **one tooth is far larger than the rest of the teeth in your mouth**, you may be worried that something in your personal and working life won't be the success you hoped it would be. **Clean teeth or teeth that glisten** are linked to strong friendships or financial security. If the **roots** of the teeth are featured, you may be thinking about the stability of your waking relationships. If the **roots are healthy**, you are satisfied with these, but if **the roots are twisted or unhealthy**, this suggests concerns in that area of your life.

■ *Idioms: show one's teeth; get one's teeth into; grit your teeth; teething troubles; long in the tooth; milk teeth; tooth fairy; cutting one's teeth.*

Body wisdom

If you look at the body in your dreams as a representation of your life and potential, the images can translate into a view of your current well being. Don't worry overly about dreams that seem to be a kind of warning; instead try to be honest with yourself, put the pieces of the puzzle together in your mind and begin to make positive changes.

BUILDINGS

C arl Jung talked about recurring dreams he had in which he would
discover parts of his house that he didn't know existed.

In these dreams he believed the house represented his personality, and the new things he discovered in the house related to new developments in his work. Many dream researchers subscribe to Jung's theory and believe that buildings in dreams represent aspects of the self, or constructions we make in our lives. The upstairs represents the conscious mind, and the lower floors and cellars the unconscious, or hidden, mind. Different parts of the building might represent different times in your life, and the attitudes and beliefs you have built from experience. The features of your dream building can also mirror features of your personality; by so doing, they reflect your character, hopes and dreams, and how you feel about yourself.

If you dream of a house or a building, ask yourself what aspect of you the building represents. Does it represent how you see yourself? Is it a symbol of your body, mind or spirit? If the house is crumbling or decaying, are you in need of some kind of psychological, spiritual or physical cleaning and renewal? If the building is burning, does this show your desire to get rid of

something that is holding you back? If the building is in ruins, do you feel worthless and manipulated by others? If the building is tall, does this suggest ambitions yet to be fulfilled? Is the house symbolic of your feelings in childhood or other past experiences? What are the conditions like in the house? Ask yourself what personal associations the buildings in your dreams have and what they represent to you.

The environment and your feeling reaction to the building in your dream will all contribute important clues as to its meaning, but it is also important to bear in mind the purpose for which the building is used in waking life. For example, castles and fortresses suggest protection and royalty, whereas factories suggest work and routine. Although high-rise buildings are believed to be phallic symbols, as a type they all have different functions: skyscrapers are homes and workplaces, lighthouses offer hope to sailors at sea, and towers isolate, elevate and imprison.

Churches and religious buildings offer us hope and quiet reflection, libraries and museums supply us with information and stimulate our minds. Courts provide social justice, whilst public buildings symbolize work, tax, bureaucratic or legal matters that need to be sorted. Hospitals are centers of healing and castles are historical icons. Houses, bungalows, flats, mansions and palaces offer different types of accommodation for different types of needs. Prisons are places for criminals to learn the consequences of their actions, and hotels provide a welcome break from home. If any of these buildings appear in your dream, this chapter will help you interpret the meaning; but for domestic buildings, homes and shops you may want to refer to HOME and MONEY AND SHOPPING. For places associated with entertainment, such as cinemas and theatres, you may want to refer to ARTS AND CRAFTS and LEISURE, and for places of work and learning consult SCHOOL AND WORK.

Building Types A to Z

ANCIENT BUILDING

The **pyramid** is said to be a focus of spiritual energy, so it if appears in your dream, your unconscious is drawing your attention to the power within. Dreams about **old or ancient buildings** refer to the past and experiences that have been lived through, such as a former life with another person. **Ruins** suggest a now irrelevant way of life or approach to life. The ruins may belong to a **castle**, and this suggests that the defenses you once built up are no longer necessary.

Mansions and palaces in dreams have a similar interpretation as **houses**, but with the emphasis on those possibilities within us that have yet to be developed and explored. There is a sense of something special or wonderful happening within yourself, as palaces are places of enchantment and treasure in fairy tales. However, palaces may also represent a warning against adopting a pretentious façade and living beyond your means.

CASTLE/CITADEL/FORTRESS

If you dream of any of these, it suggests a defensive attitude. Do you have a real fear of being overwhelmed or defeated by a group of schoolmates or colleagues? Or are you feeling so vulnerable that you are putting up emotional defenses to protect yourself? The symbol of the **castle** is that of a place where you can defend yourself from attack, so it may represent the methods you use to protect yourself from 'attack'. On the other hand, your dream may highlight your self-imposed isolation from others, and the sense of security you get from being self-reliant.

If your **stronghold came under siege**, did you identify the faces of your attackers? Are these people you know in waking life? And did your **dream defenses hold firm**? If they did, this suggests that you are successfully fending off attempts to wound or get through to your emotions. If you are a man who dreamed that you are **laying siege to a castle**, the Freudian interpretation is that it expresses your desire to have sex with a woman who has resisted your advances. The castle is also a place of historical interest, so it may suggest a need to look to the past for inspiration. It can also represent a mandala, a symmetrical pattern that symbolizes the psyche. If a **courtyard or moat** appears in the dream, this again refers to protection or the desire to feel safe and secure. The shape of the moat or courtyard will also be relevant.

CITYSCAPE

Did you dream that you were **wandering around a city**, either familiar or unfamiliar to you in waking life? If you did, were the streets friendly and welcoming, and the buildings clean and bursting with life and activity, or did you feel unwelcome, jostled about and intimidated by the place? According to Jung, places in dreams where people group together to live and work, such as **cities, towns and villages**, refer to how you perceive yourself within the community, and how well you are fitting in. So if you dreamed that you felt **happy and secure in your dream city**, the chances are you relate well to other members of the community in waking life. But if the **buildings on the sidewalk or pavement seemed to close in on you**, or you were **wandering around hopelessly lost**, perhaps you are feeling intimidated by others in waking life and have lost your sense of direction, or even identity. If the **city was abandoned** like a ghost town, does this mirror your feelings of isolation in waking life?

COMPONENTS OF A BUILDING

If you dream of a **balcony, ledge or sill**, this suggests a need for support and protection in your life. An elevator or lift in a dream usually suggests how we deal with information. If the **lift is going down**, we may be going down into our unconscious for self-understanding, whereas a **lift going up** could represent moving towards greater self-understanding. **Halls or passageways** in a dream can, for Freudians, represent passages within the body, such as the vagina or penis. On a psychological level, they can suggest how we let others invade our personal space. On a spiritual level, passages can represent the different stages of our life. A **hall** is the center of a building and to dream of **entering a hall** may therefore represent the beginnings of a journey towards self-awareness. According to dream lore, to dream of a **long hallway** suggests a period of worry ahead.

Walls in dreams indicate potential blocks to your progress, or difficulties you may be up against in waking life. They suggest obstacles that are stopping you from getting what you want. This may be something from real life or something within yourself. Perhaps you are being like a brick by refusing to show your feelings, or have come up against a brick wall with a particular problem or issue. If the **wall looks old**, this suggests the problem is old. If the **wall is made of glass**, this suggests problems with perception. If the **wall is closing in**, the dreamer may feel trapped by their current lifestyle. A **brick wall, rampart or dividing wall** all suggest the difference between everyday life and the inner psychological state. According to dream lore, if you find a **gateway through a wall**, this is a sign of good fortune. *See also* entries for doors, rooms, stairs, staircase and windows in HOME.

Exploring a building

Dreams about **exploring a building** are encouraging you to explore your own personality or resolve an ongoing conflict. In other words, the dream is encouraging you to make more of your attributes and abilities, as unexplored potential and new ideas lie within you. This is especially true if you find yourself **exploring unfamiliar rooms in a well-known house** in your dream. If the building is **run down or dilapidated**, this may suggest a personality or body in need of attention, but if the **building is well cared for and clean**, it suggests confidence and good self-esteem. A **building under attack** may suggest that someone or something is trying to break in. If a **building is under construction or being demolished**, this refers to your own ability to construct and destroy your life. If the **building is familiar**, the reference may be to the actual building itself; for example, if you dream of a **structural fault**, you might want to get the design checked out. If the building you are exploring in your dream is a **public building such as a factory, law court, prison and department store**, the building often represents the function suggested by its nature, such as work, education and healing. Bear in mind, though, that if these images appear in your dreams, they will also have personal connections and feelings associated with those buildings. For example, if a **factory feels like a museum**, both associations should be considered. Finally, consider carefully how you react to the building in your dream. Were you intimidated by it or did you feel comfortable? If the former, your dream may be warning that you are over-reaching yourself in waking life. The latter is more reassuring.

FACTORY

A **factory** in your dreams is likely to refer to conformity with society, a typical reaction to a life that lacks individuality, productivity and work. In some cases, it can also refer to the automatic functions of the body, such as breathing and digestion. A **factory on strike** may suggest an obstacle to hard work, such as lack of discipline. An **endless production line** clearly suggests frustration with your career or relationships. A dream of **waterworks** can suggest associations with water and the womb, turning the dream into a gigantic representation of the mother figure in your life. A dream of being **confined in a barracks** may be a warning that your life is too restricted, and that you are too much under the influence of someone else. If you dream of a **warehouse or other storage place**, this suggests memories, past experiences or aspects of yourself that you have put on hold; for example, career ambitions whilst you raise a child.

FARM

If a **farm** appears in your dream, you may be longing for a more simple, down-to-earth approach to life. If there is **manure in the yard**, this may point to obstacles that prevent you realizing your dream. If you dream of a **windmill**, the windmill may represent your creativity as the windmill grinds flour for bread. If you are the family breadwinner, you might identify with this dream. Images of a **stable** in your dream may suggest repressed sexuality, as horse-riding is a Freudian symbol of sex. For Jung, the horse represents humankind's harnessing of natural forces, making the stable a place where the dreamer can face these forces with confidence.

HOSPITAL

In dreams, **hospitals** can either mean a place of safety and healing if you have had a positive experience of hospitals, or vulnerability and disease if the experience was negative. Generally though, hospitals are symbols of healing, representing an aspect of yourself that longs to be pampered and cared for, relieved of the burdens of responsibilities in the waking world. If you **find hospitals threatening** in your dream, this may suggest that you feel apprehensive about putting control of yourself out of your own hands and into those of others in your waking life. If you are a **hospital patient** in your dream, this suggests a period of transition after something has not gone well, or a time of rest when you can learn from the experience and find new ways to get back on track. If you are **visiting someone in hospital**, is a part of you diseased, not well or in need of special attention? Either way, if you have a dream that focuses in some way on a hospital, this suggests that you are in need of some tender loving care, both physically and emotionally. *See also* SICKNESS AND HEALTH.

HOTEL/B&B/PUB

Dreams that highlight **hotels, bed and breakfasts, and boarding houses** suggest that you are not currently feeling secure in your situation. They can also indicate a short-term situation, relaxation and escape, or activities separate from home life. For business people, hotel dreams may refer to work. If you are about to take a vacation, your dream may simply reflect your excitement at the thought of the holiday. But if you are not going on holiday, the dream implies that you have reached a transitional stage in your life and the dream hotel mirrors how you feel about this change of circumstances. Perhaps you have recently moved to a new area, or a relationship has broken up and you are adjusting to your new single status. Was the hotel a bright, uplifting place or was it depressing and dirty? All these details will help you with the interpretation. Bear in mind, too, that hotels, although advertized as home from homes, are in fact impersonal places run by others – so do you yearn for anonymity or do you dread losing your identity? If the **hotel has a gymnasium**, this suggests challenges, finding ways to gain new skills, or concerns about your physical health and well-being.

If you were in a **public house or bar** in your dream, this suggests the sociable, easy-going side of yourself, as a bar or pub presents an arena in which you can overcome your inhibitions. If there was a **jovial atmosphere**, this can suggest a wish to be less isolated in waking life or a new, optimistic approach to life. If, however, there was a **brawl**, this can suggest repressed emotions boiling over into anger. **Drunkenness** also suggests loss of control, a desire to forget the past, or an avoidance rather than a facing of emotions. An **inn** is like a pub, but with the difference that it offers a place to sleep overnight. It also suggests a more tranquil, rural environment, perhaps pointing to your desire to deal with repressed impulses from the unconscious in a secure, secluded environment. (For dreams of **restaurants and canteens**, *see also* FOOD AND DRINK.)

HOUSE

For the psychologist Carl Jung, **building a house** was a symbol of building a self. In his autobiographical *Memories, Dreams and Reflections*, Jung described the gradual evolution of his home on Lake Zurich. Jung spent more than thirty years building this castle-like structure, and he believed that the towers and annexes represented his psyche. In dreams therefore, houses may represent your life structures or what you have created for yourself as a way of life; for example, values, attitudes and goals, or things you feel 'at home' with, or feel you can be yourself with.

When interpreting dreams of houses, how you feel about the house is of particular importance. Houses can be forbidding places, and if you feel anxious in your dream, this suggests that something about your personality is bothering you. That you

noted a **particular part of the house** in your dream may offer a clue, and the different rooms and everyday things in the house are also important as they represent different aspects of your feelings and make up. It is common to dream of **returning to a house from your past** that you knew or lived in. This dream may be nostalgic or it may reflect a longing to return to the innocence of childhood. If you dreamed of **leaving a house**, the message is that you are ready to move on in waking life. If the house in your dream **felt like it was your home**, *see also* HOME.

LAW COURT/PRISON

A **law court** in a dream may make you focus on your capacity to make fair judgments in complicated matters concerning work, friends or family members. It may also highlight your feelings of being on trial in waking life, or a sense of guilt about having broken a promise, or a moral or social law. Perhaps you are anxious about being judged by others or feel that there something that you should be punished for. If you find yourself **bundled into prison** in your dream, perhaps with the **clang of heavy gates swinging shut** in your ears, this may be drawing a parallel with your sense of confinement in waking life. So, if you have any kind of dream about prisons or being jailed, ask yourself who or what is restricting your freedom in waking life. Do you feel suffocated emotionally by your partner or parents, or do you feel trapped in a dead-end job? Or has your own shyness locked you into a self-made prison in the waking world?

Dream houses

The **front of the house and activities outside the house** represent your persona, the face you show to the world, whereas whatever is inside the house reveals your inner life. If the **house is being attacked or burgled**, this suggests criticism or social pressure from others. If the **house is burning or falling down**, this represents leaving old attitudes behind. If the **house feels cramped and dark**, there is a feeling of restriction in waking life, whilst **structural faults** suggest broken relationships or illness. If **work or repairs are being carried out** on the house, perhaps certain relationships are breaking down or health matters need to be attended to.

An **impressive big house** in dreams suggests that we are conscious of our potential. If the **house is small**, the dreamer is perhaps seeking security and freedom from responsibility. If you were **living in a bungalow** in your dream, there may be a suggestion that you are living too much on one level, both practically and emotionally. If there are **unfamiliar rooms in a well-known house**, this represents unexplored potential. If **other people are in the house**, they suggest different aspects of yourself you may feel threatened by, or other people you are involved with, or about to be involved with, in waking life. **Going into or out of the house** suggests that we may need to decide whether we need to be more introverted or extroverted. If you **go into another person's house**, this suggests that you are getting involved with that

person, perhaps being a part of their life. If you see a **loved one move into someone else's house** in your dream, this may be your fear of their infidelity, but it may also reveal a growing distance in your relationship. **Planning or altering a house, or building an annexe** may refer to a change in your lifestyle or approach to life. **Rows of houses** represent other people. According to dream lore, **country houses** suggest tranquility; **building a house**, a growth in confidence; a **new house**, a busy social life; an **empty house or moving house**, financial worries; a **big house**, good fortune, and a **small house**, misfortune.

If you are **buying a house** in your dreams this may relate to making a decision to change in waking life, or wanting to make some kind of change. Buying a house involves decision making and this points to the importance of clarifying what it is that you want in waking life. If the house in your dream is an **igloo**, this is a symbol of security and completeness and, because it is warm on the inside and cold on the outside, it points to differences between what you feel on the inside and you do and say on the outside. In general dreaming about a **flat or apartment** has the same meaning as dreaming about a house, but the interpretation depends on whether or not you have lived in an apartment or flat before. If you did, were you living alone in the flat or did you share, and what was this like? This will influence the feelings associated with the image in your dream.

Library/Museum

In dreams, a **library** can represent a storehouse of your experiences in life as well as your intellect. If the **library is well ordered**, this suggests that you handle knowledge well. If the **library is chaotic, with books missing or wrongly shelved**, this suggests that you may be suffering from information overload or have difficulty processing information. If **someone distracts you in the library** in your dream, it may suggest that the ideas being considered in waking life are not worth your attention. If you are working on your psychic and spiritual development, the library will have added significance as a place where the collective wisdom of humankind is collected. The more we develop psychically and spiritually, the more we have access to this collective wisdom – also known as intuition and the collective unconscious.

Like libraries, **museums** feed minds by giving people the opportunity to study objects from the past for their historic, scientific and artistic interest. When trying to interpret dreams about museums, any **exhibit that caught your eye** is important because it may be pointing to something from your own past that has a bearing on your present situation. If your dream involved **visiting a cinema or theatre**, refer to the relevant entries in ARTS AND CRAFTS and LEISURE.

Lighthouse

A **lighthouse** may appear in a dream as a **beacon guiding you to safety through dense fog**. Bear in mind that a beacon or lighthouse can also indicate a rocky area you should avoid, and therefore contains a warning about the direction in which you are heading. Such a dream may be urging you to rely on your own resources to avoid floundering. For Freud, the lighthouse was, of course, a phallic symbol rising above the maternal symbol of the ocean.

Religious building

Any **religious building** suggests a refuge where you can gather your thoughts and consider your beliefs. Even if you are not religious, in dreams religious buildings highlight your spiritual, peace-loving and idealistic potential. Most of us have principles we live by and these may surface in your dreams in the symbol of a religious building. If you are **walking past a church or religious building** in your dream, this suggests that you are not making contact with the best part of yourself. Is your waking life so crammed with obligations that you don't have time to explore your inner world for some much-needed reflection, meditation and contemplation? If you **entered a temple** in your dream and immediately felt enveloped in a sense of calm, was your unconscious suggesting that you would enjoy better health if you treated your body as a temple, putting your physical, emotional and spiritual welfare first? Dreams about religious buildings may also be an expression of anger against dogma; again it depends on the feelings evoked by the building in your dream. Did you feel relieved or tense? If a **vault** features in your dream, it may represent your highest spiritual ideals, as vaults often appear in churches or temples with painted stars in imitation of the vault of the heavens. A vault may also recall a crypt or burial chamber, and as such, it may conjure up thoughts of death. *See also* RELIGION.

TOWER

According to Freud, a **tower** is a phallic symbol, signifying in its sturdiness the sexual self-confidence of a male dreamer. In dreams, towers represent psychological constructions you may have built in your life, ranging from an attitude to an entire way of life. For example, a tower may be a defensive erection of inner attitudes, suggesting an imprisonment by your own anxieties or a desire to shut yourself away from the world; alternatively, it may be an attempt to reach the heights of awareness or recognition.

If you are **standing at the top of the tower** in your dream, observe how you feel

Towering above the rest

Freudian dream interpreters relate **towering structures** in dreams to phallic symbols, and therefore to macho tendencies, on account of their thrusting shape. So if you dreamed you were **living in a luxury penthouse thousands of feet above the city or that your office occupied the top floor**, could your dream have highlighted your ambitions? Do you secretly long to rise above everyone else financially, professionally and socially? Dreaming of a **spire** may indicate pride and ambition or yearning to attain spiritual heights, and an **obelisk** in a dream may be a phallic symbol. A **chimney** in a dream may be another phallic symbol especially if it was a **tall factory chimney**. In both the waking and the dream world, **skyscrapers** are symbols of elevated social and professional status and the 'greed is good creed', so if you dreamed of them, perhaps your unconscious was highlighting your waking ambition.

The most prominent and famous landmark in Paris, the city of romance, revolution and passion, is the **Eiffel Tower**. If it appears in your dream, it presents a powerful erotic symbolism, as it is a strong image of thrusting sexuality. The **clock tower**, also known as **Big Ben**, which sits alongside London's Houses of Parliament, may be a symbol of an encounter with destiny or some life-changing event. **Ticking clocks** often represent the passage of life (*see* TIME) and the clock tower combines this with the phallic form to form an image of courage and emotional development. Evoking great and solemn occasions, the **chimes** of Big Ben, or any **clock in a church tower**, relate to important life changes, such as marriage, the birth of a child or moving house, or important shifts in attitude, such as forgiveness, resolve and determination.

The Element Encyclopedia of 20,000 Dreams

Some other buildings

Airport

A desire to rise above worldly problems and responsibilities; may also be associated with high ideals. *See also* TRAVEL.

Bank

Where 'treasures' are stored; material security. If you are making a deposit, you are adding to your assets. If you are making a withdrawal, you are calling upon them.

Barn

Associated with labor. Since this is a storage place and home for animals, the dream may be implying that you have an inner storage place containing the essentials for inner growth.

Beauty parlor/hairdressers

New ideas, thoughts are cleansed, created and rearranged.

Boarding house

The essentials are provided but payment is required.

Cleaners

Clean up some aspect of your personality or have you been 'taken to the cleaners'?

Firehouse

Contains what is needed to put a fire (anger, passion) out.

Funeral parlor

Something dead needs to be laid to rest or reviewed. 'It's your funeral.'

Railroad station

Travel, change; waiting to get on the right track in life's journey. *See also* TRAVEL.

Restaurant

The nourishment is provided, but payment is needed. The type of restaurant is important. In a fast-food restaurant or cafeteria, the dreamer is required to do much to help; in an elegant setting, the basic needs are provided but more is expected in return.

School

Lessons to be learned; more growth is required; associated with school days; raise thinking to a new level.

Service station

Re-energize your body, physically, mentally and emotionally.

Store

Book store – learning, study, research; clothing store – shopping for a new means of expression; department store – temptation and choices; drugstore – healing prescriptions; health food store – healthier diet; old-fashioned grocery store – inadequate nourishment; music store – harmony; supermarket – eating and living habits. *See also* MONEY AND SHOPPING.

as you gaze down at the activity below. Were you relieved to be far removed from other people or did you feel imprisoned? Towers in dreams can also suggest an emotionally impregnable figure in the dreamer's life, for example an authoritarian father, or male authority in general. There may also be a reference to a 'tower of strength', or a person on whom you can rely for support and comfort. If your **tower has no door**, you are not in touch with your inner self. If there are **no windows**, you can't see all the good things about yourself.

An **ivory tower** suggests innocence, but it can also suggest arrogance, intellectual aloofness and the loneliness such an attitude can bring. A **square tower** suggests a pragmatic, practical approach, and a round tower suggests spiritual harmony. If the **tower is round on top of a square building,** this suggests harmony in mind, body and spirit. How you get to the tower in your dream is important in your dream. If **your steps are difficult to climb**, this suggests you are a private person. If the **door is jammed**, you are not ready to understand yourself. If the **door is bolted**, you must make the effort to go in. Once **inside the tower**, you can use other explanations in this encyclopedia to interpret what you encounter.

CHANGE AND CONFLICT

Dreams about change are common because the experience of change is an inescapable fact of life and whether the change is minor, such as a new hairstyle, or major, such as getting married, all change involves both loss and gain.

Dreams about conflict are also very widespread. This is because, in the same way as with change, we all experience conflict to some degree in our daily lives. We do not, as a result, spend all our lives feeling hostile, but every one of us experiences varying degrees of tension and anxiety.

Understanding conflicts and changes can help us manage them better, and many dream researchers believe that dreams are an invaluable tool for self-understanding. For example, Freud believed that dreams reflect hidden conflicting aspects of our personality, whilst Jung believed that the process of adapting to change or conflict was vital for survival and dreams offered an insight into that process. Adler believed dreams could solve problems, and theorists from the Gestalt school believe dreams increase self-understanding.

Dreams about change and conflict should therefore be listened to closely. They are a way of processing the thoughts and feelings surrounding that change and/or conflict and by so doing they can lead us towards psychological healing and personal growth. *See also* STAGES OF LIFE.

Change Scenarios

CELEBRATIONS

Dreams about **birthdays, weddings, anniversaries** and any other **rite of passage ceremony** all contain symbolism associated with change. Notice how you felt in the dream. How did other characters react to the change event? Was there a sense of happiness or sadness in the air? Did obstacles prevent the ceremony from running smoothly?

DISGUISES

Dreams of **yourself or other people in disguise** can often suggest change. **The wearing of a mask** relates to the appearance you present to others (as well as to yourself), and sometimes it is hard to remove the mask, perhaps because you are being forced to wear the mask by others. This may be a warning that you risk losing all sense of self. Notice who was disguised in the dream and what they were disguised as. If they were **disguised as something sinister**, perhaps this suggests fears in your everyday life. If they were **disguised as something light-hearted**, perhaps this is an element of **wish-fulfillment,** reflecting a desire to drop pretences and replace them with more fun and spontaneity in your life. According to Jungian symbolism, **wearing a veil over your head** indicates a desire to be invisible and to withdraw from the outside world.

FERTILITY

Given their associations with fertility and growth, dreams about the **birth of a baby or animal, or of tending gardens and vegetation** are associated with new beginnings and positive change for the dreamer. Dreams that involve other new beginning such as **new jobs, new houses and new relationships** are also symbolic of aspects of life change. To understand the meaning of the dream – and what particular change it is pointing to – you need to pay attention to how you feel in the dream, as well as noting any details within in.

Dream change in art

The subject of dreams and change has often been portrayed in art and culture. For example, in his classic novella *Metamorphosis*, Franz Kafka used this notion of change when Gregor Samsa awakes to find himself transformed into an insect. Surrealist artists, in particular Salvador Dali, used images of dream change to inform their work. For example, Dali's 'Metamorphosis of Narcissus' is based on the myth of Narcissus, who fell in love with his own reflection.

GOODBYE

Dreams that contain images of **death, or of saying goodbye or farewell to family and friends**, also suggest times of change. Such dreams do not mean that someone is going to die or that certain people are going to leave you, rather that a particular phase in life is coming to an end. The dream should contain clues regarding which phase in life is being referred to. If **you are the dead person or the dead person is unknown to you**, then some aspect of your personality or some issue in your daily life needs to be left behind. If a **friend dies** in your dream, perhaps that friendship has run its course, or perhaps your friend is about to get married and the nature of your friendship will change.

Labyrinth/Maze

According to Jung, the **enclosed labyrinth** is a symbol of the unconscious, and a dream of **entering a labyrinth** represents rapid change and a journey towards self-discovery. As in the Greek myth of Theseus, who entered King Minos' labyrinth in Knossos to kill the Minotaur, descent into the unconscious may sometimes involve confronting impulses we would rather ignore because they challenge or threaten us. If you see a **maze** in your dream, it may also indicate the need to find direction in life and the skills needed to negotiate change. If a **map or chart of a maze** appears in your dream, this may be a reassuring sign that you are on the right path.

Ruin/Destruction

If the dream centers on some kind of radical change such as **revolution, war, fighting or combat**, this suggests some kind of conflict in your life. **Images of destruction** can also relate to life changes that quite literally break with the past. A **house left in ruins**, for example, may suggest a family broken by divorce; **fallen trees** may symbolize a move to a new location. *See also* TREES.

Transformation

Dreams in which obvious changes occur, and **people and things are transformed into something or someone else**, suggest changes in awareness. A **landscape might change from dark to light** (negative to positive), a **person may change from male to female, or objects may take on human characteristics**. These changes are often depicted as occurring immediately in dreams, like a speeded-up movie, and they reflect changes in waking life.

Bizarre transformations of **objects into living things**, such as a **pencil turning into a snake, a doll into a donkey or a table into a swarm of wasps,** suggest untapped potential within you that can help you cope with change. To clarify what this potential is, refer to the symbolic interpretation of the objects that have been transformed. **Shape-shifter** dreams, in which **people you know suddenly transform into something else**, typically a **monster or beast,** represent unpredictable people in your waking life. For example, someone might be kind and caring towards you until they transform under the influence of alcohol. On the other hand, the shape-shifting may be some kind of moral test. Can you uncover the beauty behind the monster's mask? What lies below the outer skin of the dream beast? Try to make a connection to your waking life.

Sudden changes from winter to spring in a dream, or **from night to day**, may also suggest new directions and developments in the dreamer's life. If the other way round, and the **switch is from day to night, or spring to winter**, this may suggest the need to confront and deal with dangerous impulses. If the **landscape suddenly becomes unfamiliar** in your dream, this can point to an unwillingness or an inability to cope with the new. However, if the **new environment is welcoming and friendly** this is a positive sign. A **return to the comfort of the childhood home or a familiar environment** is widely interpreted by Freudians and Jungians as a desire to return to the security of the womb during times of change and conflict.

If **something is transfigured** in a dream, such as when an **object or person is surrounded by light**, this suggests that light has entered the person during a period of transition and they are becoming more self-aware. If **you become invisible** in your dream, it can indicate that you feel ignored in waking life – that you and your life are insignificant to others. It can also mean that you are hiding from others or yourself. If you have this type of dream, it might be time to look at how you present yourself to other people.

TRANSITION

The following dreams tend to be common during times of change or transition. A dream of **waking and getting up**, when in fact you are still asleep, may signal reluctance to face change or a new challenge – such as a new job or new relationship. Then again, perhaps this **false wakefulness** is the mind's way of preventing us from waking up, thereby exemplifying Freud's theory that the purpose of all dreams is to prolong, rather than interrupt, sleep. Dreams of a **vehicle careering out of control** suggest worries about losing all sense of direction in life, especially if you are the driver, passenger or bystander unable to influence the events.

A **rudderless, drifting raft or boat** suggests loss of direction, but some believe that sometimes not knowing where you are going can be a way of discovering your true self. A raft is an image of survival and, in some ways, this image suggests the ability to ride out the sea of troubles rather than be overwhelmed. **Strange reflections** in the mirror are often said to suggest personal identity problems during times of conflict –

if it's **your face, and your eyes are closed**, this is a refusal to confront reality and if it is **someone else's face**, this may indicate a sense of inadequacy when compared to them. **No face at all** is the ultimate identity crisis; a fear of death itself. If a **bridge** appears in your dream, this is a clear symbol of transition from the present to the unpredictable future. **Crossing the bridge** suggests that you possess the strength within to cope with life's journey and with difficult events such as moving home, divorce or a new job.

Conflict Scenarios

ABANDONMENT/FEAR/LOSS OF CONTROL

Dream images connected to feelings of abandonment, fear and loss of control all have some form of **conflict** as their theme. For example, dreams about **missing a bus, train or airplane** all point to some kind of tension in the dreamer about failing to achieve a goal. Dreams about **being abandoned or left alone by a group of loved ones** suggest feelings of anxiety about being left out, or being different from the crowd. **Anxiously searching for the right road or path** could point to fears about losing your identity. If you are **happily wandering alone** in your dream, this may suggest a feeling that the source of your problems lies outside yourself. Dreams about **anchors and lifeboats** also tell of the fight for survival in daily life. If you dream of being **lost in dense vegetation**,

The Element Encyclopedia of 20,000 Dreams

towering trees or tall reeds, you may feel that your progress is being thwarted by obstacles. As in the tale of 'Hansel and Gretel', this dream may evoke longing for the comfort and warmth of home.

ARGUMENTS

If you dreamed that you had a **heated argument with someone**, try to identify who that person was. Your dream may mirror real-life hostility between the two of you, or you may be consciously unaware of your aversion to that person or their aversion to you. Your unconscious may use the dream as an outlet to release feelings of aggression, or it may use the dream to alert your conscious self to the hidden aggression. If, however, you can find no reason for hostility between the person in your dream and yourself in waking life, then perhaps the dream argument represents an aspect of yourself – this interpretation is even more likely if you are **arguing with someone you don't know**. Try to recall what the person looked like and what the argument was about. If the dream focused on a **young person arguing with an older person**, perhaps the dream represented tension between the part of you that longs to be more spontaneous and the part of you that is a stickler for routine.

ATTACK/ATTACKER

If **you are being attacked** in your dreams, this suggests you are feeling threatened in some way, perhaps by your own impulses, or perhaps by other people and their attitude or remarks to you. If **you are the attacker** in the dream, who or what are you attacking? Attack is almost always a form of defense, so may also suggest defensiveness about some issue in, or aspect of, your life. There is also a positive side to attack, as new ideas and positive changes can threaten our old way of life and habitual way of thinking about things. If you are **attacked by an animal** in your dream, this suggests anxiety about aggression in yourself or other people. If you are **attacked by a shadowy or frightening figure**, this may depict feelings of fear and pain associated with the past. How you deal with the attack is important. If **you run from it**, the trauma is not being dealt with in waking life.

DANGER

Dreams about **earthquakes, landslides and volcanoes** all point to inner turmoil or emotional conflict that is shaking the foundation of the dreamer's world. The dream may often come close to being a nightmare, but such dreams are warning you about something that is going on in your waking life to which you need to pay attention. A dream about a **natural disaster** is unlikely to be prophetic; it is more likely to be referring to something dangerous in your waking life. For example, an **avalanche** dream may refer to oppressive forces in waking life threatening to overwhelm you – an avalanche of responsibility, for example, that accompanies the birth of a new child. If you are **swept away** in the dream, you are being urged to find something, or someone, to hold onto in waking life to regain stability. If you dreamed that the **earth was cracking open beneath you**, this threat may be echoed in changes at work or insecurity within a relationship.

An **explosion** may reflect sudden changes in waking life or the release of emotion. What damage has the explosion inflicted in the dream? If anything was broken, interpret its symbolism; if someone was clinging on to you in the dream, who are they? If you dreamed you were in danger of **thunder or lighting**, again this may refer to emotional turmoil in waking life; but a dream about being **struck by lighting** could refer to sudden insight. If you dream that you are **falling into a dark hole**, is there some situation in waking life out of which you feel you cannot climb?

Dreams featuring **alarms** may be caused by car or house alarms that go off in the night; if there is no external stimulus of this sort, and your dream features a **house alarm**, does this allude to your family? Does someone need protection at this time? Was the alarm effective in the dream? If the **alarm failed to go off**, this is an extremely significant symbol. If your dream features a **car alarm**, this may allude to some kind of rash behavior and, as men often equate cars with sexuality, you may want to consider it in this context.

Dreams can also often warn of dangers of which we may be unaware in waking life. For example if you dream of **overspending**, this may suggest you are expending too much emotion on a particular person. If you dream of **escaping from a prison to a happy landscape**, this may be a warning that you need to relax more. There are other practical warning dreams. For example, you may dream that your **car brakes fail** and in waking life find that this is indeed the case. There is usually a simple explanation as your unconscious mind may have registered the fault, but this kind of dream should not be ignored (*see* ACCIDENTS, ACTION AND ADVENTURES). Similarly dreams of **bodily aches and pains and**

other signs of poor health are also worth taking note of. *See also* SICKNESS AND HEALTH.

DISOBEDIENCE

Dreams that feature some kind of **disobedience, mutiny and rebellion** are about conflict with authority, such as a parent, a teacher, a corporation or even the government. If you were **disobedient or rebellious** in your dream, whose authority were you up against? To whom is it that you feel you need to assert your individuality and independence? On the other hand, your unconscious may have simply allowed you to give vent to feelings of resentment in the safety of the dream world. If you dreamed that you **refuse to comply with your boss**, or with someone who gives you directions in waking life, this may reflect your mounting anger or exhaustion in the face of demands and responsibilities being placed upon you.

If you felt liberated in your dream, perhaps this is a sign that you need to stand up for yourself more in waking life. If you were **involved in a mutiny**, do you long to rebel against authority? If you **went on strike**, such a dream may reflect feelings of frustration and exhaustion in waking life. If you found yourself engaged in **arm wrestling**, are you engaged in a real-life battle of wills? An alternative explanation for dreams of **rebellion against an enemy, known or unknown** is that you are in revolt against some part of yourself. Try to remember what you rebelled against in your dream and why, and see if you can draw a parallel in waking life.

The Element Encyclopedia of 20,000 Dreams

Drowning/Crawling/ Falling

Drowning in deep water suggests floundering in the depths of the unconscious. As with dreams of **pursuit or being chased**, this dream alerts you to areas of your unconscious that are creating conflict and need to be examined with care. **Falling and jumping in an attempt to escape from hostile pursuers** in a dream is a desperate escape mechanism and suggests that you might have more success if you turn at the last minute to face your enemies, having found the strength to confront them. Dreams in which you are **trying to run from something or someone** but find you cannot – perhaps because your **feet are weighed down or stuck in the mud** – can be interpreted in much the same way.

Crawling through a narrow space, **tunnel or small enclosure,** or trying to **squeeze through a tiny corridor or hall** points to your creative energies struggling to find expression; these are, however, also common-place dreams expressing anxiety about a challenging and imminent event such as a review at work, an examination or even the birth of a new baby. **Being chased, not knowing who or what is out there in the darkness, or vainly trying to push through the crowds in a busy bar, street or department store** also suggest that certain repressed aspects of your personality, or unexamined aspects of the self, demand to be dealt with. To be **trapped** in a dream signifies that you feel you are trapped by outside circumstances. To be aware of **trapping something or someone** is to try to hold onto them, and if you **trap a butterfly or animal**, you are trying to capture your inner self. Feeling trapped in dreams also suggests an inability to break free from old patterns of thought and behavior without outside help. *See also* NEGATIVE EMOTIONS.

Fighting

If you are **fighting an unknown enemy** in your dream, this may represent a struggle with the shadow side of your nature and the unwelcome aspects of your personality. For example, there might be a battle between your moral code and your sexual desire, or between your intellect and your emotional needs. Conflict can also occur between your personal drives and social, political and economic drives. The fight may also represent a battle between yourself and another person, and your conscious and unconscious needs. If the **enemy is someone you know**, perhaps you have unsuspected feelings of animosity towards them. A **fight between a younger and an older person** in your dream may suggest a rivalry between the dreamer and authority.

A **fight between people of the same age** may represent the struggle for recognition or sibling rivalry. Similar interpretations can be applied to any kind of **struggle** in your dream. Such fights usually depict a fight for freedom, independence or the truth. Your unconscious may also be urging you to work out why there is a conflict, and may be suggesting that there is a more subtle way of dealing with it than with fists. According to Freudians, the struggle depicts the battle between your father or mother for the attention of the other parent.

▪ *Idioms: fight it out; fight like cats and dogs; looking for a fight.* See also *BAD DEEDS.*

KILLING

If you dream about **killing a person, an animal or see people or animals being killed**, this does not mean you have latent violent tendencies. Instead it can mean the death of thoughts and actions that have been restricting your personal growth. A **deliberate act of murder** might suggest hostility, with the identity of the victim and murderer assisting with the interpretation. **Killing an authority figure** typically suggests a desire to escape social or personal constraints. **Killing a parent** points to unresolved childhood conflicts, perhaps deep-seated resentments that have not been expressed. If the parent was of the opposite sex, Freudians might consider it as evidence of the Oedipus complex. A dream of **poison** – either **poisoning someone or being poisoned yourself** – may refer to some underhand action we are taking or which is being taken against us. Look for clues in the dream. Who or what is being poisoned? Is someone you know in waking life poisoning your attitude unbeknownst to you? What is the color of the poison? Are you poisoning yourself in some way?

VIOLENCE

If you have a dream where the **conflict contains gruesome, explicit images of violence**, try to relate these to your waking life. If you can't think of any waking parallels, consider the identity of your opponent in the dream? Is this someone you recognize or is it a hidden part of yourself? Was your opponent serious or light-hearted? Was anyone hurt in the dream? Was the conflict resolved and how so? Any violence in dreams is a reflection of your own inner feelings about yourself and sometimes about the situation around you. Seeing yourself as a **victim of self-imposed violence** suggests self-blame, perhaps related to the end of a relationship or the death of a loved one, both of which you may feel could have been avoidable had you had acted differently. Dream violence towards yourself may also express low self-esteem, self-loathing and destructive urges that should be dealt with before they erupt into waking life.

If, on the other hand, you are **lashing out at others** in your dream, this may reflect your struggle to fight the undesirable impulses within yourself. **Violence towards an old person** can indicate resentment against authority. **Violence towards a child** may indicate the dreamer's inability to accept and express the child within themselves. If you dreamed that **you were attacked or threatened with attack**, it may be a warning of an attack in waking life. This may not be a physical attack but an attack on your integrity or character.

War

People who have been in a **war** situation may be plagued by dreams that recall their ordeals, but for those who have never seen war, such dreams usually refer to **private battles** raging either within themselves, or between themselves and other people. Are such battles necessary, or would reconciliation be better than victory? Are you being too hard on yourself? Carl Jung believed dreams of war to represent a conflict between the conscious and unconscious minds, which is a struggle between the deep instinctive forces and the rules of conscious conduct. However, sometimes turmoil is needed in order for the personality to develop and grow. If you can accept the part of yourself that is trying to find expression, you may be able to draw up a peace settlement. Anger, sorrow or pity are usually found in dreams about war; whichever of these emotions you feel will show the feeling or action in waking life that has provoked the dream.

The clue to the dream's subject may be found in the identity of the opposing armies, or the landscape, in the soldier's clothing and the course of the battle may be suggesting a similar action in waking life. Which army did you belong to? If it was a **savage army**, perhaps your dreaming mind is suggesting that your true allegiance lies with your instincts, but if you belong to a **modern, sophisticated army**, the dream may be telling you that your inclination is to follow the rule of your intellect. If you witnessed the **outcome of the battle** in your dream, or **admired the victorious army and its winning tactics**, this may give you an indication of how best to resolve the conflict within yourself.

Although war and battle dreams may indicate disagreement between two individuals, they may also point to explosive disagreements between certain groups of people in your life; for example, disagreements in the workplace or differing opinions within the family. Your dreaming mind may be warning you that you will soon be entangled in that conflict and this is especially so if a **battlefield** features in your dream. The battlefield may indicate the area of conflict and your dream may be indicating whether you should take sides or act as peacemaker. A battlefield scene may also represent your working environment or a

Particular weapons

If you can identify the weapon used in your dream and the symbolic meaning associated with it, you can get a better idea of what your real problem might be.

Axe

This can be both creative and destructive, as it is often used to separate the valuable from the worthless. An **axe or hatchet** can be a symbol of emotional readiness to cut out dead wood so you can free yourself from whatever is holding you back. If the **axe belongs to an executioner**, do you have a tendency for excessive self-criticism?

Bladed weapons

Although **daggers and knives** are symbols of violence – indicating concealed hostility towards someone – they are also symbols of male self-esteem and can stand for the secure presence of a father in waking life. But if a **dagger or knife is used against you** in your dream, this may suggest a threat from someone or a reminder that you are being confronted with a dangerous or precarious situation in waking life, as in 'being on a knife's edge'. A knife has the ability to cut into things and perhaps pinpoint what is bothering you or what needs to be cut out.

Swords

Swords feature in legend, religion and mythology and are often wielded to subdue evil forces, representing the triumph of good over evil. Swords can also denote kingship, as exemplified by 'Excalibur', the sword of King Arthur, suggesting justice or the highest source of authority. Being double-edged, swords can evoke feelings of guilt or remorse, but they also suggest spiritual strength and, like axes, the ability to cut away what is non-essential. The **sword when sheathed** may be a symbol of the self within the body. The **lance** shares the symbolism of the sword, but its phallic shape often points to sexual issues.

> *Idioms: put one's knife in; on a knife edge; under the knife (surgery); cut it out; cut the atmosphere with a knife; double-edged sword; cross swords; sword hanging by a thread (threats hanging over you); Sword of Damocles.*

Bow and arrow

The **bow and arrow** can be a symbol of tension, especially sexual tension, as in Cupid's bow. If the **arrow is fired to the skies**, this can express a wish to devote yourself to a higher purpose. Arrows also suggest being pierced by some intense emotion, or being hurt by someone. Were you the target or were you taking aim? Did the arrow hit or fall short? Was it a **poisoned arrow**? Arrows are also used symbolically to point the way, so an arrow in your dream can direct you to the right choice, perhaps relating to a decision you need to make in waking life.

Bullet/Ammunition

Bullets or ammunition can suggest verbal attacks in the context of dream conflicts. If the ammunition belongs to someone else, this represents things that you feel other people can use against you, such as lies, anger and so on. If you have the ammunition, it can represent assets you have that can build your confidence, things you could say or do to wound others if you had to. If you **run out or don't have any ammunition**, you may be feeling hopeless about a situation and unable to defend your position.

Explosive

Bullets, cannonballs, bombs and mines all explode on detonation or impact. If you fired any of these, your dreaming mind is warning you that you are in danger of exploding with frustration or anger. Are you currently on a short emotional fuse and in danger of detonating with burning anger? What was your target in the dream? This may help you understand what triggered your anger. On the other hand, could an explosive situation be building up around you? Again, if your **firepower ran out**, this could indicate lack of ammunition in a conflict in your waking life; perhaps there just isn't enough reason for you to be involved.

Gun

Guns, pistols or rifles in a man's dream typically suggest male sexuality and defenses used against emotions. The unconscious may have selected this weapon to denote his sexual performance and if he fires blanks concerns about failing virility may be indicated. But because a person can feel impotent in other areas of life a misfiring gun may also suggest general feelings of powerlessness. If a **gun appears in a woman's dream**, it may indicate her desire to be more assertive sexually. If you are **shooting the gun** in the dream, you may be behaving in quite an aggressive way in waking life. Are you defending yourself in the dream or shooting for pleasure? If you are **shot by a gun**, you may be feeling wounded or the target of criticism or hurtful comments in waking life. If you shoot the gun in your dream, this suggests anxiety about expressing emotions or hidden hostility. **Bayonets** are thrusting weapons used in conjunction with guns, and in dreams they suggest extreme danger and a desire for total control, either aimed at someone else or directed against you.

■ *Idioms: shot in the arm; shot in the dark; shot to pieces; long shot.*

Nuclear bomb

If the **cloud from a nuclear bomb** appears in your dream this is a terrible symbol of utter destruction. However, its shape will be significant; if it appears in **mushroom form**, it can also be a symbol of regeneration and renewal after the destruction. *See also* DISASTERS.

battle you are waging with yourself, such as the battle to give up smoking, the struggle to keep to a diet and so on.

If you dream of war, rather than simply a battle, different interpretations are appropriate. War has a more global effect that one-to-one combat or fighting, and this would suggest that you need to be more conscious of the effect your actions have on others. The outcome of war should be the establishment of order, and dreams of **wars coming to an end** can have a positive interpretation, suggesting that this natural process is taking place on an inner level.

■ *Idioms: in the wars; on the war path; war of nerves; declare war; battle stations; battle your way through; battle scarred.*

WARFARE

If, in your dream, you were part of a **regiment**, this may suggest that you feel safe in numbers, as a part of a crowd or group of people. If you feel sorrow or guilt or resentment, this may reflect your attitude to the group of people you associate yourself with in waking life. Taking part in **guerrilla actions** suggests secret plans in waking life, whilst a preoccupation with a **helmet and protective clothing** may mirror a desire to 'take cover' in waking life. A dream in which an **invasion** takes place may be symbolic of an invasion of your space in waking life, either real or psychological. If a **tank** appears in your battle, this is an aggressive phallic symbol. It can also suggest an attack on convention and an indiscriminate flattening of all those who stand in your way. The **torpedo** also symbolizes male sexuality but, unlike the tank, it delivers destruction by stealth. **High-tech missiles, cannon, field guns and other forms of artillery** also present variations on the phallic symbol. On the other hand, they may also symbolize obstacles or 'hot shots' you feel are against you as you pursue your goals. This may be particularly the case if you are a woman in a stereotypically male profession.

If an **air raid** takes place in your dream, this indicates emotional attack from people or feelings you have about the events around you. A **bomb** suggests an explosive situation or sudden events that have produced anxiety. It can also suggest your own anxiety. If an **underground mine** figures in your dream, this can suggest bringing to consciousness potential and innate wisdom. A dream **explosion with billowing clouds** graphically mirrors the damaging consequences of exploding with pent-up fury or tension in waking life.

■ *Idioms: I feel blitzed; come as a bombshell; put a bomb under someone; earn a bomb.*

WEAPONS

Weapons in dreams appear for numerous reasons. They are associated with aggression and hostility towards someone, perhaps you. They can be a warning that you need to take defensive action against something or someone that poses a real threat to you. They may also represent a secret desire within you to hurt someone. If you dream of **using a weapon against someone**, do you harbor hidden anger and aggression that you have not expressed in waking life? If you do not know the person you are attacking, your weapon and victim

The Element Encyclopedia of 20,000 Dreams

may be symbolic representations of aspects of yourself you do not like or find hard to deal with. You may have inner conflicts that need to be resolved, or 'killed off'. If so, what does your **unknown victim** look like, and how does he, she or it react to the threat? All this may provide you with important clues. If you have a **weapon used against you** in a dream this may suggest that you have done something to upset people around you or it may be that you feel you have become the victim of circumstances. If **you are shot** in the dream, this may be referring to internalized aggression, past hurt or a fear of being hurt.

According to Freud, almost every weapon is a phallic symbol and many dream researchers still subscribe to this view. If a **man dreams he is attacking a woman with a weapon or hunting a woman**, it may reveal an equivocal attitude towards women. A **woman who dreams of being attacked** may be expressing sexual insecurity or a fear of men. **Weapons or firearms that malfunction** in dreams or fail to work may indicate a sense of powerlessness to handle challenges in daily life. They may also suggest anxiety about sexual performance or an inability to express ideas confidently to other people. If a **work tool or other object is used as an offensive weapon**, this suggests a skill or authority that has turned against you, as might happen if a teacher was taking advantage of a pupil. The atmosphere of the dream will provide the best clue for analysis, but ancient dream oracles suggest that this dream generally means you have enemies who pretend to be friends. In other words, 'watch your back'.

CLOTHES AND IMAGE

Dreams about clothes are very common and they usually tell you something about your self-image.

In waking life, clothes protect, conceal and reveal and so in dreams they depict the façade, or persona, you create for other people; by so doing, they tell you where you may be vulnerable or exposed in waking life. The colors and condition of your dream clothes are especially important as they may symbolize how you are feeling about yourself, or how others perceive you. For example, if you were dressed in brightly colored designer clothes and were basking in the admiration of others, this may indicate good self-esteem, whereas if you were dressed in dark, shabby-looking garments in dreamland, and you felt miserable and self-conscious, it may be that this is how you are feeling in the real world.

Dreams about clothes can often focus on whether you are wearing the right outfit for the right occasion. For example, you may turn up at a party dressed totally inappropriately, you may have problems getting dressed, or you may find yourself walking naked down a busy street. Such dreams are rarely about sex and more about feelings of vulnerability, although they are sometimes about freedom from inhibitions. *See also* COLORS.

Clothing Scenarios

DRESSING IN OTHER PEOPLE'S CLOTHES

Clothes are the protective layer that keeps you warm, but they are also a way to express your personality or hide imperfections. In dreams, what you wear is often a symbol of your self-image or inner self, and if you dress in **clothes that obviously belong to other people**, this is a clear sign that you have problems accepting yourself as you truly are. It can, on the other hand, suggest admiration for the person whose clothes you are wearing.

For Jungians, wearing **clothes of the opposite sex** may signal the dreamer's need to express the anima (female aspects of the male nature) or the animus (male aspects of the female nature). For Freudians, a **child dressing up in adult clothes**, particularly if the clothes are those of the opposite sex, may suggest childhood rivalry with one parent for the affections of the opposite sex parent. If you are simply **changing outfit** in your dream, this may suggest altering your mode of behavior, role or mood. If you astonish yourself by **shopping for, buying and wearing unusual clothes** in your dream that you would never normally wear in waking life, then your unconscious may have been suggesting that you have become too set in your ways and outlook, and that it is time to open your mind up to new opinions. Is it time for you to break out of your rut and for other people to sit up and notice you?

On the other hand if you dress casually in waking life and dream of wearing a **business suit**, your unconscious may be urging you to adopt a more business-like approach. If you were surprised by the color of the clothes in your dream – either your own or those belonging to someone else – then see if that color has significance for you (*see* COLORS). If you find yourself **dressed in expensive designer clothes** you couldn't normally afford, this may also be simple wish-fulfillment, especially if you are fashion conscious.

EXPOSURE

If you **expose yourself** in your dream, either deliberately or by accident, you need to ask yourself why this happened. In your waking life, are you too open, too naïve, too trusting, or not open or trusting enough? If you feel embarrassed in the dream, then the chances are you feel that you are already exposed or in danger of being exposed in some way in waking life. If, on the other hand, you are enjoying your freedom from social constraint, then your unconscious may be urging you to be more open or free from convention in waking life. Exposing yourself in a dream may also have something to do with truthfulness; perhaps you need to be more honest and direct in waking life.

NAKEDNESS

One of the most common and often embarrassing dreams is to find yourself **naked in a public place, wearing only your underwear or clothes that are see-through**. Nakedness may represent a longing to return to childhood innocence, as the dream represents the real you, stripped of pretence and social conditioning. Do you have a desire to be seen for who you are or to reveal your essential personality without having to create a façade? Another interpretation is that nakedness expresses a latent exhibitionism or simply a desire for sex. Freud once stated that his favorite dream was of being naked in a crowd of strangers.

From a Freudian perspective, a **naked female** is usually an expression of sexual desire for dreamers – men or women – who are sexually attracted to women. Freudians see the **naked male** in much the same light as the naked female, as an expression of sexual desire for men. In Jungian terms, nakedness suggests aspirations for love and rebirth, or a desire to attain spiritual awareness and to renounce the material world. According to this interpretation, nakedness is also an expression of beauty, creativity and divinity. Ancient gods such as Venus, goddess of beauty, and Diana, the goddess of the hunt, are often depicted naked.

A **naked child** is particularly associated with the Jungian archetype of the divine child, and more generally with innocence and lack of inhibition. If you are **covering up a child's nakedness** in the dream, this indicates a general discomfort with emotional expression. Many psychologists favor the interpretation that dreams of nakedness highlight feelings of vulnerability. Such dreams may be interpreted as a fear of sexual relationships, but they are more likely to signify fears and anxieties about yourself, and the way you appear to others. Perhaps you feel failure or rejection if you reveal your true self. In your waking life, you therefore need to overcome feelings of vulnerability and learn to be more self-confident.

Being **partly dressed** in a dream may suggest that you are not prepared for what lies ahead. It might be wise to re-examine your plans and your future. If the **people in the dream seem unaware that you are underdressed or naked**, this suggests that you shouldn't worry about showing your real self to others. It may also signify that you are not worried about what others think of you, or that you long to show sides of your true personality to others. To dream of being ashamed or frightened may indicate a fear of showing your real feelings. If, on the other hand, you are **disgusted by your own, or another person's, nakedness, or other people are disgusted with your own nakedness**, this suggests anxiety about discovering the naked truth about yourself, another person or a situation.

If you positively **welcome the nakedness of other people** in your dream, it may express a frustration with what, in waking life, you perceive to be their affected behavior – you wish they could be more natural.

It may also suggest that you can see through people and see them for who they are. If you are sufficiently secure within your own self-image in waking life, you will not be afraid of being stripped in public in a dream. For example, dreaming of **appearing naked in a strip show** could suggest that you are anxious about being misunderstood, or that you welcome the opportunity to express and reveal yourself.

A state of undress

If you have a dream in which nakedness features strongly, or if you dream of appearing underdressed in public, ask yourself if you want others to see you as you really are in waking life. Examine how other people respond to you in the dream, as their reaction and behavior may be holding you back. Often these dreams reveal a fear of exposure, so ask yourself if you feel guilty about something. Have you recently been pretending, or even lying, about something you don't want others to discover? Also ask yourself if you fear that a plan or a concept you are offering to others will be met with disapproval. You should also pay attention to your feelings in the dream about being naked or underdressed. Do you feel pleasure at being free of inhibitions, or do you feel anxious and vulnerable?

The Element Encyclopedia of 20,000 Dreams

According to dream lore, if a **girl dreams of being naked**, this means that she will soon hear about a terrible scandal. Some gypsies, however, believe that nakedness dreams are a sign of good fortune, particularly if the dreamer was **walking naked under the stars**. Ancient dream dictionaries say that to dream of a **naked woman** was lucky, as it foretold unexpected honors. It was also thought to be unlucky to dream of **too many clothes**, since this meant you lacked the necessities of life, whilst to dream of **new clothes** suggested a domestic tiff. *See also* NEGATIVE EMOTIONS.

Undressing and dressing

Clothes can act as protection against being touched, so in dreams they can represent protection against the real self being approached. Clothes also conceal and reveal, so if you are **undressing or dressing** in your dream, what parts of your body are you covering up? In revealing certain parts of you, your dream may show in which sorts of ways you are vulnerable. If you are **putting on your clothes** in your dream, this suggests that you are making progress in waking life and moving forward positively. If you are **undressing**, this suggests that you wish to get to the truth of a situation. It may also indicate the shedding of old beliefs and inhibitions.

If you are **unable to get undressed** in your dream or **feel overdressed**, this may suggest difficulties in changing attitudes or self-image; it may also indicate an avoidance of intimacy. If you **receive clothes as a gift**, you may get helpful advice from another person; if you are **buying clothes**, this signifies your determination to make a fresh start in waking life. Ancient dream oracles considered dreams of undressing to indicate an impending mistake in business affairs unless advice was listened to.

Uniform

A **uniform** such as that of a sailor, soldier, and policeman carries with it the association of that profession. So, if you dream of wearing a **policeman's uniform**, it may indicate feelings of having to establish law and order, or needing to keep a watchful eye on your community. If you are wearing an **army uniform**, are you someone with a need for more rules and greater self-discipline? If you are wearing your **work clothes**, this suggests you are working at something, or is revealing of your attitudes concerning work. For school clothes, *see also* SCHOOL AND WORK.

Washing clothes

Washing may represent some kind of inner cleaning in which you get rid of attitudes and habits that are holding you back. If you are **washing clothes** in your dream, this symbolizes an improvement in the way you present yourself to the world. If you are **washing underwear**, this may indicate the resolution of feelings of sexual insecurity. If you are **washing someone else's clothes**, this may indicate your desire to help that person feel better about themselves. According to ancient dream oracles, **washing clothes and yourself** was a sign of good fortune, but **stained clothes and taking a bath fully clothed** indicated misfortune.

Problems with clothing

Clothing that is **incongruous to the situation** might be a comment on your view of your position in society. Have you found your proper place? Are you comfortable with it? **Inadequate, untidy or inappropriate clothing** that makes you feel uncomfortable or embarrassed indicates that you feel uncomfortable or ill prepared to fit in with people's expectations. Are you deliberately not conforming to what is expected of you, or are you trying too hard to adopt a certain role?

Clothing that is **too tight, too small or dating back to childhood** suggests that something about your current attitude or approach is holding you back. It may also suggest that you are aiming for more than you can achieve in the present circumstances. For Freudians, **tight clothing** may indicate a preoccupation with the breasts and buttocks whose shape they reveal. The dreamer wearing **loose clothing** may be attempting to conceal their true self, but it may also represent a yearning to be free of inhibitions.

If you are wearing **formal clothes when everyone else is dressed casually,** perhaps you have ideas above your station; alternatively, the dream may be a warning against snobbery. On the other hand, being **sloppily dressed in a formal setting** may be suggesting that your behavior is damaging your prospects. It is also common to dream about being **unable to find a suitable outfit or searching frantically for appropriate clothes**; such dreams reflect anxiety about being adequately prepared to meet the obligations and demands placed upon you.

Dreamers dressed in **shabby clothes, rags or clothes that have rips and tears** may be projecting an image of inferiority or low self-esteem, and the dream may be a warning to build their confidence. A dream of a **jumper, cardigan or other woolen garment unraveling** may indicate a growing sense of disillusionment with some aspect of your waking life. The unraveling may be a sign that it is time to look to a new direction for inspiration.

If you are aware in your dream of a **problem with your clothing**, this is a positive sign as it suggests that you are already aware of tensions that are affecting you in waking life. If you are **unaware that you are dressed inappropriately** and only notice this on waking, your unconscious is pointing to the source of feelings you have not yet understood. Finally, if you dream that you are wearing **clothes remarkably different from your normal wardrobe**, the implication is that you are ill at ease with your self-image. The color, style and texture of your clothes may be able to tell you which area of your life needs to be remolded.

What to Wear A to Z

APRON/OVERALLS

Aprons and overalls in a dream can suggest getting to work on family suggestions or secrecy. If you are wearing such garments, what part of you are you covering up in waking life? Or are you about to undertake an extremely difficult – and messy – task? If you are wearing an item of **clothing as camouflage**, what are you hiding?

ARMOR

If you are dressed in **armor** in your dream, do you need to protect yourself against something or someone? In donning such heavy attire, you are better protected but you also restrict your movement; perhaps your unconscious is telling you that it might be better to open up about what is troubling you, instead of keeping it a closely guarded secret. If **chains** feature alongside the armor, this is a symbol of enslavement and unhappiness with your current commitments. If your **chains break or are** broken, this is a positive sign.

BELT/BUCKLE

A **belt** is symbol of support and, as such, it indicates anxieties about keeping up a public face. A belt is also a bond that holds tightly and restricts freedom of movement, so if you **loosen a belt** in your dream are you ready to loosen up and free yourself from inhibitions? Or are you afraid you might be caught with your pants down? A **carefully buttoned-up coat or an item displaying buckles** also suggests restraint, whereas an **open-necked shirt or casual clothing** may refer to lack of inhibition. Be attentive to idioms such as 'belt up' and 'tighten one's belt'.

BOOT/SHOE/SOCK

Is there someone in waking life that you wish to give the boot to? **Boots and shoes** are what we wear to protect our feet and give us good contact with the ground, so if they feature in your dream, do you need to make a special effort to keep in touch with reality?

What kind of shoes appeared in the dream? If they were **hiking boots**, perhaps you long to travel and explore? If your dream shoes were **shoddy**, are you feeling down-trodden in waking life? If you were **walking over someone** in your dream, especially if you were wearing **heavy clogs**, is this literally true in waking life? Whose feelings are you treading on with your heavy feet? Shoes often represent your chosen way of life in dreams or the character traits developed to deal with life. If the shoes belong to a particular role or activity, for example **ballet shoes** for dancers or **nurses' shoes** for those in the caring professions, this may indicate a need for the qualities of that role or activity. More generally, **shoes and garters** in dreams have also traditionally represented sexuality.

If you are **changing boots or shoes**, has there been a recent change in circumstances as in 'the boot is on the other foot'? If you are **taking off your shoes** in the dream, it might suggest that you are leaving your past behind and feel open to change. If your **shoes are painful** because they pinch and rub, is your freedom of movement being restricted in the waking world? Or have you been feeling a financial pinch recently? If you are **wearing someone else's shoes**, your unconscious may have been urging you not to judge someone so quickly, because if you walked in their shoes you would understand how hard it is for them to make progress. If you are **walking without shoes**, you may be going through a rough patch or you may simply feel like letting go of your everyday responsibilities. And because of the association between shoes, shopping and sex, dreams about shoes may also simply be erotic wish-fulfillment fantasies. In ancient dream lore, **lacing up shoes** in a dream was a well-known symbol of death, as were **shoes on a table**.

Socks in dreams often represent the cleanness or untidiness of a person, and therefore depict some kind of judgment about what sort of person they are or, if the socks are yours, how you see yourself. Socks can also be associated with warmth and protection, or with certain roles such as those that **football, tennis or hiking socks** represent; expressions such as 'pull your socks up' or 'knocked my socks off' suggest a motivating or powerful experience. If the **socks are full of holes** in your dream, this may suggest that you feel demoralized in some way. If, however, you were **waving a sock** to someone, were you warning them, as might be suggested by the phrase 'sock it to them', or were you trying to get them to impress you, as might be suggested by 'sock it to me'?

Coat/Cloak/Jacket/Suit

If a **coat** features in your dream, this probably suggests the self you present in public; for example, you may be outspoken in public but your partner will know that, deep down, you are shy. An **overcoat** suggests protectiveness and not showing intimacy or vulnerability; what in waking life are you trying to ward off? **Fear of losing your coat** can suggest fear of letting your guard down. If the **coat is too short or not warm enough**, you may be craving more love and affection than you are getting in waking life. According to Freud, the **cloak** is a symbol of female sexuality, but may also represent secrecy and concealment. If a **jacket** features in your dream, this suggests the degree of formality with which you present yourself to others. A **raincoat** may suggest tears or the release of emotion. If you are wearing a **suit** in your dream, this suggests the image you or other people have of you; the way you present yourself to others and different kinds of suits – **wetsuits, bathing suit** – represent different attitudes and situations.

▪ *Idioms: cloak and dagger; dragged by one's coat-tails; up one's sleeve; coat of many colors.*

Dress/Skirt/Trousers

Many women wear **trousers or jeans** today, and so a dream that either men or women have featuring a **dress or skirt** may suggest a desire for both sexes to express their feminine side. It could also be a symbol of the mother and the security of her nurture. The colors and length of the skirt will say a lot about what is being done

The Element Encyclopedia of 20,000 Dreams

with sexuality in a social sense. A **woman wearing trousers** may – in line with the idiom 'wear the trousers' – express a fear of being dominated by a woman. In general, **trousers** in a dream suggest masculinity, whilst **jeans** suggest socialized sexuality. If you are wearing **shorts**, you may be outgrowing former pleasures and need to look to new experiences for your entertainment. On the other hand you may just be longing for the carefree days of holiday summer sun.

Fashion

Dreams in which **fashion** appears as a general theme may relate to how you feel about yourself in waking life. Do you feel dowdy, out of date and old-fashioned? If you see **models on a catwalk** and admire them, find out why you found them attractive; if you want to be a model, such a dream may be wish-fulfillment. If you are **looking at a mannequin in the window of a department store**, was your dream suggesting that you, or someone you know, lacks character? A dream in which you are **looking in the mirror** also expresses concern with your self-image. As we see ourselves in reverse in a mirror, the dream may be asking you to see yourself in a new way. If the **mirror was cracked or dirty**, the dream may be suggesting a certain amount of self-deception in waking life, but if the **mirror is clear and bright** and you notice blemishes you hadn't noticed before, the dream indicates self-honesty and the making of appropriate decisions in life.

Glove

If your dream highlights gloves is there a particular person or situation in waking life you need to handle with extra special care? Or do you need to protect yourself in some way. Are you keeping your hands clean and avoiding dirty business? Freud associated **gloves** (into which hands are inserted) with sexuality and with birth control. Traditionally, a glove was a symbol of purity in women, and **picking up a glove** would have the same meaning as picking up a handkerchief dropped by a woman – an invitation to intimacy. If you **take your gloves off** in your dream, this may suggest a desire for more honesty in waking life. If you **took your right-hand glove off in order to shake hands with someone**, your dream reveals your real feelings for that person. If you **put on a pair of gloves** in your dream, could it be that you are worried about revealing your hand? Or is someone in waking life behaving so unpredictably that you feel you have to treat them with kid gloves?

Handbag/Briefcase/Purse/ Wallet

If you **lose any of these** in your dream, your unconscious may simply be urging you to be more careful with your finances in waking life. Handbags for women and briefcases for men are highly personal items, carrying everyday and emergency objects, not to mention address books and keys, and if you lose either in a dream it might suggest that you are feeling anxious about your identity in waking life. On the other hand, if you were **looking through someone else's bag**, you may be curious to know more about them in waking life. As symbols of femininity, **handbags and purses** in dreams may also refer to female sexuality.

Hat/Cap/Hood/Turban

For Jung, hats symbolized thought, so if you are **changing hats** in your dream, this may be a sign of personal growth where long-held views are old hat and new ideas are developing. Freud, on the other hand, believed that the hat was a sexual symbol. Nowadays it is more likely to be seen as a symbol of authority, although if you **take your hat off to someone** in your dream, you are showing them your respect. In general, dream **hats** suggest intelligence and aspirations − your thinking cap − because they are worn on the head. If your hat is **taller or grander than everyone else's** in the dream, what could the aim of your unconscious be to set you apart in this way? Did you tip your hat in the dream or, perhaps because you have been accused of having ideas above your station, was it knocked off? If you are wearing a **crown**, do you feel that you deserve the acclaim of others in waking life?

Headgear is also associated with allegiance to a profession, team or particular roles in life; for example, a **judge's wig** suggests justice. Your dream may be suggesting that you can learn much from the qualities displayed by that role. If the hat is a **helmet**, this is a symbol of protection. A dream of wearing a **hood** may suggest secrecy and concealment. Although they also hint at flirtatious behavior, **fans** don't protect but hide the face, as do **veils** (which furthermore have connotations with grief and mystery) and hoods (which also have connotations with death), so if any of these accessories feature in your dream, see if you can make any connections with your waking world. From whom or what are you trying to hide? For the devout Muslim or Sikh, **turbans** are symbols of authority, strength and dignity; for those outside these religions, the turban may be associated with the mysteries of the East, and thus can represent spiritual aspirations, as well as a sense of the exotic and a desire for more excitement in everyday life. It may also draw the dreamer's attention to a male authority figure.

■ *Idioms: drop of a hat; eat one's hat; hang on to your hat; under your hat; old hat.*

Jewelry

Jewels represent qualities that we most value in ourselves and others and to see them set in a **necklace, bracelet, ring, earring or other item of jewelry** suggests attributes we cherish within ourselves and others. If you are **given an item of jewelry** in your dream, this shows that you have the support of others, but if **you give the jewelry**, it suggests that you feel you have something to offer to other people. If you **find jewelry**, your success will be due to your own efforts. If the **jewelry has a particular history**, such as a family heirloom or the first piece of jewelry given by a partner, then it represents what you feel about family tradition, or your partner. Jewelry can also indicate love that is given or received. Very often it can represent how you feel about yourself, and for it to appear in a dream as something valuable or cheap gives you an indication of your self-esteem.

The Element Encyclopedia of 20,000 Dreams

Items of jewelry

In dreams, items of **jewelry** represent a special and precious value or quality, such as love, loyalty, inner beauty, friendship or purity. Whether you are single or married, **receiving a gift of jewelry** in your dream denotes the love and the appreciation of the giver, so the purpose of such a dream may simply be to confirm or fulfill your desire for the love and affection of that person.

For centuries, a **ring or band** has been the symbol of marriage and partnership, and when a ring appears in your dream, it may represent commitment, fulfillment and completion. It may also signify a need for greater sexual fulfillment or commitment in a relationship. Another interpretation is that the ring represents your essential self and wholeness, as the circle of a ring is never-ending and self-perpetuating. **Bangles and bracelets** also suggest wholeness and eternity through their circular shape. A **wedding ring** suggests a union and a promise, a **ring belonging to the family** suggests old traditions, whilst an **engagement ring** suggests a temporary promise of devotion. An **eternity ring** would suggest that this promise is more permanent. Quite differently, a **signet ring** would indicate something that has been, or needs to be, sealed.

Necklaces arose from the wearing of a chain of office and therefore in dreams they suggest a dignity and honor bestowed on the wearer. **Seeing someone wearing a necklace** suggests a personal breakthrough. If you **lose a necklace**, you may have been careless recently, but if you **find a necklace**, you have much to be grateful for. If you **steal a necklace**, you should be careful not to take what isn't yours. If you are **given a necklace and it breaks**, this suggests that there is a weak link in a relationship. **Wearing a beautiful necklace** is wish-fulfillment, but if the **necklace is heavy**, you may feel dragged down and restricted in waking life, with heavy responsibilities.

Dreaming of wearing a **crown or tiara** suggests that you are being congratulated in some way in waking life, or deserve to be. If the **brooch** in your dream was one of your own, your personal associations with the brooch, who gave it to you and what it means to you, should be your first consideration. If it was being admired in your dream, you may be feeling pleased with yourself. Bear in mind a brooch is sometimes called a pin, so is someone trying to pin something on you or to blame you unfairly. Dream **earrings** may be drawing your attention to your ears. In waking life, are you getting the message from someone? Do you need to keep your ears open during waking hours? *See also* CRYSTALS, GEMSTONES AND ROCKS.

It may also give an indication of how others feel about you.

MAKE-UP

Make-up in dreams signifies the appearance we present to others, as well as the ability to change the impression we make on others. If you are a woman and you were **pleased with your make-up** in your dream, your unconscious may be signaling your waking confidence about your appearance. The opposite is true if you **disliked your dream make-up**. We wear make-up for many reasons to enhance our appearance, to disguise spots and to attract other people. If you are **applying make-up** in your dream, what are you trying to hide from others or yourself? If you are **painting yourself with body paint** in your dream, this is more intimate than wearing a disguise and may relate to your most intimate feelings; the color you are using will be significant.

Your dream may also have focused on one aspect of your face – your **lips**, for instance. If so, what are you trying to say in waking life? In Freudian terms, **lipstick** suggests passionate sexuality, particularly if the dream features a long stick of lipstick caressing lips that represent female genitalia. A **woman dreaming of using lipstick** signals a desire to attract the attention of a potential lover, but for a **man to dream of using lipstick** indicates that he might adopt a more feminine approach to a problem in his waking life, perhaps by trusting his instincts more. If the **lipstick appears to be smearing**, this may suggest a fear of sexuality or sexual violence. Whether you are a man or woman, if the dream scenario portrayed you as **anxiously trying to cover spots and blemishes**, are you trying to present a different face to others in waking life?

If you have a **suntan** in your dream, or are **applying suntan cream**, your dream may be warning you that you are at risk of getting burned in waking life, or that you are paying too much attention to your appearance. Decorating your body with a **tattoo** has a similar meaning to body paint, but the important difference is whether or not the tattoo is permanent or temporary. If the **tattoo was temporary**, do you need to pay more attention to your image? If the tattoo was a **name or a symbol**, the reference may not be to the image but to your desire to create a permanent memory in waking life. If you are having a **tattoo removed** in your dream, you need to accept that some things in life are difficult and painful to move away from. And what motif is your tattoo in the dream and for which part of the body was it destined? The symbolism of both motif and body part will be significant.

MASK/COSTUME

Masks suggest the deceptive appearance we present to others in waking life. If you see a **pair of masks**, this can symbolize your inherent duality – in Jungian terms, the opposed forces of light and shadow that exist within each one of us. Dreams that feature **costumes, fancy dress or drag** suggest that you are attempting to disguise some aspect of your personality. Dreams of **transvestism** – deliberately dressing in clothes of the opposite sex – are unlikely to be about sexual preference but more about the need to balance the masculine and feminine aspects of your personality. If you

The Element Encyclopedia of 20,000 Dreams

helpful. However, it may be – because of an experience you have had with it – that a particular color transcends a Jungian meaning

Dream colors have symbolic associations attached to them but, as is the case for all dream images, their meaning can vary from person to person because you may have your own personal and special associations with that particular color. It's important to bear these associations in mind. Ask yourself whether the color reminds you of anything or anyone: a specific person, a body part, a childhood toy or some other object? For example, the color red may remind you of the first bike you ever rode, which was red, or the bunch of red roses your partner gave you on your first date together.

In a nutshell, the message from your unconscious when color features in your dream may be connected to your personal association with that shade, or it may have archetypal significance. Take a look at this chapter for some clues to its symbolic meaning and to ascertain your personal association. In this context, it might help to think about how you would describe the color to someone who is blind. What personal feelings and thoughts arise when you think of red, blue or yellow, for example? Bear in mind that as well as human emotions, colors also emphasize and reflect positive or negative forces in your life; so when you are considering the implications of color in a dream, you also need to think about where they appear: on animals, trees, birds, people, yourself and so on. As with all dream interpretations, trust your gut reactions first and look for the associations that make sense to you.

The Color Directory

BEIGE

Beige represents the basics, the essentials and the barest form. It may also indicate your objective, unbiased position. Everything related to this color denotes neutrality and detachment, and if it appears in a dream, it may signify an absence of communication or passion in waking life. Keywords: neutral, bland and detached.

BLACK

Black is viewed as a symbol of death and mourning in many cultures, and when it appears in dreams it is linked with feelings of sadness, loss and even passivity. Its appearance may also represent the death of old ideas, or some other aspect of change. Another possible explanation is that it represents a hidden or rejected aspect of the dreamer, as it is also the color of mystery, the unconscious and sometimes even protection. Some dream analysts refer to the shadowy effects of black in dreams, suggesting that they are symbols of the dreamer's shadow or of an unfulfilled part of their life. It may therefore symbolize absolute recklessness and disregard of life, without considering or caring about the consequences. If **black predominates** in a dream, consider taking a rational and reasonable approach in waking life.

A **black coffin** in a dream may represent the end of a friendship and the dream

Black and white dreams

To dream in **black and white** suggests that you need to be more objective in formulating your decisions. You may be a little too unyielding in your thought processes, and thus need to find some sort of balance between two opposing views. Consider the views and opinions of others. Alternatively, black and white dreams may be a sign of depression or sadness. You may feel that there is not enough excitement in your life.

It is a quite commonly held belief that we only dream in black and white, but many people are able to identify tones of color in their dreams. If this is the case, why is it believed that we only dream in black and white? It may be because dreams that appear to be black and white only appear so because the color is not relevant. This doesn't necessarily mean, however, that such dreams are in black and white. Black and white is a function of television when the color information is removed, but the same is not true of the mind. For example, grass might not be green in a dream, but it's not gray as it is in a black and white movie; the color simply is not relevant and your unconscious isn't highlighting it. This non-relevance fools the conscious mind on waking up into concluding that, by implication, the dream must have been in black and white.

may force the dreamer to re-evaluate the friendship, or let it go. A **black funeral** may suggest difficulties in, or the need for a new approach to, a relationship or work issue, as the current approach is doomed. Or are you grieving for a phase or aspect of your life that has recently come to an end? As stated above, black often represents the death of new ideas, so could your dream be telling you to prepare for the transition? **Black animals** that appear in dreams are usually associated with notions of temptation, unconscious drives and urges, whilst **black clothes and underwear** are a symbol of hidden or unconscious feelings, or sexuality. A **night dream scene shrouded in darkness** may relate to a certain lack of direction in your waking life. According to traditional symbolism, black is also associated with wickedness, so if you are **menaced by a person wearing black** in your dream, could the dream be a depiction of your darkest fears. Do you worry that someone is a threat to you or are you your own worst enemy? Keywords: the unknown, the unconscious, danger, mystery, darkness, death, mourning, hate and malice.

The Element Encyclopedia of 20,000 Dreams

Blue

Blue is a cool, calming color, often used for relaxation and meditation. Historically, it bears associations with spirituality and is representative of truth, intellect, and justice. Within the world of dreams, blue is often thought to be a symbol of the conscious mind, especially if the dream features **blue skies**. A **shimmering bright blue** may suggest feelings of well-being and tranquility. **Muddy shades of blue** may denote depression or moodiness. A **darker shade of blue** points more to the unconscious and a readiness to liberate yourself from repressed feelings. **Dark angry blue** may suggest feelings of isolation and an undependable character. If you see **anyone wearing dark blue** in your dream, it should act as a general warning not to be too trusting in waking life. If someone **paints with the color blue on you**, you may be deceived by someone you trusted.

Clear blue water in a dream is often interpreted as a sign that the dreamer should pay attention to their emotional needs because blue, as with color in general, is a symbol of the emotions. The appearance of a **blue precious stone** may indicate freedom from a particular burden in waking life. **Blue clothes** are linked to notions of masculinity and the male part of the dreamer's psyche. **Pale blue** is traditionally the color in which baby boys are clothed, so, if you are about to become a parent, could you be thinking about a baby son? **Light blue** reflects the vastness of space, the sky and the infinite possibilities of spiritual development. It represents moral values and high standards, open-mindedness, intellect and steadfastness of purpose, so, if you have decided on a particular course of action, its appearance in your dream may be a positive signal from your unconscious that you should trust your decision.

Blue birds represent hope and liberation. **Blue smoke** is connected to new projects and a **beautiful blue vase** may suggest that you are in a state of emotional contentment. When this color appears in your dreams, it is probably a message from your subconscious telling you to relax, think things through and take things one step at a time. Depending on the context of your dream, the color blue may also be a metaphor of 'being blue' and feeling sad; you may, however, want to take off 'into the blue' to enjoy a more adventurous, unpredictable existence? Keywords: truth, intellect, communication, wisdom, heaven, eternity, devotion, tranquility, loyalty and openness.

Brown

Most of us associate the color **brown** with the earth, and this is its leading significance in dreams. If, for example, you dreamed of **walking on a brown surface**, you may be longing for a more down-to-earth lifestyle, as earthiness can represent a character trait. The **warmer the tone of brown** that was featured in your dream, the more likely it is that the reference was to nature, whether that is in the natural world or to a natural, unaffected personality. If the **brown is drab**, this may reflect your own sense of melancholy and feeling of oppression, perhaps due to obligations and responsibilities. Brown is also the color of commitment or self-sufficiency, so your dream may be urging you to work hard and take control today, if you want to achieve anything tomorrow. Although brown generally draws its symbolism from the earth as a source of fertility and rejuvenation, it can on occasion symbolize the melancholy of rotting leaves. For Freudians, brown is the color of excrement, indicating not only the anal fixation of an orderly and obsessive character, but also a repressed desire for artistic creativity. Keywords: Worldliness, practicality, domestic and physical comfort, conservatism, and a materialistic character.

Coloring

To dream that you are **coloring in a picture** may be an expression of your hidden, creative talents and your ability to look on the bright side of life. To dream about a **coloring book** indicates your wish to return to a time in life when you had few responsibilities or worries. It also represents innocence. *See also* ARTS AND CRAFTS.

GOLD

To dream of the color **gold** is often connected with wealth and prosperity, but note that the reference may be to other forms of wealth, such as emotional or spiritual riches. Some dream analysts suggest that dreams featuring gold are linked to growth, maturity and aging. It is helpful if you noticed what exactly was covered in gold in your dream, as it may represent

something that is valuable or of deep significance to you. Was everything in gold, or was it just one item? Was the gold out of reach, or could you touch it? The context of the dream will help you with the interpretation. Perhaps there was an element of wish-fulfillment or a degree of envy about someone else's wealth? Keywords: wealth, success, precious, valuable and refined.

GREEN

Green is the color of nature. It is also the color of other forms of growth and flourishing development. If green appears in your dream, are you experiencing new growth? On the positive side, green is linked to feelings of calm and hope, but on the negative side it is associated with jealousy. Green is the color displayed by growing and healthy vegetation and foliage, and it quite clearly indicates natural growth or the mental relaxation gained from being close to nature. So if you were **surrounded by lush green vegetation** in your dream, could your unconscious have been urging you to pay more attention to the environment around you, or to become more environmentally friendly? Consider, too, the other associations that are often made with this color; could your unconscious be telling you that your approach is naïve, immature or green? Could you do with an injection of freshness and hope in your life? Or have you become a victim of the green-eyed monster: jealousy?

If **darker shades of green** appear in relation to a certain person, is it because you are jealous or envious of them or something of theirs? Dark green also tends to indicate cheating, deceit and selfishness. **Muddier shades of dark green** sometimes point to envy and greed, as well as a stubborn or self-opinionated attitude. Alternatively, have you been given the green light to go ahead with some business or family venture? A **green field** could indicate inner feelings of calm. **Green fruits** may suggest that a current project is not quite ripe and that patience is needed until the time is right to begin. **Green vegetables** could also be associated with the idea of personal health or growth. **Green eyes** have traditionally been linked to feelings of jealousy. Were the eyes your own or someone else's? A **green path** may be linked to a physical or emotional journey. **Lighter shades of green tending towards blue** represent healing. This color is also representative of money. Keywords: positive change, growth, healing, vitality, serenity, money, wealth and jealousy.

GRAY

As **gray** lies between white and black in the color spectrum, it may indicate ambiguity or detachment when it features in a dream; this may be referring to someone you know, an aspect of yourself, or a lifestyle that lacks vibrancy and passion.

ORANGE

Orange has many associations, in particular with generosity and optimism. It is considered to be a color of warmth, thoughtfulness, wisdom and sociability, and it is connected with sunshine and light. Orange or **saffron** indicates a person with a strong spiritual presence. If you have been discouraged in your search for spiritual enlightenment, the presence of orange in your dream may suggest that your patience will be rewarded. If you are **dressed in orange**, this may underline your desire to shun materialism in favor of spiritualism. Dreams in which orange features are often taken as signs of positive change within the dreamer's life, but it is important to point out that orange also has associations with mistrust, uncertainty and doubt.

Muddier shades of orange may be representative of this uncertainty, and in a dream they may be urging you to be more thoughtful about a particular person or situation. **Orange surfaces and staircases** in dreams may represent positive journeys. If an **orange object** caught your dreaming eye, could it have reflected your own upbeat outlook, or could it have been urging you to transform your life for the better by being more positive, sociable and outgoing? For example, an **orange hat** may suggest an optimistic new way of thinking. An **orange flower** may suggest a sense of contentment with life. An **orange fist** may suggest anger, hostility and aggression. Keywords: friendliness, courtesy, lively, sociability, and an out-going nature. You may want to expand your horizons and look into new interests.

PINK

Pink is traditionally associated with young girls, romantic love and well-being (it is said that you are 'in the pink' when you feel at your best). If pink features in your dream, do any of the above reflect the circumstances or hopes and dreams in your waking life? In particular, pink is associated with unconditional love and some dream interpreters link the color with powers of healing or with the heart *chakra* (a center of spiritual

Color connections

When remembering the colors in your dreams, it is important to recall if the colors were **bright and vivid, or muted and faded,** as the strength of the colors may be linked directly to your emotions and emotional needs at the time of the dream. Rich, clear colors may signify inner strength or a sense of well-being, whereas weak colors may represent feelings of being jaded or washed out in some way.

There is a clear difference between **light and dark** in the dream, especially if it features an indoor location. **Darkness** can mean that your situation is unclear or confused; it could also suggest being in unknown or difficult territory, or it may represent a secret part of yourself or a part that you do not know. Another interpretation suggests depression or the darker aspects of life. **Light** is the opposite. Light represents clearness, insight and enlightenment, and can signify the light at the end of the tunnel or seeing the light. It also has much to do with confidence. To feel lighter suggests feeling good about yourself. If the **light is very bright,** it can suggest the development of intuition or insight. If your dream took place in the **bright daytime sunshine or in the shadow of a dark night,** your memory of the dream will be tinged with optimism, associated with the light and bright-ness, or pessimism, associated with the darkness.

If a **gray and faded shade of green** appeared in your dream, this may be referring to the dullness of your waking life. On the other hand, if the **green was bright and vivid,** it may be suggesting a period of new growth. Background colors therefore play an important part in creating the ambience or feel of the dream and in influencing your reaction to it. For example, if you have a **favorite or least-favorite color,** its appearance in your dream may also reinforce your positive and negative reaction to it.

In some instances, you may find yourself trying to interpret a dream but the details have faded from your memory; that is apart from the **glittering dark blue suit** your friend was wearing. Why would your unconscious have dressed your friend in this way? The answer may lie in the archetypal symbolic meaning of blue, or your personal association with it. Indeed, any color that was highlighted in your dream may have been sending you a message from your unconscious; your task is to try to make a link between what that color means to you, the context in which it appeared, your real-life circumstances and the symbolic connotations associated with that particular color.

energy). A **pink window or door** may therefore suggest an unexplored opportunity for happiness. **Pink clothes** may suggest that the dreamer longs to be wrapped in love by someone in waking life. **Pink flowers** suggest positive and loving friendships. A **pink face** may be a sign of emotional honesty. A **pink cupboard** may be related to the idea that you are storing love for someone, perhaps waiting for the right moment to reveal and express it. Keywords: love, joy, sweetness, happiness, affection, kindness. Being in love or healing through love is also implied with this color.

PURPLE

Purple is traditionally associated with royalty and the legal profession. In dreams, therefore, purple is indicative of loyalty, authority and justice. And because purple shades tinge the sky just before dawn and nightfall – times that were once thought to be imbued with mysterious and otherworldly powers – **violet, indigo and any shade of purple** are thought to possess profoundly spiritual or religious qualities. Whenever they appear in a dream, they may be seen as indicating compassion, deep intuitive wisdom and, by implication, inner peace. If anyone you know was **wearing purple** in your dream, could this have reflected your admiration and respect for their spiritual or regal qualities? Or did these clothes irritate you because of that person's self aggrandizement, or because you feel subservient to some authority figure or institution in your life? On the other hand, could the dream have been suggesting that you, or someone you know, is being a 'shrinking violet', i.e. shy and modest?

Purple everyday objects in dreams could also indicate the need for more openness and honesty in your dealings with others. **Darker shades of violet** may suggest misunderstandings or obstacles that need to be overcome. Violet is also a spiritual color, and **brighter shades of violet** in a dream are associated with inspiration and stimulation. If violet features in your dream, have you been feeling as if you cannot relate to anyone? Could your dream possibly be trying to give you added inspiration with regard to a new project? Keywords: devotion, healing abilities, loving, kindness, and compassion. It is also the color of royalty, high rank, and dignity.

RED

In waking life **red** is associated with fire, heat, blood and passion. In dreams, these 'hot' themes are often mirrored and the interpretation is typically connected with passion, energy or vitality. Red is also associated with anger and rage towards something or someone, and, through its association with fire, can represent danger and prohibition. This is reflected in the red 'stop' signs of many countries' traffic-control systems. The color also indicates the angry urge to fight back and, if you are experiencing such violent emotions and you dream of red, take it as a warning to exercise restraint, or the consequences will be tragic. Revenge or retaliation is not advisable.

If red features in your dream, perhaps you should consider the tone that was being used. **Lighter shades of red** can be representative of excitement (especially sexual), passion, energy, and life. However, **deeper** or 'weighed-down' shades of red may be indicative of the overheated emotions of lust and anger, and the impulsive desire for revenge. Notice again how the 'stop' sign is red; red can thus be seen as a hint from your subconscious to stop acting in a particular way.

Because red is the color of blood, it may also denote physical strength, vital energy and the life force which, depending on the context of the dream, may be ebbing away or throbbing with life. A **red heart** may stand for deep-seated sexual energy or desire in waking life, **red ears** may suggest embarrassment or guilt, whilst a **red nose** is often thought to indicate an inquisitive nature. **Red flames** are believed to indicate the threat of danger, **red wine** is often linked to feelings of satisfaction and contentment, and a **red rose** is typically tied to the idea of romance and passion. Who was holding the red rose in your dream? Other considerations to take into account include whether the red in your dream suggests being 'in the red' (in debt), or brings to mind a person who holds socialists beliefs (a red). It can also refer to a scarlet (sexually permissive) woman, or to waving the proverbial red flag at something, or someone, who provoked you. Keywords: danger, shame, sexual impulses, passion and urges. Perhaps you need to stop and think about your actions.

SILVER

Silver in dreams is often related to skill, new beginnings and luck. In some cases, a dream that features silver may tell the dreamer of some ambition or aspiration. Try to notice what type of silver appeared in the dream. If it was **polished silver and you can see your reflection**, the dream may be inviting you to take a step back and reflect on your progress. If the dream features **shimmering silver**, your unconscious may have been highlighting subtle, feminine characteristics associated with silver and the moon, such as intuition. Silver may also indicate old, but precious memories, and occasionally sadness. Keywords: justice, purity, reflection, intuition and protective energy.

WHITE

White is often regarded as the color of purity, truth, goodness and hope, perhaps best represented by the virginal bride. Within a Western context, seeing this color in your dreams may therefore be a message from your subconscious urging you to discover the truth of a situation, or to find your own truth. It is also the color of completeness and innocence. Questions to ask yourself if white appears in your dream: is your dream encouraging you to see the truth or could your dream be hinting at a fresh start to some aspect of your life?

If **white appeared in your dream in connection with someone you know**, your dream may have reflected your faith in that person's goodness, or perhaps you feel that in some respects this person can show you a better way. In addition, whilst black or darkness obscures surroundings, white or brightness illuminates them, which is why it can denote transparency and truth. If you dreamed of being **bathed in white light**, your unconscious may have been indicating a sudden burst of self-knowledge that will enable you to put the past behind you and make a fresh start in the world. If, however, the feeling in your dream that featured white was one of sadness or frustration, could the suggestion have been that you are tired of your colorless waking life and long for more excitement and color?

A **white sky** may be wishful thinking for a purer, simpler life, a **white room** may symbolize a state of calm or a sense of peace, whilst **white trees** could be connected to a deep-rooted wish to make a fresh start and end a difficult personal conflict. A **white book** may be a symbol of insight and knowledge, and a **white hand** the beginning of a new friendship. **White food or drink** is linked to notions of emotional purity, and if the food or drink is tainted in any way, this may suggest that the dreamer is in need of cleansing in some aspect of their emotional life. However, bear in mind that in many Eastern cultures, white is associated with death and mourning. As an absence of color, white may therefore evoke desolation or the bloodless, lifeless corpse or ghost. Keywords: purity, perfection, peace, innocence, dignity, cleanliness, awareness, and new beginnings. You may be experiencing a reawakening or have a fresh outlook on life.

Yellow

Yellow in dreams is often thought to be a symbol of the intellect and the ability to think clearly. Therefore a dream that features yellow may indicate the dreamer's thought processes, suggesting that they are thinking clearly. On the other hand, it may suggest someone who has no positive goals and who is drifting along in life. If this is the case, the unconscious is urging the dreamer to take steps towards improving their self-confidence so that they can move forward in life.

The traditional association with yellow, however, is cowardice and in dreams, **muddier shades of yellow** may mean blocked intuition, betrayal and treachery, as well as feelings of fear and cowardice. If the dream features **bright yellow**, this can suggest sunniness, joy and optimism in waking life. Yellow, like orange and gold, is associated with the sun and because the sun lights up our world and gives us warmth, these colors often impart a contented, sunny mood. Therefore if bright yellow features strongly in your dream, your unconscious may be encouraging you to cheer up. As a powerful source of energy, the sun also symbolizes intelligence and enlightenment, so if anyone in your dream was **wearing yellow**, it may have been drawing attention to their intellectual and energetic character. Could the dream have been urging you to adopt some of these qualities in waking life?

A **yellow bird or animal** may be tied to the notion of being liberated from some aspect of your life. **Yellow food or drink** may point to the need for extra sustenance to give you a physical or mental energy boost. **Yellow flowers and plants** are usually linking to creativity and change. Does this color appear in your dreams constantly in association with a certain symbol? If it does, then maybe you will find joy in association with that symbol if you allow yourself to. Keywords: The color yellow has both positive and negative connotations. If the dream is a pleasant one, then the color yellow is symbolic of intellect, energy, agility, happiness, harmony, and wisdom. On the other hand, if the dream is an unpleasant one, then the color represents cowardice and indecision.

Other color associations and trigger words

Amber: ancient wisdom, knowledge.

Amethyst: transition to spiritual awareness, higher knowledge, insight.

Apple Green: powers of healing.

Apricot: admiration.

Aquamarine: communication, expanded awareness.

Avocado Green: new beginnings.

Azure: honesty, sincerity.

Blue Green: spiritual healing.

Blue Gray: fear of new ideas.

Blue Purple: idealism.

Blue Violet: honor, spiritual truth, devotion, inspiration.

Brick Red: selfishness.

Bright Green: uplifting.

Bright Orange: health, vitality.

Bright Purple: spiritual insight.

Bright Red: courage.

Bright Yellow: enlightened intellect, sense of fun.

Burgundy: wealth, success, elegance, prosperity; in dreams, indicative of your potential power, or your desire for power and recognition.

Caramel: career goals, aspirations.

Charcoal Gray: depression.

Claret: self-determination.

Clear: clarity.

Clear Brown: avarice.

Clear Red: high energy.

Cloudy Orange: confusion.

Cloudy Red: greed, cruelty.

Cobalt Blue: intuition

Copper: fertility, career maneuvers, passion, money goals.

Coral: friendship, friends.

Cranberry Red: love, passion, energy, enthusiasm, courage.

Cream: acceptance, tolerance, maturity.

Crimson: optimistic, reckless, mournful.

Dark Brown: materialistic approach to life, wistfulness, melancholy, indecision, fatigue.

Dark Green: jealousy, rivalry, ambition, greed, insecurity, selfishness.

Dark Gray: energy and guidance for problems to come.

Dark Orange: distrust, deceit.

Dark Pink: gentle and unconditional love, thankfulness.

Dark Purple: deep devotion, deep compassion, vision.

Dark Red: high energy, strong determination, strong passion, anger, aggression.

Dark Turquoise: heightening of communication, sensitivity and creativity.

Dark Yellow: caution, jealousy, deceit.

Deep Blue: high spiritual attainment.

Deep Crimson: shame.

Deep Gold: prosperity.

Deep Orange: pride.

Deep Pink: marriage, mature love, trust, thankfulness.

Deep Red: unconscious beauty.

Dirty Green: envy, spite, illness, jealousy.

Dull Gray Brown: selfishness.

Dull Yellow: false optimism.

Dusty Pink: sexual desire.

Electric Blue: individuality, originality, encourages uniqueness, stimulates the need for behaving with humanity, creating innovation.

Emerald Green: money, prosperity, peace of mind.

Fuchsia: connection to spirituality and meditation, readiness to let go of old attitudes, preparedness for change.

Golden Brown: friendship, illumination, wisdom.

Golden Orange: self-control.

Golden Yellow: joy, gladness.

Green Gray: envy, deceit, fear.

Green Yellow: jealousy, anger, sickness, discord, cowardice.

Gray Brown: selfishness.

Hot Pink: sex, lust.

Imperial Purple: dreams, aspirations.

Indian Red: leadership, valor.

Indigo: spirituality, deceit.

Ivory: superiority, slightly tainted purity.

Jade: charitable nature.

Lavender: intuition, dignity, spiritual growth, equilibrium, daintiness, nostalgia, femininity, soothing, affection and devotion.

Leaden Gray: meanness, lack of imagination.

Lemon: stimulates and vitalizes the brain. Cleansing.

Lemon Green: a liar, a cheat.

Lemon Yellow: strong sense of direction in life.

Light Blue: hope, faith, harmony, peace, tranquility, forgiveness, fidelity, honesty, patience, devotion.

Light Green: youth, potential, vitality, health.

Light Gray: fear.

Light Pink: sexual love, love, romance, grace, joy.

Light Purple: increased psychic power, spiritual prowess, fantasy, romance.

Light Red: happiness, courage, success.

Light Violet: enchantment.

Light Yellow: high wisdom, intellect.

Lilac: acceptance of responsibility, awakening, enchantment.

Lime Green: abundance.

Magenta: emotional healing.

Maroon: sacrifice, courage, bravery, heroism, strength.

Mauve: cooperation, trust, and self-confidence.

Midnight Blue: damaged pride, protection.

Mint Green: financial gain.

Muddy Orange: pride, vanity.

Muddy Pink: immaturity.

Mustard: difficulty in rationalizing, jealousy,

Navy Blue: strong emotions, self-pity, wallowing.

Off White: realism, peace of mind.

Olive: Peace, natural wisdom, uniformity.

Olive Green: natural wisdom, harmony, need for peace in your environment.

Opal: transformation.

Opaque: grounded awareness.

Orange Brown: self-indulgence, sloth, laziness, immorality, perversion, ignorance.

Orange Red: sexuality, energy.

Orchid: physical energy, happiness, power, healing.

Pale Blue: sensitivity.

Pale Green: empathy, sympathy, weakness.

Pale Peach: modesty.

Pale Pink: true love.

Pale Primrose: great intellectual power.

Pale Yellow: shyness.

Peach: innocent love intermixed with wisdom, gentle strength, protection, confidence, communication.

Pearl: spiritual mediums.

Pink Red: outrage, imagination, innovation.

Primrose: optimism.

Quartz: protection and purification.

Red Brown: subdued emotions, deep anger, temperamental.

Rosy Pink: unselfish love.

Royal Blue: promoting laughter and joviality, loyalty, confidence, friendship, success.

Ruby Red: passionate love, passionate anger.

Sable: constancy, prudence, wisdom, abstinence and sobriety.

Salmon: knowledge.

Salmon Pink: job satisfaction.

Sapphire Blue: broader perception, inner peace, spiritual healing.

Scarlet: lust, excitement, sexuality, physical vigor, vibrancy, ostentation, manipulation, courage, passion, volatility.

Sea Green: emotional healing and protection, calming influence, dynamic motivation.

Silver Blue: deep wisdom, intuition, opportunities.

Silver Gray: meditation, relaxation.

Sky Blue: increased psychic ability, lucid dreaming, hope, restfulness, peace.

Spring Green: children, fertility.

Sunlight Yellow: creativity, warmth, optimism.

Teal: trustworthiness, devotion, healing, spiritual guidance and teaching.

Tomato Red: pride.

Turquoise: healing power, natural energy, the sun, fire, prosperity, peace, generosity, growth.

Vermilion: creativity.

Violet Red: passion, sex.

Yellow Green: jealousy, anger, sickness, discord, cowardice.

Yellow Orange: intellectual.

CRYSTALS, GEMSTONES AND ROCKS

Many dream analysts believe that when a specific stone, jewel, mineral, metal or rock is highlighted in your dream, it represents the self or the core, unique part of yourself that is charged with personal significance.

According to Freud, rocks and stones are obvious phallic symbols on account of their hardness. The appearance of rocks, stones and metals in dreams for Jungians, however, has a different interpretation inspired by Jung's interest in alchemy. Alchemy is the ancient art of transmuting base metals into gold but it is not just about this transformation. It can also be viewed as a system of self-initiation. Jung was amazed to find that the images and operations he encountered in old alchemy texts related strongly to his theories of psychoanalysis and the unconscious. He saw in alchemy a metaphor for the process of individuation or personal transformation, and the morphing and mutating imagery of that process which emerges from the stream of consciousness. For Jungians, therefore, the appearance of rocks, stones, metals and jewels in dreams are potent and powerful symbols of a person's basic nature, heart and soul, and of their potential for personal transformation. *See also* NATURE AND THE SEASONS; PLACES.

Minerals

ALCHEMY

According to Jung, **alchemical practice** is a tangible display of the process of individuation – the balancing between the conscious and unconscious sides in the individual – which aims to produce a psychic equilibrium, a point where an individual becomes whole and has realized what Jung defined as their 'Self'. In other words, alchemy is not only about changing base metal into gold, but also about psychological change; of turning a human being's focus from base materialism into angelic gold. If this symbol appears in your dreams, consider what in your life is changing or needs changing. Your dreaming mind is encouraging you to change for the better.

CRYSTAL

In dreams, the appearance of a **crystal** suggests clarity or breaking through to higher levels of consciousness. It may also suggest purity or something that is clearly understood as in 'crystal clear'. Crystals are also associated with healing properties, so in dreams they may be symbolic of something that has enormous healing capabilities. If you were **looking into a crystal ball** in your dream, what you see is most likely to be wish-fulfillment or a reflection of your hidden fears. To dream of **coral** has a significant meaning in dreams, since coral comes from the depths of the sea; it may therefore relate to your deepest hopes and fears.

A crystal is an earth compound – a **mineral or gemstone**. Both ancient cultures and modern science have utilized the mysterious qualities of crystals, which have the ability to receive and transmit energy. If a specific crystal appears in your dream it may therefore be highlighting a particular quality: **Amber**: balance; **Amethyst**: spiritual awareness, transmutation, healing; **Aquamarine**: purification, healing, calming; **Bloodstone**: courage, physical energy; **Calcite**: balance, peaceful meditation; **Carnelian**: sex, self-esteem, creativity; **Fluorite**: healing, releasing unwanted energies; **Hematite**: encouraging will-power, concentration; **Herkimer diamond**: dream recall; **Jade**: fertility, wisdom, tranquility; **Lapis lazuli**: communication, healing; **Malachite**: protection,

money; **Moonstone**: love, psychic awareness, femininity; **Obsidian**: inner growth, psychic development; **Opal**: passion, love, and emotional expression; **Quartz**: change, focus; **Red jasper**: compassion; **Rhodolite**: love; **Rose quartz**: love, compassion; **Tiger's eye**: empowerment, willpower, courage, clarity; **Topaz**: new beginnings; **Tourmaline**: healing, balance; **Turquoise**: balance, friendship, positive thinking.

METAL

In dreams, **metal** represents strength, material power and force. It can also suggest strength of will, perhaps unbending emotions or a hard or unfeeling nature. Any metal appearing in a dream therefore suggests basic abilities and attributes, but also hardness of feeling or emotional coldness.

Aluminum or aluminum foil signifies a need for reflection or introspection. Perhaps you need a change in perspective. **Bronze** suggests the blending of different aspects of your life, whilst also portraying recognition for perseverance and the successful completion of your goals. **Copper** suggests intelligence, an outgoing nature or the need to communicate something important.

Gold is a symbol of what is precious or valued in your life. **Finding gold** indicates that you are discovering and expressing these characteristics in your life; **burying gold** means you are hiding something. Associated with the sun and victory, gold may also represent life, completion and renewal. For alchemists, gold represents the spiritual treasure that was gained by transforming the spirit. If the **gold is cheap**, this suggests something you value but that does

The Element Encyclopedia of 20,000 Dreams

Dreaming with crystals

Crystal enthusiasts believe that **dreaming with crystals** can not only enhance healing and transformation but can also enhance your dream state in many ways, depending on the type of crystal and how it is used. The results can be enlightening, enriching and therapeutic. Below is a list of some of the crystals you might use. It is important to stress, however, that the following guidelines are based on conjecture and anecdotal experience only:

Love and romance

Rose quartz and jade are thought to be good crystals or stones for dreams in which love is the issue at hand. Place either crystal (or both) under your pillow. The energies of these stones are thought to encourage dreams that are loving and filled with positive vibrations.

Money and prosperity

Citrine is a powerful, healing quartz that is thought to be an excellent crystal for bringing about wealth in body, mind and spirit. Known as the merchant stone, it is believed to attract abundance in ways that fortify balance, whether that balance is sought in the home, the bank account, the body, mind or spirit.

Problem solving

Clear quartz is considered the best crystal for issues you need to work through while sleeping. Before you go to sleep, hold the quartz in your hand and spend a while meditating the issue on your mind, with the express request to solve your issue via your dreams. Then place the quartz under your pillow. You may find that when you awake you will be more focused, grounded and that the issue that was previously bothering you is now crystal clear.

Stress release and insomnia

Amethyst is thought to be an excellent stone for relieving you of the stress of the day. A relaxing crystal, it also helps with insomnia and headaches. Take a glove and place it over your left 'receiving' hand before retiring to bed. Slip a small amethyst crystal into the glove to increase your chances of good dream recall, a good night's rest and stress release.

not deserve your respect. If the **gold is tarnished**, this suggests something beautiful in you that has been neglected.

When the metal **iron** appears in a dream, it usually suggests strength and determination but it can also suggest emotional coldness. If you are using a **clothes iron**, is there something in your life you are trying to smooth over? In dreams, the appearance of **lead** suggests a situation in your waking life that is burdening you and leaving you heavy-hearted. Lead as in a lead pencil also has associations with masculinity. **Mercury** in dreams implies a fluctuating situation or vacillation within yourself over a particular problem. To dream of **nickel** suggests the need for a new approach to replace an old one. It can also suggest small steps you need to take to help you reach your goal.

Platinum in dreams is a symbol of a life aspect that stimulates multiple opportunities, whilst **silver** has a double meaning: on a practical level it suggests finance or money, but on a psychological level it represents the qualities of the moon or the need to follow your intuition. Spiritually, silver is said to represent the feminine aspect, whilst gold is the masculine. If **polished silver** has the properties of a mirror so your dream may be suggesting that you need to reflect on some waking situation.

Steel in dreams is a symbol of strength and endurance, whereas **tin** is a symbol of something or someone inferior in your life that is not of the quality it should be; tin may also indicate low self-esteem. Bear in mind, too, that certain metals are also associated with certain planets: Sun–gold; Moon–silver; Mercury–quicksilver; Venus–copper; Mars–iron; Jupiter–tin; Saturn–lead.

MINERAL

A **mineral** is a non-living crystal solid found in nature that is not made from plants or animals. Minerals are the most common non-manmade materials on Earth. There are many different types of minerals. Rocks and pencil lead are made of minerals, and even the street you walk on every day is made of minerals! Minerals can be very helpful too; you need minerals in your food to keep healthy. In dreams, therefore, minerals represent life's essentials or the bare necessities.

Mineral oil connotes a soothing aspect or factor that eases rough aspects in your life. **Mineral water** illustrates what is essential in life; that which is basic. To dream of **mines or mining** represents your unconscious physical and mental activities. If you are **digging in the mine**, this indicates that you are digging within your experiences, memories or deeper levels of consciousness to bring up the treasure and valuable resources buried within. A **miner's hat** typifies light shed on ideas, concepts or perceptions. A **mineshaft** stands for heightened awareness, an inner knowing, whilst **mining or digging for gold** may suggest financial aspirations and goals.

STONE/ROCK

If a **rock or stone** featured in your dream, it is important to take into account the context of your dream and your emotions when trying to understand the message from your dreaming mind. Bearing in mind that dream stones can represent your very heart and soul, pay attention to what the rock looked like and what attracted you to it. For example, if you **admired the stone**, this suggests emotional strength; but if you **picked up a pebble at random and flung it at someone or something**, the stone could represent your coldness of heart, the hard feelings you are harboring against someone or your attempts to keep others at an emotional distance.

Dreaming of **stone or a stone floor or path** can suggest emotional inhibition or coldness as well as stability and durability. If you are **carving stone** in your dream, you may be trying to make a lasting impression on the world. If **stone is broken up** in your dream, you may be experiencing extreme emotional hurt. Being **turned into stone** means hardening your approach or attitude, and if **stones are thrown at you**, this could suggest feelings of guilt for a misdemeanor. There is also the drug association to consider, as in being 'stoned'.

To dream of a **rock or rocky landscape** suggests security, reliability and stability in real life. You need to stand rock-like and not be dissuaded from your purpose. **Seaside rock** may remind you of childhood or of carefree times. Alternatively, like stones, rocks are associated with coldness, rigidity, barriers and stubbornness; your dream may be highlighting these qualities within yourself. Consider also whether you have found yourself between a rock and a hard place in waking life?

Precious Stones

GEMSTONE

Because of the different colors in gemstones and the different things associated with them, they can all have slightly different meanings when they appear in dreams. If a specific gemstone or precious stone appears in your dream, try to work out what that stone means to you. Was it your **birth stone** or the birth stone of someone you know? You should also consider its color. The texture and any associations or myths connected should also help with your interpretation. It would be impossible to list all precious and semi-precious gemstones, but the following associations with some of the most well-known gemstones should give you some guidelines regarding interpretation; but please note that it is always worth your while to do your own research

Purple has long been considered a royal color so it is not surprising that **amethyst** has been so much in demand during history. Fine amethysts are featured in the British Crown Jewels and were also a favorite of Catherine the Great and Egyptian royalty. Amethyst, transparent purple quartz, is the most important quartz variety used in jewelry. Leonardo Da Vinci wrote that amethyst was able to dissipate evil thoughts and quicken the intelligence, and in dreams the appearance of amethyst suggests healing and transcendence. The gemstone is also a symbol of sobriety and remorse, due to the legend of the origin of amethyst. Dionysus, the god of intoxication, was angered one day by an insult from a mere mortal and swore revenge on the next mortal that crossed his path, creating fierce tigers to carry out his wish. Along came unsuspecting Amethyst, a beautiful young maiden on her way to pay tribute to the goddess Diana. Diana turned Amethyst into a stature of pure crystalline quartz to protect her from the brutal claws of the tigers. Dionysus wept tears of wine in remorse for his action at the sight of the beautiful statue. The god's tears stained the quartz purple, creating the gem we know today.

Diamond is the symbol of incorruptibility, integrity, perfection and wisdom, so if you dream of it, these may be themes that would repay further investigation in your interpretation. But your dream may also be hinting that you need to look at various facets of a problem. There is also the association with human greed. As a symbol of fertility and regeneration, **emerald** in dreams suggests personal growth and a connection with the natural in life. The green of the emerald is the color of life and of the springtime, which comes round again and again. But emerald is also the traditional color of beauty and of constant love. In ancient Rome, green was the color of Venus, the goddess of beauty and love. In dreams, emerald can convey harmony, love of Nature and elemental joie de vivre.

According to Chinese legend, **jade** is the sperm of the Celestial dragon that fell to earth; it therefore represents a union between heaven and earth. In the West, jade is more likely to bear the symbolism of its color green. It may also appear in dream word-play. Is there something in your waking life about which you feel jaded

and would like to change? In gemstone therapy, it is said that jade stimulates creativity and mental agility on the one hand, whilst also having a balancing and harmonizing effect.

A symbol of the inner world of fantasies and dreams, **opal** stands for intuitive awareness. All of nature's splendor seems to be reflected in the manifold opulence of fine opals: fire and lightning, all the colors of the rainbow and the soft shine of far seas. Almost ninety-five per cent of all fine opals come from the dry and remote outback deserts of Australia. For ages, people have believed in the healing power of opals. It is reported to be able to cure depression and to help its wearer find true and lasting love. The fantastic color-play of opals may reflect changing emotions and moods; either your own or of the people around you. For example, the sparkling images of **boulder opal**, the vivid light flashes of **black opal** or the soft shine of **milk opal** characterize the colorful world of this fascinating gemstone.

Rubies are a symbol of emotion, passion, empathy and reaching out to others. The most important characteristic about this valuable stone is its color. There is of course a reason for this: the name 'Ruby' was derived from the Latin word 'rubens', meaning 'red'. The red of rubies is in a class of its own, being peculiarly warm and fiery. Two magical elements are associated with the symbolism of this color: fire and blood, implying warmth and life for mankind. In the light of this, ruby-red is not just any old color red; it is the epitome of the color: hot, passionate and powerful. Like no other gemstone, ruby is the perfect symbol of powerful feelings. To dream of a **ring set with a precious**

The Element Encyclopedia of 20,000 Dreams

ruby does not symbolize a calm and moderate sympathy that one might feel for someone else, but rather the passionate and unbridled love which two people feel for each other.

Sapphires are symbols of hope, joy and aspiration, and blue is the color most often association with this precious stone. This color is also linked to emotions such as sympathy and harmony, friendship and loyalty. These emotions are permanent and reliable – they are emotions in which overwhelming and fiery passion is not the main element, but rather composure, mutual understanding and unshakeable trust. Sapphire blue has thus become a color related to anything permanent and reliable, and this is one of the reasons why women in many countries settle on sapphire for their engagement rings. Sapphire symbolizes loyalty and faithfulness, whilst at the same time expressing love and yearning. The most famous musical example for this melancholic shade of blue can be found in George Gershwin's 'Rhapsody in Blue'. Sapphire's blue color is also evoked where clear competence and controlled brainwork are the issue. After all, the first computer ever to wrangle a victory from a chess grandmaster and world champion was named 'Deep Blue'.

In many cultures of the Old and New World **turquoise** has for thousands of years been appreciated as a holy stone, a good-luck charm or a talisman. In Asia and Europe, turquoise is often worn as protection against the evil eye and its exquisite shade of blue is associated with heaven. In dreams it can represent healing and higher aspirations.

Birth stones

Ancient talismans were believed to have magical powers to protect the wearer. Talismans for protection and healing are often engraved on stones corresponding to the signs of the Zodiac. So if any of the following stones feature in your dreams are they referring to a specific date or month, the characteristics of your Zodiac sign or someone you know?

Aries (21 March–19 April) – topaz
Taurus (20 April–20 May) – garnet
Gemini (21 May–21 June) – emerald
Cancer (22 June–22 July) – sapphire
Leo (23 July–23 August) – diamond
Virgo (24 August–22 September) – zircon
Libra (23 September–23 October) – agate
Scorpio (24 October–21 November) – amethyst
Sagittarius (22 November–21 December) – beryl
Capricorn (22 December–19 January) – onyx
Aquarius (20 January–18 February) – jasper
Pisces (19 February–20 March) – ruby

Jewel/Jewelry

In dreams, **jewels** represent the qualities you value in yourself and others in waking life; they also represent the lasting and precious parts of yourself that connect you with others. Most of the time, dreams about jewels are pleasant and reassuring, as they have their basis in wish-fulfillment. If **jewelry is given to you** in a dream, this is a sign of high self-esteem; **loss of jewelry** suggests the opposite. If a **specific item of jewelry** is highlighted in your dream, your feelings about how you acquired it, from whom you acquired it and what the feelings mean to you should be your first consideration. If the **jewelry was being admired**, you may be feeling pleased with yourself.

The **pearl** is a Freudian symbol of female sexuality, especially when seen embedded within an oyster or when adorning a woman's neck in a pearl necklace. For Jung, pearls express a dreamer's aspiration to purity and personal spiritual transformation. Alternatively, dreams of pearls may be highlighting a 'pearl of wisdom' someone has to offer, or the inner wisdom and beauty that has emerged from the trials of life.

DISASTERS

When nature pushes the elements to the extreme, the result is often explosive.

Volcanoes and lightning create fire, an unstable earth unleashes quakes and avalanches, water creates floods and drought, and air stirs hurricanes and typhoons into furious motion. Man-made disasters also create explosive and devastating results. People's lives are tragically ended or irreparably damaged in seconds, panic and fear take over, and the best and worst of human nature is exposed. It is small wonder, then, that the unconscious often employs the symbols of catastrophe and disaster to provide striking and memorable dream images or messages.

Dreams of disaster, such as those involving earthquakes and plane crashes, can be extremely detailed, intense, colorful and vivid. You may wake up terrified and concerned for your safety, or for the safety of loved ones. To dream of any kind of disaster is always unsettling, but it is important to point out that such dreams are rarely prophetic or precognitive; it is much more likely that they are an expression of your hidden fears or anxieties concerning events you feel are beyond your control. A disaster dream may be expressing anxiety

about what the future will bring, or highlighting the fact that you are trying to do too many things, or trying to please too many people, at the expense of your own peace of mind. On the other hand, disaster dreams can also reveal great inner change and growth, but this change and growth may make you feel temporarily uncertain of yourself, your direction in life and your position in the world.

Group disaster dreams can be particularly frightening and they may even recur, making it easier to assume that they might be warnings of actual events. Although there are rare exceptions, it is important to point out that vehicles and locations crowded with people who experience disaster are usually symbolic, reflecting our experience with a social influence or a real-life group. For example, if you dream of being in a bus crash that leaves you dazed and miles from home, you may be feeling increasingly disillusioned and detached from the goals of your place of work; your hopes of achieving satisfaction in that area of your life may in fact be already wrecked. Your dreaming mind may be telling you that you have gone as far as you can with that group of people, or course of action, and it is time to change your approach or lifestyle.

In some instances, dreams about disaster that involve surroundings or people you know may be a simple warning. For example, you may have forgotten that your car is due for a service, but your unconscious remembers and tries to draw your attention to this oversight in a dream in which you are driving your car and the brakes suddenly fail. If you have lived through a natural or man-made disaster, your dream may also be recalling the horrific events in an attempt to help you come to terms with the trauma. According to Gestalt therapists, dreams that repeat a disturbing event or focus on disaster scenarios following an experience of physical or emotional trauma are reminding the dreamer that there is an emotional scar that needs attention and healing.

Finally, when trying to interpret any dream that involved a natural disaster, remember that if you live in an area that is prone to them your dream may simply be reflecting your anxiety about being caught up in such a catastrophe. The same applies to man-made disasters, such as terrorist attacks or train crashes. Your dream may be triggered by the climate of fear, and intense media coverage and speculation that now surround these tragic events. See also ACCIDENTS, ACTION AND ADVENTURES; NIGHTMARES.

Natural and Man-made Disasters

AVALANCHE

If you dreamed of an **avalanche**, your unconscious is warning you that the foundations of your waking life are under threat. Or maybe you just feel snowed under by responsibilities, or overwhelmed by the avalanche of work your boss requires of you? If you dreamed of being **caught in the middle of an avalanche**, this suggests you are feeling overwhelmed by circumstances, but if you **witnessed an avalanche**, you are currently experiencing a destructive force in your life. The dream is urging you to assume control and take precautionary steps to protect yourself from danger. An avalanche dislodges snow and ice, so your dream may have expressed your fear of someone else's hostility or emotional coldness, and the impact this has in the real world. Snow is white (the color of innocence), so you should also consider whether you are disguising some action in waking life.

CHASM/ABYSS

If the **deep, precipitous sides of a chasm or large hole threaten to engulf and swallow you up** in a dream, or if an **abyss suddenly opens up** in front of you, transforming a previously pleasant scene into a terrifying one, could your unconscious have been warning you that your position in waking life is not as stable as you might think and that you could be facing unexpected mishaps or pitfalls? Chasms and holes in dreams always suggest an element of the unknown or something in some way risky, and they urge the dreamer to make a decision one way or another in waking life. Perhaps you dreamed of **teetering on the brink of a ravine**, petrified that you would lose your footing? Such a dream may be warning you that you are in danger of falling into an emotional black hole, out of which you feel powerless to emerge. Also, because the earth is a symbol of the archetypal mother, **devouring chasms** may represent a devouring maternal figure in your life, intent on dominating you or dragging you under.

CHOKING

Dreams in which you are **fighting to breathe** are usually to do with a sense that the external environment, or your inner attitudes or fears, are threatening to kill your pleasure in living. Dreams in which you feel you are being **choked or strangled** may suggest that that there is something in waking life that is choking, strangling or squeezing the life out of you – a job, a relationship or a situation. You feel stifled by people or circumstances and are not in control of either. Choking in dreams also suggests an inability to express yourself properly in waking life. There may be some kind of conflict or indecision about whether or not you should speak out or hold your tongue.

If you **struggled to breathe in a smoggy or smoke-filled atmosphere** of a polluted dream environment, this could suggest that you are finding your real-life circumstances claustrophobic and stifling

to your individuality and personal growth. Or do you feel that the demands of your job or lifestyle are killing your curiosity and creativity? If you were **strangled by someone**, this suggests you may be holding back feelings as most of our feelings create sounds, such as laughter or crying; an attack on the neck is thus an attempt to stifle these emotions. Whatever you decide caused you to fight for air in your dream, be it a positive or a negative influence, your unconscious was probably warning you to broaden your horizons and let some metaphorical 'fresh air' into your life. *See also* NIGHTMARES.

CRASH/SHIPWRECK

If you are involved in (or die) in a **train, bus, car, bike or airplane accident** in your dream, whether or not you were driving the vehicle that crashed is significant. If you were not driving, the dream may be urging you to take control of your life; if you were driving, the dream is urging you to alter your course or change your plans in waking life to avert disaster.

If you dreamed that you were in a **ship and the water was coming overboard and submerging you**, the traditional association of water with emotion suggests that you are being overwhelmed by emotion. If this is the case, the dream is urging you to try a more logical and rational approach to your problems. If you were **attempting to save other people in your shipwreck**, think about what, or who, they may represent in waking life. If it was a **child**, it may represent a part of yourself you are trying to develop that might act as a counterbalance to your powerful emotions. Dreams about a **shipwreck** can be associated with your life course, or work life. The dream is suggesting that something going on in your present life experience may be making you feel isolated, abandoned, or on the verge of some kind of a catastrophe or tragedy. Those who have this kind of dream are often going through a transitional period in their lives, such as a graduation or engagement. The ship therefore represents your goal, but the journey has become out of control and the horror of being dragged down by the ship captures a sense of the horror of being dragged down by traditions and expectations. This kind of dream isn't a prediction of failure in your relationship or career; it simply indicates that details surrounding it are threatening to obscure the happiness and satisfaction you are hoping for. *See also* ACCIDENTS, ACTION AND ADVENTURES.

EARTHQUAKE

Dreams about **earthquakes**, in which the ground cracks open beneath your feet and your surroundings crash around you, can be seen as attempts to prepare you for big changes in your waking life. This is because earth symbolically represents the stability and security of your personality, and dream earthquakes signal that your emotional foundation is being – or is about to be – shaken to the core, bringing the structure of your waking world crashing down around you. Try to make a connection between your dream and your waking life. Are there signs that you might lose your job or that your relationship is in trouble? Such events would shake the foundations of your life, but remember that when the rubble has been cleared away, reconstruction can begin. You may find

that rebuilding your life makes you a stronger person because you can build on the ruins of your past by learning from your mistakes.

FIRE

The elements often have important roles in disaster dreams. In a dream, **fire** can be a purifying influence, it can relate to anger, or it might be suggestive of destruction. It may also relate to the fact that you are being consumed by a passion in waking life. In any event, its appearance in your dream may suggest that something in your life (most likely related to work or home) is in the midst of considerable change. Such a dream may be a warning – especially if you are trying unsuccessfully to smother the flames. The dream would be reassuring if a **house or room was catching fire and you could control the flames**, for here is a symbol of controlled passion. The dream is reassuring you that you are, or can be, in control of your life.

Disaster dreams in which you see **people engulfed in a burning building** should make you consider both your reaction and your personal connection with the disaster – if any. If you are merely a **spectator** in the dream, too scared to move or offer your help, you should ask yourself whether you are equally fearful of life, or whether you are less forceful than you need to be. If any of your **friends, colleagues or family members are trapped in the building and you know you should help them**, your dream may be telling you to take a more active part in their lives. If you dreamed that **you were in the burning building or that the building was falling down around you**, consider whether your

The Element Encyclopedia of 20,000 Dreams

life is also collapsing around you. To dream of being **burned alive** may express your fears of a new relationship or phase of life. Finally if you are **fire-fighting** in your dream, this is a positive sign as it shows you are putting up a fight in real life.

FLOOD/DROUGHT/FAMINE/ TSUNAMI

Flood dreams are frightening, but they also suggest a release of energy or pent-up frustration that needs to be set free before progress can be made. To be in the **middle of a flood** indicates that you are being overwhelmed by these feelings, whilst **watching a flood** suggests you are watching yourself. If you are not good at expressing yourself verbally, dreaming of a flood may help you come to terms with your anxieties and insecurities. If you dream of being **drowned**, it suggests you are in danger of being overwhelmed by emotions you cannot handle or that you are fearful of allowing your emotions free expression. Drowning may also indicate an inability to handle stress and a feeling that you have no control. The natural disasters of **flooding, tsunami and drought** indicate great hardship for the dreamer, but they also offer hope. For example, if you dream that you are **immersed in rising water or that your house is flooded**, this indicates the emergence of a personal crisis. However, if adequate precautions are put in place, or you heed warning signs of impending disaster, it is possible to avert or overcome the disaster. Similarly, a dream in which **you endure a drought** portends misfortune, and scant reward for your effort, but the dreamer can take comfort that this difficult time will pass, leaving you wiser and better prepared for any future crises with which life may surprise you.

Tidal waves or tsunamis often represent a cascade of emotion or impending change in your life. It is not unusual for someone struggling with a tough situation, such as the loss of a job, illness in the family and so on, to dream of being threatened by a tidal wave. A tidal wave in this instance depicts the emotional devastation that occurs when situations change in unexpected, or unwanted, ways. Whether the wave represents emotion, change, or something or someone else, to you the implication is that you are in the thick of it now and you have little to gain by running away or denying it. Your best approach is to ride the wave, accept that you feel overwhelmed for a while, but know that this isn't permanent as the storm will run its course and you'll emerge wiser and stronger.

Famine and drought dreams can also indicate that you are emotionally drained in waking life. If you are **hungry** in your dream, your needs or demands, physically, emotionally and mentally are not being met. **Starvation** dreams also indicate that something within yourself is not being given due attention; aspects of yourself are being impoverished and ignored. Perhaps your partner is draining you and you are feeling exhausted. If scenes of **poverty** feature in your dream, this often indicates feelings of being inadequate, or negative emotions depriving you of your well-being. On the other hand, dreams about **starvation and poverty** may be hinting at your humanitarian qualities, and could be suggesting that you could do more for charity.

Hurricane/Tornado

Although it might be possible to dream about a major weather disaster before it occurred, it is much more likely that you are dreaming about some kind of emotional turmoil occurring in your waking life. In fact, dreams of tornadoes are often symbolic of ongoing verbal arguments, fighting and emotional tension occurring in a relationship. A tornado is made up of wind moving very fast, just as air comes out of one's mouth very fast during an argument. With this in mind, the next time one of these 'tornado' dreams occur, look at what has just taken place in your waking life. Have you just had an argument with someone? Has someone had an argument with you? Overall, the presence of tornadoes or hurricanes in dream land suggests that you are an extremely emotional person and that either you (or those around you) are prone to emotional outbursts. Alternatively, you may feel as if you are being swept along by forces beyond your control – perhaps someone's passion. A hurricane can also represent the power of your own passion, or passionate belief, which picks you up and carries you along.

Life-and-death Struggle

Life-and-death struggles are common in dreams, but in some cases these dreams end with a struggle to avoid catastrophe. These are the sorts of dream in which **almost every stranger turns out to be an enemy**. Even the **landscape of these dreams is laden with death traps, sharp ravines, wild fires, dangerous animals** and so on. If you have this kind of dream, the chances are you are fighting for survival in some aspect of your waking life. On the other hand, you may be the kind of person who makes ordinary choices and decisions as if their survival were at stake. For example, small disappointments or minor upsets send you into meltdown and you are frequently dissatisfied if some invisible inner standard has not been met. If you are prone to life-and-death dreams, your unconscious is urging you to find a kind of security that cannot be lost. In other words, you need to look at things that are intangible and reside in your spirit and in your emotions, because everything else – since it is out of your control – is at risk. You need to develop greater flexibility and tolerance, and by so doing you can find contentment and peace.

If your life-and-death battle involves a **war scene**, the emphasis shifts. Despite war's disturbing and destructive nature, it can sometimes be represented as a cleansing process that represents a victory of good over evil. However, in dreams war is generally regarded as a warning that dangerous times lie ahead, as well as indicating inner conflicts and deep-seated grievances. An important aid for interpreting dreams of warfare is to remember whether you were on the winning or losing side. If you were **on the winning side**, this suggests you are on the right track. If you were **on the losing side**, what can you learn from the tactics of the winning side? Surprisingly, to dream that you are **wounded in battle** denotes that you have finally been accepted by your peers.

Lightning/Storm/Thunder

Hearing thunder in a dream can warn of a potential emotional outburst. If the

thunder is in the distance, there may still be time to regain control of a difficult situation. Spiritually, the rumblings of thunder can demonstrate deep anger. Because **lightning** has long been considered the prerogative of the gods and a symbol of communication between the world of gods and that of human beings, if lightning appears in your dream or you are **struck by a thunderbolt**, this suggests intuition, inspiration and the sudden awakening of psychic powers. In general, lightning in a dream indicates unexpected changes that are taking place, or are about to take place. These changes may be to your routine or to the way you think.

Lightning can also indicate strong, passionate love that can strike suddenly and unexpectedly. Alternatively, lightning in a dream can indicate a discharge of tension, or a necessary but destructive act on your part in order to make progress. Spiritually, lightning can denote sudden enlightenment or personal growth. If a **storm** – with or without thunder and lightning – appears in your dream, this indicates personal emotional outbursts as the storm allows the dreamer to release emotion and clear the air. But if the **storm is approaching**, this indicates a sense of difficult times ahead, and of anger or passion about someone or something that has built up, but which has not yet been expressed.

MAN-MADE DISASTER

Disaster dreams typically indicate that something is terribly wrong with your life or about to go wrong if the current situation remains unchanged. They will tell you that a job, a relationship, a religion, or a conscious attitude is not good for you and is leading you to crisis. If the disaster in the dream is specifically **man-made** and not natural, such as a **terrorist attack, or a plane, train, car, or bus crash**, this image may be urging you to change an attitude or belief system before the situation in waking life becomes perilous. These dreams are telling you that you are not in a safe place and you need to move away from it.

Oftentimes, the unconscious will use cultural symbols and images to bring to mind some thematic experience or situation. For example, to dream of the **attack on the World Trade Center** can be symbolic of a tragedy, a horrendous situation, an attack, or the destruction of one's working environment. Similarly, any form of **terrorist attack** can be symbolic of an intrusive invasion of your personal space in waking life, a violent clash of opinions or cruel, sadistic and cowardly behavior.

If you dreamed of making a **panic-stricken call to the emergency services**, could your unconscious have been highlighting your fear that an emotional trauma has devastated your world, or is about to, and that you urgently need help? A dream focusing on a **disaster in your home** may be saying something about your attitude to life. It might be that you are ready to make important changes that will involve destroying what you have built up over the years, or it could be a warning that your present, or planned, actions could prove disastrous in the long run. Much depends on your reaction. Supposing that you dreamed your **house was falling down**; if you were relieved, unconcerned or walked away from the ruins, you are ready to move on and leave the past behind you. You may have had a dream that focused on **man-made environmental pollution and the** disease, destruction, decay and death to which this leads. If you have had such a dream, the dream is urging you to avoid an attitude, thought or emotion that is not good for you, now or in the future.

Other people's attitudes and beliefs may also be contaminating the way you think and feel, and this can sometimes be shown in dreams about **toxic waste or poisons**. On the other hand your dream may be urging you to become more environmentally aware. If **demolition** features in the dream, it can highlight either self-inflicted trauma or changes in your life, depending on the circumstances of the dream. If you are carrying out the demolition, you should be in control, but if someone else is, you may feel powerless in the face of change. You may also be conscious of a build-up of tension within you that can only by released by a breakdown of old attitudes and approaches.

Nuclear war/End-of-the-world scenarios

Although you could interpret your dreams literally, a much more likely interpretation is a symbolic one. In this respect, dreams about **nuclear war, the earth exploding, stars and planets falling from the sky, or the superpowers declaring war on each other** would be a symbol for the 'end of the world' as you know it – in other words, some kind of personal upheaval that would completely change your life. Amongst such events, one should consider: the divorce of your parents, having to move house, ending your time at one school and going to another, having your best friend move and so on. Whatever has changed in your life has rocked your sense of things and your

peace of mind on a global level. Therefore, rest assured, the dream is probably not about the end of the world, but is instead about a big change in your world. Whatever and however your life has been up until now, it has changed and it will never be the same again; the positive message that you take from such a dream is that you will emerge from this destruction into a fresh, new phase.

Feeling dramatically out of control in your personal life can trigger **apocalypse dreams**. These may be caused by hormones in adolescence, the menopause or andropause, the death of a loved one (especially a parent), or divorce and other significant relationship losses. The dream visions of the world ending are an escape mechanism to avoid dealing with a world so dramatically changed by new circumstances. In some cases, world-ending dreams feature **the dreamer alone amongst generally unrecognized figures**, reflecting the dreamer's sense of isolation in waking life. When interpreting this type of dream, you should ask yourself, 'How is the world ending and who is to blame?' This dream may be calling for you to protect yourself against a risk that takes you well outside your comfort zone, to become more involved in a particular cause, or to think again about the rationale of your fears.

If you are religious in waking life, you may have a dream in which **significant icons of your faith initiate, or withstand, the massive destruction**. Another scenario is that **adherents to your religious or belief system are identified in a particular way and thereby survive the destruction**. In these dreams, the world is often reordered. Often, these dreams will accompany a time in the dreamer's life

The Element Encyclopedia of 20,000 Dreams

when they feel that the entire world is against them, and it is only their association with something larger than themselves that can provide a resolution to the struggles being faced.

PRECOGNITIVE DREAMS

Carl Jung believed that the unconscious could be revealed through dreams, premonitions or synchronistic experiences. Most often these revelations would be of a personal nature, commenting on the life experiences of the individual. There were also times, however, when the unconscious might deliver a message to the conscious mind that addressed collective issues and events. It is often difficult to distinguish which revelations contain an individual message and which are of collective import. Even if these two types can be differentiated, the full meanings and ramifications of such 'collective dreams' are often known only after the fact. But there is still value in paying attention to these dream images, which in many cases presage something yet to come.

A dream that seemingly includes knowledge about the future which cannot be inferred from actually available information is referred to as a **precognitive dream**. For example, you may dream of your **friend being involved in a skiing accident**, only to discover a week later that this has actually happened when your friend calls you to say they have broken their leg. Precognitive dreams have been reported throughout history; famous examples are the Pharaoh's dream of seven fat and seven thin cows, and Bishop Lanyi's dream of the assassination of Archduke Franz Ferdinand, the event that triggered World War I.

Most studies indicate that women report more precognitive dreams than men, while the frequency of precognitive dreaming declines with age. Precognitive dreams tend to focus on the possibility of **accidents or disaster**. Though they are generally considered symbolic of psychological processes, some precognitive dreams and **nightmares** are intended as guidance or warnings on a very practical level. For example, if you were to dream about the **brakes failing on your car**, it might help to ponder whether you are figuratively having trouble 'slowing yourself down' in your life, however, it also wouldn't hurt to check the actual brakes on your automobile in waking life. In the great majority of cases dreams about some kind of disaster or the death or murder of yourself or a loved one, warn of current behavior trends, courses of action, or decisions which may soon become detrimental unless you change them. There are however, extremely rare occasions when a dream occurs that does appear to accurately and inexplicably predict a future event; although this event may not always be about an important world event or news item and is more likely to be about normal every day events, such as who you might bump into on the way to work. How and why this occurs is unknown but if it does occur it could indicate potential psychic or clairvoyant ability in the dreamer.

VOLCANIC ERUPTIONS

Early dream oracles linked dreams about volcanoes with passionate but deceitful love. An eighteenth-century almanac claimed that if a **woman dreamed of an active volcano**, she would be driven by greed to 'ensnare a husband by wantonly

Precognitive disaster dreams

The following precognitive disaster dreams certainly challenge our preconceptions and rational explanations about how the world and the dreaming mind relate to one another.

In his book *Recollections of Abraham Lincoln, 1847–1865*, Ward Hill Lamon relates a dream Lincoln had shortly before his death. In the dream, Lincoln heard a group of people mournfully weeping downstairs in the White House, but when he went to investigate, he found no mourners, although their desperate weeping continued. Upon entering the East Room he discovered a corpse wrapped in funeral vestments. Demanding of one of the soldiers stationed there, 'Who is dead in the White House?,' he received the reply, 'The President. He was killed by an assassin.'

A day before the SS *Titanic*'s demise, a woman on the infamous ship dreamt of the horrible event that was to occur the next day. She told her husband, who scoffed at her worries and ignored her pleas. However, the dream so affected her that she secretly prepared herself the night before and had all her children sleep in their warm clothes in order to be ready at a moment's notice. During the night, after the ship struck the iceberg, she and her children were rescued and escaped the sinking ship. Her husband, sadly, went down with more than 1,500 people.

In 1914, one hundred and twenty Newfoundland sealers were abandoned on an ice-floe in the North Atlantic during winter. The incompetence of the ship's captain, and of other crew members, meant that the missing men were not noticed for two days and two nights. By the time they were rescued, more than half were dead. It was the worst disaster to strike the Newfoundland sealing community in many years. However, the disaster did not come without warning. One of the fifty-five survivors later told of a dream he had two weeks before the disaster. According to Cassie Brown's report on the disaster: 'John Howlet had suffered a chilling nightmare weeks before. In his dream he was on a mountain of ice, lost and freezing. He was alone, terribly and frighteningly alone, but everywhere he wandered there were vague, indefinable "things" on the ice around him – things with no particular shape that he could make out. He found himself walking among those things, unable to find his way, wondering what they were and dreading them. In his dream he was counting, counting, counting … He was still counting the white mounds when he awoke, shivering and terribly depressed.'

Unfortunately, even this dream did not make him avoid joining the crew of the ship, *Newfoundland*, most of whom would be dead in a matter of days. It was only afterwards he realized that the bodies covered with snow were the white mounds from his dream.

In his autobiography, Jung recounts

disturbing dreams and visions in 1913. In one vision he witnessed a monstrous flood covering Germany and realized a catastrophe was in progress. 'I saw the mighty yellow waves, the floating rubble of civilization, and the drowned bodies of uncounted thousands. Then the whole sea turned to blood.' Jung said he was perplexed and nauseated, assuming this vision was personal. It was not until World War I broke out a year later that he realized its collective nature. This irrational experience led Jung to conclude that each person's unconscious possesses not only a personal, but also a collective, dimension.

Probably one of the best-established and most reputable cases of premonitions of disaster comes from the grim events that occurred on 21 October 1966 in Aberfan, Wales. On that day, 116 children and twenty-eight adults were killed when a large mountain of coal collapsed and buried a small section of the town of Aberfan, including an elementary school filled with children. The disaster touched nearly every family in the town and effectively extinguished an entire generation of children. After the disaster, the reports of premonitions began to flood in. The mother of one of the deceased students reported that her ten-year-old child (who died in the disaster) had a dream the night before which foretold the disaster. The child told her mother, 'I dreamed I went to school and there was no school there. Something black had come down all over it.'

The reports of precognitive dreams literally came from all over Wales and England. One lady had a nightmare that she suffocated in 'deep blackness'. Another dreamed of a small child being buried by a large landslide. Another clearly saw a schoolhouse be buried by an avalanche of coal, and rescue workers digging frantically for survivors. Another woke up from a nightmare in which she was being buried alive. On the morning of the disaster, Mrs Sybil Brown woke from a dream in which she saw children being overcome by 'a black, billowing mass'. Probably the clearest of the premonitions was reported by a man in north-west England who claimed that the night before the disaster he had a dream which consisted only of letters being spelled out in dazzling light: A–B–E–R–F–A–N. At the time, the dream had no meaning to him. Hours later, he would realize with horror what it meant.

An interesting phenomenon occurred in the aftermath of the terrorist plane attacks that destroyed the World Trade Center and damaged the Pentagon on 11 September 2001: numerous people came forward with reports of vivid dreams they'd had of these disasters in advance. The dreams were filled with images that later took place: planes crashing into buildings, planes crashing on the ground, tall buildings collapsing, flames shooting out of buildings, people running covered in gray ash, and feelings of panic, mass death and war. These nightmarish dreams were so realistic that many people awoke from them in terror and sweat.

The question most often raised about precognitive disaster dreams is, if so many people dreamed in advance of these disasters, why could nothing have been done to prevent them? The answer is that most people who have precognitive dreams only realize that they have had them after the events the dreams foretold have taken place, and they see how their dreams matched the events. Other dreamers, especially those who have periodic or frequent precognitive dreams, usually do not dream enough

specific details to know exactly v going to happen, where, and Some may only have a sense of that 'something terrible' is goi happen, usually soon. For exam dream that a tall building is colla would not have sparked the imm connection that terrorists were go fly planes into the World Trade Center on the morning of 11 September 2001. A dream analyst would more likely interpret the image dream within the context of the dreamer's life, suggesting that the dream reflected emotional turmoil within the dreamer's life.

flaunting her charms'. In dream-lore today, volcanoes are generally thought to represent strong emotions, possibly carnal desire, held in check but bubbling away just below the surface to be released in a violent eruption of pent-up fury. In other words, hot passions are aroused, and care should be taken in case they erupt without warning into violent or dangerous behavior. If you dreamed of **visiting or living by a volcano** – perhaps a famous one such as Mount Saint Helen's – and then having to run for your life as it suddenly erupted and spewed molten lava into your path, this dream may be referring to a struggle in waking life to suppress your mounting fury. Your unconscious may have used this dramatic image to warn you that you won't be able to contain your anger for much

longer. What is especially telling about the volcano is its unpredictability; it could erupt at any time. If the **lava** is prominent in the dream, feelings will run deep, but if the **lava has cooled**, there has been a deep passion which has now cooled off. If the explosiveness is more noticeable than the lava, anger may be more prominent. On the other hand, your dream may have reflected the volatile temper of someone you live or work with in waking life, and your fear of being at the receiving end of their anger. Or is a torrent of fiery emotion about to explode in waking life? If it is, or might be, the experience can be devastating and yet also cathartic. To dream of an **extinct volcano** can indicate that passions have been killed off or a difficult situation has ended.

ELEMENTS

The elements are common symbols in dreams, expressing the entire range of human characteristics.

They are divided into solid (earth), liquid (water), vapor (air) and energy (fire), and the ancient philosophers believed that these four elements sustained the world and influenced personality. According to Empedocles, a Greek philosopher, scientist and healer who lived in Sicily in the fifth century BC, all matter, including humankind, is comprised of four 'roots', or the elements of earth, air, fire and water. In astrology, the elements symbolize the four essential human qualities: earth for fertility; water for emotion; air for intelligence and fire for ambition. Since we know that Carl Jung studied mystical literature, astrology and alchemy, it is possible to conclude that his conceptualization of intuition, sensation, thinking and feeling as basic archetypes, or components of personality, is a derivation of Empedocles' ancient theories about fire, earth, air and water.

When the elements feature in dreams, many dream analysts believe they represent the state of your psychological well-being. Listed below you'll find the specific symbolism and dream-lore interpretation typically associated with each element. *See also* NATURE AND THE SEASONS; WEATHER.

The Element of Earth

The earth has ancient associations with the human body and personality.

According to astrological theory, people born under the earth signs of Taurus, Capricorn and Virgo are thought to have predominantly 'earthy' characteristics, such as emotional solidity, materialism, practicality and patience. Jungian analysts regard the earth as a symbol for sensation. In dreams, earth often represents the things you take for granted – yet rely on – in life, such as your body, the processes of life, and your family or cultural background. Earth also represents the past, the fallen leaves of your experience from which soil, new structures of self, are built.

Dreams associated with the earth, therefore, such as **lying on the ground**, may show that you need to be more grounded, practical and realistic in waking life. You may need to concentrate on worldly matters rather than flights of fantasy. To dream of the **planet earth** may be a symbol of your true self. If you were **gardening** in your dream, creativity is probably indicated; the dream may be referring to your psychological growth and increasing emotional or financial security.

■ *Idioms: down to earth; grounded; go to earth; like nothing on earth.* **See also** NATURE AND SEASONS; TREES.

DIGGING/GROWING/WATERING

Just as the physical earth is made up of past events – the trees and leaves, the plants and creatures that have lived and crumbled into the dust of the soil – so the earth of your dream represents the past on which your present depends and your future is built. Therefore, **digging** into it will tend to uncover things – most often feelings – you have buried there from your past. The earth is also your mother. It represents the soil, the genetic material, and the background from which you have sprung. It is the womb of the past from which you are born. In other words, it is both the physical material from which things grow as well as the overall environment in which something new can grow.

So if you are digging in your dream, is there something you need to learn about your past? Or is there something you want to find out, a vital piece of information that will complete the picture? If you are **uncovering an** object or old bones, then you are probably becoming conscious of long buried memories and feelings from your past. If you are **trying to bury something**, what are you trying to cover up or hide in waking life? Bear in mind the expressions associated with digging, too. Is someone having a dig at you in waking life? Did your dream reflect your entrenched, firmly held opinions? Or was your unconscious urging you to adopt a more down-to-earth approach? If you are a gardener, you will know that although the earth is the giver of sustenance, security and new life, each life cycle also has an end, so when earth figures in a dream, it may also indicate the end of a phase in life and the beginning of a new one.

A dream about **digging, watering or feeding** the earth may therefore suggest your desire to begin a new phase. It could also depict your fear of unpalatable hidden truths being exposed in waking life. Anything **growing from the earth** in your dream shows something that has developed from the possibilities of your life, and who you are. If your dream depicted you **planting a seed**, try to make a connection with your waking life. The dream seeds may refer to the planting of an intellectual or creative concept that has the potential to grow if placed in fertile ground and cared for. Then again, planting dreams may refer to your thoughts about starting a family. A dream of **healthy crops** may suggest that your waking ventures or family are flourishing. If what you are taking from the earth is **vegetables or things to eat,** these are the fruits of your past efforts, and suggest benefits arising in your life. If, however, the earth in your dream is **barren and nothing is growing**, this could indicate that you are emotionally and physically exhausted by the demands of waking life.

GOING UNDERGROUND

If you dream of being **underground**, this may suggest a desire for personal transformation – the death of the old to make way for the new. If you experience the nightmare of being **buried alive**, do you feel that others are suffocating your individuality in waking life and there is no way out? If in your dream you suspect that someone has **deliberately buried you alive**, your unconscious may be trying to alert you to hidden hostility from that person towards you in waking life. If you managed to escape, try to remember whether you stumbled across anything significant; this may hold the key to transforming your situation so you can step out of the darkness into daylight in waking life. To **come up out of the earth or a grave** suggests some kind of rebirth, new insights or a new period of your life. Being in a **tunnel, cave, chamber or mine** shows you exploring what is usually beneath the surface of your mind, such as unacknowledged insights or feelings. This is a journey into your unconscious. Remember the rules here are different to those in everyday life. Here you create your own environment, your own traps and freedom out of your own fears, hopes and desires.

If the dream **hole** was of your own making in the dream, what was its purpose? Freudians equate holes in dreams with vaginas, so – if you are a man – your dream may have been imbued with sexual innuendo. Whatever your sex, because the vagina leads to the womb it may be that you long to shut yourself away, or withdraw for a while from the unpleasantness of your waking life. On the other hand, your dream may be highlighting those of your 'underground' tastes or secret longings that are unexpressed in real life. There is another explanation for dreams about **burrowing underground or entering tunnels and caverns**. The tunnel is a symbol of transition and the bowels of the earth a symbol of the unconscious, so your dream may denote your search for some kind of transformation. What you saw or heard in the cavern or tunnel is therefore significant. If you **saw light or made your way to the end of the tunnel** in your dream, the implication is that you will find the inspiration you need in waking life.

MUD/SAND/SOIL

What is the quality of the earth in your dream? Is it richly fertile or a wasteland? **Sandy soil** suggests uncertainty; **red earth**, hard work and toil, and **rich, dark soil**, satisfaction. **Soft soil** links with the need for mothering or tactile contact. **Parched or barren ground** is, however, a sign of inner conflict or exhaustion, suggesting that you should search your dreamscape for signs of hope. **Sand** in a dream suggests instability and lack of security, especially if you see it together with the sea. If the **sands are shifting**, you may feel uncertain about what you want from life. If you see **sand in an hourglass**, you are conscious of time running out. If you are **building sandcastles** in your dream, this suggests that the structure of your life lacks permanence.

Mud symbolizes creation in many religions, specifically the creation of mankind. In the Bible, God molded Adam from a

Earth's features

Cave

Like a womb, a **cave** protects and conceals. It is associated with mystery, danger and the unconscious. While the cave may appear frightening, an exploration may reveal exciting things. If you **enter the cave** in your dream, this suggests change and a deeper understanding of yourself. If you are **too afraid to enter**, there may be aspects of yourself that you don't want to acknowledge. Or do you feel that you are about to cave in or give way to someone else?

Chasm

Chasms or bottomless pits typically indicate a lack of spirituality and a desire for illumination. Sometimes, the only way to find joy is to sink to the bottom and experience the pit of despair first.

Cliff

The high vantage point of a **cliff** offers the opportunity for a wider bird's-eye view, even if it may be frightening to be so exposed. If you dream about being on a cliff, it may relate to an important decision or a difficult situation. You may need to take a risk by overcoming fears and stepping into the unknown.

Desert

A **desert** may reflect feelings of isolation, being in a place that has no interest for you or a desire to get away and have some time to yourself. Or it could be hinting at things you have deserted or left behind. Although we think of deserts as barren places, they are in fact teeming with underground life, so is your life a bit like a desert – desolate on the surface but rich underneath?

Forest/Woodland

Forests are dark and mysterious. They symbolize the unknown and the unconscious. This archetype appears in many myths – characters get lost in the wood or forest, only to discover great treasure or wisdom, as well as great dangers. Dreams about **woodland** and forests often have a lot to do with feeling lost and being unable to find the right path or direction. *See also* TREES AND PLANTS.

Mountain

Mountains are where earth and heaven are said to meet, and this is why so many mountains are regarded as sacred places. They symbolize aspiration, renunciation of worldly desires and the search for higher potential. In dreams, mountains represent challenges and choices. If you are **climbing a mountain**, you are challenging your own fears. If you **reach the top**, you feel that you have achieved your goal. To **fall down a mountain** suggests carelessness in your waking life. If you are **broken into pieces by a fall**, it may suggest that your heart and your head are not working together in harmony.

lump of clay and breathed life into him, and it is traditionally to clay and dust that human beings return. Ancient dream interpretation suggested that to dream of mud foretold finding great riches, while a dream in which you **sank in mud** would lead to a rapid recovery from illness. From a psychological viewpoint, mud represents the fundamental substance of life, which handled properly has potential for growth, but handled badly can drag you down. Mud in dreams can also represent past experiences – or your perception of them – as something that is holding you back, or in which you are stuck. Clear as mud paradoxically means that something is not clear at all. Are you unclear about a situation in which you are involved? *See also* CRYSTALS, GEMSTONES AND ROCKS; TREES.

SHAKY, SLIPPERY AND SOLID GROUND

A dream of **standing on solid ground** may mirror your own feelings of groundedness in daily life, but a dream in which the **ground gives way under your feet** or you have to **dodge pitfalls or open manhole covers** mirrors your current sense of insecurity in waking life. When the earth opens up in your dream, consider what it is you are afraid of falling into, or what might open up for all to see? If you **lose your balance** in your dream and **fall into a huge pit or hole**, are you on the verge of 'putting your foot in it' or making a huge blunder ('being wrong footed') in real life? If you find yourself **slipping and stumbling** in your dream and are **covered in mud**, do you feel as if you are making mistakes and your reputation has been dragged through the mud, or have you been the victim of

mud-slinging or bad words in the waking world. Alternatively, do you feel somehow soiled and grubby? If your dream depicted a **pig happily rolling in the mud**, do you need to take a more down-to-earth approach in waking life? If your dream depicted you being **sucked into the ground or into mud**, do you feel caught in a situation that is draining you and about which you feel powerless to do anything? Ask yourself who, or what, the mud or sand in the dream may have represented. Is anyone, or anything, in your life dragging you down? Or have you become a prisoner of your own inhibitions, so that you are stuck in the mud?

If you find yourself **off the ground** in your dream, this may suggest that you are losing connection with your roots of family or culture, or living in a state of mind that does not connect you with everyday reality. This lack of grounding may also be occasionally shown as **being on a high building**. Finally, if the **earth is soft and difficult to walk on**, you are probably finding your present life hard to deal with. Negative emotions are bogging you down. But if the **earth is dry and firm**, then you are feeling on firm ground as far as relationships and creativity are concerned. *See also* DISASTERS.

The Element of Air

You can't see air but it is crucial for your survival and well-being.

The element of air is associated with the Zodiac signs Gemini, Libra and Aquarius.

For Jungian analysts, air seeks to establish itself in the realm of the intellect; it is through the process of thinking that we develop ideas and communicate. Air contributes inventiveness, originality, creativity and versatility to the personality. It gives that feeling of freedom and objectivity, and the ability to appreciate the differences between people. In dreams, air encourages you to let your thoughts soar, helping you to realize your full potential.

When air's influence is exaggerated in a person, we see them as living in a dream world full of unrealistic goals and flights of fancy. Air should seek to maintain practicality and develop consistency in dealing with the real world. You cannot live without air, so when it appears in your dreams, consider its quality. Is it **foggy, misty, clear or polluted**? The answer will give you an idea of the atmosphere that surrounds you in waking life. If you are outdoors in your dream and conscious of the clarity and coolness of the air, your dreaming mind may be urging you to give freedom to your thoughts. Or perhaps you feel released from a recent problem or situation. Air may also refer to the way in which you behave. Are you putting on airs and graces, or behaving in a superior way that demeans other people?

BREATH

Breathing indicates the presence of life, so in your dream the condition or speed of your **breathing** may depict your pace of life. If you are **holding your breath**, this suggests fear and stress. If you are **panting or breathing fast**, this suggests excitement and stimulation. If you are **underwater or not breathing at all**, this reproduces

the condition of the womb and indicates a need to escape from waking reality. To dream of **breathing warm air** denotes the possible onset of trouble, whilst breathing cold air foretells strength and courage. If you are **feeling stifled by stale air or oppressive humidity**, this indicates an ill-advised friendship that isn't encouraging the dreamer to fulfill his or her potential. Or perhaps you feel stifled by your current circumstances in waking life. Alternatively could you be feeling breathless with anticipation? If you dreamed of **taking in great gulps of invigorating air**, your dream may be urging you to clear the air – resolve a tense situation – in your waking life, or it may have been referring to a sense of freedom and lightness.

DRIFTING/BALLOON/KITE/ PARACHUTE

An awareness of **drifting through the air** in your dream may signal a similar lack of direction in waking life, but if you found yourself **drifting towards dark clouds**, could this be a warning that you are about to hit a potentially dangerous situation? Or were you terrified that you would plunge to earth in your dream? If you were, your unconscious may be reflecting your fear of losing control in waking life. If a **parachute** suddenly appeared to help you land safely, perhaps you need to lower your aspirations, thereby escaping from an exciting but ultimately perilous situation.

If you find yourself **flying in a hot-air balloon** in your dream, do you long to rise above or overcome problems that are tying down your waking life? Although you may have no sense of direction, flying in a hot-air balloon does allow you to take an

The Element Encyclopedia of 20,000 Dreams

overview of the situation, rather than letting your vision become bogged down with petty details. If you dreamed that you **clutched a balloon, let it go and watched it drift skyward wondering where it will go**, your unconscious may be commenting on your own lack of direction or focus. On the other hand it may simply imply your desire to coast for a while through life. A dream of **flying a kite** may suggest that, although your feet are on the ground, you are starting to control your aspirations and direct them to a higher place. If the **kite disappeared from view or snapped from its string**, then this may suggest that you have been overambitious and that your vision has lost touch with reality.

SOARING

Air often appears in dreams as the medium through which we fly. Dreaming of **soaring or flying** through the air may therefore have mirrored your own quest for spiritual or intellectual inspiration or achievement. According to Freud, flying dreams express the urge to enjoy unlimited sexual freedom and to indulge in sexual experimentation. Although this may have meaning and relevance to you, another explanation is that you yearn to feel as free as a bird. Or perhaps you have risen to new heights in an area of your life. If, however, you dream of **losing the air** that sustains your flight, this suggests a loss of freedom, objectivity or even confidence.

The Element of Water

In dreams, **water** is a common theme and its association with the fluid of the womb and its role in evolution make it an archetypal symbol in the dreamer's emotional life.

Water is also a symbol of the spiritual life force. In most cultures there are tales of healing waters and in dreams, as in baptism, to be immersed in water is to be spiritually cleansed. As the governing element of the Zodiac signs of Cancer, Scorpio and Pisces, it is said to endow people born under that sign with the feminine qualities of gentleness and changeability.

Dreams of **entering water** suggest refreshment, healing and beginning something new. **Deep water, pools and lakes** are symbols of the unconscious or of being out of your depth, while **shallow water** represents a lack of energy. To dream of **drawing water from a tap or well, or to be drinking it** is in general a positive and creative sign. However, to **spill water** suggests setbacks. **Flowing water** signifies peace and security. To be **immersed in water** suggests pregnancy and birth or new beginnings, and **coming out of water** also suggests a fresh start. **Fast-flowing water** suggests lively encounters and fast-moving action; **deep, still water** suggests hidden depths, whilst also possibly warning against a person of few words with a hidden agenda. If you **see your reflection in water**, this suggests the transient nature of life since the reflection can easily be lost.

Features of the Sky

Sky/Cloud

If the **sky** is a dominant feature in your dream, you may be thinking about the purpose of your life. A **star-studded night** sky may represent the unconscious, whereas the **daytime sky** may represent cosmic, rather than ordinary, awareness, giving you an insight into your place in the world. If the **sky is dark**, this reflects moodiness and hardship but if the **sky is bright**, joy and the prospect of a respite from worries are heralded. The sky can also signify what is unattainable and beyond your reach. Jung regarded the night sky as highly significant in dreams because the symbolism of the constellations and the signs of the zodiac are archetypal representations of the inner world of the unconscious. According to traditional dream-lore, to dream of a **red sky** predicts disaster for the nation, to dream of a **cloudy sky** spells misfortune, whilst to dream of a **blue sky** brings good luck.

Clouds in dreams can either indicate feelings of joy and inspiration, or they can suggest that you are feeling overshadowed by someone or something. Furthermore, they suggest that you may be suffering from a hidden depression.

Wind

To dream of the **wind** suggests unsettled emotions and indecisiveness, but it may also indicate intellect and the beginnings of self-awareness. You may feel the need to make changes in your life. How you interpret the dream will depend on the force of the wind. For instance, a **breeze** would suggest gentleness and the beginnings of a new idea. A **gale** might represent something about which we feel strongly and the **north wind** would suggest a threat to security. If **smoke is carried on the air**, obscuring your view, you should consider the implications. In waking life, are you being forced into a situation in which you are being forced to reconsider ideas that you previously refused to contemplate? *See also* SPACE AND SCIENCE; WEATHER.

The imagery may serve as a caution against trusting unworthy friends or projects.

If, in your dream, the **water is dirty or muddy**, it means your feelings are influenced by outer circumstances, worries, material problems, or values. If, however, the water is **clear and sparkling**, it symbolizes faith, honesty, hope and joy. Have you dreamed of **boiling water**? If you have, this may indicate the need to let off some steam. Is anything welling up that needs your attention? If you are **on the water**, for example in a **boat,** this suggests lack of emotional commitment, whilst to be **in the water but not moving** suggests fatigue. If you dream of the **elements of water and air clashing** – such as strong winds creating a stormy sea – the symbolism suggests you might be contemplating human emotion in general, with all its ebb and flow from rage to calm and rage again. Finally, don't forget that dreams featuring water may simply be triggered by raging thirst or a full bladder while you sleep.

ICE/ICEBERG

Just as water symbolizes the emotional life in general, **ice and icebergs** in dreams represent frozen emotions. Only when the ice melts can water flow. If you are **falling through ice** in your dream, this suggests a breakthrough of emotion, although the experience will be uncomfortable. An iceberg denotes a significant problem that is blocking your progress in waking life. Could it symbolize a difficult problem you have put on ice or tried to avoid but now have no option but to confront? If you dreamed of **walking carefully over a frozen lake or pond**, could the message have been that you are walking on thin ice

in waking life or that someone is making your feel so vulnerable in waking life that you are treading carefully around them?

The **tip of an iceberg** reveals only a small part of a larger mass; in dreams, therefore, an iceberg may symbolize the visible part of a problem, acting as a warning to the dreamer to think more deeply about something. In addition, icebergs are impressive and beautiful, so their hidden depths may be overlooked. If an iceberg appears in your dream, ask yourself if you have hidden your feelings so well that people aren't aware of them. Are you hiding how you really feel? On the other hand, are you being icy towards someone or is someone giving you the cold shoulder?

OCEAN/SEA

Dream **oceans and seas** represent the unconscious emotions, instincts or urges that are influencing your attitude, approach and reactions in waking life. Perhaps their most symbolic associations are with the unconscious mind, and with the ebb and flow of feelings that can sometimes build up into a tidal wave of emotion. The state of the sea in your dream is highly significant: a **shallow sea** suggests lack of emotion, a **stormy sea** suggests passion and a **calm sea** suggests peace.

The ocean and the sea are also a symbol of the feminine principle, so a dream of being **overwhelmed by a wave** may suggest that you are being smothered or dominated by a woman in your life, whilst **calmly floating in the sea or surfing the waves** suggests a good relationship with yourself, and perhaps with a woman. If you are **struggling against the tide**, this is a

Diving/Drowning/ Floating/Swimming

Dreams of **diving, floating and swimming** usually hint at your current emotional state or the need to tap into the resources of your unconscious mind. If you are **diving into water** in your dream, this represents trying to find parts of yourself that have been repressed. Dreams in which you are **floating in warm water safely and calmly** are amongst the most comforting and secure you can have. They may reflect a longing to be able to coast effortlessly through life, letting worries wash over you. But if you felt uneasy, such dreams may be mirroring your concern that you lack direction and power in waking life, and are just treading water as opportunities fly past you.

If you have a dream in which you are **swimming calmly and happily through calm waters**, this suggests a positive attitude to your waking life, as things are going well, or 'swimmingly', for you, and you feel in your element, be it at school, work or home. If, however, you dream that you are **struggling against a current**, it suggests inner conflict and the force of opinion against you in the waking world. In your dream, did you swim with the tide or continue with your struggle? If you found yourself **out of your depth** when you went swimming, this may mirror a sense of being out of your emotional depth. **Drowning** suggests that your emotions are overwhelming and engulfing you. If a **lifeboat** appears, you believe your unconscious can throw you an emotional lifeline.

Where water is contained in a space, such as a **bath or swimming pool**, it signifies controlled emotion and restraint. A dream **shower or bath** in which you wash yourself may refer to a need to cleanse your emotions of negative influences, whilst a **Jacuzzi** may have sexual connotations. Being in a **swimming pool** may remind you of the importance of relaxation. A **surreal underwater scene**, in which you meet and interact with family and friends, may suggest that you have been too busy to take the time to connect emotionally with loved ones. It might be wise to slow down and devote more quality time to them in the real world.

sign that you are not making the progress you had anticipated, but that you are nonetheless gaining strength and wisdom from the struggle. If a **sea monster emerges from the depths**, could this symbolize unconscious fear or even an aspect of yourself that is being repressed in waking life?

■ *Idioms: lost at sea; plenty more fish in the sea; all at sea; watered down.*

The Element Encyclopedia of 20,000 Dreams

Rain

If you are **drenched by rain** in your dream, this may be suggesting that you tend to overreact and be guided by your emotions in waking life. If, however, you were **shielded by an umbrella**, this may suggest that you are protecting yourself from your emotions. *See also* WEATHER.

River/Bridge/Canal/Dam/ Reservoir

Rivers and streams always represent the way you live your life, as well as the way you see your life. Did you dream of a **meandering river or one that was direct**? The first would suggest emotional ups and downs, whilst the second would suggest emotional calm. Dreams of being **carried along by a river or stream** can refer to the passage of life from birth to death, but they are more likely to refer to your emotional life. How you felt in the dream will indicate the meaning; were you frightened, happy or excited? If the **river is rushing by**, this may suggest that you feel life is moving too quickly. If it the **river is static**, your unconscious may have been commenting on your lack of drive and direction.

If you **threw a stone in the river**, did the **ripples** that formed echo your sense of going around in circles in waking life? The river depicts the richness or poverty of your life energy, so if you are **crossing a river** in your dream, this suggests you are in the process of making great changes in your life. If you are **in the water to cross**, it means you will feel a lot of emotions in the process of change. If you see **someone else cross the river or fall into the river**, this may refer to your feelings about aging and the passage of time. If the **river is contaminated**, this suggests that you are holding back your feelings in waking life and not doing the best you can for yourself. If you were in a **river- or steamboat** in your dream, this may refer to the circumstances that surround you, for example your family or home life. The context of the dream and how you feel will all help you with the interpretation. Was the boat solid and safe like a steamer, or fragile like a canoe or a dingy?

Canals, dams and reservoirs are all designed to regulate water flow and in dreams they suggest conscious attempts to control emotion; how effective they are at directing the water mirrors how effective you have become at controlling your emotions in waking life. A canal may also symbolize the birth canal and thus represent a desire for children. Because reservoirs are where water is collected and stored, if one features in your dream, could it be commenting on your own emotional reserves? The **water level of the reservoir** in this dream is important. If it is high, your emotional resources are abundant but if it is low, you may be feeling emotionally drained by the demands of others. In dreams, dams also suggest control over your emotions, and their effectiveness in your dream will say a lot about your emotional health. If, in your dream, you were **standing on a bridge watching the water flow beneath you**, you could be ready to leave the past behind – as suggested by water under the bridge – since you are at a turning point in your life (the bridge is a symbol of transition). *See also* TRAVEL.

STILL WATERS RUN DEEP

Unlike rivers and seas, **lakes, lagoons, pools, ponds and puddles** are typically still, so if they feature in your dream, they could be reflecting your emotional calm. If a **lagoon appears mysteriously**, reminding you that still waters run deep, this could be referring to your own hidden strengths or weaknesses. Some dream researchers believe that lagoons in dreams are symbols of the womb, so perhaps when they appear in a dream, you are longing to retreat to a safe haven. If you are a woman, they may refer to a desire for children and if you are a man, a longing for intimacy. Dream ponds can also reflect your unconscious personality, facets of which will be represented by the creatures who live in it. If your dream **pond is lifeless and stagnant**, is your emotional life currently unfulfilling? If you **watched a fish swim to the surface**, could it have represented the emergence of your intuition? If the **pool suddenly transforms into a whirlpool or maelstrom**, this suggests emotional turbulence or confusion in waking life.

WASHING

If you are **washing yourself, or someone or something else** in a dream using water, this suggests the cleansing of negative feelings such as despair or self-doubt. Is it time to clean up your act or perhaps get started on a project you have been postponing? Dreams of **washing your hair** suggest you are thinking of changing your attitude or the way you present yourself to others; if you are **washing a vagina or penis**, it could mean that you are dealing with the results of a pent-up sexuality, whilst if you are

washing your hands, you may be trying to get rid of feelings about something you have done or been involved with. If you dream of **hanging up washing**, it suggests that you are allowing change to come into your life, as well as letting other people see your new attitudes.

WATERFALL/FOUNTAIN/ SPRING/RAPIDS/WELL

Dreams of a **waterfall or rapids** may be referring to birth, especially ones in which you are **swept along in a warm stream of water through a tunnel and emerge into a pool or lagoon**, as it is thought that we all carry the memory of birth in our unconscious. On the other hand, the dancing waters may be reflecting your sense of happiness and exuberance in waking life. A dream of a **fountain** (suggests womanhood) or a **hosepipe** (suggests manhood) may have a sexual connotation. If the **jet was weak**, then it may suggest that sexual desire is not matched by emotional commitment (or the other way round) A **steady flow of water** is probably symbolic of confidence in waking life.

In dreamland, **springs** can represent a source of untapped creativity and they can also hint at wisdom, because another name for spring is fount, suggesting 'fount of all knowledge'. **Wells** in dreams can hint at emotional rebirth or good fortune, as wishing wells have been credited with wish-fulfillment for centuries. So if you dreamed of **drawing water from a well**, what is it that you long for? Because wells are sources of water, it could be that your waking life has become emotionally dry and that you are thirsting for a revival of feeling.

The Element of Fire

Fire is often considered the most fearsome and powerful of the four elements because it not only devours, causing pain and destruction, it also purifies, cleanses and illuminates.

In dreams, **fire** is a potent symbol of the passion of strong emotion and burning love, as well as of new beginnings. It has many different and conflicting meanings, and interpretation is sometimes difficult. **Standing in, or being in, flames** can therefore suggest the burning out of old attitudes or experiences to make way for the new; but such a dream could also represent your fears of a new phase in life, your own personal suffering for your beliefs, or that you are consumed by destructive emotions, such as passion or envy. Sometimes interpretation is easier; for example, if a **house is burning down** or there is a **forest fire**, this suggests you are consumed by passion. The exact interpretation will depend on whether the fire is being controlled or not. If fire figures in your dream, consider whether your emotions have got out of control. Are you being a hot head? Is your passion burning?

A **controlled dream fire** can also symbolize security. The **fireplace or hearth** is the heart of the home and the center of warmth, and to dream of it may show that you feel comfortable with yourself. Freud said that fire was a symbol of the libido and passion, and to dream of poking a fire represented sexual arousal. Jung, on the other hand, said that fire suggested intuition and psychological transformation. Just as the alchemists used fire to transform base metal into gold, so fire is a symbol for personal growth. It destroys the past but lights the way for the future. It is the eternal flame in the temple of the soul and from the fire the phoenix of hope arises. Baptism by fire signifies a new awareness of spiritual power and transformation. Sometimes fire can be a warning of illness. It is also associated with the astrological signs of Aries, Leo and Sagittarius. If a **fire is put out by** water, this suggests physical energy being restrained by the cooler processes of thought.

▪ *Idioms: too hot to handle; you burn me up; hothead; old flame; the burning bush; fired up; burning interest; fan the flames.*

CANDLE

The small **flame of a candle** can spread considerable light, so if it appears in your dream, it may be suggesting that only a small amount of energy will achieve the same results in waking life. And because the light of a candle illuminates, your dreaming mind may be focused on intellectual or spiritual development. If you are **blowing out your candle**, this could suggest the ending of a phase or relationship in waking life. If you **put the candle out with spit or urine**, is this a symbol of your disgust at, or disapproval of, a person or viewpoint in waking life?

Cooking

If you used fire to **cook** something in your dream, try to remember what you are cooking. It might symbolize an idea or a plan, or it may refer to your career or lifestyle. A **barbecue** may refer to your social life. A **brazier** is used for warmth and comfort, so what in your waking life could use a little of that?

Firework/Explosion/ Inferno

If you watched a fantastic **firework display** in your dream, are you feeling particularly good about yourself right now? Has there been a personal triumph? Or should you interpret the dream sexually, as fireworks are symbols of sexual climax in the movies. On the other hand, fireworks may denote explosions of furious rage and any dream explosion may reflect pent-up fury or frustration that is building up in waking life. Is there something in waking life that is making you tense and angry? Dreams in which you watch helplessly as a **raging inferno destroys your home** may be warnings from your unconscious to fit a smoke alarm in your home or office, but they may also have highlighted your current overheated emotional stage. It is important to ask yourself who or what is provoking your rage and whether the full force of your anger is about to be unleashed in waking life. And what would the results of the **explosion** be – devastation that all you have worked for has gone up in smoke, or liberation that you have burned your bridges and can arise energized from the ashes?

To dream of a **fireman** represents self-control and your ability to deal with your energies, burning desires or emotional emergencies in the waking world. To dream that **you caused a fire** may be a warning from your unconscious that you are playing with fire and may be in danger of getting your fingers burned if you go ahead with a certain project or get involved with a certain person. If you find **yourself on fire**, your passions may be consuming you and you may feel hopeless and trapped in waking life. If, however, you managed to **put a fire out**, this shows that you are asserting control over the fire raging within you. If **someone else started a fire**, your unconscious may have been telling you to watch that person carefully in waking life or to carry out some simple safety checks.

Furnace/Forge

The **furnace** is a powerful symbol of creativity as all the fire's energy is devoted to one specific task. If you are using **fire to forge something**, such as a tool, your dream may be hinting that you should use your creativity and passion more in waking life. Have you developed a burning interest in something or someone recently and isn't it time to pour your energy into making it a reality?

Lighting a fire

If you dreamed of **lighting a fire**, what sort of fire was it and who else was there? **Kindling a fire** represents a summoning of energy, so the context of the fire in your dream should always be taken into consideration. Where are you focusing your energy? If the **fire spreads out of control** in your dream, this may indicate that your

The Element Encyclopedia of 20,000 Dreams

Smoke/Ashes/Embers

Smoke, embers and ashes are associated with fire in dreams but they also have their own associations. If **clouds of black, choking smoke** appear and there is no fire, what are you missing in waking life as there is no smoke without fire? **Smoke and smoking** in dreams typically suggest a feeling of danger and if you are smoking, you are trying to control your anxiety. Smoke can also represent passion that has not yet flared into being. Contradictory interpretations are that smoke signifies cleansing and purification, as with incense, or contamination.

If you watched the **glowing embers of a dying fire** in your dream, this may suggest either that a passion is dying out, or a fondness for someone or something just won't die out. It could also suggest that underneath your calm exterior you are smoldering with anger and resentment. If you were **raking over the ashes** in your dream, upon which aspect of your past are you reflecting? Ashes in a dream often indicate penitence and sorrow, and the feeling that there is nothing more than can be, as the ashes or memories are all we have left. The important thing now is to learn from the experience. And bear in mind that your unconscious may also use the dream images of smoke, ember and ashes to warn you that you are at risk of physical or emotional burnout.

emotions are in danger of running out of control too. If you succeed in **controlling the blaze**, this suggests you are in control of your waking life. Also pay attention to what was being burned in your dream and what the fire was feeding on, as the other symbols in the dream may help with your interpretation. For example, if you were **burning your clothes**, is it time to brighten up your image?

A **fire burning in a domestic hearth** is likely to point to your private life, whilst a **bonfire or beacon** has more public significance as a symbol of communication. **Lighting a stove** to cook a meal for family and friends suggests concern for your loved ones, and **lighting a candle for a meal or curling up in front of a log cabin's roaring fire** may suggest sexual heat.

TENDING A FIRE

In dreams in which you are **tending a fire**, try to remember how much attention it needed from you; did it burn vigorously or did you have to fan it, stoke and feed it fuel to keep it alight? If you **had to keep it alight**, perhaps some passion or desire in your waking life is flickering or waning, and you need to take action to energize it; or have the demands of your working life forced you to neglect your real passions, be they people or interests. Remember lighting fire dreams represent the birth of creative energy, so how you tend and control the fire is significant. If you are **conscious of the flame of the fire**, this suggests an awareness of your own strength and energy. If you are **aware of the heat of the fire**, you are aware of someone else's strong feelings.

EVERYDAY THINGS

Although you may have your share of fantasy dream scenarios, the chances are your dreams will also be littered with everyday items and situations you are familiar with in real life.

Perhaps you have come into contact with one particular item or situation more often than any other, this familiarity explaining its appearance in your dream. According to Christopher Evans, a British psychologist and computer scientist, the appearance of everyday things in dreams is simply the brain's way of processing and arranging information. Most dream analysts, however, find this explanation unconvincing and argue that everyday things in dreams contain symbolic values and may represent far more than their everyday function might suggest. The ways in which common items are used and everyday situations are experienced in dreams have enormous significance, as does the context or scenario in which they appear. In other words, everyday images in dreams operate in much the same way as all symbols and their appearance in dreams is a testimony to their shared, as well as to their individual, meaning. In this chapter, some of the most common everyday items and experiences you may encounter in your dreams will be explored.

Everyday Items

CONTAINER

Boxes, drawers, wardrobes and other storage containers in dreams may relate to feelings of safety, security and containment. They may also suggest that you are storing too much emotional baggage and need to lighten your load. An **empty container** may suggest that you are in need of emotional support or fulfillment. If a dream **container is well organized** with room to spare, you may be feeling comfortable in the way you organize your life. If, however, the **box is disorganized and overcrowded with items**, this can symbolize a sense of being overburdened with daily tasks or with emotions. It is worth remembering whether any items were offloaded in order to make the box easier to use.

CUTLERY

As food is associated with emotion, a dream of **eating with cutlery that is old, rusty or inadequate or wrongly used** (for example, trying to eat soup with a fork) may suggest you are attempting to satisfy your emotions in an inappropriate way. If, in your dream, the **spoons, knives and forks are shiny and glittering**, this could indicate a contented home life. Forks are often associated with social interaction and they may indicate a future event you are looking forward to. They may also suggest trying to get to the root of problems. A **rusty or twisted knife** in a dream can indicate relationship or family problems. If both a **knife and a fork** appear in your dream, they may represent the masculine and feminine elements of your personality, and how you express and balance the two in waking life. If a **spoon** appeared in your dream and you saw a distorted picture of yourself reflected in it, this suggests a distorted view of yourself. If you were **eating or drinking anything from the spoon** in your dreams, this may relate to someone, or something, in waking life that you want to protect. If the **spoon contains medicine**, there may be an unpleasant lesson for you to learn, or swallow, in waking life.

DISH/DRINK/FOOD/GLASS

In dreams, a **dish** usually represents food that needs to be eaten now, and thus represents ideas or projects that should be tackled immediately. Jungians often see a **drinking glass or wineglass** as a symbol of the mythical Holy Grail, offering the dreamer spiritual sustenance. For Freudians, to dream of **drinking from a glass** expresses sexual desire, as like other receptacles, the glass symbolizes the female genitals. A **broken drinking glass** can represent loss of virginity. **Food and drink** are everyday items that regularly feature in dreams. In general, they are regarded as positive signs, but there are so many possible interpretations when food or drink – or eating and drinking – feature in a dream that a whole chapter has been devoted to the subject later on. See FOOD AND DRINK.

GARBAGE

Dreams in which **you throw away garbage** may be connected to a desire to rid yourself of emotional and physical waste. Try to work out what the dream is referring to and dispose of it. If, however, the dream **garbage was being thrown out by friends or loved ones**, then perhaps other people are doing your dirty work for you. There may also be a suggestion that you need help ridding yourself of something damaging. If you **throw something precious out** in your dream, you are not appreciating someone close to you or are taking them for granted. If you are **covered in garbage**, you may be afraid of some form of humiliation or feel emotionally burdened in waking life.

The presence of **dirt** in your dream will also refer to something distasteful in your waking life. Bear in mind, though, that such a dream may not be completely negative, as we use **manure or fertilizer** to encourage growth. The allusion may therefore be to some action that is disagreeable but will yield results. **Excrement or feces** in dreams has a different meaning, indicating that you are purging yourself of something or someone in waking life that is poisonous to you. A dream of **pollution** also refers to something that is damaging to you – emotionally and physically – if you do not avoid or dispose of it. Dreams of **splashing through a** puddle or being covered with soot may refer to mild irritations in waking life. A **drain** disposes of excess water and if it appears in your dream, it may suggest that you are feeling drained emotionally.

Household items

Dreams that feature **brooms** are considered to be a sign of good fortune, suggesting that you are making a clean sweep in your waking life. The dream may be urging you to sweep out something from your past, so pay attention to what you are sweeping up. If the **broom is damaged**, you may be suffering from low self-esteem or feelings of insecurity. If the **broom is being used outside**, are you taking too much interest in the outside world and neglecting what is really important to you?

Dreams of **scissors** can be related to decisiveness and cutting out unwanted emotional aspects of the dreamer's life. If the **scissors are unused**, this can express a desire to begin a new relationship or make an existing one stronger. Dream scissors may also suggest that you are dividing your attention among too many people. If you are **cutting with scissors**, you are in the process of making an important decision. Another interpretation for scissors is that they are a symbol of sexuality, either male or female, depending on whether they are open or closed. A **knot** in a dream symbolizes the various ties in your life and relationships with others. If you **carefully untie a knot** in your dream, this suggests a readiness to deal with a problem, rather

than ignoring it by impatiently cutting the knot in two. The knot also has sexual symbolism, representing a couple's personal and sexual union.

Dream **envelopes** suggest messages to or from the dreamer. If the **envelope is open**, this signifies daily problems that can be tackled but if the **envelope is closed**, it may be harder to solve the problems. If the **envelope is bulging**, you may be feeling that your life is overburdened with worries and emotional expectations from those around you. A **ladder** in your dream may relate to work in your home, such as painting, but if you cannot make a practical connection, try and think of the purpose of the dream ladder. How is it being used? Like **elevators and stairs**, ladders in dreams relate to your progress or lack of it. *See also* HOME.

Mirror/Lighting

As a symbol of the mind, the **mirror** suggests the art of reflection, looking at the reality of who you are, or seeing yourself in a new or different way. If a mirror appears in your dream, do you need to reflect on something that is bothering you? If you **saw your reflection**, were you happy with what you saw or do you want to make changes? **Light** in dreams symbolizes intuition or inner guidance, so if you dream of lights or **light bulbs**, consider their shape. Are they candles flaring upward or is the light contained in a bulb? Is the light flickering or steady, and what does this represent for you right now? If you are carrying a **light that flares** in your dream, does this mean you have a flair for something, a talent you are not using? Or does it mean you are about to flare up and have an angry

Furniture items

Specific furniture items can indicate the attitudes, beliefs and notions with which you furnish your mind and self-image; you might be, for example, an antique fancier or a lover of novelty. The purpose to which they are put may also be sending you a message; if you dream of a **chair or sofa** do you need to take it easy? If you focused on a **light bulb**, are you in need of illumination? If you have **excess furniture** in your dream, is your lifestyle overcrowded?

Bed

In dreams, **beds** symbolize intimacy and relationships, but also your need to get away from the world and withdraw into yourself to enjoy healing rest. Sometimes they represent sleep and dreams, and meeting your unconscious. Consider in addition the well-known saying, 'you've made your bed, now lie in it.'

■ *Idioms: bed of nails; go to bed; make your bed and lie in it; test bed.*

Carpet/Mat/Rug

In some instances, these can indicate the state of your finances; so bare floorboards, for example, would indicate hardship. Alternatively, do you feel as if you are being walked on or something is being covered up? Pay attention to the color and design; these may reflect how satisfied you feel with yourself. A **carpet with a distinct floral design**, for example, may be an optimistic symbol of a garden, but if the pattern is of a **labyrinth or maze**, perhaps you feel trapped and confused in your waking life.

■ *Idioms: sweep under the carpet; roll out the red carpet; rug pulled from under your feet; carpet burn.*

Chair

This image suggests rest and receptivity as well as escapism. If you are in a group, watch where your **chair** is placed, as it could indicate your status within the group. If you are pushing an invalid in a wheelchair, is this a weak or sick aspect of yourself? Chairs are also associated with female sexuality. A **broken chair or one that collapses under the dreamer** may suggest the end of a sexual relationship. A dream of a **cushion** may be suggesting ways of protecting yourself; the color of the cushion will help you decide from what it is you need protection. A **sofa or couch** is where you sit and relax with others, and let your guard down. When it is called a couch, it may refer to the way we sometimes 'couch' information, presenting it in a more acceptable way. Is there a need to do this in waking life?

Cupboard/Closet/Wardrobe

If you dreamed of **opening a cupboard door to find that it opened into an empty room or a room you hadn't**

seen before, your dreaming mind is telling you that you are ready for new challenges in life. The time is right to begin a new project or make a change. The dream can also suggest hidden memories and emotions, suggestive of the 'skeleton in the cupboard'. If the **cupboard is open, closed or you are trapped in it**, this indicates how open or closed you are to other people and the possibility of change. To see a **closet** in your dream symbolizes something in your life that you have kept hidden. It may also signify an unveiling of previously hidden aspects of yourself as in 'coming out of the closet'. **Storing clothes in the wardrobe or dressing room** may express the image you want to present to the outside world – or in Jungian terminology, the persona. A **locked wardrobe** indicates a desire for privacy, whereas a **wardrobe overflowing** with clothes suggests extravagance.

Curtain

Closing curtains or drapes in your dream may mean that you are unable to face up to a certain situation or problem, or that you do not know what is going on around you. On the other hand, it may mean that you are being secretive and do not want other people to know how you are feeling. Dreams that feature **closed curtains** can suggest a sense that you are trying to block out a problem in waking life, or perhaps feel the need for secrecy relating to a certain issue. If the **curtains are open** in your dream, you may be feeling generous or ready to share information.

Table

This symbolizes your social connection with others. If the **table is bare**, it suggests that you are giving very little of yourself. If the **table is expensive or of good quality**, it suggests high-quality relationships with others; **your place at the table** refers to your self-image and a **dressing table** refers to your attempts to create a good social image. Alternatively dream tables can also indicate the need for hard work and perseverance to achieve your goals.

■ *Idioms: lay your cards on the tale; table talk; table hopping.*

Rearranging furniture

A dream in which you are moving furniture around, or trying to make it fit into a small place, may be a reflection on the way you are trying to cope with your present circumstances in waking life. Are you managing to fit everything in? If a **chair is placed upon a table** in your dream, this can suggest a new relationship with someone of the opposite sex.

outburst? As mentioned above, light is the symbol of life, knowledge and enlightenment and in dreams, **casting a bright light** may present an optimistic image of your well-being, but if it is **flickering**, this suggests uncertainty. A **light that is unlit** may be a symbol of ignorance. If you use a **flashlight or torch** in your dream, this suggests you are trying to seek out truth and integrity in a corrupt situation.

Money/Handbag/Jewelry/Purse/Wallet

Money, cash or coins in dreams are often thought to be a sign of emotional transactions. If you **give money away**, this suggests a generosity of spirit or it might reflect emotional ties that are expected of you at present. **Receiving money** can suggest the acceptance of emotional support or the emotional needs of the dreamer. **Borrowing money** can be a warning to hold back as far as financial plans are concerned and to explore all aspects of the deal before going ahead. **Making a payment, signing a check or using a credit card** are thought to be positive signs that things are going to plan. The notion of **saving and investing** in dreams may refer to the need to prepare yourself emotionally for situations and relationships that need your attention.

A **wallet, purse or pocketbook containing personal items** may relate to your private world, the kind of person you are and your interests. If you dream of an **expensive designer purse or bag**, you may feel a need to have a more glamorous image. A **worn purse** may symbolize feelings of being worn out and shabby. Do you need to brighten up your identity so that you look and feel brighter? Your dream wallet may symbolize your private thoughts and desires, hidden from public view. Is your wallet full or empty? Are you worried that someone has got too close to you or on the contrary are you seeking greater intimacy? A **bag** in your dream may symbolically carry your hopes for the future. A **heavy bag** suggests more projects than you can handle, whilst an **empty bag** – far from meaning that you have no hope – suggests that you wish to search for new ideas. Frequently associated with fruit, a **basket** may evoke images of fertility and sexuality. Depending on what's in the basket, it can suggest youthful energy or ripe maturity.

Finally, items of **jewelry** are symbols of wishes and wish-fulfillment. If you are **given a gift of jewelry** in your dream, you may be experiencing a sense of recognition in waking life. **Viewing a rare jewel** from a distance may be a sign that you have failed to understand the importance or meaning of an event or relationship. **Losing a jewel** may reflect fears of personal or financial loss in waking life. *See also* CRYSTALS, GEMSTONES AND ROCKS; MONEY AND SHOPPING.

Soap

Soap is a mundane symbol of cleanliness, most obviously symbolizing feelings of guilt that you want to wash away. It could also simply reflect a need to create more order in your life. If you were threatened in childhood with having your **mouth washed out with soap** when you spoke out of turn, to dream of the same may be warning you about casual obscenity.

The Element Encyclopedia of 20,000 Dreams

Tool

Dreams in which machinery or tools feature, or in which we are using an implement, can relate to you in a number of ways. For example, you may be the **bulldozer** in your dream, clearing away everything before you. A **plow or dredger** may be referring to a problem you have in waking life. If an **engine is not starting** in your dream, could this be referring to a project that is having troubles getting started? A **wheelbarrow** represents progress and the clearing of unwanted material, but it is a vehicle that cannot move unless you push it, hence its association with energy and action. If the **barrow is filled with household objects**, it may suggest a break from the past.

A **crutch** in your dream may refer to your partner's support. A **needle** that is impossible to thread refers to a tricky situation. A **pin** may be a problem you are trying to pin down or understand. If the **pin falls out of its cushion**, this suggests confusion. A dream of **pins and needles together** may relate to a sense of nervous anticipation in waking life. A **hairpin** may be a highly charged dream image of female sexuality, owing to its arched shape and the classic seductive symbol of taking out a hairpin to release the hair. Dreams about **razors** could suggest that you should get rid of some unattractive characteristic in waking life.

Nails in dreams may be symbols of persecution, punishment and suffering, due to their association with the Crucifixion. **Nuts and bolts** draw your attention to the practicality of a project. A **hammer driving in a nail** may be seen as a symbol of willpower, the forceful energy that directs the dreamer's judgment. According to Freudians, dreams that feature tools are more often than not linked to masculinity and male characteristics. The phallic nature of their shape is used as justification for this explanation. For example, **a drill, hammer, nail or needle** can all be seen as phallic symbols; in particular, a **needle being threaded** can be seen as representing the loss of virginity.

Jungians regard tools as implements that dig and hide and so they could be tied to elements hidden away in the unconscious of the dreamer. The action of the tool and what you are doing with the tool may provide a clue to its meaning. For example, a dream **spade** may suggest that something is emotionally hidden and the dream may be urging you to reopen this chapter or leave whatever is buried. A **lever** is used to enhance strength. If the dream tool was a **plow**, the dreamer may be in the process of turning over their problems and seeing them from a new angle. **Corkscrews** may represent the uncorking of a new idea or plan. If the corkscrew was difficult to use, then the new project may encounter problems. If, however, it was easy to use this suggests that the new project will be successful. If you were using a **screw**, this could be referring to some creative work or a project you are planning, and your desire to give your work added security and stability. If everything fitted and went smoothly in your dream, you are making progress in real life and your dream is reassuring you.

Everyday Situations

BROKEN GLASS

Dreams of **walking on broken glass, seeing or being surrounded by shards of glass** or, even worse (and far from everyday), **having to eat broken glass** may represent cutting words or wounding experiences. The vivid image in the dream is designed to draw your attention to a pain that you may have been denying in waking life. It can also refer to something clear and pure that has been broken, suggesting the shattering of expectations. Typically, such dreams are linked to personal, rather than career, conflicts. If you have such a dream, has something in your waking life changed dramatically and has that change caused you pain? If you are **eating the glass**, this suggests that you are taking in the painful experience, but it may be asked whether you are trying to swallow rather than acknowledge your pain. If you are **walking on glass**, consider how your direction in life is causing you pain.

BURGLARY

You may dream that a **burglar is trying to get into your house**; eventually he gets in and you frantically try to hide or call for help. But all to no avail. If you have this dream, it suggests that something surprising has entered your life and is creating tension. The house symbolizes you and the intruder is someone who has crossed the line into your territory, shaking things up.

Career changes or new relationships may trigger this dream, as it is drawing your attention to potential drawbacks in a situation that you may not yet be ready to acknowledge.

CAR PARK

Dream **car parks** are often difficult to navigate and all too often cars will go missing. Such dreams tend to occur when you are making an important decision in your waking life concerning your career and life path. Getting **lost in the car park** suggests confusion and if your **car goes missing**, you may feel that you have lost your identity in the struggle to succeed and meet expectations. The car park itself could be seen as the illusion of the good life. You can make all the right moves to get ahead but in the process you may find that something important is missing.

CHEWING GUM

In this dream you may find yourself **endlessly chewing gum and unable to spit it out. When you try to get rid of the gum, it simply gets bigger in your mouth, and if you try to spit it out you may find that you spit out parts of your mouth**. This dream indicates frustration and overload. Objects you put in your mouth represent things you are trying to assimilate and indigestible items suggest experiences that are both hard to stomach in waking life and contain little nourishment. The gum represents an activity that takes up a lot of your time and energy but provides little satisfaction. The desire to spit it out suggests your desire to be rid of it but you are unable to do so because of

The Element Encyclopedia of **20,000** *Dreams*

commitments or obligations in waking life. If you have this dream, you may have bitten off more than you can chew and the dream's message is that you should find ways to ease your burden, such as asking for help, delegating tasks or saying no more.

COMPUTER AND PERIPHERALS

Computers are symbols of the brain and your thinking processes, therefore **computer malfunctions or problems** suggest errors in thinking, faulty logic or distortions in the way you are approaching a current issue. Pay attention to your response in this dream, as it may provide a clue to how you can tackle real-life problems that are frustrating you. The **hard drive** of your computer may be associated with the functional, driven part of your personality, the **screen** with the image you have of yourself and the world, the **printer** with the manifestation of your plans and the **software** as your creativity. **Blank sheets of paper** in your dream may be a symbol of either hope or despair; the opportunity to create or the sense that you have no fresh ideas. **Paper that is crumbled up or torn** can suggest the rejection of outdated ideas.

CONDOM

As a symbol of protection, **condoms** in dreams symbolize both physical and psychological protection from vulnerability in intimate relationships. If a condom features in your dream, it might help to see it not only as a reminder that you are using appropriate contraception, but also as a warning to check you are dealing with loved ones in a caring and respectful way. *See also* SEX AND EROTICA.

FACTORY/OFFICE/PROCESSING PLANT

To dream of these types of building, filled with people slaving away on computers, production lines or machines, might be a reflection of the obsessive worker part of your personality and any anxieties that you may feel about being a workaholic. The conditions in the **factory, office or plant** will symbolize the health of your creative drive. If the conditions are hideous like those in a sweatshop, are you working in a highly paid job that discourages your spirit? If the factory is high-tech or manic, consider how it reflects your love of the work you do. *See also* SCHOOL AND WORK.

HOSPITAL

If a **hospital** features in your dream, your unconscious may be sending you a message about some part of your life that deserves care, attention or is even in need of healing. The elements in the hospital that support or dismiss your needs reflect things in your life that are affecting your well-being. If the **nurses, doctors and receptionists are rude and dismissive**, this may represent your own refusal to acknowledge your needs. **Operations and procedures that fail** can suggest attempts to solve problems with quick fixes. If you can think about what would improve your situation in your dream, this may give you some indication of a possible way forward. *See also* HEALTH AND SICKNESS.

The ten most common dreams

Anthropologists, psychologists and dream analysts often find similar themes in dreams that appear to transcend all generations and cultures. Whilst not all experts agree on the same list and frequency, the list below is representative of what are generally accepted as common dream themes. You'll notice that both fantasy and contemporary scenarios appear in the list, and when it comes to interpretation, both the surreal and the everyday can be rich sources of symbolism.

1. Being chased or attacked

Many people dream of being pursued or attacked, although who or what is attacking or doing the pursuing varies from place to place. These dreams are a natural response to life stress; it could be that events are catching up with you or perhaps you trying to run away from something.

2. Being lost or trapped

In these very common dreams, you're lost and feeling desperate. You may be buried alive or locked in a cage. You dream of not being able to move; you're powerless to scream or breathe. Or you may feel desperate for the toilet and unable to find one. These dreams may occur when you feel confusion or conflict about how to act in waking life.

3. Being injured, ill or dying

Such dreams may involve deaths of famous people, your parents or children, a lover and even yourself. When you dream about an accidental death of any person, that person's death symbolizes something in you that is no longer functioning. It can also suggest new beginnings; out with the old and in with the new. Another common scenario under this theme is of teeth falling out or crumbling. This might have a physical origin in people gritting or grinding teeth during sleep. Freud suggested that dreams of teeth falling out are related to fears of castration, but women have this dream as often as men. Other psychologists believe the dream reflects anxiety about your appearance and how others perceive you.

4. Car or other vehicle trouble

An out-of-control vehicle is a fairly common nightmare among all people and ages, whether or not the dreamers actually drive. Such a dream may occur when the dreamer feels events in waking life are out of control.

5. House or property, loss or damage

In these dreams, your house is damaged or destroyed by fire, water or other causes. These dreams may surface because you feel that some valuable aspect of waking life is at risk. Dreams about losing a wallet, watch or cherished piece of jewelry, such as a wedding ring, also fall into this category. Meanings vary depending on what is lost or damaged. The flip side of this is that dreams about discovering new spaces or rooms in your home, or dreams about repairs or improvements are also common. These dreams may occur when you feel that some valuable aspect of waking life is improving.

6. Poor test or other poor performance

You've probably dreamed of arriving for a test and found the exam has already started. Or you search fruitlessly for the examination room. This is a common dream that can occur years after school or college; it usually occurs when you feel you are somehow being 'tested' in waking life. Some psychologists think the dreams can denote anxiety about sexual performance.

7. Falling or flying?

Falling is one of the most common dreams among people of all ages, and may be a reflection of feeling insecure, helpless or of having no support or solid grounding. Some people may actually fall from their beds during this dream. Dreaming about drowning is less common, and often occurs when a person feels overwhelmed. Dreams about flying, swimming or dancing are the flip side of falling or drowning dreams. Such optimistic dreams inspire, as the dreamer is lifted to spiritual heights or is filled with creative notions. Pleasurable swimming may mean freely

exploring your depths; dreams of dance may be a metaphor for moving freely through your life.

8. Being naked in public or inappropriately dressed.

This is a common dream scenario that occurs at all ages, even with children. The dreams involve feelings of exposure and vulnerability, and often include an element of embarrassment or shame. On the other hand, dreams of wearing a special outfit may suggest you feel good about your body or your life.

9. Missing the train or connection

You rush to catch a departing bus, train, airplane or ship, only to find it has left without you. These dreams reflect feelings that you are missing out on something in waking life. Machine or telephone malfunction dreams are another variation on this theme, often occurring when you feel anxious about making an emotional connection or when you feel you're losing touch with someone.

10. Natural or man-made disasters

You're confronted with overwhelming floods, tidal waves, earthquakes, volcanic eruptions, tornadoes, hurricanes, bombings or chemical warfare. These dreams may depict personal problems raging out of control. Dreams of vibrant flowers, verdant hillsides or uplifting music that leaves the dreamer feeling inspired are the flip side of disaster dreams.

LEFT AND RIGHT

You may have a dream in which **left and right** become significant. If this is the case, bear in mind that if you are right-handed, the right hemisphere of the brain is thought to control the left side of the body and this part of the brain is instinctive, artistic and intuitive. The **left side of the body** therefore indicates these qualities and in dreams represents the parts of yourself that are less expressed, such as the unconscious. In right-handed people, the left hemisphere of the brain is thought to control the right side of the body, and this part of the brain is believed to be logical and functional. The **right side of the body** therefore represents the dominant, conscious and well-expressed side of yourself. Dreams can also use a play on what is right or left to suggest opposites or conflicts within yourself. The left usually suggests the external world of activity and the environment, whilst the right parts of your unconscious suggest struggling to express yourself. A few people might also find that in some dreams one side of their body represent the feelings and attitudes they absorbed from their mother, and the other side what they absorbed from their father.

PHONE WON'T WORK

In this kind of dream you are in a situation in which you urgently need to call for help but, maddeningly, the **phone won't work**. Either the line is dead, the buttons don't work or you get through to the wrong person or end up with an operator who cuts you off. You try to explain your situation but no one is willing to help. During these

types of dream, tension levels are high. **Phones and mobile phones** in dreams represent your ability to communicate and dreams about phone trouble typically occur when things are reaching crisis point in waking life. You may be finding it hard to get your message across and to get the help you need. If the **operator puts you on hold or ignores you**, it is more likely that you have been ignoring your own needs for rest, outside help or relaxation. The message this dream is trying to convey to you is that it is time to pay closer attention to something that you may have been putting off; this may involve asking for qualified help and support. Phone dreams are usually signals to be honest with yourself and listen to your intuition. A variation of this dream is the **email error on your computer screen**, indicating an inability to communicate with someone important in your life. Freudians might see phallic symbolism if you are using a **mobile phone**, suggesting that once again sex is the root of the problem. *See also* MEDIA AND TECHNOLOGY.

SHOPPING CENTER/MALL

Shopping centers or malls are associated with making choices and in many dreams they serve as the backdrop for meeting friends, or trying to find the right item for yourself or someone else. Typically, these dreams feature friends and sales people; this suggests that such dreams aren't associated with work but are about your social life. If you **encounter obstacles or get assistance on your dream shopping trip**, these may symbolize real-life forces, both internal and external, that play a role in the choices you make in waking life and the

The Element Encyclopedia of 20,000 Dreams

satisfaction you experience. Women and teenagers tend to have this kind of dream more often than men or children, and the theme for these dreams tends to be choice and identity, and the ability to stay true to yourself whilst also satisfying the needs of others. *See also* MONEY AND SHOPPING.

TOXIN

Toxic substances, such as **cigarette smoke, controlled drugs and alcohol** and other environmental toxins that can make you ill and pollute the environment often represent emotional toxins that render situations poisonous to you. If you do not smoke in everyday life and find yourself **lighting up in your dream and enjoying it,** this suggests an addictive pattern in real life that may be related to unhealthy eating patterns or even relationships. In some cases, the image can represent unhealthy thinking patterns, such as anger, jealousy or obstinacy. Knowing that your unconscious has sent you this warning should be enough encouragement to take a look at what is trying to control you and reduce the risks involved. A desire for sex may be expressed in the dream imagery of a **cigarette placed between the lips and cupped in the hands when being lit,** whilst a **stubbed-out cigarette** may signal the end of a love affair. **Lighting a match** could express the dreamer's desire for enlightenment and spiritual love, **matches that refuse to light** express spiritual doubt and **dead matches** symbolize loss of faith. A **cigar**'s oral and masculine associations have been related to latent male homosexuality, although the cigar-smoking Freud discouraged overdoing this sexual symbolism with his famous comment, 'sometimes a cigar is just a cigar'.

WISH-FULLFILLMENT

We all have aspirations and desires, and we may learn to stifle and even forget them because they seem impossible. Our dreaming mind, however, does not forget. The most typical dreams that are **wish-fulfillment** are ones that reflect our hopes in an obvious way. For example, if you are feeling tired and run down you may dream of **being on a beach in Hawaii.** If you are attracted to someone in real life, you may dream about **making love to them.** If you are apprehensive about retiring or getting older, you may dream of **being a teenager or baby again.** If you are having financial troubles, you may dream of being **surrounded by piles of cash or winning the lottery.** If you long to get married, you may dream of your **wedding day or honeymoon.** If your fantasy is sexual variety, you may dream about **visiting a prostitute or gigolo.** If you have your sights set on a promotion, you may dream of **being the boss.** If you long to make your mark on the world, you may dream of **becoming prime minister.** If you want to be famous, you may dream of yourself **on the red carpet, writing a best-seller or singing before an audience of thousands of screaming fans.** If you dream of **buying something you want or need in waking life,** this is simple wish-fulfillment but the dream is reminding you that satisfying your desires may cost you. If you were **buying food** in your dream, you may be trying to buy someone's affection in waking life.

FAMILY

Family relationships have been studied and written about for centuries, from the brothers Cain and Abel, through Joseph the favored son, to evil stepmothers in fairy stories and Mrs Robinson in *The Graduate*.

Whilst whole schools of family therapy have been developed to help address the issues that emerge within a family context, it is worthwhile looking at one theory of a child's development into an adult as it sheds much light on dreams about the family. This is Jung's theory of the process of 'individuation', one of his most interesting and important theories. In short, individuation refers to the processes involved in becoming a self-aware and independent human being. The area of being to which we refer when we say 'I' or 'me' is our sense of self, which Jung calls the ego. A vital part of the process of individuation is to meet and integrate, or become independent of, your childhood patterns. This includes desire for the love of the parent of the opposite sex, rivalry mingled with dependence with the parent of the same sex, and the move away from total dependence on both parents.

An absence of a father's or mother's love can be especially traumatic, as parents are the soil out of which your sense of self must emerge. And even if your parents are no longer alive or you never had a relationship with them, their impact on your psyche can be just as profound. Without a doubt, parents are powerful, emotive figures in dreams but a person's identity cannot gain any real independence while still dominated by these internal forces. Psychologically, this struggle for individuality should take place within the safety of the family unit. Unfortunately this does not always happen and in dreams, images of family members may be manipulated so that issues and conflicts that have been unresolved during Jung's process of individuation can be worked out.

Family dreams are so common because most of the conflicts and problems in your waking life are experienced first within a psychological environment laid down by your family. It is as if a pattern has been imprinted that will continue to appear until it is broken willingly. The way you were brought up has such a profound effect on your psychological health that any dream you have of family members will probably have a unique and highly specific meaning to you, depending on what your family means to you, your own experience of family life and other related attitudes. Because there is such variety here, you will need first to define your present relationship and feelings about the member of your family that features in the dream.

Individual family members can represent the various archetypes in your dreams. For example, the father can represent the masculine principle of authority and discipline, whilst the mother represents the feminine principle of nurturing and protection. In many instances, dreams featuring your family members can be reassuring. They may give you confidence and guidance, as well as a feeling that you are supported and loved. On the other hand, they may also highlight current or long-term problems within your family or personal relationships. Because they can replicate values, attitudes and emotional or social responses towards living that you have absorbed from your family, all future relationships outside the family are influenced in some way by the ones you first develop within your family. In times of stress, therefore, your dreams might use scenarios involving family members to try and put things right or reveal and confirm the conflict.

Bear in mind that each dream about a family member must be considered in context, and what the idea of a family means to you may not mean the same to another person. For example, Western concepts such as individuation, sibling rivalry or Freud's Oedipus complex would make no sense in those cultures where an uncle or grandparent is considered no less significant than mothers or fathers. *See also* RELATIONSHIPS.

Family Scenarios

CONFLICT

If you dream of an **argument or rivalry with one of your parents**, it suggests that you may be questioning yourself in some way. When a child is born it moves from self-involvement to an exclusive relationship with the mother and father; later on the child has a need for a third relationship with another person outside the family, and often this third relationship can cause the child to question their own validity as a person. Dream images of conflicts with parents therefore suggest that this issue still needs to be resolved so that successful relationships can be established outside the home. If you dream of **someone you know outside the family arguing or in conflict with a member of your family**, this may suggest that you have not yet learned to establish what your needs are. Learning to love outside the family is a sign of independence and maturity. The figure of a **family member disrupting or preventing intimacy with a friend or loved one** in your dream suggests that family loyalties are getting in the way of your development and fulfillment in everyday life.

CONFUSION

Dreams in which **body parts of family members are confused** – for example your sister's head on your father's body – suggest that you may be having problems deciding which family member is the most important for you. Dreams in which a **family member doesn't arrive when expected or appears unexpectedly** suggest that the relationship between you and that family member needs to be better understood so that trust can develop. Dreams in which **family members are injured, distorted or suffering in some way** may reflect your fear or anxiety for that person. Dreams of an **incestuous relationship with a family member** suggest that the dreamer has become over involved with that person; the dream has appeared to warn that if this over involvement continues, the consequences will be damaging to your development.

The personality of family members in your dreams may also be transformed. For example, parents who have been difficult in waking life may appear tolerant and loving in your dream. This may be an attempt by your dreaming mind to counter the negative consequences of their cold attitude towards you when you were a child. A **negative dream of a partner** when all seems well in waking life may be a warning that there is an underlying problem in your relationship with them. Examine the context of your partner's misbehavior in the dream as your unconscious may have noticed a flaw in your relationship that you are unable or unwilling to recognize in waking life. Remember, however, that the dream may relate to another negative area of your life; your partner may represent someone or something else important to you in your dream. *See also* Divorce dreams entry in RELATIONSHIPS.

DEATH OF A FAMILY MEMBER OR PARTNER

A close family member has died and the remaining family are attending the funeral. Everyone, including you, is crying. Such dreams can be very unnerving because you may worry that something is going to happen to a family member but, contrary to your fears, dreams of death are often a reflection of change, rather than death. Changes that bring some era to a close or cause shifts in family roles, such as going to college, getting married or starting a family, are likely to trigger death dreams. Think of these dreams as a rite of passage. Your relationship with the person in your dream has not died but it will be different, because something is different in your life. Another explanation of the dream death of a family member or spouse, is to consider what aspect of yourself that person represents and what you may be rejecting or repressing.

For example, to dream of your **mother dying** could represent the death of your own motherly nature. Perhaps you should try to be more caring and maternal, or perhaps something or someone should be nurtured instead of ignored. Alternatively, you may be expressing hidden feelings for that person. Do you secretly resent or wish to be independent of him or her? Such dreams may also represent a positive or negative change in your relationship or attitude toward that particular person. Yet another interpretation suggests that dreams of being **prostrate with grief at your father's or mother's funeral** can be an emotional dress rehearsal staged by your unconscious to prepare you for the devastation you may feel when your parent

The Element Encyclopedia of 20,000 Dreams

really does die. Such dreams tend to be more common in women, especially concerning the death of a partner, as statistically women live longer than men.

Dreaming of a **relative or partner who is dead in waking life** is, not surprisingly, quite common. After all, that person may have played a big part in your life, and their influence and memories are still very much alive in you. It is not unusual to have disturbing dreams for some period after the death of a loved one; it is equally common not to be able to dream about the husband or wife at all, or to see the partner in the distance but be unable to get any nearer. Such dreams of dead people are expressive of attempts by your dreaming mind to help you make the transition from external reality to internal memories, or to deal with feelings, guilt or anger in connection with the person who died. *See also* SPIRITS AND GHOSTS.

ORPHANED/ADOPTED/ FOSTERED

If you dream of being an **orphaned, adopted or fostered child**, this usually suggests that your relationships with members of your family in waking life have created some sense of loss and rejection in you. Dreaming of having **lost your parents or being rejected by your parents so you become an orphan, adopted or fostered child** may denote that you feel you didn't get their unconditional love and attention, and that you have to find your own way in the world without their support. Alternatively you may feel as if you are an outsider in the relationship to your family. Perhaps you have been excluded or perhaps you have little in common with them. Do

you consider yourself rejected or at odds with the rest of your family? Whatever the reason, your dream may be suggesting to you that you need to create a surrogate family to get the support you need; this may be with your friends or your partner, and they will be able to help you feel loved, secure and accepted for who you are.

Another explanation of such dreams is that it is time for you to be more independent and self-reliant by moving away from your parents. When life forces you into permanently or temporarily losing your parents, either by death or by other circumstances such as foreign travel, you may experience dreams of being orphaned. The dream might not refer to your relationship with your family at all, but might be telling you that you are feeling abandoned, unloved, rejected and misunderstood by your partner, friends or colleagues in waking life. If this is the case, the dream connects to feelings of belonging or not belonging in waking life. If you are **looking after an orphan** in your dream, you are attempting to heal that part of you that feels unloved.

PARENTS

During the early years of your waking life it is likely that you were physically and emotionally dependent on one or both of your **parents** or, if either or both were absent, on an alternative mother or father figure. As you emerged into adolescence and adulthood, the chances are you became less reliant on them, yet memories of that early dependency usually remain with you on a conscious or unconscious level. Because your parents had such a great influence over you at a time when your personality was developing and you began to assert your individuality and independence, your feelings towards them will remain intense.

Dreams that feature your parents can have numerous interpretations but the key to understanding them depends on the feelings you associate with your parents, particularly those when you where a child and your parents were the center of your universe. When your dream parents are true to character, the message of your dream is usually easy to understand. For example, if your **parents appeared in your dream with words of encouragement and love** and they were, or are, this warm and loving in real life, then your dream may simply indicate that you are feeling insecure and in need of validation or unconditional love. Perhaps you dreamt that your **parents scolded you about your recent poor performance at work** and you have memories of them chiding you harshly over poor grades at school? If this is the case, it may be that your dream is highlighting your dissatisfaction at not living up to the standards your parents instilled in you.

If your **parents appear together** in your dream, this indicates the rules and codes you learned as a child that still speak to you from within. If you are **hurting, killing, burying or trying to avoid a parent** in your dream, this suggests a desire to be free from restraints and values gathered from your parents. You may feel shocked by such a dream, but it is in fact a healthy sign of emerging independence as when your dream parents die or are beaten, you can inherit the power gained from what was good in your relationship.

Dreams in which your **parents appear foolish, drunk or disorderly** have a similar interpretation; they are a means of gaining independence from internalized values. Dreams in which your **parents are crushing you** are fairly easy to interpret, suggesting that you need to break away from childhood behavior patterns and develop as an individual. Dreams in which **parents die or are dead already** can be interpreted the same way. When a **parent appears in your environment, home or workplace** in your dream and there is no sense of tension, this indicates that you have learned to develop your sense of self and can accept your parents as friends.

Frequent appearances by one or both parents in dreams may be a sign that you have not thrown off an infantile overdependence on them. Jung cites a young man's dream in which the man's **father appeared as a drunken driver**, smashing his car into a wall. This was the exact opposite of the man's real father, who was a most respectable person, and who was rightly – but far too greatly – respected by the son. What the unconscious was doing through the dream was dethroning the father in order to enable the son to achieve a proper sense of himself as a person in his own right, with his own unique destiny and values. So if your **dreams regularly feature your parents,** this may suggest that you are more dependent on them than is healthy at this stage in your life. Dreams in which your **parents hurl abuse at you or behave inappropriately** may therefore be trying to shock you into taking your mother or father off their pedestal so you can give yourself some much-needed emotional independence and freedom.

Whether or not your parent's behavior in real life mirrors their behavior in its dreamland negative, **reoccurring dreams**

The Element Encyclopedia of 20,000 Dreams

about parents often raise the question of whether it is time for you to become more independent and strike out on your own, regardless of what your parents may think is best for you in waking life. If you **behaved inappropriately towards your parents** in your dream, for example swearing at them, listing their faults or even murdering them, such a dream is likely to be a safety valve that enables you to let off tension that you may have been repressing in waking life. It is also likely to be an indication that you need to break free of parental control and take charge of your destiny. Finally, if an interpretation of the appearance of your mother and father still eludes you, it may be that your anima (if you are a man who dreamed of your mother) and your animus (if you are a woman who dreamed of your father) may be making an appearance; alternatively, it may be that another archetype has disguised itself as one of your parents.

SIBLING RIVALRY

The appearance of **siblings** in your dream may be a direct representation of them or it may actually stand for something else in your life. Some dream analysts believe that all dream characters represent aspects of yourself. So when interpreting dreams that feature images of your siblings, try to bear in mind these different layers of potential meaning. A dream in which your **brother or sister is seen in a negative light** may denote unresolved childhood feelings towards that sibling in waking life. According to Jung, dreams of a sibling often recall childhood competition for our parent's love and the dream **death of a sibling** may show how intense this rivalry

is. However, as even Freud suggested, this rivalry may be just a memory and may not relate to your waking relationship with your brother or sister. Dreams in which you are **arguing or fighting with your sibling** suggest feelings of doubt and insecurity, perhaps as to whether you were loved enough within your family.

Bear in mind that in dreams, siblings can also represent the shadow. This is because it is easier to project the negative or hidden side of our personality onto another member of the family than it is onto a non-relative, and siblings tend to be the closest to you in age and experience. Your dreams may be an attempt by your unconscious to resolve this projection before it creates problems in waking life. When dreams of the **opposite sex sibling** occur, this may also be an expression of your anima or animus archetype. It could represent the tension – or union – of opposites in some way; your dreaming mind may be trying to create harmony and balance in your life by pointing to some aspect of yourself. For example, if your dream **sister was incredibly rude**, the dream may be highlighting your own feelings of guilt about being rude to some one. Alternatively, such a dream may be urging you to be more assertive in waking life. The same would apply if you dream of **siblings or step-siblings but don't have any brother or sisters** in waking life, or if your **sibling behaves completely out of character** in the dream. If your **dream casts someone you know as your brother or sister**, this may be because you have brotherly or sisterly feelings for them, with all the associations of rivalry and platonic love that such a relationship implies.

SUFFOCATION/SEPARATION

Dreams of **suffocation or being crushed** often relate to your feelings concerning separation and attachment in waking life, and as such, point to experiences of childhood and family. Such dreams often occur at times of change, such as leaving home for the first time, getting married or at times of illness and death. Dreams of suffocation can also tell of fears of being overwhelmed, dominated or drowned by a powerful figure, who is likely to be a family figure. Two influential psychoanalysts – John Bowlby and Donald Winnicott – have written extensively about the concept of separation and attachment. They suggested that a large proportion of anxieties and mental health problems are associated with separation between infant and mother in childhood. Their suggestion is that separation is not only distressing for a baby but can also cause anxieties in later life. They proposed that premature separation can lead to insecurity, which can lead to hostility, and that this hostility can interfere with the processes determining subsequent growth and development. All of this is said to trigger mourning at an age when a child is too young to manage such feelings, meaning that a child may be stuck in a state of despair or depression. Dreams of **suffocation, separation, loss and abandonment** may therefore be informative as they can tell the dreamer of an unresolved separation in their family. This is when feelings of mourning or hostility towards the parent or other family figure have not yet been explored or dealt with.

Separation anxiety occurs when we have to confront the prospect of being separated from someone who is considered essential to our physical or emotional survival. Typically, separation anxiety occurs in relation to family members or partners, as these are the people with whom we normally have the closest relationships; the anxiety may often be reflected in nightmares and disturbing dreams. Although normal in childhood – when a child is absolutely dependent upon the parent to provide for its needs – separation anxiety in adulthood, when the presence of another person is used in defense against some other form of anxiety, is considered detrimental to a person's emotional development. **Dreams of suffocation or nightmare scenarios involving the separation, death or loss of a family member or spouse** are often triggered by separation anxiety and in many instances they can offer clues to help manage and resolve these feelings in waking life. *See also* NIGHTMARES.

TRANSFORMATION

A man's first close relationship with a woman is with his mother, so a dream in which his **mother transforms into another woman** can be symbolic of a kind of growth, as it shows that he can let his mother go. Depending on the circumstances of the dream, this transition indicates some kind of positive or negative change in his perception of women. By the same token, a woman's first relationship with a man is typically with her father or brother and to progress onto fuller relationships she must learn to walk away from those relationships. Therefore if she dreams that her **father transforms into another man**, this indicates some kind of positive or negative change in her perception of men,

The Element Encyclopedia of 20,000 Dreams

Jung's first dream

Jung himself apparently went through a difficult separation from his mother in early childhood that had repercussions for his social health later in life. Jung's mother was said to have experienced a depressive illness at this time, which resulted in a separation of several months from Jung when he was three years old. In her absence, Jung was cared for by his aunt but he was troubled by the separation and his anxiety is reflected in the lack of maternal protectiveness in a dream he recalled from this period and published in his autobiographical *Memories, Dreams, Reflections*. As well as his relationship to his mother, this dream – which occurred when Jung was just three or four years old – reveals much about his family, culture and life, as well as about his relationship with his mother and father.

'In the dream I was in this meadow. Suddenly I discovered a dark, rectangular, stone-lined hole in the ground. I had never seen it before. I ran forward curiously and peered down into it. Then I saw a stone stairway leading down. Hesitantly and fearfully, I descended. At the bottom was a doorway with a round arch, closed off by a green curtain. It was a big, heavy curtain of worked stuff like brocade, and it looked very sumptuous. Curious to see what might be hidden behind, I pushed it aside. I saw before me in the dim light a rectangular chamber about thirty feet long. The ceiling was arched and of hewn stone. The floor was laid with flagstones, and in the center a red carpet ran from the entrance to a low platform. On this platform stood a wonderfully rich golden throne. I am not certain, but perhaps a red cushion lay on the seat. It was a magnificent throne, a real king's throne in a fairy tale. Something was standing on it which I thought at first was a tree trunk twelve to fifteen feet high and about one and a half to two feet thick. It was a huge thing, reaching almost to the ceiling. But it was of a curious composition: it was made of skin and naked flesh, and on top there was something like a rounded head with no face and no hair. On the very top of the head was a single eye, gazing motionlessly upward.

It was fairly light in the room, although there were no windows and no apparent source of light. Above the head, however, was an aura of brightness. The thing did not move, yet I had the feeling that it might at any moment crawl off the throne like a worm and creep toward me. I was paralyzed with terror. At that moment I heard from outside and above me my mother's voice. She called out, "Yes, just look at him. That is the man-eater!" That intensified my terror still more, and I awoke sweating and scared to death …'

Later in his life Jung wrote the following about his reaction to this childhood dream. 'From then on I always felt mistrustful when the word "love" was spoken. The feeling I associated with "woman" was for a long time of innate unreliability. Father on the other hand meant reliability and powerlessness.'

although much depends on the circumstances of the dream and the woman's feelings about it.

Dreams in which **parents, family members or partners behave completely out of character** – for example, **your gentle mother transforms into a cruel tyrant or your teetotal father transforms into a raging alcoholic** – can be extremely unsettling, as they turn what you regard as accepted truths on their heads. Such dreams have little to do with real-life family members or loved ones; far more are they to do with unresolved aspects of either your life or yourself that you need to confront and work on in order to find fulfillment. In such cases, your unconscious mind may have conjured up parental or family archetypes to bring neglected issues to your attention or to warn you of an authority figure who presents a threat to you in waking life. For example, perhaps the **controlling father** in your dream represents your boss who is stifling your individuality, or your **nurturing dream mother** is telling you to mother yourself or someone close to you.

Individual Family Members

ANCESTORS/EXTENDED FAMILY

Dreams that feature your **ancestors** in some way indicate the web of cultural and family influences from which your personality has arisen. If a **particular ancestor** is highlighted, then you need to explore your personal associations with that person. For example, your great-aunt could have been renowned for her psychic abilities, so a dream about her might represent that intuitive tendency in you. **Family scenes** in your dream may represent feelings of security and unity, or a desire for this in your waking life. The appearance of your **whole family together** in a dream can indicate that you are yearning for the security and togetherness of childhood and home. On the other hand, if you dream that you **see your family but are not present among them or are ignored by them**, perhaps you feel emotionally distant from them at present. The appearance or mention of your **family name** in dreamland calls attention to your heritage or family situation. If **family planning** is a feature of your dream, this suggests the need to take responsibility for your future. A **family room** suggests congeniality. Members of the **extended family** (such as **cousins, aunts, uncles, nieces and nephews**) usually appear in a dream as an aspect of yourself relevant to the person you dreamed about. For example, if your cousin is shy in waking life, his appearance in a dream may refer to the inhibited part of yourself.

To dream of a **family tree** may indicate your true spiritual heritage, providing you with a record of your origins and your place in the overall scheme of things; alternatively, if you believe in reincarnation, particularly genetic reincarnation, it may represent your own past lives. If you are finding it difficult to analyze the meaning of your dream, it may be that your unconscious has cast a feminine or masculine archetype in the role of the relation. To determine if this is the case, ask yourself if your dream uncle has more in common

The Element Encyclopedia of 20,000 Dreams

with the archetypal wise old man than your father's brother, or if your dream niece has more in common with the archetypal amazon or huntress.

Aunt/Uncle

For Jungians, an **aunt** may represent the anima (feminine aspect) of a male dreamer and the **uncle** the animus (masculine aspect) of a female dreamer. Uncles and aunts in dreams can also be symbols of your unconscious feelings towards your mother or father. The most general characteristic of dreams that feature your aunt is that they depict an aspect of yourself. For many people an aunt is a role model, so if she figures in your dream, she is commenting on the success or failure of certain strategies you may be using in your waking life. An uncle may also be a role model and, however you feel about him in waking life, your dream may use him to make a comment on the success or failure of strategies you may be using in waking life. For example, if you think of your uncle as a failure or a success, ask yourself what it is in yourself that you consider to be a failure or a success.

Brother/Sister

In dreams, **brothers** tend to depict an aspect of yourself rather than the brother himself. They can also represent the characteristics you like or dislike about your own siblings and the dream may be telling you something about those particular characteristics in yourself. An **older brother** can represent experience and authority, whilst **younger brothers** can suggest vulnerability and, in some instances,

immaturity. If a **woman dreams of a younger brother**, it can express either her own or her brother's rivalry or vulnerability, but if she dreams of an **older brother**, it might signify her extrovert self.

The **sister** in dreams usually represents the feeling, expressive side of your personality and you can make contact with that side of yourself by understanding your sister's personality. If a **man dreams of older sisters**, it can represent anxiety but also caring. If the **sister is younger**, however, she can symbolize the vulnerable side of the male dreamer. If a **woman dreams of younger sisters**, it can suggest rivalry, but if she dreams of **older sisters**, she may be concerned about her own practicality.

■ *Idioms: big brother; brother-in-arms; blood brother; sisters under the skin; sister (nun).*

Daughter/Son

The most likely explanation for dreams about your **children** is that you are worried about them in some way or that you need to see certain issues from their point of view. If you dreamed that you were a **parent but you have no children in waking life**, this could be wish-fulfillment or your dream child may have represented a new idea, project or commitment. Alternatively, a dream **son or daughter** may represent one of the many archetypes that are facets of the masculine and feminine principles. Dreams parents may have in which the **relationship with a daughter is highlighted** tend to represent the health of the relationship between the mother and the father, as the child is the result of that relationship. For example, a **sick daughter** in a dream could suggest that the relationship is unhealthy.

Dreaming about your daughter often relates to how you feel about her. Is she an adventurous creative person? If so, then the dream will usually be depicting your pride in her achievements, or your own feelings of creativity and risk-taking. Is she an anxious or introverted person, and are you worried about her? If so, then the dream is either about your own urges to withdraw, or your feelings of concern for her. If you are a **mother dreaming of your daughter**, it could represent the support you get from her or any ties you feel to her through being her parent. It may also be referring to your own feelings and difficulties at her age that might be surfacing at the time of your dream. You might even be feeling her as a competitor because of her youth.

If you are a **father dreaming of your daughter**, it usually represents your feelings and your more feminine or receptive side. So problems in the dream could suggest you are having difficulty allowing your feelings to express themselves in waking life. Your daughter could also depict difficult feelings – more often not self-recrimination – you have about mistakes you have made in your relationship with her mother. When your daughter starts dating, dreaming of her might also point out the struggle you have to let go. Dreams about **someone else's daughter** often indicate the nature of your feelings about your own daughter.

A **son**, like a daughter, is the fruit of your relationship with your partner; as such, in your dreams he can represent the state of your relationship with his father or mother. On the other hand, he can represent the need for the dreamer to express themselves. He can also suggest the youthful, playful part of yourself or your own potential. Dreams about your son may also have no symbolic meaning at all, and are simply about your own son. Are you worried about him? If you are a **mother dreaming of your son**, it can indicate ambition and hope. If you are a **father dreaming of your son**, it can suggest unfulfilled hopes and dreams. Dreams about **someone else's son** can indicate feelings about your own son. If you are **killing your son** in a dream, try not to be shocked; it reflects your anxiety about your son making a move towards independence. Traditionally, it is fortunate to dream about your son. If you dream of **your son getting married**, there will be financial worries (easily explained by the cost of the up-and-coming wedding!).

FATHER

The **father** represents the archetypal symbol of worldly authority and competence. For a **man to dream of a father figure** suggests that he may be searching for a role model, whether negative or positive. According to Freud, dreams that feature **hostility towards the father figure** could be explained by the Oedipus complex. Freud claimed that the ancient Greek myth of Oedipus was a symbolic representation of the psychological development of the male individual. He thought that children between the ages of four and seven went through a phase during which they developed an incestuous desire for the parent of the opposite sex; a young boy would therefore have feelings of resentment towards his father, whom he saw as a rival. Normally the Oedipus complex resolves itself by puberty, but in Freud's view, the failure to achieve freedom from parental influence could result in the Oedipus complex lasting into later years. If it does, it should be fairly apparent from the content of some of your dreams, especially if you are **attacking, insulting or feeling envious towards your father**.

Jung also believed the symbol of the father played a vital psychological role in waking life. He thought that a **man dreaming of hostility towards his father** was a positive sign, as it showed that the unconscious was dethroning the father so as to enable the dreamer to achieve a sense of self and be a person in his own right. A **woman dreaming of a father figure** is often dreaming of the pattern upon which all her future relationships are based; her dreams may encourage her to work out a more appropriate way to have mature relationships. The more difficult the relationship with her father, the harder this may be.

For men, a father may represent the conscience, or in Freudian terms, the super-ego. If this is the case, bear in mind that your father's prohibitions and commands will probably represent either conventional moral options that may lack relevance to your true nature or 'destiny', or irrational fears and feelings of guilt that began to take shape in early childhood. Of course, a dream about your father may simply express your current feelings for him and issues surrounding your relationship with him. The presence of your father may be a straightforward representation of him, or of the way you see or remember him. In any case, the reason for your father appearing in the dream will be shown by the part he plays in the dream story. For example if, in the dream, your **father features as a protector**, it may be that you need to 'grow up' and rely on your own resources.

GRANDPARENT

The appearance of **grandparents** in dreams can highlight your attitude towards them, as well as representing the traditions and beliefs handed down to you by them or your feelings about old age and death. It is often said that parents do not know if they have done a good job raising their children until their children have children of their own. As grandparents are often seen by children to be more sympathetic figures than parents in dreams, they may stand for wisdom, intuition or the desire for an untroubled relationship with your father and mother. Your dream grandparent may have appeared to remind you of the happy times you shared in childhood. Apart from reflecting a yearning for the security of childhood, dreaming of either of your grandparents may suggest that you are in urgent need of their guidance and experience as you face life's dilemmas and pitfalls.

If you don't associate the grandparent with impartial wisdom, ask yourself whether he or she may have been an archetype in disguise, especially the priest or priestess, or wise old woman or wise old man. Whichever archetype seems to fit your grandparent, their advice will help set you on the right path; the very appearance of a **family elder** in a dream indicates that you should look to the past for inspiration and solutions to your current problems. The key may be an ancestral trait you have inherited or an actual event in your family's history that has parallels with your waking situation.

To dream of a **grandparent who has died** will usually be reassuring, telling you that you have inherited some of their wisdom. For Jungians, the grandfather may symbolize the wise old man; he can appear in various forms such as king, wizard, prophet, teacher, guru or priest. The grandmother may likewise symbolize the great mother archetype, which may appear as a goddess, wise old woman, prophet or teacher. Jung called these figures 'mana personalities', from the Melanesian word for 'the divine'. These are symbols of the power and the wisdom that lies in the deepest part of the psyche, and dreams that contain mana figures represent a time of great spiritual progress and opportunity in waking life.

Husband

To dream of your **husband** may simply be a dream about your relationship and your unconscious feelings about it. On the other hand, he may also represent the male side of your personality (animus) or your father. A woman's view of herself will have been formed by her connection with her father and any subsequent relationship will be colored by that attachment. If doubts about validity and intimacy are not properly resolved in her waking life, they will appear in dreams about the **loss or death of her husband**. They may also be projected onto other women's husbands in dreams. If your **husband goes missing in your dream or you can't find him while out with him**, your unconscious may be referring to the well-known statistic that most men die before women.

If your **husband is dead** in both your dream and in your waking life, this refers to the memories you have shared with him. If **another woman's husband** appears, this may refer to a desire for a relationship outside your current one. If you are **having sex with your husband** in your dream, this can be a wonderful indicator of how you are feeling about your sexual and emotional relationship with him. If your **first husband** appears in your dreams, this represents nostalgia for the past, or more obliquely, competition for your current husband. *See also* Gay relationships in RELATIONSHIPS.

Mother

A dream about your **mother** may be telling you something about your relationship with your mother. Mother-attachment may be so strong that the development of your own individuality has been stalled. Gaining inner independence from your mother is the first great step towards realizing your true self. The mother may symbolize the unconscious, intuitive part of yourself. This, however, can take a positive or a negative form. She may appear as a **kindly mother or aunt**, or as a **place such as a cave, church or garden**; all these images represent the qualities of growth, nourishment and fertility. In her negative form, a mother may appear as a **witch or a dragon**, and represent dark, destructive tendencies that can devour and destroy.

Freud believed that the Greek myths of Oedipus and Electra symbolized psychological conditions. Oedipus killed his father and married his mother and Freud claimed this represented a boy's incestuous desire for his mother and his jealousy towards his father. Electra desired her father and was jealous of her mother. A girl may therefore

The Element Encyclopedia of 20,000 Dreams

In-laws and step families

Archetypes may appear in your dreams in the disguise of in-laws or step-relations. For example, your mother-in-law or stepmother may appear as the **devouring mother**, and your father-in-law or stepfather as the **warrior or villain**. If dreams about in-laws or step-parents are negative, this typically suggests feelings of insecurity, rivalry and mistrust that naturally arise when a newcomer enters the family and exerts influence over you. However well-meaning their intentions, they will always feel like a threat to your individuality at the beginning.

Stepfather

To see your stepfather in your dream symbolizes authority. It suggests that you need to be more self-reliant. Consider also your waking relationship with your stepfather. If you **do not have a** stepfather in real life, this dream may indicate issues of tension or disappointment with your father.

Stepmother

To dream about your stepmother in your dream suggests that you are seeking to develop your own individuality. You want comfort and guidance, but you may have to create that for yourself. If you **don't have a stepmother in real life**, this dream may be a signal that you are following the wrong path. Or, you may be having issues of abandonment or disagreement with your real mother.

Step children

To dream about your step children suggests that you are developing your nurturing, caring side. If you **don't have step children in real life** this may suggest that your nurturing caring side isn't being expressed in waking life.

Step-brothers and step-sisters

To dream about **step-brothers and step-sisters** suggests close male and female friends in waking life. If you do not have step-brothers and step-sisters in waking life, this may indicate a lack of intimacy and connection in your current social circle. *See also* RELATIONSHIPS.

believe she has been castrated by her mother and is an incomplete male. According to Freud this gave rise to penis envy; the root cause of women's so-called feelings of inferiority. Freud's Oedipus complex theory is no longer accepted today but there is no doubt that the mother relationship is the first pivotal relationship in a child's life and it should be a nurturing, loving and supportive one. Jungians associate her with the **Great mother archetype** that influences our psychological growth. Each of us has a fundamental, perhaps instinctive drive to bond with a woman at birth and if that bonding does not happen much of what would be considered normal development cannot or does not take place. So mother sometimes represents the survival instinct and what happens in those early years of trying to becoming independent of such needs. In a man's life if these needs are not met this may result in dependent relationships with older women or inability to commit long term to a relationship. In a woman's life her relationship with her mother will impact all other relationships and if it is lacking in some way she may find herself nurturing needy males or in forming unsatisfying relationships with both men and women. Scenarios involving the mother figure in dreams are therefore one way of working through and moving forward from these issues. Of course, a dream about your mother could also be just that: a straightforward depiction of the woman who gave us life. How

she appears may point to issues in your upbringing or current relationship. Is she proud of you or angry?

WIFE

As with women dreaming about their husbands, to dream of your **wife** may simply be a dream about your relationship and your unconscious feelings about it. This dream may be about your real partner or it may represent the feminine side of your personality. According to Freudians, the way you relate to your wife in your dream may contain elements reminiscent of your relationship with your mother.

If you find yourself in a **love triangle** in your dream this indicates a difficult conflict of interests and shifting feelings within a relationship. If your **first wife** appears in your dreams this represents the past; competition for the second wife. If a **widow** appears in your dreams, this represents fears about the break-up of your relationship, or even the desire to break a relationship. It can also suggest feelings of loneliness or loss. If you are a **married woman dreaming about being a widow**, this indicates fears about losing your husband or a desire to be free of him. **Unmarried women dreaming of, or meeting, a widow** might indicate anxieties about a relationship or the prospect of one. *See also* Gay relationships in RELATIONSHIPS.

FAMOUS PEOPLE

If some celebrity or famous person appears in your dream, they may be there to express something about you or someone close to you.

According to Freudians, such dreams are pure wish-fulfillment, with the celebrity representing either what you want to be or your desire for more recognition in waking life. By contrast, Jungians consider that dreams of celebrities represent archetypes and aspects of your personality that are still buried in your unconscious. If so, your dreaming mind is encouraging you to incorporate those desired qualities that you see in the famous person into your conscious life, because they are already present – latent – in you. On the other hand, the famous person may represent your shadow or hidden side: a part of your personality, or a behavior pattern, that you have refused to acknowledge – for example, aggressiveness or a will to dominate.

In short, celebrities in dreams often symbolize those hidden qualities upon which you need to turn the spotlight. Whenever you dream of becoming famous, or meeting someone famous or powerful, quickly write down a couple of positives and a couple of negatives about that person. Don't think too much. Then ask yourself, 'Do I see any of these qualities in myself right now? Are they qualities that I want to develop? What can I learn from the dream about myself and my life from this person?' *See also* ARCHETYPES; PEOPLE.

The Fame Game

BEING FAMOUS

In dreams in which you are **famous, or achieving fame within a chosen field**, your dreaming mind may be urging you to recognize and give yourself more credit for your achievements. In waking life you may be very shy but in dreams you can achieve things you never thought yourself capable of achieving. The ego is a powerful tool and your need for recognition arises from it. If, however, you are to move forward with your life and reach your full potential, you have to believe in yourself and a dream about fame allows you to accept the possibility that you are more powerful than you think.

On the other hand, a dream in which you are famous would be considered wish-fulfillment by Freudians, reflecting a yearning for more attention and recognition in waking life. It could also, however, reflect the fact that more people recognize your waking behavior (for good or ill) than you realize. Dreaming of being a famous person or celebrity is quite common for adolescents, reflecting their desire to be part of a talented and admired group of people. Such dreams show a strong urge to find a place within a group that is emotionally secure and creatively satisfying.

CELEBRITIES

Our fascination and adoration of favorite **celebrities** stems from a desire to emulate their positive qualities or talents. We admire them for their beauty and creative talent, and sometimes for their humanitarian work and political activism. Frequently we feel that these people are doing something that we would love to do but cannot because we have neither the opportunity nor the self-confidence. Whether you yearn to be as good looking, rich or powerful as the star that ascended from your unconscious depths into your dreamland, or whether you simply have a crush on them, such dreams are typically a wish-fulfillment response of your unconscious to your desires.

As well as giving you temporary gratification and adding a hint of glamor to your life (perhaps in compensation for anxieties about your personal appearance or boredom with the routine of your life), your dream celebrity may have had another purpose. A dream of **Clint Eastwood or John Wayne** or other celebrated icons of

manliness may, if you are a man, have been acting out your anima; if you are a woman, your animus may have been **Marilyn Monroe or Audrey Hepburn**. Any of these stars may have highlighted personal qualities that you greatly admire, would like to possess or are relevant to your current situation. For example, if you dreamed of **Nelson Mandela**, would you like – or do you need – to become more compassionate, patient and tolerant? It may also be that you long to change your direction in life and your dreaming mind has summoned up a representative to encourage and inspire you to follow your dreams.

If you secretly yearn to be a singer/songwriter, a dream of **sharing the stage with a top group and together sending the crowd wild** may encourage you to pursue your vision. Finally, bear in mind that whenever a celebrity appears in your dream, they are typically someone you have admired for a long time; such a dream may also suggest that you want some of the recognition that routinely comes their way. Maybe your role in waking life is hidden from view? Being **singled out by a celebrity** in your dream – no doubt to the envy of your dream friends who suddenly see you with new admiring eyes – suggests that you somehow feel undervalued in your waking life or taken for granted by those around you.

MEETING A FAMOUS PERSON

Famous people appear in dreamland just as they do in the media. On the death of **Diana, Princess of Wales**, thousands of people described how they had dreamed of her. During his presidency, **Bill Clinton** was also an extremely common dream

Questions to ask yourself if dreaming of celebrities

To fully understand the message of a dream in which a celebrity features you need to hone in on the quality they represent and decide whether it pertains to someone you know, or to some aspect of yourself. First you need to consider the outstanding trait for which that celebrity is famous, then you need to think about what makes that person stand out for you. For example if you dream of **Madonna**, why didn't your dreaming mind select another female singer, for example **Shirley Bassey**? What is it about Madonna that inspires you? Is it her drive, her ambition, her feistiness or her ability to reinvent herself? Try to spell out in your mind the qualities this person stands for and what trait is being shown. Then consider the implications. Celebrity dreams may seem sweet or even corny, but they do have a powerful energy. If you think the celebrity represents a quality in yourself you'd like to foster, don't assume you have to copy them and follow their life path. Remember dreams only depict the essence of something; the way you choose to put that energy to work, and how it appears in your life, is entirely up to you.

figure in the United States. His vitality and leadership ability seemed to strike a chord with men and women alike. As they sorted through power issues in themselves and others, dreams of the president offered a forum to explore the dynamics involved. Whenever there is a major event involving someone famous or someone charismatic dominating public awareness, you can expect an upsurge in this type of dream.

Getting to meet your hero or heroine is usually an expression of a wish-fulfillment dream. Typically, the **celebrity appears as a friend and gives helpful advice**. The famous person may be living or from the past, but in your dream you regard them as your best friend. They may even visit you in your home in recognition of the special bond between you. If you dream of meeting a famous person, ask yourself if you would like more recognition for your star qualities in your waking life. If this doesn't apply, ask yourself what the famous person means to you. What psychological characteristics and traits does this person symbolize to you?

Famous people in our dreams are telling us to 'Go for it!' by integrating the positive qualities we admire in them into our own personalities. Reflect upon what this person symbolizes for you. The primary qualities you admire may not necessarily be fame, beauty or money. You may place greater value on psychological aspects such as their drive or even recovery from an addiction or tragedy. Get in touch with these aspects of yourself and work to bring them into focus and manifestation. In some cases dreams of meeting famous people don't highlight feelings of inferiority in waking life they can empower you and add real value. For example, to dream of meeting, talking or even helping a person such as the late **Mother Teresa** might plant the kernel of an idea into your mind that you might find great satisfaction in voluntary work of charitable donation.

If you dream of **meeting the prime minister or president or running for high office**, the dream's interpretation depends on how you rate the value of politicians in society. If you dream of **meeting a famous writer, such as Jane Austen, Charles Dickens or J. K. Rowling**, perhaps you have always longed to write a book or perhaps you want to express yourself better in waking life so your opinions can influence or stimulate other people. If you dream of **being a great composer such as Mozart or Beethoven**, do you yearn for passion and creativity in your waking life? Mozart represents the tragic image of a great artist cut down in their prime. Mozart also represents effortless beauty achieved through dedication and hard work. Ludwig von Beethoven was a musician of extraordinary talent and his heroic ability to challenge convention and create timeless beauty out of adversity makes his story extraordinary.

If you dream of **meeting a great artist, such as Vincent Van Gogh or Leonardo da Vinci**, perhaps you have an artistic talent you need to nurture or simply feel that your life should be more creative. Dreams that feature Leonardo da Vinci may evoke in you a desire to share the secrets of his genius. Perhaps you yearn to understand life's mysteries? If **Picasso** appears in your dreams, perhaps in conjunction with his famous cubist paintings in which he has broken down a face or a body into its various facets, the dream image may express a need to understand all aspects of

your life, observe them separately and then put them together to make sense of them all. To dream of Picasso suggests the importance of observing life's complexity even if you cannot understand it. Whatever famous or influential person you meet, or become, your dreams are all ones of aspiration and striving to achieve your ideals. *See also* PEOPLE; ROLES.

Sex with famous people

Dream analysts tend to describe dreams about sex with famous people as simple wish-fulfillment. For example, an aspiring athlete may dream of **having sex with a famous sporting hero**. But someone who has no talent for sport might also dream of making love with a sporting icon. The quality that is desired here might be the sporting legend's ability under intense pressure. In some cases, the famous people you might be romantically involved with in your dreams are really stand-ins for people who aren't so famous, the people in your everyday life. *See also* SEX.

HISTORICAL FIGURES

Historical figures typically represent the kind of person you would like to be or could be, as people in dreams often represent aspects of yourself of which you may be unaware. The historical figure you dream about can come from any time period; you need to look for character traits and attributes, experiences and achievements either good or bad that have meaning and relevance to you. If you dream of **Tutankhamen**, for example, the beautiful golden face of this young pharaoh may suggest the delights of youth and early promise; on the other hand, that the body is embalmed for all eternity may suggest that you are denied the right to express yourself. The association with 'mummy' suggests that your parents might not be allowing you the freedom you need.

If you dream of **Julius Caesar** – someone famous for being brutally betrayed and assassinated by his followers – this image may suggest that your hostility towards someone, however justified, is a betrayal. Caesar also warns against alienating others through ambition and pride. If you dream of **Nero**, the Roman emperor, it could be that you are worried by your own, or someone else's, life of debauchery and random, cruel decisions. To dream of **Cleopatra** is a stark warning of the dangers of balancing love with ambition and power; she famously combined sex appeal, political cunning, beauty and ambition to influence her Roman lovers, Caesar and Mark Anthony. The warning in the dream comes from the fact that she ultimately died from a self-inflicted serpent bite.

For Jungians, 'good queen Bess' or **Queen Elizabeth I** may evoke the archetypal image of the great mother, combining earthly power with spiritual exaltation. Also significant is the fact that Elizabeth, as the Virgin Queen, renounced her sexuality for her country. **George Washington** was a brave soldier and honest leader, and presents an image of the archetypal father figure. Freudians might perhaps see his felling of the infamous cherry tree, because 'he could never tell a lie', as an acknowledgement of repressed sexuality. The famous French leader **Napoleon** was a liberator yet also a tyrant, and in dreams may be the symbol of a dictator or overbearing father figure. As a role model of justice with wisdom and compassion, **Abraham Lincoln** may evoke the wise old man archetype with its ability to impart knowledge and inspire; his assassination, which he predicted in a dream, adds elements of sacrifice and intuition to his symbolism. The head of the Catholic Church, the **Pope**, may also represent the archetypal wise old man.

As the ultimate villain of the twentieth century, **Adolf Hitler** reminds you that dark urges are not fictional characteristics but very much alive in human nature. Jungians would see in him and other brutal dictators, such as **Stalin, Mao Tse-Tung or Pol Pot**, the archetypal shadow figure. **Winston Churchill**, by contrast, is a shining example of the triumph of wisdom, experience and indomitable will, as his greatest glory only came when many thought his career was over. A symbol of strength and persistence, he is also an ideal father figure: tough and gruff, but also fair, courageous and protective. The dream image of **John F. Kennedy** is a symbol of the archetypal free-spirited hero, but he may also indicate voracious sexual appetites.

The appearance of **Carl Jung** in your dreams may be reassuring you if you share his view that dreams are a powerful way to gather new insights on the path to spiritual self-fulfillment. If **Freud** appears in your dreams, he may represent the image of the psychoanalyst listening to your anxieties. You may speak to your dream analyst about things you keep from others – and even yourself – in waking life. For dreams such as **being present at a famous event in world history**, such as the Battle of Waterloo or the first moon landing, *see* TIME.

ROYALTY

Dreaming of meeting a famous person, whether a **king, queen, prince or princess**, has particular significance because it can indicate your desire for recognition, admiration and respect in waking life. Your dreaming mind has chosen someone acknowledged to be of the highest social rank to fulfill this craving. The dream is an attempt to redress the balance but it may be a signal of low self-esteem, so it is important to heed the message and take steps to boost your self-confidence in waking life. If **Elizabeth II** features in your dream, this is a mother archetype, although the troubles of her family may have tainted this image. **Diana, Princess of Wales** has become a symbol of the wronged and martyred heroine, the maiden held captive by social constraints.

Influential People in World History

Certain key figures in human history have had such an impact on world history that your unconscious may have stored the information – perhaps from school or college days, or even from a documentary or media report – and then drawn upon that knowledge to create an image that can encourage, teach or inspire you in dreamland. The list below contains some of the world's most influential figures and gives keywords to trigger personal associations. Please note that the list is by no means comprehensive or definitive; if the influential person in your dreams isn't listed here or in this chapter and you want to find associations that have meaning and relevance to you, it might be worthwhile reading their biography or autobiography, or investigating their life story and significance to world history.

Alexander the Great: conqueror, empire building, warrior archetype

Aristotle: influential Greek philosopher, the importance of asking questions and challenging conventional thought

Bell, Alexander Graham: inventor of telephone, communication, networking

Bonaparte, Napoleon: French emperor, tactician, warrior archetype, exile

Columbus, Christopher: explorer, led Europe to the Americas, new territories to discover, new potential

Confucius: the founder of Confucianism, wise old man archetype

Copernicus, Nicolas: priest, astronomer, taught heliocentricity, the world revolves around the sun

Daguerre, Louis: pioneer of photography, vision, impressions, image change

Darwin, Charles: biologist, formulated theory of evolution, survival of the fittest

Descartes, René: rationalist philosopher and mathematician, logic, reason, I think therefore I am

Edison, Thomas: inventor of light bulb, illumination, insight

Einstein, Albert: physicist, theory of relativity, greatness achieved by power of the mind

Fermi, Enrico: father of atomic bomb, ultimate weapon of destruction, the last resort

Fleming, Alexander: penicillin, advances in bacteriology, immunology and chemotherapy, strengthening your defenses

Ford, Henry: industrialist, revolutionized mass production, the repetition of the production line

Galilei, Galileo: Catholic astronomer, accurately described heliocentric solar system, visionary, conflict of authority with freedom of thought

Gutenberg, Johann: developed movable type, printed Bibles, communication, the printed word

Machiavelli, Niccolò: author of *The Prince*, archetype of the manipulator

Marconi, Guglielmo: inventor of the radio, communication, words, reaching a large audience

Marx, Karl: social philosopher, Marxist communism, class struggle

Michelangelo: painter; sculptor, architect, diversity, energy, talent

Moses: God's messenger, leader of people out of slavery

Muhammad: Prophet of Islam, founder of major world religion, military and political leader, pure ideals, indomitable will

Newton, Isaac: physicist, theory of universal gravitation, laws of motion, universe working like clockwork

St Paul: proselytizer of Christianity, dogma, tradition, rules and regulations

Plato: Greek philosopher, intellectual focus on spiritual concepts rather than physical elements of life

Shakespeare, William: playwright, understanding of complete range of human emotions, stupendous output

Voltaire: writer and philosopher, crusade against tyranny and bigotry, the importance of tolerance

Washington, George: first president of the United States of America, the basic rights of the individual, David versus Goliath

Watt, James: developer of steam engine, new possibilities, travel

William the Conqueror: first King of modern England, beginning a new project, invasion

Wright, Orville and Wilbur: Inventors of airplane, longing to escape, fly away or reach new heights

Good and Evil People in Dreams

Now and again your dreaming mind may conjure up powerful images of notoriously evil people to warn you against the destructive effects of negative forces in yourself, or in some aspect of your waking life. These people embody the classic shadow or villain archetype. Similarly, your dreaming mind may come up with images of people celebrated for their incredible compassion and goodness; your unconscious may have chosen such people to inspire and encourage you to find healing within, or to reach out to others with compassion. Such images

Influential figures in your dreams

Artists and entertainers

This diverse group of stars has won fans and spawned imitators around the world. If they appear in your dreams they can enlighten and inspire us to follow our dreams.

Business icons

Salesmanship, creativity and sheer brashness are qualities the world's most influential business brains share. If they appear in your dreams could they be urging you to go ahead with that idea, create that business or push ahead with your career.

Heroes

Some people right wrongs, play through pain, offer spiritual solace or simply inspire us with their remarkable talents. Their appearance in a dream can be a potent source of inspiration and encouragement.

Movers and shakers

Whether to conquer space or remake the political world, certain people create the big ideas of our time. If they feature in your dreams they could be urging you to take a risk and challenge yourself or convention in waking life.

Revolutionaries and leaders

Warriors and peacemakers, dictators and democrats, terrorists and holy men – these are the men and women who had, or have, the clout and power to change our world. In dreams, they signal the need for some kind of dramatic change in your waking life or, at the very least, a shift in attitude or approach.

are typically archetypal symbols of the teacher and healer.

The following list is merely a starting point, being far from comprehensive, but if any of these well-known figures appear in your dreams, try to find out why. They are such vivid and colorful examples of the potential power of good or evil in waking life that their appearance in dreamland should be taken extremely seriously as a powerful message from your unconscious.

GOOD

Buddhism, far more than Christianity or Islam, has a very strong pacifist element. The orientation toward non-violence has played a significant role in the political history of Buddhist countries. In dreams, the **Buddha** characterizes the highest spiritual attainment; enlightenment and the true wisdom that accompanies it. The **Dalai Lama** is head of the dominant Dgelugs-pa order of Tibetan Buddhists and,

The Element Encyclopedia of 20,000 Dreams

until 1959, both spiritual and temporal ruler of Tibet. In 1989 he was awarded the Nobel Prize for Peace in recognition of his non-violent campaign to end Chinese domination of Tibet. In dreams, a meeting with the Dalai Lama suggests a message of justice, peace and inner strength.

In dreams, **Jesus Christ** symbolizes love, a high spiritual messenger or someone who sacrifices everything for a goal, whilst **Mother Teresa** is the archetypal mother figure who characterizes selfless love, compassion and giving aid. Once Mother Teresa was asked how she could continue visiting the terminally ill, day after day after day, feeding them, wiping their brows, giving them comfort as they lay dying. She said, 'It's not hard, because in each one I see the face of Christ in one of His more distressing disguises.' **Abraham Lincoln** paved the way to freeing the slaves from oppression, and so in dreams he represents integrity and things of which you should be proud.

Martin Luther King was an American clergyman, Nobel Prize winner, a prominent advocate of non-violent protest and one of the principal leaders of the American civil rights movement. His 'I have a dream' speech is known the world over and in dreamland the appearance of King himself may be urging you to commit yourself to a cause and strive to achieve your dreams. A similar figure is **Mahatma Gandhi**, an Indian nationalist leader who established his country's independence from Britain through a non-violent revolution. If Gandhi appears in dreams, he characterizes living spirituality or fighting for spiritual principles.

EVIL

History suffers from no shortage of evil figures. Amongst the most cruel and appalling must be numbered such figures as **Genghis Khan**, the leader of the pitiless Mongol hordes who swept across Europe from the East. Another is **Tomas de Torquemada**, whose name is synonymous with the Christian Inquisition's horror, religious bigotry and cruel fanaticism. Of similar repute is **Ivan the Terrible**, the grand prince of Moscow and the first to be proclaimed Tsar of Russia. Through cruelty and torture, his reign saw the completion of the construction of a centrally administered Russian state and the creation of an empire that included non-Slav states.

Perhaps unequalled in the annals of human depravity is the name of **Adolf Hitler**; a symbol of insanity, pure evil and Machiavellian cynicism, if he appears in your dreams, it is worth asking what, or whom, is being tarred with one of the blackest names history can produce. If you dream of **Adolf Eichmann**, a man responsible for organizing the shipping of Jews to the extermination camps in Poland in World War II and a powerful symbol of a fanatical obedience to an unjust cause, it may be that you are doing something for someone else that deeply toubles your conscience.

Mao Tse-Tung was responsible for the deaths of millions of his countrymen and his 'Cultural Revolution' led to the destruction of much of China's cultural heritage and the imprisonment of a huge number of Chinese intellectuals, amongst other social chaos. If he makes an appearance in dreams, it may be a warning against the dangers of personality over substance, and the total disregard for tradition and experience.

The final member of the triumvirate of hugely powerful and hugely evil leaders in the twentieth century is **Joseph Stalin**, who brought about the deaths of more than 20 million of his own people while holding the Soviet Union in an iron grip for during the middle part of last century. As with Hitler and Mao, Stalin is potent symbol of negativity, repression and cruelty.

The Element Encyclopedia of 20,000 Dreams

FLOWERS

The fragile loveliness of flowers, their bright colors, exquisite shapes and fragrant scents have meant they have long been regarded as a symbol of the spiritual self and pure inner beauty.

This is why, apart from enjoying them ourselves, we use flowers as gestures of love, reassurance and sympathy and why we often give them to people we like, love or admire. It is generally in one or other of these contexts that flowers appear in your dreams. When flowers are in bloom their beauty is vibrant and colorful but also fleeting and fragile, because as soon as a flower bursts from its bud into full bloom it is in the process of dying to make way for the next generation of flowers. As such, flowers in dreams can also be symbols of hope and optimism, as well as of the cycle of birth and death.

In his practice, Carl Jung observed that the dreams his patients reported consistently contained geometric shapes, such as circles, squares and triangles. A close look at a flower reveals that it is similarly composed of repeated shapes and patterns, reminiscent of the mandalas used in the Eastern religions that represent the wholeness of the spirit unfolding like a blossoming flower. The Buddha observed that the lilies floating in a pond were in various stages of development, just as each individual is in various stages of spiritual development. Some rose above muddy conditions to thrive whilst others struggled to survive.

In helping you discern their particular meaning, the color and condition of the flowers in your dream may be as significant as the flowers themselves. For example, red roses speak of romance and beauty whilst white roses speak of purity, spirit and healing. To dream about new blossoms suggests the opening of the inner self. To dream about a healthy flower represents healthy vitality, and to dream about a wilted flower represents a low energy or life force. Dreaming of an expansive field of beautiful wildflowers may symbolize freedom and uninhibited growth. Flowers growing through concrete or popping up through the snow might symbolize a strong spirit whilst flowers growing in the spring indicate new growth and beginnings. Flowers are often present in dreams of departed loved ones, symbolizing the natural cycle of life and death. Reflect upon the personal significance of the flower to determine its meaning in your dream. Take note, too, if the flowers have unusual colors; a friend giving you green roses, for example, may be jealous of your romantic attachments. *See also* COLORS; NATURE AND THE SEASONS; SHAPES; TREES.

Dream Flowers

FLOWERS IN BLOOM

Flowers that are blossoming in dreams may symbolize the flowering of an idea or new relationship, or that a new phase in your life has begun. According to Freud, flowers are a female symbol, because of their cup-shaped blossoms and because a bee enters them in order to fertilize them. A **flower in male dreams** may therefore represent women in general or a particular woman. They can also represent an idea that has been fertilized in your mind. **Pink or white blossom** may also be a symbol of innocence in a dream and if the image of **blossom fluttering down to the grass** appears, this may signify the passing of innocence. When interpreting your dream, remember that a bloom is a plant's reproductive structure, the carpel containing the female reproductive organ, and the stamen the male. So if your dreaming mind focused on a flower, the reference may also be sexual. And if the flower that bloomed in your dream was one that you recognize, its personal or symbolic meaning may have further relevance for you in waking life.

If, in your dream, the **flowers were particularly colorful**, this signifies kindness, compassion, gentleness, pleasure, beauty, and gain. Your dream may be an expression of love, joy and happiness. The colors of your dream flower may also be significant, as would their shape. Alternatively, dream flowers may denote a particular time, season or day of special significance to the dreamer or may relate to a specific sign of the Zodiac (see box on page 247). Keywords: Symbolic of beauty and inner development, puberty, coming into flower, seeing the beauty in a situation, violating, plundering or removing innocence and beauty from something, deflowering it, a homonym for flour.

GARDEN FLOWERS

In general, **cultivated flowers** symbolize how we can influence and control our development, whilst **wild flowers and weeds** symbolize spontaneity and how nature's abundance comes in all shapes and varieties. If you were **planting flowers in rows** in a garden or see **formally arranged flowers in a flower bed**, this could be suggesting that your life is a little too organized and lacking in spontaneity. Although it could also indicate that your personal life needs putting in order, in general flowers appearing in a dream garden suggest that your life lacks vibrancy and you are too preoccupied with the practical business of earning a living. A dream of an **inviting, flower-filled garden scene** may be encouraging your waking self to relax. If you dreamed that you were **lounging lazily in a garden surrounded by flower-filled borders**, your unconscious may have been mirroring your sense of

Zodiac signs and flowers

Zodiac Sign	Dates	Flower
AQUARIUS	20 Jan.–18 Feb.	Daffodil and Primrose
PISCES	19 Feb.–20 Mar.	Freesia and Cineraria
ARIES	21 Mar.–20 Apr.	Tulip and Calceolaria
TAURUS	21 Apr.–20 May	Iris and Hydrangea
GEMINI	21 May–20 Jun.	Alstromeria and Geranium
CANCER	21 Jun.–21 Jul.	Rose and Gloxinia
LEO	22 Jul.–21 Aug.	Carnation and Begonia
VIRGO	22 Aug.–22 Sep.	Gladiolus and Chrysanthemum
LIBRA	23 Sep.–22 Oct.	Dahlia and Cyclamen
SCORPIO	23 Oct.–21 Nov.	Gerbera and African Violet
SAGITTARIUS	22 Nov.–20 Dec.	Anemone and Azalea
CAPRICORN	21 Dec.–19 Jan.	Chrysanthemum and Poinsettia

satisfaction with your waking life but also may have been encouraging you to take the time to enjoy life's simple pleasures.

If the **flowers in the garden are dead, wilting or attacked by a worm or grub**, this conveys a message of regret and danger. If **flowers are strewn across your garden, your house or even yourself**, this suggests that your life contains a great deal of pleasure and fulfillment. If you were **watering or feeding the flowers in the garden** or anywhere else in your dream, this suggests that you need to work on a relationship. Did you dream that **your garden suddenly became parched and you were rushing to find water to feed the flowers**? If this was the case, perhaps a dream like this is implying that you need to pay more attention to those around you, as your close personal relationships – symbolized by the drought-stricken flowers – are in urgent need of nourishment and rejuvenation.

GIVING AND RECEIVING FLOWERS

If you dream of **sending someone flowers or presenting or receiving flowers or a bouquet**, try to identify who the other person in the dream is. It may be someone you admire, love or respect, someone from whom you desire admiration, love or respect, or someone who has more regard for you than you realize. According to dream-lore, to dream that you receive a bouquet of flowers represents respect, approval, admiration and reward. If you can't identify the person in your dream, this suggests that your self-esteem needs a boost. A **garland of flowers given or received** has similar, though more formal, associations. If you are **sending or receiving a wreath of flowers**, this may be connected with feelings of guilt, hostility of loss that you need come to terms with. If you are **giving dead flowers** in your dream, this represents something you want cut out of your life because you no longer have anything more than dead feelings towards it.

WILD, CUT OR ARTIFICIAL FLOWERS

In dreams, **wild flowers** represent freedom, freshness and natural beauty, symbolizing a disregard for the highly organized beauty of **artificial flower beds or plastic flowers**. If **many flowers are growing** in your dream, this indicates feelings of well-being and optimism. The opposite will be the case if the flowers are dying or wilting. Do nature's simple charms have great meaning for you, with your dream of wild flowers indicating the need for a simpler life? Or do you feel you are about to flower and fulfill your potential? Dreamers **picking wild flowers** may be turning away from their partner.

Cut flowers are unable to give pleasure in their natural setting and therefore may suggest artificiality and appearance over substance. Because flowers are a symbol of sexuality, **fake or artificial flowers** in a dream may suggest that those whom you think of as friends are actually showing you a false face or persona. On the other hand, **flowers in a vase** suggest a showcasing of your inner beauty or something that facilitates your personal development. If you were **arranging flowers in a vase or in a floral arrangement**, try to remember if you did so carelessly or with great care. The positioning of flowers in dream floral arrangements can indicate how we unconsciously relate to others. If your **arrangement was artless or careless**, you have a casual approach to relationships with others that may leave others feeling unimportant to you. If you took **extreme care with the arrangement**, this can either indicate a positive, caring approach to relationships with others or controlling and manipulative tendencies. And if **dried flowers** appeared in your dream, this suggests that past relationships may be more important to you than the people with whom you are currently interacting in waking life.

WITHERED OR DEAD FLOWERS

To see **withered or dead flowers** in your dream denotes disappointments and gloomy situations. You may not be utilizing your full potential and talents. If you **receive wilted blooms** in dreamland as a gift from someone you know, think about the nature of your relationship with that person; your unconscious might have detected that the relationship is weakening. Similarly, if you are **pricked by a hidden thorn in a bunch of roses given by colleague who was congratulating you** in a dream scenario, is it possible that they are concealing real feelings of resentment towards you in waking life? If you **gave a bunch of dead flowers to a difficult or strict former schoolteacher**, could this highlight your extreme dislike of that person? To see **flowers blooming in barren soil**, however, signifies that your energy and cheerful nature will enable you to overcome your grievances.

The anatomy of a flower

Bud

If you dream of **flower-buds** in the middle of winter, your unconscious may be mirroring your longing for spring and warmth. It might relate to a budding relationship, a potential talent waiting to be developed, or to someone close to you. The unconscious can sometimes use buds or seeds to symbolize unborn children, the potential germination of an idea. If **you picked or nipped your bud** this could be urging you to nip something in the bud. If the **bud looked plump and ready to flower** this could mirror a potential development in your life. To recap: a flower-bud represents new beginnings and your potential, whilst an opening or blossoming flower indicates development and fulfillment. So, a **magnificent bloom** could reflect your sense of satisfaction and fulfillment at having realized your potential? If you feel that you are past your prime, a **bloom that is losing its petals** may echo your sense of regret and loss.

Bulb

A **flower bulb** is likely to indicate something that can expand and express its magnificence. It refers to the budding of talent in your life, or the realization of future plans.

Petal

Petals are a magnified emphasis of the presented flower. They can celebrate a marriage or unity of any kind. The shape or number of petals reflect a flowering aspect or the displaying of true colors. **Petals falling from a flower** may represent making way for a new phase.

Pollen

Pollen indicates elements in your life that enhance positive aspects, although it can also be associated with irritation for hay fever sufferers.

Seed

Seeds reflect the potential of a new beginning or growth. If you **scatter seed on barren earth**, you may be wasting your energy on something. Seeds can represent sperm or the ovum, although botanically, pollen is the equivalent of sperm.

Stalk/Stem

The **stalk** represents the supporting factor of an element or issue. Is it healthy and strong, or weak and thin?

Thorn

Thorns on your body may symbolize feeling a need to protect yourself, something to be avoided or merely 'a thorn in your side'. For a Christian, thorns may suggest sacrifice and eventual redemption.

Individual Flower Meanings

If a specific type of flower appears in your dream, the first step on your road to interpreting it is to find out whether it awakens a personal association. For example, **daisies** may trigger happy memories of childhood when you spent hours in the sunshine with your friends making daisy chains, whereas **lilies** may trigger unhappy memories because they bedecked a loved one's funeral. If, however, the **flower in your dream evoked no special memory**, then your unconscious may have tapped into the universal symbolism associated with certain flowers. In past times, each individual flower had a traditional meaning and your unconscious may be accessing this knowledge to illustrate a point or convey a message to you. This is especially true if you are given flowers or are giving flowers to another person.

If you are intrigued by the possibility that a specific flower in your dream may be sending you a message, the information below may help. It might also be worth researching the medicinal, historical and secular associations of the flower, as well as its spiritual symbolism. Another tip is to take the name of the dream flower into consideration as your dreaming mind may, for example, have featured a **rose** to remind you of a special friend called Rose, or if you dreamed of a **bleeding heart** wilting, is someone close to you heading for a broken heart? Don't forget, however, that a specific flower may have individual meanings for you, so if the emphasis in your dream seems to be on one particular species, try to recognize any possible personal connections first.

ANEMONE

Anemones are known as wind flowers and are named after the Greek god of the wind, Anemos. The **red anemone** is said to have sprung from the spot where a drop of blood fell from the god Adonis, who represents death and rebirth. In dreams this represents mental awareness/acuity.

BLUEBELL

Bluebells thrive in woodlands and, like all flowers with bells, they represent the bringing of news to the dreamer; before the introduction of modern communication systems, bells were traditionally rung throughout Europe to announce news.

BUTTERCUP

Often associated with the carefree days of childhood buttercups with their bright yellow head represent simple pleasures and the shining optimism of the golden **sun.**

CARNATION

In dreams, the **carnation** may refer to passion but is more likely to refer to the part of yourself that is socially correct and overly concerned about appearances.

The Element Encyclopedia of 20,000 Dreams

Chrysanthemum

The **chrysanthemum** is an autumnal flower and its petals evoke the rays of the sun. If this flower appears in your dream, it may suggest longevity and mature wisdom. In traditional Chinese belief, the chrysanthemum also symbolizes the virtue of scholarly retirement, so your unconscious may have been urging you to study harder for an exam that you may be facing in the real world. On the other hand, because the chrysanthemum appears on Japan's imperial crest, does Japan hold any significance for you?

Clover

This three-leaved plant evokes feelings of well-being and security, as suggested by the phrase 'living in clover'. A **four-leaved clover** is a universal symbol of good luck and if it appears in a dream, it may reveal optimism or overreliance on chance.

Cornflower

As **cornflowers** are a delicious shade of blue, the color symbolism may suggest calmness and serenity. On the other hand, cornflowers are often presented as **dried flowers**, suggesting that an aspect of the dreamer's life has been crushed, damaged or destroyed.

Daffodil/Narcissus

The cheerful yellow petals of the **daffodil** bring brightness to spring, when it is one of the first flowers to appear, showing that winter is over. Because of this it is a symbol of hope and renewal. Therefore if a daffodil appears in your dream, you may be entering a new phase of your life. On the other hand, you may urgently need an injection of cheerfulness and optimism to brighten your life. The smaller form of daffodil, traditionally known as the **narcissus**, warns against self-centeredness and not to confuse shadow for substance.

Daisy

Plucking petals from a daisy may indicate being undecided or unsure of something. It can also indicate a need to lighten up, or it may be slang for a homosexual or something that is excellent. On the other hand, daisies are often regarded as childhood flowers; if they appear as **daisy chains, bracelets or necklaces**, it may suggest a desire for the security and innocence of childhood. Another interpretation indicates that something is dead, buried or needing to be released, as in pushing up the daisies.

Forget-me-not

A symbol of lovers or friends who are separated, the **forget-me-not** relates to your personal relationships. Do you feel that a lover or friend has been less interested than normal or is neglecting you?

Foxglove

The elegant **foxglove** is known as the flower of insincerity. Within the bright exterior of the foxglove is a substance called digitalis, a natural heart stimulant that is used as a cardiac medicine but can kill if given in high doses. This is why the foxglove is sometimes called dead man's fingers. Do you need some form of stimulation for the heart? Foxgloves are also called finger flowers because the flowers are like the fingers of a glove. When you dream of foxglove, think of the significance of a glove; a glove can protect, as well as conceal, a hand. Is there something you are trying to keep hidden? You should also consider the symbolism of the fox. Are you being stealthily or crafty in pursuit of your desires, or are you foxed or puzzled about anything at the moment?

GERANIUM

The **geranium** is a symbol of a renewed sense of optimism, so if you dream of one, a recent quarrel may not be as serious as you originally thought.

IRIS

In Greek mythology, the gods let down a bridge or rainbow between earth and heaven so that the goddess Iris of the rainbow could act as a go-between to ease discord between men and gods. Dreams of **irises** may therefore be referring to your role as a peacemaker or the need for you to make peace with someone. In addition, the iris is often depicted as a *fleur-de-lis*, a symbol of France that shares the symbolism of the lily, indicating purity, peace and resurrection. The tall stem and swordlike leaves of the iris add male sexuality to the female bloom; as a result, the Iris is often associated with the animus or masculine aspect of femininity. The common **yellow iris** is often called the **flag iris**. If you dream of a yellow iris, it may mean that you want to call attention to, or flag, something about which you are concerned. On the other hand, does your dream iris refer to

the iris in your eye? Are you seeing clearly what is going on around you?

LILY

If you dreamed of a **lily**, you may associate it with a wedding (where it denotes hope and innocence) or a funeral (where it denotes mourning); in dreams, lilies are also associated with purity, peace and rebirth. It is the sacred flower of all the virgin goddesses in mythology. Christ told the Jews that Solomon, their monarch, dressed in all his sumptuous finery, could not equal the majesty of the lilies and told them to consider the lilies of the field – beautiful but unadorned. The beautiful **white arum lily** is associated with death or transformation. **Lily of the valley**, also known as **fairy bells**, was associated with witches as it was used for healing, so your dream could be linked to some form of healing. If you dream of **lilies in a church**, could they be linked to a wedding or a funeral? Or does the image you need to project in waking life need to be more elegant, cool and remote? On the other hand, they may also indicate being lily-livered or cowardly.

LOTUS/WATER LILY

The **lotus or water lily** was regarded in ancient Egyptian mythology as the primal flower, the source of creation. In Buddhism, it is the symbol of the individual's spiritual development, of consciousness rising from the muddy depths of ignorance and opening to the full glory of enlightenment. The Buddhist **thousand-petalled lotus** symbolizes the final revelation and enlightenment. Both associations may apply to a dream of this flower. The dream may refer to a spiritual transformation or to a birth within. Are you using all aspects of your creative power or does you dream lotus inspire renewed interest in spirituality? Does it suggest the lotus position from yoga to you? A **lotus fruit** may also represent being forgetful.

Orchid

The **orchid** derives its name from the minor Greek God Orchis, meaning testicle; as a result, the orchid is often considered to be a symbol of fertility. Its fragile beauty has also made it an image of perfection, admiration and wealth, evoking feelings of sexuality in dreams. Consider also the riches and beauty surrounding you. Do your dream orchids symbolize a sexual relationship? Orchids need great care if they are to flower – and if they do, the flowers may last for months on end – so do you feel that, like an orchid, a relationship of a project of yours needs special care to reach its full potential?

Pansy

The **pansy**, also called Cupid's delight, love in idleness and heartsease, represents undying love.

Poppy

The **poppy** is a symbol of death and regeneration. Remembrance Sunday is known as Poppy Day in Britain because people wear plastic or paper poppies as an act of remembrance for those compatriots who have died serving their country in war. In the United States, Veteran's Day serves the same

purpose and people likewise wear poppies for remembrance. Sleep and unconsciousness are also associated with the poppy. This is because opium, from which morphine and heroin is made, is extracted from the unripe seed-head of the opium poppy. Are you in need of rest and relaxation? Are you getting enough sleep? Because the poppy produces an abundance of seeds, the flower is also associated with fertility and new beginnings.

Rose

The **rose** is universally used to symbolize love and passion. As the flower of many goddesses, it also suggests femininity, beauty and fertility. In dreams, roses typically suggest romance, given that they symbolize your heart, the love and beauty that you hold within and your inner rose. Common everyday idioms might point to other general interpretations. To be in a 'bed of roses' can indicate a situation of ease, luxury or comfort; to do something 'under the rose' suggests a meeting conducted privately or secretly; 'smelling the roses' hints at an appreciation of beauty, whilst 'coming up roses' might mean a good outcome or a prosperous turnout.

Be sensitive to the different meanings that both roses and colors have in different countries or regions. **White roses** are generally thought of as symbols of purity and virginity, so if you dream of them it may represent a yearning for innocence. But white is also the shade of mourning in many parts of Asia, so for some dreamers the image may provoke the quite different feelings of loss or bereavement. The **red rose** may symbolize desire and passion, but it is also the national flower of England, although both the white rose and the mixed **white and red Tudor rose** are sometimes used as well. In the United States, different roses have very different functions: yellow roses are given for friendship, white roses are the flowers of weddings, whilst red roses are appropriate at funerals.

Symbolic meaning of roses

Red rose: love and respect
Yellow rose: joy and friendship
White rose: innocence, purity, and secrecy. (Hint: When it's time to propose marriage, choose an all-white bouquet to show the purity of your intentions and add some ivy to express your promise of fidelity.)
Dark pink rose: thankfulness
Pale pink rose: grace and joy (these flowers are particularly suited for newborns and weddings)
Light peach rose: modesty
Coral rose: desire
Orange rose: fascination

Roses, their constituent parts and the places they grow can therefore suggest a host of often contradictory meanings. A **rose garden** is a symbol of paradise, so if you dream of being in a rose garden, this may indicate happiness in your waking life. Roses, however, also possess **thorns**. In dreams, a rose with thorns may indicate a thorny problem with which you need to grapple to gain the reward promised by the rose. In this context, a dream of thorny roses may indicate conflict within a romantic relationship. Does a fragment of your dream conceal a thorn or danger that is a threat to you? Finally, if **you are given roses** in a dream, consider their number and color. **Twelve red roses** may be a sign that the giver is in love with you.

SNOWDROP

One of the first flowers of spring, the dainty white **snowdrop** symbolizes hope, new life and fresh opportunities after a period of darkness. In Victorian Britain, the snowdrop was called the flower of friendship because it pushes through the snow each spring, acting as a sign that winter is coming to an end. If a snowdrop appears in your dream, could this represent a glimmer of hope after a difficult time? Have you been unwell and are you finally feeling better now?

SUNFLOWER

A symbol of the sun, and representing prosperity, abundance and brightness, the **sunflower** may indicate your inner light, joy or self-expression in a dream. However, as the sunflower always turns in the direction of the sun, it may also indicate an over-reliance on the advice and guidance of others. Along with the lotus, however, this flower is most often associated with insight, intuition and optimism.

Dream it with flowers

In Victorian America and Europe, flowers were attributed with specific meanings by young men and women who used them during courtship to send messages to each other, whether in a forthright manner or by more clandestine means. Straightforward romantic or poetic thoughts were conveyed by the presentation of a single bloom, whilst lengthier messages were communicated by larger arrangements.

Love and happiness were not the only feelings expressed by these floral epistles. Infidelity, jealousy, disdain and rejection were also expressed by a suitably chosen bloom. Whilst a simple flower may have been sent to a young lady to propose marriage, another seemingly innocuous blossom may have been sent in response, telling the gentleman caller to 'get lost'. The color of the flower was extremely significant; to cite a few examples, red usually meant love, yellow indicated friendship, lavender suggested enchantment, and orange fascination.

As far as dream interpretation goes, the list of meanings is seemingly endless, as nearly every flower has been attributed with a specific meaning at some point in time. In Victorian times, the range of available flowers was limited, and so certain flowers had specific meanings; today, with so many flower choices, there are no rules – it's the sentiment and personal association that gives the flower meaning to you in a dream. For those interested in the historic or generally accepted meanings of flowers, the list below has been compiled from a variety of different sources, including the American Society of Florists.

Historic and generally accepted meanings of flowers

Acacia: concealed love, chaste love
Agapanthis: secret love
Alstroemeria: aspiration
Amaryllis: pride, drama
Ambrosia: your love is returned
Anemone: sincerity, fragility
Apple blossom: promises
Arbutus: Thee only do I love
Aster: symbol of love, daintiness, contentment
Azalea: take care of yourself for me, abundance, symbol of womanhood (China)

Baby's breath: festivity
Bachelor's button: anticipation
Begonia: deep thoughts
Bells of Ireland: good luck
Bittersweet: truth
Black-eyed Susan: encouragement
Bluebell: humility

Cactus: endurance
Caladium: great joy, delight
Camellia (general): graciousness, good-luck gift for a man
Camellia (pink): passionate longing
Camellia (red): a flame in the heart
Camellia (white): admiration

Carnation (general): fascination, women, love

Carnation (pink): gratitude, I'll never forget you

Carnation (purple): caprice, whimsy

Carnation (red): passion, drama, admiration

Carnation (solid color): affirmation

Carnation (striped): refusal, sorry I can't be with you, wish I could be with you

Carnation (white): sweetness and loveliness, innocence, pure love, remembrance, woman's good-luck gift

Carnation (yellow): cheerful for all occasions (except in matters of the heart, when it means rejection)

Cattail: peace, prosperity

Chrysanthemum (general): cheerfulness, rest

Chrysanthemum (bronze): excitement

Chrysanthemum (red): sharing

Chrysanthemum (white): truth

Chrysanthemum (yellow): slighted love, secret admirer

Cosmos: peace

Crocus: foresight, cheerfulness, gladness

Cyclamen: resignation, good-bye

Daffodil: chivalry, respect, regard, unrequited love

Daisy: innocence, loyalty, loveliness, purity

Dandelion: faithfulness, happiness

Delphinium: boldness

Fern: magic, fascination, confidence, shelter

Fir: time

Flax: domestic symbol

Forget-me-not: true love, good memories

Forsythia: anticipation

Freesia: full of spirit, trust

Gardenia: joy

Geranium: comfort

Ginger: pride

Gladioli: sincerity, strength of character, flower of the gladiators

Gloxinia: love at first sight

Heather (lavender): admiration, solitude

Heather (white): protection, wishes will come true

Holly: defense, domestic happiness

Honeysuckle: happiness

Hyacinth (general): sincerity

Hyacinth (blue): constancy

Hyacinth (purple): sorrow

Hyacinth (red/pink): play

Hyacinth (white): loveliness

Hyacinth (yellow): jealousy

Hydrangea: perseverance

Iris: inspiration

Ivy: wedded love, fidelity, friendship, affection

Jasmine: grace and elegance

Jonquil: desire for affection returned

Larkspur: beautiful spirit

Lavender: distrust

Lily (calla): regal beauty

Lily (day): enthusiasm, emblem for mother (China)

Lily (Eucharis): charms
Lily (tiger): wealth, pride
Lily (white): virginity, purity, majesty
Lily (yellow): I'm walking on air
Lily of the valley: sweetness, return to happiness, humility

Magnolia: nobility
Marigold: jealousy
Monkshood: beware, a deadly foe is near
Moss: maternal love, charity
Myrtle: love, emblem of marriage

Narcissus: egotism
Nasturtium: conquest, victory in battle

Oleander: caution
Orange blossom: innocence, eternal love, marriage and fruitfulness
Orange mock: deceit
Orchid (general): love, beauty, refinement, symbol for many children (China)
Orchid (Cattleya): mature charm

Palm leaves: victory, success
Passion flower: burning passion
Peony: healing, happy life, happy marriage
Petunia: resentment, anger
Pine: hope, pity
Poppy (general): eternal sleep, consolation, imagination
Poppy (red): pleasure
Poppy (white): consolation
Poppy (yellow): wealth, success
Primrose: longing
Primrose (evening): inconstancy

Queen Anne's lace: delicate femininity

Ranunculus: radiance
Rhododendron: beware
Rose (bridal): happiness, love
Rose (dark crimson): mourning
Rose (Hibiscus): delicate beauty
Rose (leaf): you may hope
Rose (pink): friendship
Rose (red): love, I love you
Rose (tea): I'll remember always
Rose (thornless): love at first sight
Rose (white): innocence and purity
Rose (white and red mixed): unity, flower emblem of England
Rose (yellow): decrease of love, jealousy
Rosebud (general): beauty and youth
Rosebud (moss): confessions of love
Rosebud (red): pure and lovely
Rosebud (white): girlhood
Roses (bouquet of mature blooms): gratitude
Roses (single full bloom): I love you, I still love you

Smilax: loveliness
Snapdragon: presumption
Spider flower: run away with me
Star of Bethlehem: hope
Statice: success
Stephanotis: happiness in marriage, desire to travel
Stock: bonds of affection, you'll always be beautiful to me
Sunflower: pride, sunshine, adoration
Sweetpea: shyness, thank you for a lovely time

Tulip (general): love, flower emblem of Holland
Tulip (pink): caring
Tulip (purple): royalty
Tulip (red): declaration of love
Tulip (variegated): beautiful eyes
Tulip (white): forgiveness
Tulip (yellow): passionate longing

Violet (general): modesty, faithfulness
Violet (blue): watchfulness, faithfulness, I'll always be true

Violet (white): adventure, risk taking
Viscaria: celebration

Wisteria: welcome, steadfast

Zinnia (magenta): lasting affection, thoughts of friends
Zinnia (mixed): thinking (or in memory) of an absent friend
Zinnia (scarlet): constancy
Zinnia (white): goodness
Zinnia (yellow): daily remembrance

TULIP

The colorful **tulip** is a symbol of fertility. It is the emblem of the Turkish House of Osman and the national flower of Holland, where over 5000 varieties are grown for export all over the world. In Chinese symbolism, the tulip is associated with harmony and refinement, often suggesting the perfect man. If a tulip appears in your dream, is this a sign that you need more color in your life? Or are there links with Holland, Turkey or China in your dream?

FOOD
AND DRINK

As food and drink are important and familiar to us, it is no surprise that eating or drinking often features in our dreams.

In some cases, dreams that focus on food and drink may arise out of nocturnal hunger or thirst but, more often than not, such dreams provide symbols that refer to other appetites; these could be, for example, our desire for spiritual, emotional and intellectual nourishment, or for sensory or sexual gratification. For Freud, food represented sexuality because he considered the mouth to be the primary erogenous zone. Most dream analysts, however, follow Jung's lead and suggest that dream food represents the qualities you are taking in, or need to take in, to yourself for personal, emotional and spiritual development. In other words, the dream is trying to compensate for your feeling of being malnourished in some aspect of your waking life and it could be pointing to a physical, intellectual, spiritual or emotional source for this hunger.

Dreams of being thirsty, drinking or drunk, cooking, comfort eating or dining out, fasting or gorging can send you powerful messages about your current state of psychological well-being. If a specific food was highlighted in your dream, this might also be significant; different types of food can mean different things. As always when interpreting dream images, it is important to examine what your personal associations with that food are first.

Food Scenarios

COOKING

If you were **cooking** in your dreams, the chances are that your family or partner rely on you to give them comfort and support; it may be, however, that you do not, or cannot, give these to them, and so your unconscious might be urging you to do so. How did you feel when you prepared the meal; contented or resentful? Because a cook transforms raw materials into something edible, is there something you are cooking up in real life, a plan that has been simmering in your mind? If you were **baking**, what have you been cooking in your dream oven? An idea, perhaps, or could your dream image be expressing your desire for children, as in the phrase 'bun in the oven'?

If **someone else was cooking for you or helping you in the kitchen**, you may regard this person as a source of emotional support. A **cookbook** denotes the many opportunities and ways you can use to reach your goals. To dream of a **cookery school** represents a means of becoming aware of the many ways you can offer your help and support to others in life.

DIETING

A dream of **abstinence from eating** may suggest that you have been taking on too much in waking life. If you dream of **being on a diet**, you may be telling yourself to limit your emotional involvement in someone or something. If you suddenly **ballooned to obesity** in your dream or became **waif-like and starving**, such scenarios all point to poor body image. If you aren't preoccupied with your weight in waking life, such dreams may suggest a feeling of being dragged down by weighty problems that you long to shed. Or perhaps you are indulging yourself or getting obsessed with a hobby or a job and your waking life has become unhealthily unbalanced. On the other hand, if you are studying, you may feel as if you have taken in so much information that you are fit to burst.

If you are **too thin** in your dream, have you been starved of vital nourishment recently – intellectual, emotional, sexual or spiritual – in waking life? If someone is **withholding food from you in the dream or preventing you from eating in some way**, they may be the cause of emotional malnourishment or are perhaps trying to

protect you from self-destructive habits. If you **suffer from food poisoning** in your dream, is there anyone you know who might be trying to poison your mind by feeding it toxic thoughts? Or are you poisoning yourself with an unhealthy diet and lifestyle, perhaps with little or no exercise and a high alcohol, nicotine, caffeine, sugar, salt, additive and saturated fat intake?

EATING

Freud associated **eating** with sexuality insisting, for example, that dreams about **fruit** were always about women's breasts or buttocks. But it is true to say that dreams about eating do often have a sexual implication. The ancients believed that, because of their shapes, certain types of fruit and vegetable were aphrodisiacs; these associations linger to this day. Your physical actions in the dream may also be significant; **sucking and licking food**, for example, probably have a sexual reference. **Biting and chewing food** can also have a sexual reference, but they may also refer to your ability to absorb new information. Eating might, in addition, represent a need to be more body conscious or grounded in material reality.

To dream that you are **eating alone** signifies loss, loneliness and depression. Alternatively, eating alone may reflect your independent nature. Also consider the pun, 'what's eating you up?' in reference to any anxiety that you may be feeling. To dream that you are **eating with others** denotes prosperous undertakings, personal gain and joyous spirits. To dream that you are **overeating** suggests that you have an indulgent sexuality or lifestyle, or that you

The Element Encyclopedia of 20,000 Dreams

Dining out

Restaurant

Eating out in **restaurants** is often part of a couple's courting rituals, so dream meals that are cozy and enjoyable reflect good social relationships, and, if you were **enjoying an intimate meal for two**, your desire for an intimate relationship. If the person you were dining with is someone you know, this suggests your desire to get closer to them, sexually, emotionally or intellectually. Further clues are hidden in the dream scenario. What kind of food were you eating? If you were **eating oysters and sucking fruit,** this may denote a desire for a sexual relationship but if you **felt your tongue tingle** in your mouth, this may suggest a need for verbal or intellectual stimulation.

Your dream dining experience will reveal not only the quality of your physical diet, but also the kinds of beliefs, behavior and attitudes with which you fill your life. What kind of restaurant are you in? Is it humble, exotic, shabby or expensive? Have you chosen to eat in a **down-to-earth cafeteria, canteen or café**? Or have you decided to eat on the go and grab a **takeaway** because you are in a hurry? What is the service like in the restaurant and is the quality of the food good? All this will speak volumes about the way you live your life at the current time.

Being **turned away from a restaurant** suggests frustration and disap-pointment, as well as a sense of social isolation. To dream that **someone clears away the food before you have finished eating** indicates problems and issues concerning those who may be dependent upon you in some way. If you see yourself in the role of a **waiter or waitress**, the quality of service you provide may express concern about the way you relate to people outside your family circle; you may have a tendency, for example, of being overfamiliar, effi-cient, clumsy or polite. If you see your-self in the role of **restaurant critic**, this will usually symbolize yourself criticiz-ing the quality of what you fill your life with. To dream of **studying the menu** could indicate various options in waking life. Were you confused or decisive in your dream menu choice, as this may refer to your waking attitude to a deci-sion you need to make?

Bar/Pub/Tavern

Bars, pubs and taverns are dreamland places in which you can overcome your inhibitions. What is the atmosphere like? If it is friendly, your dreaming mind may be urging you to overcome your isolation. If the atmosphere is **pleasant and upbeat**, this suggests you are feeling optimistic about your future but if **drunkenness or a brawl** occurs, are you about to boil over with uncon-trolled anger, or is a situation in your waking life getting out of control?

have been expending too much emotion and effort recently; dreams of **not eating enough**, on the other hand, signify a denial of sexual needs or a lack of fulfillment in your waking life.

Dreaming of **eating in uncomfortable or frightening surroundings** may represent unhappiness with your relationships. Dreams of **desperately seeking food or even becoming food yourself** may underline the message that you have voracious appetites in waking life that are not being satisfied. Your hunger may be a symbolic cry for more attention, love, power or status. An alternative explanation is that eating suggests qualities you are assimilating or making part of yourself. This may refer to nourishment of the emotions, senses or the mind. Hunger sharpens the appetite, so ask yourself what it is you are hungry for. Could it be the comfort of a fulfilling relationship, a stimulating job or is it food for thought, such as intellectual stimulation? What is currently missing from your real life that is important for your emotional well-being? What wets your appetite for life?

The type of food you are eating is important, as is its quality. If you were **eating leftovers** in your dream, are you losing out in some way in waking life? If you enjoy a dream **dinner with friends**, are you feeding off other people's ideas? If you were attending a **banquet or feast**, are you feeling comfortable with yourself and your lifestyle right now? Were you being force-fed or was the food taken away? All these details will help you relate the particular type of food or drink to an appetite or desire in waking life.

■ *Idioms: what's eating you up; eaten away; eaten up with; eat dirt; eat humble pie; eat like a horse; eat your heart out; eat out of your hand; eat out of house and home; proof of the pudding is in the eating; dog eat dog.*

Food for Thought

The following foods have specific symbolic meanings but remember that whatever you eat in a dream is likely to correspond with your food preferences in waking life first and foremost; so, for example, if you hate mustard but find that it tastes good in a dream, this may refer to a difficult experience that is good for you. The interpretation would differ if you loved mustard perhaps suggesting a period of overindulgence. *See also* VEGETABLES AND FRUIT for the symbolic significance of vegetables, fruit, nuts and seeds.

BISCUITS/COOKIES

In dreams, these treats suggest small rewards. To dream that you are **stealing biscuits or cookies** signifies that you will let trivial problems and minor disputes annoy you. To dream that you are **baking biscuits or cookies** signifies feelings of optimism or an increase in productivity. A **cookie cutter** stands for repetitiveness and lack of original thought. A **cookie jar** connotes goals you are trying to reach, whilst **crackers** in dreams suggest small benefits or considerations.

The Element Encyclopedia of 20,000 Dreams

Bread

To see **bread** in your dream represents the basic needs of life, or aspects of things or people that sustain you. Bread may also signify the positive qualities and great things you have learned on your journey of life. A **breadbasket** denotes those aspects of life that contribute to your sustenance, a **breadboard** refers to life aspects that support your livelihood, whilst a **breadbox** portrays the energy you put into your livelihood. **Breadcrumbs** suggest a tiny amount of something and a **breadline** denotes a lack of emotional necessities. A **bread machine** suggests the ease of making a living or that which comes easily to you, whereas a **bread mold** suggests a possible need to change jobs or approach your existing job in a new way. A **breadstick** represents things that you may overlook in real life, whilst a **breadwinner** characterizes someone who does the work.

Breakfast/Lunch/Supper

If the foods in your dream are **breakfast foods** such as cereal and toast, these may suggest your attitude to a new project. It is worth recalling how these foods were eaten. Was there an atmosphere of calm or was the meal rushed? This can have implications for how you are feeling about a new stage in your life. Alternatively, your mind may already be thinking ahead about what to make for breakfast in the morning. It is not uncommon for your fleeting thoughts to be incorporated into your dream.

If a **lunch** features in your dreams, this implies a need to take time out from your daily efforts to revitalize yourself. The appearance of a dream **lunchbox** could be urging you to get as much done as possible or economize financially. **Supper** pertains to a need to revitalize and energize yourself, whereas **dinner** connotes your main source of nourishment. The **dinnerware** used will portray your personal perspective towards nourishing yourself. A **dinner dance** suggests the joyful, nourishing benefits. A **dining room** usually suggests a concentrated and enjoyable manner of being nourished, whereas a **dining car** corresponds to a need to pay attention to your emotional needs whilst on your life journey. If you enjoy a **snack** in your dream this implies rejuvenation or the re-energizing of yourself.

Butter

To see or taste **butter** in your dream suggests that you are looking to be gratified in some area of your life. It suggests the richness of simplicity and the unaffected perspectives that come with it. You need to indulge yourself in life's simple pleasures. **Bread and butter** mean your livelihood, that which provides your basic needs, whilst **butter and eggs** represent optimism. **Butterball** portrays excess, an overblown or fattened aspect of yourself, whereas a **butter churn** denotes aspects that create life's simple riches. **Buttermilk** refers to life's spiritual rich rewards. **Butternut** points to receptivity to others and **butterscotch flavor** suggests something that has a rich flavor to it, rich as in emotional intelligence. Be aware too of the phrase 'butter fingers', which suggests that you have let something slip through your fingers and denotes a need to get a grasp on some important aspect of life. **Margarine** implies an effective substitute for the dreamer to use.

CAKE

To see a **cake** in your dream suggests that you are learning, or need to learn, to share and delegate your workload instead of trying to do everything yourself. Cakes also indicate the feeling of not getting your fair share. On the other hand, the dream may represent your accomplishments and achievements. Consider also the metaphor a 'piece of cake' or some situation that is easy. To see a **partially eaten cake** in your dream signifies missed and lost opportunities. To dream that you are **buying a cake** suggests that you have accepted the rewards and recognition you deserve for your work, and are learning to enjoy your moment in the spotlight. A dream **cake pan** refers to that which assists you in achieving your goals, and a **cakewalk** suggests a sure thing, something that is easy to accomplish. To see a **birthday cake** in your dream represents your willingness to let people in and share your life with others. If you see a cake that isn't a **birthday cake**, this pertains to a shared goal. Did you get your slice? To dream that you are **baking muffins** denotes that you are a hard worker and will reap the fruits of your labor. To dream that you are **eating muffins** represents the factors in your life that make you feel secure.

CHEESE

To see **cheese** in your dream indicates potential profit and gain in waking life. **Cheese spread** denotes a false impression or something which is a poor substitute for the original. **Cheesecake**, on the other hand, suggests a rich reward and the expectation of satisfying outcomes to events that lie ahead.

CHOCOLATE

According to Freud, to see **chocolate** in your dream signifies self-reward. It also denotes that you may be indulging in too many excesses and need to practice some restraint, as chocolate is a temporary pleasure that might bring guilt and other negative effects later on.

CORN

To see **corn** in your dream signifies abundance, growth and fertility. Also consider the pun that something is 'corny'. **Cornbread and corn on the cob** represent nourishment through personal efforts. **Corn chips** signify small benefits in life, a **cornfield** signifies an abundance of inner strength, **cornflakes and corn oil** suggest motivation and new beginnings, whilst **cornflour** stands for inner strength.

DESSERT

To see a tasty **dessert** in your dream represents indulgence, celebration, reward, or temptation. You are enjoying the good things in life. Whenever you dream of savoring sweet treats such as **honey, biscuits, pies, cakes or desserts**, your unconscious may be expressing satisfaction with your circumstances at present or, in some cases, compensating you for their bitterness. To dream that you are eating **raisins** could suggest a damaging lack of self-confidence but it could also suggest nourishing benefits that are as unexpected as they are welcome. If **molasses** features in your dream, this defines a factor in your life that can provide much-needed energy or motivation; this factor may well appear as a result of the hospitality of others. To see **popcorn** in your dream suggests that you are full of ideas. It may also indicate that you have developed an idea that is now accomplished and ready to make its mark on the world.

Egg

To see or eat **eggs** in your dream symbolizes fertility, birth, new beginnings and your creative potential. To find a **nest filled with eggs** in your dream signifies some financial gain; the bigger and more abundant the eggs, the more significant the gain. To see an **egg hatching** could refer to a new idea gestating in your mind. To see **cracked or broken eggs** in your dream denotes potential misfortunes and feelings of vulnerability. Alternatively, it could mean that you may be breaking out of your shell and being comfortable with who you are. To see **brightly colored eggs** in your dream symbolizes celebration of a happy event, but to dream of **rotten eggs** signifies loss. You may have allowed some situation to take a turn for the worse. To see **fish eggs** in your dream represents an idea that has emerged from your unconscious.

Consider also the verbal expressions associated with eggs. Are you putting all your eggs in one basket by taking an all-or-nothing gamble? Or have you had egg all over your face when you did something recently that made you look stupid. Dream **omelets** suggest aspects connected to something in waking life with which you are directly associated. It may signify a mixing up or blending of elements regarding a relationship, situation, event or perspective.

Fish

In dreams, **fish** symbolize spiritual aspects of your life, so to be eating a fish in your dream suggests a desire for spiritual nourishment and inspiration. **Fish oil** stands for a highly beneficial characteristic or element. Consider also the word association of 'fishy', meaning suspicion and a questioning sense regarding something. To see **shrimps** in your dream suggests that you are feeling overpowered and insignificant. *See also* REPTILES, FISH AND AMPHIBIANS.

Frozen Food

Different types of food can symbolize a wide range of things. Generally, **frozen foods** may be a reflection of your cold emotions and frigid ways. They could also signify hidden potential that is not being utilized or from which you have not benefited.

Fruit

To see **fruit** in your dream most often points to the nourishing and beneficial effects of using your talents to help others. To see **green fruit** in your dream denotes your hastiness and impatience, whilst to see **ripe red fruit** denotes lust and sexuality. To see a **fruit basket** signifies help given or received. To **see or eat rotting or bitter fruit** suggests that you are missing opportunities for personal growth and pleasure. To dream that you **buy or sell fruit** signifies personal satisfaction but it may also imply much business but insufficient financial reward. A **fruit cocktail** constitutes a multitude of benefits but a **fruitcake** may suggest a lack of logic and reason. *See also* VEGETABLES AND FRUIT.

ICE CREAM

To dream that you are **eating ice cream** denotes pleasure and satisfaction with your life. On the other hand, dream ice cream may also indicate double standards; someone who is aware of the truth but doesn't act upon their knowledge. To dream that you are eating **ice cream that is tasteless, sour or melting** signifies sorrow, disillusionment, or betrayal. An **ice cream cone** implies spiritual aspirations that are internalized but not shared with others. An **ice cream maker** illustrates your ability to grow spiritually but that you have few opportunities to express this growth. An **ice cream parlor** applies to opportunities to share your spirituality. An **ice cream sandwich** suggests spirituality that is hidden by physical or material aspects. An **ice cream soda** implies spirituality that is not demonstrated to others.

LEGUMES

To see **legumes, peas or beans** in your dream symbolizes small annoyances and minor problems. Recall what the legume was associated with in the dream. **Pea soup** pertains to a cloudy perspective or unclear view, whilst to see **lentils** in your dream signifies that your surroundings are emotionally straining.

LOLLIPOP

To **see or lick a lollipop or gobstopper** in your dream indicates surprises, new experiences and adventures that are long lasting.

It also represents indulgence, sensuality and the pleasant aspects of life. Alternatively, the lollipop may be a pun for 'sucker', and thus suggests someone who is easily manipulated. Your dreaming mind may be warning you to proceed with caution in some relationship or situation.

MEAT

To see **raw meat** in your dream refers to solid basics and highly nourishing elements. To see **cooked meat** in your dream may suggest that you will see others obtain the object for which you have been striving. To dream that you are **eating meat** signifies that you are getting to the heart of the matter. Consider also whether you have been chewing over a meaty or substantial piece of information in your waking life. If **beef** figured in your dream, are you in a stew, or troubled by something? Alternatively, if you **carved the meat**, even though you may be a vegetarian, could you be yearning to savor the sins of the flesh? And if you relished the taste of a dream **curry**, do you long to spice up your life?

Meat and potatoes in your dream suggest a preference for the basics or bare essentials of an issue. **Meatballs** indicate irrationality or the times when you lose your reason. A **meat loaf** represents the combining of basic ideas or elements. A **meat packing house** illustrates the quality of the fundamental concepts or basic ideas that you have digested. Recall the condition of the factory; was it clean, or were there rodents and bugs? Consider also the type of meat you eat. If you are eating dream **beef** this may warn you against the ready acceptance of new (raw) ideas. **Chicken**

The Element Encyclopedia of 20,000 Dreams

points to a lack of faith or confidence in oneself. If you are eating **lamb**, do you long for spiritual sustenance? To dream that you are eating **ham** signifies over-emotionalism, dramatics and theatrics.

Oatmeal

In dreams, grains such as **oats** suggest life aspects that have the ability to bring emotional, mental or spiritual nourishment. To dream that you are **eating oatmeal** signifies something in life that comforts and nourishes you. To dream that you are **cooking and serving oatmeal** signifies that you are comforting and nourishing to others. To see **rye or fields of rye** in your dream symbolizes rejuvenation and prosperity in your future. To see or eat **rye bread** in your dream foretells of a cheerful and tranquil home.

Oil

If you dream of **cooking oil**, this indicates a lack of abrasiveness and friction, because oil is a substance that soothes and eases, an essential element to keep things going smoothly. If you **drizzled oil over your dream food**, are you trying to smooth things over in waking life or are you pouring oil over troubled waters, perhaps because you are trying to keep the peace in some way?

Oyster

To dream that you are eating **oysters** signifies that you will lose all your senses and morality in the pursuit of low pleasures and indulgences. To see oysters in your dream symbolizes beauty, wealth, wisdom, and a laid-back atmosphere. On the other hand, dream oysters can also represent shyness or social anxiety, reflecting your inner fears of anything new or of having to interact with others. It can also indicate the wisdom gained from deep introspection and the resolution of inner conflicts.

Pasta

If **pasta** features in your dream, this suggests a basic or important aspect of your life. If you see **pasta, noodles or macaroni in large quantities** it may also suggest a need to economize, and save money. A **pasta fork** stands for a desire to stop an issue becoming complicated by keeping the elements separate.

Pepper

To dream about **pepper** suggests that you need to make some kind of response or decision in waking life. Alternatively, it may indicate that you need to put a little more spice and variety in your life. It may also indicate that there is something that is bothering or irritating you; your dream may be trying to point to the source.

Pie/Pizza

Dream **pies** indicate potential reward for your hard work. They also suggest that you may have been reaching beyond your abilities or they could be a metaphor for getting your fair share, as in your 'piece of the pie'. To see or eat **pizza** in your dream may represent abundance, choices and variety in waking life. Alternatively, it may indicate that you are lacking in, or feeling deprived of, something.

POTATO

To see **potatoes** in your dream symbolizes an essential or basic element in your life, since potatoes are basic nourishment. It may also suggest laziness or stupidity. To see or eat **mashed potatoes** in your dream, suggests that you are experiencing concern over your financial affairs. **Potato skin** relates to the most potent aspect of a situation or the place where the greater number of benefits can be found. To see or eat **crisps or potato chips** in your dream symbolizes overindulgent behavior. It can also relate to the various methods you use to satisfy a basic need. To see a **pretzel** in your dream symbolizes twisted perceptions or confused thought processes concerning a relationship or situation in waking life. It may indicate that you are preoccupied with some complex issue and are not sure how to handle it.

PRESERVE/PICKLE

To dream that you are eating **marmalade or preserves** reflects a tendency to maintain fundamental elements of something, not losing sight of all of an issue's various factors. To dream that you are **making marmalade** denotes an unhappy domestic life. To dream that you are eating **jam** signifies a troubling situation but, by contrast, to dream that you are **making jam** suggests a happy home life. Consider also the pun 'caught in a jam', which means that you may find yourself in something of a fix. To dream that you are eating **jelly or jelly beans** refers to small blessings that may be overlooked in waking life. A **jelly roll** suggests a person who is superficial and frivolous. To see a **pickle or gherkin** in

your dream signifies some anxiety, fear or realization that must be faced, accepted or resolved. Are you in a pickle in the real world? Alternatively, a pickle may be seen as a symbol for the penis.

RICE

To see **grains of rice** in your dream is a symbol of success, prosperity, luck, fertility and warm friendships. To dream that you are **cooking rice** signifies that new responsibilities could bring you much joy. To see **rice mixed with dirt** in your dream signifies illness and separation from friends. Other cereal crops such as **maize, wheat and corn** have a shared symbolic significance when they appear in dreams, one that emphasizes the message denoted by the harvest of dream fruit (*see* VEGETABLES AND FRUIT). If the **crop appeared healthy and plentiful** and you enjoyed eating or tasting it in your dream, this is a reflection of your optimism that will reap a rich harvest or rewards in waking life. But if the **crop was blighted or scarce**, you are probably unconsciously aware that there are hard times ahead.

SALT

To see **salt** in your dream represents added flavor and a new-found flair for the varied experiences of life. Salt is said to be the essence of life, so if you dreamed of **sprinkling salt all over your food**, what is essential in your life? You may be experiencing an elevated sense of individual worthiness and an increased zest in your life. Alternatively, salt also symbolizes dependability, truth, dedication and longevity. If **salt and pepper** figure in a dream this signifies duality and a balance of positive and negative elements. A **salt shaker** relates to an opportunity you may have recently had to improve a situation or a relationship.

SANDWICH

To see a **sandwich** in your dream suggests that a lot of pressure and stress is being put on you. It represents a boxed-in feeling such as may be provoked by a situation, relationship or belief that has a confining effect. It also reflects your ability to do two things at once. To see or eat a **fish sandwich** in your dream indicates conflict between your spiritual beliefs and what is practical.

SPICE/CONDIMENT/HERB

To dream of **spices or herbs** suggests you need more variety in your life. You need to look at a situation or relationship from a different perspective. To dream of **growing herbs** suggests self-advancement through hard work but the dream may also refer to your health. Many herbs have symbolic meanings that go back centuries and, as a result, most individual herbs have specific symbolic meaning in dream lore (*see* box on page 270).

For example, the ancient Romans offered wreaths of **bay leaves** as a symbol of triumph and peace, and they also used to strew **rose petals**, a symbol of both love and victory, on the paths of wedding parties and victors of war. In Britain, **rosemary** was called 'Rose of Mary' in memory of the Virgin Mary, and in Shakespeare's *Hamlet*, Ophelia says, 'There's rosemary, that's for remembrance, pray you love, remember.' In accordance with this association of rosemary with remembrance, the herb was once placed on the graves of loved ones. To see **sage** in your dream constitutes rejuvenating elements in your life, but it could also signal the need to be 'sage', or wise, when taking a decision that is preoccupying your waking mind. **Majoram** is thought to absolve and purify, **rue** reflects the bitterness of loss, whilst **thyme** is seen to represent 'love forsaken'. If **garlic** features in your dream, this refers to your personal defenses against negative aspects or forces in your life. The dream may, in addition, have referred to garlic's medicinal properties and the need to take better care of your health in waking life.

To dream that you are eating **gravy** suggests that something in your life will happen more easily than you expected. Alternatively, it may suggest health problems and business disappointments. To dream of **vinegar** indicates worrisome and negative matters in real life; it may indicate that are the object of jealousy. If **ketchup** features in your dream, this suggests that you need to spice something up in waking life. To see **mustard** in your dream signifies a desire to improve your prospects in life. On the other hand, it could denote some hasty action for which you are suffering and now bitterly regret. Or are you hoping to 'cut the mustard' and satisfy your own expectations in a forthcoming challenge in real life? **Mustard seeds** will most often indicate a new idea and your desire to plant, tend and realize its harvest.

Herbs and symbolism

This is by no means a complete list of the symbolic meanings of each herb but it offers a good starting point. If a specific herb features strongly in your dream, you may want to investigate the historical, religious, medicinal and cultural significance of that particular herb to enrich your interpretation.

Aloe: healing, protection, grief, bitterness, affection
Angelica: inspiration, magic
Bay: glory, honor, reward
Calendula: sacred affection, joy, remembrance, grief
Chamomile: energy in adversity, patience, long life, wisdom
Chives: usefulness, why do you weep?
Dandelion: faithfulness, happiness
Dianthus: dignity, woman's love, symbol of Mother's Day
Dill: preservation, good spirits
Dogwood: love undiminished by adversity, durability
Elder: compassion, bad luck, zeal
Fennel: strength, worthy of praise, flattery
Garlic: protection, strength, healing
Grass: submission, utility, usefulness
Iris: wisdom, faith, valor
Ivy: patience, fidelity, undying love, eternal life

Lavender: housewifely virtue, acknowledgment
Lily of the valley: contentment, return of happiness, let's make up
Marjoram: joy, happiness
Mint: eternal refreshment, wisdom, virtue
Mugwort: be not weary, tranquility, happiness
Mustard: faith, indifference
Nasturtium: patriotism, victory in battle
Pansy: happy thoughts, meditation
Parsley: useful knowledge, feast, joy, victory
Rose: love, victory
Rosemary: remembrance, love, loyalty, fidelity
Saffron: beware of success
Sage: wisdom, long life, immortality, high esteem
Sassafras: foundation, considered choices
Sunflower: haughtiness, loftiness, pride, pure thoughts
Thyme: activity, bravery, courage, strength
Violet: humility, devotion, faithfulness, forgiveness
Yew: immortality, sorrow
Yucca: opportunity, fidelity
Zinnia: thoughts of missing friends

SUGAR

In dreams, **sugar** expresses an energizing element in your life or it may indicate a highly desirable aspect of something, a sweet benefit or a pleasing outcome. To see **syrup** in your dream symbolizes sentimentality and nostalgia. Alternatively, you may have found yourself in a sticky situation. If you are using an **artificial sweetener** in your dream, this suggests an effort to be optimistic and upbeat that is not working very well.

SWEETS/CANDY

To see or eat **sweets or candy** in your dream symbolizes the joys, sweetness and special treats of life. It also represents indulgence, sensuality or forbidden pleasures. Is life sweet at the moment? A **sweet-shop or candy store** indicates the varied methods that are available for experiencing life's joys. A **sweet wrapper** suggests recently experienced joys that should not be so easily forgotten.

VEGETABLES

To see **vegetables** in your dream signifies your need for spiritual nourishment. It may also suggest that you are lacking in some essential nutrients, whether these be physical, emotional, social or intellectual. To see **withered vegetables** in your dream denotes sadness. If you are a **vegetarian** in your dream, this represents a separate opinion or attitude. A **vegetable steamer** denotes the preserving of important elements. *See also* VEGETABLES AND FRUIT.

Thinking about Drinking

ALCOHOL

Dreams that feature **alcohol** can be interpreted in two ways. They could be a warning that you need to take it easy or they could be a suggestion that your life needs more stimulation and excitement. If, however, a **drunk** appeared in your dream or you got **drunk and had a hangover**, this may suggest that you have been overdoing it recently. It can also refer to the way you deal with difficult feelings by drowning them in drink. On the other hand, do you feel drunk with success and if you do, is your unconscious warning you to reign in your exuberance as it is unsettling to those around you? Don't forget the Latin phrase *'in vino veritas'* (wine reveals the truth) and pay attention to what you and other people say in your dream over a glass of wine or beer.

To see **whisky** in bottles symbolizes your alertness, carefulness and protective nature. If you are **drinking alone**, this signifies a selfishness that is driving friends away. To dream of drinking **wine** refers to festivity, celebration, and companionship. To dream that you are **breaking wine bottles** signifies over-indulgence and lack of control.

COFFEE/LEMONADE/MILK/TEA

In waking life **coffee** is a stimulant, so do you need to inject more energy into your waking life? Coffee may also represent sociability, friendship, the giving and sharing of affection or a social life that is in need of reviving. If you are drinking **tea** in your dream, this may represent some stimulating idea, hope, person or contact. It can also suggest a need for relaxation. To dream that you are **drinking water** represents your need for emotional and spiritual refreshment, and to dream that you are **drinking lemonade** signifies that you have the ability to accomplish great things from very little.

If you yourself made, or were given, a **mug of warm milk** in your dream, your dreaming mind is offering you a sensation of warmth, comfort and security, perhaps to compensate for circumstances that are stressful or demanding in waking life. Your dream may also have reminded you of your need to be nurtured and cherished by a maternal figure, a provider of human kindness. Milk is a basic food that can also be drunk and in a dream it may refer to some deep-seated emotional need. If you are a **woman feeding milk to a child or animal** in your dream, this may refer to your desire to mother a person, an animal or protect in some way. Another explanation is that it may represent semen and your desire for a

sexual relationship. To **spill milk** in your dream symbolizes a loss of faith, opportunity, and trust. It may indicate that your friends will cause you much temporary disappointment and unhappiness. To dream of **sour or impure milk** denotes small problems that will torment you, but to dream that you are **bathing in milk** denotes a stable circle of reliable and pleasant friends. Finally, to dream that you are **choking on milk** indicates that you are being overprotected; perhaps you are feeling smothered in some relationship.

DRINKING

If you are **drinking** in your dream, this connects with feelings of thirsting or longing. It suggests that you will find a satisfaction of your longings, either emotionally, physically or spiritually. It can also denote absorbing something, taking nourishment and, by so doing, it points to a change in some way. If you are **thirsty** in your dream, it may be that you are thirsty as you sleep; if this doesn't apply, a dream thirst suggests that you may be feeling emotionally parched in waking life, as **water** is a symbol of the emotions. Generally, if you are **drinking something sweet**, this may suggest a longing for more affection in waking life, whilst dreaming of a **stronger drink** may suggest a need for more energy or a stronger approach to a problem.

The Element Encyclopedia of 20,000 Dreams

FOREIGN COUNTRIES

Should you find yourself visiting, observing, holidaying or living in a foreign country in your dreams, your dream is placing the spotlight on attitudes and emotional climates that are different to yours.

Such dreams can also represent meeting an aspect of yourself that is unknown or foreign; the unfamiliar. If you feel contented in your dream, this suggests excitement about new opportunities in waking life. If, however, you feel insecure and vulnerable, and long to return to the familiar, this is widely interpreted by both Freudians and Jungians as a desire to return to the security of the womb in times of difficulty.

Your associations, beliefs or opinions about a certain country also need to be explored. Do any aspects of your life connect with what appears in the dream? For example, have you previously visited or worked in the country featured in your dream or do you know someone who lives there? What is the main action in the dream, and what is your role in it? Are you meeting things – perhaps for the first time – that you fear in your dream; how do they make you feel? What are the symbols in the dream and can you make any connections with your waking circumstances? *See also* PLACES; TRAVEL.

Foreigners

ABROAD

If you are **going abroad or are abroad** in your dream, your unconscious is thinking about your own personal freedom or your ability to move freely around the your inner and outer worlds. Your dream is giving you an understanding of your feelings towards the widening of your horizons or the making of changes in your life. Pay attention to how you feel in the dream, as this will help you interpret it. The dream could also be about a need to escape from, or leave, a situation, as suggested by the phrase for having a holiday abroad – 'getting away from it all'. If **someone or something arrives from abroad**, this represents a change or something new happening in your life. Someone of the **opposite sex arriving from abroad**

Flags and their symbolism

The way in which a **flag** is treated in your dream may represent the feelings you have towards the country that flag represents. If it is **dirty, burned, torn or trampled on**, this may suggest anger against those who have attacked the country or anger against the country itself. A **sea of waving flags in a crowd** may suggest benign patriotism or a sense of foreboding about excessively strong nationalism. If the **flag is unknown**, it may be a tribal emblem of your entire network of family and friends. Do you feel supported by them or neglected? Your positive or negative attitudes towards the flag in your dream may reveal your unconscious feelings on this issue. As always, the colors of your particular flag – whether or not the flag is known to you or associated with a country you have been to – will be significant.

As far as the universal symbolism for flags is concerned, you can ascribe meaning to certain symbols, but bear in mind that your personal associations should be considered first. For example, the **cross** in the flags of Greece, the Scandinavian countries and Britain is a symbol of Christianity, but it may be telling you something else. Similarly, the **Arabic writing** on the flag of Saudi Arabia saying 'There is no god but God, Mohammed is His Messenger' and 'God is Great' on the flag of Iraq are also **Islamic messages. The Star of David** on the flag of Israel is an ancient Jewish symbol.

Religious symbolism can also be expressed via color. **Green** is often used in the flags of Arab and Islamic countries, such as Libya, Pakistan and Saudi Arabia; the flags of Kuwait, Jordan and Palestine all contain a green stripe. The flags of Turkey, Tunisia and Pakistan include the crescent moon, another traditional Islamic symbol. Communist-derived flags may include a **hammer and sickle**, as in the flag of the former USSR and the current flag of Angola, or a **red background**, such as the flags of China and Vietnam. The **eagle** has been used as a national or imperial symbol since the times of the Roman Empire, which was a huge and enduring Christian territory for over a millennium. Consequently, many Christian, imperial and other aspiring successors and hopefuls have adopted similar emblems, including Germany, Egypt, Russia and the Orthodox Christian Church.

Other symbols in flags can be self-explanatory, such as the 'R' in the middle of the old Rwanda flag, or they can be explained by the history, geography or flora and fauna of a country, such as the cedar tree in the flag of Lebanon.

indicates hopes for a new relationship or the need for new life to be injected into a current relationship. The dream may also be slang – 'a broad' – expressing desire for a particular female.

FOREIGNER/FOREIGN
LANGUAGES

According to dream-lore, **friendly foreigners** in dreams are symbols of good luck, but a person in your dream who is **foreign or who speaks an unfamiliar language** may represent a part of yourself that you do not fully understand or accept. You may be neglecting important feelings or talents, or the dream may be mirroring a sense of frustration caused by problems in communicating with someone in waking life. The latter is often the case when you dream of a **letter that is illegible or written in a foreign language**, although such a dream could also suggest frustration with not being able to solve some difficult issue in waking life.

Whilst **hearing foreign or strange languages** in a dream can suggest misunderstandings, it can also be symbolic of some kind of communication from within, something important that has not yet become clear enough for us to understand or put into words. If you pay attention to the strange language, the next stage of understanding will follow. In spiritualism, hearing strange language is communication from discarnate beings.

UNFAMILIAR COUNTRIES

If, in your dream, you find yourself in a **country where everything seems strange and nothing seems familiar**, this may suggest that you have difficulties in coping with change. However, if the **people are friendly and welcoming**, this may point to the stimulation and satisfaction of a new opportunity in waking life. If you dream of a **particular country but have never been there before**, you might be imagining that you lived there in a past life. Alternatively, such a dream could represent the unknown within yourself, your dream journey representing an exploration of your unconscious.

Your dreams may use foreign countries in many ways to comment on your situation in waking life. For example, if you have bills to pay, the dream may be set in a tax haven such as **Switzerland**; if it is about your instincts, it may be set in some tropical jungle. Unless you have personal associations with the country in your dreams, if your dream is about a **cold country, such as Poland or Russia**, such a dream may be about your emotional life, with cold countries representing the need for more warmth in your life. In much the same way, **hot countries**, such as those in **Africa or southern Asia**, may represent passion. More specifically, you may associate **France** with love, **Italy** with glamor, **Germany** with efficiency, **Spain** with passion, the **USA** with self-reliance, **Belgium** with dullness, and all the other clichés with which we stereotype foreigners and foreign countries.

Foreign Places and Peoples

If your dream highlighted a specific foreign country the brief information below concerning the various countries, continents and parts of the world may help you with the interpretation. It will also apply to a foreigner you encounter in your dream or recognize as being from a particular country or region. For example, if you meet a French person in your dream, the interpretation for France would apply. See if any of the details given about the location, shape on a map, landscape, history or associations with a particular country trigger a personal association for you. You also need to pay attention to how you feel in the dream, as this will aid you with the interpretation. It would be impossible to list every single country; the list below is by no means comprehensive and simply designed to get you thinking along the right lines. If the country or foreign person you dreamed about isn't in the alphabetical list, or if you want to know more it might be worth your while doing some investigation of your own. Finally, your dream country will belong to a specific continent or region; see if there are not wider issues at stake than merely those suggested by the country itself.

COUNTRIES, REGIONS AND AREAS

Afghanistan is a war-torn country bordered on the north by Turkmenistan, Uzbekistan, and Tajikistan, on the extreme north-east by China, on the east and south by Pakistan, and by Iran on the west. The dominant religion is Islam, and in recent years Afghanistan has been the scene of war, conflict and disorder, although signs of economic and financial stability are emerging. If Afghanistan appears in your dreams, your unconscious may have been using the intense media coverage in recent years as raw material, the battle-scarred landscape acting as a symbol for insecurity and conflict in your waking life. On the other hand, it may have been using it to represent hope and new beginnings.

Alaska is a breathtakingly beautiful state in the north-west of the United States that is plunged into almost total darkness for several months every year. If it appears in your dreams, it may either suggest untapped natural talents that are yet to be discovered or the need to take time for careful reflection. The **Alaska Highway** signifies a rugged path with a road that isn't as rough as might be expected.

Albania is situated on the eastern shore of the Adriatic Sea, with Montenegro and Serbia to the north, Macedonia to the east and Greece to the south. Still largely agricultural, Albania is one of the poorest countries in Europe and in dreams it may suggest that you are neglecting an aspect of your life or not giving yourself sufficient emotional and spiritual nourishment.

Algeria is bordered on the west by Morocco and Western Sahara and on the east by Tunisia and Libya. The Saharan region, which constitutes over three-quarters of the land area of the country, is almost completely uninhabited. In dreams, **hot sandy regions such as the Sahara**, suggest a life-stage or condition in which you need a reserve of strength and a good deal of perseverance. It could also suggest a period of emotional drought in your life. Perhaps you have been working too hard recently and have neglected your loved ones?

Andorra nestles high in the Pyrenees mountains on the French–Spanish border and is a popular tourist and winter sports destination, and a wealthy international commercial center. Its banking facilities, low taxes and lack of customs duties make it an appealing place in which to do business. Do any of these associations have meaning for you?

While tourism and financial services have turned **Antigua** into one of the more prosperous countries in the Caribbean, law enforcement officials see it as a major center of money laundering, drugs trafficking and arms smuggling. If Antigua features in your dreams, it's possible that there are dishonest or underhand dealings in your waking life and your dreaming mind is trying to alert you to them.

For many people **Argentina** is associated with the life and times of Eva Duarte de Perón (Evita) and her enormous courage, charisma and popularity with the working classes. Although she never held a government post, Evita acted as de facto minister of health and labor in the 1940s and 1950s, establishing a national charitable organization and awarding generous wage increases to the unions. Dreams that feature Argentina could be urging you to make a stand and fight for what you believe in. If you are a football fan, however, you may be thinking of the 'Hand of God'; has someone been cheating you recently?

Austria includes much of the mountainous territory of the eastern Alps. The country contains many snowfields, glaciers and snow-capped peaks. The Danube is the principal river, and woodlands cover nearly half of the country. Could any of these natural features have significance for you as symbols in your dream? If the focus isn't on the landscape, Austria is the land of Mozart, Johann Strauss, Freud and Klimt; the country is also, like Germany and Switzerland, well known for its attention to detail and a tendency to strive for perfection.

The Bahamas are an archipelago of about 700 islands and 2,400 uninhabited islets and cays lying fifty miles off the east coast of Florida. Only about thirty of the islands are inhabited; the most important is New Providence on which the capital, Nassau, is situated. Other islands include Grand Bahama, Abaco, Eleuthera, Andros, Cat Island and San Salvador (or Watling's Island). In dreams, the Bahamas may indicate holidays, the importance of rest, relaxation and fun and a desire to get away from it all.

Bangladesh, on the northern coast of the Bay of Bengal, is surrounded by India, with a small common border with Myanmar in the south-east. Tropical monsoons, frequent floods and cyclones inflict heavy damage in the delta region. The dramatic climate and landscape of Bangladesh, as well as its close association with India, may hold the key for interpretation if it features in your dream.

An island in the Atlantic about 300 miles north of Venezuela, **Barbados** is circled by fine beaches and narrow coastal plains. In dreams it conjures up images of sunshine, sand and relaxation. Are you in urgent need of some of this in your waking life?

Located in western Europe, **Belgium** has about forty miles of seacoast on the

North Sea. In dreams it can indicate hospitality or a willingness to help others. It can also reflect a desire for more sweetness or quality in your waking life as in the association with the Belgium Chocolates.

If you find yourself lost in the **Bermuda Triangle** in your dreams, this suggests vacillation and confusion in waking life.

Bosnia and Herzegovina make up a triangular-shaped republic on the Balkan peninsula. Since the time of the Roman Empire, the Balkans has been a crossroads of religions and civilizations, so in dreams it could be urging you to find a common ground with another person or adopt a unified approach to a particular situation in your waking life.

Brazil covers nearly half of South America and is the continent's largest country. Brazil may be divided into the Brazilian Highlands, or plateau, in the south and the Amazon River Basin in the north. Over a third of Brazil is drained by the Amazon and its more than 200 tributaries. In dreams, the **Amazon jungle** conjures up images of confusion, danger and the unexpected. The **river Amazon** conjures up images of a path thwart with dangers.

About the size of Delaware, **Brunei** is an independent sultanate on the north-west coast of the island of Borneo in the South China Sea, wedged between the Malaysian states of Sabah and Sarawak. Brunei has one of the highest per capita incomes in Asia, and the Sultan of Brunei is believed to be one of the richest men in the world; so if Brunei features in your dream, it may well be referring to your desire for a life of luxury and opulence in waking life.

Bulgaria shares borders with Serbia, Macedonia, Romania, Greece and Turkey. The Maritsa is Bulgaria's principal river, and the river Danube also flows through the country. In dreams, Bulgaria may indicate strength of character or a strong constitution.

Burma is located in south-east Asia, bordering the Andaman Sea and the Bay of Bengal, between Bangladesh and Thailand. Does this area have any special significance to you or someone you know in waking life? The association with Burmese cats, a breed of cat known for its expressive, outgoing and appealing personality may also be of significance.

Covering most of the northern part of the North American continent and with an area larger than that of the United States, **Canada** has an extremely varied landscape and topography. Canada is a federation of ten provinces (Alberta, British Columbia, Manitoba, New Brunswick, Newfoundland and Labrador, Nova Scotia, Ontario, Prince Edward Island, Quebec, and Saskatchewan) and three territories (Northwest Territories, Yukon and Nunavut). If your dream should feature Canada in some way, this probably relates to a diversity of inherent talents that your dreaming mind is encouraging you to express in waking life.

Situated south of Peru and west of Bolivia and Argentina, **Chile** fills a narrow 1,800-mile strip between the Andes and the Pacific. If you find yourself in Chile in your dreams, this may relate to situations or relationships in your life that could develop into hot ones due to the 'chili' word association. If this doesn't apply, other associations include the strong Roman Catholic bias of the country, the symbolism of the arid Atacama Desert and a strong feminine principle embodied by socialist Michelle Bachelet who won 53% of the vote in the March 2006 presidential elections.

The vast and highly populated country of **China** might suggest the duality of fragile treasures and mass-produced products – or delicate elements in your life being interspersed with common, unremarkable and mundane events – when it appears in dreams. **China syndrome** is a symbol that seriously warns of the destructive effects caused by uncontrolled emotions, **Chinatown** refers to the absorption of seemingly foreign aspects into your belief system, whilst **Chinese puzzle** denotes confusion and difficulty in finding solutions to a problem. (Bordering China, **North Korea** currently stands for oppression and **South Korea** suggests a tenuous position or situation.)

Colombia is bordered on the north-west by Panama, on the east by Venezuela and Brazil, and on the south-west by Peru and Ecuador. Despite its dramatic and varied landscape, Colombia is chiefly known for its drug trafficking, corruption and high crime rate. In May 2004, the UN announced that Colombia's 39-year-long drug war had created the worst humanitarian crisis in the Western Hemisphere. More than two million people have been forced to leave their homes and several Indian tribes are close to extinction. If Colombia features in your dream, your unconscious may be trying to warn you of unethical or dangerous activities going on around you.

Costa Rica has the reputation of being one of the most stable, prosperous, and least corrupt Latin American countries, although in 2004, three former Costa Rican presidents were investigated on corruption charges. If Costa Rica features in your dreams, this may relate to some kind of fall from grace or deviance in waking life. On

the other hand, it could represent energy, vitality and prosperity.

The largest island of the West Indies group, **Cuba** is famous for its history, tropical beaches, salsa music, nightlife, architecture, cigars, art and diversity of cultures; in dreams, it may be encouraging you to liven up your daily routine with a little adventure and excitement. On the other hand, you might be thinking of the American prisoner base at Guantanamo Bay, which, depending on your politics, has quite different meanings.

The third-largest island in the Mediterranean, **Cyprus** lies off the southern coast of Turkey and the western shore of Syria. Should the country feature in some way in your dream, there may be associations with the **cypress tree**, which stands for grief or mourning. On the other hand, it may relate to the need for more tranquility and peace in your waking life.

The **Czech Republic**'s central European landscape is dominated by the Bohemian Massif, which rises to heights of 3,000 feet above sea level. This ring of mountains encircles a large elevated basin, the Bohemian Plateau. In dreams, this country suggests strong traditions and a personal sense of noble heritage.

Smallest of the Scandinavian countries **Denmark** occupies the Jutland peninsula, a lowland area. In dreams it typically suggests a tolerance or acceptance of another person's unique individuality.

The **Dominican Republic** was explored by Columbus on his first voyage in 1492. He named it *La Española*, and his son, Diego, was its first viceroy. The capital, Santo Domingo, founded in 1496, is the oldest European settlement in the Western Hemisphere. In dreams, it could

Continents and Foreign Cities

Africa

Uncluttered thoughts and ideas; instinct, intuition and hidden or secret mysteries.

North America

Perseverance and free expression of individuality.

South America

Positive and negative hidden aspects to benefits that appear bright.

Asia

Symbol of spirituality and the search for hidden truth.

Australia

Congeniality and friendship.

Europe

Diversity of ideas and perspectives.

North Pole/Arctic

Seeking balance, higher conceptual aspects to focus on.

South Pole/Antarctic

Basic elements of an issue or concept that are difficult to discover.

Foreign cities in dreams have similar interpretations as foreign countries in general, but by choosing a specific city, your dreaming mind is drawing your attention to something about that city that is of particular significance or meaning to you. This list is solely designed to give you some pointers, so if your dream city doesn't appear here, or you want to find out more, it might be worthwhile to do some additional research on the history, culture and significance of specific cities that appear in your dreams. *See also* LANDSCAPES.

Bangkok

Busy, crowded and beautiful, **Bangkok** is a mixture of old and new and famous for its Buddhist temples. In dreams, it could be urging you to use your past experience to deal with a present situation.

Barcelona

Barcelona is one of the world's most dynamic, cosmopolitan cities – and one of the most progressive. Widely famous for its architectural attractions, Barcelona lives on the edge of fashion, design and music, and its dining and nightlife reflect the same cutting-edge modern tastes. Could a dream of this Catalan city be urging you to revamp your image or add some variety to your life?

Berlin

The **Berlin Wall** signifies the destruction of walls built to separate or segregate peoples; if you dream about it, have you recently enjoyed the fruits of some thaw in relations with a disliked figure in your life – or in yourself?

Istanbul

Historically, **Istanbul** is famous as one of the most besieged cities in the world, so could a dream set in Istanbul mirror conflict or invasion of personal space in your waking life?

London

Tradition, history and monarchy are associated with London. Do any of these meanings have significance to you?

Los Angeles

Hollywood and movies dominate associations with **Los Angeles**, so could you be yearning for more attention or action in waking life?

Moscow

The capital of Russia, **Moscow** can be a very cold place and if it features in your dreams, perhaps you have been a little cold or distant lately. Is it time to bring warmth and emotional depth into your life?

New York

Excitement, opportunities, shopping and glamor are all associated with **New York**; on the other hand, it has always been associated with crime, and is now – after 9/11 – associated with terror and destruction as well. Try to work out the associations that have meaning for you.

Paris

Along with Venice, **Paris** is the capital most associated with love and romance, so could you be longing for more passion in your waking life?

Rome

Famous for its glorious art and architecture, **Rome** is a center of culture and beauty. Your dreaming mind may be urging you to explore your creativity if Rome features in your dreams.

Tokyo

Well known for its shopping and business potential, **Tokyo** is a city associated with industry, business, risk, success and opportunity. Do these associations have meanings for you?

suggest strong traditions but it may also suggest financial hardship mirroring the economic crisis of the Republic.

Egypt, at the north-east corner of Africa on the Mediterranean Sea, is bordered on the west by Libya, on the south by the Sudan, and on the east by the Red Sea and Israel. Egypt is divided into two unequal, extremely arid regions by the landscape's dominant feature, the north-ward-flowing river Nile. In dreams, Egypt is generally a sign of the spiritual life and conveys a spiritually related message of some kind. It can also suggest a yearning to learn more about human history.

Ethiopia is in east-central Africa, bordered on the west by the Sudan, on the east by Somalia and Djibouti, on the south by Kenya, and on the north-east by Eritrea. In dreams, perhaps fuelled by media campaigns and reports, Ethiopia can be a symbol of famine, malnourishment and emotional need.

With its revolutionary history and reputation as the country of love and romance, **France** suggests passion in dreams and the inner strength to fight for what you believe in. The **Eiffel Tower** suggests recognition of past achievements, as well as being a notable phallic symbol.

Located in central Europe, **Germany** is made up of the North German Plain, the Central German Uplands (Mittelgebirge), and the Southern German Highlands. Germany's major rivers are the Danube, the Elbe, the Oder, the Weser and the Rhine. In dreams, Germany is a symbol of fortitude, discipline and renewal, but it can also suggest hardship, injustice and fanaticism due to lingering associations with Hitler and the atrocities of World War II.

Located in south-east Europe, **Greece** represents the origins of democracy and the practice of philosophy. If it features in your dream, the associations with Greek mythology and the gods of Olympus suggest desirable attributes and talents; on the other hand, it may simply mean that you are stressed and need a holiday.

This central European country is a fertile, rolling plain lying east of the river Danube and is drained by the Danube and Tisza rivers. In dreams, it signifies pride in ethnic traditions and strength of character. It can also be associated with emotional or physical malnourishment, as in the word association with 'hunger'.

Iceland lies in the North Atlantic Ocean east of Greenland and just touches the Arctic Circle. It is one of the most volcanic regions in the world. Much of the country is covered by snowfields and glaciers, and most of the people live in the small part of the island that is made up of fertile coastland. The Gulf Stream keeps Iceland's climate milder than one would expect from an island near the Arctic Circle. In dreams, it can refer to largeness of character, self-reliance and fortitude. It may also refer to emotional frigidity that needs to be thawed or, because Iceland is volcanic, hidden passions lurking beneath a calm or cool exterior.

India occupies most of the sub-continent of India in south Asia. It borders on China in the north-east, Pakistan on the west, Nepal and Bhutan on the north, and Burma and Bangladesh on the east. As one of the most densely populated countries in the world, it exemplifies a wealth of spiritual diversity, as well as ritualistic spiritual beliefs. It is also one of the poorest countries in the world, so to dream of it may also

The Element Encyclopedia of 20,000 Dreams

suggest emotional malnourishment or financial worries.

Indonesia is an archipelago in south-east Asia consisting of 17,000 islands (6,000 inhabited) and straddles the equator. The largest islands are Sumatra, Java (the most populous), Bali, Kalimantan (Indonesia's part of Borneo), Sulawesi (Celebes), the Nusa Tenggara islands, the Moluccas Islands, and Irian Jaya (also called West Papua), the western part of New Guinea. Indonesia, part of the 'ring of fire', has the largest number of active volcanoes in the world. Earthquakes are frequent and this symbolic association may help you with your interpretation.

Iraq is a Middle Eastern country ripped apart by conflict, bitterness and fanatical devotion to religion. If it should appear in your dreams, it may be expressing your concern for the future of world peace, but may also be mirroring conflict, tension and hostility in your waking life.

Israel lies at the eastern end of the Mediterranean Sea. It is bordered by Egypt on the west, Syria and Jordan on the east, and Lebanon on the north. Its maritime plain is extremely fertile. A country at present suffering from religious conflict between the various inhabitants of the country, Israel, and particularly Jerusalem, are traditionally associated with all three of the Abrahamic religions: Judaism, Islam and Christianity.

Slightly larger than the state of Arizona, **Italy** is a long peninsula, shaped like a boot, surrounded on the west by the Tyrrhenian Sea and on the east by the Adriatic. The fashion capital of the world, Italy is a symbol of glamor and emotional expressiveness.

An archipelago in the Pacific, **Japan** is separated from the east coast of Asia by the Sea of Japan. Japan's four main islands are Honshu, Hokkaido, Kyushu, and Shikoku. In dreams, it may indicate spiritual tranquility or the need for it in waking life.

The Middle Eastern kingdom of **Jordan** is bordered on the west by Israel and the Dead Sea, on the north by Syria, on the east by Iraq, and on the south by Saudi Arabia. Traditionally associated with Christianity, it is currently a hotbed of religious and political tensions, and in dreams may refer to inner conflict, or some kind of hostility and tension directed towards you in waking life.

Kenya lies across the Equator in east-central Africa, on the coast of the Indian Ocean. Well known for its wildlife and safari adventures, if Kenya features in your dreams it could indicate a lack of adventure and excitement in your waking life. It may also refer to your instincts and be urging you to follow your intuition.

Mexico is bordered by the United States to the north, Belize and Guatemala to the southeast and is about one-fifth the size of the United States. In dreams, it can suggest a readiness to express your emotions and opinions. This may come as a message to make sure you have your say or it could be suggesting that you should hold your tongue. The dream may also be referring to the strong determination and fortitude of a meek-appearing friend, as in the Mexican hairless dog breed.

On the coast of the North Sea, the **Netherlands** is renowned for its **tulips**, windmills and dykes, as well as for its sexual openness and belief in the freedom of speech, thought and action. In dreams, it may be encouraging you to explore your sexuality or to express yourself more openly.

Located to the south-east of Australia, **New Zealand** consists of two main islands and a number of smaller outlying islands so scattered that they range from the tropical to the polar. In dreams it suggests diversity but also pastoral respite.

Situated in the western part of the Scandinavian peninsula, **Norway** is a country renowned for its fjords, the quality of its goods and for its sound economy. In dreams, it may be encouraging you to make more quality choices in your daily life and take better care of yourself by eating healthily, and by getting regular exercise and fresh air.

The **Philippines** are an archipelago of over 7,000 islands lying about 500 miles off the south-east coast of Asia. In dreams, the Philippines may stand for hidden hazards and the need to watch out for the unexpected in waking life.

Located in north-central Europe, the cold winters in **Poland** may mirror a lack of emotional warmth in your waking life; but the country could also stand for a hearty character and loyalty to tradition and family.

Portugal occupies the western part of the Iberian peninsula. In dreams, it refers to emotional expressiveness and the ease with which one can share feelings openly with others. If your dream is set in Portugal perhaps your unconscious is encouraging you to open up to others.

Romania is in south-east Europe and if this country features in your dreams, could it be drawing your attention to the symbol of the vampire? Is someone you know, or something you are doing, in waking life draining the life out of you?

Russia occupies most of eastern Europe and northern Asia, stretching from the Baltic Sea in the west to the Pacific Ocean in the east, and from the Arctic Ocean in the north to the Black Sea and the Caucasus in the south. If it features in your dreams, it could be referring to emotional coldness in waking life, but it could also symbolize perseverance, a strong character and a struggle to express your individuality that is eventually successful.

Saudi Arabia occupies most of the Arabian Peninsula, with the Red Sea and the Gulf of Aqaba to the west and the Persian Gulf to the east. In dreams, it signifies power gained through wealth.

Spain occupies most of the Iberian peninsula, which it shares with Portugal. In dreams, it suggests strong traditions. Bear in mind too, the association with bulls and fighting.

Sweden, which occupies the eastern part of the Scandinavian peninsula, is the fourth-largest country in Europe and may represent tolerance for individuality if it features in your dream.

Switzerland, in central Europe, is the land of the Alps. In dreams, it suggests neutrality and a tendency to stay out of another's affairs; it may also represent the presence of a fine skill.

Turkey is at the north-east end of the Mediterranean Sea in south-east Europe and south-west Asia. Should images of **Turkey** or of Turkish visitors feature in your dream, this may refer to hidden intelligence or quiet wisdom behind an unlikely exterior.

The **United Kingdom**, consisting of **Great Britain (England, Wales,** and **Scotland)** and **Northern Ireland** is a constitutional monarchy and parliamentary democracy, with a queen and a parliament that has two houses: the House of Lords and the House of Commons, which has 651 popularly elected members. In dreams, England can represent good friendship, lush green countryside, a tendency to adhere to social mores and tradition, and a glorification of past achievements and history. Northern Ireland is separated from Great Britain by the Irish Sea; frequently in the news for the religious tensions that still exist, this beautiful country is a symbol of undiscovered possibilities, as well as of inner conflict. It can also relate to undiscovered aspects of reality, unproven aspects of reality or the range of possibilities open to you. Scotland refers to a proud heritage and Wales denotes good heartedness and unpretentiousness.

The **United States** is a federal republic consisting of fifty states. In dreams, it stands for diversity and openness to possibilities, as well as open-mindedness, hope and new beginnings. The **American dream** refers to basic life goals or basic rights common to everyone. In other words, the good life that is without ties to country, class or ethnicity.

GATHERINGS

Groups or gatherings of people in a dream usually depict how you relate to other people in waking life.

According to a Jungian interpretation, social gatherings suggest different aspects of yourself in waking life. In all large gatherings of people there is usually a strong emotional charge of either good feelings and generosity of spirit, or tension, conflict and stress. If you find yourself part of a gathering in your dream, you can begin your interpretation by considering the basic atmosphere and feeling of the occasion.

Whether you are celebrating a special occasion in your dream, catching up with friends or colleagues or being bustled along in a busy, crowded street, the people who surround you, your reaction to them, their reaction to you and the events that occurred in the dream all suggest your personal likes and dislikes. These preferences refer to the people with whom you mix, to your self-perceived status within your family, social and professional life, as well as to your self-confidence, insecurity and individuality. Bear in mind that such dreams can also be full of surprises; you may find the people or yourself in your dream gatherings behaving out of character.

If you are confused about the meaning of your dream, this chapter is designed to help; but you may also find it useful to refer to the chapters on FAMILY, PEOPLE and RELATIONSHIPS.

Family and Social Gatherings

FAMILY OCCASION

Dreams that focus on **happy family get-togethers, celebrations, anniversaries, meals or meetings** could be explained as wish-fulfillment, nostalgia or even anticipation. Perhaps your dreaming mind is recalling a happy event from the past or mourning the loss of those happy times when the family was all together. You may also be looking forward to meeting up with your family in the future. If the **family dream is stressful**, however, your dreaming mind may have conjured up images of

Celebrations

Dream **celebrations** tend to reflect feelings of satisfaction you may have about yourself in waking life. If images of **Christmas, Easter, New Year or Thanksgiving** appear in your dream, your dreaming mind may be prompting you to pay more attention to your spiritual beliefs. If **Christmas is disappointing or forgotten** in your dreams, perhaps you need to lower your expectations in waking life. If you were taking part in a **carnival or procession** in your dream, who or what was in the procession or carnival? Were you getting involved in the action or missing out on what your waking life has to offer? If your dream **festival** was celebrating someone or something, who or what was being celebrated may hold the key to the interpretation.

If you dream of a **village fete**, it is well to recall that these events often involve some rivalry and competition; perhaps this is significant to your interpretation. To dream of **any occasion for rejoicing, such as a graduation, birthday party, promotion or investiture** is a positive sign of an upbeat mood. If you are **not joining in with the fun**, consider whether you need to brighten up your outlook on life. In general, dream celebrations present us with images of what life could be like if you got that promotion, passed that examination or got the partner of your dreams. They are good examples of wish-fulfillment in dreams. **Chilled champagne, finger food, piñatas and brightly colored decorations** are all symbols of celebration that may emphasize an elated waking mood in dreamland.

real or imagined **family arguments, disagreements, tensions and grudges** to highlight and bring to your attention those unresolved tensions associated with your family life that are still holding you back in your waking life; for example, sibling rivalry or lack of respect for authority or the parent figure. Alternatively if your family life is healthy and happy, and you still have dreams in which family arguments occur, your dreaming mind may conjure up such images to highlight possible feelings of insecurity; perhaps you feel that you are failing to live up to the standards and expectations of your relatives.

FRIENDS

Dreams which feature your **friends or groups of friends** highlight your feelings about them in waking life. If the **friends are people you do not know**, they may represent your inner wisdom or intuition; the character of the friends will tell you what aspect of yourself they display. In dreams, **friends behaving inappropriately** can also represent your shadow self – the aspect of your personality that you are denying or have rejected. By portraying your shadow aspect as a friend or group of friends, your dreaming mind may be urging you to integrate neglected parts of your personality and restore inner harmony. You may have a dream in which a **group of friends or people you know behave like total strangers to you**, despite your efforts to remind them that you know each other. Such dreams are symbols of low self-confidence, but they can also suggest that you are trying too hard to be popular or to make a friendship work, because the desire for friendship is one-sided: your own.

PARTY

If you dream of **hosting a group of people at a social event or party**, this may express a desire to show affection to those close to you in your waking life. Pay attention to who is or isn't present, as it may indicate who or what is missing from your life. If you **wrote invitations, gave presents, hosted or invited people you don't like**, this suggests that you have been neglecting your social life and need to revitalize it. If **you invited people you like**, this suggests that you need to have more fun in your life. Being **showered with gifts or attention at a party** may be a wish-fulfillment dream. Dream **parties and social events** may also reflect a desire to widen your social circle or forge new work contacts.

If **you were the life and soul of the party or event**, this indicates a longing to be popular, self-assured and socially confident. Pay attention to how you behave at the party and how you interact with others as it will be commenting on your social skills. If you **confidently mixed with everyone at a New Year's party**, this is a positive message but if you were a **shy wallflower**, your dreaming mind may have been suggesting that you should try to interact more. **Conversations at parties with someone you know** suggest a desire to get to know that person more; if you **do not know the person**, your dreaming mind is encouraging you to discover hidden aspects of yourself. If someone **gatecrashes your party**, this could reflect your feelings towards someone who is pestering you in waking life or hindering your progress.

Festive gathering at restaurants will also have relevance to your waking relationships. Pay attention to who is attending and if the atmosphere is pleasant; this could indicate the people that you feel sustain you emotionally or who you wish would perform this role. If you are the family cook in waking life, your dream may also have been urging you to treat yourself. If **wine was served at the meal**, this suggests relaxation but if **champagne was served**, celebration. If you are **puzzling over menu choices** in your dream, this may be reflecting uncertainty in your waking life or the number of tempting choices available to you.

Work Gatherings

CONFERENCE/CONVENTION

If your dream contained images of **conferences or conventions**, your unconscious may be suggesting that you listen to the

The Element Encyclopedia of 20,000 Dreams

opinions of other people and become more open-minded. If you were **speaking at such a gathering**, pay attention to the reaction of the audience as it will indicate how well other people are reacting to you in real life. For example, if the **audience walked out or fell asleep**, this is a negative sign. If, however, they **applauded you at a public meeting**, this may symbolize a breakthrough or recognition in some area of your waking life. If you **stuttered your way through a speech or left the stage feeling humiliated**, your unconscious was probably reflecting your anxiety about your work performance or a future event at which you are obliged to speak in waking life.

Meeting

If your unconscious **calls a dream meeting** with the people with whom you work in waking life, it may be commenting on your relationship with them. You may find in such dreams that **work colleagues or bosses behave out of character**; for example, a **timid colleague is loud and aggressive or a supportive boss becomes a tyrant**; if this is the case, your unconscious could have been warning you to watch out for these people as they may not be what they seem in waking life. To dream that you are **attending a reception** suggests the possibility of, or desire for, pleasant engagements and social gatherings.

Clubs, Groups and Crowds

Club/Tribe/Secret order

Being part of a group is a fundamental human urge and it can express itself in dreams that feature large groups or people. Being a member of a **club or gang** gives you a sense of security, as it is a meeting a group of people with a common interest, goal or purpose. If your **social dream was pleasant**, it can suggest that you are feeling secure and happy in your current social situation. If the dream was unpleasant, however, and you were **rejected or thrown out of your club**, you may be feeling that your goals and opinions are not the same as those of other people in your life. We often hate to feel different from our friends and so any dream in which you were a **part of a tribe or secret order with elaborate ritual and rules** may be questioning how much you are expressing your individuality in waking life. If you are **chased by a gang or yob** in your dream this is similar to dreams of being chased by a monster and the gang or yob should be faced. Consider who or what the gang or yob represents to you.

Commune/Community

In waking life, **communes and communities** are gatherings of like-minded people who, being often prepared to sacrifice personal material gain for social ends, often work for scant pay; if you are in a **dream**

commune or community, do you feel a little exploited in your working situation or taken advantage of in some way? Your dream may also be expressing your sense of concern for the common good. Perhaps you are thinking about undertaking some kind of volunteer work or your dreaming mind is urging you to do so.

Miscellaneous groups

Being part of a **church congregation** in your dream may be in some way connected to your moral attitude. Your mood, attitude and reaction to the service will be important when interpreting the dream. If you were part of a **regiment, orchestra or dance troop** in your dream, this suggests a need for more discipline and communicative action in waking life. The people involved may also represent the people with whom you are working in real life. Was everyone in time, marching with purpose or keeping in step? If your dreams take you back to **school, college or university reunions**, your dream may be suggesting that you are in need of greater intellectual challenge and stimulation in waking life, and that you need to open your mind. If you were attending a **political rally** this suggests some anger in your waking life that needs to be worked through.

CROWD

A number of possible interpretations for dreams of **crowds** suggest themselves. These range from a need for a feeling of unity or belonging; a sense of suffocation, feeling stifled or crowded out; a desire for anonymity and to blend into the crowd; a sense of feeling like a stranger, that you are misplaced or too much going on in your life. The details of your dream should help provide the meaning. In dreams, crowds can also express how well you relate to other people, particularly in a social sense. They may also indicate how well you hide yourself, hide aspects of yourself or attempt to avoid responsibility.

A **large crowd** can suggest information overload, a crowd of problems or finding yourself in a situation that overwhelms you. A dream of **feeling at one with a crowd** – such as watching or singing along at a match or game in a sport's arena – may have been emphasizing the security you derive from being with like-minded people. If, however, you **do not feel at one with the crowd**, your dreaming mind may be urging you to assert your individuality. If you **transformed into a cheerleader**, your unconscious may have been highlighting the euphoria that you feel in waking life from being at one with the people around you. The **denser and more claustrophobic the crowd** in your dream, the greater and more demanding the problems in your waking life may seem; if you **find a way out of the crowd or take control of it**, your dream interpretation will be positive. If you are **trampled down in the crowd** in your dream, this suggests that you need a great deal of help. Perhaps you are working too hard, caring for a sick relative or the

Dream group

Whilst individual dream work is rewarding and necessary to the growth of your understanding of dreams, you can sometimes overlook or be bewildered by certain aspects of your dreams. These are the natural limitations imposed by your blindspots, or over-involvement with the dream itself. These blindspots are those of your beliefs and values that are held as unchangeable; the over-involvement with the dream occurs when your emotional reaction to the dream or the dream images is still fresh enough that the necessary perspective one needs for some of the dreamwork can be missing. Other people can usually avoid these limitations because they are not directly connected to the dream material. They approach the dream with fresh eyes and ears, and with sufficient difference in life experience that they can provide the distance necessary for an accurate interpretation.

In short – even when using this encyclopedia – you may find that you get stuck every now and again when interpreting your dreams. If this happens, you may want to share your dreams with a dream partner. Another approach would be to join a dream group that meets weekly or monthly.

Most of us have dream partners, and we don't even know it. Friends, partners, co-workers: all of them have probably heard us say at one time or another: 'I had the strangest dream last night!' Such interaction is normal, and can be helpful and insightful; there can be problems, however, especially if your dream partner appears in an unfavorable light in your dream, or disturbing images appear in your dream that might make for uncomfortable listening.

A **dream group** is a group of people who meet on a regular basis to share and help each another understand the meaning of their dreams. A group may consist of two or up to twelve members, although from five to seven individuals in this type of group works very well. Some are professionally facilitated or led by a well-experienced dreamworker; others are leaderless or egalitarian. Some 'organizers' of the group charge a fee for participation; others don't.

Each group has its own unique ethics and procedures, often based on those processes developed for doing dream group work over the past few decades. One of the most popular is Dr Montague Ullman's 'If it were my dream' technique, or variations on that theme. Most groups don't try to mimic the dream analysis or interpretation that would take place in a therapeutic situation; the intent is rather to provide a safe environment in which to allow a dreamer to be respectfully heard and questioned, respectfully listening to the dreamer, questioning them and ultimately helping them to come to a better understanding of what their dream is communicating.

Sharing dreams with a partner or with a group can be beneficial to everyone. But when you are dealing with something of such a personal nature, there have to be guidelines:

Everyone has to remember that dream sharing is NOT therapy.

No matter how tempting, do not interpret anyone else's dream for them. All you will be doing is reflecting your own feelings about the dream.

Respect the dreamer's experience of the dream, no matter how much you may personally disagree.

For the partnership or group's work to be successful, the dreamers must feel comfortable enough to express as much (or as little) of their emotions as they want. Remember that the dreamer is vulnerable, and go to all lengths to ensure confidentiality.

Treat the dreamer with gentleness. When the dreamer wants to stop a discussion, they must be able to without feeling an excuse is necessary. Never pressure a dreamer to talk, no matter how helpful you may think it would be.

problems you are facing are too overwhelming to deal with alone.

In dreams, **unknown people in crowds or gatherings** often represent aspects of yourself, such as your attitudes, strengths and anxieties. As social relationships are important for personal well-being and survival, such dreams also help you clarify your way of interacting with society in general. Are you in contact with the people in your dreams? Do you conform or rebel? Do you like the people in your dream and what do they mean to you? Questions like these will throw light on the meaning of your dream. Such dreams can also depict what public opinion thinks of you, so pay attention to the reaction of the people in the crowds.

GOOD DEEDS

Positive experiences are usually less common in dreams than negative experiences; but when they do appear, their purpose is to compensate, inspire, encourage and motivate.

According to Jung, dreams are a compensation for what is going on in daily life. They can serve as a positive or negative compensation. In this way, they attempt to balance the psyche. For example, if you experience unhappiness in daily life, you may have a positive, uplifting dream of happiness and contentment. There may also be an element of wish-fulfillment. For example, if you are in financial trouble in your waking life, you may have an exciting dream about winning the lottery.

As well as serving a compensatory or wish-fulfillment function, your dreaming mind may conjure up images of courage, bravery or tenderness in dreams to highlight the need for you to be equally courageous, brave or tender in your waking life. Dreams that feature kindness, love, goodness and purity also highlight qualities that you might want to consider nurturing within yourself. And if you see yourself acting like a saint or a hero in your dreams, the message may be that if you follow the example set in your dream you may find a way to overcome obstacles that are holding

you back so you can move forward in certain areas of your life. *See also* BAD DEEDS; FAMILY; RELATIONSHIPS; SEX.

Acts of Courage

BRAVERY

Acts of **bravery** in your dream tap into the archetypal hero and, if they appear in your dream, your unconscious is urging you either to accept help when it is offered or to discover courage within yourself. In other words, your dreaming mind is urging you to find the hero inside yourself.

RESCUE

If you had a dream in which your very own **knight in shining armor appeared to fight off and rescue you from danger**, try to identify your rescuer. Was it someone

Archetypal healing dreams

Jung thought that dreams tell us things about ourselves that we might not already know, giving us information that contrasts with our conscious understanding of our feelings, thoughts and desires. Jung also believed that dreams can help us find our true vocation and life purpose. Those who listen to this inner guidance often find new directions in life that set them on a course of great fulfillment and happiness. In other words, dreams can have a healing function.

Archetypal symbols in our dreams, Jung taught, are especially important as they carry potent healing energy, enabling us to change on inner levels that bypass pure intellect. The unconscious mind actually 'speaks' in symbols – symbols are its language – so we accomplish change most powerfully when we communicate with the inner self using archetypal symbols instead of words. Let us say, for example, that you have an exceptionally clear and vivid dream about a **robed, bearded figure** – a typical image of the wise old man – and he is **floating outside the windows of your home**. Since the home often represents yourself, the dream might make you aware that you are seeing wisdom outside of yourself instead of within. But the presence of the archetypal symbol also tells us that our higher self seeks to intervene!

Or let's say you dreamed of a **valiant hero or heroine rescuing you from extreme danger**. You may be hoping to be rescued by someone in your waking life. Your dreaming mind is urging you to accept assistance if it is given to you; it may also be urging you to find the hero or heroine, in other words courage, within yourself. Or you might have an archetypal dream of a **mother bear**. In the dream, this archetype of the great mother might be cuffing her young or refusing to feed them. Such a scene would give you important information about how you are nurturing others or yourself. Perhaps you neglected your basic needs. In some way, you are not 'mothering yourself' in a healthy and beneficial manner; your higher self seeks to call this to your attention.

On the other hand, in a time of loneliness in your life, you might dream of being held and comforted by a great mother figure – and wake up from the dream feeling energized and ready to go on. The great mother in your dream, in a very real way, 'kissed it and made it better'. In looking at these two views of the mother, you can see the opposite sides that Jung pointed out were an essential aspect of all archetypes. It is through integrating this duality that you can become whole and at peace.

you know or know of, or was it a stranger? Who was rescued, and who or what were they or you rescued from? If the **rescuer was someone you know**, your unconscious may have been underlining your reliance on them or hinting that they could soon play an important part in your life. If the **rescuer was a stranger, a celebrity or superhuman being (or even you)**, your dreaming mind is prompting you to admire and adopt these qualities in your waking life. The dream intention is to inspire and encourage you to be as brave and as decisive as the heroic archetype that appeared in your dream when you confront a challenge in your waking life. Try also to identify who or what was rescued as this could help you identify what in your life needs rescuing. Identifying whom or what you or the hero is battling against will also help you identify what is threatening you in real life; this will give you an opportunity to save it. If your **hero gave you words of wisdom** in your dream, pay attention to them too, as they may provide you with rich insight into your current situation.

Acts of Kindness

COMPASSION

You may have had a dream in which **someone was uncharacteristically compassionate, merciful or generous towards you or someone else**. If this is the case, your dreaming mind may have conjured up this scenario to alert you to the need to rise above negativity and pessimism so that you can recognize and possibly adopt more compassion and selflessness in your own life. If your dream benefactor was an archetypal figure such as the **mother, father, high priestess or priest**, this dream may have been particularly inspirational and uplifting. Your unconscious may also be urging you to respect other people despite their faults and to stop judging and start understanding more.

GRATITUDE

If **someone helped you out or gave you something of great value** in your dream, pay attention to how you felt when receiving their help, attention or charity as this will be the key to the interpretation. If you felt **unworthy**, your unconscious is urging you to boost your self-esteem or is perhaps highlighting feelings of guilt. If you are **forgiven** in your dream, who forgave you and what were you forgiven for? Also if you are **given gifts**, these represent something you think you need in waking life. If **you are the person being charitable**, the message remains the same.

KINDNESS

If **acts of kindness** fill your dreams – for example, **someone does you a favor, you do one for them, you give money to charity or help someone in need** – such dreams may be prompting you to ask for or give assistance when dealing with a problem. In other words, your unconscious would like you to ask for or give help when it is needed.

Positive Signs

AUSPICIOUS DREAM

In China and Tibet, dreams that are a sign of good fortune are called 'auspicious dreams'. These may include dreams of **holy or famous people, a clear lake, a spotlessly white cloth, climbing a mountain or fruit-laden tree, or receiving good food and gifts**. Tibetans believe that dreams occurring before midnight are benign and usually forgotten. If a dream comes just before dawn between about three or four o'clock in the morning – when the mind is vivid and clear – it is especially important. Always bear in mind when trying to pinpoint auspicious symbols in dreams for the purposes of interpretation that the meaning of symbols can vary from culture to culture; what is auspicious in one country might be considered to be a sign of misfortune in another. *See also* SYMBOLS.

GOOD LUCK SUPERSTITION

Good luck superstitions have been around for centuries and vary from culture to culture. Here are some of the most common and their appearance in your dream can, depending on the context and mood of the dream, be a positive sign: **Fingers Crossed. Knock on wood. Sneezing three times before breakfast. Meeting three sheep. Looking at the new moon over your right shoulder. A four-leaved clover. Spilling wine while proposing a toast. Putting a dress on inside out. Nine peas in a peapod. Hearing crickets singing. Picking up a pin. Dropping a glove. A horseshoe. Peacock feathers. Cutting your hair during a storm. Sleeping facing south. White heather. Picking up a pencil in the street. Breaking clear and uncolored glass. Walking in the rain. Sleeping on un-ironed sheets. Avoiding cracks in the sidewalk. An itch on the top of your head. Scissors hanging on a hook. A ladybird on you. Carrying an acorn on your person will ensure good luck and longevity! Picking up a piece of coal that has fallen in your path. Black cat. To have one's garments caught up by a bush or briar when out walking promises monetary gain. New enterprises will be fortunate if begun at the time of the new Moon. You meet the same person twice when out on business. Dolphins swimming near a ship. A naked woman on board a boat is said to calm the seas. Setting out to play golf on a rainy day. Rabbit's foot. See a penny, pick it up.**

POSITIVE ACTIVITY

If your dreaming mind depicted you engaged in positive activities such as **beginning a new health regime or hobby you love, losing weight, cutting out smoking and alcohol, spring cleaning, sorting out your wardrobe, volunteering for charity work, washing your car, mowing the lawn, picking up litter, holding a door open for the person behind you**, the message may be that you need to undertake similar action in your waking life. If you cannot draw a parallel between your dream and your waking life, ask yourself which positive actions you need to take in your life. Has your general outlook on life become

Spiritual or mystical dreams

Tibetan Buddhists call these 'dreams of clarity' because such dreams go beyond everyday situations and concerns into a space of 'the divine'. You may wake up from such a dream with a feeling of awe and unreality, knowing that something special and mystical has transpired. The more you focus on the spiritual aspects of your waking life, the more likely it is that you will have a mystical, visionary or spiritual dream. The Tibetan dream yoga tradition, in common with other Eastern practices, encourages daily meditation and other self-awareness rituals to help clear the mind so that you may be open to receiving spiritual dreams during sleep.

Spiritual dreams are often categorized in several ways: **Numinous dreams** are dreams in which you can achieve practically anything, since you possess 'numen', or divine power. **Transpersonal dreams** are those in which you go beyond personal concerns into a concern for the needs of all humanity. **Transcendent and spiritual dreams** are those in which you make contact with higher or divine knowledge; in such dreams, you might interact with angels, spirits, gurus or other divine messengers and learn profound lessons about ultimate human values, such as compassion, courage and self-discipline.

Scrooge's dream in *A Christmas Carol* is a classic example of a spiritual dream. As was the case with Scrooge, a spiritual dream leaves you feeling inspired, motivated, filled with hope and at peace. Many dream experts believe that these special dreams have the ability to give your life new meaning and offer a higher perspective on life in general. Spiritual dreams stand out and are rarely forgotten. It is not uncommon to glean incredible insight from this type of dream, information that assists you in various areas throughout the rest of your life. Spiritual dreams are most likely to occur during the following periods in your life:

1. Before a significant change.
2. Before or during a shift in your perception about yourself and your life.
3. After a commitment to something meaningful has been expressed and is genuinely being pursued.
4. Following a major loss or change.
5. When becoming more aware of yourself, your circumstances, your life.
6. During emotional and spiritual breakthroughs, such as taking a class, attending therapy, practicing yoga or meditation.
7. During a recovery process.

Spiritual dream symbol

How do you know when you are having a spiritual dream? Spiritual dreams tend to be more intense and colorful than other dreams, leaving you with feelings of awe and wonder. Certain symbols are also likely to appear. These include: **Light, bright colors, candles, clear** water. **Higher-self figures: wizard, angel, fairy, old man. Spiritual or religious books, cross, star, Sun, Moon, lotus, mandala, labyrinth, rainbow, sea, rose, stone, tree, mountain top,** **music or any symbol that has spiritual significance to you**. Many spiritual symbols are also archetypes, since they carry universal meaning. *See also* ARCHETYPES.

cynical and jaded; is it time to freshen your attitudes up in some way?

TOUCHING

If you had a dream in which you **express your affection physically (a kiss, a hand squeeze or a reassuring touch) with no ulterior motive**, your dreaming mind is drawing your attention to warm and positive feelings in your life, either coming from yourself towards someone or coming from someone to you. A dream of **massage** could symbolize your yearning for greater emotional and physical intimacy in waking life. Alternatively, **enjoying or giving a massage** in your dream may also suggest that you are feeling relaxed and happy in a relationship, or that you need to take some time out to relax, unwind and pamper yourself.

SIGN/SYMBOL

Dream symbols can have both positive and negative associations but some dream symbols do tend to have more positive associations than negative and these include: **Acorn**: To dream of an acorn indicates a huge growth process from small beginnings. **Advice**: Receiving advice in a dream means you should consider guidance from within. **Angels**: often considered to be divine messengers. **Artist**: This dream image urges you to recognize the artist within you. **Ascension**: A breakthrough in your waking life. **Bamboo**: Good breeding, long life and a fulfilling old age. **Basket that is full**: Symbol of abundance. **Birds**: Symbol of freedom and liberation. **Birth**: Symbol of new beginnings. **Blue skies**: Symbol of optimism. **Breeze**: Symbol of love and contentment. **Cup**: Symbol of intuitive information: **Daisy**: Symbol of innocence and purity. **Death**: Symbol of new beginnings. **Dove**: Symbol of peace. **Eagle**: Symbol of inspiration and strength. **Easter egg**: Symbol of potential. **Garland**: Symbol of distinction or honor. **Honey**: Symbol of pleasure and sweetness. **Knight**: The guiding principle of your life; the spirit guiding the physical. **Light**: Symbol of inspiration and illumination. **Mandala**: Sacred shape of unity and healing. **Pyramid**: Symbol of power, wonder and regeneration. **Rainbow**: Symbol of hope and redemption. **Summer**: Symbol of good times in life. **Yes**: Occasionally in your dream you may become aware that you are saying 'yes', and this is an instinctive acceptance of the need for personal growth; **Yin Yang**: Symbol of balance and harmony.

The Element Encyclopedia of 20,000 Dreams

HOME

Dreams about houses and homes usually symbolize your emotional and psychological self or center, in other words yourself.

Dream homes say very little about your real-life residence; instead, they say a great deal about your present circumstances, your perspective on life and the challenges you are currently facing. According to Jung, all of your experiences, stages of development, and parts of your conscious and unconscious life may be represented by dream homes. When trying to analyze the house in your dream, consider how it is kept and its condition, color and shape. The rooms in the house relate to facets of your personality and experience. Many people are amazed at the detail of their dream home. From the wallpaper patterns to the position of the dining room table, every detail seems planned and almost familiar, even though it may bear little or no resemblance to their real-life home. So when a dream shows you living in a particular home or setting, your dreaming mind is letting you know this is where you are coming from right now and this is how things are affecting you.

Dreams of being at home also suggest returning to a place in which you feel safe, a sanctuary where you can be yourself without fear of reprisal. Spiritualists speak of going home when they are approaching death, as they believe the physical state is a temporary one. *See also* BUILDINGS.

Your Dream House

ATTIC

To see an **attic** in your dream represents past memories and experiences. It can also highlight family patterns of behavior and attitudes that have been handed down to you. To see a **cluttered attic** is a sign urging you to organize your mind and thoughts, but an **overly neat and tidy attic** may suggest an approach to life that is too formal and timid. **Ghosts in the attic** represent memories that haunt you, whilst a jumble of **unused clothes and equipment** reflects unused energy. In some cases, particularly those in which your dream attic is radiant and heavenly, your attic may represent your higher self but in general, such dreams refer to stored material. Whatever your dream attic contains, consider it a clue to making your present circumstances more rewarding.

BACKYARD

In dreams, the **backyard** represents the parts of your life that are taken for granted, the parts that are so familiar you have forgotten they are there. If you dream of **something pleasant in your backyard**, this represents hidden potential waiting to be used without needing much effort; but if **something ugly is present**, this suggests an intrusive energy in your home life that may be draining you. *See also* Garden entry in PLACES.

BALCONY

To dream of a **balcony** suggests a need for an objective viewpoint. You need to take a step back, move away from involvement and try to see the bigger picture; it may also suggest a need for sunshine and relaxation. For lovers, to dream of saying **sad adieus on a balcony** signifies passionate attachment to each other. Alternatively, the balcony is a classic Freudian symbol of women's breasts; if you dream of **standing on a balcony**, it might represent a wish to return to your mother's breasts.

BASEMENT/CELLAR

Even though **basements** are becoming less common in newly built houses, they are still common in dreams. To dream that you are in a basement symbolizes being deep down in your unconscious mind, in the psychological storage space where you sort through things you are finding hard to understand. A basement is the place where you've shelved aspects of yourself that aren't matching your ambitions in waking life. A basement can also indicate the power that is available to you provided you are willing to make use of it, or the way in which your current attitudes are derived from past assumptions and family legends.

To dream that the **basement is in disarray and messy** signifies some confusion which you need to sort out. It may also represent your perceived faults and shortcomings. Wine is traditionally kept in the **cellar** and the contents of your unconscious can similarly harbor special treats that you can bring out on special occasions. Try to decide if your dreaming mind took you into the cellar to confront an issue in your life or to make good use of talents you have been suppressing.

BATHROOM

To dream that you are in the **bathroom** relates to your instinctual urges. You may be experiencing some sort of burdensome feelings and need to 'relieve yourself'. Alternatively, it may symbolize purification and self-renewal; you need to cleanse yourself, both emotionally and psychologically. To dream that you **cannot find the bathroom** signifies that you are having difficulties in releasing and expressing your emotions. You may also have overcommitted yourself and are neglecting your own needs. **Plumbing problems in your dream bathroom** may reflect trouble in processing your feelings. Do you feel swamped right now? **Flooding in the bathroom** suggests emotions that are both out of control and out of character.

BEDROOM

To dream that you are in the **bedroom** signifies aspects of yourself that you keep private. This room is where you rest, where you retreat, and where you sleep and become unconscious. You may even be dreaming in the same bedroom as the one that appears in your dream. The bedroom is also suggestive of sex, love and romance, but just as often reflects aspects of your life that are particularly private to you alone.

CHILDHOOD HOME/HOME FROM THE PAST

If your **childhood home or a home from the past** continually features in your dreams, this does not necessarily mean you are stuck in the past or long to return to the security of childhood. The homes in which you once lived can become symbols of certain factors that shaped the person you have now become. Perhaps the most common past home dream is that of **living in the house you lived in when you were a child**. There may be major changes to the structure of the house, there may be people there that you hadn't met when you lived there, but you know that house more intimately than any other. It is a true reflection of yourself and the storehouse for all your emotions, both positive and negative. The house in which you grew up always has a huge influence on your psychology. Your house gives you boundaries and it is the place where you go to feel safe, its every corner a reflection of your mind. It is the symbol of your family, connections and traditions.

Your dream childhood home can help give you clues about your current situation and help you examine your personality. What kind of house was it? Was it a large or small house, and did you think it was the same size when you were young? Are you still living in the same house? How many floors did it have? How many windows? What was its shape? Most of us live in square houses with corners, but some people's houses are round with no corners. Some suggest this may have a profound effect on a person's psychology because circles represent infinity and thus no restrictions. Can you remember what colors your house was painted in; how do those colors affect your feelings now? If something good always happened to you in a certain room, the color of that room may still make you happy for the rest of your life. Was there a place in your house where you went if you were miserable, or a place where something bad happened? What were the colors and shapes that were involved? Is it a dark place or a light place?

Although you are by no means doomed to repeat past mistakes, your dreaming mind may use your first home as an important reference throughout your life and you may often find yourself trying to work through current issues in the setting of this childhood home. Try to think of such dreams as an opportunity to reflect on your basic beliefs about home and family. Are you repeating patterns from your childhood in a current relationship and situation? Can your dream help you relate the past to your present life and to your life in the future?

DOOR/KEYHOLE

In dream-lore, to **pass through a door and enter a house** is a decisive and symbolic action as the door represents the passage from one state of being to another. Freud and Jung agreed that the house signified the self and the body, but disagreed about the doors of a house. For Freud, doors are dream images representing the body's orifices, whilst for Jung, doors express the dreamer's relationship to their conscious and unconscious world. According to Jungians, a **door opening outwards** suggests a need to open up to others, whereas a **door opening inwards** suggests the need for greater reflection or a desire to explore the inner self.

In general, most dream analysts believe that **entering through a door** signifies new opportunities that will be presented to you. Doors and doorways represent an opportunity for either positive or negative change. You may be entering into a new stage in your life, moving from one level of consciousness to another. If your dreaming mind portrayed you as **stepping through a door**, it signals your willingness to embrace change and the unknown, whilst **letting someone in through the door** indicates your willingness to interact with them. If you were **faced by a confusing number of doors**, you may be feeling overwhelmed by choices in life and unsure which opening is right for you. If you simply **can't find the door to escape through** in your dream, then perhaps you feel unable to express yourself in waking life. To dream of **locked doors** signifies opportunities that are denied, unavailable to you or ones on which you have missed out. Also consider who or what you are shutting out of your life if your dream features a door; perhaps as one dream door closes, another will open ...

More specifically, a **front door** usually symbolizes unfamiliar outside circumstances – if a **doormat** features in your dream as well, you may be allowing others to walk all over you in real life – while a **backdoor** stands for the more familiar traffic of people we already know. Unwanted changes in your life are often depicted in dreams as **intruders or strangers at the door**, and if you are beginning a new relationship and themes of **burglary or home invasion** appear in your dreams, this does not necessarily mean your partner is dangerous; the dream may be providing an early warning of undercurrents in your relationship that are not nourishing to you. In some instances, the **dark stranger at the door** represents an aspect of yourself that is self-critical and self-destructive.

Another dream featuring doors is that of being **locked out or being unable to enter your home because you have lost your key**. This image reflects a situation in which you are being prevented from accessing your talent, drive and energy. You have been locked out from the best part of yourself but the situation can be easily corrected by remembering your key next time, or finding another way in. In most cases, the key indicates willingness to change and to experiment with alternatives. **Keyholes** in dreams allow you to view that which is otherwise concealed; if this image appears in your dream, ask yourself whether your privacy is being invaded in some way or whether you are prying into affairs that are no concern of yours. A **rusty key** may indicate talents that are being neglected. Freud viewed the key as a phallus and saw potent sexual symbolism in the trio of key, door and the door's subsequent opening. Finally, to dream that you **hear or ring a door bell** foretells of unexpected news.

The Element Encyclopedia of 20,000 Dreams

Driveway/Fence

To **see or drive up to a driveway** in your dream symbolizes an end to your journey, and therefore generally represents security and rest. It may also denote your path toward achieving inner peace and toward finding your spirituality. Take into account **how easy or hard is it to gain access to your house** as this will show the barriers you may have put up to prevent other people getting close to you. It may be that you have become too open to the demands of others and need to be more self-contained.

To see a **fence** in your dream signifies an obstacle or barrier that may be standing in your path. Are you feeling fenced in? To dream that you are **climbing to the top of a fence** indicates success and the development of your potential. To dream that you are **building a fence** signifies secrecy, withdrawal and an intense need for privacy. There might also be someone with whom you need to **mend fences** in waking life? To dream that you **fall from a fence** suggests that you may have overcommitted yourself in waking life. To see **animals jumping over a fence into an enclosure** could mean that you are unable to control your instincts and emotions.

Floor

To see the **floor** in your dream represents those things that support you. It may also represent the division between your unconscious and conscious mind. To see a **polished, wooden floor** in your dream indicates that you are fully aware of your unconscious but not tapping into its potential, whilst to see a **slanted floor** foretells that you are deviating too far from your original plans and goals. For Jungians, the **floors or storeys** of a house represent your unconscious and conscious aspirations. In general, the **attic** represents the intellect, the **ground floor** the conscious mind and the **basement** the unconscious. The appearance, style and condition of each floor will be significant. Are they easy and welcoming on the eye or intimidating and confused? **Difficulty getting from one floor of the house to another** suggests difficulties progressing spiritually.

Garage

To dream that you are in a **garage** indicates how you store and relate to your personal talents, abilities and ambitions. If you are **repairing a car in the garage**, perhaps your ability to motivate yourself needs a boost or an MOT. On the other hand, if you dream of a **garage as a shelter for a car**, this is a dream symbol of female sexuality; if you are **fixing your car**, this may suggest sexual problems or inhibitions. To dream that you are **pulling your car into the garage** represents the security and stability that is brought about by your accomplishments and efforts. To dream that you are **opening the garage door** denotes that you have made a decision about a matter, perhaps one relating to a long-term goal. On the other hand, if you are **closing the garage door**, it suggests that you are putting off your goals for the sake of others around you.

Guest/Neighbor

If you dreamed that you had **guests around at your home**, much of the interpretation will depend on how you felt about them.

Did you welcome them and enjoy their company, or were you reluctant to let them in? Did they cross your threshold? The **welcome guest** may represent the beginning of an important project that you are ready to work on, whilst the **unwelcome guest** could stand for something or someone you do not want to face up to in waking life. In dreams, **neighbors** can be a help or a hindrance and this may mirror your feelings towards them in waking life. You should also consider whether there is something or someone important you are neglecting.

Hallway/Corridor/Passage

To see a **hallway** in your dream symbolizes the beginning of a path that you are taking in life or a journey of self-exploration into the unknown. In some dreams, **passages, corridors or hallways can stretch endlessly into the distance, with hundreds of doors on either side**; in other dreams, they are **so small you have to crouch down, or are so bewilderingly complex you get lost**. Such dreams represent the way you feel about the choices and options open to you in life and it give you an invaluable vista onto what you believe to be possible and necessary. **Halls** in dreams also illustrate how you meet and relate to other people in real life.

Home

If the house that featured in your dream was your actual **home** and some aspect of it was highlighted, you need to decide whether your dream was literal (if you were **clearing out a cupboard**, is this on your 'to do' list?) or whether it relates to some

aspect of yourself (could the same dream be telling you to sort things through and reassess your priorities?). The **foundations of the house** symbolize the basic attitudes and processes upon which your life is built. If your dream house represents yourself, what did your dream tell you about your foundations and structure? Were they sturdy and able to withstand bad conditions, or were they in danger of collapsing?

If your **home is damaged** in your dream, first consider whether you are worried about the condition of your home in real life; if you find that you are not worried about it all as you have just had a positive surveyor's report, then consider the dream's symbolic meaning. If the **walls or fences were damaged**, this would allow outside elements to get through, so perhaps you feel vulnerable or undermined in waking life. **Broken doors** also indicate vulnerability and an inability to maintain boundaries. **Broken windows** leave you open to intruders and may affect your view of things.

Houses in dreams often represent parts of your mind or personality, so if you dream of **leaving your current home to live in another house**, this simply reflects your awareness of different parts of your personality. Maybe you have been moving from one part of yourself to another, trying out different aspects of yourself? Maybe you are trying to decide who you really are? To dream that your **house is broken into** suggests that you are feeling violated. It may refer to a particular relationship or current situation in your life. Alternatively, it indicates that some unconscious material is attempting to make itself known, because some aspects of yourself have been denied. If your **dream home is burgled**, this may symbolize something you valued that has been taken away from you, leaving you feeling violated. Are you taking care of all of your valuables in your life, including yourself? Is someone trying to breach your personal defenses?

HOUSE

To be living in a **house** in your dream, even one that isn't at all like your home, also represents yourself. Jung once called the house the 'mansion of the soul', and most dream analysts believe that houses in dreams become holistic symbols of yourself; your mind, body, spirit and your past, present and future. If you were **buying or building a house** in your dream, perhaps you are considering making a dramatic change to your life, even to the extent of rebuilding it. If your dreams focus on **paying the rent or the mortgage** and this isn't a problem in waking life, then they are highlighting a responsibility in waking life that you find a burden. An **abandoned house in disrepair** may suggest emotional and physical neglect, whilst a **house that is shuttered up** might suggest being blind to what is going on around you. Dreams of an **unfinished house** should motivate rather than be a cause of despair, as life is a constant work-in-progress. A **half-built house** suggests what you need to acquire to further your personal development; perhaps more windows to give you a better perspective. A **damaged blind or broken lock** in your dream can highlight lack of privacy or your perceived vulnerability. A **house in bad repair** can denote the need to heal a family rift.

Even the most bizarre dream homes reflect the psychological territory you are living in right now, even if that 'home' is a **medieval dungeon, a tropical island, a prisoner-of-war camp or a train station**. If you dreamed of living in a **bizarre or fictional setting**, consider the condition and qualities of that situation. Is it cramped, crowded or lonely? Your new dream home can give you valuable information about how your current circumstances are affecting you and how you relate to others. If you are restricted or limited in your dream territory, ask yourself if you are creating those restrictions by your reaction or if the situation is creating it. To see an **old, run-down house** in your dream represents your old beliefs, attitudes and how you used to think or feel. A situation in your current life may be bringing about those same old attitudes and feelings. Alternatively, the old house may symbolize your need to update your mode of thinking. If your dream **house is unfurnished**, this may suggest a bleak self, devoid of feeling; an **empty house**, however, may indicate new opportunities.

To dream of a **haunted house** signifies unfinished emotional business, related to your childhood family, dead relatives, or repressed memories and feelings. To see a **glass house** in your dream signifies that appearances in waking life may be deceptive. To dream that you are **living in a glass house** signifies the threatened loss of your reputation. To see a **mansion** in your dream suggests that you need to grow in some way or other; if **servants are waiting on you**, this indicates undue vanity. You may feel that your current situation or relationship is in a rut and want to expand and develop your potential. If you see yourself **living in a cottage**, this signifies a longing for a gentler more spontaneous way of life.

Home improvement/Housework

If your dream hasn't been triggered by a television home makeover show, making improvements to your home may symbolize making improvements to yourself. Are there any jobs that you feel need to be done right now? Could you do with a coat of paint to brighten yourself up with a fresh new color? If you dream of **building an extension**, do you want or need to expand your horizons? Putting on a **new roof** may relate to raising your expectations, whilst **applying a coat of varnish or paint** can suggest a desire to disguise your own self-perceived flaws. It can also indicate the desire to gloss over problems in a relationship.

Whitewash may represent your attempts to cover up something that causes you embarrassment, whether relating to your own feelings of guilt or your suspicion that others are not what they seem. **Clearing or laying** down new paths or foundations may relate to new approaches to life. If **household breakages** feature in your dream this may represent flawed ideas. A cracked cup can symbolize lost love. A dream of **breaking things in the house** may suggest anger or despair.

Dreams of **housework** in general suggest keeping your internal house in order, perhaps by taking time to clarify or define motives, opinions and feelings about others; they also stand for the cleaning out of non-functional or negative attitudes, thoughts and experiences. To dream that you are **cleaning your house with a broom or dustpan and brush** signifies your need to clear out your thoughts and get rid of old ways. You are seeking self-improvement. If you, or a **cleaner**, are cleaning, this may also recall memories of your mother. Alternatively, the house being cleaned may symbolize the self and a need to give extra care and attention to neglected aspects of your personality. When compared with sweeping up, **vacuum cleaning** suggests both a definite desire to do away once and for all with the effects of a past action, and a definite desire to move on and put the past behind you.

To dream of **cleaning windows** suggests that you are trying to get a clearer view of the world around you. Using a **washing machine** may suggest it is time to confront old issues that are destroying your peace of mind. The water may also point to deep-seated childhood issues that need to come out in the wash. **Hanging your clothes out to dry** may suggest a yearning for the lost innocence of childhood or a desire for uninhibited sexuality. If you are **washing the dishes in your dream kitchen**, this may suggest a desire to wash away feelings of shame or disgust, or a wish to deny responsibility for something.

An **ancient house** could refer to a previous life in some way connected with your present existence. If you are **living in a tent or mobile caravan** in your dream, do you feel weighed down by the routine of your life? Would you like to travel, move house, get back to nature or try the life of a nomad for a while? If you imagine your **house is in amongst skyscrapers in the city**, this suggests a preoccupation with financial matters, perhaps at the expense of your personal life. The opposite is true if your **house is in a village** in your dream.

Whether your dream home is an igloo or a mansion, pay attention to the details of the dream as it will be like a documentary featuring the interaction of your past beliefs, current challenges and recent situations. If you don't like what you see, it is important to understand that you are in charge of your life; sometimes making small changes may be all that is needed to bring big results. Ancient dream-lore has many interpretations for dreams about houses and homes but here are the most typical: **country house**, tranquility ahead; **building a house**, you will be self-confident; **new house**, a busy social life; **empty house**, low income; **moving house**, worries about money.

KITCHEN

To see a **kitchen** in your dream signifies your need for emotional nourishment. The kitchen is the emotional heart of the home and when you are trying to sort through your feelings you may dream of it. Kitchens are also places of experimentation and magic where you can create new dishes out of existing ingredients. Did the kitchen encourage you to linger by offering rich food for thought or was it a barren room that had no temptations or stimuli on offer? Pay attention to the condition and layout of your dream kitchen. If it is **cramped and cluttered**, you may have taken on too many emotional problems that belong to others. If the **kitchen is bare**, your life may be lacking in emotional intimacy.

Kitchen imagery often reflects the need to work through your current problems by listening to your heart and recognizing what really matters to you in your waking life. Assume that all the people and elements present in your kitchen dreams are clues to help you develop your full potential. If you dream of the **scullery**, this room – used for the storage of kitchen utensils and doing messy kitchen work – could be another symbol of your mind, the storehouse of your unconscious.

LIVING ROOM

To dream that you are in the **living room or lounge** represents the image that you portray to others and the way in which you go about your life. It is representative of your basic beliefs about yourself and who you are, as – like the bedroom – this is a room in which you tend to relax and be yourself. If your dream **living room is crowded, cramped and full of strange furniture**, this suggests a lack of privacy. If it is taken up with **office furniture**, this suggests absorption with career. Don't assume that a **trashed living room or even a coffin in the middle of it** mean that you are on the path to self-destruction. Dreams such as these are pointing to qualities within yourself that can be changed or corrected by adjustments to your attitude and approach to life. When a living room

Something cooking in the kitchen

Male and female sexuality, as well as family life in general, are symbolized by the utensils and vessels used in cooking. The **cooking fire or oven** is traditionally the focus of the household and can symbolize the deepest center of your being; something **burning in the kitchen** should therefore alert you to problems in your family life. If you are **preparing a meal in your dream kitchen**, this may suggest a quest for love and affection. If you are **frying food** in your dream, there is the constant risk of getting burned; the **smoke billowing around your kitchen** may be warning you that a problem could get worse if you avoid it or don't deal with it. **Cinders or a grate** in your dream kitchen can represent ruined hopes as well as the potential of projects yet to be born.

If you dream of a **kettle**, even though its spout it is a symbol of male sexuality, it suggests that someone can get hurt if passions are not handled carefully. On the other hand, it could also indicate your present mood: steamed up and about to explode. At the other extreme, the image of a **broken kettle** may mirror feelings of emptiness, as if all zest for life has gone. If you are **cooking with pots and pans**, the association is with male or female sexuality, depending on whether the **pot or the handle** is featured.

When a **cup** is seen to represent female sexuality, **drinking out of it** is erotic wish-fulfillment. If it is **hurled across a room by a man**, it may express fear of, or anger towards, female sexuality; if by a woman, the dream suggests that the dreamer is using sex as a weapon. For Jungians, the cup is a homely symbol of the abundance of life's opportunities; it is also a symbol of self-realization in that it is an echo of the Holy Grail. A **full or overflowing cup** often symbolizes excitement and new opportunities, but an **empty or smashed cup** indicates the opposite.

Cutlery in dreams may suggest a desire for domestic security or the taming of aggression. **Spoons** may have a similar symbolism to cups, but they can also represent a desire to be spoon-fed. A **teaspoon** may be telling you to take things in one step at a time. A **silver spoon** may refer to someone you envy. A **colander or sieve** may be seen as standing for the process of developing a new outlook on life and sifting out unhelpful attitudes and ideas. *See also* EVERYDAY THINGS.

features in your dream, take notice of those things that make it special or pleasant, as these are things within you that make your life rewarding. If the room is **ugly, leaky or damaged**, consider what parts of your life these dream images represent and how they can be cleaned up, repaired or changed.

PASSAGEWAY

To discover **secret passageways** in your dream is often a sign that something new and exciting is occurring in your waking life. It may refer to new opportunities, a new relationship or a new attitude toward life. If you **wake up before fully exploring these passageways**, then it suggests that you may not know how to go about taking advantage of these opportunities or how to move forward with a relationship. Perhaps the newness and uncertainty of this discovery also makes you a little more cautious.

PATIO/PORCH

To dream that you are in the **patio** suggests your openness toward a particular situation. To dream that the **doors to the patio are opened** represents your receptive state of mind. If the **doors are closed**, then it indicates that you are not being open-minded enough in waking life. Because the front of your home is symbolically much like your face, to dream of a **porch** represents your personality, your social self, your façade and how you portray yourself to others. It is the portion of your life on display to others. Whatever happens on your porch in your dream is something that has become quite public, suggesting that you feel exposed in some way. Consider the condition and size of the porch. To dream of an **enclosed porch** suggests your tendency to distance yourself from others and your desire for privacy. To dream of an **open porch** signifies your outgoing nature and welcoming attitude.

ROOF/CEILING/CHIMNEY

A **roof** symbolizes protection, security, shelter in general, or the family home under which you find shelter and comfort. Consider the state of your roof – is it in good condition, weatherproof and complete, or is it in need of repair? If the latter, do you need to think something through more carefully? In architecture, particularly in churches and temples, the roof symbolizes the dome of heaven, so if a **leaky roof** features in your dream, one interpretation might be that an awareness of your unconscious is slowly making itself known to you. Typically, leaky roofs in dreams warn that the very structure of your life is on the verge of collapsing on top of you unless changes are made in your waking life. To see a roof is also an overview of how you see yourself and who you think you are.

To dream that you **are on a roof** symbolizes excitement and creativity. To dream that you are **falling off a roof** signifies that you may not have a firm grip and solid foundation on your advanced position. Consider also the expression 'to hit the roof', which means you have become enraged. Are you angry at the moment? To have a **slate missing** means to be a little slow, so are you missing the point of something? To see a **ceiling** in your dream represents your mental or spiritual perspective.

Chimneys in dreams generally symbolize warmth, tradition and family values. The condition of the chimney reflects how we deal with our inner emotions and warmth. If your dream contained a **smoking chimney**, its smoke signal imparts a message of emotional warmth. The image of a dream chimney is, in addition, laden with sexuality, male and female, depending on whether the chimney is viewed from the outside or from the inside.

SECRET ROOM

If you discover a **room that has been long forgotten containing fascinating things** in your dream, this suggests a neglected part of your life that your dreaming mind is trying to encourage you to reclaim. It is telling you that it is not too late to go back to college, learn a skill and so on. If, however, the room you dream about is a **forbidden room**, the interpretation depends on what you find behind the door, assuming that you have the courage to enter. In most cases, the images in the room will be frightening, as they reflect insights you find hard to swallow in waking life; by bringing these insights to your attention, your dreaming mind is helping you understand the dynamics involved, helping you face and deal with that which you find frightening in real life. If you find a **new room** in your dream, remember that it relates to uncovering new aspects of yourself, either positive or negative. Think about the function of that room. If it is a **bathroom**, this refers to bathing, hygiene, elimination and cleansing. If it is a **bedroom** it suggests rest and intimacy, whilst if it is a **dining room**, it suggests feeding yourself and interacting with others.

STAIRS/STAIRCASE

According to Jung, **stairs** are a clear symbol of psychological growth, whereas Freud attributed phallic symbolism to the image. In general, dreams stairs are thought to represent feelings in connection with achievement, failure, climbing and falling. To dream that you are **walking up a flight of stairs** indicates that you are achieving a higher level of understanding. You are making progress in your journey, whether it is a spiritual, emotional or material one. To dream that you are **walking down a flight of stairs** suggests that you are descending into your unconscious. It also refers to setbacks that you will experience in your life. To see **spiral or winding stairs** signify growth and/or rebirth.

If you are **running up a staircase** in your dream home, this suggests an attempt to escape from an unconscious urge by taking refuge in the abstract or intellectual. If you are **running up the stairs in fear**, this suggests a lack of confidence, a fear of failing or not being capable in some way. If you are **running up the stairs with pleasure**, then it suggests exuberance, and a possible change in your feelings and situation. If you are **going down the stairs in fear**, a loss of belief in your own ability is implied. If you **trip on the stairs**, this may suggest problems you have brought upon yourself by meddling in the affairs of other people.

A dream often experienced by children is that of **skimming down stairs**; this dream feels almost like flying down the stairs, the feet just touching the edge of the stairs every so often, creating an exhilarating sense of pleasure. The reason for the dream is that it represents a task – the

The Element Encyclopedia of 20,000 Dreams

climbing of stairs – that once seemed daunting to a toddler, but which now has been mastered, giving rise to the sense of effortless achievement symbolized by 'skimming'. Finally, using an **escalator instead of stairs** in your home, or anywhere else, may express a certain lack of emotional commitment to a person or project in waking life. A dream of **walking against the direction of the escalator** suggests frustration at a lack of personal progress.

Toilet

To see a **toilet** in your dream symbolizes a release of emotions or getting rid of something in your life that is useless. To see a **clogged toilet** in your dream signifies that you are holding something in or keeping your feelings to yourself. Your emotions have been pent up for too long. To see an **overflowing toilet** in your dream denotes your desire to express your emotions fully. Dreams featuring problems with toilets – such as **toilets that are too dirty to use or broken toilet seats** – can indicate that you want to eliminate waste material but are frustrated in some way. Such dreams may be urging you to clean yourself up emotionally. If, however, your dream home **toilet is a pleasure to use**, this may represent healthy self-expression and the symbolic release of outdated aspects of your life. *See also* Toilet and elimination dreams in BODY.

Wall

To see a **wall** in your dream signifies protection, limitations, obstacles and boundaries. When they are well maintained, walls can give privacy. When they are damaged, however, they can let anyone or anything through. A wall may also symbolize a barrier obstructing your progress; you may have become accustomed to your old habits and way of thinking, and the wall symbolizes your own inertia. Whilst a 'wall of silence' is a term used to describe problems with communication, there is also the saying 'walls have ears', so have you heard something inappropriate recently? Perhaps you have 'hit a brick wall' and feel you can make no more progress? Similarly do you feel as if you are 'banging your head against a brick wall'?

To dream that you **jump over a wall** suggests that you will overcome tough obstacles and eventually succeed. To dream that you **demolish or break down a wall** indicates that you are breaking through obstacles and overcoming your limitations. If you see a **wall crumble**, this suggests that you have easily risen above your problems and overcome your barriers. To dream that you are **building a wall** represents a bad relationship or some childhood trauma. It also suggests that you putting barriers up in waking life. To dream that you are being **thrown or shot through a wall** literally means that you need to break down those walls that you have put up around you. You need to venture out and explore.

Window

For Jungians, **windows** offer a view of the outside world. To see windows in your dream signifies points of view, perspectives, insights and the eyes through which you view life. If you are **looking through the window**, then it signifies your outlook on life, your consciousness, awareness and intuition. Windows are made of glass which

Glass

Glass in dreams represents the hidden but powerful feelings and social barriers we use in everyday life. These include caution, inhibition, disinterest, pride and the fear of being hurt. **Frosted or smoked glass** suggests parts of yourself that you are keeping hidden from others. It can also indicate an obscure or unclear view of a situation. Occasionally it relates to death, the very real yet obscure experience we all face. If you dream of **breaking glass**, what barrier or restraint are you breaking through? Could it mean that your emotions might be shattered? **Breaking something made of glass** might symbolize the breaking up of a relationship, the shattering of an illusion or simply that you or someone else are broken-hearted.

Glass may not always be very visible, so it may represent hidden dangers; if you dream of **stepping on broken glass**, it suggests that you are being careless about your direction in life or your present situation; if it is being done without heed to injury, walking on glass represents self-inflicted pain. If you dream of **glasses as in spectacles**, this refers to your ability to see or understand something or someone clearly. The image may also refer to the mask you use to hide behind, as with sunglasses. Terms like 'short-sighted' or 'long-sighted' help us understand the use of glasses in a dream.

can be transparent, giving a clear view; but they can also be opaque, the view being obscured by thick, colored or distorted glass. Can you relate this to your view of a situation? The 'pane' in window pane may indicate a different sort of pain, so consider whether you need to be more clear-sighted about something that is troubling you.

To see **shut, shattered or broken windows** in your dream suggests a closed mind. **Opening a window** may represent a willingness to let in new ideas or fresh air into a life that has become stale. **Looking in through the window** symbolizes insight, but it may also – as in the story of 'The Little Match Girl' – suggest that you have been left out in the cold whilst others enjoy the warmth denied to you inside. **Looking out of a window** may represent your outlook and how you feel about your life. Eyes are sometimes called the windows of the soul. Whilst, for Freudians, a **smashed window** represents female sexuality, to Jungians it suggests a feeling of disillusionment with the world. Whenever you dream of a window, ask yourself what it reveals about the perspective you have on a current situation or whether it seems to hint that a broader, more open-minded perspective is required. But if a **house contained no windows or if drapes obscured your view out of them**, it is likely that you have a shuttered outlook on life, preferring to live in your own world.

The Element Encyclopedia of 20,000 Dreams

INSECTS AND ARACHNIDS

Insects are often considered to be irritating pests and harbingers of disease and infection in the waking world.

According to Jungians, the general interpretation of insects in dreams closely follows the way they are perceived in real life: as irritating and potentially dangerous creatures that often attack in great numbers. Some insects do, however, have qualities we can admire and although still able to annoy us, they can set a helpful example when they appear in dreams. Use your common sense and some general impressions about the specific insect when interpreting your dream. For example, if you dream about bees stinging you, think about some of your relationships; if ants appear, then consider you social interactions and work ethic. If you dream about wasps, are you in some kind of danger? Bear in mind, though, that dreams featuring insects are generally warning you of some poisonous or dangerous influence in your waking life.

Insects can also represent irritating, small problems in daily life with which you feel powerless to deal or feelings you would rather do without. These might be feelings of guilt or regret, or something that you cannot quite recognize tugging at your conscience. More often than not, insects represent negative feelings; they can symbolize how life requires you to form a brittle shell; they can also sometimes completely replace your own body, as in Franz Kafka's novella *Metamorphosis*.

Arachnids – here comprising scorpions, spiders and ticks – often have a different symbolism; many people suffer from severe phobias for spiders in particular. If you are fearful of spiders in the waking world, they will quite often simply represent something of which you are terrified in your subconscious.

Insect A to Z

ANT

The positive aspect of **ants** lies in their incredible industry, organization and persistence. Whenever they appear in a dream, whether as positive or negative creatures, they suggest that hard work and persistence will make a difference in your life. The negative aspect of ants comes out in their robotic nature; dreaming of **thousands of ants moving in rigid, pre-determined patterns** can suggest you need more variety in your waking life. In this regard, you may feel that your life is too structured and orderly. Ants can also indicate that you are feeling neglected and insignificant in your waking life or that petty things are annoying you. Cooperation may be the only way to achieve your desires. Dreaming of a **column of ants** is another image reflecting the importance of hard graft and teamwork in real life. An **anthill** in your dream may symbolize the workplace.

BEE

Bees represent productivity and the importance of group energy but they can also indicate frantic internal chatter. The **noise and sting of bees** can represent a cycle of worry and conflict. To see bees in your dream symbolizes good luck as a group, but weakness as an individual; dreams of bees are common when you are going through an experience that is laden with social expectations, such as a wedding. Bees, like ants, are symbolic of work and industry, as suggested by the phrase 'busy as a bee'. To dream that you are **stung by a bee** signifies unexpected misfortune; you may be unaware of trouble brewing around you. It can also indicate acting to fend off those who are trying to hinder your progress. Being **attacked by a swarm of bees** suggests that you may be creating a situation that has become uncontrollable and that you need to find ways of calming your inner chatter.

To dream of **bees making honey** offers the encouraging prospect of potential happiness and success in waking life. The sweetness of honey has long been identified with visions of happiness and well-being; in classical myth, honey was the food of the gods, and milk and honey flows in the Promised Land of the Old Testament. However, to **kill or injure a bee** in your dream indicates the loss of something important to you. To dream of a **queen bee** refers to your need to feel, or be, superior in some way; it might also mean that at some level you are aware of the need for hard work and industry. Spiritually, the bee symbolizes immortality, rebirth and order.

■ *Idioms: hive of activity; bee in your bonnet.*

BEETLE/LADYBIRD

To see a **beetle** in your dream indicates that some destructive influences may be at work in your waking life. You may also feel that your values and beliefs are being compromised. If you dream of a **scarab beetle** – a creature worshipped by the ancient Egyptians as a symbol of creation – this symbolizes your ability to survive, adapt and change. You may, however, be anxious about death and aging, and so it might also be a dream about immortality. Quite by contrast, to see a **ladybird** in your dream is symbolic of good fortune and happiness.

BUTTERFLY

To see a **butterfly** in your dream denotes creativity, romance, joy and spirituality. You may be undergoing a transformation or rebirth in your way of thinking. To see a

beautiful colorful butterfly in your dream denotes the positive impression you hope to make at a future social gathering or in some aspect of your life. It may also indicate your love of freedom and a refusal to be tied down. For Jung, the butterfly was a symbol of the whole psyche – as it was for the Greeks, to whom the word '*psyche*' meant both butterfly and soul. If you have recently been bereaved, you may have felt comforted by dream in which a **butterfly flutters up into the sky**; this may represent the soul of someone who has died, as the departing soul is traditionally said to assume the form of a butterfly. Your unconscious may have been signaling to you that your loved one's spirit has been liberated. Remember, too, that a butterfly can represent your own soul and, if you are currently feeling overburdened in waking life, then this may be a wish-fulfillment dream.

Swarm of insects

Swarms of insects in dream can depict instinctual urges in life, such as sexual urges. Swarms may also represent small children or the sperm swarming toward the ovum, and therefore may be suggesting issues to do with pregnancy. The power of the group can additionally be suggested by a swarm; where one insect seems to be moving aimlessly, large numbers do not. Your dream swarm might be telling you that you can often only succeed in changing matters by group effort. As Jiminy Cricket suggests, insects can also represent your conscience, guilt and feelings you might want to forget; perhaps insects represent these areas because they live their lives in our house and garden largely unseen, although we sometimes sense their presence. In this sense, a swarm might represent being overwhelmed with guilt.

If you see a **swarm of insects around you**, this suggests malicious rumors are being spread about you, but if you manage to **kill the insects or escape**, you will find an easy remedy for your problems. If **insects are taking something apart in your dream**, this suggests you may be in the phase of ending something and you need to complete that process before starting something new. If the **insects have invaded your food or contaminated something** in your dream, consider whether your lifestyle is a healthy one. A dream of **killing or spraying insects** may also recall childhood hostility towards a sibling that may persist into later life. If the **insects are flying off**, this may represent children leaving home or the end of a particular problem that has been upsetting you.

CATERPILLAR

To see a **caterpillar or grub** in your dream signifies a challenging stage in your own personal growth and development. You are on the right path but have not yet reached your goal. Your dream is warning you that you must undergo a complete metamorphosis to grow into something more beautiful and realize your full potential.

CENTIPEDE

To see a **centipede** in your dream refers to modest beginnings that can take you further and higher than you initially expected; the implication is that you should return to your roots for inspiration and energy. In their negative aspect, centipedes suggest fears and doubts that hinder you from making progress and achieving your goals. You need to stop thinking negative thoughts. The numerous legs of the creature represent the variety of ways that limiting beliefs and self-criticism can move with us from childhood into every stage of later life. Your dream is alerting you to these thought patterns and urging you to cast them aside, as they are quite small in comparison with the force of your intelligence and spirit.

COCKROACH

To see **cockroaches** in your dream represents an undesirable aspect of yourself that you need to confront. Alternatively, they may be a pun for smoking marijuana – the 'roach' is the filter – or pointing to a problem with your health or personal hygiene. They might even be referring to the low-life company that you are keeping in waking hours. On a positive note, cockroaches may also be symbolic of tenacity and longevity, or may be signifying your need for renewal, rejuvenation and self-cleansing of your psychological, emotional, or spiritual being.

CRICKET/GRASSHOPPER/ LOCUST

To see **crickets** in your dream represents the need for introspection. You need to pay attention to Jiminy Cricket, your conscience. To **hear crickets** in your dream suggests that you are letting minor things bother you. To see a **grasshopper** in your dream foretells of enemies that will threaten your interest, disappointments in business or illness. To draw other people's attention to a grasshopper signifies your indiscretion in dispatching your private business. Because we associate grasshoppers and crickets with the lazy days of summer, to dream of them may be often be more positive than is suggested by the interpretations above; your dream may simply have been wish-fulfillment. It could also have been a comment on your grasshopper mind: the inability to focus on anything for long before turning to something else.

The image of a plague of **locusts** is so strong in human thought that even in dreams it can present retribution for some wrongdoing in waking life. Dreams of locusts could mirror the horde of ugly problems that have been plaguing you in your waking hours. To see locusts in your dream could also signify scattered thoughts that need direction if they are to make an impact in your waking life.

The Element Encyclopedia of 20,000 Dreams

DRAGONFLY

To see a **dragonfly** in your dream symbolizes changes. It may also indicate that something in your life may not be as it seems. To dream that you are **eating a dragonfly** suggests that you are consumed by some sort of passion, even at the risk of offending or hurting another person's feelings.

FLEA

To see **fleas** in your dream signifies that you will be provoked into anger and manipulated into retaliation by someone close to you. Fleas are also celebrated for their ability to jump from one body to another. Do you have the kind of mind that can leap quickly from subject to subject? To dream that **fleas bite you** may signify vicious rumors by false friends that slander your character.

FLY/BLOODSUCKER

Unless a real **fly** is trapped in your bedroom and your unconscious incorporated its annoying noise into your dream, flies in dreams evoke images of persistence, speed and relentless pursuit; they may also symbolize nagging, unwelcome people that you know or the need to be aware of certain negative aspects in your life. In addition, a fly can also represent limiting ideas or an unproductive use of energy; someone might be a 'fly in the ointment' and ruining things for you. If a **fly settles on the wall** in your dream, do you wish you could discover the details about something or if everyone in your dream is swatting away flies for you do you feel smart as in no flies on him?

Blood-sucking insects such as **gnats, midges or mosquitoes** may represent instincts from the unconscious, the water from which they are bred and the darkness in which they thrive. Symbols of irritation, gnats, midges and mosquitoes, like flies, violate the intimacy of their victims and feed off their blood. Is there someone in your waking life who is sucking you dry and draining you of energy?

HORNET

If a **hornets' nest** appears in your dreams, perhaps there is something you need to steer clear of in waking life. Hornets represent people and situations that bring threats with them; they are a symbol of trouble waiting to happen or festering beneath the surface. Have you 'stirred up a hornet's nest'? If you have been short-tempered lately and have a dream of a hornets' nest, look for the problem in the way you think about yourself because hornets nest in high places. Occasionally a **hornet** may represent busy thinking and over-activity; your dreaming mind may be sending you the image to encourage you to calm down and take things one step at a time. To dream that you are **stung by a hornet** is an indication of revenge and vengeful attitudes. It may also represent some stinging remark.

INSECT

In their positive aspect, **insects** in your dream represent the power of small things to create big results; they may be encouraging you to focus on the details and work in harmony with others. If you are a person who likes to work alone, your dream may be urging you to ask for help. On the negative side, insects can represent people, situations or behavior that irritate you. You need to stop trying to brush things aside and deal with whatever it is that is bothering you.

To dream of a **solitary insect** may be a message from your inner self. That your inner self should employ such an unlikely ambassador is a reflection of your (very unwise) contempt for your inner self, as shown perhaps in the way you exclude it from your conscious life. (Remember the cricket in Pinocchio's adventures?) A **solitary insect** may also imply something or someone that is 'bugging' or even threatening you. It might also suggest you are feeling insignificant, like an ant in the mass of other ants. More positively, a solitary insect can appear in dreams as a reminder of instinctive behavior.

If you are **stung by an insect or insects** in your dream, this suggests anxiety and grief caused by your own obstinacy; the dream is trying to prick you into taking positive action. The sting may also be an emotional one. Someone may have hurt you or gossip may have stung you. Have you been stung or hurt by someone's criticism, or was the dream referring to a sting or swindle someone is about to perpetrate in waking life?

LEECH/LOUSE

To **see or be bitten by leeches** in your dream refers to something in your life — people, habits, or negative emotions — that is draining the energy and vigor out of you. Alternatively, if your **body is covered in leeches**, then you are feeling disgusted by your own body or repulsed by something you have done. To see **lice** in your dream signifies frustration, distress and feelings of guilt. You may also be feeling emotionally or physically unclean. Alternatively, the lice may represent a person, situation or relationship from which you would like to distance yourself. You may be feeling used or taken advantage of.

MOTH

The polar opposite in dreams to the butterfly, the **moth** symbolizes those dark and uncontrollable urges from the unconscious that plague our efforts at transformation and self-awareness in real life. The moth is largely associated with night-time and therefore indicates the hidden or darker aspects of your personality. To see a moth in your dream indicates that unseen damage will not become apparent until it is too late. Such a dream is telling you that it is important to pay attention to minor details and not overlook things or others. Alternatively, the moth may symbolize your weaknesses, character flaws or a dangerous attraction to someone who is not good for you, as the image of a moth flying too close to the flame indicates. **Moths flying out of clothes** in your dream may indicate old arguments and hurts that need to be addressed. Pay attention to the item of clothing that the moths attack; a coat, for example, might symbolize protection. More positively, however, to dream of **a moth emerging from darkness** signifies growing self-awareness in real life.

Insect miscellany

Earwig

An old superstition says that **earwigs** crawl into the ears of sleeping people; this is why they are associated with anxiety and fear in dreams. They can, however, also suggest secrets revealed by a loved one or close friend.

Maggot

To see **maggots** in your dream represents your anxieties about death. It may also be indicative of some issue or problem that you have been rejecting and that is now 'eating away' at you.

Praying Mantis

If the stately but dangerous **praying mantis** steps into your dream, this suggests that you are in a destructive relationship. It may also indicate that you are preying on others.

Termite/Tick

To see **termites** suggests that you may be feeling undermined in waking life, as termites, along with **woodworm, and the larvae of death watch and furniture beetles**, can undermine the very foundation of your home – a Jungian symbol of the self. If **ticks** appear in your dream, it might indicate that something is slowly draining the energy and strength out of you; this might be a relationship or a job, or maybe someone is sucking the life and energy out of you. The dream may also be a pun on being 'ticked off' and thus represent your feelings of being annoyed or irritated.

Weevil

To see a **weevil** in your dream signifies some kind of loss in waking life.

SCORPION

To see a **scorpion** in your dream represents a situation in your waking life which may have been painful or hurtful. It is also indicative of destructive feelings, 'stinging' remarks, bitter words or negative thoughts being expressed by, or aimed against, yourself; remember that the scorpion has a sting in its tale. Your dream forewarns of a self-destructive and self-defeating path. The scorpion is also a symbol of death and rebirth, suggesting that you need to get rid of the old and make room for something new. To see **scorpions floating in water** suggests that you need to let go of some pain and learn to accept the situation. You may be going through the three-step process of denial, acceptance and finally moving on. Alternatively, dreams of scorpions may also represent a person who is born under the Zodiac sign for Scorpio.

SLUG

Slugs rarely appear in a positive light in dreams and are often symbols of prejudice. Consider whether you have been denying some part of yourself; if you have, accepting that part might be the best medicine. Slugs are also associated with sticky, difficult situations, or emotions with which you would rather not deal. The only way to remove the problem is to deal with it slowly and carefully. Try to overcome your reluctance to handle a situation and let go of your wish that it will just go away. The situation will prove much easier and less painful to deal with if you proceed with awareness and care.

SPIDER

In their positive aspect, **spiders** represent the feminine capacity for creating something beautiful that has not existed before. Spider energy is also connected with patience and success through skill. On the negative side, spiders represent small or hairy things that create big fears and a dream featuring scary spiders may be associated with personal fears to which your dreaming mind believes you are overreacting. To see a spider in your dream can also indicate that you are feeling like an outsider in some situation or that you may want to keep your distance.

A spider may represent a fear, or something or someone who makes you feel vulnerable. Perhaps you feel trapped or entangled by emotions or fears from which you cannot escape. Alternatively, are you a spider trying to trap someone else in your web or is someone trying to trap you? Freud believed that dream spiders represent the devouring mother who consumes her children through possessiveness or the ability to arouse guilt. Try to get to know, not only your mother, but more importantly, what your mother means to you. One way of doing this is to converse with the spider: hold it in your mind and ask it searching questions. Or perhaps you are feeling trapped by another relationship in your life?

Dreams of a spider in your bed may suggest that intimacy with a loved one is triggering a lack of self-confidence and fears about being vulnerable and exploited. The spider can also depict any emotions you don't want to 'handle', such as those surrounding a spouse leaving. It can suggest that you want to ensnare someone or something, or that you are feeling trapped yourself. It may even represent the most basic survival instincts in us – can I eat, or will I be eaten by this person or situation? Superstitions dating back to the Middle Ages claim that it is a good sign to dream of spiders. To see a **black widow** in your dream suggests fear or uncertainty regarding a relationship. You may feel confined, trapped or suffocated in this relationship. You may even feel hostility toward your partner. Because the female black widow has the reputation of devouring its mate, it thus also symbolizes feminine power and domination over men.

WASP

To see a **wasp** in your dream signifies angry thoughts and feelings. Perhaps your unconscious is alerting you to someone in your waking life who has a waspish or bad-tempered character and from whom you expect a stinging rebuke? To dream that

Web

If the image of a **spider's web** appears in your dream, it can represent a sticky situation in which you have found yourself, feeling caught up in something that might trap you or being trapped by the power of someone else's emotions or expectations. It can also imply a web of lies, as well as the connections linking you with other people, events and the world. You might find this link to be supportive or threatening. Another interpretation associates the web with the circle of life and the symbol of the Mandala; the center of the web suggests a merging back into the primal energy of life. **Spider's webs in a dusty house** suggest a need to spring clean, or deal with old memories and the past. Sometimes the web made by a spider is a cocoon, and so is protective. Often this relates to very delicate processes of change going on in us, perhaps ones which need us to be a little withdrawn or protected from the world in order for the process to work out and mature. If your dreaming self walked into a **room obscured by cobwebs**, ask yourself how that pertains to you. Have you been withdrawing from life recently and is it time to blow away the cobwebs and become more active again?

you are **stung by a wasp** symbolizes for Jungians a dangerous attack by the instincts. To dream that you **kill a wasp** signifies your fearlessness in warding off your enemies and maintaining your principles and rights. If **wasps are building a nest in your dream roof** this may indicate difficulties with spiritual progress.

WORM

Freudians might regard the **worm** as a phallic symbol, and according to your reaction, worms in general may represent a sense of threat. To see a worm in your dream also represents weakness and general negativity; you have a very low opinion of yourself or of someone in your life. To dream that the **worm is crawling on your body** indicates that you feel someone around you is taking advantage of you and feeding off your kind-heartedness. If the **worm is bigger than you** in your dream, this suggests a real sense of inferiority. There are also associations with death and rebirth, as being 'given to the worms' is a metaphor for death.

To dream that you have **ringworm** is urging you to take better care of your health and boost your immunity with a healthy diet and regular exercise. To have or see a **tapeworm** in your dream likewise forewarns of poor health if you do not take better care of yourself. If the floorboards in your dreams bore the signs of **woodworm**, could your unconscious have been warning you that unless you take action, something or someone troublesome will crawl out of the woodwork, ultimately causing things to collapse around you?

LEISURE

If one of your favorite leisure activities featured in your dream, your unconscious may have chosen this image to send you a useful message.

Your dreaming mind may have been urging you to take some time out of your busy schedule for the things you love to do. It could also have been suggesting ways in which you could improve your experience or become more accomplished at it. If, however, the leisure activity in your dream is something you wouldn't dream of doing during your waking hours, then the chances are that your unconscious was referring to your current approach to life. For example, dreams in which you are playing chess may emphasize your concern with intellectual development or competition. For Freudians, dreams that feature a preoccupation with leisure pursuits are potent symbols of sexual excitement. Jungians, however, would see dream leisure activities as a mirror of your spiritual aspirations. The associations between your dream scenario and your waking situation will often be clear, but if you are uncertain about what is meant by your dream, this chapter may be of assistance to you. *See also* ACCIDENTS, ACTION AND ADVENTURES; ARTS AND CRAFTS; EVERYDAY THINGS.

Sporting Scenes

BOXING/MARTIAL ART

If you dreamed of **boxing, wrestling or practicing any kind of martial art, such as karate, judo or kick boxing**, your dream may have had either hostile or defensive undertones. The violence of boxing or martial arts reveals a repressed hostility towards someone or something in your waking life. A **knockout** can indicate a guilty wish to inflict punishment or pain. Your dream may also be urging you to adopt a more calculated or self-disciplined approach to a certain threat or challenge in real life. At its most basic, boxing is an endurance sport; in dreams, it can suggest a period of uncertainty during which your intuitive and rational halves will be in conflict with each other. Your dream is telling you that if you have self-discipline and patience, you can develop inner strength and resilience.

KEEPING FIT

A dream in which you were **keeping fit by working out** – whether it was in the **gym with weights or on an exercise machine, or following an exercise video at home** – may be commenting on your real-life need to gain or lose weight. If you already take good care of yourself and exercise regularly, your dreaming mind could have been encouraging you to build up a different kind of strength and stamina; not necessarily physical, but emotional or intellectual. Alternatively, keep-fit dreams could have been commenting on how you are feeling in real life. For example, if you were **running on a treadmill**, do you feel that you are expending a lot of energy but actually getting nowhere? If you were **lifting weights**, do you feel you are shouldering a burden in waking life? If a **fitness instructor is yelling at your exhausted dream self**, do you feel that you are being pushed beyond your limits by someone who has authority over you in real life? Dreams in which you are **practicing or watching yoga** may be urging you to take a more flexible approach to life. They may also be encouraging you to step back from outward activity for a while to explore your inner motivations.

SOLO COMPETITOR

If you dreamed of being an individual competitor in a game of **tennis or golf** or engaging in solo activities such as **running or gymnastics**, your dreaming mind may have been turning the spotlight on your self-sufficiency. If you can remember who your opponent was in your dream, is this someone you are battling against in real life? Did you **serve ace after ace** in your dream or **hit that elusive hole-in-one**? If so, then your unconscious is referring to what you feel is an outstanding performance or ability in waking life. Are other people there to admire your success or is your triumph a lonely one in your dream? If, however, you **missed a shot or putt**, this suggests that your current lack of discipline or dedication is weakening your chances of success in the real world. Unless you can find focus and dedication, you may end up being the loser. If you performed badly in your dream because your **racket or club had a fault or broke into pieces** your unconscious may have been advising you to update the tools of your trade because they are slowing you down or hindering your progress.

The sexual symbolism of **fencing** is impossible to ignore given the thrusting nature of many of the moves. The focal point of the dream may well be when the **opponent takes off their mask** to reveal who you have been fighting. Is your mystery opponent a person you know in waking life or your own unconscious hostile urges? A dream in which you play a **friendly game of golf**, enjoying both the game and the company, is a positive sign that suggests a sense of contentment in your waking life. However, to **record a poor score** suggests that something or someone in your real life is trying to undermine you. To dream of a **tee** will most often point to an irritating element in your life or something you want to put behind you or get rid of.

To have a dream about **gymnastics or to become a gymnast** in your dream reveals a desire for greater self-expression and flexibility; it is, however, important to achieve a balance between what is achievable and what is unrealistic. To dream of being a **diver** suggests a course of action that has to be followed through, no matter what.

SPORTING ACTIVITY

Dreams which relate to **sporting activities in general** are usually positive but they can also reveal your competitive spirit. They should not be taken literally, as they rarely relate to sporting prowess; they are used by your dreaming mind as a metaphor in your waking life to represent your attitude to winning and losing, and how you play the game of life. Whatever your chosen sport, to see yourself **winning fairly and cleanly** without resorting to cheating is an empowering symbol that should have a positive influence on your waking life. As a dream message, it is important for you to defeat your dream competitors in as honest a way as possible; so dreams of **winning by cheating or competing against people who are weaker than you** suggest a disheartening struggle ahead, as fair play is a crucial concept for your dreaming mind.

A dream of performing on an **athletics track** may refer to how you feel your performance rates when compared with others in waking life. Are you way ahead of the rest or struggling to keep in the race? Whether you were **performing the high jump or throwing a javelin or taking part in a relay** in your dream, if you were powerful and successful, your unconscious may have been indicating how successfully and rapidly you are advancing in waking life towards achieving your goals. Dreams that feature **running, cycling, skiing and skating** may also be commenting on your

progress, or lack of it, in waking life. For example, if you dreamed of **putting on a pair of skating boots**, perhaps your unconscious is urging you to put your skates on and make an extra effort; or perhaps you need to be aware of the metaphorical phrase, 'skating on thin ice'. If you dreamed of **cycling or running down a bumpy road**, have you hit a difficult patch in waking life? If you dreamed of **skiing down a piste and tumbling headlong down the slope**, are you in danger of losing control in waking life? **Going down a mountain** is a classic Freudian symbol of sexual intercourse but with the added thrills and anxiety implied by skiing. For Jungians, dreams of **yachting or regattas** may suggest exploration of the unconscious. For Freudians, such dreams recall memories and longings for the mother's womb.

TEAM GAME

Most dreams in which you are playing a **team game** reflect how well you feel you are performing within a group situation in waking life, whether it is among your family and friends, or – more typically – in relation to colleagues at work. So if you dreamed of **playing football, basketball, hockey, netball, rugby or volleyball**, pay attention to how you are reacting or playing in the team. Are you the weak link? Are you lazy? Are you the one who pulls the team together? Are you a good sport? Do you play fairly, or do you cheat and break the rules? Do you respect authority and the decision of the referee or judges? Are you a team player or only concerned about your own performance? The answer to questions such as these will prove helpful if they are considered in the context of your participation in group dynamics in waking life.

Dreams that feature **baseball** can be littered with sexual symbols such as the bat, the ball and the gloves. According to Freudians, such dreams – and this would be true of all games containing **umpires or referees** – might be an oblique reference to a challenge you have made to a father figure, as represented by the umpire. The **white outfits worn in the game of cricket** may suggest a yearning for childhood innocence; the friendly, relaxed and languid nature of the game might reveal a longing to withdraw from a fiercely competitive environment, whether at home or at work. The intense passions of **football**, whether in the form of rugby, soccer or gridiron, may symbolize sexual excitement; scoring a goal or a try, for example, might symbolize orgasm. Jungians, however, would see dream football as a mirror of the dreamer's spiritual aspirations. Some team sports seem unlikely topics for a dream but your dreaming mind may select them specifically for their symbolism. To dream that you are part of a **rowing team**, for example, stresses the importance of collective effort and pulling together as a team.

Games Scenarios

BOARD GAME

Games in dreamland symbolize the manner in which the dreamer is approaching life. Individual games, such as **solitaire**, will indicate your tendency for self-absorption, where excelling or enjoyment is a significant motive. Interactive games, such as **chess**, indicate that competition is a significant motive for you. In either case, the dream will be highlighting your thought processes, mental skills and dexterity. In general, dream **board and card games** indicate how you are rising to a particular challenge in your waking life or how successfully you are playing the hand that fate has dealt you.

Little physical effort is required when playing board and card games, so games of this nature tend to focus on your intellectual performance or ability to think and react quickly. Pay attention to the tactics you use whilst playing and to your overall strategy. Were you calm and controlled with a set of tactics, or were you out of control? Was your game defensive or offensive? What is the dream telling you about your ability to respond to external stimuli in the directing of directing of your life? Are you self-motivated, continually striving to better your skill, or do you rely on competition for motivation? Your answer to questions such as these will tell you much about your current approach to waking life.

Consider too the colors of the pieces or cards you were using and what they might signify. For example, if you were playing with **white chess pieces**, do you associate yourself with kindness and your opponent with malevolence? If you are **accused of cheating** in your dream, are you deceiving anyone in waking life? Games in which **pieces are moved around a board at the throw of a dice** are often designed to mirror life's challenges and this is often what they represent in dreams, suggesting fears or concerns about factors you can't

Dice

The ultimate symbols of chance, dream **dice** clearly suggest that you feel that chance rather than your personal abilities will determine the outcome in your life. Dreams of dice may also suggest doubts about the fairness or uniformity of life and concerns as to whether the universe is subject to anything other than the forces of chance. To be **playing with dice** in your dream suggests that you are taking chances in your life. If **someone else is rolling the dice**, then you are leaving your fate in the hands of others, and running your life according to their rules and not your own. An eighteenth-century American almanac declared dice to be made from 'dead men's bones' and to **roll dice and win** foretold losses far greater than you could afford to bear. To **lose at dice**, however, points to profitable opportunities developing in the near future.

control. The **game board** reveals the moves you make in life and a **games room** stands for a meeting place in which plans and strategies are devised. A **game show** cautions against a desire to consider yourself intellectually superior.

Specific dreams may have their own symbolism; for example sexuality in **snakes and ladders** and the repercussions of your actions in games that require **dominos**. A

game of **backgammon** may point to your desire to resolve the secrets of your unconscious (the inner table) before time or the other player stops you. **Pool, billiards or snooker** suggest clever scheming, combined with the skill to accomplish a goal. The condition of the **poolroom** will give you a clue as to whether this refers to healthy competition or dirty dealings, whilst the **pool table** refers to the issue or subject of your plans.

CARD GAME

If you **hold all the aces or win a game of poker** with a royal flush are you feeling certain that you have a real advantage in the real world, of which those around you are unaware because you are holding your cards close to your chest or being secretive? There are many colloquial expressions associated with cards that your unconscious may be using to relay a message to you. For example, did you 'play your cards right'? Did you 'lay your cards on the table', thereby revealing your intentions? If you did, your dreaming mind may be encouraging you to be more open about your intentions in real life. If you had an 'ace up your sleeve', are you biding your time? In dreamlore, the old proverb 'lucky in cards, unlucky in love' may filter through into your dreams; some believe that to dream of a **winning hand** is indicative of unrequited love. Other authorities urge a careful rethink of finances to anyone who experiences a dream win. If you **focused on a particular card**, does this have a particular relevance for you in waking life?

Some dream analysts believe that particular suits have particular meanings that can aid dream interpretation. **Hearts** can suggest joy, happiness, love and romance. **Diamonds** highlight money concerns but also insights and aspirations. **Clubs** highlight knowledge, intellect and achieving goals. **Spades** represent the difficulties of life and warn of obstacles ahead that you will need endurance to overcome. If the **joker** appears in your dream, your unconscious may be drawing your attention to someone in your life – perhaps you yourself – who is fooling around

CHESS

In Jungian terminology, the game of **chess** represents the dreamer's conscious (white pieces) and unconscious (black pieces). Chess originally signified the war between good and evil, so in dreams it can express the conflict within or the need for some kind of strategy in your waking life. The game is a symbol of the battle between light and dark; this may represent a moral dilemma you are facing in waking life. The game is also rich in the symbolism of sexual rivalry and so dreams that feature chess lend themselves well to a Freudian interpretation: chess is won by killing the father figure, the piece most capable of killing him being the mother queen.

Consider the symbolism of the color of the pieces you choose and whether they were black of white. You may also want to consider the symbolism of the pieces you handle or move in your dream. For example, the **king** may represent someone who needs defending in waking life. If you are using **pawns**, do you feel as if you are being manipulated in waking life? Consider also the implication of making a **good or bad move** in your dream and your life; if someone **checkmates** you, who or what is

trying to restrict your movements in waking life? If, however, **you are the person who checkmates**, this suggests that you have your eye on your goals in waking life and have the strategy you need to succeed in achieving them. To dream of **winning a chess match** points to a highly analytical mind. **Losing at chess** indicates that you may have overstretched your abilities and need to lower your expectations.

GAMBLING

If your unconscious depicted you as **rolling a dice and hoping for a six**, does this suggests that you feel as if your destiny is not in your hands but in the hands of fate, or that the direction your life will take is out of your control? Or are you dicing with death and taking a big risk in your life? Any dream in which you are **gambling** may be considered a warning that you are risking something for which you have worked in real life and that the odds are stacked against you. On the other hand, if your gamble came off in dreamland and you **won a bet or money**, perhaps your dreaming mind is encouraging you to be a little less cautious in waking life and take a chance on something as it has the potential to yield great reward. This does not have to be the lottery or a horse race; it could be an emotional investment. **Winning a large amount of money on the lottery** in dreamland is a common wish-fulfillment dream. The dream may also be warning you that if you hope to achieve your goals without any effort expended on your part, your chances of success are minimal. Freudians relate **lottery or money** dreams to anal preoccupation and the desire to break with miserliness.

Playing cards in dreams

Long before people used cards to play games, they were used to foretell the future. In fact, playing cards were invented for divination rather than for entertainment. Bear in mind that dreams comment on future possibilities rather than predict the future, but if a **particular card is highlighted** in your dream, the following traditional divinatory meanings may suggest possible situations you might like to encourage or avoid in your waking life.

First of all, the suits are associated with the four elements as follows: Hearts – Water; Clubs – Fire; Diamonds – Earth; Spades – Air. The individual card meanings are as follows:

Ace of Hearts: Love and happiness; a particularly favorable card that indicates troubles lifting.

King of Hearts: A fair-haired man with a good nature; or a man with water signs predominating in his chart; fair, helpful advice. Affectionate, caring man. This man helps you out without much talk; his actions reveal his kindness and concern.

Queen of Hearts: A fair-haired woman with a good nature; or a woman with water signs predominating in her chart; kind advice. Affectionate, caring woman. This card can sometimes indicate the mother or a mother figure.

Jack of Hearts: A warm-hearted friend; a fair-haired youth; or a young person with water signs predominating in their chart; often points to a younger admirer.

10 of Hearts: Good luck; success; this is an important card that suggests good fortune after difficulty.

9 of Hearts: The card of wishes; a wish or dream fulfilled.

8 of Hearts: Unexpected gift or visit; an invitation to a party.

7 of Hearts: Someone whose interest in you is unreliable; someone with fickle affections for you; can indicate lovesickness.

6 of Hearts: A sudden wave of good luck; someone takes care of you or takes a warm interest in you.

5 of Hearts: Jealousy; some ill-will from people around you.

4 of Hearts: Travel; change of home or business.

3 of Hearts: Love and happiness; can also indicate emotional problems and an inability to decide who to love.

2 of Hearts: A warm partnership or engagement; a very favorable card that indicates strength and support coming from a partner.

Ace of Clubs: Wealth, prosperity, unexpected money; can also suggest mismanagement of money.

King of Clubs: Dark-haired, kind-hearted man; or a man with fire predominating in his chart; a generous, spirited man.

Queen of Clubs: Dark-haired, confident woman; or a woman with fire predominating in her chart; she may give you good advice.

Jack of Clubs: A dark-haired or fiery youth; a popular youth who is good-hearted and playful; can also indicate an admirer.

10 of Clubs: Business success; good luck with money; a trip taken now may result in a new friend or love interest.

9 of Clubs: Achievement; sometimes a wealthy marriage or sudden windfall.

8 of Clubs: Work or business problems that may have to do with jealousy.

7 of Clubs: Business success, although there may be problems with the opposite sex; a change in business that may have been expected or earned, such as a promotion.

6 of Clubs: Financial aid or success.

5 of Clubs: New friendships or alliances are made.

4 of Clubs: Beware of dishonesty or deceit; avoid blind acceptance of others at this time.

3 of Clubs: Love and happiness; successful marriage; a favorable long-term proposition; a second chance, often in an economic sense.

2 of Clubs: Obstacles to success; malicious gossip.

Ace of Spades: Misfortune; sometimes associated with a difficult ending.

King of Spades: Dark-haired man; or a man with air predominating in his chart; an ambitious, perhaps self-serving, man.

Queen of Spades: Widowed or divorced woman; a woman with air predominating in her chart.

Jack of Spades: A youth who is demanding or jealous.

10 of Spades: Worry; bad news.

9 of Spades: Misfortune; a personal low.

8 of Spades: Temptation; danger; upsets.

7 of Spades: Advice that is best not taken; loss; there is some obstacle to success, and this indicates that obstacles may be coming from within you.

6 of Spades: Small changes and improvements.

5 of Spades: Opposition and obstacles that are temporary; a blessing in disguise; sometimes indicates a negative or depressed person.

4 of Spades: Small worries; problems; financial difficulties, personal lows.

3 of Spades: Breaks or conflict in relationships.

2 of Spades: Deceit; may also warn against possible infidelity or separation.

Ace of Diamonds: Change; a message, often about money, and usually good news.

King of Diamonds: Fair-haired or graying man; a man with earth predominating in his chart; a man of authority, status, or influence.

Queen of Diamonds: Fair-haired woman; a woman with earth predominating in her chart; a gossip.

Jack of Diamonds: A youth, possibly in uniform; a jealous person who may be unreliable; a person who brings news, generally negative, but relatively minor.

10 of Diamonds: A change in financial status, often for the better.

9 of Diamonds: A new business deal; travel; restlessness; a change of residence.

8 of Diamonds: New job; change in job situation; the young or the old may find love on a trip.

7 of Diamonds: An argument concerning finances or employment, generally expected to be resolved happily.

6 of Diamonds: Relationship problems; arguments; separation.

5 of Diamonds: Happiness and success; a change for the better; a birth, or good news for a child; a good time to start new projects.

4 of Diamonds: Financial upswing; an older person may give good advice.

3 of Diamonds: A legal letter; be tactful with others in order to avoid disputes.

2 of Diamonds: A business partnership; a change in relationship; gossip.

Making any kind of wager or bet in your dream may stand for a gamble you are taking in waking life. Your dreaming mind is urging you to weigh up the odds and consider how much you are risking. The rhythmic gallop of the horses may symbolise sexual intercourse and if you are **betting on a horse** in your dream, this may reflect the emotional weight of success or failure as far as a relationship is concerned. **Playing for high stakes at poker** in your dream can imply that you are being too impressionable and emotionally insecure in your personal relationships, whilst to **play poker with strangers** indicates a lack of emotional connection in your life. If you **visit a fortune teller** in your dream, this expresses concern about your future prospects; if you are a skeptic, such a dream may represent a crisis of faith in the powers of reason.

Light Entertainment

CINEMA

If you dreamed of **watching a film**, your unconscious may have been alerting you to a charade or drama unfolding around you in waking life. Watching a film may also add a veneer of glamor to aspects of your life from which you ought to distance yourself. Such a dream may be urging you to create that distance, warning you to stop denying responsibility for your actions in waking life. If you dream of **going to the cinema**, pay attention to what you are actually watching as it could have relevance for your waking life. For example, if you **dreamed in black and white**, do you need to add romance or color to your life? **Action and adventure films** suggest escapism. If **acting, music making, dance or a visit to the circus** feature in your dream, *see* ARTS AND CRAFTS. *See also* MEDIA AND TECHNOLOGY.

FAIRGROUND

If your dreaming mind conjured up an image of a **fairground**, it may have been commenting on your response to waking life. For example, if you dreamed of **taking a rollercoaster ride**, are you feeling apprehensive or sick of the dramatic ups and downs in your life recently? If you were **spinning on a carousel**, do you feel as if you are going round and round in circles and making no progress in waking life? Or does your carousel dream feature sexual

symbolism, with images of **horses and flying** and a desire to return to the sexual innocence of childhood? If you dreamed of **swaying gently in a carriage on a Ferris wheel looking down at the world below**, your dreaming mind may be encouraging you to take an overview of the bigger picture of your life.

If you were **interested in or involved with a puppet show** in your dream, this may be a warning that somebody is trying to manipulate you in waking life and pull your strings. **Swings** are an image of childhood freedom and may have a similar interpretation to dreams of flying. If you are using the Freudian interpretation of swings as images of sexual intercourse, the person or thing who is pushing the swing in your dream will be significant. Dreams of **playing on a seesaw** have the same sexual associations.

TOY

Dreams that feature **childhood toys** can be either encouraging or discouraging, depending on how you feel in your dream. On the one hand if you dreamed of **playing happily in a toy shop** for hours and hours, your dreaming mind may be reminding you of the importance of having fun every now and again, and playing childish or adult games. Has fun or relaxation been missing from your life recently? On the other hand, if you **feel bored by your dream toys**, then perhaps it is time to put your energy to productive use. Dream toys may also express a wish to assert control over your adult life at a time when you may be having problems.

Breaking toys may express your frustration with problems you find hard to resolve. If toy dreams suggest asserting control over problems, dreams which feature **puppets or dolls** are about asserting control over other people. Dreams about dolls can express your feelings and beliefs about your parents but they may also represent your feelings about being manipulated by people close to you in waking life. To dream of a **rocking horse** bears the same symbolism as a dreaming of horses in general, but it can also express a yearning for the comfort and security of childhood with its gentle, rocking motion. One of the most ancient and well-known toys, the **spinning top** may suggest a trance-like state or meditative frame of mind in which you look into the depths of your unconscious. The wailing sound it produces may also be associated with sorrow and bereavement. **Cuddly toys, especially teddy bears**, illustrate comforting and soothing aspects of your life. *See also* Toy entry in BIRTH AND CHILDHOOD.

Vacation Time

HOLIDAY

If you are **traveling towards a holiday destination** in your dream, this may suggest disillusionment with your current daily routine. If you are making a **hectic dash to the airport or enjoying first-class perks on your journey**, this can point to whether or not you feel anxious or calm about your current circumstances. If you have **packed too many bags for your dream holiday**, this may suggest clinging onto worries and issues that burden you.

Baggage in dreams tends to symbolize material or psychological concerns, so if you have **no baggage at all** in your dream, your unconscious may be urging you to leave your emotional baggage behind so you can move forward feeling lighter and less encumbered. If you dream of **losing your baggage**, is that good or bad for you? Does it offer you an opportunity to start afresh? If your dream **baggage is very elegant and all items match**, does it suggest a need to make a good impression on others or an overdeveloped concern with outward appearances?

If a **ticket for going on holiday** features in your dream, this expresses opportunity. The dream image conjures up wishes associated with travel or taking a risk in some aspect of your life. If you **lose your ticket** in your dream, this suggests anxiety about losing the chance of new opportunities in your emotional and professional life in the real world. **Taking your camera on your dream holiday** may indicate the need to preserve, hold onto or remember an important event or person in your life. **Forgetting your camera** means that you are forgetting what is important in your life.

ON THE BEACH

A dream in which you are **lying sunning yourself on an idyllic beach with rolling sand, gentle waves and warm tropical sunshine** may represent simple wish-fulfillment and a longing to escape the daily grind of your routine and responsibilities. Another interpretation, the Freudian one, suggests that events on dream beaches can highlight your anxieties. For example, dreams of **burying any authority figure in**

Hobbies

Dreams that feature **hobbies** relate to your interests and how you relax. Each hobby will have its own interpretation. Some of the more popular hobbies are listed below, but there are countless more.

Camping

Camping refers to a temporary return to a calmer emotional state. It may be suggesting that if you were more tolerant, the frequency and number of your current conflicts might be reduced. Alternatively, it could indicate the need to balance work with relaxation. If **camping gear** features in your dream, this suggests the need to equip yourself with more tools to achieve a less stressful state of mind. A **campfire** denotes an inner peacefulness or tranquility.

Hunting/Fishing

Dreams of **hunting** relate to the killing of innocence or the search for something important. Surrounding dreamscape details and the type of animal you are hunting will clarify the meaning. **Fishing** suggests an exploration of your unconscious. *See also* REPTILES, FISH AND AMPHIBIANS.

Reading

This relates to the gathering or recalling of knowledge or information; the key is to recall what was read. **Books** in dreams tend to relate to things you have learned from experience. They can also reflect the world of imagination and escape. Alternatively, they can relate to your ability to learn from the opinions and experience of others. Dreams about **writing** pertain to a desire to express inner thoughts, ideas or sensitivities. If you **suffer from writer's block**, this may point to confusion and an absence of inspiration. *See also* LETTERS AND COMMUNICATION.

Stamp Collecting

This indicates recognition of the value of something or someone. If a **specific stamp is highlighted**, this refers to the value of communications. Try to recall the image on the stamp.

TV Watching

What you are **watching on TV** will reveal the current quality and state of your perspective on life. A **cartoon** would represent immaturity; **news** with keeping current with daily events. The key is what you are watching. *See also* MEDIA AND TECHNOLOGY.

For spending time with family and children, *see* FAMILY; RELATIONSHIPS. For gardening, *see* PLACES: NATURE AND THE SEASONS. For painting, listening to music, amateur dramatics, singing, dancing, and arts and crafts, *see* ARTS AND CRAFTS. For visiting foreign countries, driving around, and working on cars, *see* FOREIGN COUNTRIES; TRAVEL. For animals, *see* ANIMALS; PETS.

the sand may be symbolic of the Oedipal murder of the father figure, whilst castration may be represented by **tall sand castles being washed away by the incoming tide** of the feminine or maternal sea. If you dreamed of **taking a dip in the sea**, pay attention to how you felt.

Beaches are places where water meets the earth, or, in symbolic terms, where the unconscious meets the rational mind. If you dream of **emerging from the water**, for example, this may signal an end of a period of emotional conflict in your waking life. Do you feel emotionally stronger or emotionally battered by the experience? If you **stayed on the shore**, do you prefer to remain on the firmness of land and reason, rather than venturing into the perilous depths of the sea or the unconscious mind? **Bathing whilst on holiday** lends itself to a Freudian interpretation as a dream symbol of birth or of the desire to return to the mother's womb. If the **sea washed away your footprints in the sand** in your dream, is there something in your past from which you wish to move away so you can make a fresh start? If the **sand in your dream starts to shift so you lose your footing**, could this mirror a concern that the foundations of your life are about to give way?

Holiday dreams can often contain **romantic scenes in an arbor or other sheltered retreat such as a cave**. Such dreams can suggest a longing for romance but they can also suggest frustration with aspects of your current relationship or love life, as well as a need for adventure and freedom of responsibility from daily chores. If you dream of a **holiday from hell** in which you are given **poor accommodation, are double booked or experience terrible weather or food**, such a dream can warn against over idealism. It also suggests that negative thinking and pessimism will destroy the quality of your life if you allow them to continue. In dreams, **desert islands** may be symbols of loss or a general sense of emotional insecurity. Alternatively, they may also express a yearning for solitude, clarity, simplicity and time alone to reflect and work out your priorities.

The Element Encyclopedia of 20,000 Dreams

LETTERS AND COMMUNICATION

Dreams are a unique form of communication; a way for your dreaming self to communicate with you.

Sometimes the messages contained within dreams can be obscure and difficult to interpret but if your dream contains symbols of communication, such as letters, handwriting, telephones or emails, its meaning may be easier to interpret. Often these symbols are entwined with a wealth of other images but sometimes you may wake with a lingering image of them as the main item in your dream.

Both Carl Jung and Fritz Perls believed that each dream symbol is an aspect of your true self and that communication symbols, in particular, contain useful messages from your unconscious. When trying to interpret these messages, first consider whether the communication makes a clear reference to your waking life or triggers other associations for you. The next thing to consider is the form the communication took and what this suggests. For example, a phone call suggests something more informal than a telegram. If the communication was coded, does that imply a close connection or a lack of understanding? Considering all these aspects in their context along with the other symbols in your dream may help with

the interpretation. *See also* NUMBERS; SOUNDS.

Communication and its Elements

ADDRESS

In dreams, your **address** represents your present life style or status, whilst **another person's address** suggests some kind of contact with that person. **Past addresses** indicate the person you once were. If you **forget or lose your address** in your dream, this suggests a loss of connection or understanding. Your dream is reflecting your real life confusion about who you are, where you are going and how you connect and communicate with others. If you had a dream in which you were **going through your address book and deleting or checking names**, your unconscious was probably sorting the people in your life into those with whom you wish to remain in contact and those whom you want to leave behind. Were there any surprise messages from your unconscious about any particular perople if you had this dream?

ALPHABET

The **alphabet** in dreams may refer to childhood or to basic lessons in life. To see **letters of the alphabet** in your dream symbolizes any object, animal, place or person associated with or resembling that particular letter. For example, the letter 'T' may refer to a type of intersection in a road or a person you know called Tom. Alternatively, you may still be trying to understand some concept or emotion that is still in the primitive stages. For some possible interpretations when certain letters of the alphabet feature in your dreams, see the box on page 337. Bear in mind, however, that your personal associations with the letter need to be considered first.

DOCUMENT

If **formal documents or deeds** – such as **birth, marriage or death certificates, wills and deeds** – appear in your dream, this may express an important turning point in your life or your feelings about key events in your life. **Burning or destroying these documents** indicates closure. **Contracts** in dreams symbolize a personal or professional commitment in waking life. **Tearing up the documents** may suggest your desire to be free from an obligation.

EMAIL/FAX/TEXTING

Although dreams in which you **write and send an email** can have a similar interpreta-

tion to those when you write and send a letter, the important difference here is urgency. **Sending an email** may suggest that you need to make a fast decision in waking life. **Deleting an email** indicates that you need to think things through more carefully. **Hitting the delete button** may suggest that you want to remove an uncomfortable person or situation from your life. If an email, **fax or text message** appears in your dream this may be a message from your dreaming mind to attend to some communication as soon as possible. Such dreams represent your desire to move on speedily with a current project. Alternatively electronic communication or texts can also express your desire to go on the record and publicly state your intentions. As always pay attention to the content of your message. *See also* MEDIA AND TECHNOLOGY.

ENVELOPE

According to Freud, an envelope is a symbol of female sexuality and **putting a letter into an envelope** represents sexual intercourse. If the **envelope is left unopened**, this may represent virginity or sexual repression. **Leaving a letter unopened** in an envelope may also suggest that you are not taking advantage of an opportunity in real life. In dreamland, as in real life, envelopes are symbols of mystery and we can never be really sure of what they contain until we open them. If you are awaiting news about something or someone and dream of **holding an envelope in your hand**, your dream is probably just reflecting your anticipation. If you **open the letter and discovered either positive or negative news**, don't read too much into it; your unconscious was

The Element Encyclopedia of 20,000 Dreams

Possible dream associations for the letters of the alphabet

A

First letter of the alphabet. The corresponding letter of the Greek alphabet is alpha. Alpha and omega, the last letter of the Greek alphabet, symbolize the beginning and the end and, in the New Testament, Christ. In musical notation, the letter is the symbol of a note in the scale. The symbol can also refer to a blood group, a vitamin, the months August and April, or any word, place, sound or name represented by the letter 'a'. In education, a grade of A typically represents the highest score that students can achieve.

B

Any word, name, place or sound represented by the letter 'b'. The second in a series. Something shaped like the letter B. The second best or second highest in quality or rank. A mark of 'B' on a term paper. A written or printed mark representing this note. A string, key, or pipe tuned to the pitch of this tone. One of the four major blood groups in the ABO system. The symbol for the chemical Boron.

C

Any word, name, place or sound represented by the letter 'c'. The third in a series. Something shaped like the letter 'c'. The third best or third highest in quality or rank; a mark of C on a term paper. The first tone in the scale of C major or the third tone in the relative minor scale. Symbol for the element carbon and the Roman numeral 100. A circled 'c' represents copyright or ownership.

D

Any word, name, place or sound represented by the letter 'd'. The fourth in a series. Something shaped like the letter 'd'. The lowest passing grade given to a student in a school or college. A string, key, or pipe tuned to the pitch of this note. In Roman numerals, the number 500.

E

Any word, name, place or sound represented by the letter 'e'. The fifth in a series. Something shaped like the letter 'e'. In education, a grade that indicates a 'fail'. A string, key, or pipe tuned to the pitch of this note. The hypothesized traditional source of those narrative portions of the Pentateuch in which God is referred to as Elohim, so therefore a word of great power. In weather forecasting and geography, E stands for east, one of the four cardinal directions.

F

Any word, name, place or sound represented by the letter 'f'. The sixth in a series. Something shaped like the letter 'f'. In education, a grade that indicates a 'fail'. A string, key, or pipe tuned to the pitch of this note. In chemistry, F is the symbol of the element fluorine.

G

Any word, name, place or sound represented by the letter 'g'. The seventh in a series. Something shaped like the letter 'g'. A string, key, or pipe tuned to the pitch of this note. In physics, G stands for the gravitational constant, the force that brings you back to earth.

H

Any word, name, place or sound represented by the letter 'h'. The eighth in a series. Something shaped like the letter 'h'. In chemistry, H is the symbol for the element hydrogen.

I

Any name, word, place or sound represented by the letter 'i'. The ninth in a series. Something shaped like the letter 'i'. A symbol for the self, the person you are.

J

Any word, name, place or sound represented by the letter 'j'. Symbol of January, June and July or the Jack in a deck of cards. The tenth in a series. Something shaped like the letter 'j'. The hypothesized traditional source of those portions of the Pentateuch in which God is referred to with the Tetragrammaton rather than as Elohim, therefore a letter of power.

K

Any name, word, place or sound represented by the letter 'k'. The 11th in a series. Something shaped like the letter 'k'. In chemistry, K is the symbol for the element potassium. In law, K is a symbol for contract and in baseball for a strike-out.

L

Any name, word, place or sound presented by the letter 'l'. The 12th in a series. Something shaped like a 'k'. In the movie *Men In Black*, agent 'L' (as in 'elle', French for 'she') is the lead female character.

M

Any name, word, place, or sound represented by the letter 'm'. The 13th in a series. Something shaped like the letter 'm'. In information systems, M is often used as the abbreviation for the male sex in personal data records. In calendars, M is often an abbreviation for Monday, or for the months March or May. In French, and some English works by French authors, M. is an abbreviation for *Monsieur*.

N

Any word, name, place or sound represented by the letter 'n'. The 14th in a series. Something shaped like the letter 'n'. In weather forecasting and geography, N stands for north, one of the four cardinal directions. In calendars, N is often an abbreviation for the month November. In chemistry, N is the symbol for nitrogen.

O

Any word, name, place or sound represented by the letter 'o'. The 15th in a series. Something shaped like the letter 'o'. One of the four major blood groups in the ABO system. Zero or nothing. In chemistry, O is the symbol of the element oxygen, essential for life.

P

Any word, name, place or sound represented by the letter 'p'. Symbol for the smallest unit of the British currency, the penny. The 16th in a series. Something shaped like the letter 'p'. In chess, P is a symbol for the pawn. In chemistry, P is the symbol for phosphorus, something that spontaneously combusts at room temperature.

Q

Any word, name, place or sound represented by the letter 'q'. The 17th in a series. Something shaped like the letter 'q'. A hypothetical lost manuscript, consisting largely of sayings of Jesus, that is believed to have been the source of passages in the gospels of Matthew and Luke. In chess, Q is a symbol for the queen. It is also the symbol for a question, as in

R

Any word, name, place, or sound represented by the letter 'r'. The 18th in a series. Something shaped like the letter 'r'. In film, R is a rating given by film classification boards meaning 'restricted'. R is sometimes used as a symbol for river.

S

Any word, name, place or sound represented by the letter 's'. Symbol of the snake. The 19th in a series. Something shaped like the letter 's'. In chemistry, S is the symbol of the element sulfur. In weather forecasting and geography, S stands for south, one of the four cardinal directions.

T

Any word, name, place or sound represented by the letter 't'. The 20th in a series. Something shaped like the letter 't'. In calendars, T is often an abbreviation for Tuesday or Thursday. In propositional logic, T is the symbol for true.

U

Any word, name, place or sound represented by the letter 'u'. The 21st in a series. Something shaped like the letter 'u'. A grade that indicates an unsatisfactory status. In communication, U is an abbreviation for the word 'you' in SMS or instant messaging.

V

Any word, name, place or sound represented by the letter 'v'. The 22nd in a series. Something shaped like the letter 'v'. V is for Victory. In computing, V is an operation on a semaphore, used for process synchronization. In grammar, v is an abbreviation for verb or action.

W

Any word, name, place or sound represented by the letter 'w'. The 23rd in a series. Something shaped like the letter 'w'. In weather forecasting and geography, W stands for west, one of the four cardinal directions.

X

Any word, name, place or sound represented by the letter 'x'. The 24th in a series. Something shaped like the letter 'x'. A mark inscribed to represent the signature of someone who is unable to sign their name. An unknown or unnamed factor, thing or person. To delete, cancel, or obliterate with a series of Xs. Often used with the word 'out'. In films, X used to be the rating given to films suitable for an adult-only audience. A symbol for Christ, as in Xmas. In genetics, X denotes the X chromosome and XX denotes female in the XY sex-determination system

Y

Any name, word, place or sound represented by the letter 'y'. The 25th in a series. Something shaped like the letter 'y'. In genetics, Y denotes the Y or male chromosome and XY denotes male in the XY sex-determination system. In Internet slang, 'why' is commonly denoted by Y due to the similarity in pronunciation.

Z

Any word, name, place or sound represented by the letter 'z'. The 26th or last place in a series. Something shaped like the letter 'z'. In cartoons, multiple Zs are slang for sleep. In mathematics, z denotes a complex variable.

probably just mirroring your fears or fulfilling your deepest wishes. In other words, your dream may come true in waking life but it also may not.

If you had a dream in which you **received an envelope and recognized the handwriting of an old friend**, this may reflect your desire to see them again. If you are struggling financially and dreamed of **shoving envelopes into the dustbin**, this message from your unconscious is a warning that if you continue to ignore your financial situation, your unconscious will continue to send you such dreams until you deal with the problem in real life.

GUEST/VISITOR

If the **guest or visitor in your dream is known to you**, then perhaps you are expecting some important news to reach you or perhaps there is something you need to know about that person. If the **guest or visitor was not known to you or they make you feel uneasy**, perhaps you are concerned about an unwanted interference in your life. If **you are the guest or visitor**, this suggests that you are looking to broaden your horizons or gain new experience. If the **guest or visitor outstayed their welcome**, think about your current relationships; are some of them past their sell-by-date? If **you were the guest that** people wanted to leave, perhaps you are being insensitive in some sphere of your life.

HANDSHAKE/GREETING

A **handshake** is a familiar form of **greeting** in many parts of the world. If your dream **handshake was strong**, this suggests that you are feeling positive about your life at present. If the **handshake was weak**, this suggests you may be in need of an energy boost. If **someone offers you their hand then withdraws it quickly**, you may be feeling distrustful of that person. If the **greeting was a hug**, try to recall how you felt about that greeting. Did you feel warm and comfortable, or uneasy and unnatural? If you felt secure, then this suggests you are feeling appreciated in everyday life; if you felt uneasy, this suggests you are feeling isolated and unsupported.

HANDWRITING

To dream that you are **writing by hand** represents your self-expression and creativity. Consider the symbolism of what you are writing by hand and how it relates to your waking life. Pay attention also to the style of writing you are using and the patterns revealed by your handwriting. Graphology is the scientific method of identifying, evaluating and understanding a person's personality through their handwriting. Graphologists believe that handwriting, just like dreams, can reveal hundreds of elements of a person's personality and character; these includes glimpses into the subconscious mind, emotional responsiveness, intellect, energy, fears and defenses, motivations, imagination, integrity, aptitudes and even sex drives. If you are **reading handwriting** in your dream, pay attention to that too, as it may reveal much about the person who wrote it. For example, if you **recognize your sister's handwriting and it appeared shaky**, could it be revealing her vulnerability; if any words **were underlined or capitalized**, did they underline or emphasize the message of your dream?

INTERVIEW

Dreams in which you are **being interviewed** are extremely common, especially if you are applying for a job in real life. Such dreams may reflect your true fears about the interview process but if you are not applying for a job, the dream image suggests that you are feeling uncertain about a path you have chosen in waking life. If, in your dream, you are **told that you have or have not got the job**, this shows how well you feel you are coping with a current project. If you are **late for your interview or miss it**, this indicates that you feel you have missed out on an opportunity. If you are **giving a presentation** in your dream, consider your feelings about the task. If you enjoyed it, you may feel that you are a good communicator; if you were terrified, you may doubt your ability. If **you are the interviewer**, you may be looking to solve a problem in waking life. Who were you interviewing, what did they represent and how might this help you in waking life?

LANGUAGE

If you find yourself being talked to in a **language you don't understand or that doesn't make sense**, the dream may tell of your concerns about missing the point in

Features of handwriting in dreams

Professional graphologists can recognize several hundred handwriting features which they believe reveal aspects of a person's character. Here are some basic handwriting features that may help you interpret the message hidden in the handwriting in your dream:

Size

Large handwriting can mean a friendly and sociable personality, or that the writer puts on an act of confidence – this behavior might not be exhibited to strangers. **Small handwriting** is generally an indicator of a detailed, academic and technical personality.

Line slope

Writing which rises shows optimism and cheerfulness; if it **sags downwards**, it shows physical and mental weariness.

Slant

Right slant indicates a more extrovert kind of person. **Upright** handwriting suggests independence. **A left slant** tendency shows emotion and reserve.

Spacing between words

This indicates social attitudes towards others. **Close words** are a sign of sociability; **large spaces between words** indicate a person who is most comfortable alone.

The three cases

The three cases represent the three aspects of our personality: the **upper case** represents our higher or spiritual self, the **middle case** our mental and social approach to life, and the **lower case** our physical aptitudes and attitudes. The upper case is the area in which the extended up strokes are found in tall letters like b, d, h and t. The middle case is the central region occupied by letters with neither long up strokes nor down strokes, such as a, c, e, m, n, o, etc. The lower case is the area occupied by down stroke letters such as g, j, p, etc. Look where the emphasis of the writing is as this is where the emphasis of the personality lies.

Some other simple indicators

Large upper loops are a sign of emotion; **uneven upper loops** show mood swings; **closed 'e's** show secrecy; **stand-alone or properly formed 's's** at word ends show independence; **angular central cases** show an interest in ideas rather than people; **uncompleted letter cases** show a casual nature with a tendency to gossip; **rounded central cases** show an interest in people; **omitted 'i' dots and 't' cross strokes** show forgetfulness and carelessness. The position and style of 'i' dots show different things: if the **dot is ahead**, this means an active mind; if the **dot is behind**, it shows a thoughtful nature; if **positions vary**, this means a distracted mind; if it is **flicked,** this shows a sense of humor and if it is **directly above and in line,** it means an exacting personality.

regard to some element in your waking life. If you are **speaking in a new language**, this suggest that you need to broaden your horizons. Perhaps you need to take on a new challenge or embark on a new adventure. If an **interpreter** appears in your dream, this may suggest that you need to have something explained to you. If **you are doing the interpreting yourself**, perhaps someone in your life is relying too heavily on you in social situations and this is placing too much responsibility on you.

If your **speech is broken or you cannot get the words out** in your dream, this reveals insecurity about your communication skills. If **code language** is involved in your dream, try to remember the code signals and see if they have any relevance to your waking life. Finally, if **you or a character in your dream says something totally out of character or unexpected**, this may be giving rise to something you aren't yet ready to say to yourself or to hear. For example, if your **best friend tells you that you are going to fail your driving test**, perhaps this indicates that your friend isn't as supportive of you as you like to think they are. Alternatively, these surprising words may reflect your own self-doubt, or that old issues and negative voices from your past are coming back to haunt you.

LETTER/PARCEL/POSTCARD/ TELEGRAM

The **arrival of a letter** in your dream represents a realization, usually about someone else, or news about yourself. Your reaction to the letter is important. Did you feel anxious, resigned or happy? How you opened the letter is also significant. Did you open it eagerly or did you put it aside unwilling to open it? Whenever a letter appears in your dream, your dreaming mind is telling you that something needs your attention in waking life. Dreaming about **receiving letters**, just as in daily life, usually represents receiving news, information or messages from someone specific, from your unconscious or from the world at large. You may be coming into greater awareness about some aspect of your life or yourself. If your dream **letters remain unopened**, this may represent missed opportunities. If the **letter is black around the edges**, this may refer to your feelings about death.

If the **letter is from a particular person**, this suggests specific feelings or thoughts concerning the person the letter is from. If you get to **read the letter** in your dream, try to see if the text has any bearing on your waking life. If the **letter came from abroad**, you may be thinking of traveling or are thinking of someone who lives abroad. To dream of **writing a letter** may tell you of the need to communicate information to someone; a dream of **writing several letters** may tell you that there are many people you wish to make contact with. If you dream of **sending a letter**, this may be a prompt to contact the person to whom you are posting the letter or to impart information to them. **Incomprehensible or unintelligible letters** may suggest frustration at being unable to solve some problem. A **letter that turns out to be a blank page** is a clear sign that you should stop waiting for other people to take the initiative and take the initiative yourself. An **anonymous letter** can be a message from your unconscious that you need to slow down and reflect on your actions in waking life. While handwriting in a dream letter can reveal personal feelings or communications, a **typewritten or word-processed communication** implies a more impersonal communication.

Dreams of **sending a telegram** may occur during times of stagnation or routine in your professional life and may serve as an urgent stimulus to change. Alternatively, dreaming of **receiving a telegram** may express an urgent yearning to make contact with someone. Because of their indiscreet and fun nature, dreaming of **postcards** may suggest that you need to be more open with those around you. According to Freud, **parcels** may symbolize female sexuality. If you are **excited about opening a parcel**, this may suggest the heady thrill of a new relationship, but if you **do not want to open a parcel**, this may express a fear of intimacy with others.

NOTICE/MESSAGE

Dreams that feature **notices or messages** are often seen as wake-up calls to the dreamer, implying that they need to be more aware of what is going on around them. Is there something or someone in your everyday life that you need to take note of? If the **notice appeared on your fridge door**, the message may be concerning your home life but if the **notice appeared on a notice board**, it may relate to school, college or work. If you are the one **pinning up a message**, this suggests that you are the one who wishes to communicate with someone but haven't yet found the right time. If you **can't read the message on the notice board**, then perhaps you are feeling left out of a particular social group or need to branch out on your own.

POSTMAN

A dream **postman who passes you by without giving you a letter** may indicate feelings of disappointment. If you **run after the postman**, this suggests that you are determined to create your own luck and if **you see yourself as a postman**, perhaps you feel that you deserve to be given more responsibility. If you regard people who deliver mail as impartial go-betweens, the image of a postman may be linked for you with a person in waking life, perhaps yourself, who is acting as an intermediary. If you dreamed that the **postman was someone you know, such as your father, who handed you a letter in your sister's handwriting**, perhaps your dream is reflecting real life with your father playing the role of mediator between you and your sister.

SECRET MESSAGE

In waking life, **secret messages or codes** are used to convey important information as speedily as possible and to keep secrets from outsiders or enemies. Any dream in which you were **sent a code that you could decipher** may therefore indicate the need for speed and secrecy when communicating with someone in waking life. If, however, you were **unable to understand the code**, this suggests that you are finding it impossible to understand someone in real life. The secret message in your dream may also appear in the form of an anagram (a word puzzle in which you rearrange the letters of the original word or phrases).

Homonyms are words that sound alike but have different spellings and meanings and polysemy refers to single words that have many meanings. These word-plays are

The Element Encyclopedia of 20,000 Dreams

common in dreams. For example, the words 'tale' (story) and 'tail' (backside), or 'navel' (belly button) or 'naval' (navy) are examples of homonyms. The word 'suit' is polysemous as it can mean something you wear, one fourth of a pack of cards or as acceptable (as in 'suits me fine'). If your dream messages don't make sense, look for hidden codes. Write the mystery message or word down on a piece of paper and try to see if there are any words that sound the same but mean something different. Can you rearrange the letters to form different words or another phrase? In most cases, if you play around with the words you'll discover their secrets.

SPEECH

If you were **making a speech** in your dream, what you are saying may have bearing on what is currently happening in your life. If you **spoke angrily or wearily**, this may show how you are feeling about something or someone. If you are **nervous before your speech**, there is something you need to say or some information you need to impart but feel apprehensive about doing so. Pay attention also to the way in which your speech was received. If you were **cheered and clapped**, you feel confident and upbeat, but if you were **booed and jeered**, you feel uncertain and lacking in confidence. If **close friends or family were in the audience applauding**, you are feeling supported or appreciated by them. If you listen to a **speech by someone else**, were they saying anything that might be relevant to you in waking life? If the **speaker was famous**, this might be wishfulfillment but also might reflect concern with an issue or feeling that they represent to you. *See also* Speaking entry in SOUNDS.

VERBAL COMMUNICATION

Telephones and cellphones in dreams are symbols of instant communication in both the real world and dreamland. The message of your dream in which you picked up the phone to call someone almost certainly indicates that you are thinking about them and need to communicate something to them. If you had a **telephone conversation that was one sided and you couldn't get a word in**, does this mirror how you feel about someone in waking life or was your unconscious simply urging you to be more assertive in waking life? Alternatively, was your unconscious drawing your attention to your own tendency to monopolize conversations? Dreaming of phone or cellphone conversations may also be reminding you to say or do something in waking life; the context of your dream and the symbols within it may give you a clue as to what that 'something' is.

If, in your dream, **you dialed a number and nobody picked up the phone**, do you feel that nobody is listening to your point of view in waking life? Similarly if you dreamed of **making a call to the emergency services**, could your unconscious be expressing your fear about someone or something in your waking life or that you are in urgent need of support or help.

WORDS

Sometimes in dreams a special word is emphasized. Some words, such as 'peace' and 'joy', can be symbols of creative power and can therefore be used in meditation to rebuild the emotional and mental attitudes or conditions surrounding the word. Dreams may also give you letters and numbers to decipher, such as on a dream **car number plate**.

Talking in your Sleep

Talking whilst asleep is a relatively common sleep disorder. The subject matter being talked about tends to be harmless. It may also make no sense at all. At other times, the content may be vulgar or even offensive to a listener. The talking can occur many times and might be quite loud, disrupting the sleep of a bed partner or roommate. Sleeptalking may occur in any stage of NREM or REM sleep and, because of this, some dream experts believe that talking or walking in your sleep could simply be an attempt to act out your dream. The reason for sleepwalking and sleeptalking could be the firing of motor and speech mechanisms in the brain, but no conclusive evidence for this has been found.

During the course of a normal night of sleep, the human brain switches between deep and light sleep, and dreaming sleep, several times; confusional arousals occur when the brain becomes divided, literally, between sleeping and waking. Part of the brain wakes up, but another part remains deeply asleep. During a confusional arousal, a sleeper may talk, sit up in bed, scream, or even leave the bed and wander around – the proverbial sleepwalking, although that is less common than sleeptalking. Because development of the sleep stage switching mechanism occurs during the period from infancy to about ten years old, confusional arousals are most common in this age group. Current research confirms the validity of popular lore about sleeptalkers and sleepwalkers – that one should not attempt to awaken them. Despite the open eyes, despite the calm or agitated talking, sleeptalkers are deeply asleep. The recommended strategy is that there is no need to yell or try to wake up someone who is sleeptalking; just make sure they are safe and comfortable. In the morning, the sleeper will not remember their episode. *See also* Sleep disorders entry in NIGHTMARES.

Are the letters or words in your dream intelligible or are they a throwback to a language you once learned or heard or simply don't understand at all? Some people say such images are evidence of past lives emerging into your dream life but most dream analysts believe they are symbolic representations of parts of yourself that you simply can't understand or communicate with. Is the sound or the meaning of the word significant? As always it is important to try to decipher the confusing aspects of your dream. You might find that speaking the phrase aloud or sounding the letters after you wake up jogs some unexpected realizations. Sometimes confusing phrases when spoken aloud can suddenly make sense.

If the word you read or hear in your dream is **your name**, it is likely that your attention is being drawn to the person you

The Element Encyclopedia of 20,000 Dreams

are. You may also want to do some research on the true meaning of your name, as some believe it teaches the most important lesson we need to learn in life. If you are **aware of other people's names** in your dreams, you may be aware of the qualities that person has and it is these qualities you need to be looking at. If you don't know any person by that name again it might be worth your while considering what the traditional meaning of that name is. If the **name of a place** comes up, what are your associations with it? Consider also if there is some word-play on names.

WORD GAME

Sometimes your dreaming mind will use visual, verbal or colloquial puns to get a point across. For example, if your dream contained images of **hands**, this could indicate that you are in need of a helping hand or that you are feeling handled or manipulated. Other possible puns might include: an airplane (are you feeling plain?); first in the queue (are you being up front?); dreaming of a highway bypass (are you concerned about being bypassed in life?) and so on. The list is practically endless. The idea is to start looking for puns in your dreams based on visual images, words, people's names and common sayings.

Also look out for verbal slips in dreams in which you express strange or unacceptable thoughts or urges. These slips happen in everyday speech as well as in our dreams and, according to Freud, such slips can tell us something about our unconscious wishes. In real life, they may appear as verbal slips; in dreams, however, they can appear in images of the unexpected, embarrassing but secretly true feelings you may have.

WRITING

Writing is a means of communication. In dreams, it may be a symbol of communicating with others but it mostly represents communication with oneself. If you are **writing in a dream or reading someone else's writing**, it may suggest an unconscious effort to become aware of forces or issues in life. Take note that writing is a secondary form of communication. **Speaking** is more direct and less cumbersome for most. Thus, the written message

The traditional meaning of some popular names

Abigail: Source of joy
Andrew: Manly
Ashley: A former surname meaning 'ash tree clearing'
Christopher: Christ-bearer
Daniel: God is my judge
Elizabeth: God's oath
Emily: Ambitious
Emma: Ancestress
Ethan: Firm
Hannah: Blessed by God
Isabella: Consecrated to God
Jacob: Conqueror
Joseph: God multiplies
Joshua: God is my salvation
Michael: Like God
Matthew: Gift of the Lord
Olivia: Symbol of peace
Samantha: Listener
William: Determined guardian

Telepathic messages in dreams

There is one form of communication that requires no paper, pen, computer or phone: thought transference or telepathy. Although the jury is still out as to whether telepathy is a real phenomenon or not, there is plenty of anecdotal evidence to suggest that it is; you may have experienced it yourself in dreams. For example, if you had a dream of your **much-loved cousin being badly injured in a car crash,** and then woke to receive news that he had been involved in such a car crash during the night, your cousin may have communicated his pain telepathically to you. In most cases, telepathy is thought to occur between two people who have a very close or empathetic relationship and the sender may often be unaware of transmitting their emotions to the receiver. The most common published accounts of telepathy and ESP are between lovers or family members, and focus on a life-threatening injury or death. Psychics believe these people are able to tune into each other's frequencies as they are so close to each other emotionally; a twin brother, for example, will sense the pain of his twin sister. In times of crisis, we send out our message and those who are in tune will pick it up. Another example of dream telepathy is called shared dreaming, in which people try to meet up with each other in dreamland or to dream of the same landscape.

in your dream may be disguised or may be less genuine than other forms of receiving information from the unconscious.

You may be trying to figure something out and this might be the first step in that process. Sometimes the instrument you are using when writing is important. For example, a **pencil** would suggest the information is less permanent than it would be if you were using a **permanent marker**; a **typewriter or word processor** would suggest business rather than personal communications. If you dream of **leaning over to write on a blank sheet** of paper, this suggests an opportunity to make a fresh start and if you are **holding a pen,** you have found a means to express your thoughts. Were you writing to someone you know or starting to write a novel? Whatever you were writing and whoever it was for, the message implicit in dream writing is that you have an urge to communicate either to someone in particular or to a wider audience. An **ink blot** in a dream suggests that you have doubts about something or someone in waking life. The **shape of the blot** may be significant if you can recall it. If **tears smudge your writing,** this may suggest feelings of guilt towards someone or emotional difficulties.

The Element Encyclopedia of 20,000 Dreams

LOSS AND FRUSTRATION

Some dreams leave us with a painful sense of loss; dreams that take us back to happy times in the past, for example, or dreams of being abandoned, lost or bereaved.

In some instances, such dreams can reflect feelings of regret about actual events or people you have lost but more often they are a symbol for something missing in your life; perhaps direction, confidence or intimacy or even a sense of personal identity. Another explanation suggests that such dreams are a warning that you are in danger of losing something important. Perhaps you have not been valuing or appreciating an aspect of your life enough. Finally, a dream of losing something or someone important can also suggest lost opportunities, past relationships or, according to Jungian analysis, forgotten aspects of yourself. Your personal associations to the thing you lose will give you clues as to the emotional meaning and possible interpretation of your dream.

Dreams that leave you with a sense of frustration or anxiety are very common; you will almost certainly experience this kind of dream at some time or other, especially during times of stress in waking life. The stress may be triggered by an exam, a job interview, a relationship breaking up or

fears of failing; this stress can express itself in dreams of falling or being confined, or dreams of feeling frustrated by a machine that doesn't work or finding yourself naked in the middle of a busy street. According to Freud, such dreams are inspired by sexual frustration or anxiety, but most dream analysts believe that they stem from deep-seated feelings of inadequacy or frustration in all areas of your waking life, not just the sexual. Another thing to consider is whether the frustration in the dream was 'because' of something. In other words, did it happen because you took a wrong direction, because you went along with a particular person or because you didn't listen to advice? If you are able to pinpoint a cause or reason try to define what the 'because' factor is in your everyday life.

However, disturbing, upsetting or frustrating such dreams can be they are not meant to cause more anxiety. Your dreaming mind has conjured up these images to enlighten and strengthen you. Whenever you have a dream that leaves you with feelings of loss, regret or frustration, try to pinpoint exactly what caused you the most anxiety in your dream as this may hold the key to understanding the root of your fear. If you are able to understand the message of your unconscious, you will feel that you are in a better position to face your fears or at least to find ways to manage it if you are unable to conquer it.

This chapter covers some aspects of loss and frustration but there are countless others. For example, you can lose weight, hair, teeth, vision, smell, possessions, friends, your freedom, your personality, your children, a body part or even your own life in a dream. Dreams of being chased, paralyzed, imprisoned or missing a train can all refer to stressful situations in your waking life. Refer to the relevant entry in the index for the significance of other dream symbols of frustration and loss. *See also* NEGATIVE EMOTIONS.

Loss

ABANDONMENT

Dreams in which you are **abandoned by a loved one or left feeling lost and helpless** can hark back to archetypal childhood fears of being abandoned by those on whom you were totally dependent for physical and emotional nourishment, such as your parents or the people who raised you. As adults, this fear can manifest in dreams of being abandoned or rejected by parents, friends, family or people you care about. If you had this kind of dream, you may be feeling insecure about the love and respect

the person in your dream has for you. Alternatively, your dreaming mind could be reliving the actual pain of a relationship break up. If this is the case, you haven't resolved your feelings about the break up; the message of your dream may be to face up to the loss, think positively and take control of your life again. If you felt liberated in your dream when you were abandoned by a friend or partner, your dreaming mind is telling you that your break up is not the disaster you feel it might be; in fact it could be a liberating experience.

CROWD

The dream scenario of **losing someone you love in a crowd** is typically associated with the grieving process. It is not uncommon for bereaved people to feel, in addition to their sorrow, that their loved one has abandoned them. It might be, however, that the person lost in the crowd could represent a part of yourself you are unable to connect with. Dreams of **trying in vain to struggle through crowds in a busy shopping centre or sports arena** suggest conflict or barriers between your conscious and unconscious mind. **Oppressive crowds** between you and your goal indicate that you are not satisfying your unconscious desires.

DEBT/BANKRUPTCY

Dreams in which you are **bankrupt or heavily in debt** may reflect real-life financial concerns but there are other explanations which have little to do with money. A dream debt may, for example, be a debt of gratitude that you need to pay to someone. Is there someone to whom you feel indebted? Dreams of **going bankrupt or**

Grief and bereavement

Dreams in which you woke up crying or feeling sad because you have had a dream in which you were **bereaved** can be a cathartic experience, helping you work through grief towards accepting the loss of a loved one in real life. If, however, you were **grieving for someone who is still alive and healthy** in your dream, have you neglected your responsibilities towards that person or is your dreaming mind using the death of a loved one as a symbol of something that needs to end in your waking life? What is it about you or your life that the deceased person in your dream could be representing? Inhibition or recklessness perhaps? Or could the deceased represent a quality that has departed from your life, such as fun or relaxation? You may also fear that your relationship with this person might actually end in waking life. Whatever the identity of the deceased person, dreams of being bereaved also bring up issues of loneliness. Perhaps you feel that your partner is neglecting you or you feel you are losing touch with your friends. Such dreams may be urging you to make a conscious effort to reconnect with other people.

A house is often interpreted as a symbol of the dreamer and represents the place from which you withdraw to live your inner life. **A dark, cold or empty house** can symbolize a profound sense of loss, suggesting that you feel deprived of emotional warmth. Images of **ashes and dust** in dreams are also often associated with the loss of a treasured person or thing in waking life. If you dream of an **empty purse**, you are mourning – through a classic symbol of death and bereavement –for the comfort and happiness we all crave. On a literal level, however, it may signify that you overvalue material things in life. *See also* LIFE STAGES; SPIRITS AND GHOSTS.

ending up in poverty often refer to the loss of personal qualities rather than to financial disaster. Ask yourself what your lost finances could symbolize: the love of your partner, for example, the respect of your colleagues at work or your own physical energy. Whatever it is you have lost, your dreaming mind is urging you to take the appropriate steps to prevent a breakdown or crash in your waking life. *See also* MONEY AND SHOPPING.

FAREWELL

Dreams that feature **farewells or final goodbyes** tend to have the same significance as dreams of bereavement. If you were saying goodbye to someone in your dream, ask yourself if that relationship is coming to an end, at risk of coming to an end or whether you need to say goodbye to some aspect of your life that you connect with that person. Dreams in which a **loved** one recedes into the distance and eventually disappears from sight suggest feelings of grief mixed with resentment. On the other hand, dreams in which a **loved one waves goodbye happily from a distance** suggest you are reconciling yourself to the reality of your loss.

HOMESICKNESS/NOSTALGIA

Dreams from which you wake up with a sense of **unhappiness, regret and nostalgia for the past** occur for two reasons. The first is to compensate for unhappiness in your present circumstances by reminding you of past happiness and the possibility of enjoying that kind of happiness again. The second is to help you come to face up to painful memories and come to terms with the past. If you were **awash with homesickness** in your dream, try to pinpoint exactly what it was that you were missing. The answer may tell you what your unconscious has identified as lacking in your real life. Perhaps it was a sense of belonging, a sense of fun or childhood innocence and spontaneity.

INCONGRUOUS EMOTIONS

If, in your dream, you are **attending a cheerful, fun occasion such as a party, festival or dance and feel intensely and inappropriately sad**, this may indicate your need to turn away from distractions and confront your sense of life. Similarly, if you experience **inappropriate happiness or elation at a dream funeral or death**, this might point to your being in a state of denial in order to protect yourself from the reality of a personal loss.

LONELINESS

Dreams about **being alone** often refer to the solitary life you might be leading, but they can also refer to those times when you need to strike out in a new direction, separating yourself from your friends and family in a non-social context. To dream that you are **alone in a crowd** may imply that you are isolated from those around you, whilst **being alone in a landscape** may suggest that you prefer to make decisions by yourself. A dream of being an **astronaut on a solitary space walk** may refer to deep feelings of being alone or going it alone. If you dreamed you were **alone in a garden or the countryside**, a more tolerable – even pleasurable – form of solitude may be being referred to. Finding yourself **alone as a child** is a powerful image of loneliness, emotional vulnerability and feeling lost. *See also* RELATIONSHIPS.

LOSING SOMETHING

If you **lose something** in your dream, this suggests that you have become distracted in waking life and have lost sight of what really matters. Ask yourself what it is you have lost and what it may symbolize. It may be an opportunity, a relationship, a way of thinking or even your own identity. Do you no longer feel as if you belong somewhere? Alternatively, the image may be a symbol of something that is missing from your life that you never had in the first place. For example, if **you lost your car**, you may have lost a sense of direction; if **you lost money**, you may feel you've lost your self-confidence or something you value about yourself; if **you lost your key**, have you forgotten a solution to a problem or

The Element Encyclopedia of 20,000 Dreams

perhaps the key to self-knowledge? If you simply can't work out what significance your lost object has to you, it might help to do a free association exercise (write down the first 10 or so words that immediately come to mind in relation to that symbol) to decipher the lost object's symbolism, to decipher what it is that you need to find.

If you dream that you are **recovering lost property**, the nature of the property recovered, together with the feelings of relief and joy it brings, will indicate the focus of your dream. For example, if you **recover your purse**, this is linked to identity and a renewed sense of self. If you **recover your wallet**, this is linked to finances. Do you now feel in a stronger position? If you **recover a camera** are you trying to hold on to memories or seeking a false sense of security? If you recover **lost clothes** are you seeking a new self image? If you recover **shoes** are you recovering your footing? If you recover your **lost phone** are you re-establishing communication with some one?

LOSS OF BODY PARTS

Because the body often represents the self, **loss of body parts or injuries to your body** in dreamland can symbolize the emotional pain of losing parts of yourself. A dream that **some part of your body is amputated** can leave you with a feeling of irreplaceable loss. Such images may refer to the loss of a loved one but they can also appear when what you have lost is less tangible – for example, the love or respect of someone or your own self-respect. Psychologists give the name 'fragmentation' to the process when you give up parts of yourself in order to fit in with or please others. This is something we all do, but if your own true nature is overly censored, the unconscious may send out warning signals about what you stand to lose by the denial of aspects of yourself.

Dreams in which you **lose a hand or a foot, are missing an internal organ or have a body part disappear or fall off** are therefore often signs that some part of your potential is being lost due to the path you have chosen. The common dream of **losing teeth** may reflect waking problems but can also symbolize loss, the break up of relationships, moving house, moving away or any other change which involves the ending of one phase in life and the beginning of another. If the **teeth become loose but stay in your mouth choking you**, this could mean that you are holding something back or keeping your thoughts and feelings to yourself; the price is some form of damage to yourself. A dream in which you **lose your virginity** is a reflection of the loss of childhood innocence. What have you lost recently in waking life that has damaged your previous system of beliefs? *See also* BODY; SICKNESS AND HEALTH.

LOST

Dreams in which you are **lost** link with feelings of confusion, lack of direction or conflict. The dream environment in which you are lost will define what the confusion or conflict is about. Sometimes this lost feeling arises because there are issues or changes in your life that you have not acknowledged or do not want to acknowledge. If you have this dream, ask yourself in what sense you have lost your way. Have you lost your identity, are you confused about your career goals or unable to make clear decisions? Do you feel as if you have no direction in life? Identifying the problem area and considering your options should help you get right back on track. In spiritual terms, you do not know what you are looking for until you find it and the search for lost objects represents the search for enlightenment. Some psychologists believe that dreams about being lost may also signify a new beginning as they express the anxiety of leaving behind the old and familiar.

Dreams in which you are **lost in a maze or labyrinth** are classic symbols of difficulty or confusion in various areas of your life. Dreams in which **someone else is lost** represent issues or feelings regarding that person that are unresolved; they can also indicate a lost opportunity. Consider also whether there are aspects of the person you have dreamed you have lost within your own self. Perhaps you need to recapture and re-acknowledge those aspects. To dream of **losing your partner** is a common dream for people in long-term relationships, showing that you are exploring their possible death. It is not a prediction, only an awareness of a situation that may or may not occur whilst you are still alive or together with them. Dreams in which you are **happily wandering alone in a desert, forest or unknown land** may be prompted by feelings that the source of all your problems lies outside yourself. Your dreaming mind is urging you to look within for the answers.

Lost purse or wallet

In this dream, you are out somewhere and suddenly discover you have **lost your purse or wallet** and start to panic. You may try to retrace your steps but can't find it and the problem gets worse when you realize you have also lost your keys and money. The loss of a dream purse or wallet suggests that change is occurring in your life and you are experiencing it largely with a sense of loss, confusion and even as a threat to your being. Your dreaming mind is urging you to reconnect with the things in life that bring you reassurance and joy, and to look towards the future with optimism instead of panic.

Redundancy

Dreams in which you are **fired from your job, dismissed by your employer or refused work** may reflect insecurities about the regard in which you are held by the people with whom you work. On the other hand, your dream may reflect your sense of redundancy in another area of your life. Perhaps your children have grown up and you don't feel needed as a parent anymore. If your position at work is uncertain in your waking life, your dreaming mind may also be preparing you for the inevitable and highlighting the importance of being prepared. If you did actually lose your job and your dreaming mind keeps reminding you of your sense of rejection, then you need to work through your feelings and move forward with your life.

The Element Encyclopedia of 20,000 Dreams

Frustration

Communication Breakdown

If you **hear a message in a dream which you know to be important but simply cannot understand, even if it is in your own language**, this is a clear symbol of frustration in waking life. A similar scenario would be if you are **trying to explain something to someone but cannot make yourself understood**. Both dreams speak of times in your life when, for some reason, communication is blocked, or you are misreading the emotions of someone or they are misreading you.

If you dream that you have **muddled your words**, this suggests a vain struggle to attract the attention of someone in your dream. The inability to say the right words when you meet them may symbolize feelings of inadequacy in real life or a deep sense of frustration that the important people in your life, or the people you respect and admire, do not appreciate or even notice you. One of the most distressing scenarios in a dream is when you **try to talk or cry out but have no voice**. If you have such a dream, try to work out who is not hearing you in waking life; do you need to listen more and give your voice a rest?

Tripping up in public, forgetting your words when giving a speech, treading on someone's toes in a dance, or spilling food and drink over a VIP can all betray a deep sense of social inadequacy, even with regard to people close to you. Perhaps your ineptitude masks an element of defiance, expressing your feelings of frustration with the stifling rules and norms of social convention. If **someone you know appears in a dream but you find yourself unable to recognize them**, this suggests feelings of frustration or ambivalence towards that person in waking life. A similar sense is conveyed if you are **looking on as a spy whilst a friend or lover commits a crime, or an illicit or compromising act**.

Confinement

Your frustration at the restrictions life puts upon you can often spill over into your dreams. Although depressing, pay attention to the details of such dreams as they may contain hints as to how to overcome these restrictions. If you dreamt of being **locked up, restrained or confined in some way by locks, ropes, chains or impossibly tight clothes**, this might reflect feelings of great frustration in your waking life. Such dreams typically indicate that you are feeling frustrated because someone or something in your life is preventing you from realizing your potential or your ambitions. If you saw who was trying to confine you in your dream, they may represent the person who is making you feel trapped. Alternatively, you may be feeling trapped by some obligation, situation, deadening job or stifling relationship from which there is no escape. Your unconscious is urging you to find a solution and break free.

If you are **gagged** in your dream, this is a sign that something or someone has taken away your freedom of expression. If you are **chained up or locked up in a cell**, such symbols could represent your own inhibitions; if this is the case, your unconscious is again urging you to break free from your self-imposed shackles. You may be fearful of making a decision in case you make the wrong one and, if this is indeed the case, your dreaming self is depicting you bound and fettered as a way of telling you that sometimes in life you need to take a risk and make a judgment call. Dreams in which you are **confined in a small space but still able to move or crawl** may point to the struggle of your creative energies to find expression in waking life. Is something or someone repressing your energy and is it time for you to break free? Dreams in which you are **crawling through a tunnel** also express anxieties about a challenging event in your waking life.

If you dream of **falling into a pit**, this is a reference in waking life to something or someone who is restricting your movements or thought. If you **fall into a trap**, the implication is that this desperate situation may be partly your own fault. A dream in which you are **caught in a net** may, however, have erotic connotations, as the symbol of the net is connected with feminine power. If your **horse is in reins or a harness** in your dream, because the horse is traditionally a symbol of life and may represent an aspect of your personality, the reference may be to some frustration or confinement in waking life; this might be self-imposed or imposed by someone else, but either way it is preventing the full expression of your personality.

DEAD END

If you **come to a dead end** in your dream, your unconscious is telling you there is no way of escaping your fears, even though

you feel that it is vital for you to flee. The same interpretation applies a number of similar dreams; whether you are **caught in quicksand, forced to carry an impossibly heavy weight, suddenly become paralyzed, find yourself rooted to the spot and powerless to do anything, or find that your feet have become heavy or stuck in the mud when trying to flee someone or something**. If you have such disturbing dreams it is possible that you are facing some kind of emotional crisis in your life that requires a drastic decision; for example, whether you should leave your partner or not.

If you are **being chased**, identifying who or what was chasing you or why you need to escape may help you decide what course of action to take in real life. If you don't know who the person chasing you is, this may stand for certain unpalatable aspects of your personality which have been repressed but which are now forcing you to deal with them. Alternatively, your unconscious may be reflecting on your feelings of powerlessness in regard to a difficult situation in your waking life. Do you feel as if you are caught between a rock and a hard place?

FAILURE

Failure themes can occur in dreams about **missing trains, muddling words, losing a race or game, or failing an examination**. Very often a sense of failure arises in a dream because you have been comparing yourself with someone or something else in some way. It is therefore helpful to consider exactly what comparisons mean or provide. You may also have been feeling some level of competitiveness. Alternatively, failure in

Sleep paralysis

There may be a physical cause for dreams in which you find yourself **unable to move or sense anything**; it is called sleep paralysis. During REM sleep when dreams are most frequent, your brain shuts down your body's nerve impulses, notably to the limbs, to prevent you from acting out the drama of your dreams. However, should you gain some awareness during sleep paralysis, your unconscious mind may mirror your physical actions in your dream. There may also be a physical cause for some **falling** dreams; such dreams may be triggered by a muscular spasm called a myoclonic jerk that typically occurs just before you are fully asleep. Dreams in which you **suddenly step into nothingness** are believed to be associated with myoclonic jerks.

dreams might not be interpreted as a lack of energy or power, if, for example, **cars fail to start or lights fail to work**. Fear of failure often originates in childhood and stems from fear of punishment by parents or carers or the withdrawal of love and this fear can linger into adulthood.

If your dreams often feature themes of failure or missed opportunities, instead of focusing on what is wrong with your life, try to lay more emphasis on what is right whilst ridding yourself of the negative 'glass half empty' perspective on life. **Losing a race** in your dream, especially if you were **pipped at the post**, indicates the frustration and sometimes humiliation of realizing the limits of your potential.

FALLING

Dreams of **falling** are extremely common. They may be prompted by your fear of heights in waking life. If this isn't the case, falling dreams may be your dreaming mind's way of drawing your attention to feelings of frustration and loss of control. In which area of your life do you feel you are 'falling down', slipping or losing your place? Are you anxious about schoolwork, your love life, your career or your domestic life? Dreams of falling can be associated with feelings of loss of control or letting yourself down; sometimes the sensation is so terrifying that your conscious mind jerks you awake mid-flight. If, in your dream, you **fall and were unharmed**, this is a clear sign that your current situation is less uncertain than you think. Whatever the scenario in your dream, if falling is a part of it, your unconscious is urging you to identify the source of your feelings of uncertainty and try to find a solution even if that means accepting something less than you hoped for, or accepting your limitations. *See also* AMBITION AND SUCCESS.

FRUSTRATING TASK

The frustration of everyday chores at home and work can sometimes translate into images of **impossible tasks** in dreams, such as **building an enormous house of cards or painting a wall with a toothbrush**. In some cases, humiliating and pointless dream tasks are conjured up by your dreaming mind to teach you a lesson in humility. *See also* PUZZLES.

HOT PURSUIT

Dreams in which you are being **chased or pursued** show that you feel threatened by someone or something in life. The key to such dreams is to discover the identity of your pursuer. If you know the person or the sphere of life they represent, try to work out why you should be feeling intimidated by them in the real world. If you didn't recognize the person, it is possible that they represent aspects of yourself about which you are in denial or from which you are trying to escape; such an interpretation is particularly likely if they are of the same sex and their appearance repulsed you. The attacker may have been your shadow, representing your dependence, neediness, jealousy, greed or lust. Your unconscious is encouraging you to come to terms with this quality within yourself and deal with it.

If a **monster, animal or anything non-human was chasing you**, this symbolizes internal fears rather than external threats. Such creatures generally represent your aggressive animal or instinctual nature which you need to learn to control. **Not knowing who or what is out there in the darkness trying to get you** is a classic anxiety or frustration dream often experienced if you are about to begin therapy; the anxiety is provoked by your realization that the therapist might reveal unexamined areas of yourself. Whoever or whatever your pursuer symbolizes, remember that they represent a challenge you need to face in order for it to be neutralized. As with dreams of pursuit, if you are **drowning or**

struggling to breathe in your dream, you may be experiencing feelings of panic and uncertainty in waking life. Such a dream also alerts you to areas of your unconscious that need to be confronted.

INAPPROPRIATE ATTIRE

Dreams in which you are **inappropriately dressed or underdressed when everyone else is appropriately dressed for the occasion** are classic metaphors for feelings of frustration and uncertainty in your waking life. Perhaps you arrive at your dream party wearing formal dress and everyone else is in shorts. If you are **underdressed**, it suggests that you feel out of place or are falling short of other people's standards. If you are **overdressed**, a misplaced air of superiority is indicated. Such dreams also reflect your insecurity about your social position and how other people regard you. If you were **completely naked whilst everyone else was dressed**, did you feel liberated or mortified?

The clothes we wear in dreams are aspects of our persona, so when they are stripped away they enable you to see yourself for who you really are; in other words, the absence of clothes reveals not only your body, but also your true self. If you **felt embarrassed** in your dream, do you feel vulnerable about exposing your true self or feel that it is lacking in some way? Are you afraid of being rejected if you show others what you truly feel? What are you afraid of exposing about yourself? If, however, you **felt liberated**, perhaps it is time to throw away your pretences and reveal to others who you truly are. If **nobody other than yourself noticed your nudity**, your unconscious is comforting you by letting you know that it is safe to reveal your feelings in the real world. Another symbol of frustration in dreams is **being refused a restaurant table**, especially if there are plenty of spare tables in the restaurant. Such a dream, with its association with food and social interaction, may express a sense of social inadequacy.

LATE

Dreams in which you are **late for a train, bus, plane, appointment, interview or date despite your best efforts to be on time** often signify your anger and frustration at having missed an important opportunity in waking life. If someone or something was responsible for making you late, try to identify who or what it was. Dreams in which you are **anxiously checking your watch but still miss the bus** may also be warning you that you are both mentally and physically exhausted; this is especially true if you were too tired to summon up the extra energy needed to get to where you needed to be. If you have such a dream, ask yourself whether you feel frustrated about missing an opportunity in your life and try to identify what that opportunity was. Dreams in which you **miss a bus, boat or any other travel connection** may also suggest that you feel others are moving ahead of you and leaving you lagging behind. Dreams of **running after a departing train** are very common. According to Freud, trains are classic phallic symbols, suggesting a sexual cause behind frustration expressed in the dream. *See also* TIME.

MALFUNCTIONING MACHINE

Dreams in which your **car breaks down, your computer crashes or your phone won't work** occur for two possible reasons. First of all, your dreaming mind may be warning you to take precautionary steps, such as installing anti-virus software on your computer or making sure your car is regularly serviced, so as to avert potential problems in the future. If this isn't the case, the malfunction could be a symbol for an aspect of yourself that isn't working properly. A car, for example, could symbolize your energy or drive, and, if it breaks down, your lack of it. Are you in danger of running out of control? If a **fuse blows** in your dream, are you about to explode with frustration over someone or something?

TEST/EXAM

Dreams of **tests** of any kind can indicate some form of self-assessment. If you are a student or about to take some kind of test or exam in waking life, dreams in which you are actually **sitting the exam** are common; in these dreams you typically feel unprepared or unable to answer the questions or perform the required components. Such dreams are simply expressing your fear of failure. If you are not a student or about to take an exam, this type of dream is usually a metaphor for some kind of difficult situation you are facing in your professional life or career. You feel that your performance will be judged by others and the dream reflects your lack of confidence in yourself. This type of fear-of-failure dream can also occur for other types of challenges you may face in waking life, ranging from driving tests and auditions to job interviews and presentations.

More often than not, you will be judged in these dreams by an audience's reaction; that reaction is often negative. If the **audience starts booing or catcalling you** in your dream, try to remember who the audience was and what you were humiliated for. Ask yourself whether the condemnation was justified or whether the evaluators or adjudicators in your dream were actually self-critical aspects of yourself. If you **stammered in front of your dream audience or adjudicator**, this underlines your feelings of uncertainty and lack of self-confidence. **Medical tests** may be alerting you to the need to watch your health. A **driving test** may suggest a test of confidence or ability, and a **written test** an examination of your understanding of a certain situation. **Testing something yourself** in your dream means that you are trying to establish some kind of standard; alternatively, it might suggest that you are testing your own resolve.

WAITING

Dreams in which you are **waiting for something or someone** suggest a sense of anticipation in real life; they may also indicate that you are looking towards other people to help you move forward in life or make decisions. If you are **impatient** in your dream, then you have high expectations but if you are **waiting patiently**, you believe things happen in their own good time. Dreams in which you are stuck in a **stationary traffic jam or in a broken-down car** may express frustration about a relationship that seems to be lacking in direction or going nowhere. Such dreams, like that of **not being able to find a parking spot**, suggest an inability to find your true identity in life.

Dreams in which you are **waiting for test results, lying in front of a doctor or waiting in the dentist's chair dreading what is about to happen to you** may reflect real concern if you have a health problem and are awaiting the results of a scan or test. If this isn't the case, such dreams are telling you that an unavoidable ordeal lies ahead and you need the strength to face it. Alternatively, your unconscious may be aware of a potential problem with your health or teeth and is trying to encourage you to consult your doctor or dentist for a check-up.

The Element Encyclopedia of 20,000 Dreams

MEDIA AND TECHNOLOGY

Almost all of us have dreams directly related to things we are involved with in our waking lives, so it is not surprising that we dream about computers, television, telephones and the media.

If you dream that your hard drive is crashing, do you wake up just before the Fatal System Error message appears? What would be the meaning of a dream about a cursor that was frozen, not flashing, on a blank screen? And in scrutinizing nightmares about phones that won't work in times of extreme emergency, are there times when a hard drive is really just a hard drive? In other words, is your dream a reflection of your day-to-day preoccupation with computers, televisions or mobile phones or does it have a deeper meaning?

As computers, televisions and phones leach deeper into our unconscious, accounts of anxiety-filled dreams about them are becoming increasingly common. According to Jungians, the computer as a symbol of the advance of technology is fast becoming its own archetype. In this chapter we'll take a look at some of the most common dreams about the media and modern technology, and what they might signify to you. *See also* EVERYDAY THINGS; LETTERS AND COMMUNICATION; NIGHTMARES.

Computer Technology

COMPUTER/COMPUTER DISC

A **computer** is a symbol of the rational unemotional part of your mind, but it can also suggest your personal potential or abilities, your memories and stored information, and even your unexplored potential. The computer and other high-tech gadgetry are such a part of our lives now that their meaning depends very much on the other images in your dream. If you work a lot with computers, they may simply be a means to an end but they may also be a reminder of your potential or abilities. **Keyboards** have replaced **typewriters** and are – along with **slots for floppy disks, CD-ROMs and DVDs** – Freudian symbols of female sexuality. **Computer screens or monitors** are associated by Jungians with the search for knowledge in cyberspace, whilst **computer hackers** are associated with Jung's trickster archetype in their ability to bring chaos to order. The **computer hard drive** can represent conscious, physical and material side of you, with the **software** representing your inner self and the **curser and mouse** the direction your life needs to take. If a **cursor is frozen or a hard drive crashes** in your dream, this could suggest obstacles and blockages that stop you progressing in waking life. *See also* EVERYDAY THINGS.

EMAIL/TEXTING

Email and texting are a symbol of communication and connection in dreams; this connection may be through your thoughts and intuition, and not simply through physical links such as the telephone. In general, these modern methods of communication mean communication is faster. So if an email or text appears in your dream, this is a message that something needs to be attended to as soon as possible in your waking life. Such dreams are positive, expressing a desire to move forward swiftly but they can also be a sign that you should be cautious when embarking on a new project or plan, and not jump in at the first opportunity.

INTERNET

A powerful symbol of limitless possibilities, dreams of the **Internet** reflect your desire for variety in life and interest in exploring different modes of interaction. If you dream of **cookies, virus or spam**, these might be symbols of small irritations or niggling concerns that, left unchecked, could cause big damage.

MODEM

As with dreams of the telephone, dreams of **modems** are about communicating or reaching out to others, but it is less personal or specific. It is more about reaching out in general and how you manage your contacts with the world via media, technology and business. Images of modems in dreams may also refer to your wider awareness or intuition. **PlayStation/X box/Computer games**: Modern symbol indicating a desire for instant happiness and success without making the necessary effort.

ROBOT

A symbol of habit or responses that are automatic or not thought about, the **robot** in some dreams is linked with the future and how we feel about it. It also can suggest being on the defensive and being guarded about your feelings, in the sense of the robot's metal plating defending it against hurt. Dreams in which **robots or computers take over the world** suggest anxiety about the spread of technology destroying traditional ways of life. It also suggests extreme loss of sensitivity.

TELEPHONE/FAX

In dreams, **telephones** are symbols of communication or the desire to make contact with an aspect of yourself or someone else. If you were **speaking on the phone**, try to recall to whom you were speaking and what the conversation was about. If you **repeatedly dial a number but cannot get through**, this suggests an element of frustration in your life. If a

The Element Encyclopedia of 20,000 Dreams

telephone rings continually but remains unanswered in a dream, there is a chance that you may be ignoring some issue or problem in your life by refusing to hear or see it. If you are **contacted by telephone**, this suggests information is available to you that you do not consciously know.

If you go to a **telephone box but find no telephone inside**, this suggests that you are missing some vital clue or piece of information that would help you in waking life. If the **telephone is larger than usual**, this may represent yourself but it may also be an indication that you will soon need to convey an important message. If you dream of a **telephone answering machine**, this may be tied to the notion of passing or avoiding responsibility for something you need to do in waking life.

A **cell phone** has similar associations with a telephone, but with the added association of urgency or emergency or fear of being left out or not included in your close circle of friends. If you **cannot or will not answer your phone** in your dream, this suggests that people are finding it hard to get through to you; you may also be feeling alone and vulnerable in waking life. If an **emergency call** figures in your dream, this suggests that you or someone you know is reaching out for help. It could also indicate some kind of moral dilemma.

If you **know the telephone number you are ringing** in your dream, it suggests an attempt to communicate with the person whose number it is. If you **do not know the number**, it may be that the numbers are significant. Some people believe that dreaming of **receiving a telephone call** is lucky. If you dream of **making a call**, it suggests that there will be postponements and delays in waking life. **Long-distance calls** are said to bring happiness. **Fax machines and faxes** may represent unexpected things arising out of your unconscious or the need to communicate with someone. *See also* EVERYDAY THINGS; NUMBERS.

Media

ADVERTISEMENTS

You cannot escape **advertisements** in daily life and you may well find that they pop up in your dreams too. If an advertisement does feature in your dream, its purpose will be to highlight your aspirations – so pay particular attention to the content of the advert. What or who was it trying to sell? If your dreaming mind lingered over the advert for **shoes, a fast car, holiday or any other object of your desire**, your unconscious may simply be reflecting your waking obsession with it. If the dream highlighted **cosmetics or clothes**, your dreaming mind may be encouraging you to change your image in some way in waking life.

MUSIC PLAYER

Records, cassettes, and CDs can simply represent the pleasure you feel when you listen to music but they can also, depending on your personal associations with the music being played, suggest the unconscious impressions you are responding to or the impressions you would like to give to others about yourself. Dreams of **personal**

stereos or iPods may suggest a desire to concentrate on your intuition and shut out the noise and confusion of the outside world. A dream of **wearing a personal stereo and using earphones** may also warn against an excessive need for privacy and avoidance of interaction with other people.

Cameras and camcorders

If you had a dream in which you were **using a camera, camcorder and you were taking photographs or filming an event or person from your waking life,** this most likely mirrors your sense that time is passing fast and your desire to capture a moment in time before it is gone. In dreams, **cameras and camcorders** are symbols of committing something to memory and they often appear at times of exam stress, expressing your wish to have a photographic memory that can absorb and retain information quickly. If you find yourself **studying a specific photograph or film** that you have taken in your dream, this suggests that something in your waking life may have escaped your attention and you need to re-examine it in more detail. A dream of using a **tape recorder** may have a similar interpretation to dreams of using a camera or camcorder, in that you wish to remember the chatter and noise that is currently filling your life. If you **hit any of the buttons on your camera, tape recorder or camcorder,** this may express a wish to pause, rewind or fast-forward to the past or the future.

If you dreamed of **recording your thoughts on a Dictaphone,** this may be to ensure that you remember them when you awake. If you dreamed of **peering through a camera lens and become frustrated because everything was out of focus and you couldn't get it into focus,** the suggestion may be that you are not seeing things as clearly as you should in waking life. Perhaps your mind is clouded with emotions and you have lost sight of the truth. If you fitted a **wide-angle lens to your camera or adjusted the focus** to improve your vision, the implication may be that you need to take a broader view of your waking situation. Pay attention also to the **image you are filming or photographing** and ask yourself whether you are portraying it accurately; this will indicate whether you have an accurate or distorted view-point in waking life. Finally, do not forget that **cameras and camcorders** are also tools used by artists and creative people to produce beautiful shots or thought-provoking films, so if you dreamed of **feeling happy when using your camera or camcorder,** this could suggest that you are neglecting your creative talent in waking life. *See also* TIME.

The Element Encyclopedia of 20,000 Dreams

NEWS

Radio, television and newspapers keep us up to date with world events and when these kinds of media appear in your dreams, their function is typically to send you a message about your current circumstances from your unconscious mind. Your waking reaction to a **news broadcast** typically holds true in dreams, but in the latter the broadcasting authority is your unconscious mind trying to transmit a message to you. Did you dream that you were **driving along or pottering about at home with the radio or television on in the background, when a newsflash drew your attention**? If so try to pay attention to the headlines and see if you can find any links to your waking world. The message may have been coded in the language of dreams. For example, a **war bulletin** or report could warn of conflict at home or work.

NEWSPAPER/MAGAZINE

These, like books, are symbols of information and knowledge but because their contents are more temporary and disposable, they don't tend to share the symbolism of wisdom with books. The main function of **newspaper**s in waking life is to keep you informed and that is why they can have the same meaning as **radio or news bulletins**. So if you dreamed of **passing a news stand and seeing a headline**, the message of that headline may have personal significance for you. If, on the other hand, you dreamed of **scanning the newspaper for a news item or advertizement**, this may indicate your anticipation or desire to hear some kind of news or result in waking life. Alternatively a dream in which you are **flipping through a magazine** may suggest that you have become bored with your life and that you are looking for stimulation. If you remember **pausing over a specific article** in your dream, perhaps your unconscious is urging you to consider its message or to take time out of your routine to enjoy yourself. Another interpretation would be that your dreaming mind is urging you to update your knowledge or outlook on life and learn more about the opinions of other people.

RADIO/TELEVISION

A **television** may represent your mind with its stream of thoughts, and a **radio** your inner voice with its communications. The **programs** you watch and listen to are intimate and objective representations of what is going on in your mind, so pay particular attention to what is on your dream television or radio. If you dreamed of **adjusting a radio dial or television remote control to find a particular station or channel**, perhaps your dreaming mind portrayed you as trying to tune into your intuition. A dream in which you **channel surf** may suggest your waking restlessness or boredom. As well as helping us stay abreast of current events, radios and televisions also offer mental stimulation and **DVDs and VCRs** allow us to record anything we want at a time that suits us.

If you dreamed of listening to a **radio broadcast, TV program or trying to record a specific program**, always try to recall its subject matter. If it was a faithful replica of a something you saw and heard on television or radio last night, your dreaming mind is simply playing out the images again in your sleep or perhaps reproving you for watching rather than living life. If it was a **variation of the program's theme or you felt deeply involved with the program** (which may or may not have been an exact rerun of the original), the chances are that it reveals a facet of your waking life, or news from within yourself. Did you identify with one of the characters, or with a specific situation or topic in the show, because you have found yourself in a similar state in the past or fear that you will in the future? Alternatively, if you dream about **radio or television program but do not feel that involved in the action**, your unconscious could be providing you with light relief from waking anxiety.

If you **see yourself on TV**, your unconscious may be attempting to communicate emotions and ideas that you feel unable to express in waking life. The image may also arise from a desire for attention or recognition from the people in your life. If you received **static instead of a clear signal**, this suggests an inability to make contact with your innermost thoughts. The image would be intensified if you watched a **DVD recording of a program**, as this indicates memories that are recorded or deeply embedded in your unconscious.

The purpose of TV or radio programs such as talk shows, soap operas or movies – is to entertain, enlighten and divert us from our everyday lives. Your unconscious may have used the **plot or situation from an entertainment show** of this kind and used it as a vehicle to replay an event in your past or to act out a current concern. Modern dream superstition suggests that if you enjoy dreaming about watching television, you will be successful in life; but if you are bored or upset by what you see, you will be led astray as your lack of concentration will mean you are unable to achieve success.

MIND, BODY, SPIRIT

Dreams focusing on the Zodiac or other ancient mystic arts, such as alchemy or Tarot, have much to say about the human condition.

According to Jung, you are tapping into what he called the 'collective unconscious' when mystical images surface in your dream. The collective unconscious refers to that part of a person's unconscious mind which is common to all human beings and which arises through our shared instincts, experiences and culture. It contains forms, archetypes or symbols that are manifested by all people in all cultures. They are said to exist prior to experience, and are in this sense instinctual.

In addition, ancient mystical symbols can also show scenes, facts or situations that reveal your everyday worries. Bear in mind, too, that the child within each of us might see almost any process of life as mysterious. In addition, love has what some call a mysterious magical quality, as we often feel completely changed when its spell is upon us.

Remember that a dream can unify your body, mind and spirit. It provides a means for self-exploration. When mystic or magical symbols appear in your dream they are often a clear reference to your aspirations and the underlying – some might say spiritual – forces of your being. *See also* RELIGION; SPIRITS AND GHOSTS; SURREALISM AND FANTASY

The Magical Arts

MAGIC

If **magic** featured in your dream, you need to bear in mind the nature of your attitude towards the mysterious arts in waking life. Do you regard anything magical as evil and dangerous, or do you believe that the powers of witchcraft can be used as a force for good? Alternatively, have you been influenced by reading or watching *The Lord of the Rings* or the Harry Potter books, in which magic can be used for both good and evil purposes? Whatever your attitude towards the magical arts in waking life, you need to bear in mind that it will influence the meaning of your dream. Whether you actually believe in magic or not, you were probably first introduced to the magical arts in childhood fairy tales; vestiges of your childhood belief will linger in your unconscious mind, surfacing now and again in dreams in which you are exposed to things you can neither understand nor explain.

For example, you may sense that someone doesn't like you or wishes you harm; in your dreams, this person may appear as a **witch or evil sorcerer**. If you are **using magic** in your dream to make something happen, this is pure wish-fulfillment. On the other hand, depending on whether or not you feel empowered or afraid in the dream, it can suggest that you are capable of controlling the situation you are in by utilizing your intuition. If you had a dream in which you were **standing in a magic circle**, this is a symbol of protection against evil forces. If you are **using a wand or watching a witch or wizard use a wand**, it is probable that the wand is a phallic symbol and conductor of energy. **Pentagrams and hexagrams** are symbols of defense against outside forces and a **broomstick**'s significance may lie in its phallic shape, as well as in its ability to help a rider take flight. **Cauldrons** can denote both the womb and the mystical powers of regeneration. A **hex** wards off evil and **spells** symbolize your deepest desires or fears, depending on the nature of the spell being cast. *See also* SPIRITS AND GHOSTS.

MAGICIAN/HYPNOTIST

If someone transforms into a **sinister magician or evil sorcerer** in your dream, it is likely that your dreaming mind has identified someone you know in waking life with the archetypal black magician, a self-obsessed, power-hungry person who will stop at nothing to get what he wants. On the other hand if the person in dream materialized as a **witch doctor, shaman, white magician, guru or high priest**, this suggests that you are in urgent need of advice and inspiration in waking life. Perhaps there is an older person in your life whom you regard as a mentor and whose advice you should follow. However, if your dreaming mind conjured up an image of a **conjurer, hypnotist or stage magician** whose success owes little to magic and everything to sleight of hand, this image may be warning you of someone or something in your life that is not trustworthy or is manipulating you in some way.

WITCH

If a woman you know in your waking life transforms into a **sorceress, priestess or witch** in your dream, this means that some woman in your waking life inspires feelings of uneasiness or mistrust in you. If you dreamed of stumbling upon a **coven of witches** in your dream, did you recognize any of them in waking life? If you did you may suspect them of being in a secret pact in waking life that is either benign or malignant. If you do not recognize them, this suggests a need for protection, concealment or togetherness in real life. *See also* SPIRITS AND GHOSTS.

The Element Encyclopedia of 20,000 Dreams

The Mystical Arts

ALCHEMY

Alchemy is a quest for inner perfection symbolized by the element gold; analytical psychologists believe that gold and many other alchemical symbols present themselves to us in dreams. According to Jung, the secret art of alchemy was a system of symbols that could bring about the transformation of the personality from its base state (lead) to its exalted state (gold). Alchemical symbols in dreams are therefore archetypal images from your unconscious, and if you dream of alchemy you may be undergoing a period of positive, but sometimes difficult, inner transformation. The message is that by combining your intuition with your intelligence you will achieve great energy and be capable of many things. In short, your dream suggests the healing power within you that can bring about transformation.

ASTROLOGY

To dream about **astrology** suggests that you are concerned about your current situation and how it will affect your future chances of development. If you are given an **astrological forecast or see your horoscope** in your dream, this may offer a significant message which should be analyzed closely to see how it relates to your life. A dream **astrologer** often represents your intuition or unconscious insights into yourself and others; there may be a link with your need for a sense of destiny or direction. But perhaps you do not believe in astrology, in which case your dream might be suggesting you are being misled in some way.

Astrology can enter your dream world in ways that you have probably never imagined. The celestial messages may come through symbols, numbers, archetypes, elements, planets, gemstones, body parts, plants, colors and places associated with a particular sign of the Zodiac. It is also possible that symbols in your dreams can be connected to astrological ideas relating to your own birth chart or people connected to you. A person appearing in a dream can be an aspect of your psyche, show an attitude or quality, represent the real person, be a symbol, or a combination of all of these. Similarly, several other elements can have meaning if you are able to crack the code. For example, if you dream you are a **warrior charging into battle**, this is definitely an Aries theme. At critical times of transformation in your life you can dream of the astrological event that is thought to correspond to what is actually happening. For example, when you experience a **Saturn Return**, which according to astrologers is a time of coming of age and maturing that only happens once every twenty-nine years (between the ages of 28–30, 57–59, 86–88), you might dream of **climbing a mountain and reaching the top of the first peak**. If you dream of a particular Zodiac sign or symbol, *see* Zodiac signs below. *See also* SPACE AND SCIENCE.

CHAKRA

In Hinduism and its spiritual systems of yoga, in some related Eastern cultures, as well as in some segments of the New Age

Chinese astrology

The Chinese Zodiac is based on the year rather than the month as in the Western system of astrology. If you dream of a particular **Chinese Zodiac symbol**, such as a rat or snake, you might want to consider these characteristics and try to apply them to yourself or others.

Rat [1900, 1912, 1924, 1936, 1948, 1960, 1972, 1984, 1996, 2008, 2020]

People born in the year of the **Rat** are often energetic and tenacious. They are capable of being generous and lovable, and are good listeners when one is needed, Rats can, however, also be manipulative and power-hungry creatures, so those befriending them must be wary of these tendencies.

Buffalo [1901, 1913, 1925, 1937, 1949, 1961, 1973, 1985, 1997, 2009, 2021]

Those born under the sign of the **Buffalo** (also known as the Ox) are usually hard-working, methodical and patient people. Though they can often be found in positions of leadership, they can sometimes be loners. People born in the year of the Buffalo can also be stubborn to the point of being rigid, and at worst they can be jealous or vindictive.

Tiger [1902, 1914, 1926, 1938, 1950, 1962, 1974, 1986, 1998, 2010, 2022]

The **Tiger** is a noble, courageous creature, as can be the people born under this sign. They are protective and passionate as well, which complements their sensi-tivity. Tigers can be hot-headed at times, even to the extent of becoming quarrelsome and acting rashly or hastily. These characteristics can lead to vain, uncompromising or unruly folk.

Cat [1903, 1915, 1927, 1939, 1951, 1963, 1975, 1987, 1999, 2011, 2023]

Those born in the year of the **Cat** (sometimes known as the **Rabbit**) are often refined and socially adept, which makes them all the better to have as friends. These clever folk can sometimes be seen as a bit old-fashioned or even aloof, and at worst they can be thin-skinned and devious.

Dragon [1904, 1916, 1928, 1940, 1952, 1964, 1976, 1988, 2000, 2012, 2024]

To be born in the year of the **Dragon** is to be a spirited and scrupulous individual. People tend to admire the enthusiasm and the vital, generous nature of the Dragon. However, as a fire-breathing creature, the Dragon can be overbearing, loud-mouthed and irritable. Generous and independent, the scrupulous Dragon can be a demanding person to be around.

Snake [1905, 1917, 1929, 1941, 1953, 1965, 1977, 1989, 2001, 2013, 2025]

Those born in the year of the **Snake** can be wise and understated, and are often soft-spoken, placid and compassionate souls. Snakes can have an air of intelligence about them that could be related to their good breeding or philosophical minds. But beware of angering a Snake; they can be vengeful, fickle and possessive, and they are often sore losers.

Horse [1906, 1918, 1930, 1942, 1954, 1966, 1978, 1990, 2002, 2014, 2026]

People born in the year of the **Horse** are often athletic, independent and skilful. These powerful, hard-working folk are not only quick on their feet but are also quick with their tongues. Horses make quite charming friends because of their wittiness and upbeat moods on most days. They can be rebellious and tactless at times, even ruthless when they lose their tempers.

Goat [1907, 1919, 1931, 1943, 1955, 1967, 1979, 1991, 2003, 2015, 2027]

The year of the **Goat** gives rise to peaceful, sweet-natured people who tend to be well-mannered and artistic. These intelligent folk can be kind-hearted and persevering when a cause motivates them. However, a Goat can also be intrusive, irresponsible and inclined towards melancholy.

Monkey [1908, 1920, 1932, 1944, 1956, 1968, 1980, 1992, 2004, 2016, 2028]

Those born in the year of the **Monkey** are often known for their intelligence and problem-solving abilities, which could explain why they make such good businessmen. They can be witty and captivating, but at worst they can be vain, untrustworthy or immature.

Rooster [1909, 1921, 1933, 1945, 1957, 1969, 1981, 1993, 2005, 2017, 2029]

The year of the **Rooster** brings forth enthusiastic, self-assured people. Roosters are quite industrious, and they often have a conservative streak that clashes with the more adventurous side of their nature. Whilst these people can be very resourceful, they can also be difficult to work with or be around because of their tendency to nit-pick and brag. At their worst, Roosters are brazen and untrusting.

Dog [1910, 1922, 1934, 1946, 1958, 1970, 1982, 1994, 2006, 2018, 2030]

Loyal, discreet and dutiful people are often born in the year of the **Dog**, making them excellent prospects as friends. They can be intelligent and selfless as well, but they can also be introverted, critical and defensive, and at their worst, Dogs are cynical and grim.

Pig [1911, 1923, 1935, 1947, 1959, 1971, 1983, 1995, 2007, 2019, 2031]

People born in the year of the **Pig** are often peace-loving, accommodating and sociable folk. Pigs have a sensual side that often shows their love of indulgence. Whilst they can be intelligent, some Pigs are naïve, which allows less scrupulous individuals to take advantage of them. Gullibility and insecurity can be a dangerous combination for Pigs at times.

movement – and to some degree, the distinctly different New Thought movement – **chakra** is thought to be an energy node in the human body. The seven main chakras are described as being aligned in an ascending column from the base of the spine (the first chakra) to the top of the head (the seventh chakra). Each chakra is associated with a certain color, multiple specific functions, an aspect of consciousness, a classical element and other distinguishing characteristics. If you dream of chakras, the following list of things associated with the seven chakras may help.

1st Chakra: perineum, red, earth, survival, grounding, stillness, elephant, earth. **2nd Chakra**: lower abdomen, orange, water, emotions, sexuality, desire, tears, crocodile, moon. **3rd Chakra**: solar plexus, yellow, fire, will, power, anger, joy, laughter, ram, sun. **4th Chakra**: heart, green, air, love, balance, compassion, antelope. **5th Chakra**: blue, throat, ether, sound, communication, creativity, expansion, excitement, deer. **6th Chakra**: third eye or adjna centre, indigo, forehead, light, clairvoyance, psychic abilities, imagination, dreaming, owl. **7th Chakra**: top of head, violet, thought, spiritual connection, understanding, knowing, bliss, God.

Feng Shui

Feng Shui is the art of mindfully organizing your environment – whether it is your living or working space – so it brings you good fortune and harmony in life. In dreams, Feng Shui stands for a desire to achieve harmony; there may, however, also me a suggestion that you follow the ideas of others instead of making changes according to how you feel about organizing your life.

Fortune telling

To dream that **you have your fortune told** in a dream, either by **astrology, palm reading, tarot or crystal ball**, suggests that your current situation feels uncertain and you are in need of guidance. You may also have an important decision to make in waking life but the message of your dream is that there is no easy answer and that hasty decisions should not be made.

Guru

If a **guru** appears in your dream, this indicates your connection with the whole of life, with collective wisdom or the collective unconscious. A guru is not concerned with the material world but with the realization of your eternal nature and life as it connects with the whole. Thus the guru in dreams will usually guide you towards greater self understanding, a deeper relationship with himself or herself, and instruct you in any necessary disciplines of mind and body. There will, where necessary, be a gradual unfolding to you of the inner meanings of ancient scriptures. If you reach a stage in your dreams in which **you become the guru**, this suggests spiritual transformation of the most powerful and dramatic kind.

Lucky sign

If various objects, amulets or talismans that traditionally symbolize luck appear in your dream, such as **horseshoes, pebbles and four-leaved clovers** appear in your dream, this is a positive sign. Bear in mind, however, that the nature of luck is that it always changes, so you need to appreciate what you have or move quickly to capitalize on your current good fortune. The following list is by no means comprehensive but mentions some of the well-known symbols of good fortune. If your lucky charm doesn't appear here, your dreaming mind might still be sending you a positive message; it might also be urging you to strengthen your defenses or protect yourself in areas of your personality or your life where you may appear vulnerable.

Ankh: An ancient Egyptian symbol resembling a cross with a loop at the top. It symbolizes the power of life and cosmic knowledge, and is the oldest and most popular amulet or religious symbol used by the Egyptians. When worn, carried or featured in any other way in your dream, the ankh symbolizes good health, as well as promoting fertility and the powers of intuition. **Arrowhead**: In waking life, those who believe in lucky charms carry an arrowhead for protection against enemies, bad luck, hexes, jealousy, evil spirits and all other negative forces. They may place an arrowhead over their front door or under the doormat to prevent burglars from breaking into their homes, and keep one in their car to help guard against accidents and theft. If an arrowhead appears in your dream, this is a powerful symbol of the need for protection and security in your life. **Crescent moon**: A sacred symbol of the Goddess, and also a symbol of magic, fertility and the secret powers of nature. Believers often wear a piece of pink quartz shaped like a crescent moon as a love charm to attract a lover or soulmate. **Four-leaved clover**: In waking life, it is thought that fortune will smile on you if you carry a four-leaved clover, or if you wear a pin, ring or pendant shaped like one. The four-leaved clover is

believed to be the most powerful of all lucky charms and was used by the ancient Druids as a charm against evil and to attain clairvoyant powers. **Garlic**: This aromatic bulb is one of the oldest and most famous forms of natural protection against evil forces, and is used throughout the world in a variety of ways to keep away vampires, sorcerers, demonic spirits and all other forms of evil. It is also used by many witches and shamans as a healing amulet. **Horn**: The gold horn is a popular necklace-charm worn by Italians as an amulet against the evil eye. When worn by a man, the horn – an ancient and obvious phallic symbol – increases sex appeal and promotes male virility. **Horseshoe**: This is a well-known good luck symbol in many parts of the world. According to superstition, nail an iron horseshoe over your door with the convex side pointing up for protection against sorcery, bad luck and the evil eye. For good luck, believers nail it over their door with the convex side pointing down. If a horseshoe appears in your dream, this is a positive sign suggesting good health and positive energy in your life. **Rabbit's foot**: perhaps the most used good-luck charm in modern times, this is usually carried on a keychain or worn on a necklace to ward off accidents and evil, and to increase good luck, happiness and fertility. **Skeleton key**: Wear an old skeleton key on a chain around your neck as an amulet to open the doors of opportunity and success, guard against the evil eye, and repel sorcery and all evil spirits. **Skull and crossbones**: A symbol of death once used by pirates and, more recently, as a warning label on poisons, the skull and crossbones can be used as a powerful amulet to protect the wearer against evil forces. It possesses the power to reverse any hex or curse and return the evil to the person who cast it upon you. This symbol is also popular among gamblers, as it is believed to keep their good luck from turning bad. **Unicorn**: The unicorn is an ancient symbol of chastity and protection, and its fabled horn was said to be used in medieval times as an amulet to detect poisons in the food or drink of kings, queens and popes. To promote fertility or increase sexual magnetism, believers wear any type of jewelry shaped like a unicorn. The symbol of this magnificent mystical creature also pierces the plans of enemies and keeps the wearer safe from all evil forces. **Wishbone**: Believers wear gold wishbone-shaped jewelry – or even an actual turkey or chicken wishbone on a necklace – as an amulet to attract good luck, and to make wishes and dreams come true.

New Age

To dream of **walking into a New Age festival or bookshop, to participate in a New Age ritual or visit a place closely linked with New Age ways of thinking such as Glastonbury or Stonehenge,** corresponds to new things, new people and new places in your life. You may even be taking on a new identity and developing new strengths. Your dream is urging you to use and build on your past experience to create a new and exciting future for yourself. If you feel anxious in your dream, this signifies that you are feeling out of place in some situation.

Palmistry

To notice your **palm** in your dream suggests that you hold all the knowledge you need in your own hands. You need to reach out and utilize your full potential. To dream that you are having your **palms read** represents your current life goals and ambitions, and the need for you to focus on where you are heading.

Pendulum

To see a **pendulum** in your dream represents your desire to be closer or more intimate with someone. The dream may also indicate that you are feeling emotionally touched by some situation or by someone. To see the back-and-forth swinging of a pendulum suggests that you are experiencing some conflict or difficulty; It might also suggest that you are confused about making an important decision in your life and that you may be afraid of change. People around you are anxiously awaiting your decision but your dreaming mind is urging you to take your time and not make rash or hasty decisions.

Tarot

Symbols are the language of the subconscious mind, and both **Tarot** and dreams speak to us in exactly the same way, in the language of symbols. Some dream experts believe it is a natural marriage to combine Tarot and dreams to at once deepen and enhance the understanding of dream symbols whilst also expanding one's understanding of Tarot.

Jung saw all the Tarot images as being 'descended from the archetypes of transfor-

lude several of
were encoun-
uation process,
al maturation
g of the physical
adow, the anima
old man. The
ls representing
s of transforma-
hero, the mother,
birth. In Jung's
hese archetypes
nic components of
the unconscious that affect the human
psyche in many different ways. To dream of
a **Tarot reading** indicates your current
situation and state of mind. It means that
you are open to the idea of exploring your
unconscious thoughts and feelings. Pay
attention to what the Tarot cards revealed.

The deck of cards known as the Tarot is
divided into two parts: the Major Arcana
and the Minor Arcana (the word 'Arcana' is
from the Latin word for 'secret'). The
Major Arcana consists of twenty-two
cards, each separately titled. These cards
depict symbolic figures, such as the Fool,
the Magician, the High Priestess and the
Empress, elements of nature such as the
Star, the Moon and the Sun, and human
experiences on the spiritual journey, as well
as joys, hopes, fears and sorrows. The
symbols are drawn from legend, and from
universal symbolism and magical belief.
Typically, the Major Arcana are subject to
broad interpretations. In essence they are
archetypes and their sequence from naught
to twenty-one is believed to represent the
soul's journey to awareness, the process of
becoming whole or the alchemical process
of spiritual transformation. They represent
the stages of a person's individual passage

through life, from non-existence, birth,
love, marriage, death, spiritual ascension
and back to non-existence again.

Most of the cards in the Minor Arcana
represent everyday concerns, events or
qualities. The Minor Arcana is a combination of four suits; each suit is comprised of
cards numbered from one to ten, plus the
court cards of Page, Knight, Queen and
King. The four suits of the Minor Arcana
are most commonly known as Cups,
Pentacles, Wands and Swords; from these
suits it can clearly be seen that the Minor
Arcana is the ancestor of our modern
playing cards with their corresponding
suits of Hearts, Diamonds, Clubs and
Spades. Each suit of the Minor Arcana has a
meaning. Traditionally the Wands represent fire, inspiration, spirituality, action,
initiative, and the psyche. The Swords
signify air, determination, strength, faith
and conquering of fear. The Cups symbolize water, emotions, purity, and your
outlook towards life and the future. Finally,
the Pentacles denote finances, social influence, worldly knowledge, and your connection with nature and earth. Consider these
general meanings of the Major and Minor
Arcana and the four Tarot suits, as well as
the individual meanings of the cards.

TAROT CARDS

If a **specific tarot card** appears in your
dream the following abbreviated list of the
classic meanings of each card might help
with your interpretation:

The Major Arcana

0 – **The Fool**
A jester figure representing impulse, birth
and youth, sometimes shown beginning a

journey and accompanied by a dog. If this card appears in your dreams, it stands for a new start and infinite possibilities. When it appears, you might be about to make a move, not just to a new home, but to a new job or way of thinking. There is more than just change, renewal and a brand new beginning in the Fool; there's also movement, and a fresh, exciting new time. But the card carries a little bark of warning as well. Stop daydreaming and fantasizing and watch your step, lest you fall and end up looking the fool.

1 – The Magician

Sometimes shown as a juggler or illusionist at a fair, sometimes playing with the symbols of the four suits, representing consciousness, a sense of self-control and dexterity. In dreams, this card might be telling you that you will have a vision, an idea or a magical mental image of whatever it is you most want, whether it is the solution to a problem, a successful career or a fulfilling love life.

2 – High Priestess

Shown as a female religious leader, representing women's liberation, wisdom, independence and psychic development. The High Priestess is the card of knowledge, instinct and the supernatural. She offers secret knowledge, like the moon on a dark night, so that you can find your path in life. She sits between the pillars of dark and light, consciousness and unconsciousness, waxing and waning. All secret knowledge is hers.

3 – Empress

Shown as a queen on a throne or as the mother goddess, she represents illumination, intelligence, understanding, maternity and creativity. The Empress is a creator, be it the creation of life, of romance, of art or business. This card tells you that if you want your new romance, career, business or creation to grow into all it can be, you have to pay attention to it, baby it and be willing to let it take those first steps when it is ready. Most of all, like any pregnant mother or good gardener, you have to be patient. All things need time to gestate and sprout.

4 – Emperor

Sometimes shown as a king on a throne holding a sphere and scepter, he represents sight, vision, realization, power and strength. In the best of circumstances, he signifies the leader that everyone wants to follow because he rules with intelligence and enthusiasm. But sometimes that throne can also be a trap, a responsibility that has the Emperor feeling restless, bored and discontent.

5 – Hierophant or Pope

A religious leader, sometimes shown as the Pope seated on a throne, he represents the link between God and man, and symbolizes spiritual discovery, the father, transcendence, and the teacher. The Hierophant's only problem is that he can be stubborn. At his best, he is wise and soothing, offering much-needed advice; at his worst, he is an unbending traditionalist.

6 – Lovers

Shown as two people surrounded by cupids, flowerbeds, they represent struggle, beauty, sovereignty and, union. Above all, this card is a symbol of choice. Love is a force that makes you choose and decide for reasons you often can't understand; it makes you surrender control to a higher power. When this card appears in a dream, you are being told to trust your instincts, to choose this career, challenge, person or thing to which or whom you are so strongly drawn, no matter how scary, how difficult, irrational or troublesome.

7 – Chariot

Sometimes shown as warriors parading triumphant in chariot or an icon of a hero being paraded around, it represents victory, the domination of humankind over nature, power, war and self-control. If this card appears in your dream, it suggests that control is required over opposing emotions, wants, needs, people or circumstances; it is urging you to bring them together and give them a single direction, your direction. The card can indicate new motivation or inspiration that gets a stagnant situation moving again.

8 – Strength or Lust

Represents love as a source of strength, endurance, will to survive, strong desires and perseverance. In dreams, this card suggests that you can control not only the situation, but also yourself. It is a card about anger and impulse management, about creative answers, leadership and maintaining your integrity. It can also stand for a steadfast friend.

9 – Hermit

Often shown as a hermit holding an hour-glass, the hermit represents withdrawa solitude, abandonment of convention inner conviction and a preoccupation v details,. This is not a time for sociali the card indicates, instead, a desire for and solitude. Nor is it a time for discussion or decisions; it is a time to organize, ruminate and take stock. I may be feelings of frustration and discontent during this time of withdrawal. But such times lead to enlightenment, illumination and clarity.

10 – Wheel of Fortune

Represents karma, reincarnation, the consequences of chance happenings, cycles, optimism and generosity. This card can mean movement, change and evolution, but its primary meaning is that such changes will seem to come out of the blue as a stroke of good, unexpected fortune.

11 – Justice

Often shown as 'lady justice' (blindfolded with scale), representing decision, equilibrium. Justice is about cold, objective balance through reason or natural force. This is the card that tells a person they can't keep smoking and drinking without consequences to their health. It is the card that advises cutting out waste and insists that you make adjustments, do whatever is necessary to bring things back into balance, physically, emotionally, socially and spiritually.

12 – Hanged Man

Represents sacrifice, violence, transition. Sometimes you need to sacrifice cherished positions, opening yourself to other truths and other perspectives in order to find solutions. One thing is certain; whether the insight is great or small, spiritual or mundane, once you have been the Hanged Man in your dreams, you never see things in quite the same way again.

13 – Death
Often shown as a skeleton or the Grim Reaper, this card represents stagnation and routine, but also fresh starts, a clean slate, liberation and renewal. This is a time of change, a time for something to end, but also a time for something new to begin. You may feel sad, empty or low, but that will help you rise again, like a phoenix from the ashes. Death is not the end. It is only the precursor to resurrection.

14 – Temperance
This card represents enthusiasm, moderation, truthfulness, the mixing of opposite ingredients in proper proportion, and working together. Temperance may, at first glance, be a warning to 'temper' or modify your behavior, to cut your wine with water. But it may also be a reminder that seemingly irreconcilable opposites may not be irreconcilable at all.

15 – The Devil
Perhaps the most misunderstood of all the major Arcana, the Devil is not really 'Satan' at all, but Pan, the half-goat nature god, or Dionysus, the god of wine and licentiousness. This card represents superficiality, confusion, ignorance, apathy, limitations, frustrations and sexual problems. These are gods of pleasure and abandonment, of wild behavior and unbridled desires. This card is about ambition, but is also synonymous with temptation and addiction. On

the flip side, however, the card can be a warning to someone who is too restrained, someone who never allows themselves to get passionate, messy or wild – or even ambitious.

16 – The Tower:
Representing spiritual awakening, destiny, often shown as a 'house of god' or a ruins, the Tower is a card about war. This war is between the tangled structures of lies and the lightning flash of truth. If this card appears in your dreams, you can expect to be shaken up or to be blinded by a shocking revelation. It sometimes takes such a shock to make you see a truth that you refuse to confront, or to challenge and destroy beliefs that are well constructed and deeply defended. What is most important to remember is that the tearing down of this structure, however painful, makes room for something new to be built.

17 – The Star
Often shown as a woman kneeling on a sea shore, this card suggests clarity of vision and spiritual insight, and represents meditation, inspiration, hope, immortality. Most importantly, it suggests that unexpected help will be coming, but that help is only the first step. The star only reveals the future. It is up to you to find your way to that future.

18 – The Moon
A card that is connected with sleep, and so both with dreams and with nightmares, the Moon represents illusion, self-deception, confusion and the growth of intuition. It is a scary card in that it warns that there might be hidden enemies, tricks and falsehoods. It should also be remembered that

The Element Encyclopedia of 20,000 Dreams

this is a card of great creativity, of powerful magic, primal feelings and intuition. If this image appears in your dreams, you may be going through a time of emotional and mental trial. This time however, can also result in great creativity, psychic powers, visions and insight. You can and should trust your intuition.

19 – The Sun

Just as the moon symbolized inspiration from the unconscious or from dreams, this card symbolizes discoveries made fully conscious whilst wide awake, and represents enlightenment, clarity, understanding, comprehension, wisdom, happiness and splendor. It is a card of intellect, clarity of mind, and feelings of youthful energy, as well as symbolizing science and math, beautifully constructed music and carefully reasoned philosophy.

20 – Judgment

Often showing angels blowing trumpets, this card represents awakening to something new and rebirth. There are wounds from the past that may not have healed and Judgment advises you to finally face these, recognize that the past is past, and put them to rest, absolutely and irrevocably. This is also a card of healing, quite literally from an accident or illness, as well as a card signaling great transformation, renewal and change.

21 – The World or Universe

Simply put, this card tells you that a successful conclusion to a long-term project is in sight, and that it will be accompanied by well-earned praise, celebration and success. It represents completion, reward, perfection, a unity of positive and negative, and, on a more mundane level, the World card indicates travel. These are not short business trips, but long, fantastic trips. This is a wonderful card of wholeness, perfection, satisfaction and happiness.

The Minor Arcana

Wands

Ace: New starts, new business idea, rush of energy.
Two: Planning for the future, anxiety, working partnership.
Three: Business success, leading a group.
Four: House move, success.
Five: Trouble and strife, especially petty fighting.
Six: Public success, recognition.
Seven: Fighting for your vision, competition.
Eight: Communications, quick movement.
Nine: Last-minute problems, self-protection.
Ten: Success which brings many burdens.
Page: News of work or business, new interests.
Knight: Travel and action, a red or fair-haired youth.
Queen: A business-like or active woman, a red or fair-haired woman.
King: An active and influential man, a red or fair-haired man.

Cups

Ace: A message of love, the start of a romance, doing something for love, creativity.
Two: A happy relationship or partnership.
Three: Partying and celebrating.
Four: Boredom and apathy, the grass always seems greener on the other side of the fence.

Five: Depression and regret.

Six: Simple joys, something or someone from the past.

Seven: Confusion, too many choices, dreams and illusions.

Eight: Leaving something behind, change of lifestyle.

Nine: Dreams come true.

Ten: Good luck and happiness, satisfaction.

Page: A new friendship, news of something or someone dear to your heart.

Knight: A proposal or invitation, a good-natured, brown-haired youth with light eyes.

Queen: An intuitive woman, a kindly brown-haired woman with light eyes.

King: A gentle man, a healer, a good advisor, a good-natured, brown-haired man with light eyes.

Suit of Swords

Ace: Crisis point, success through difficulties.

Two: Sitting on the fence, balance, waiting.

Three: Anxiety, unhappiness, separation.

Four: Rest, hospital, withdrawal.

Five: Fighting for the wrong things, arguments, being forced to recognize your limitations.

Six: Moving away from troubles.

Seven: Deception, theft, non-confrontation.

Eight: Feeling trapped, standstill, restrictions.

Nine: Anxiety, worries, mental anguish.

Ten: Misfortune and endings, failure.

Page: Spying, email or telephone call, brash new idea.

Knight: Upsetting changes, arguments, a dark-haired youth with gray eyes.

Queen: A widow, an unscrupulous woman, a dark-haired woman with gray eyes.

King: An ambitious and authoritative man, a lawyer or doctor, a dark-haired man with gray eyes.

Pentacles/Coins

Ace: Money and security, health.

Two: Juggling time and money, cautiousness.

Three: New job or work, success in work.

Four: Success but unwillingness to move forward or change.

Five: Ill health, financial losses, loss of self-esteem.

Six: Receiving and giving help, financial or otherwise.

Seven: Making adjustments in your plans and being prepared to do the hard work.

Eight: New job, studies, working with a hobby.

Nine: Success from your own efforts, security.

Ten: Money and property, the countryside, inheritance.

Page: News about money or a job, study for a job.

Knight: Cautious person working towards a goal, a dark-haired youth with dark eyes.

Queen: Self-confident and practical woman, a dark-haired woman with dark eyes.

King: An honest and practical man, a dark-haired man with dark eyes.

Sun signs and dreams

The Sun signs of astrology can appear in dreams, through the following correspondences: *See also* SPACE AND SCIENCE.

Aries (21 March–19 April) is the cardinal fire sign, and is dynamic and action oriented. Associated with: **soldiers, angry people, athletes; the ram; the owl; Mars; red; tiger lily; ruby; number one; head, brain, eyes, face, teeth; and typical dreams might be set in stadiums or battlefields**. The best-known symbol for this first sign of the Zodiac in Western astrology is the **ram**, the ruling planet is **Mars**. Aries is influenced by the fire element. People born under the sign of Aries tend to be enterprising, impulsive, warm-hearted and confident free spirits who say what they mean and mean what they say, but they can also be impatient, rash, tactless, excitable and bossy.

Taurus (20 April–20 May) is the fixed earth sign, and is solid, dependable and sensual. Associated with: **singers, lovers, gardeners, models; the bull; Venus; red-orange; mallow; topaz; number two; the neck area, voice, ears, thyroid and cerebellum; and dreams set in a luxurious home or a beautiful setting**. The best-known symbol of Taurus is the **bull** and the ruling planet is **Venus**. Taureans are influenced by the earth element. Those born under the sign of Taurus are persistent, reliable, loyal and patient individuals with a discriminating taste for quality and the good things in life. The downside is that they can at times be lazy, materialistic and moody.

Gemini (21 May–21 June) is the mutable air sign, and is changeable, social and a coordinator. Associated with: **teachers, talkers, writers, twins; magpies; orange; Mercury; orchid; tourmaline; number three; arms, hands, shoulders, lungs, thymus, nervous system, speech; and typical dream settings might be high-up places**. The **twins** are the best-known symbol for Gemini and the ruling planet is **Mercury**. Geminis are influenced by the air element. Those born under Gemini are intellectual, natural communicators but they can also be inconsistent and flighty at times. Their endearing zest for ideas and something new sometimes makes committing to anyone and anything problematic.

Cancer (22 June–22 July) is the cardinal water sign, and is shy, self-protective and nurturing. Associated with: **chefs, mothers, carers; crab; turtle; Moon; yellow-orange; lotus; amber; moonstone; number four; stomach, esophagus, pancreas, breasts, womb, ribs, digestive system; and a typical dream setting is of a cottage by the sea**. The best-known symbol for Cancer is the **crab** and the ruling planet is the **Moon**. Cancerians are influenced by the water element. Those born under Cancer tend to be emotional and empathetic with a wacky sense of humor, but they can be oversensitive and insecure at times.

Leo (23 July–22 August) is the fixed fire sign, and is outgoing, an entertainer and warm. Associated with: **actors, salespeople, motivational speakers; lion; Sun; yellow; Sunflower; cat's eye; number five; the heart, spinal cord, circulation, spleen, pulse; and a typical dream setting is a stage**. The best-known symbol for Leo is the **lion** and the ruling planet is the **Sun**. Leo is influenced by the fire element. Those born under Leo tend to be courageous, vivacious, energetic and natural leaders but they can also be prone to arrogance and be attention seeking.

Virgo (23 August–22 September) is the mutable earth sign, and is reserved, particular and intelligent. Associated with: **dieticians, auditors, priestesses; virgin; Mercury; yellow-green; narcissus; peridot; number six; assimilation, food and diet, intestines, bowels, nails; and dream surroundings that are orderly and neat**. The best-known symbol of Virgo is the **virgin** and the ruling planet is **Mercury**. Virgos are influenced by the earth element. Those born under Virgo tend to be meticulous, disciplined and analytical. They can appear cool and reserved, but great sensitivity lies behind the detached exterior.

Libra (23 September–23 October) is the cardinal air sign, and is elegant, refined and cultured. Associated with: **princes or princesses, artists, musicians; scales; elephant; Venus; green; aloe; emerald; number seven; adrenals, kidneys, lumbar region, skin; and the ideal dream landscape is a rose garden**. The **scales** are the best-known symbol of Libra and the ruling planet is **Venus**. Librans are influenced by the air element. Those born under Libra tend to be peace-loving, agreeable, harmonious people but their natural ability to understand the viewpoint of everyone and fit in everywhere can be interpreted as insecurity and indecisiveness.

Scorpio (24 October–21 November) is the fixed water sign, and is introverted, intense, and magnetic. Associated with: **Grim Reaper; dark figures, exotic people; scorpion; eagle; phoenix; Mars; Pluto; blue-green; cactus; turquoise; number eight; bladder, genitals, colon, prostate, uterus, sex organs; and a typical dream setting would be a bedroom**. The best-known symbol of Scorpio is the **scorpion** and the ruling planets are **Mars and Pluto**. Scorpios are influenced by the water element. Those born under Scorpio tend to be passionate, focused, sensitive and sensual, but they can also be secretive and destructive.

Sagittarius (22 November–21 December) is the mutable fire sign, and is adventurous, curious and wise. Associated with: **hunters, horseback riders, explorers; archery; Centaur; Jupiter; blue; rush; jacinth; number nine; hips, thighs, arteries, base of spine, pelvis; and a typical dream setting would be scenes around a campfire**. The best-known symbol for Sagittarius is the **archer** and the ruling planet is **Jupiter**. Sagittarians are influenced by the fire element. Those born under Sagittarius tend to be unconventional, idealistic and visionary with a need to seek spiritual enlightenment, but they can also be reckless and ruthless.

Capricorn (22 December–19 January) is the cardinal earth sign, and is conservative, organized and determined. Associated with: **mountain climbers, accountants, bankers; mountain goat; Saturn; indigo; hemp; jet; number ten; bones, skeleton, joints, cartilage; and a dream setting might be an old house at the top of a hill**. The best-known symbol of Capricorn is the **goat** and the ruling planet is **Saturn**. Capricorns are influenced by the earth element. Those born under the sign of Capricorn are persistent, cautious, self-disciplined, warm-hearted and stable, but they can also at times be mean and inflexible.

Aquarius (20 January–18 February) is the fixed air sign, and is humanitarian, unique and interesting. Associated with **electricians, conductors, Eskimos; water bearer; man; star; Uranus; violet; olive; chalcedony; number eleven, ankles, calves, circulation, breath, eyesight; and a dream setting might be a cold place or planet**. The best-known symbol of Aquarius is the **water carrier** and the ruling planets are **Saturn and Uranus**. Aquarius is influenced by the air element. Those born under the sign of Aquarius tend to be idealistic, intellectual, generous, altruistic and unconventional, but they can also be unpredictable and emotionally detached at times.

Pisces (19 February–20 March) is the mutable water sign, and is dreamy, imaginative and otherworldly. Associated with: **religious teachers, monks and nuns, photographers; fish; dolphin; Neptune; red-violet; poppy; pearl; number twelve; feet, toes, lymph glands; and a typical dream setting might be a cathedral**. The best-known symbol of Pisces is **two fish** and the ruling planets are **Jupiter and Neptune**. Pisceans are influenced by the water element. Those born under the sign of Pisces tend to be intuitive, sensitive and spiritual but they can also be dreamy, impractical and impressionable at times.

ZODIAC SIGNS

The **Zodiac** may come into dreams in numerous ways. If you are a fan of astrology in waking life, dreams of the Zodiac often reflect your desire for a fuller understanding of the world. If you are not a serious fan of astrology, to see the Zodiac in your dream represents the various aspects of your conscious being. If you dream of a particular **Zodiac sign or symbol**, you should consider these characteristics and either apply them to yourself or others. Each sign, such as Cancer, Leo and Pisces, has a stereotypical meaning to illustrate various facets of life and human personality traits. Think also about the Zodiac symbol and the gems, numbers and other elements associated with it.

MONEY AND SHOPPING

Money in dreams represents things of great value to you, but such dreams are not necessarily about monetary value.

For Jung, money is a symbol of the power required to achieve spiritual objectives. According to Freud, it is a symbol of an orderly or obsessive personality. If symbols associated with money, riches and wealth – such as cash, precious jewels, treasure, expensive houses and cars, and winning lottery tickets – appear in your dreams, try to identify what money means to you in a non-materialistic sense. That this symbol appears in your dreams suggests that you need to assess what is important to you in life, as well as being aware of what price you are prepared to pay for your actions and desires.

It may be that gold does not represent the precious metal to you, but rather someone who has a heart of gold or who is a winner, just as a dream of treasure might represent the people you love in your life, a wealth of knowledge or a treasury of ideas. Do you associate money with freedom, power, desirability or your own personal worth? Do you believe that money can buy you happiness? Thinking about such questions should help you identify the things you really value in your waking life and you

may in turn start to question the real value of your previous goals and aspirations. *See also* CRYSTALS, GEMSTONES AND ROCKS; EVERYDAY THINGS.

Money, Money, Money!

BANK

Banks and vaults in dreams represent your psychological potential. Your unconscious may be urging you to start using your inner reserves and energy rather than locking your talents away. On the other hand, your dream may simply be highlighting your need for financial security. If you dream of **robbing a bank**, it may suggest that you are depleting your inner resources. If, in your dream, you were **depositing money in a bank**, this suggests feelings of security in waking life, although such a dream may also contain an element of wish-fulfillment.

Banking in dreams can refer to something you are storing within yourself; perhaps you are withholding emotion or important information. Freudians would regard dreams of **safes or strongboxes** as representing female sexuality, since these things usually contain valuables. As places for hoarding things, they may also suggest greed or an inflexible approach to life. Money is a symbol of spiritual power for Jungians, so the safe or strongbox may represent a storehouse of insights into your unconscious mind.

CASH/MONEY

The appearance of **cash or money** in your dream represents those things you value in life, or perhaps your feelings of self-confidence. It can also signify, your energy, personal resources or what you feel about yourself. In some cases, dreams of cash or money link in with feelings of hardship or misery associated with the struggle to survive or pay your way. For Jung, money appears in dreams as a symbol of spiritual power and represents your ability to achieve your goals; in many dreams, money can depict your personal sense of power to change things or the power you feel you have over others; what you pay in order to satisfy your desires or actions can also relate to sexuality and self-giving.

For Freud, money is a symbol of excrement and dreams of **hoarding money** express an anal fixation, perhaps caused by the parents mishandling the dreamer's toilet training in childhood. Such dreams may therefore suggest an obsessively orderly and obstinate personality. Dreams of a **pile of coins** are especially potent symbols of anal preoccupations.

Most modern dream analysts believe that dream money or cash is a symbol of security, although it may also indicate things of intrinsic value to you or the way in which you value yourself. Whenever you dream of money and those things with which it is associated – such as **shopping, writing checks, banks, investments, prizes or wills** – you should consider whether they are commenting on the importance of things with a non-materialistic value in your waking life. Bear in mind, too, that money can represent emotional transactions in waking life.

Giving money may signify a generosity of spirit or kindness, or it may reflect emotional ties. **Receiving money** can suggest the acceptance of emotional support, whilst **borrowing money** may be a warning to pay attention to your current spending levels. Dreaming of a **lack of money** can suggest a lack of qualifications or the need to achieve a desired goal and **hoarding money** can indicate selfishness. **Finding money** suggests that you are realizing something valuable or gaining power; such a dream is often accompanied by a feeling of release from stress. **Holding on to money** in your dream signifies feeling insecure, or being 'tight' emotionally or sexually; it is also a symbol of not using your power to get what you want. **Losing money** is a symbol of losing power or opportunity, or can simply represent the pain of loss. **Not having enough money** indicates a sense of being inadequate or may even be reminding a man about his failing potency. **Stolen money** represents feelings of guilt about gaining power, a sense that you do not deserve what you get; it may also reveal a sense of feeling cheated or feeling that others are taking us for granted. Perhaps you have given yourself cheaply in sex or in a relationship. According to ancient dream-lore, it was considered fortunate to dream of **receiving or finding money**, with some traditions going further and saying that a dream of finding money means a birth. Money dreams, of course, may simply reflect anxieties about your finances.

CHECK

Signing a check, signing a contract or making a payment are generally regarded as positive signs in your dreams, indicating that certain of your plans are going to schedule. **Writing a check** is a deliberate action; what is important here is not so much the check, but your attitude towards it. If you **wrote a check in your dream for an amount you knew you could not afford**, you may be feeling guilty about someone or something in waking life. This may relate to money but it may also relate to your recent actions towards someone.

A dream **demand for payment** represents the personal investment you need to make in order to move forward with your life. **Making a payment or paying a bill** emphasizes the effort needed to achieve your goals but also reminds you that you only get out of life what you put into it. If you find your **pockets empty or your credit card rejected when you are trying to pay the bill**, this highlights feelings of inadequacy; it may also be a warning not to squander your resources. **Paying with cash instead of a credit card or check** may suggest impatience to progress and **receiving payment** reflects your sense of being rewarded in some way. As a house is often regarded by dream analysts as a symbol of the self, **paying rent or your mortgage** in your dreams suggests a need to preserve your independence or integrity. Alternatively, if the dream stresses that you are a **tenant and not a house-owner**, this may suggest your unease with yourself or uncertainty concerning a current situation.

COIN/BANKNOTE

If **coins were running through your hands** in your dream, are you being extravagant or excessive in waking life or wasting time on things you know are not good for you? Your dream may be urging you to be more careful. If you are **surrounded by piles of banknotes** in your dreams, this may be simple wish-fulfillment if you are experiencing financial worries. On the other hand, the banknotes may not just refer to financial concerns, but also to sexual or emotional deficiencies.

CREDIT CARD

If a **credit card** appears in your dreams, this symbolizes your feelings about money and the satisfaction, pleasure, security it can bring, as well as the uncertainties. It may also represent your ability to get what you want in life. **Having or getting a credit card** symbolizes your sense of personal power in the waking world and the ease with which you make money. **Losing a credit card or having it rejected** in your dreams signifies uncertainty about your financial future and may reflect the feeling of stress to which getting your needs in life can often lead.

DEBT

In your dreams, **debts** may represent something you owe to yourself, such as time to relax, but they may also be a symbol of the debt that others owe you. For example, do you feel that you deserve more respect, consideration or attention from others in waking life? On perhaps you are in debt to someone or are in danger of becoming emotionally bankrupt or destitute?

A dream in which you were **bankrupt or refused admission to something because you did not have enough money** is a symbol of frustration in waking life. The lack of money in your dream could indicate people who are interfering in your life, obstacles standing in your way or your own lack of confidence. Dreams of **going bankrupt or becoming a pauper** may also refer to the loss of cherished non-financial resources, such as talents, looks or friends. If such a dream traumatized you, ask yourself what your lost dream riches could symbolize: the love of your friends, your self-respect or your energy reserves? Your dream may be urging you to take some kind of action to avert a real-life financial, emotional, physical or professional decline. If you have a dream in which you **leave valuables with a pawnbroker**, this represents the sacrifices you are prepared to make in order to achieve your goals. The pawnbroker may also represent someone whom we admire but whose advice or example is questionable; a pawnbroker can also serve as a symbol of low self-esteem.

Investment

The notion of **saving and investing** in dreams may have practical or emotional implications. These may relate to the need to save for your future or equally may be making some reference to the need to prepare yourself emotionally for situations or people that need your attention and time. Dream investments represent an outlay of some kind allied to an element of risk or uncertainty. Are you taking an emotional or business risk? Your dream may be guiding or warning you, or summing up the situation in some way.

If your dreaming mind homed in on a **solitary egg in a bird's nest**, it may have represented your nest egg or funds you have been saving. If you have a dream of **losing vast amounts of money on the stock market** – an image of a **ruined man or a man on the verge of suicide** may appear – this represents feelings of great disappointment or disenchantment with an aspect of your life in which you feel you have invested a great deal of time and energy.

MISER/BEGGAR

If the character of a **miser** appears in your dream, ask yourself if it refers to you. The dream image may not necessarily be referring to your attitude towards money; it may be telling you about your miserly approach to others. Are you always taking and not giving back in return? **Beggars** in dreams could refer to aspects of yourself or an area of your life that is in some way lacking or deficient. Do you need an intellectual challenge or are you feeling lonely?

Pension

In dreamland, **pensions** are generally associated with aging or old age, so if you had a dream in which you were **collecting your pension or setting up a pension**, your dreaming mind may be urging you to do just that. If you **received your pension payout** in your dreams, pay attention to how you felt about it. Did you feel delighted or lost? The answer will tell you not just about your attitude to aging, but about your attitude to work and whether you are working to live or living to work.

Salary

Dreams that feature a **wage or salary** refer to your potential in waking life; **how you spend your wage** indicates how you are developing your potential in waking life. The income in your dreams may represent your goals in life but it can also suggest job satisfaction, depending on whether or not you feel you are being fairly paid in your dream. If you dreamed of being paid in any way – be it a **wage, salary, bonus check or cash** – remember that money in dreams often symbolizes something of worth, so your attitude towards receiving the money is extremely important. If you **felt angry because you were paid a derisory sum**, you may be feeling undervalued in waking life or you may feel that someone is cheating you out of your rightful reward. If, however, you **accepted the derisory sum without complaint**, this suggests that your self-esteem is in need of a boost. If you dreamed of **receiving a pay check for a vast amount of money**, your dream was probably simple wish-fulfillment, referring either to your desire never to have to work for money again or to your desire to be recognized in some way.

Digging for treasure

Finding money in a dream, or digging or searching for treasure or riches can suggest power, independence and security. It may have a literal interpretation, telling you that now is a good time to start a new financial venture, but more often than not it symbolizes discovering parts of yourself that have been neglected or repressed. The treasure in your dream may symbolize things you want from life but can also suggest the treasure lying within you, maybe something that has been neglected or repressed such as a positive attitude, self-respect or a talent of some kind. Ancient dream-lore disagrees with more modern interpretations of this kind of dream, suggesting that it indicates that someone you have loved and trusted is not worthy of your love. If, however, you dream of **finding gold**, then this is usually a good sign.

Shops and Shopping

MARKET

The colorful and varied array of goods for sale in an **open-air market** represents the huge range of choices that are available to you in waking life and this kind of dream is most likely to appear at times of great change in your life, such as starting a new job or a new relationship. If you hear the many **cries of market sellers or street vendors**, this may express your fears of losing direction in waking life. Dreams of **being in a market** suggest your ability to cope with the demands and social interactions of daily life. If, however, the **atmosphere in the market is closed in and intense**, this may suggest feelings of confusion

Bear in mind that markets are also places of buying and selling, so they can give you an indication of how highly you value yourself and your talents, and whether you feel you have something you can sell or there is something you want to buy. **Busy market** dreams may simply suggest that you need to spend more time with other people. The exotic atmosphere of a dream **bazaar or souk** represents the desire to seek out new and exciting experiences, whilst **haggling merchants** can represent people in your life who are extremely demanding.

SELLING

Selling is all about persuasion and buying is all about acceptance. Selling is about persuading people to have things they did not know they needed, so you need to bear that in mind if an **item is up for sale** in your dream. **Street peddlers, hawkers or door-to-door salesman** are all symbols of possible dishonesty; if they appear in your dream, you should weigh up the pros and cons of some new undertaking or the motives of someone close to you. **Trading** in dreams symbolizes interaction and communication and if this image appears in your dream, you may be considering what personal qualities you have to offer someone or what they have to offer you.

SHOP

In dreams, **shops** suggest what you want or think you need in waking life. If you are in a **shop you know**, then you are aware of what you want from life, but if it is an **unfamiliar shop**, then you need to open your mind to new possibilities. Shops and stores are places of interaction, whether this is the exchange of money and goods, or the communication between the salesperson and the shopper. In dreams, they therefore represent things you desire in life and the manner in which you go about getting these things. A **supermarket**, for instance, suggests a wide range of choices, a **village store** represents the essential things in life, whilst a store or website selling a range of odds and ends – such as an **antiques store, an auction site on the Internet or even a car-boot sale** – suggests the small details of everyday life that are often overlooked. Your dream may be urging you to pay attention to these.

If your dream was quite mundane and you saw yourself doing your **weekly grocery shop**, then your dreaming mind may simply have been processing a memory or reminding you that you need to go shopping. Alternatively, such a dream may be suggesting that you are taking good care of your basic emotional needs. If, however, you had a dream in which you **could not decide what to buy**, this may be referring to some kind of confusion or indecision in waking life. If someone you know in your dream **transformed into a sales assistant**, your dreaming mind may have been commenting on the emotional cost of your relationship with them.

Bear in mind, too, that whilst **stores, supermarkets and shopping malls** are places of opportunity and choice, they also threaten potential exclusion and humiliation if you do not possess the necessary funds; your feelings about going on your dream shopping trip should indicate whether or not you are feeling empowered or denied in your waking life. If you dream that a **shop is closed or that you have insufficient money**, this may indicate that you feel the things you want from life are unattainable. Your dream may be telling you to lower your expectations and set more realistic goals. Finally, if your idea of heaven is to go on an **exclusive shopping trip and spend loads of cash in luxury stores**, then a dream of having a day doing just that may be simple wish-fulfillment.

SHOPPING

Shopping often represents the possibilities in life, the decisions you can make, the variety of attitudes or activities from which you can choose, or something for which you are searching. The image of shopping presents a view of your life's prospects and opportunities; it also represents the exchanges you are prepared to make to satisfy your desires. What you are shopping for may be relevant. If you are **shopping for food**, you need sustenance but if you are **shopping for clothes**, you need protection. **How much you buy** in your dream may indicate your ability to take advantage of opportunities.

Not finding the item you want or discovering that the store has sold out of it may express frustration at not getting what you want out of life. A much-reported shopping dream involves the **panic at closing time**. Not being able to buy all you want before the shops close suggests anxiety that life is too short to achieve all your ambitions. **Shop windows** are symbols of opportunities in waking life that may be out of reach. The image may evoke frustration or envy that you are missing out on the good things in life, but it can also remind you that you still have the choice to seek out more accessible and affordable items.

Nature and the Seasons

Dreams that feature images of natural settings relate to those parts of your being that are natural or not molded by conscious ambitions and desires.

In the earliest religions, nature was thought to be alive with a multitude of spirits. The nature spirits were worshipped in order to maintain a harmony with them. Civilization and the advance of technology have inhibited our contact with those elemental energies and spirits. Your dreaming mind may, however, take you on a journey to the realm of nature spirits where you can explore or confront various elements of your unconscious. To go into nature in your dreams is therefore to go into the wilderness of your unconscious where you will encounter primordial instincts. For Freudians, these basic instincts would be sexual, whilst Jung would see natural settings as symbolic of the nurturing but sometimes harsh mother archetype.

Dreams of nature may also reflect your sense of being grounded or connected to Mother Earth. The dream environment may represent your core essence, unaffected by personality traits, your bare nature or something that comes naturally to you and is second nature. Finally, the great outdoors is usually seen as a surrounding that is supposed to bring relaxation and have a calming, nurturing effect on people; your dream may therefore be prompting you to take some time out from your busy routine. *See also* ELEMENTS; FLOWERS; PLACES; TREES; WEATHER.

Natural Features

COUNTRYSIDE

A blissfully peaceful landscape of **meadows, trees and perhaps a brook and birds singing sweetly** may express a wish for the good life for those who live in urban areas. If the **weather turns bad**, this may warn against unrealistic fantasies and expectations. A **view or vista of the countryside from a window suggests** aspirations to a more natural way of life.

Field

When you dream of **green fields**, it serves as a symbol for freedom and happiness. You may also experience a time of growth. It may also mean that you have a love of nature. Dreams of **lush fields with crops ripe for the harvest** suggest ideas and creativity waiting to be explored and utilized. If the **fields or farmland is reduced to stubble**, your dreaming mind may be suggesting that you have reaped the reward of past efforts and it is time to plant new seeds of creativity. **Barren fields** suggest a pessimistic attitude to life's challenges. If the image is of a **tranquil, flower-filled meadow**, then your dreaming mind may be urging you to take some time out. Drawing on Christian symbolism, the image of **grain, wheat or other crops** represents the renewal of life after death.

Forest/Wood

When **forests or woods** appear in your dream, they are representations of life, fertility, as well as a period of rejuvenation. They are also a reference to the season of spring. Sometimes they may refer to an unknown part of your life. You may have to learn to trust your instincts. If you are **taking a walk through a forest**, it may mean that any hardships that you have recently endured will lead to the success that you seek. The darkness and concentration of trees, plants, animals and other creatures in a forest make it a powerful symbol of the unconscious and its instincts. Jung saw dreams of **fear of entering or simply being in a forest** as indicative of the dreamer's anxiety about what might be found within the unconscious. For Freud, dreaming of **entering the forest** is a symbol of the sexual act. If you are **lost within a thick forest**, you may be in need of some direction in your waking life. *See also* PLACES.

Mountain

Major obstacles and challenges within your life are represented by mountains in dreams. If you appear on the **top of the mountain**, it means that you have conquered any obstacles or that you have reached goals that you have set for yourself. The style in which you are climbing the mountain will tell you how well you are dealing with problems, and any difficulties you may encounter on the way, such as **falling rocks, avalanches or cut ropes**, will all possess a significance.

Mountains are also a symbol for spiritual truth. If you are **climbing a mountain** in your dream, it signifies that you are a determined and ambitious person. **Falling off a mountain** in your dream means that you are tempted to give up on things when the going gets tough. According to Freud, the image of a mountain in a dream represents female sexuality, because their profile resembles a woman's breast. A dreamer feeling **anxious about climbing a mountain** in a dream may be expressing sexual anxiety and **standing on top of a mountain** can indicate feelings of domination. For Jung, the **view from mountain tops** symbolizes an overview of your progress and **looking at a peak from below** indicates the vast challenge offered by the process of self-discovery. Because **hills and gentle slopes** lack the challenge of steep rocky or icy mountains, in dreams hills indicate that the task of self-discovery may be easier than you think. *See also* AMBITION AND SUCCESS.

NATURAL GROUND

In dreams, being aware of the **ground you are walking on** in a natural setting suggests a need to ground or earth yourself. It is also a symbol of your true essence and can suggest a need to deal with or face reality, come back down to earth. If you are **walking on clay**, for example, this stresses the importance of resilience on your life's path. The symbolism of **grass** in dreams may come from its green color, which is a symbol of renewal and revitalizing energy. According to Freudians, grass is a symbol of pubic hair. A dream of **lying in the grass** may express a simple desire for relaxation or, like other dreams of **soft grass, sand, moss or water**, a desire to return to the comfort and security of the mother's womb. If you were **cutting grass in your dream**, is there an aspect of your life that needs to be restricted or cut back on? If you were **gathering grass to make hay**, the dream may be urging you to make the most of a situation in waking life and to seize the day. *See also* Garden entry in PLACES.

A mixture of earth and water, **mud** is usually associated with the ground that hinders progress and dirties the feet. In many dreams, feelings are intensified as you try to escape from someone or something but cannot move forward because the mud or clay is pulling you back.

PLANTS

Plants are symbols of the power of nature and, in the words of Jung, are 'regarded with awe and contemplated with philosophical wonderment'. Dreams that feature plants can send powerful messages. Plants embody the life force in dreams and represent the union of earth, water and heaven. Ancient peoples thought that each species of plant had specific qualities and this ancestral lore has produced symbolism and interpretation that is still used in dream analysis today.

Plants, and herbs in particular, have many ancient associations. **Climbing plants and honeysuckle** symbolize ambition; **ground elder** suggests powerful ambition. Although **deadly nightshade** is no longer considered a murder weapon, its association with death is still strong. Is there someone against whom you harbor strong feelings? **Thistles and brambles** are prickly symbols that hint at antagonism on your own part or on the part of others. If you dream of **weeds**, they are a powerful symbol of lies and falsehoods. *See also* FLOWERS; TREES.

RIVER/LAKE

In dreams, **rivers** indicate the eternal change and flow of life, serving as a reminder that change and renewal can be something refreshing, strong and not to be feared. **Streams and brooks** are gentler images of change. A **riverbank** may represent the security of the conscious mind if you go swimming or paddling in the river of the unconscious. If your dream reveals an image of yourself **contemplating on the river bank**, pay attention to how you feel. Are you anxious or feeling confident? If an artificial **embankment or levee** appears in your dream, this may be a sign that you need to build stronger defenses as you are in danger of being submerged by unconscious desires.

The Element Encyclopedia of 20,000 Dreams

Herbs

Many **herbs** have symbolic meanings that go back centuries. For example, the ancient Romans offered wreaths of bay leaves as a symbol of triumph and peace. Earlier, bay was a sacred plant for Greeks and considered to be a protector from disease, witchcraft and lightning. In Britain, rosemary was called 'Rose of Mary' in memory of the Virgin Mary; in Shakespeare's Hamlet, Ophelia says, 'There's rosemary, that's for remembrance, pray you love, remember.' This is by no means a complete list of the symbolic meanings of each herb in your dreams. Bear in mind that the symbolism of herbs is inextricably tied to culture and religion; your personal associations also need to be taken into account.

Aloe: healing, protection, grief, bitterness, affection
Angelica: inspiration, magic
Basil: sweetness, kindness, deep affection
Bay: glory, honor, reward
Calendula: joy, remembrance, grief
Chamomile: energy in adversity, patience, long life, wisdom
Chives: usefulness
Dandelion: faithfulness, happiness

Dill: preservation, good spirits
Dock leaves: used to soothe the irritation caused by nettles, so in dreams they suggest how you should approach a difficult situation in waking life
Fennel: strength, worthy of praise, flattery
Garlic: protection, strength, healing
Lavender: housewifely virtue, acknowledgment
Lily of the Valley: contentment, return of happiness, let's make up
Marjoram: joy, happiness
Mint: eternal refreshment, wisdom, virtue
Mugwort: tranquility, happiness
Mustard: faith, indifference
Parsley: useful knowledge, feast, joy, victory
Rosemary: remembrance, love, loyalty, fidelity
Saffron: beware of success; all is not what it seems
Sage: wisdom, self-esteem
Sassafras: foundation, considered choices
Thyme: activity, bravery, courage, strength

In dreams, **lakes** are symbols of the unconscious. What lurks beneath the water? If you dream of **fishing, swimming or sailing** on the lake, this can suggest contentment; if you are drowning, this suggests anxiety. For Jung, a lake, like the sea and the river, is a symbol of the mother archetype. A dream **pond** can suggest hidden depths. When you see a **swamp** in your dream, it is referring to a part of your life that is dark and hidden, or to something that is holding you back. If you see a **marsh**, this may refer to anxieties that undermine your confidence in waking life. A **spring** is an image of beginnings and, as such, it symbolizes maternity in dreams as well as purity and clear, clean water. According to Freudians, the image can suggest joyful sexuality. Jungians might see dreams springs as an image of the inner life or spiritual beginnings. A **waterfall** unites images of female and male sexuality with the foam of the tumbling waters evocative of the sensations of orgasm. Alternatively, the turbulence of the waterfall can represent powerful changes in your life. *See also* ELEMENTS; PLACES.

TRIBAL PEOPLES

Any dream which contains **tribal peoples** living in harmony with nature is making you aware of how simple the structure of life really is when you strip away whatever is not essential. They are a symbol of the easy expression of your natural feelings and wilder self, rather than your civilized self. **Native culture** is also a structured management of power in that every person is aware of their place and function in life; this aspect may be relevant in dreams about tribal peoples. In the spiritual sense, tribal peoples represent a closeness to nature and the earth – something you need to understand if you are to develop spiritually.

VALLEY

In dreams, a **valley** is a symbol of fertility and abundance as it brings together the elements of earth and water. Another interpretation suggests that a valley represents the journey of self-discovery. If the valley in your dream is a rugged and steep **ravine or gorge** with a river running along the bottom and trees lining its slopes, this can be a metaphor for sexuality and the adventure, dangers and excitement this promises. A **steep canyon** in your dream may represent maternal domination. If you dream of a **cliff**, this may be referring to a newfound awareness, as well as a new attitude.

The Seasons

The words of Ecclesiastes, 'to everything there is a season and a time for every purpose under heaven', echo in many facets of dream-lore. The seasons of the year over the ages have come to represent the natural progression of your life, representing change and renewal, as well as your state of mind. They also relate to the four elements: winter represents earth; spring symbolizes rain or water; summer, heat and fire; and the winds of autumn, air.

The Element Encyclopedia of 20,000 Dreams

Months of the year

When dreaming about a particular month, a dreamer should explore some of the outside influences that could have triggered such a dream choice. Upcoming birthdays, anniversaries, holidays, festivities such as Easter or Christmas or special events could be the cause of dreaming about a particular month, as well as other dates that hold a special significance. But there may also be additional reasons why a certain month may appear in a dream.

January

The name given to the month of **January** is derived from the ancient Roman god Janus who presided over the gate to the New Year. Janus protected the Gate of Heaven and was known as the 'Lord of Beginnings'; he is often symbolized by an image of a face that is simultaneously looking forwards and backwards. This symbolism can easily be associated with the month, as for many the start of a new year suggests out with the old and in with the new. It is the time when many reflect on events of the previous year and make resolutions to redress or improve some aspect of daily life or personal philosophy. As part of the astrological calendar, this is the month of the Zodiac signs of Capricorn (22 December–19 January) and Aquarius (20 January–18 February) and shares their symbolic associations.

February

A dream centered on the month of **February** could signify testing situations that will demand all of your resources, as well as self-discipline and possibly even health concerns. The name 'February' is believed to have been derived from the name 'Februa', taken from the Roman 'Festival of Purification'. The root 'februo' means 'I purify by sacrifice.' **Valentine's Day** dreams stand for the celebration of those you care about and may occur if you are not expressing your feelings sufficiently. This is the month of the Zodiac signs of Aquarius (20 January–18 February) and Pisces (19 February–20 March) and shares their symbolic associations.

March

Mars was the Roman god of war, and fertility was the inspiration for the name 'March', so dreams in which **March** is the focus may concern conflict or the need to initiate plans or steps towards a desired goal. It is the month of the Zodiac signs of Pisces (19 February–20 March) and Aries (21 March–19 April) and shares their symbolic associations. March is a time of spirituality and the influence of the feminine aspects of nature within all faiths. At the same time, the Zodiac sign of Aries brings the power of the masculine, the sun, the seed, and also the determination and strength to succeed.

April

This is the month of the Zodiac signs of Aries (21 March–19 April) and Taurus (20 April–20 May) and shares their symbolic associations. Dreams featuring the month of **April** may suggest happiness, pleasure and the need to begin working towards your desired goal in life. To dream of **April Fool's Day** reveals something foolish done by yourself or someone you know. Images of **Easter** signify triumph over problems in your waking life. **Easter baskets, eggs and bunnies** signify optimism and hope for a positive outcome to events.

May

This is the month of the Zodiac signs of Taurus (20 April–20 May) and Gemini (21 May–21 June) and shares their symbolic associations. Dreams featuring the month of **May** tend to signify prosperity, as well as upcoming waves of rejoicing or pleasure and happiness.

June

According to the Celtic calendar, this is a time associated with natural healing of the body and of the spirit. When a dream focuses on the month of **June**, this suggests a time of positive renewal or the desire to begin afresh in some way. This is the month of Zodiac signs of Gemini (21 May–21 June) and Cancer (22 June–22 July) and shares their symbolic associations.

July

July is most commonly associated with the healing properties and sanctity of water. This may be due to the fact that July is a month of warmth, of the sun, of scorching heat and the dryness of the land that comes with the dreaded drought. This is the month of Zodiac signs of Cancer (22 June–22 July) and Leo (23 July–23 August) and shares their associations. In dreams, it suggests a time for self-examination and reflection.

August

August has historically been considered to be a lucky month and the ideal time to repair mistakes made in the past. This is the month of the Zodiac signs of Leo (23 July–23 August) and Virgo (24 August–22 September) and shares their symbolic associations.

September

This is the month of Zodiac signs of Virgo (24 August–22 September) and Libra (23 September–23 October) and shares their symbolic associations. In dreams, **September** represents a waning period or a winding down.

October

At this time of year, perhaps more than any other, according to the Celtic and pagan calendar, the natural and the supernatural were greatly enhanced, with many rituals taking place such as All Hallow's Eve or Hallowe'en (31 October) This is the month of the Zodiac signs of Libra (24 September–23 October) and Scorpio (24 October–21 November) and shares their symbolic associations. In dreams, **October** represents a time to unite conflicting aspects within yourself or to reaffirm personal bonds. To dream of **harvest festivals** suggests the fruits of shared gifts and the inner joy when you reach out to help others.

November

This is the month of the Zodiac signs of Scorpio (24 October–21 November) and Sagittarius (22 November–21 December) and shares their symbolic associations. In dreams, **November** suggests a time to count your blessings, discard the negative and appreciate the positive elements in your life.

December

In Celtic traditions, **December** was a time to keep light alive in the darkness, to maintain the burning fires and was a time for families to reunite as the light began to return following the winter solstice. This is the month of the Zodiac signs of Sagittarius (22 November–21 December) and Capricorn (22 December–19 January) and shares their symbolic associations. In dreams, this month stands for a period or rest, renewal and reflection. Images of Christmas in dreams, including **Christmas cards, lights, gifts, trees, ornaments, puddings and stockings**, stand for a major spiritual awakening and growth, or the sharing of spiritual gifts and joy. *See also* Zodiac signs entry in MIND, BODY, SPIRIT; TIME.

Autumn

Dreams dealing with the **autumn** mean that a series of ups and downs may be experienced, but the transformations that are felt may be crucial to your personal growth. This time may represent a maturing of your ideas. It is also a time when one cycle ends and trees bear fruit, so it may suggest the fruition of a plan. Autumn may also symbolize middle age. Bear in mind too that Keats's 'season of mists and mellow fruitfulness' conjures up images of poetry even in dreams. If you dream of autumn your dreaming mind is urging you to reap what you sow and appreciate your blessings.

Spring

Dreaming of the **spring season** means that new beginnings are in the future. It is a symbol of optimism and rebirth, and may represent new ways of thinking or behaving, or a new project. It is also a symbol of youth, childhood innocence and first love. However, because spring is the first of the seasons, it may also be warning against enthusiastic optimism, leading you into making unnecessary mistakes.

Summer

A dream of the **summer** season signifies growth, emotional fulfillment and maturity, as well as relaxation and vacations. It is also a symbol of adulthood. To dream of **summer appearing unseasonably early** warns you to guard against relying on luck when you know that hard work and dedication are the ingredients for success.

Winter

For those living in the Northern hemisphere, a dream involving the winter season signifies a time of rest and contemplation but your dream may also be suggesting that your life is barren and empty. It may also symbolize old age or a time during which you need to look back on your life and try to learn from both your mistakes and your successes. If this is your favorite time of the year, the dream may hint to an upcoming holiday vacation.

NEGATIVE EMOTIONS

It is important to note that the feelings you experience in dreams are not symbols of something else but are reflections of your real feelings.

The emotion may be symbolically represented or experienced in the dream or later on in the form of the emotions you experience after awakening. Most dream analysts believe that the emotional atmosphere and feeling of a dream are important clues for its interpretation. This is because when a symbol or dream scenario arouses a particular emotion, your dreaming mind is suggesting to you that this is an emotion that you need to either suppress or, more typically, release in waking life. According to Jung, dreams are a wonderful way of identifying repressed emotions and feelings, and, by so doing, they can encourage emotional and spiritual wholeness and healing.

Negative emotions, such as fear, anger and sadness, tend to occur more often in dreams than pleasant emotions. Fear and anxiety are the most commonly expressed emotions in dreams. Anger ranks next. As the language of dreams is symbolic, you might have trouble identifying what triggered your negative dream in some cases. If this is the case, consulting CHANGE AND CONFLICT, DISASTERS, NIGHTMARES, LOSS AND FRUSTRATION, SPIRITS AND GHOSTS and STAGES OF LIFE or other dream entries that inspire negative emotions or situations may help. *See also* POSITIVE EMOTIONS.

Negative Energies

ANGER

In a dream scenario, anger may express the tension between your conscious and unconscious urges. The aggressor in the dream will often represent the part of you that is demanding to be acknowledged. Freud spoke of an aggressive drive which he believed revealed itself in all walks of life and in all types of people. He believed that the aggressive drive was just as much present in sex as in war. Alfred Adler (1870–1937), an early disciple of Freud, believed that anger was the most fundamental force of the psyche and, if repressed, it could express itself in dream images of anger and aggression. Whatever may be the trigger, anger is one of the most common emotions to express itself in dreams, either by physical violence or by using symbols of anger such as weapons. Such dreams are likely to continue until the trigger for your anger is discovered and dealt with.

If a person has recurring dreams in which they are **assaulting, raping or attacking someone**, this suggests deep-rooted sexual problems that they might want to talk over with a doctor. A single dream in which aggression, sexual or otherwise, occurs is not so worrying and is actually quite typical. Such a dream will be expressing negative feelings of anger, hostility, rejection, embarrassment or envy that have probably been repressed in waking life. Dreams of **assassination or murder** have the same interpretation. Dreams in which you are **evicting someone from their home or your home** suggests that there is something in your life you are angry about and of which you desire to be rid. This may be some characteristic within yourself or another person. Dreams that focus on **ambushing** may have the same theme but in this case there may be something about the person or thing being ambushed that you want to possess yourself.

Libel dreams in which you are attacking someone verbally may suggest that you are spreading vicious rumors or someone is spreading them about you. Any dream in which you have a **feud, dispute or attack** suggests either a disagreement with someone in your waking life or inner conflict with an aspect of your character. Dreams in which you are **rebelling against someone or something** have the same interpretation. Pay attention to the

atmosphere of your dream as it may reveal much about your emotional state at present. The dream may also be describing your feelings of being threatened.

Catharsis

Your dreams may often be cathartic vehicles to help you resolve difficult and painful emotions. The basic idea of **catharsis** is to purge or let off steam. It is thought that if a person is angry, letting off steam can help them feel better and reduce the likelihood of aggression. Many films, plays and books contain cathartic scenes in which various characters express intense feelings of rage, anger, guilt or hostility and, by so doing, resolve the key issues in their lives. Catharsis also occurs in dreams; your unconscious conjures up various scenarios in which negative emotions are expressed or acted out. It is urging you to face up to difficult feelings and take action to resolve them in your real life.

BETRAYAL

To dream that you have been **betrayed** represents your suspicions about a particular person, relationship or situation. This dream often occurs when you are having feelings of insecurity and are faced with major commitments in your life at the same time. To dream that you are **confused** may reflect your true confused state of mind.

Isolate the single element in your dream that is confusing to you and analyze its meaning. Alternatively, dreams of confusion may suggest that you are being pulled in opposite directions or do not know which viewpoint is right.

EMBARRASSMENT

To dream that you are **embarrassed** signifies hidden weaknesses and fears that you are not acknowledging in your waking life. You may feel that your self-confidence has been undermined. Such a dream also suggests insecurities about your sexuality. To dream that you are **emotionless** suggests that you are closing yourself off from those around you. You may be neglecting your own feelings and should start paying more attention to them. If you dream of **tearful farewells, partings or frantic escapes** you may be feeling relief, sadness or a mixture of both about leaving something or someone behind in your waking life. Perhaps you have left your job, ended a relationship or moved out of your parent's house. The dream is referring to a phase of your life that is over. If you **escaped from someone or something** in your dream, try to identify what you were escaping from. If the escape was successful, this may suggest that you have resolved emotional problems and made progress.

FEAR

In the majority of cases, dreams that make you feel scared, terrified, anxious or afraid in some way are described as nightmares, but some dreams can express your waking fears or anxieties in symbolic and thought-provoking ways. In some cases they may show you how to confront or face your fears. Dreams in which you are **falling, drowning, being chased, crushed or captured** may occur when you have done something of which you feel ashamed or that you know is wrong; your dream is a form of self-punishment. Other dream researchers believe that such dreams are caused by the suppression of forbidden or hidden instincts. Discussing such dreams with others may help to ease your fears.

Any dream in which you are **attacked or pursued** is also a representation of fear; you should try to identify who or what is attacking or chasing you. Facing your dream demons may help to understand and resolve them in waking life. Dreams in which you are being **attacked or threatened by animals** are sending a clear message that you have suppressed your instincts too much and need to be more natural, or loosen up, in waking life. Dreams in which an **intruder breaks into your house** are extremely common and they also express a fear or concern about a specific person or situation in your waking life. Try to identify the intruder, as this will give you a clue to the interpretation. If you experience **paranoia** in your dream, or have an **irrational fear in your dream of going mad or insane**, this will reflect an uncertain situation in your waking life.

FRUSTRATION

To dream that you feel **frustrated** represents your difficulty in coping with a situation in your daily life. It may reflect your concerns that your life is not going in the direction you want. Be aware of associated feelings of anger when feelings of frustration feature in your dream.

GUILT

Dreams can often remind you of things about which you should or already feel **guilty** in real life; they remind you of mistakes you may have made or offences you have carried out against others or your true self. If you wake from a dream and feel you have **committed a crime and are worried you might be found out**, this suggests you should feel guilty because you are concealing aspects of your true nature and not being true to yourself in waking life. Dreams in which you **commit adultery or bigamy** may be wish-fulfillment but they may also be an expression of guilt, even if you have only thoughts of being unfaithful in waking life. Dreams in which you are **paying alimony** may not refer to divorce but to the fact that you need to pay for some misconduct in waking life. Dreams in which you are a **criminal or have committed a crime** also refer to some misdeed in waking life and, if a **penalty is exacted**, this will be based on your feelings of guilt and how severely you feel you ought to be punished.

So, if you are **sentenced to prison or execution** in your dream or **beaten up** or find yourself actually facing the **hangman, electric chair, lethal injection, firing squad or the guillotine**, this suggests strong feelings of regret. Alternatively, it may also mean that you are going to change your life and make a new start. **Fines** in dreams tends to refer to minor misdemeanors but bear in mind that money in dreams can sometimes be related to emotion; if you are pursued by a **bailiff or debt collector**, for example, this may indicate that you owe something to someone, perhaps affection, in waking life. If you dreamed you were **shoplifting**, your dreaming mind may be reminding you of a minor offence you have committed in waking life but if you are involved in **serious theft** your dreaming mind is warning you that there will be serious consequences for your actions if you are discovered. If you dream that you are **blackmailing someone or they are trying to blackmail you**, consider whether you are trying to force the affection of someone in waking life by threatening to leave them or by bribing them?

If you **appear in court** in your dream, this is another sign of guilt for some action or offence you feel you have committed in waking life. Try to identify who was judging you. If the **judge was a famous person and the press are present or you are lynched by a mob**, you may feel condemned, not by yourself or another person, but by everyone you know. Dreams in which you have an **allergy or a reaction to something you have eaten or put on or worked with** are also expressions of guilt. Dreams in which you are **confessing to a priest or condemned from the pulpit by a preacher** are also symbols of guilt in waking life; they suggest your desire to absolve yourself or rectify a situation. If you dream of being **forgiven**, this will be very comforting.

Dreams in which **someone who has died appears in tears or is hostile to you** may be suggesting that you feel guilty about your behavior towards that person when they were alive. Your dreaming mind has conjured up this image to encourage you to think about that person in waking life and perhaps admit your faults or misdeeds towards them. If your dream leads you into temptation, for example

succumbing to the charms of an irre-sistible stranger if you are in a settled relationship, this may reflect unconscious, hidden desires; it may also be warning you that you will be easily tempted when opportunity presents itself. Finally, bear in mind that when feelings of guilt are experienced in your dream, they may be telling of repressed anger towards you or another person in real life. Dreams of anger may equally be connected to experiences of guilt, so be alert and careful when you try to interpret them. Whatever you feel angry or guilty about in your dream, you may find that the only way to regain your peace of mind is to put things right or make amends or new resolutions in your waking life.

Horror/Panic

If you are **overcome with feelings of panic, fear and horror** in a nightmare dream scenario, try to identify what it was that horrified you. Your dream may be reflecting a phobia you have in waking life; your unconscious is not trying to torture you but is encouraging you to confront that particular fear. If you have a recurring dream of this nature, try to urge your dreaming self not to panic or run away but to face the spiders, ghosts, vampires or whatever fills you with dread. You may find that this puts an end to the dream once and for all. If the cause of your dread is not so clear cut – for example, **you are talking with a friend and suddenly feel anxious** in your dream – your dreaming mind may be telling you that there is something about this person you fear at an unconscious level in waking life. You may feel that your friend is undermining you all the time with silly jokes about your weight or appearance. If,

on the other hand, a **hideous monster is about to devour you** in your dream, this is a clear symbol of something you fear; your dreaming mind is telling you that, unless you deal with your anger, jealously or guilt will consume you.

Hostility

If you are **hurling verbal abuse at someone** in a dream, this may be urging you to put your energy to better use. If **someone is hurling abuse at you**, consider if you are accusing yourself of something in waking life or if you have made someone angry. If **fury is expressed vocally** in your dream, consider what is being said as it may contain a clue to your agitation. If you **use or see weapons** in dreams, these are clear symbols of aggression and heated emotions. The type of weapon featuring in your dream should help you understand what it represents in your waking life. If you know the person who is attacking you, then your dream may reflect genuine hostility between the two of you. If you do not know the person, the dream may represent your lack of control over a situation in your waking life or feelings of insecurity.

Consider also if this person could have been your shadow. Ask yourself what it is about this person that you dislike. Because your unconscious sometimes projects characteristics or qualities that you dislike in yourself onto others, in your dreams your dreaming mind may be sending you a message that you should acknowledge this hidden aspect of yourself and come to terms with it. If you are **threatened or make a threat** in your dream, were you accusing yourself of something? Have you made mistakes or been inconsiderate lately?

Take a note of your attitude in the dream as it could tell you a lot about your attitude towards being intimidated in real life. Do you cringe in fear or stand up for yourself? If a **physical fight or dispute** features in your dream, this may be between different aspects of your character or two different arguments that you need to balance. If there is a clear winner in your dream, you need to think about what message your dreaming mind is sending you about the correct course of action to take.

If **explosions** feature in your dreams, they may be symbols of your feelings of anger and hostility in waking life. On the other hand, the image may also be suggesting that you are bottling up your action and now is the time to express yourself before you lose control in your waking life. If you were **lighting a fuse that triggered an explosion or taking part in a demolition** in your dream, you may want to destroy an aspect of your life. This may refer to a situation you are finding difficult to resolve or negative aspects of your character that you would like to replace with positive qualities. Images of a **bursting dam, an erupting volcano or an avalanche of snow or rocks** may also warn of emotional explosions overwhelming your self-control; they are all a sign that you should express how you feel. More positively, such dreams may point to a release of creative energy. Hidden anger towards someone can also be revealed by **sudden discharges of gas or flames from a container** – a **bottle, box or container** in dreams often represent feelings that are bottled up. Other hate-filled images such as **acid thrown in someone's face, a decapitated loved one or throwing rotten eggs at someone** can reveal that you urgently need to deal with

your pent-up rage. *See also* CHANGE AND CONFLICT.

INSECURITY

There may be areas of your waking life in which you feel insecure or unsure of yourself. You may be aware of some of these areas but in other cases you may be repressing your anxiety. Repressing any emotion is damaging and to grow stronger emotionally you should try to recognize and understand it. Dreams can help you with this process. Dreams in which you **missed a bus or plane or miss an appointment** may be reflecting your fear of being late. They may also be suggesting feelings of uncertainty in your waking life. If **someone makes you late**, that person may be part of the reason for your insecurity. If you are angry with yourself in your dream, you may be angry with yourself about missing opportunities in waking life.

Any dream in which your safety is threatened by **natural disasters, such as floods, storms or earthquakes**, may be a sign of feelings of insecurity in waking life. Scan your dream for any clues as to who or what is dragging you down, killing you or giving you reason to hope. Is there a **lighthouse, lifeboat or coastguard** in sight? Dreams in which you are **abroad and unable to understand the language or culture** are classic symbols of uncertainty about new situations in your waking life, as are dreams in which you are constantly **outbid in an auction**. Try to identify what you were bidding for as it might help you understand what is worrying or bothering you. Dreams in which you **consult a therapist, psychiatrist, psychologist, counselor or fortune teller** are telling you

Phobias/fears

Phobias and fears in dreams tend to signify feelings of inadequacy, uncertainty and lack of self-confidence in waking life. Every person will have their own unique fears but the list below contains the dream meanings of some common fears:

Accidents: Inability to focus on the here and now

Aging: Lack of appreciation for the natural stages of life

Alcohol: Doubts regarding your self-control

Aloneness: Low self-esteem and the need for others to validate you

Amnesia: Insecurity about your identity

Animals: Basic instincts that are threatening to spill over into your waking life

Ants: Inability to cooperate with others

Bacteria: fear of being affected by others

Baldness: fear of losing the ability to think clearly

Beards: Suspicion over what someone is hiding

Bedtime: Fear of dying before certain goals are accomplished

Beggars: Fear of appearing helpless or difficult feelings when faced with another person's neediness

Birds: Fear of freedom or success

Black/dark: Fear of what you do not understand

Blindness: Dread of losing your perceptive skills

Blood: Dread of losing your inner strength

Blushing: Fear of embarrassment

Body odor: Dread of offending others

Books: Fear of the opinions or criticism of others

Brain disease: Fear of losing your reason

Buildings, high: Fear of being forced into a situation in which you feel you have no control

Bullets: Fear of loss of self-control

Burglars: Sense of vulnerability

Buried alive: Fear that a pending plan will not have a chance to prove itself

Cancer: Fear of negativity, poor health

Cats: Fear of loss of independence

Childbirth: Fear of change or new beginnings

Children: Fear of the child within

Clocks: Fear of falling behind in your schedule or commitments

Clowns: Fear of letting your guard down

Coitus/sex: Fear of getting close to another person

Cold: Fear of becoming lazy or apathetic

Color: Fear of standing out

Computers: Fear of learning new things

Confined spaces: Fear of getting into situations in which you feel trapped

Constipation: Feeling unable to express yourself

Cooking: Aversion to planning things

Cross: Fear of being reminded of sacrifices you need to make or have made

Dancing: Dislike of showing emotion

Daylight: Fear of exposure

Death/corpses: Refusal to accept reality

Decisions: Fear of taking responsibility

Demon/goblin: Fear of life's negatives

Dentists: Fear of someone changing your mind

Disease: Fear of problems

Doctor: Aversion to the opinions of others

Dolls: Tendency to look at the motives of others with suspicion

Electricity: Dislike of control from anyone but yourself

Empty rooms: Suggests lack of vision

Fat/gaining weight: Fear of loss of self-control

Fire: Fear of emotional outbursts

Fish: Revulsion towards anything associated with religion or spiritual growth

Floods: Fear of being emotionally overwhelmed

Flowers: Denial of your talents

Flying: Fear of expressing your opinions

Food: Fear of nourishing an aspect of yourself

Gay/lesbian: Fear of human diversity or traits different to yourself

Ghosts: Fear of your past returning to haunt you

Gold: Inability to handle money

Hallowe'en: Dread of discovering hidden aspects of another person's character

Heat: This suggests procrastination and the avoidance of challenge

Heights: Reluctance to advance due to fear of failure

Hell: Fear of depression

Horses: Fear of others seeing your own wild nature

Hospitals: Fear of change

Houses: Fears about personal security

Hurricanes/tornados: Aversion to fanaticism

Injections: Fear of the new and different invading your personal space

Insanity: Fear of losing grip on reality

Insects: Inability to deal with life's irritations

Jumping: Fear of becoming impatient

Lightning/thunder: Reluctance to experience new insights

Machinery: desire to avoid assistance

Medicine: Lack of trust

Men: Distrust of men or problems accepting masculine traits within yourself

Mice: Worry over something invading or upsetting your routine

Mirrors: Apprehension over facing yourself or knowing yourself

Money: Avoidance of responsibility

Myths: Fear of hearing the truth about a situation

Night: This implies someone with an overactive imagination

Noise: Someone who is easily distracted

Old people: Fear of aging or mortality

Open spaces: Fear of exposure

Opposite sex: Being out of touch with your opposite gender characteristics

Outer space: Feeling helpless and weightless

Pain: Fear of being hurt in waking life

Performing: Panic about being watched or judged

Plant: Fear of not using your natural talents and not measuring up to expectations

Railways/trains: Fear of not being able to change direction

Relatives: Fear of others knowing things about you

Reptiles: Fear of what you do not understand

Ridicule: Fear of being criticized

School: Fear of the inability to reach your potential

Shadows: Suspicions about all sorts of things

Snakes: Fear of what you do not understand

Speaking aloud: Fear of being criticized for speaking your mind

Speed: The need to take things slower

Spiders: Fear of being manipulated by others

Stairs: Fear of moving forward

Stuttering: Fear of not being able to express yourself

Swallowing: Fear of being gullible

Technology: Distrust over advancements

Telephones: Aversion to communication without being able to read the other's body language

Tests: Trepidation about your ability or competence; fear of failure

Tombstones: Fear of facing your mortality

Ugliness: Inability to face reality

Walking: Fear of being independent

Wind: Fear of showing emotion

Women: Fear of not being accepted by others or inability to accept feminine traits within yourself.

that you are not feeling as in control of a particular situation in your waking life as you feel you ought to. You may also feel unsure about who to turn to for advice.

Jealousy/Envy

To dream that you are **jealous of another's fortune** signifies your own misfortune and difficulties in climbing the social ladder. To dream that you are **jealous of another person** signifies that such feelings may be carried over from your waking life; something about this person makes you feel inadequate. Try to identify what exactly you are jealous of and ask yourself whether this is a quality you should nurture within yourself. If you dream that **someone is jealous of you**, your dreaming mind may be telling you that this person harbors hostile feelings against you.

Rejection

To dream that you are **rejecting something** indicates that there are feelings, ideas, people or situations in your waking life with which you feel you cannot cope or want to be rid of. Your dream may be suggesting that there is a great deal of clutter in your life that you need to reject or dispose of; this clutter can be old habits, worn-out opinions, or old objects and clothes. Does your self-image or your wardrobe – or both – need a makeover? Alternatively, you may be refusing to accept a situation that is being imposed and forced upon you.

To dream that **you are being rejected** signifies a lack of self-belief. If you dreamed of **your partner leaving you**, this reflects feelings of insecurity about the strength and consistency of their affection for you in real life. If **you do the leaving**, however, your unconscious is alerting you to negative emotions that person arouses in you. It may be, however, that your dreaming self rejected your shadow; a quality within yourself you dislike. If you dream of **losing a treasured object, item of jewelry or even a pet or childhood toy you value highly**, it may be a warning that someone or something in your waking life is draining you. This may be something within yourself – perhaps your possessive nature – but it may also be referring to your talents, and whether or not you are making enough use of them. *See also* LOSS AND FRUSTRATION.

Sadness

If you feel **sad, melancholy, morose or depressed** in your dream or **wake up with feelings of sadness**, your unconscious has used your dream as an outlet through which to release feelings of despair and sadness. Shedding dream tears may be a cathartic experience if you have buried feelings of grief or sadness, and do not wish to put yourself through the pain of dealing with them. If, however, you find yourself **repeatedly unhappy or grief-stricken** in your dreams, your unconscious may be expressing the onset of depression; such dreams are likely to continue unless you seek professional help.

NIGHTMARES

Nightmares draw your attention to the many hidden fears that may be preventing you from moving forward.

In general, nightmares are those dreams that are painful, unpleasant and frightening. Dream analysts have reported two kinds of nightmares: those in which you wake up with a general sense of fear but you can't recall what it was that scared you – this is often called a night terror – and those which involve you waking up from a vivid dream at its most frightening or threatening part. Technically, the former is not a nightmare, whilst the latter is.

Many people in the nineteenth century still blamed nightmares on indigestion and it was only with the publication of Freud's ideas that they became seen as the expression of unfulfilled wishes and sexual anxiety. Jung described them as part of humankind's 'collective unconscious' and said the helplessness we feel in nightmares is a memory of the fears experienced by primitive peoples. Today, most dream interpreters believe these disturbing dreams are sent to warn the conscious mind that something is being blocked or ignored. Rather than putting the nightmare out of your mind because it was such an unpleasant experience, it is important to make efforts to interpret and confront the nightmare imagery in order to identify the waking cause.

The hallmark of a nightmare is that it is frightening. It is often long, detailed and amongst the easiest of dreams to remember. Nightmares often occur when hidden feelings of guilt, self-doubt, anxiety, anger, worry and insecurity are pushed out of your waking thoughts and repressed. In typical nightmares, you may feel as if you are being buried alive, suffocated, drowned or chased by a murderer. Dreams from which you awake with feelings of intense distress or anxiety usually occur towards the end of a night's sleep. There is no common element and everyone has their own type of nightmare, probably produced by our own hidden fears. Many psychologists – some of them trained in the Freudian and Jungian traditions – believe that nightmares, like all dreams, carry a host of coded meaning within them, and that they are the psyche's way of alerting us that something is wrong or unresolved in our waking lives.

From this perspective, nightmares are seen as arising from our deepest fears, frustrations and repressions. They are, however, an opportunity for you to discover which part of yourself is threatening to destroy your own happiness. If you do have a nightmare, try to find out what exactly it is that you fear so much that you have tried to push it away into your unconscious. The stage of your dreaming mind offers you a safe place to enact and work through challenging or scary ideas or situations. When you have a nightmare, your unconscious world is sending you a loud message that you have no choice but to wake up. Examining the content of your nightmares will usually give you clues to the troubling issues or events that you are not ready to face consciously.

When you wake up from a nightmare, take a few moments to orient yourself to the reality that, no matter how frightening the events of the dream, they are not real and cannot harm you. Try to remember as many details as you can, because nightmares are windows into the worries and fears that plague your mind; as a consequence, you don't want to dismiss them out of hand. One way to help you figure out what your nightmare means is to try and continue the story when you are awake. This gives you a chance to rewrite the dream plot from the point of view of the menacing character or object in your dream. According to ancient dream-lore, if you can overcome what is frightening you in your dream, you can overcome the things that frighten you in waking life. *See also* DISASTERS; NEGATIVE EMOTIONS; SPIRITS AND GHOSTS; STAGES OF LIFE; SURREALISM AND FANTASY.

It's a Nightmare!

BEING CHASED OR HUNTED DOWN

The most common type of nightmare or bad dream is the one in which you are being **chased or hunted down by something or someone**. According to Jung, being chased or stalked as prey is a primal memory of your human collective unconscious and may refer to early times in the history of humankind when it was common to be chased, often to the death, by an animal. If **you are being chased** in your dream it is important to think about who or what was chasing you, and then ask yourself whether there is anyone or anything in your life that reminds you of your pursuer.

DESTRUCTION/LOSS OF CONTROL

Dreams of **your own death or the death of a loved one** do not mean that you or someone you love are going to die; they do, however, require you to take stock of your health and the way you manage your life. Many dream experts believe that dreaming of your own death can signify a rebirth, the shedding of the old and a new beginning. In many cases, these dreams represent being involved in painful relationships or unhealthy habits or situations that have a destructive effect on you. Dreams of actually **killing or murdering someone or being killed or murdered yourself** in a dream are not very common, but if you do experience such dreams they may indicate deep and unresolved emotional and psycho-

The history and science of nightmares

In ancient times, **nightmares** were thought to be caused by evil spirits. The word, in fact, derives from a Scandinavian legend in which a 'nacht-mara' – the 'mara' being a female demon – came and sat on the sleeper's chest at night, leaving him with a heavy, suffocating sensation of being awake but paralyzed. Nightmares have been known to inspire great artists: John Henry Fuseli's 1781 painting 'The Nightmare' caused a sensation with its depiction of an incubus crouching on the body of a sleeping woman. John Newton – a slave trader and the composer of the hymn 'Amazing Grace' – became an abolitionist after a nightmare in which he saw 'all of Europe consumed in a great raging fire' whilst he was the captain of a slave ship. Robert Louis Stevenson's *Dr Jekyll and Mr Hyde* was inspired, in part, by a nightmare. Elias Howe, who invented the sewing machine, came up with the breakthrough concept of a needle with a hole at the pointed end after he had a nightmare in which jungle warriors brandished spears that had holes in their blades.

As we have seen, both Freud and Jung had theories regarding nightmares: Freud tried to explain them as the expression of unfulfilled wishes, whilst Jung described them as part of humankind's 'collective unconscious' and argued that the helplessness we feel in nightmares is a memory of the fears experienced by primitive peoples. Today, in medical textbooks, nightmares are most commonly defined as a disturbing dream that results in at least a partial awakening.

Nightmares, in common with most dreams, occur during REM stages of sleep and they generally cause the dreamer to wake up. If you don't wake up, the dream is not technically a nightmare and could be described as a bad dream. Nightmares are often characterized by the following symptoms: a sense of fear and dread that lingers for hours or days after the dream upon awakening; the ability to recall all or part of a dream scene; in most cases the dreamer is threatened or actually harmed in some way; a recognition of powerful images in the dream or the repetition of the dream itself for months or even years after; and a physical paralysis or lack of muscle tone called atonia which signifies REM sleep.

Drugs, alcohol, lack of sleep and spicy food can alter the quality and quantity of REM sleep and perhaps trigger nightmares but there is no hard evidence to support this. Whilst these things can increase the risk of nightmares, the mundane struggles in daily life are generally thought to be the cause of most nightmares. Sleep researchers have discovered that long-standing nightmare sufferers tend to be emotional, creative, sensitive but prone to depression.

Modern sleep researchers have identified the following causes for nightmares:

- Unconscious memory of intense emotions such as that of a child being abandoned by its mother. Many people have had the experience of feeling trapped in a difficult situation – a terrible marriage or another situation they want to get out of – and nightmares can hark back to that situation, mirroring the intense feelings of being trapped associated with it.
- Intense experiences produced by external situations, such as involvement in war or being a victim of assault. Trauma, surgery, a death in the family, crime and accidents can also cause them to proliferate.
- Many nightmares in adults arise from fears connected with repressed internal drives or from fears concerning the process of growth and change.
- Threats to self-esteem. People may be faced by or fear the loss of something important to them, such as the failure of a relationship or the loss of a child, being seen to fail at work or not being able to cope with life in other ways. Nightmares may arise out of feelings of inferiority or loss of self-confidence.
- Some sleep researchers consider the occasional nightmare to be a natural response to stress; the dream is seen to be the body's way of practicing its 'fight or flee' response, providing us with a way to work through aggressive feelings in a safe way, given that the body's muscles are essentially paralyzed during REM sleep.

logical conflicts that are interfering with your emotional and psychological health in waking life. There is a part of you that feels dead or out of control or there is a part of your life that you wish would disappear. Such dreams of murder or killing can also express violent and powerful rage. What is making you feel so angry in waking life?

Dreams that present you with undisguised imagery – **the roof falling in on you, or your car stalling on a motorway** – may be warning signals to pay greater attention to the care and maintenance of yourself and the things around you. Other common images in nightmares and bad dreams include: **menacing strangers, clifftops, dark woods, alleys, forests, heights and depths, land or sea storms, earthquakes, tidal waves, terrorist attacks, outbreaks of disease, friends or family who suddenly become cruel, dangerous, old or ugly, guns, knives and other weapons threatening you, car or plane crashes and being lost**. All these scary images leave you with a sense that your place in the world is uncertain or shifting. You are out of control in a big way and your sense of self is eroding. Dreams in which your whole world is rocked or changed are clear symbols of fear, anxiety and a crisis in confidence. Dreams in which you **sink slowly but inevitably into**

The Element Encyclopedia of 20,000 Dreams

quicksand or are swallowed by an angry lion usually represent feelings of being overwhelmed in waking life. Dreams in which you are **drowning** have a similar interpretation. *See also* STAGES OF LIFE.

MONSTER

If you dream of being **hunted by a savage and terrible monster** of any kind, you might want to try and face it if the dream recurs. Mystery is not so terrifying once it is identified and understood, since it becomes something you can recognize and therefore deal with. If you do recognize your personal monster, you might also want to try and engage it in a dialogue. A classic way to interpret a difficult dream such as this was devised by Dr Frederick Perls, the distinguished Gestalt therapist. Take two chairs and place them opposite each other. You sit in one and imagine your dream monster or enemy in the other chair. Move between the chairs as you first ask and answer the questions. Try asking your dream monster what it wants, why it is in your dreams and why it is chasing you. The process may take some time, but eventually you (as the dream) may deliver a message that speaks to you. When that happens, you may find it easier to face your fears and interpret your dream. By understanding nasty nightmare animals, as well as people, places or things, you may be able to harness their energy and take back into your self those parts of your personality you have been trying to disown.

Animals in dreams reflect the animal or instinctual part of your nature, so if the **fierce animal terrorizing you** in a dream is a tiger, lion or snake, consider what this animal represents to you and what it says about your psychological state. Are you confining, restricting or subduing an important part of yourself? If you begin to get answers to these questions, you may find that the animals in your dreams become less fierce and threatening. It might also help to draw or write a description of your animal. Of course, your personal associations to the specific animals is of great importance here.

If your **shadow** – the part of yourself that you keep hidden – appears in your dreams as a **monster, fierce animal, murderer, vampire, werewolf, ghost or other sinister threatening being**, this may be a positive thing; it is your dreaming mind's way of reintroducing the parts of yourself you are repressing in an effort to make you whole. *See also* ANIMALS; SPIRITS AND GHOSTS; SURREALISM AND FANTASY.

PARALYSIS

One of the most terrifying and anxiety forms of nightmare is the one that involves some kind of **paralysis** where you cannot move. Dreams of being paralyzed are in fact a part of REM sleep, during which the majority of us are unable to move. A person tossing and turning in their sleep is not having a nightmare. The simplest interpretation of a dream in which you are paralyzed is that you are unable to move forward and feel pinned down or paralyzed in some aspect of your life. The dream may also be an expression of some kind of conflict; you may be unable to choose between two possible courses of action or be caught in a situation that restricts you.

Night terrors

Night terrors are not nightmares. In fact they are not even dreams. Also known as sleep terrors, night terrors occur during non-REM sleep, not during REM sleep when the majority of us dream. They typically occur within the first few hours of going to sleep. The person may wake up for about twenty seconds and in most cases settle back to sleep. There is typically an increase in heart rate, blood pressure and respiration. There will also be a classic physiological response to fear, with dilated pupils, confusion or panic and sweat. Subjects may scream or yell during an episode and flail their arms and legs around or sit upright in bed. In adults, alcohol, stress, fever or lack of sleep may trigger night terrors and they are believed to have their basis in a purely biological function.

If the terror wakes the sleeper up, they may recall a single image of terror but if they fall back to sleep there is unlikely to be any recall of the feeling. If you or someone you know experiences more than three or four episodes of night terror a month, then you or they might be suffering from an anxiety disorder. It is important to consult a doctor if this is the case. Night terrors tend to be most common in children between the ages of three and eight, and most sleep experts urge parents and carers not to rush to their child to try and wake and comfort them as this can intensify or aggravate the night terror. You should instead let the night terror run its course and the child will rarely recall the event in the morning. There is not much evidence that night terrors reflect deep psychological problems and occasional night terrors are considered quite normal in young children. *See also* Sleep paralysis, and Incubus and succubus entries in SPIRITS AND GHOSTS.

POST-TRAUMATIC STRESS NIGHTMARE

If you have experienced a traumatic event, for example an attack, accident or disaster, such as an earthquake, you may find that your dreaming mind recalls the horror of that event but as time passes the nightmares tend to become less intense. In general, they have little meaning other than your memory of it and are an attempt by your dreaming mind to help you deal with the original horror. **Post-traumatic stress nightmares** are usually different from other nightmares as the content of the dream will closely resemble a traumatic event that happened in their waking lives.

POWs from World War II and concentration camp survivors have been known to suffer post-traumatic stress nightmares for up to fifty years after the event. Unlike 'normal' nightmares, these dreamers can experience significant physical symptoms during REM sleep and non-REM sleep, such as an increase in respiration and heart rate, muscle twitches and more than one arousal. Adults might experience other traumatic events in their lives, such as the loss of a loved one or bankruptcy, and these events can also continue to play out in dreams over the years in the form of nightmares. The more standard anxiety nightmare dreamers, however, have nightmares that relate to work, school or relationship stresses. The threat here isn't to your life but to your self-confidence and sense of self.

PUNISHMENT

Your dreaming mind may from time to time inflict **punishment** on you for thoughts and actions of which your waking self disapproves. In most cases, the dream symbols will be disproportionate to the 'crime'. For example, if you have spoken thoughtlessly about a friend, you may find yourself being **executed** as you have murdered your friend's good name. Your dreams may also reflect your belief that someone else deserves to be punished and the criminal being caught in your dream may be someone else, not you.

An **angry mob** can suggest aspects of your own personality, as well as public opinion. If you dream of being **lynched**, ask yourself whether you have been behaving appropriately in waking life. Whatever the instrument of punishment or torture in your dreams, be it the **gallows, cane, guillotine, gibbet or birch**, you need to identify who is being punished and why they are being punished. Bear in mind, too, that the

inflicting of punishment, especially if it is a **beating**, may reflect a tendency towards masochism. Those dream interpreters that draw on Jung's theory that nightmares are concerned with the shadow consider scary dreams to be a form of self-punishment for the cravings and desires you suppress during the day.

If you dream that you are **back at school and forced to stay after a lesson in detention** because you have not worked or listened properly, this may suggest that you are not absorbing information or paying significant attention to something important in your waking life. The ultimate image of punishment in dreams is **hell**, so if you dream of being **condemned to hell, suffering eternal torment or are damned forever**, this may be a reference to a mistake you have made in waking life, or something you have said or done and the force with which you are rebuking or warning yourself.

RECURRING NIGHTMARE

Nightmares often depict issues that threaten your emotional safety and well-being and you may find yourself dreaming of the same event, person, situation or setting over and over and over again. One theory holds that **dreams with recurring themes** may coincide with life stages or are an underlying response to the psychological stresses of events such as divorce or the loss of a loved one. Women tend to report recurring dreams more than men. For example, the thing young children fear the most is abandonment, as without the love and protection of their parents or carers they would die. Later, as they begin to crawl, then walk, then run, they fear bodily harm. Some dream analysts believe that these two issues – fear of bodily harm and abandonment – recur again and again in a person's life. A forty-year-old woman who discovers her husband has had an affair may, for example, dream of an **earthquake and her inability to find a place of safety**. This relates to fears of being abandoned.

Recurring nightmare dreams may be an indication that the dreaming mind is trying to present troublesome emotions or situations to a conscious mind that is somehow stuck in a habitual feeling state or response. The dream is encouraging the dreamer to find ways of resolving the trauma or difficulty underlying the dream.

VIOLENCE

Are you the bloody victim or the violent murderer in your dream? If **you are the perpetrator of violence, crime, arguments or disruption** in your dream, you need to identify which part of yourself or someone you know it is that you are angry at or want to kill off. If **you are the victim of the anger or violence of someone else** in your dream, this may suggest feelings of guilt about thoughts or actions you have had or made in waking life. If your dreams are often violent, disturbing and consistently terrifying to the degree that they are damaging the quality of your waking life, you should consider seeing a therapist to talk about them.

The Element Encyclopedia of 20,000 Dreams

NUMBERS

When numbers feature significantly in your dream they can either have a personal or a symbolic association.

Should numbers appear in your dreams, first make a note of any personal associations you may have with that particular number, as it may have relevance in your waking world. For example, numbers can represent your age, the number of your house, the number of your children and their birth order. They can also represent time, days, weeks, years and lucky or unlucky numbers.

Your mind may often retain the significance of a number even if you do not consciously remember it yourself. Your memory is a database that stores all kinds of numbers of personal significance: pin numbers, post codes, license plate numbers, as well as dates of birthdays and anniversaries, be they personal or of global significance such as 6/6/1944 (D-Day) or 9/11/2001. So when you dream of a number, consider any connections you have with it as its significance in dreamland may not be immediately clear. By bringing a specific number to your attention, your dreaming mind may have been prompting your conscious mind to remember something that happened on that particular date

or in the house you lived in that had that particular number; it might, however, have been reminding you to call a friend with that phone number or to remember an appointment on that day.

If you cannot figure out any personal associations, the next step is to see whether you can see symbolic meanings for individual numbers. If your number has more than one digit, reduce it to single numbers: e.g. $451 = 4 + 5 + 1 = 10 = 1$, or $1965 = 1 + 9 + 6 + 5 = 21 = 2 + 1 = 3$, and see whether the single number carries any meaning for you according to the symbolic interpretations given in this chapter.

Numbers have some kind of symbolic significance within all cultures, religions and belief systems of the world. Since humans could first count, numbers have had a fascinating, mysterious and even mystical significance. Early man found in numbers realizations of inner qualities, spiritual understanding, unconscious wisdom and even magic. For Freud, numbers reveal their meaning through each individual dreamer's free association. In myth, legend and fairy tale numbers play an important role and these ancient associations – which Jung called 'root symbols' – are expressed in dreams. According to Jung, numbers therefore represent 'archetypal energies of the collective unconscious' and the various stages of spiritual growth.

Alternatively, the order in which numbers are given in your dream may be significant in terms of helping you to prioritize events or projects in your life. Dream numbers may also suggest time running out, as in 'your days are numbered' or the need for you to make a calculated move. Alternatively numbers in dreams may refer simply to multiplicity or size, as in a crowd of events, a big experience, or some kind of realization that has many facets or involves many people.

Also worth noting is the idea that odd numbers are considered to be aggressive, 'masculine' active powers, whilst even numbers are considered to be more 'feminine,' tranquil and passive. *See also* LETTERS AND COMMUNICATION; MIND, BODY, SPIRIT; SHAPES; TIME.

The Number Directory

ZERO

In dreams, **zero** denotes timelessness, super-consciousness, eternity and absolute freedom. It also symbolizes spirituality. Because it is linked in shape with seeds and eggs, it also suggests potential yet to be realized. If zero appears to the right of other numbers, it multiplies them by ten and therefore indicates abundance or infinite potential and possibilities. Alternatively, a zero is without value or substance on its own and may be a symbol of desolation and loneliness. The more mystic interpretation suggests that zero is a symbol of the unconscious, the feminine and the great mother archetype. In Tarot, zero is the unnumbered card, the Fool, which is also a symbol of the unconscious mind. Its associated shape is the circle or the mandala.

ONE

One stands for individuality, solitude, the ego, leadership, single-mindedness, resolve, originality and being a winner. This number suggests a need for action and is imbued with masculine virility and determination. It also suggests uniformity that is imposed at the expense of individuality, as well as stubbornness and conceit. One can also represent the beginning of something and creative potential, partly because it is the first number of others that follow and partly because it can also symbolize an erect phallus, pointing to sexual desire. In addition it may refer to yourself, as in 'one is not amused', or to the number-one person in your life or unity. Was your dreaming mind urging you to look out for number one with this dream image? In Tarot, one is the number of the Juggler or Magician and is a symbol of the conscious mind or will. Its associated shape is a point.

TWO

Two stands for diversity, partnership, soul and receptivity. It can also symbolize double weakness or double strength, and

Fractions

Quarter: Possible interpretations include: showing mercy or pity to a defeated opponent, giving quarter to them; dividing something into any number of smaller units, quartering it; accommodation, abode, living quarters; something that is in close proximity or being engaged in combat, close quarters.

Half: A half of a circle in your dream may represent being diametrically opposed to something. If the image of half features strongly, it may also indicate lack of thoroughness, doing things by halves or something carried out to an excessive degree e.g. being too clever by half. Another interpretation suggests something that is incomplete, imperfect, having vague intention, not being fully committed to something or having half a mind to do it. Sharing expenses or 'going halves' is another possible interpretation. It may also symbolize the number two, as a third might symbolize the number three, fourth four, fifth five, sixth six and so on.

two sides to an argument. Two represents duality, as in male and female, mother and father, yin and yang, heaven and earth. Two is the number of dialogue rather than monologue, and it suggests harmony and interaction between the unconscious and conscious mind. On the other hand, two can also suggest division and separation, ambiguity of meaning (being in two minds), or ambivalence or indecision over some issue or person. The number of the Tarot's High Priestess, the card of feminine intuition and insight is associated with the number two.

THREE

Considered by the ancient Greeks to be the perfect number, **three** represents the union of mind, body and spirit and for Christians it is a symbol of Father, Son and Holy Ghost. Three signifies life, freedom, vitality, inner strength, completion, imagination, creativity, energy and self-exploration. Three stands for trilogy, as in the past, present, and future or father, mother, and child. For Freud, three is a symbol of the male genitals. It can also indicate impatience, overconfidence and relationship troubles, as in 'three is a crowd'. Its shape is the triangle, which is a symbol of the creative force. Three is the number of the Empress Tarot card, which represents the feminine principles of fertility and nurture.

FOUR

Four denotes stability, physical limitations, inadaptability, hard labor and earthly things, as in the four corners of the earth. It also stands for materialistic matters, practicality, responsibility and the importance of getting things done. It is thought to encompass the essence of the material world – the four points of the compass, the four seasons, the four elements, the four members of the nuclear family; father, mother, son and daughter – and therefore also implies strength, stability, order, harmony and wholeness. For Jungians, four can represent personal growth, as it represents Jung's 'quaternity' of thoughts (conscious and unconscious), feelings, senses and intuitions. It is the number of the Emperor in the Tarot deck, a symbol of masculine strength and resolve – and its associated shape is the square.

FIVE

Five represents your persuasiveness, a daring or bold nature, action or the five human senses. This number may reflect changes in direction, irresponsibility, rashness, unreliability and inconsistency. **Five** is a symbol of the human species: the five senses, five fingers, five toes and the five points of your body in harmony with the cosmos – feet on the ground, arms stretched to the skies, head communicating to the heavens. It therefore represents striving to transcend earthly limitations to establish a link between heaven and earth. The number five is also associated with the Tarot Pope, the card that denotes spiritual wisdom. Its shape or symbol is the five-pointed pentagram.

SIX

Six is a symbol of cooperation, balance, tranquility, perfection, warmth and love. Through its amplification of the number three, it is also a symbol of creation and choice, and the number of psychic intuition, your sixth sense. It may also represent a struggle between good and evil or the spiritual and the material as symbolized by the six-pointed star in alchemy, which is composed of two opposed triangles, one pointing to heaven and the other to hell. Its

associated Tarot card is the Lovers, which symbolizes choice.

SEVEN

This is the number of mental perfection, healing, completion, music and the attainment of high spirituality. **Seven** is a sacred number for many peoples, being the number of the rhythm of life (the world was created in seven days) and the passing of time (seven days in a week). Life is also said to run in seven-year cycles in the West; adulthood is traditionally celebrated on the twenty-first birthday and in Judaism a boy adopts adult responsibilities at the age of fourteen. Numerologists believe that seven is a number that possesses cosmic energy because it was once believed that there were seven planets in the cosmos. In dreams, the number seven could also suggest the possibility of the seven-year itch, the urge to be unfaithful or make a hasty decision. As the number of the Chariot in Tarot, seven can symbolize drive that is controlled and directed.

EIGHT

Eight stands for power of authority, success, karma, material gains, regeneration and wealth. Eight is a multiple of four and has a similar significance of wholeness; but eight, when it is placed on its side by mathematicians, also symbolizes infinity – apart from zero, eight is the only Arabic number to have no beginning and no end. When the number eight appears in your dream, trust your instincts and intuition. In Tarot, eight is the symbol of Justice, symbolizing impartial wisdom. The Chinese believe that eight is very lucky and

The Element Encyclopedia of 20,000 Dreams

Numerology

Numerology is the age-old study of numbers according to numerical principles established by the ancient Greek philosopher and mathematician Pythagoras, the Kabala (ancient mystical tradition of Judaism) and Tarot. It attributes a number to each letter so that both words and numbers can be studied for their mystical meaning. In numerological divination, all numbers are reduced to a number between 1 and 9 and each number is also associated with each letter of the alphabet. Any number larger than 9 can be reduced to a single number by adding all the digits together; for example, the number 821 becomes 8 + 2 + 1 = 11; then 1 + 1 = 2. The qualities of 821 are equivalent to the symbolic number 2. Using the single digit as a guide, the patterns of different dates and a person's name can then be analyzed to define character and to predict the future. Holy books such as the Bible are packed with numerological references. When the numerological equivalents of a person's name and birth date are added together, the numbers obtained are thought to tell a great deal about a person's character, skills and destiny. Dreams often use principles of numerology in the same way and the art of numerology is sometimes applied to dreams for divinatory purposes.

In numerology all numbers correspond to the letters of the alphabet as follows:

1 = A, J, S
2 = B, K, T
3 = C, L, U
4 = D, M, V
5 = E, N, W
6 = F, O, X
7 = G, P, Y
8 = H, Q, Z
9 = I, R

The human qualities associated with each number are:

1 Independent, creative, ambitious, extrovert, innovator
Downside: Can be selfish and have tunnel vision

2 Sensitive, domestic, imaginative, musical, attractive
Downside: can be timid and gullible

3 Scientific, powerful, seeker of knowledge, multitalented, communicator
Downside: Can be superficial and hedonistic

4 Practical, stable, dependable, honest, trustworthy, homemaker
Downside: Can be stubborn and overly serious

5 Energetic, sensual, daring, experienced
Downside: Can find it hard to commit

6 Perfection seeker, creative, compassionate, calm
Downside: Can be super-sensitive and overemotional

7 Intellectual, philosophical, imaginative (psychic)
   Downside: Can be impractical, secretive and unapproachable
8 Materially successful, just, trustful, businesslike
   Downside: Can be opinionated, impatient and intolerant
9 Spiritual, humanitarian, healer, free
   Downside: Can be self-serving, possessive and volatile.

Numerologists believe no number is better or worse than another. All the numbers have incredible power potential as well as a downside. The downside simply suggests challenges associated with a particular number and if these challenges are faced and overcome, they can be a source of incredible strength. *See also* LETTERS AND COMMUNICATION.

can bring food fortune. It can represent regeneration and new beginnings.

NINE

As it is the last sign digit, **nine** can suggest reconciliation, completion and the accomplishment of a creative task. As three times three, it has a sacred wholeness as the number of total perfection and balance. In the West, nine is considered to be the number of eternity; in India, it is the number of God and Yogi who will leave the wheel of birth and death. In dreams, the number nine suggests the end of one cycle and the beginning of another but it can also suggest lack of concentration. Pregnancy is usually of nine-months' duration, so your dreaming mind may be suggesting a preoccupation with birth and babies. Nine is the number of the Hermit card in the Tarot pack and as such can suggest solitude and introspection.

TEN

Ten corresponds to closure, great strength, and gains. In the Jewish and Christian traditions, ten is the symbol of law, the Ten Commandments governing human relations between each other and with God. As the sum of 1, 2, 3 and 4, ten is considered a perfect number, integrating creation, movement, humanity and stability. Ten is associated with the Tarot Wheel of Fortune, a card that suggests change and opportunity.

DOUBLE DIGITS

In Tarot and in dreams, the significance of numbers does not stop at ten. In most cases, the number can be reduced to a single digit number as described above, but certain numbers have additional associations. **Eleven** is associated with the power of the intellect and the Tarot card Strength. It stands for intuition, mastery in a particular domain, spirituality, enlightenment and

The Element Encyclopedia of 20,000 Dreams

capacity to achieve. Eleven is also traditionally a symbol of transgression, as it goes beyond the law, represented by ten. St Augustine called eleven 'the coat of arms of sin'. Eleven can also suggest anxieties about a deadline, as in 'the eleventh hour'.

Twelve has a spiritual significance because of the Jesus' twelve disciples and in dreams it may represent a revelation of truth. There are also twelve months in a year, so the number twelve in a dream may be urging you to enjoy your success and prepare for the future. Twelve is the number of the Hangman, a Tarot card symbolizing the sacrifice of ego, or new outlooks and perspectives.

Thirteen is traditionally an unlucky number and it may cause anxiety if you are superstitious. But it is also a symbol of optimism, completeness and new hope. For Mexicans, thirteen is a lucky number since their Pre-Colombian ancestors worshipped thirteen gods and thirteen heavenly bodies. Thirteen is the number of the Death card in a Tarot reading and it represents transition and rebirth. In dreams, thirteen is a paradoxical number meaning death and birth, end and beginning, and change and transition. It is symbolic of obstacles standing in your way that you must overcome to achieve your goals.

Fourteen is associated with the Tarot card Temperance, representing balance, harmony and equilibrium; it signifies the unexpected and your need to adapt to ever-changing circumstances. It is also symbolic of over-indulgence and giving in to your desires. **Fifteen** is the number of the Devil, a Tarot card symbolizing the need to resist temptation or break free from restrictions. The number **sixteen** is linked to the Tower, a Tarot card that suggests a struggle for

freedom; it also symbolizes innocence, vulnerability, tenderness, destruction of the old and the birth of the new. **Seventeen** represents the Star, or renewed hope, in a Tarot deck; **eighteen** is the number of the Moon in the Tarot deck, which warns against illusion and confusion; it also warns against treachery, deception and lies; **nineteen** denotes the Sun, a symbol of success and happiness in the Tarot deck; it indicates independence and the overcoming of personal struggles. You will find that you often have to stand up for yourself.

Twenty is associated with Judgment; a Tarot card of assessment and new beginnings and **twenty-one** represents the World, in a Tarot deck, a symbol of unity. According to numerologists the number **Twenty-one** represents a turning point in your life. It is also associated with the responsibilities to which you need to own up. **Twenty-two** denotes mental powers and knowledge. It also indicates that you are goal-oriented and practical. The number **twenty-four** symbolizes rewards, happiness, love, money, success and creativity. **Twenty-six** symbolizes the earth, and the law of cause and effect. **Thirty-three** is a symbol of personal and spiritual growth. The number **thirty-nine** symbolizes understanding and thoughtfulness. **Forty** denotes a period of cleansing, preparation and growth. **Forty-four** refers to a sacred union or divine marriage. **Fifty** stands for all that is sacred in your life. **Sixty** is associated with time. It may refer to time running out or longevity.

Generally, rather than sending an archetypal or symbolic message, **double digits** in your dreams may also have been referring to your age, or the passing of time or times in your life from which you can draw inspiration or from which you are reluctant to depart.

MASTER NUMBER

There are three double digit numbers that require special emphasis. These are the numbers **eleven, twenty-two and thirty-three**. They are called master numbers because they are thought to possess huge potential. Eleven is the most intuitive of all the numbers and it suggests powerful illumination. Twenty-two suggests the realization of your goals. Thirty-three is a powerful symbol of personal wisdom and understanding.

MINUS NUMBER

If **negative or minus numbers** appear in your dream, they are not necessarily negative symbols. In some instances they may contain a message to look back to a past time or situation and evaluate it more objectively. Perhaps you need to take a few steps back from a situation or to revisit things, as glitches may still need to be sorted out. On the other hand, negative numbers may reveal a sense of negativity and could be a wake-up call for you to start thinking more positively.

TRIPLE DIGITS

The larger the number in your dream, the greater amount of yourself may be involved; big numbers represent things that are impressive or mean a lot to you. A **hundred** is a symbol of completion, a full century and a more powerful representation of those qualities associated with the number 10. **666**, the number of the Beast, is mentioned in the Book of Revelations in the New Testament. In some interpretations of Christian eschatology, the 'Beast' is believed to refer to an entity controlled by the Antichrist and the number is even today considered unlucky or a sign of evil by some people. In the Jewish tradition, however, the number 666 is considered a mystical and holy number and is considered to be God's number. It also refers to creation, since the world was created in six days. If the number **9/11** appears in your dream, your unconscious may have been using these numbers to draw a parallel with the shock and devastation you felt on that terrible day of death and destruction, and your similar reaction to the events currently rocking your world.

If the number **thousand** appears in your dream, it may be associated with the Millennium and the coming of the Messiah, or it may signify some other form of spiritual awakening. It is also a symbol of vastness and the immortality of love. Once you start dreaming of **millions, billions or even larger numbers**, these numbers are so vast they take you beyond the personal. They are also associated with riches of some sort, not necessarily financial.

PEOPLE

From a Jungian perspective, people in dreams reflect the dreamer's inner life, sometimes showing the various parts of the dreamer's personality.

Many people assume that when they 'see' another person in their dreams, that the dream was meant for that person. This is rarely the case. People in your dreams can appear as themselves, particularly if they are people you know or have known; your dreaming mind may introduce them to highlight a specific quality or character you need to be aware of in them. Many dream analysts, however, believe that the majority of people seen in dreams are a subjective representative rather than an objective one. Each type of person throws some light on some aspect of *your* life – be it your relationships, your hopes and fears, or aspects of your personality that you need to learn to control or cultivate.

Whenever you encounter another person in your dream, ask yourself these two questions: what is a single word that describes my current opinion of the person, and what is the person doing in the dream that I am doing in real-life? The person is chosen in the dream for their symbolic representation. We all come to associate certain people with certain actions or characteristics. If they are known to you,

consider what the dream is saying about that person as a reflection of a part of you. There may also be emotional considerations that arise through your dreaming mind's choice of that particular person. For these, ask more questions: are there parts of that person that I admire, that I envy, of which I am jealous? What is it that I feel for the person in the dream? In many cases, the feelings that your interaction with people in your dreams gives you will be those that you are becoming aware of in real life.

People in dreams are most typically connected to hidden or repressed aspects of your character. They can raise issues that you would rather forget. If you can listen to your dream characters, they may be able to help you deal with conflict or confusion in your waking life and help you achieve balance. Whatever the case, in order to achieve an understanding of the people in your dreams it is important to consider the atmosphere, the role that each character played, the feelings that you experienced in your dream and your waking associations with these people. In short, if people figure in your dreams ask yourself what these people say about the hidden aspects of yourself. Try to work out what or whom each person in your dream makes you think of. In that way you will be able to discover the deeper meanings and associations.

Many of the people in your dreams will remind you of family members, partners, loved ones or yourself at various stages of your life; if this is the case, refer to the relevant entries in the BIRTH AND CHILDHOOD, FAMILY, STAGES OF LIFE and RELATIONSHIPS chapters. If your dream images are of famous people or people from other countries, refer to the FAMOUS PEOPLE and FOREIGN COUNTRIES chapters. For more information about professional people at work in dreams, refer to the SCHOOL AND WORK chapter. Bear in mind that your dreaming mind may also weave aspects of yourself into dream archetypes, such as the stranger, the hero, the fool, the hermit and the wise man or woman, who are all trying to convey a certain message to you. If this is the case, turn to the chapter on ARCHETYPES. For occasions or situations when people group or gather together, see GATHERINGS. Finally, according to ancient dream-lore, as long as the people you meet in your dreams are friendly and well presented, good fortune can be expected.

The People of your Dreams

AUTHORITY FIGURE

Most of us typically rebel against authority at some time in our lives but when **authority figures** appear in your dreams as themselves or as archetypal figures, they command our attention and respect, and remind us to behave responsibly. Your concept of authority is most likely to have developed through your relationship with your parents in early life and depending on how you were treated by them, your view of authority will either be of an inspirational helper or a judgmental disciplinarian. In dreams, authority figures will therefore appear for several reasons. One reason may be to act as a voice of conscience, rebuking you for wrong thoughts or actions, and attempting to lead you back to what is expected of you. Another may be to advise or help you decide on the best course of action. A third is to remind you of your duty to be fair and kind to yourself and to others.

BEGGAR

In dreams, **beggars** are symbols of low self-esteem as they depend on others for support. They may also represent a form of self-abasement and can remind you of the vanity of material concerns. **Beggars, hobos and vagrants** may also send a caution that you need to change some aspect of your life or you too might end up with nothing. In most cases, this nothing will not refer to material concerns but rather to emotional loneliness or to the fact that you have starved a part of your personality into destitution. The clue may lie in the identity of the beggar in your dream. If the **beggar is someone you know**, have you been denying that person affection? If, however, the **beggar is unknown**, then perhaps you have been neglected your essential need for stimulation or affection in waking life.

Tramps share a similar symbolism to beggars but also represent a desire for freedom from routine; **gypsies** are a more powerful representation of this yearning for change, travel, adventure and a change of routine. The appearance of a dream **gypsy fortune teller** may suggest unexplored creativity.

COMPOSITE CHARACTER

In a similar way to composite animals, **composite people** in dreams will emphasize and draw your attention to particular characteristics and qualities within you. Human beings are many-faceted creatures and such a dream may be suggesting that a better understanding of a situation can be obtained by putting yourself in the position of someone else or seeing things from their point of view.

FRIEND

If a **friend** appears in your dream, pay attention to how they behave. If they **communicate with you in a familiar way**, your dream may simply be reflecting the important part your friend plays in your life. If, however, your **friend acts out of** **character or oddly**, your unconscious may be warning you about an aspect of their character that makes you feel uneasy. On the other hand, your dream may be warning you that it is you rather than your friend that the dream is depicting, as the dreaming mind tends to project aspects of yourself onto people you are close to in waking life in order to make you aware of aspects of your personality that are being neglected or suppressed. If you have a dream in which a **friend suddenly turns on you or even tries to kill you**, this image may have been sent to tell you that this particular friend is not all that they seem to be in real life.

MAN

The appearance of a **man** in dreams can identify the shadow for a man and the animus, or masculine aspects, within a woman's personality. A **white-haired older man who seems holy** can be a symbol of your inner wisdom or represent the father archetype in dreams. If a **large man** appears it suggests that your beliefs have more strength and certainty than you realize. A **woman dreaming of a man** suggests the more logical side of her nature. If you **know the man in your dream**, then you may be trying to work out the nature of your relationship with him. If, however, you **do not know the man**, then the image represents the masculine part of your personality that you do not recognize. If the **man is handsome**, he represents action, conviction and assertiveness and other heroic archetype qualities.

Dream authority figures

Father figure

For some people it was the **father** who was the ultimate arbiter of discipline and authority when growing up and any appearance of your father in your dreams may remind you of punishments he may have dished out in the past. If the father figure was absent when you were growing up or your father never punished you severely or unfairly, your unconscious may summon up a father archetype to bring to your attention immature attitudes that are holding you back.

Your **older brother, uncle or boss** may assume the dream role of the archetypal father, a benevolent provider and protector who uses his authority fairly and wisely; in dreams, such figures may appear to dispense invaluable advice. Bear in mind, though, that the father figure can also abuse his authority and if **father figures appear as brutes** in your dreams, they may have been pointing to your own brutishness and selfishness. If you had an authoritarian father, a well-known dictator such as **Hitler, Stalin or Chairman Mao** may appear in your dreams representing that relationship.

If you dream about your **boss**, this may simply suggest anxieties you have about your work. Dream bosses, however, can also represent aspects of your father and dreams of being fired can recall parental rejection. If you **ask for a raise** in your dream, this expresses a need for more attention and love in waking life, whilst a friendly boss reveals a longing for less responsibility. If **you are the boss** in your dreams, this represents your desire for more dominance in a waking relationship. If you **rebel against your boss** in your dream, this can be a positive sign, as rebelling against parental authority or challenging authority that is dictatorial and unjust is a healthy part of growing up and becoming a self-confident adult.

Houses are often represented as images of the dreamer; so a dream of a **landlord or landlady,** or someone else who actually owns your dream house, may suggest you are not feeling in control of your waking life; or perhaps someone, such as a partner or parent, is being overly dominant.

Head of state

Whether it is a **president, king or queen**, the symbolic role of the head of state is to act as the father or mother of the nation and your unconscious may therefore summon such an image into your dream to represent the **mother or father archetype** to guide you or alert you to disruptive or dictatorial behavior within yourself. If you dream of being **knighted, praised or singled out** in some way by a visiting head of state, this may suggest that you feel unappreciated by those around you in your waking life. Alternatively, depending on the context of the dream and your relationship with your parents or boss in waking life, a dream head of state may also represent your relationship with your actual parent or boss.

The Law

Dreams of being **tried or sentenced by a judge or law court** express feelings of guilt about something you have thought, said or done in waking life. But if you **feel you are innocent and your dream portrays you as guilty**, this represents your waking sense of indignation that you have been a victim of injustice or feel that you have been judged unfairly. If, however, you **played the part of the judge** in your dream, pay attention to who was on trial and what they were on trial for. Try to see if there are any parallels with your waking life. If you were part of a **jury** in your dream, you may feel that you are part of a collective judgment in waking life or that you have joined in with others in judging someone else.

If you were **locked in a cell by a jailer you recognize**, consider whether or not that person is restricting your freedom in waking life. If the **jailer is unknown**, what part of yourself are you locking away? If **you are a jailer or prison officer**, who did you arrest and who did they represent? If the person was unknown, could you be acting as your own jailer and restricting your personal growth with fears and inhibitions? If, in your dream, **you are playing a game and the umpire or referee makes what you feel is an unfair decision**, this may concern someone who has authority over you in real life whom you feel is not treating you fairly. If, however, **you are the umpire or the referee and are struggling to impose your authority**, this may mirror your struggle in waking life to keep peace between warring aspects within yourself, or a group of people with whom you are living or working.

Uniformed and professional authorities

Uniforms are symbols of depersonalized authority in dreams, so if your dream featured images such as **soldiers in uniform or policemen on duty and you were the only one not wearing a uniform**, this may reflect your waking sense that you are falling out of line in some way or have deviated from what is expected from you. Did you try to fit in or did you assert your individuality and non-conformist nature?

If members of various **professional bodies** appeared in your dream, such as **doctors, dentists or pilots**, try to make a link with the profession they represent and the relevant area of your waking life, as your unconscious may be offering you inspirational or helpful advice. When the main point of interest in your dream is the occupation or profession, there is typically a good reason why your unconscious has highlighted that particular job. For example, members of the caring professions in dreams, such as **nurses, nuns, charity or voluntary workers**, may suggest a more compassionate side to your nature, or the side of yourself that has a vocation in life. In men, these images may suggest the importance of non-sexual relationships. For more information about specific occupations and people at work, *see* SCHOOL AND WORK.

Old people

Dreams of **old people** may refer to your parents or to life experience. They can of course reflect your feelings about aging, and how you are dealing with it. Old people in dreams also signify traditions and wisdom from the past – those things which are sacred to you or to your family. In some cases, older people may represent your parents, even though the dream figures may have no relation to them.

People from your past

Images of **people from your past** not your present can link you with that period in your life, as well as with specific memories and experiences. A **first boyfriend** in a dream, for example, would represent all the emotions and struggles you had in that relationship and what you took away from it in terms of life experience. Dreaming often of people you knew in the past would therefore suggest that past experiences or lessons are very active at the moment, or that you are reviewing those areas of your life. If you dreamed of a **reunion with someone from the past**, this suggests that you are looking back to the past too much and should be looking ahead to the future. To dream of **dead people** is a testament to the influence those people still have in your life; they may be dead, but they possess an influence on you. They may also represent your feelings about death. *See also* SPIRITS AND GHOSTS.

Silent witness/Mirror image

Unable or unwilling to speak, a **silent witness** in your dreams represents an area in your life in which you are not expressing yourself. According to Jung, favoring the intellect over your emotions or vice versa can make you speechless and unable to communicate fully and openly with other people. The only way to create intimacy in your life is to find a better balance. In dreams, **twins or mirror images of a figure** often represent two aspects of your personality. If they are **not identical**, they suggest conflict between your inner and your outer realities. If they are **identical**, they are a sign of inner harmony.

Stranger

Your dreaming mind may often conjure up images of **strangers, unknown people or people whose faces are hidden by masks** as representations of the shadow, private and sometimes shocking side of your personality. This is especially the case if the **strangers are inadequate or sinister in some way, or if they are burglars, intruders or criminals**. If such images appear, it is important not to ignore them as you need to acknowledge these dream figures as reflections of an aspect of yourself in order to face up to your fears. If you do not do so, you will continually come up against feelings of insecurity and low self-esteem in waking life. The stranger in a dream represents that part of yourself that you do not know. There may be feelings of conflict or tension but you need to deal with these dark images before you can progress in waking life. Jung referred to the shadow as the dark side of a person that you would like to keep hidden – 'the thing a person has no wish to be'. The shadow can be thought of as an instinctive and primitive side of your personality that you are trying to repress.

Dream strangers therefore generally represent aspects of your character that you either haven't consciously acknowledged or that you have neglected. This is why they appear unfamiliar or strange in your dream. How these strangers look and behave will give you an important clue to the nature of the problem area. If a **sinister figure** does appear in your dream, try not to avoid confronting it. Notice how it tries to control the action in your dream. Observe what negative aspects of yourself it may be addressing and try to address them in your waking life. Self-destructive urges are less likely to overwhelm you if you are prepared to confront them.

If dream strangers represent aspects of your personality any **spacemen, aliens or extraterrestrials** in your dream usually indicate that you are feeling threatened by alien forces or situations. Starting a dialogue with them should help you understand them better and allay your fears of the unknown. The same applies if a **foreigner** appears in your dream speaking an unfamiliar language.

WOMAN

In a **woman's dream a woman such as a family member or friend** often represents aspects of her personality that she needs to understand and nurture in waking life. In a **man's dream such a figure** represents his relationship with his own feelings and his intuitive side. It may also show how he relates to women in his life. A **goddess or holy woman** suggests the potential for compassion. **Oriental women** signify the mysterious side of the feminine, whilst an **older woman** represents the dreamer's mother or a sense of inherited wisdom. A **beautiful but unknown woman** will represent the anima in a man's dream, said by Jung to personify instinct, emotion and the capacity for love; she will represent the shadow in a woman's dream. Dressed in black, dream **widows** may represent your feelings about death, but in Freudian dream interpretation the widow, like the **hag or the crone**, suggests the loss of male energy in life and, in a man's dream, may represent unconscious fears of castration.

PETS

Animals in dreams typically represent your most basic and natural feelings and drives.

These may be anger, the need to survive, parental urges, sex or procreation, desire for recognition in the social group, maternal or paternal love, home building and spontaneous feelings of affection.

Animals represent these drives free of social convention and expectations. Dream pets also represent your basic nature but, because they are domesticated and integrated into home and social life, they carry a slightly different interpretation. They particularly indicate the desire to be loved or petted, and they are most often associated with feelings of responsibility or caring.

Your dream will indicate whether you have indeed cared for and 'house-trained' these feelings, or whether they have been caged and aren't being cared for. The action in the dream will suggest what you are doing with this aspect of your nature. According to Jung, if images of starving, out of control, violent or destructive pets and animals appear in your dreams, this indicates that you have become estranged from your instincts and closed the door to your inner nature. It may also reflect your feelings about becoming pet-like and whether or not you have become overly dependent on the demands or attentions of someone else in your waking life. *See also* ANIMALS; BIRDS; REPTILES, FISH AND AMPHIBIANS; INSECTS AND ARACHNIDS.

Dream Pets

BIRD

Freud thought that the **bird** represented the phallus and that flying represented the sexual act. Although in many countries the word 'bird' means a girl or woman, in Italy it means the male organ. In ancient myths, birds denote freedom, spiritual knowledge or wisdom gained from experience, but many dream analysts believe dream birds represent your imagination and the aspect of your mind that can travel far and wide, even if this is only in dreams.

When a **pet bird** appears in your dream, there are plenty of ways to interpret its visit. If the **bird is chirping or flying**, then it may symbolize feelings of happiness, love, joy or harmony. Sometimes it means that a weight will soon be lifted off your shoulders or that you will experience spiritual freedom in the near future. On the other hand, if the **bird is starving, injured or dying**, this may symbolize feelings of restriction and loneliness in waking life. If, in your dream, the **pet bird is caged or you are trying to put the bird in the cage**, this represents feelings of being restricted in some way, being trapped in a relationship or holding back love or affection; if there are good feelings about the caged bird, this may suggest a need to withhold or withdraw love or freedom. If you **set a bird free or a bird escapes** in your dreams, this indicates feelings of spiritual, emotional or physical freedom.

Pay attention to the **species of pet bird** in your dream too, as this may hold a clue to the interpretation. For example, **cockatiels, lovebirds, Senegals, red bellies, African grays and pionus parrots** generally have a reputation for being quiet birds and their appearance in dreams may suggest a period or introspection and reflection. **Cockatoos**, on the other hand, have one of the worst reputations for screaming, largely because they require quite a bit of attention and amusement or they clamor for it loudly. Is there an aspect of your personality that is screaming out for more attention? **Parrots** are born copycats, so is your dreaming mind urging you to be more original or to follow someone else's example? In dreams, such birds suggest that you are repeating without judgment what others have told you. Are you accepting or copying someone or something in your life without a proper process

of evaluation? Alternatively, dream parrots may also symbolize verbosity or the need to express yourself in some way. **Parakeets or budgies** can represent a lack of analytical thought or spiritual thinking, whilst **finches** are a sign of emotional maturity or the need for it. Dreaming of **canaries** suggests singing and may therefore refer to a joyful emotion. On the other hand, it may reflect your anxieties about being the focus of gossip.

To dream of **doves** reflects a peaceful nature or condition. The dove is not a pet that often features in dreams, in fact it rarely appears in the dreaming panorama at all, being quite different from pets like cats, dogs and horses that rouse strong emotions. Therefore, if a dove does appear in your dreams, your dreaming mind has conjured up a rare symbol to send you a rare message. In mythology, the dove is the bird with the sweet song that accompanies Venus; it is the symbol of a sweet creature, of a delicate strength. In dreams, pet **doves that stay with you not because they have to but because they want to** are symbols of a sentiment of deep tenderness, of the sharing of a magic moment that involves the lovers, their soul and their bodies. The dove holds in itself the sweetness of love and the elevation of the spirit, the above and the below, earth and sky. Similar in some ways to the dove is the **lovebird**; this bird is a symbol of companionship or an appreciation of other people in your life.

Bear in mind too that pet birds are messy creatures; the amount of cleaning they require is the biggest complaint heard from bird owners who are having second thoughts about their pets. If you are **cleaning up the cage of a pet bird** in your dream, this may suggest that you have perhaps taken on more responsibility than you can manage in the care of someone else or in some aspect of your life.

CAT

To see a **cat** in your dream signifies an independent spirit; they also suggest feminine sexuality, creativity and power, as well as the enigmatic, mysterious and wise part of yourself. Bear in mind, though, when interpreting your dream that your real-life reaction to cats is crucial. If you are a woman who likes cats and one appears in your dream, this may be a manifestation of one of the positive aspects of the female principle: the mother, high priestess or Amazon archetype. If you are a man, it may have been guiding your anima towards an appreciation of the feminine part of your personality. Your dream may also have been urging you to place more reliance on your instincts when dealing with a current situation.

If, however, you dislike cats or the **cat in your dream is aggressive**, then it suggests that you are having problems relating to the feminine aspect of yourself. The dream cat may have represented the more negative female archetypes of the terrible mother, siren huntress or witch. Or perhaps there is a deceitful woman in your life who is behaving cattily. Alternatively did your dream cat remind you of a pun? Are you feeling smug, like the cat who got the cream or were you being reminded that curiosity killed the cat?

If you see a **cat with no tail** in your dream, this signifies a loss of independence and lack of autonomy. To dream that a **cat is biting or scratching you** symbolizes the devouring female or perhaps you are taking and taking without giving. You may be expressing some fear or frustration, especially if something is not going as planned. Such a dream may also be a warning against treacherous people in your life or it may also represent a part of your personality that is crying out for love and attention. If a **cat is injured or killed** in your dream, your dream may be a reference to the nine lives that cats enjoy. In this regard, your dream refers to the overcoming of numerous obstacles in your waking life; the resilience of the cat represents your own inner strength and tenacity. Generally, cats are symbolic of feminine power and independence, so if one appears in your dream, have you been feeling that these characteristics are not being expressed within yourself?

If you come across a cat in your dream and **spend a great deal of effort trying to locate its owner**, it could be because you are the owner of that 'cat'. The cat is symbolic of a part of your inner self. The characteristics that cats represent can be understood by thinking about their 'essence', or the associations that we make when we think about cats. Cats are territorial animals. They are guardians of their space. They are also aloof and a part of them can never be domesticated. Culturally, there is a sexual connotation in regard to cats. Thus, in your dream you could have found that special part of yourself – the sexy, soft and curious you (the cat within). The trouble is you insist on giving it back to an elusive owner. Your dreaming mind may be urging you to claim what is rightfully yours.

A cat will have several different meanings in your dream according to its color or the color it changes into. So, for example, to see a **black cat** in your dream suggests that you should trust your instincts or intuition more. If you associate black or white cats with bad luck or misfortune, then to dream of them indicates your negative mindset (*see* COLORS). If you dreamed of a **cat in a cage** this may be a reference to your own sense of crippled independence. Kittens represent your inner child, playfulness and self-responsibility, so to dream about a **kitten** may mean that you need to take more time for yourself, have more fun, and nurture yourself and your sense of play more. According to dream-lore from the Middle Ages, it was unlucky to dream about cats because of their association with witchcraft. Prior to that, however, cats were sacred to the Egyptians as custodians of the souls of the dead.

Dog

The **dog** appears more often than any other animal in dreams. It represents your natural drives that, despite usually being well socialized, still have a tendency to revert back to their spontaneous or 'wild' state. This is particularly the case if the dog within is provoked or encouraged. Dogs can also represent those parts of yourself that you express spontaneously: your easy-flowing natural feelings; devotion, perhaps to a lover or child; fidelity and faithfulness. Like the cat, the dog can be a substitute baby for women, or represent an outlet for affection or caring. This is particularly true of dreams about **puppies**, which are a symbol of childlike playfulness or following someone about in a devoted way. In mythology, the dog has symbolized the guardian of the gates of death, or a messenger between the hidden and the visible worlds. The dog was also thought of as a guide or guardian of the hidden side of life.

If a dog appears in your dream, pay attention to whether it was aggressive or friendly. It is also important to consider what your waking feelings about dogs are, as this will have an influence on the interpretation of your dream. If you love dogs and you **enjoyed caring for or playing with your dog** in your dream, then it may be a sign that you are in need of more fun and friendship in your real life. Alternatively, because dogs are traditionally thought to be loyal, dependable, faithful friends and protectors to humans, it may be that your unconscious was highlighting these qualities within yourself or a person you know. Perhaps you are longing to have a friend you can trust and on whom you can depend.

Dogs typically represent friends and companionship in dreams, so if you dreamed of **taking out-of-control dogs for a walk with them all straining on a lead**, perhaps you are finding it hard to fit into your current circle of friends; do you feel that you have little in common with them anymore? If your **dog broke away from you or you dropped its lead** in your dream, do you fear losing the trust or loyalty of your friends? If you are **taking a dog for a walk and were holding the lead**, this suggests that you might be restraining of your aggression towards a friend or someone else; if **someone else is holding the lead**, it may be that you are feeling attacked by someone you know. If a **dog was aggressive** in your dream and you fear dogs in waking life, your unconscious may have been reflecting your waking fear. If, however, you love dogs in real life, such a dream may represent a friend who is about to turn on you in waking life – perhaps they already have.

The **loud barking of a dream dog** can signal the animal within you trying to break free. Perhaps you feel angry about someone or something and are close to exploding with rage; or is your bark worse than your bite? A **dog barking happily** shows that you are enjoying your social life. A **friendly, happy dog** shows that you have lots of good friends. A **dog barking and snarling** warns against enemies and if the dream **dog is big and powerful, as well as friendly**, it shows that you feel in need of a powerful protector. If a **dog bit you** in your dream, could this suggest an ungrateful loved one or relative who is biting the hand that feeds? Since dogs are often associated with masculine energy, if you were **attacked by a dream dog**, such a dream might represent feelings about a man or a relationship with a man. The **black dog** figures quite frequently in people's dream imagery. For some people it represents depression; for others, death.

If a dog appears in your dream you may also want to consider if your dreaming mind is speaking in puns. Do you feel 'sick as a dog' or are you 'in the doghouse', and so on? Although interpretations will vary, bear in mind that in general a dream of dogs usually has positive association.

■ *Idioms: die like a dog; dirty dog; dog-eared; dog eat dog; dog in the manger; gay dog; go to the dogs; let sleeping dogs lie.*

FERRET

Ferrets are lively, playful and easily tamed, but they need a lot of space. They can also inflict severe bites and emit a strong, musky smell. Although ferrets can appear very tame, they are not easy to look after as they often try to escape because, as a pet, they feel confined in the small places that we typically provide for them. To see a ferret in your dream may therefore suggest distrust and suspicion of others. The dream may also be a pun on the idea of 'searching' or 'ferreting around'. Before getting any pet, you should think very hard about whether you can provide everything it needs; this is especially true for ferrets, so if you dream of one, are you giving yourself or someone you know all the care and attention they or you need?

GOLDFISH

These water-dwelling creatures may represent messages from your unconscious, indicating to you how well you are navigating through your emotional waters. They could also symbolize the nourishment of body and soul, and navigation through the unknown depths of ourselves. Generally, **fish in a bowl or aquarium** suggest constricting emotional conditions in which aspects of your personality are prevented from expressing themselves. They may also refer to aspects of yourself that need to be nourished emotionally. To dream of a **goldfish bowl** may simply suggest boredom, or a lack of privacy or confidentiality.

If the fish in your dream are **goldfish**, the symbolism of gold – suggestive of the most valuable aspects of yourself – cannot be ignored. Crucial to your interpretation will be the condition of the fish and your attitude towards them. Are they enjoying their safe and secure life in captivity, or are they suffering? If the latter, is it time for you to be a little more adventurous and creative in your waking life?

The Element Encyclopedia of 20,000 Dreams

Hamster/Gerbil/Guinea pig

Hamsters are lively and clean, and most are happy to live alone. They can take time to become tame, and, because they are nocturnal, they need to have peace and quiet during the day. If a hamster appears in your dream is it **running endlessly on its wheel in frustration**? If this is the case, do you feel as if your life or a particular relationship is going nowhere? If, however, the **hamster seems content**, the dream could depict aspects of your life that give you small comforts. As hamsters tend to enjoy solitude, could your dreaming mind be urging you to rely more on your own resources. **Gerbils and guinea pigs**, on the other hand, need companionship, so in dreams they could be highlighting your need for more friends in real life.

Horse

Along with cats and dogs, the **horse** is one of the most common animal themes in dreams, particularly amongst women. Like dogs, horses are domesticated animals, and so they represent urges and drives in yourself that you have learned to harness or direct. The big difference is that the horse can carry us. **Tame, working or domesticated horses** in dreams therefore suggest energy and the sort of enthusiasm or feelings of well-being that can help to 'carry'

Equestrian issues

Black or dark horse: passions that have not been acknowledged; fear of the unknown or threatening changes.

Blinkered horse: Not allowing yourself to see what is happening around you; anxiety and worries about life.

Controlling the horse, or fear of it: Trying to control your feelings of passion and sexuality. These natural drives can motivate you or drag you along unwillingly.

Dead horse: Serious loss of energy or motivation which could lead to illness or depression; an old and dying set of habits and motivations or way of life.

Falling off horse: A sign that you are relating badly to your basic urges and needs. If you continue to deny these, poor health could be the unwelcome result.

Grooming and caring for a horse: Taking care of your basic needs such as food, shelter and sex.

Horse and carriage: The natural processes of life that carry you from birth to old age; natural forces that can move you forward either from within or as natural events.

Horse dragging the dreamer along: Impetuosity of feelings; feelings dragged along by natural urges.

Horse being playful or affectionate: Feelings of warmth and strength from within.

Horse race: The events of everyday life and your relationship with people; everyday competition and where you rate yourself in the race; what happens in the race shows how you are relating to opportunities or how you feel about your accomplishments.

Horse running freely: Allowing your emotions or sexuality free rein; a symbol of the love of life.

Horse unwilling to move or carry: Your dreaming mind is telling you that you are uncertain about the direction in which you are trying to go.

Mare: Symbol of femininity, receptiveness and fertility.

Newborn horse or pony: Symbol of refreshing energy or new motivations.

Old or worn-out horse: Current state of your feelings. You may be feeling worn out or overworked, or feel that a particular relationship has run its course.

Riding or leading horse easily: A symbol of a good relationship between your personality and your instinctive drives.

Running away from a horse or from charging cavalry: Fear of sexuality, including anxieties towards the responsibilities of parenthood and relationships; you may be avoiding the need to direct or control your feelings and urges.

Sick or dying horse: loss of health, energy and enthusiasm for life.

Stallion: Symbol of masculinity, power and virility.

Strange or unknown horse or horseman/woman: Message from the unconscious; a new opportunity or event.

Struggling to control the horse: Fighting your urges and natural drives. You may be having problems controlling your emotions or sexuality.

Tied-up horse: A symbol of inhibition. Your dreaming mind may be telling you that it is time to release your feelings and give free rein to your creativity.

Training a horse: This suggests that you are learning to direct your sexual and emotional energy.

Uneasy on ride: If this image appears in your dreams you may feel as if you are being taken for a ride or feel that your emotions are taking over your life.

White horse: An image of transformation or meeting with an expanded awareness of ourselves.

Winged horse: Shows how you can rise above your basic needs and urges to discover awareness and fulfillment beyond personal memories and experience.

Working horse: The energy or motivation needed to work. The condition of the horse will tell you how you feel about yourself in relation to your work. Do you feel you are only a workhorse or that you are being treated as such?

you through the day. According to Freud, horses are also symbols of the sexual drive, and the physical energy and life processes that 'carry' us around.

The astrological sign of Sagittarius is depicted by a half man-half horse hybrid, so a dream of horses or horses that are half human may be referring to someone born under that sign. In myths and fairy tales, horses often speak and **talking horses** in dreams may represent the voice of your unconscious – a message from your inner self. In Greek myth, horses were associated with Hades and the underworld but ancient dream-lore suggests that to dream of horses indicates that you will receive news from a distance. To dream of a **horse being shod** is thought to be extremely lucky because of the association with the horseshoe, a well-known symbol of luck. *See also* ANIMALS.

Pet

Pets are an important part of many people's lives and when a **pet from your past or present** features in your dream, your unconscious may be reflecting your feelings about that companion be they affection, regret, comfort or loss. If, however, you **don't have a pet in your waking life and you dream of one**, this may represent someone in your life who is feeling vulnerable and needs your emotional support. Another interpretation for pet dreams is that the animal depicts an aspect of your character. In your waking life you may not be aware of your deep need for affection and attention but this need will show up in your dreams when a pet appears. It is a symbol of your natural drive to give and receive love.

If you **own a pet in your dream**, your unconscious is drawing your attention to

your ability to look after someone or something more vulnerable than yourself. It is also a symbol of unconditional love, and being sensitive to the distress and needs of others. Alternatively, it may also represent an aspect of your character or personality that you feel you should use in a particular situation. If a **woman dreams of baby pets**, this may signify her desire for children; if adults of either sex dream of baby pets, it may be relating to their feelings of dependency and how they feel about not being fully in control. If **children dream about pets**, this may similarly refer to their feelings of being dependent, but will generally represent their desire for unconditional love from their parents or carers. If the **pet you dream about is familiar to you**, the interpretation will very much rest on the nature of your relationship with that particular pet.

Dreams in which you are **caring for your pet or shopping for pet supplies** show that you are paying attention to your emotional needs or making sure you get what you need. But if a **pet appears starving, uncared for and without food or water**, this suggests that you are not taking enough care of your own basic needs for affection and attention. Perhaps you are too busy and have forgotten your needs, or perhaps you are so wrapped up in caring for the needs of someone else that you have neglected your own. To dream that you are **saving the life of your pet** suggests that you are successfully acknowledging certain emotions and characteristics represented by the animal. The dream may also stem from feelings of inadequacy or feeling overwhelmed. Dreams which feature **pet shows or competitions** can suggest pride in your achievements and emotional confidence,

Strange and unusual pet

In general, when dreaming of **strange or unusual pets** that would most typically be found living in the wild, any negative associations with that particular animal, insect or reptile are replaced by positive associations. For example, the general associations with **wild rats** are extremely negative but if you dream of a **pet rat**, the associations are quite different. Pet rats in dreams suggest vulnerability, instinctive intelligence and the caring feelings. In dreams, **wild snakes** conjure up images of worries, fears and poisonous words and deeds; but if you dream of a **pet snake**, this can indicate healing and enlightenment.

Any exotic or unusual pet is like a small part of untamed nature and in dreams they can represent personal growth, untapped creative energies and a sense of new-found respect, wonder, curiosity and excitement about life and the adventures it sends your way. Take the **Madagascar hissing cockroach**, for example, which is kept by some people as a pet. The very name sends a chill up the spine of some people but those people who keep such cockroaches as pets are fascinated at the elaborate rituals these creatures have developed to defend territory, produce offspring or simply to identify themselves. So if a hissing cockroach or any other scary creature-turned-pet such as **a tarantula or Bengal tiger** appears in your dreams and you are happy to care for it, this is a sign that you are conquering your hidden fears. *See also* ANIMALS; INSECTS AND ARACHNIDS; REPTILES, FISH AND AMPHIBIANS.

but they can also suggest the potential for arrogance.

Animals symbolize the untamed and uncivilized aspects of yourself, so to dream that you are **fighting or struggling with your pet** suggests that you are trying to reject or hide your need for affection and companionship in waking life. To dream of **talking pets** suggests that you are listening to some form of superior or mystical knowledge. What the animal is saying to you will usually be some form of wisdom, particularly if the pet is very old, like a **tortoise**. Alternatively, a talking pet denotes your potential to be all that you can be.

RABBIT

Our association of **rabbits** with an ability to breed rapidly means that they are often symbols of sexuality in dreams. Rabbits are also soft and non-aggressive, so they might be depicting you or someone you know who is behaving as a docile victim, or being foolishly idealistic and passive. Alternatively, dreams of pet rabbits may suggest your desire to be petted or cared for; do you have

The Element Encyclopedia of 20,000 Dreams

a need for gentle contact and caring? The rabbit is also a symbol of sacrifice in dreams because it is so often the victim of predators; it may therefore express the hurt you might experience to the soft, vulnerable parts of your nature as you face the hard knocks of reality. If you are **hunting rabbits** in your dream, this suggests that you may be feeling criticized, attacked, 'hunted down' or hounded. It may also indicate a need to dominate others. If you dream of a **rabbit hole**, this is a symbol of self-exploration, of a going within the self into the unconscious; it might also be a symbol of returning to the womb. Are you trying to escape or avoid problems by turning within?

PLACES

Whatever happens in your dream, the landscape or setting in which the action takes place will be extremely significant to the interpretation.

When interpreting your dreamscape, bear in mind that the setting is often a vivid clue about the topic of your dream and a metaphor for a real-life situation you may be dealing with, whether external, such as relationship demands or internal, such as an inner conflict. Jung paid close attention to the details of landscape and setting in his work on dream analysis, looking for clues to the emotional condition of his patients. For example, a sunny scene might indicate optimism and a gray landscape a gloomy view on life. He believed that the purpose of dreamscapes is to mirror feelings and concepts concerning inner development.

In short, landscapes and settings in dreams refer to the feelings you have about yourself and your life, and however meaningful the other symbols in your dream may be, they only really make sense if interpreted within their context. It would be impossible to list all the possible settings here as every dream can have its own unique dreamscape. Listed below are just some of the limitless possibilities that your dreaming mind might conjure up. If you can't find your specific landscape, setting or symbol here, try looking for it under the relevant entry in the index. *See also* BUILDINGS; HOME; NATURE AND THE SEASONS; WEATHER.

Dreamscapes A to Z

ABROAD

Dreams set in **foreign lands** may suggest confusing new situations through which you must find a way. They may also suggest that you need a holiday. Dreaming that you are in the **Arctic or Antarctic** – both very cold and isolated places – may be a comment on your waking life. Dreaming of **warm climates** may be simple wish-fulfillment, but it can also suggest emotional warmth. Dreaming of an **expedition through an unknown land** may refer to the need to explore an idea, project or relationship more thoroughly. Whether or not you are successful as an explorer in your dream will be significant. If you **set up a camp** in your dream travels, this may suggest uncertainty and transience in waking life.

To dream that you are at the **docks** signifies that you are about to make a journey, either to another place or into undiscovered parts of yourself. If you are dreaming that you are in a **busy airport**, it may symbolize a longing for freedom from responsibilities; alternatively, it may mean that you are heading towards a new stage in your life, whether it is a new career goal, new relationship or new journey. If you find yourself at a **deserted airport**, it may represent plans that need to be altered or delayed. *See also* FOREIGN COUNTRIES; TRAVEL.

ALLEY/CORNER/PATH

If you appear in an **alley** within a dream, you may find yourself facing a dilemma in the near future. The image suggests that you may feel you have little choice while an **avenue, street or path** in good condition may indicate support for the direction you wish to take. **Paths** in dreams signify the direction you have decided to take in life; the type of path, and whether it is **smooth, rocky, winding or straight**, may be as important as the path itself. A **rough track** does not have a negative meaning if the journey was interesting and you felt confident in your dream about following it. A path can often represent the way you feel a relationship or situation is developing. It can also suggest a way to follow up a line of inquiry.

To dream that you are in a **corner** or see a corner signifies feelings of frustration and lack of control in making decisions. You may feel trapped and cornered in waking life. To **turn a corner** indicates that you are moving forward in your life, despite the obstacles in your path. You are no longer feeling trapped or restricted, and feel that you can handle the unexpected or new experiences. You have gained a new and positive perspective on life. To be turning a **right-handed corner** indicates a logical course of action, whilst to turn a **left-handed corner** indicates a more intuitive approach to life.

BATTLEFIELD/WAR ZONE

In dreams, **war** always denotes conflict and suggests that you need to be aware of the effect your actions are having on others. Dream **battlefields** can represent areas of conflict in your waking life, for example conflict with your partner or boss. More typically, however, a **war zone** is a picture of an internal battle raging within you. A dream of a **minefield** may be referring to a waking life full of explosive situations and potential danger. Your dream may be reflecting your concern, or urging you to call in an expert and tread with care. If you find yourself in a **trench** in your dream, this may express your fear that a current situation is not as secure as you might think. A trench may also be warning against inflexibility and entrenched views. To see or live in a **concentration camp** in your dream indicates that you are afraid of differences; you are having difficulties accepting others and the way in which they are different from you. Learn to appreciate diversity and the uniqueness in yourself and in others around you. If you actually **lived in a concentration camp**, the dream may signify a situation in your waking life which is triggering similar feelings.

CASINO

Devoted to gambling, **casinos** in dreams suggest making a game of life, in which the chances you take can have a very direct connection with real events. The image can also represent competitiveness and the desire to win at all costs. Being placed in a casino within a dream refers to the risk-taking qualities that you possess. If you are normally a passive person, the dream may be a sign that you should take a chance in your life. If you already live on the edge, the dream may suggest that you should make more careful decisions instead of relying on chance. What you are doing in your dream casino can indicate how you are playing the game of life. Are you playing recklessly and with no thought of the morrow, are you playing by the rules or are you seeking to exploit loopholes in the rules? All this can be seen as a comment on real-life situations, such as starting a business or new job. *See also* Gambling entry in LEISURE.

CASTLE

When a **castle** features in your dream, it symbolizes honor and power, as well as recognition for things that you have accomplished. Dreaming of a castle also connects to the feminine principles of enclosed and defended spaces, and it can represent problems reaching your goals or the need for more security in waking life. If you are **trapped in a castle** in your dream, this may indicate that you have problems freeing yourself from old habits or attitudes. **Trying to enter a castle** may signify obstacles that you need to overcome before you can progress in waking life. *See also* BUILDINGS.

CAVE

Dreams of **camping, resting or seeking shelter in a cave** are common in dreamland, although few of us have explored caves in waking life. In dreams, the cave, as an image of the womb, may represent sanctuary and protection from outside forces; it is a place to which you can retreat and regain your strength. **Emerging from a cave into daylight** may symbolize a new beginning, whilst **descending into a cave or catacomb** may represent a desire to explore your unconscious. **Passing through a cave** signifies a change of state and a deeper understanding of negative impulses within you. *See also* Cave, Chasm and Valley entries in NATURE AND THE SEASONS.

CHURCH/GRAVEYARD

A **church or religious building** in your dreams represents your feelings about religion; if you are not religious, it marks all that is sacred to you in your life. To see the **outside of a church** in your dream signifies sacredness and spiritual nourishment. It is representative of your value system and the things you hold sacred. To see the **inside of a church** indicates that you may experience some minor setbacks. However, whatever seems like a nuisance might eventually turn out to be a blessing in disguise.

Dreaming of a **grave or graveyard** is an indication that you must resolve or deal with your feelings concerning the inevitability of death. It may be that you are trying to deal with feelings concerning someone who has died. Alternatively, part of your personality may have been killed off or is buried – or cut off – from the outside world. To dream that **you are in a graveyard** signifies sadness, unresolved grief or ambivalent feelings about death. It can also represent those parts of yourself that you have killed off or have stopped using. From a spiritual perspective, a graveyard is not only a place of death but also a place of spiritual regeneration and rebirth. To see a **mausoleum** in your dream signifies possible health issues or anxiety about your health.

CITY

To see a **city** in your dream, whether you recognize it or not, signifies all the aspects of your social environment. The dream can also refer to your spiritual community, since a city was originally given its status because it had a cathedral. Dreaming of a **city or town that is known to you** refers to your sense of community or belonging to a group. In dreams, we often give clues as to what we require emotionally from our environment and **streets that are totally empty or crowded with expressionless hurried people** may emphasize a need for more intimacy. Dreams in which you are **lost in a crowd** can suggest the desire to blend in so attention is taken away from you. It can also indicate that you do not have a sense of your own identity at present or that you long to join a group of like-minded people.

If you have a dream set in an urban landscape, this is your dreaming mind's way of exploring your social feelings and beliefs. It can also be an expression of your work and career aspirations. Alternatively, such dreams can also represent you as a person; as Jung pointed out, cities can be a symbol of the self. In particular, he noticed that in dreams the structure of a city is often symmetrical in the shape of a mandala. Jung interpreted mandalas as an expression of the fullness of the self and wholeness. According to Jung, every town and city that is mapped to a mandala format is an expression of the human desire for wholeness; in dreams, the pattern can remind dreamers that the path to happiness is not to be found in the city but within yourself.

To dream that you are in a **deserted city or that you feel alienated from the activity of the city** suggests that you feel rejected by those around you. To see a **city in ruins** denotes that you are neglecting your social relationships and allowing them to deteriorate. This dream image can also stand for the destruction or ideals and goals. If the **ruins are ancient**, you may be yearning for an idealized past. A **walled city** may signify resistance to change and the refusal to accept or listen to new ideas. Alternatively, it may indicate a desire for seclusion so you can recharge your emotional or spiritual batteries. In contrast to the city, a dream set in a **village** may evoke a longing for simple and traditional values in waking life. It may be an attractive ideal for dreamers disillusioned with the rushed and impersonal nature of city life.

CLASSROOM

So many dreams are set in the **classroom or school** that it may be one of the most frequent dream settings. The primary focus of such dreams is on your own level of competence and how it may be reflected in the eyes of others. The theme of fitting in is perhaps why so many anxiety dreams that reflect a sense of insecurity and failure are set in schools. *See also* SCHOOL AND WORK.

COUNTRYSIDE

Country scenes in dreams refer to the forces of nature within you. When you dream of the countryside, you are putting yourself in touch with your natural, spontaneous feelings. If you have memories of feeling relaxed and happy in the country, your dream may recreate this with images of freedom and openness, urging you to clarify your own feelings about the way you are leading your life. If **country lanes** appear in your dream, this indicates a meeting with what is natural in you; in some cases, what you encounter on the path can be disturbing, such as a wolf.

In countryside dreams, **hills, mountains and slopes** are images of problems you may be encountering in your waking life; the dream will indicate how confident you are in dealing with them. Are you climbing confidently or with fear? Remember, too, that the higher the mountain in your dream, the more difficult the challenge ahead. Are you gripped by a fear of falling as you climb? This would reflect your waking fear of losing your position or your reputation. Or did you reach the **highest pinnacle of the mountain or cliff** and bask in your sense of achievement? If you dreamed of **descending a mountain**, this could indicate your desire to come down to earth or your exhaustion with your continual upwards struggle. It could also indicate a sense of regret. If you **fell down a mountain**, this mirrors fears in waking life that you are losing control of your career.

Dream impediments such as **chasms, gorges, ditches or hurdles** also indicate difficulties you need to leap or surmount. For Freudians, **climbing over a stile**, like straddling a horse, is a common dream image of sexual intercourse. A dream featuring a **boundary or frontier** may suggest challenge and criticism, or the ability to overcome problems. Dream **fences and gates** also imply restrictions of some kind, but they can also indicate a need for security in waking life. **Open plains, prairies or moorland** evoke the endless possibilities of the unconscious, both exciting and frightening at the same time. *See also* ELEMENTS and NATURE AND THE SEASONS for more information on natural dreamscapes.

COURTROOM

To dream that **you are in court listening to charges against you** signifies your struggle with issues of fear and guilt. A situation or circumstance in your life is giving your much distress and worry, and you may feel that you are being judged in some way. If your dream focuses on a **law court, a judge or justice in general**, this can indicate that your unconscious is trying to sort out right from wrong in your waking life; the moral confusion might be on a personal level or something to do with your social life. Such dreams may also be urging you to pay attention to your actions or to your attitude towards authority.

The image of a **jury** in a dream indicates struggles with peer group pressure. Perhaps you feel that others do not understand you or that you are being judged in some way? If **you are a member of a jury** in your dream, you may feel that you need

Landscapes and settings

When the **setting** of your dream is particularly prominent in your dream, it is usually trying to convey to you some kind of message from your unconscious. The setting of a dream is the environment or landscape in which the action takes place. Sometimes the place reflects your mood but it can also be a reminder of a particular time in your life or of particular people. In general, the setting signifies the environment in which the main action of your life is happening. For example, if you dream of **walking across the road in a busy city in the rain**, your dream has a completely different setting to going for a **walk in a park on a sunny day**.

Try to assign a feeling and function to the setting of your dreamscape; that busy city might convey the feeling of purpose and speed, together with the function of work; that park might suggest the feeling of relaxation and the function of refreshment. When you have defined your feeling and function, try to see what part they play in your waking life and what the other details of the dream say about them. Bear in mind, too, that you need to consider personal associations. A **countryside walk** may conjure up an image of heaven for some people but of hell for others, particularly if they suffer from severe hay fever.

Interpreting the symbolism of the dream setting can give you an insight into your own inner landscape. If the **setting is familiar**, look out for symbols of your work or home situation to decide whether the dream is about your professional or personal life. Such a scene may also take you back to childhood or a time of learning. If the **setting is not familiar, or from your past,** think about how it may relate to the emotional climate of a current situation. **Recurring landscapes** in dreams indicate feelings to which you often return; if the same scenes recur, they suggest habitual attitudes with which you approach a situation. **Recurring scenes of your past** represent a stance you developed at that time in your life. Although landscapes do tend to reflect habitual feelings rather than temporary moods, if the **landscape does change** in your dream, perhaps you need to make corresponding changes in your everyday life or in your approach to life. **Composite scenes**, consisting of many images that you recognize in one setting, are usually drawing your attention to particular qualities or moods which have relevance to the content of the dream. The **country** where your dream is set may also have significance. *See also* FOREIGN COUNTRIES.

Bear in mind, too, that the light, the weather and other features of your dream landscape all contribute to the setting and are all saying something about your mood or the feelings the dream inspires. Light is a common symbol of consciousness, so a **sunny landscape** will indicate clarity and awareness and a **bright and sunny place** will suggest fun and liveliness. **Dark places** in general represent the unconscious, although **landscapes that become dark or dreary** during the course of the dream may also refer to your subjective view of the world; for example, a **dark shadowy murky scene** signifies feelings of depression. A **place that becomes lighter and brighter during your dream** suggests possibilities and potentials, whilst the dim illumination of **moonlight** is a common symbol of intuition.

The nature of the weather in your dream will also express how you are feeling. **Bad weather** may foretell of troubles lying ahead, **rain falling** may indicate a release of tension, whilst the appearance of a **rainbow across the landscape** might suggest your troubles have found some sort of resolution. A **beautiful place** in a dream may be encouraging you to use your creative imagination in waking life, a **sheltered place** might be offering peace and security, **unknown places** could be revealing aspects of yourself of which you may be unsure and **wide open spaces** offer you a taste of freedom from confinement, whether emotional or physical.

The structure of the landscape also reflects your feelings about the content of your dream. A **landscape that is hard to travel over or live in** says much about the emotional or practical obstacles in your waking life. Your dream may have created a symbolic scenario to show you the things that are preventing you from being happy and fulfilled. What you see lying ahead of you in a dream, such as a **mountain or a flight of stairs**, is significant as it represents the challenges you have yet to face. Obstacles in dream landscapes may express your everyday concerns. For example, you may find it **impossible to cross a busy street** in your dream; the street may well be a symbol of an impending exam. If some aspect of your dream **landscape did not seem right or was out of proportion**, perhaps you are not seeing things straight in waking life. In your dream, look out for other symbols that suggest some aspect of your waking life is out of proportion; if your dream has a surreal or supernatural elements, refer to the chapter on SURREALISM AND FANTASY.

to go along with the group or go it alone regarding a certain situation in your waking life. Alternatively, do you have to make a difficult decision in real life or an unpopular judgment?

CROSSING/CORRIDOR

If you are **crossing a road** in your dream, this is an image of potential danger, fear and uncertainty in waking life. If you are **crossing a field**, you may need to bring your feelings out into the open. **Crossing a river or chasm** depicts the end of one phase

The Element Encyclopedia of 20,000 *Dreams*

or stage of life and the beginning of another. To dream that you are at a **crossroad** signifies that you have come to a point in your life where you have several options from which to choose, all of which will take you to different destinations. This dream suggests you need to make an important decision, often in relation to career or life changes. To **turn left** at the crossroad can indicate following your intuition, whilst to **turn right** can mean making logical decisions. To dream that you are **walking down a long corridor** signifies your desperation in trying to escape a repetitive situation or behavior patterns.

Desert

Your waking feelings about the **desert** will be significant here; that which is a terrible ordeal for one person may symbolize romance and escapism for another. Likewise, a **desert island** may have a romantic associations for some people, whilst for others it can mean isolation, an intense desire for privacy or a cry for solitude to end in waking life. A dream of **being alone in a desert** may signify emotional isolation or being surrounded by a sea of emotions, and dreams of **being with someone in the desert** can indicate that this particular relationship is coming to an end. Such dreams can also suggest the need – if you are to survive – to consider very carefully a course of action you are about to take. Bear in mind, too, that the desert's vast expanse and rich underground life may represent an invitation to seek out the mysteries of life beneath the surface.

Any dream that focuses on **sand** may have been highlighting the sands of time, which may be running out for you in certain aspects of your waking life. **Quicksand**, like bogs and swamps, reveals the uncertainties that can be found in even a seemingly firm reality. If you are **seeking out an oasis** in your dream, it may represent the inner fears and insecurities that you may have to deal with. When you are **resting at an oasis**, positive future business and monetary ventures may be around the corner, although it might simply be a sign that you are in need of a vacation.

Dungeon

Various types of **dungeon, prison or jail** are common dream settings and they appear at times when something or someone in your life is restricting your sense of freedom. If you have such a dream, your dreaming mind is urging you to consider whether your loss of freedom is self-enforced; it is urging you to be honest with yourself about the causes and cost of being imprisoned. Such dreams may also symbolize a deep-rooted feeling that you are not able to fully express yourself. When **someone else is seen in prison**, this refers to a part of yourself that you are unable to reveal to others and even to yourself. When **someone is released from prison** in your dream, it signifies changes that may have taken place within your life. It is also a sign that you will overcome obstacles that may be holding you back at the moment.

Fairground

Dreams that feature **fairgrounds** as their setting may represent a reconnection with the light-hearted childlike part of yourself. Your dreaming mind may be urging you to let your hair down and be less inhibited or to drop whatever constraints you may have been imposing on yourself or others. Fairgrounds are enclosed worlds devoted to pleasure, so to dream of one could also indicate that you are wrapped up in your own pleasure. Alternatively, if you experience as many pains as you do pleasures, perhaps you feel that you are on life's merry-go-round.

A lack of harmony in your life might be represented through a dream of a **carnival with outlandish objects and performers**. If you are enjoying a **carnival ride**, it is a suggestion that you may currently be going round in circles in waking life or enjoying a bunch of cheap thrills.

FARM

To be in a **farm or farmyard** in your dream suggests that you are very much in touch with the down-to-earth aspects of yourself. It also indicates a need to feel safe and looked after. Whatever animals there are in the farm will be significant to the interpretation.

FOREST

Dreams of being **lost in a forest or group of trees** tend to occur during those times when we feel lost, confused or vulnerable and are trying to find certainty. The image is symbolic shorthand for whatever you might find insecure and unsettling in waking life, but such dreams suggest that you may emerge wiser and better for the experience. A forest is often a place of testing and initiation, and always concerns coming to terms with the emotional side of yourself. In fairy tales, the **dark or enchanted forest** is a symbol of the soul

entering the unknown and therefore has much to do with the unfamiliar, the unknown and the need to find direction. A **rainforest** may represent a rich source of inspiration to one person, whilst to another it may suggest apprehension and fear. *See also* NATURE AND THE SEASONS; TREES.

HEAVEN/HELL

To see **heaven** in your dream signifies your desire to find perfect happiness. You may be trying to escape from the difficulties you are experiencing in your life, your dream serving as a medium through which you can restore your faith, optimism, and hopes. To dream of **hell**, by contrast, denotes that you may be suffering in a seemingly inescapable situation. You may have placed your decision about which course of action to take into someone else's hand. Alternatively, you may be experiencing fear and guilt about something, and are wondering what the punishment might be. *See also* RELIGION.

HIGHWAY

In dreams, any kind of **highway** represents a symbolic journey in real life; this may be related to your career, your private or your social life. Your actions on this journey will be significant. Were you caught in traffic, were you steering down a winding, dangerous road or driving the wrong way up a one-way street? Everything that occurs will be significant for your dream interpretation. To dream that you are in **parking lot** suggests that you need to slow down and take some time to relax from your daily activities. To dream that you **cannot find a parking spac**e indicates your inability to

Garden

Dreams in which a **garden** features tend to refer to your inner feelings, areas of potential growth and change, and what it is you are trying to cultivate in your life. Considering the garden's features will tell you whether you are successfully cultivating the seedlings of your potential or allowing them to become choked and killed by weeds. Gardens also reveal the inner life of the dreamer, allowing you to see what you appreciate about yourself; they also represent features of the difficult process of self-discovery, as symbolized by the tree of knowledge.

Other interpretations suggest that dreams of gardens express a desire to be closer to nature or your natural self. Sometimes, dream gardens are symmetrical with a central point; this mandala symbol represents the inner wholeness of your true self and to dream of a garden that reproduces its form may indicate inner healing after a period of unease or even illness. If your **dream garden is beautiful**, this suggests creativity and abundance in your life, whereas an **overgrown neglected garden** warns that you have neglected your personal growth. It is time to clear away the weeds and start nurturing your talents.

The garden is also the symbol of the feminine attributes and the qualities of wildness that need to be tamed in order to create order. **Closed or walled gardens**, in particular, have this significance and can represent virginity. Freud saw the garden as an image of the female genitals, with the dreamer perhaps facing the carnal temptations associated with the serpent in the Garden of Eden. If your dream **garden is square or circular in shape**, this suggests unconscious wisdom and insight. If there is a **pool in the garden** this refers to memories of childhood or hidden, unexpressed emotions.

If you are **gardening** in your dream, this indicates that you are in the act of creation; the dream may be referring to your psychological growth and increasing emotional maturity. To see a **vegetable garden** symbolizes increased prosperity will come your way through diligence and care; it also suggests stability and inner growth. To see a **flower garden** in your dream foretells of tranquility, comfort, true love and a happy home in your future. To see a **sparse, weed-infested garden** indicates that you have neglected your emotional and spiritual needs. **A garden gate** may represent a welcome invitation to a more natural environment for those detained awhile by city life. **Walking through a garden gate** may represent moving into a new phase of life; new opportunities await you. An **open gate** represents changes for the future; a **closed gate** means problems or obstacles ahead.

A conservatory or hothouse full of exotic plants symbolizes the unconscious being kept under tight control. A **fountain in the garden** is a symbol of encouragement, renewed hope and a release of creativity. A **well in the garden** may stand for your most valued talents and inner resources, but if the **well is dried up** and you cannot draw water from it, this suggests frustration at being unable to find an outlet for your talents. To see a **neat and well-** kept yard reflects your ability to maintain and organize aspects of your outside life, such as work and your social activities. To see a **messy and neglected yard** denotes those aspects of your life that are out of your control. *See also* Plants entry in NATURE AND THE SEASONS; TREES.

find your place in life. You may still be on your quest to find your talent or the niche where you belong. Alternatively, it may reflect your busy life and lack of time.

JUNGLE

Dreams of **jungles** often appear when you are pressured at work. As a more savage and untamed version of the forest, the jungle – with its creepers, wild animals and carnivorous plants – is a metaphor for the tough and confusing instincts lurking in the unconscious. It can often symbolize chaos, as in 'a jungle out there', and this chaos can be either positive or negative, depending on the interpretation of the dream. The jungle represents your unconscious urges, those areas of yourself that remain uncivilized and which need to be tamed if you are to move forward with your life. If you are **trapped in the forest** in your dream, this indicates that you are feeling trapped by negativity and fear; but if you are **surviving happily in your dream jungle**, you have overcome your fears and made sense of yourself and your environment. *See also* NATURE AND THE SEASONS.

LABORATORY/WORKSHOP

To dream that you are in a **laboratory** signifies that you are experimenting with your inner feelings, beliefs and fears; you are testing yourself in some way. Alternatively, you may be going through some sort of transformation. You may also need to use a more scientific approach to life and to develop your thinking skills. In short, you need to make an objective assessment of what is happening in your life. To see a **workshop** in you dream represents the development of your skills; you are trying to understand yourself and find out who you are. A workshop is a symbol of productivity, but it can represent group interaction and creativity since it is a place in which you are likely to meet like-minded people.

MARKET

To dream that you are in a **market, flea market or marketplace** signifies frugality. It may also indicate your ability to cope successfully with everyday life and relations with other people. Alternatively the market

The Element Encyclopedia of 20,000 Dreams

may be representative of your career and what you have to offer. It is a place of buying and selling, and can therefore give some indication of the value you place on your skills and attributes, and whether you have something to sell or are buying. On the other hand, as markets are typically busy and bustling places, your dream may simply be suggesting that you need to get out more and interact with people. To see a **barren market** in your dream signifies lack of choice. To dream that you go to a **fish market** signifies pleasure and joy, but to see **decayed and rotting fish at the fish market** denotes anxiety. To dream of a **grocery store or market** suggests that you are brainstorming for new ideas or looking for the various choices that may be out there for you. The interpretation of your dream may depend on what you are shopping for. *See also* MONEY AND SHOPPING.

ORCHARD

In dreams, **orchards** may represent how well you take care of yourself and the interpretation will depend upon whether the trees have flowers or fruit, and what type and color the fruit are. If the trees are showing **flowers or fruit**, this suggests potential success. Happiness and a sense of security are signified by a dream in which you are traveling through an **orchard filled with blossoms**. If the **orchard has been affected by a storm or is empty**, the opposite is suggested. Just like the fruit on its trees, the orchard itself may represent pregnancy. An **orchard with unripe fruit** may remind you that much work still needs to be done to achieve your objectives; **rotting fruit on the grass** may suggest that you are spoiling your chances of

success by not acting. **Vines or vineyards** in dreams can suggest fruitfulness, fertility and potential growth. To dream of a vineyard can represent a sense of optimism since it is a place where you can gather the fruits which end up as wine, a notable lifter of spirits. **Olive groves** are symbols of peace and purity, as well as triumph over adversity, and in dreams they are harbingers of a period of great creativity.

PARK

Wandering about a **park** or enjoying a **picnic** in your dream may refer to the need for temporary relief from life's harsh realities. It may be interpreted as wish-fulfillment; are you in need of some rest and relaxation? It is also important to interpret your feelings about this dream and the other symbols, particularly what you were doing and the people you were with. Park images in dreams also represent feelings that have become a matter of importance not just for yourself but for the community in which you live. Dreams in which you are visiting an **amusement park** may be a sign that you may need to incorporate more enjoyment within your life. They can also be symbolic of things that can easily distract you from your tasks. If the **amusement park is empty or seems shut down**, it signifies the need to stop taking yourself so seriously. Consider also how everything in the park is an expression of some aspect of yourself.

PARTY/POST OFFICE/THEATRE

If you are attending a **party** in your dream, it may mean that you should get out a little more and embrace life; or perhaps you need to celebrate something about yourself. If the **party you are attending is dull** or you aren't enjoying yourself for some reason, then it may be an indication that you have doubts about the social skills you possess. If you dream of a **political party rally**, it shows that you are prepared to stand up for your beliefs. When a dream is set on stage, whether it is in the form of an **opera, play or ballet**, this suggests you are working through an issue that relates to the way you are seen by others. To dream that you are in **a post office** signifies an important message from your unconscious or inner wisdom. It may relate to your need to reach out and communicate with others. You may be trying to maintain your beliefs or make contact with someone from your past. *See also* ARTS AND CRAFTS; LEISURE; LETTERS AND COMMUNICATION.

QUAGMIRE/SWAMP

To see yourself **bogged down in a quagmire** signifies your inability to meet obligations and your feeling that you are stuck in a boring routine. To see **others bogged down in a quagmire** denotes that you are being affected by the moods of others. To see a **swamp** in your dream symbolizes aspects of yourself that are repressed and dark; it also represents feelings that undermine your confidence and well-being. Perhaps you feel overwhelmed by a feeling or an emotion.

QUARRY

Dreaming of a **quarry** means that you are digging out aspects of your personality that may have been buried. If you are **seeking a quarry**, this suggests that you know what you need in real life but you still need to find it.

RESERVOIR

To see a **full reservoir** in your dream symbolizes stored-up or repressed emotions; to see an **empty reservoir** denotes that you have expended all of your energy and emotions on others.

SEASIDE

In dreams, the **seaside or beach** represents a new dimension of experience. The land symbolizes past experience and everything you have tried, and the water is the symbol of the new unlimited potential awaiting you. This image often appears in dreams when you feel you are through the worst of things; it is therefore a harbinger of hope, growth and change. *See also* On the beach in LEISURE.

TOWN

Freud saw in dream images of **towns** an all-embracing symbol of women; the symbol might be inviting or forbidding, according to whether the **streets are brightly lit or dark and empty**. For Jung, the image of a town evokes the unconscious and an urge to explore your connections with other people. For some dream analysts, the dream town – just like the dream house or city – is a representation of the self. How you feel about being in your dream town can reflect your sense of well-being or dissatisfaction in real life. If your town or city has **run-down slums or dilapidated houses**, this can represent a refusal to keep up appearances; but if the town or city is taken as a

The Element Encyclopedia of 20,000 Dreams

Your position

It is worthwhile to pay attention to the position you assume within the setting of your dream, as this can give you an indication of your stance or moral position in life or towards a certain situation. It can also give an indication as to how you are handling situations in your life. If you are **standing in a lofty position relative to other people or the landscape** in your dream, this suggests the need for a wider perspective; it can also suggest feelings of superiority, or of having risen above your station. If you are **adjacent, beside or adjoining someone or something** in your dream, this suggests a close connection with some aspect of yourself or your life; it can also suggest something you can no longer avoid. **Things that fall behind you** in a dream represent what you have left behind or of which you are unaware. **Things that are below you** represent that which you can look on from detached viewpoint. Alternatively, submissive behavior may be suggested. If **someone or something is positioned very close** to you in your dream, this indicates a situation that is imminent, near at hand or being realized now.

Things that appear in the distance refer to feelings with which you no longer strongly identify, but they may also indicate the future or the past. **Things in front of you** refer to what is being dealt with now in your waking life. **Things that are opposite you** represent resistance to the direction you want to take or the need to reconcile opposites in some way. **Things by your side** suggest supportive feelings or taking sides in some way. Something in the **wrong position** in a dream may indicate that you are going about things in the wrong way. The **upper part of anything** (of a building or a body, for instance) typically refers to your intellect and ideals, whereas the **lower part of anything** refers to the unconscious. Something **upside down** signals the need for change. Rejection or acceptance can be seen in a dream as viewing the **back or front** of something and **backward or forward motion** indicates delays or progress and whether or not you have a forward- or backward-looking approach to life. To be aware of the **center of something** in your dream is to be aware of your real self. **Horizontal things** symbolize the material world, **vertical things** symbolize the spiritual or intuitive realm, whilst **straight things** suggests a direct approach.

To be on top, trying to reach the top or being on an upper level might suggest you are assuming control and are capable of achieving the upper hand in waking life. **Going down or being underneath something** may represent the part of you that wants to hide or feels less confident. **Going north** in your dream suggests a journey into the unknown; **going south** is representative of passion and following your heart; **going east** suggests rebirth and becoming self-aware, whilst **going west** suggests the more logical side of your nature. Anything observed in dreams on the **right-hand side** usually represents your progress in waking life, as the **right-hand side** represents logic and correct behavior. **Movement to the right** can indicate that something is coming into consciousness; it can also express more masculine attributes such as dominance. The **left-hand side** is less to do with dominance or reason, and more to do with instinctive behavior and dreams, as the left-hand side expresses feminine attributes. **Indecision over whether to go left or right** in a dream suggests an inability to decide if you want to follow your obligations or your instincts in real life. *See also* BODY.

representation of the self, **seeing yourself in the slums** is an indicator of either low self-esteem or a desire to explore unknown parts of yourself.

To dream of the **gutter** signifies degradation and unhappiness with yourself or with others. To **find articles of value in the gutter** in your dream signifies that current difficulties will teach you a valuable and important lesson. On the other hand, seeing yourself in the **rich quarter or prosperous suburbs** may suggest optimism and a good level of self-esteem. If, however, you are **just passing through rich areas** in your dream, your dreaming mind may be reminding you that there is more to life than simply material satisfaction. If the **town is on a hill** in your dreams, this is a Jungian symbol of wisdom. The town's high position may also express satisfaction with your progress in waking life.

UNDERGROUND

A dream that takes place **underground or under the ocean** can be a symbol of the journey into the unconscious and lead to the discovery of unknown parts of yourself. This type of dream can also be a representation of the womb and of the possibility of rebirth. To dream that you **live underground** symbolizes a desire for greater security and peace of mind. If you dream of a **pit**, you might suffer from anxieties about female sexuality. Jungians see the pit as an image of unconscious urges that need to be explored with care. To dream that you are in a **mine** signifies that you are getting to the bottom of a particular problem, and may have even reached its core. The journey you are prepared to take to understand yourself better might be symbolized if you find yourself **traveling on the tube or the subway**; the same is true of any dreams of **tunnels**, which generally indicate the need to explore your unconscious. Such dreams may also represent the birth canal and therefore the process of birth. If

The Element Encyclopedia of 20,000 Dreams

there is **light at the end of the tunnel**, you are progressing positively but if something is **blocking the tunnel**, some past fear or experience is blocking your progress.

Zoo

To dream that you are at a **zoo** symbolizes loss of freedom, or that your abilities and talents are going unnoticed. You feel caged in by someone or something in your waking life. The zoo may also represent chaos and confusion, as implied by the common phrase 'this place is a zoo!' You may need to tidy up some situation in your life. Alternatively, dreaming of a zoo can indicate the need to understand your instincts and urges; or perhaps you feel that you are being watched in some way in waking life. Your dreaming mind may be alerting you to the importance of appropriate behavior. *See also* ANIMALS.

Positive Emotions

Your dreams can provide you with deep and powerful insights into your moods, and can be used to help you manage feelings of joy as well as sadness.

Perhaps you have woken up from a dream with feelings of euphoria or unexplained happiness, or found yourself laughing without knowing why. Every now and again your dreaming mind may give you an emotional and psychological boost by creating images in which you feel deeply secure, happy and loved. It may also conjure up images of freedom, adventure, success and excitement to spur you on. Dreams that leave you with such lingering feelings of joy and exhilaration are less common than those that leave you with feelings of dread and uncertainty. This may be because there are always constant challenges and responsibilities to face in the real world and your dreams tend to reflect your anxieties about meeting these challenges. Even though they are relatively rare, feelings of immense happiness in dreams are just as important to understand as feelings of sadness according to Jung and most other dream analysts. Joyful, uplifting dreams allow you to focus on the real-life experiences and situations that evoked them, as well as the way you feel about yourself and your life.

See also AMBITION AND SUCCESS; NEGATIVE EMOTIONS; RELATIONSHIPS; SEX.

Happiness

HAPPY

You may have had a dream in which you felt **blissfully happy and content**. Perhaps you dreamed that your **life was filled with laughter, that you were surrounded by your loved ones or felt profoundly peaceful and joyful**. If these senses and feelings mirror your current feelings in waking life, then your dream was simply reflecting your elation. If, however, you had a **joyful dream but your current waking circumstances are far from ideal** and you are feeling worried, anxious or lacking in self-confidence, your unconscious may be trying to comfort and reassure you as a way of compensating for your current unhappiness or misfortune. Your unconscious may also be trying to send you an important message that can help boost your chances of happiness in waking life. Pay attention to the details of your dream. Who or what was it that made you feel happy? Was it a person, a situation, a place or a sensation? Once you have discovered what it was that made you feel good, try to decide if your dream was a wish-fulfillment fantasy or whether the person, situation, place or sensation holds the key to your happiness.

Dreams of **flying, playing and floating** are often connected to feelings of elation, joy and happiness. Flying dreams evoke feelings of freedom, liberation and breaking free from the chains that bind you in waking life. Flying dreams can tell you of personal growth, creativity and self-discovery. They may also symbolize great joy and excitement about what lies ahead for you in the real world. If you experience what seems like **inappropriate happiness in your dream** in a setting that in the waking world would normally be sad, such as attending the funeral of someone dear to you, such a dream may point to a state of denial – in order to protect yourself from current feelings of unhappiness you may be refusing to face reality or drowning your sorrows in excessive or addictive behavior. As always, consider the context of the happiness or joy in your dream before settling on an interpretation.

HOT AND COLD

Unless your bedroom is very hot or cold or you have too many or too few bedclothes, perceptions of **being or feeling hot or cold** in a dream are associated with your emotions. For instance, a **refrigerator,** **freezer or cooler** in your dream may indicate emotional coldness or even sexual frigidity in waking life; if you subsequently have dreams of **thawing out or defrosting**, this indicates that your feelings are changing and your attitudes and emotions are becoming more relaxed. You may even have put something on ice in waking life and feel you can't make any more progress with it.

On the other hand, feelings of **heat or warmth** suggest passion for something in your waking life, or feelings of a sexual or loving nature towards someone. Remember, too, that heat is associated with fire and ice is associated with water. Dreams of a **romantic sunrise or sunset** may contain elements of wish-fulfillment, but they may also suggest feelings of inner optimism if it is a sunrise, and inner contentment with a sense of finality if it is a sunset.

LAUGHTER

You may find yourself **laughing** as you wake up from a dream; in some cases, when you recall the dream images you may realize that what you were laughing at was not very funny at all. If this happens, study all the other symbols in your dream and particularly the symbol that most made you laugh, as this will hold the key to your interpretation. The purpose of jokes is to surprise and amuse you in unexpected ways, so if you dream of **hearing or telling a joke**, your dreaming mind may be trying to draw your attention to a serious issue to which you need to pay attention in your waking life; serious things are often said in jest, even in dreams. Alternatively, **dreams of laughter** can also have a sinister side, as laughter can reveal emotions of embarrass-

Compensatory wish-fulfillment dreams

If your life is particularly difficult, you may have a dream in which you **feel blissfully carefree and happy**. If you are feeling lonely and unloved, you may have a dream in which you are **making love**. Many dream analysts describe these night-time idylls as wish-fulfillment compensatory dreams. In classic Freudian theory, dreams are thought to be vehicles for wish-fulfillment. In dreams, the dreamer can develop and satisfy complex wishes and desires that would not be allowed to seep through to consciousness in waking life. Although this theory can be quite complicated, put simply it suggests that dreams reflect your unconscious desires. For example, if you are having financial problems, you may dream of **winning the lottery**. If you are worn out after weeks of hard work, you may dream of **sunning yourself on a beach without a care in the world**. If you are worried about the way you look, you may dream of **being a supermodel**.

Bear in mind, though, that compensatory wish-fulfillment is just one explanation for uplifting dreams; the meaning of your dream will always remain personal to you. However much a dream may appear to be wish-fulfillment, it is still important to consider its many layers of meaning. Jung's theories about alchemy may also help you understand feelings of both intense joy and of sadness in your dreams. In his classic 1944 text *Psychology and Alchemy*, Jung concluded that the ancient tradition of alchemy could help us make sense of a universally valid truth – that one becomes aware of new meanings within the unconscious by seeing them mirrored in the world around us. This is the psychological phenomenon of projection – the placing of unknown and unfulfilled desires onto other people and things – a process Jung believed was often at work in dreams.

ment, fear or even a sense of paranoia, especially if **others are laughing at you**. Associated with folklore and wicked witches, if you hear **cackling** in your dream, it may be your inner voice ridiculing your grandiose pretensions.

RELEASE

You may have a dream after which you wake up **feeling exhilarated, liberated or experience a rush of excitement and a sense of freedom**. When you finally realize that it was only a dream, you may feel a crushing sense of disappointment. In dreams of this kind you may find yourself **walking out of your job or leaving your** responsibilities behind and driving into the sunset. Or perhaps you **learned to fly, were offered the lead part in a Hollywood blockbuster or discovered that you had an amazing musical talent and signed a million dollar record deal**. Whatever it was that gave you a euphoric high and helped you break through the chains that inhibit your mind and freedom in waking life, such dreams are typically wish-fulfillment escapist fantasies that compensate for the dreariness of your waking life.

On the other hand, they may also be encouraging you to shake off the shackles that bind you in waking life. Perhaps you feel burdened down with responsibilities or feel stifled in a suffocating relationship or job. Whatever it is that is sapping your energy, your dreaming mind is urging and warning you to find a more fulfilling solution or way of coping, otherwise the bitterness and disappointment you feel on waking from your dreams may become permanent.

Uplifting feeling

To dream that **you are amorous or see that others are amorous** suggests that your sense of morality may be being put to the test. Your dreaming mind may, however, be encouraging you to explore and express your sexuality or creativity. To dream that you are **showing your devotion to your loved ones or to your beliefs** serves as a reminder that nothing good in life can be gained by deceit. To dream that you are experiencing **delight** suggests that life is good for you at the moment or that you wish it could be, whilst to dream that you are **joyful** denotes harmony amongst

friends and loved ones, although — in common with many such dreams — it may also be compensatory wish-fulfillment.

To dream that you are **merry or in merry company** signifies a time of pleasant engagements and profitable affairs; but again, it could also be compensatory **wish-fulfillment**. To feel **peace** in your dream indicates an end or a resolution to an emotional issue or inner conflict. It also suggests that you have reached a new level of stability and calmness. Alternatively, the maddening quietness may refer to the calm before the storm. To dream that you have **pride** denotes that you need to stand up and fight against attacks to your integrity. You

Sweet dreams

To encourage joyful dreams, some dream experts suggest that you do some visualization exercises during the day. For example, you may want to look for flying objects during the day, such as leaves, insects, seeds, birds or kites and then try to imagine what the world looks like from their perspective. How would it feel and what would the earth look like? Another exercise to do during the day would be to imagine or picture in your mind a dream that takes you on an exciting or joyous adventure. If you do have happy, joyful dreams during the night remember how they feel and try to take some guidance from the dream.

may soon be challenged. To dream that **you are tipsy** signifies your carefree nature and jovial disposition. To see **others tipsy** in your dream denotes that you need to be careful as to choice of friends, as their actions or words may reflect on your own character.

That Loving Feeling

LOVE

Psychologists generally define **love** as an intense feeling of liking, affection or an enduring sentiment towards a person combined with a strong desire to be with that person. In dreams, sexual images are more frequent than the ephemeral images of love; it was this which encouraged Freud to develop his theories about sex and sexual energy as being more powerful in dreamland than love itself. The connection between love and the erotic is therefore often inescapable in Freudian dream analysis, and the sexual interpretation of dreams became for Freud the key to unlock their meaning.

Jung, on the other hand, saw the world of dreams and love quite differently from Freud. He rejected Freud's heavy emphasis on sex and instead saw dreams not only as a way to understand what was wrong with a person, but also as a way to encourage the creative development of a person's whole potential. Dreams could therefore be a way of improving and encouraging feelings of wholeness, love and tenderness towards oneself and others in waking life.

Most dream analysts draw on the theories of both Jung and Freud when exploring the concept of love and dreams but they also ask the question: is the person in your dream really the object of your intense feelings of love or is there another way to read the dream? For example, dreams in which you **fall in love or are reminded of the passionate early days of a relationship** may have nothing to do with actual relationships but may be urging you to inject some passion into your life. They may also suggest that you are yearning to be loved and cherished. Try to remember who or what aroused feelings of love or passion in your dream. If it was your partner and you are deeply in love in waking life, your dream may have been reaffirming your lasting affection. If, however, you are past those heady days of romance and passion, your dream may be reminding you of the chemistry that drew you to your partner and how easily it can be rekindled.

If you had a dream in which you found yourself **in love with someone who in waking life is a friend, a colleague or someone you don't really know** but see on the journey to work every morning, you may find the experience unsettling, especially if you are in a committed relationship. It is possible that you feel drawn to that person in some unconscious way but are ignoring those feelings in waking life because they are inappropriate. Our dreams are often quickly prompted by a perhaps irrational attraction; if this is the case, your dreaming mind is allowing you to experience your desires in a safe environment in which no one can be hurt. If you are not in a relationship, however, then such a dream may be urging you to acknowledge or express your feelings for

The Element Encyclopedia of 20,000 Dreams

that person. Bear in mind, too, that you may not dream of the actual person but may find them represented symbolically. For example phallic symbols, such as **spears, swords or tall buildings** may represent the man a woman is attracted to. Look also for puns concerning the object of your desire. Your lover may also be represented by an **animal such as a kitten** in your dream. In waking life, do you feel the need to be protected and adored in the same way? Alternatively, if you are not attracted to the person in your dream in any way in waking life, there may be something about them that you admire and wish to cultivate yourself: for example, a way with words, a flair for fashion, a musical talent, an exciting job or a carefree lifestyle. Try to work out with which aspect of that person's character and life your dreaming mind has pictured you falling in love. To sum up, as with most emotions, in your dreams love is usually an expression of that feeling or a compensation for not receiving it in waking life.

SYMBOLS OF LOVE

Love can be expressed in many ways in your dream and almost any symbol can be associated with it. Dreams of **adopting or looking after a child, person or animal** are often strongly associated with the idea of taking care of someone and are associated with love. To dream of **shooting an arrow** is also a love symbol. At whom or what were you shooting the arrow and whom or what do they represent? The arrow may also be a phallic symbol. As far as your emotional life is concerned, your dreams can sometimes tell you things of which you are not yet aware; it is worth paying attention to the suggestions that come to you in your sleep.

For example, if you are undecided about whether to commit to a person, dreams in which **bells feature or you hear bells chiming** appear to be hinting at marriage or a deeper emotional commitment. You may, for instance, have a dream in which the **door bell rings and your prospective husband, wife or partner is at the door**. Bear in mind, however, that dreams are not always so literal; dreams of love are more difficult to understand than overtly sexual dreams, since almost any symbol can be associated with this area of your life. Pay attention to your feelings in the dream as they can help you see your potential partners and your feelings for what they really are. So if you have a feeling of dread when the door bell rings, this probably is not a good sign.

Bear in mind, too, that dreams that contain symbols closely related to home life, such as a **beloved family object or a much-used room**, are more likely to relate to a family member and your feelings towards them than to a potential lover. It may also be helpful to see how the feelings of love are being represented in your dream. If the **emotional bond and closeness is more important than the sexual**, this may be related to baby love. If **great sexual drive and the fulfillment of your own needs is the theme along with a desire to explore and experiment**, this suggests adolescent love. Adult love is represented by a dream sense of **recognizing the needs of the partner and putting them before your own without losing your sense of direction or independence**.

TENDERNESS

Dreams can be used to explore your feelings about yourself. For example, if you see **other people touching or loving each other and feel excluded or dream that you are surrounded by loved ones**, this often expresses a need for the comfort, support and unconditional affection that you enjoy when someone is completely in love with you. Such dreams could be a strong indication that your levels of self-esteem need a boost; one way to do that is to seek out the love and support of those closest to you. Alternatively, the characters in your dream may represent aspects of yourself. Are they warm and loving or were you unable to reach or feel them because they were so self-centered?

Dreams in which you see yourself **reaching out in some way** suggest a desire for something or someone you do not have; this may either be an emotional or a physical absence. Your dream may also be telling you that you are trying to manipulate circumstances or control others with your emotional neediness. This is particularly relevant if your efforts to reach out and touch others are rejected or received with distaste. **Witnessing a dream betrothal, wedding or engagement** is another variation of the wish-fulfillment compensatory dream. Lastly, dreams in which you are **in love with someone** – it could be anyone you know or do not know in waking life – **but your feelings are not reciprocated** are less positive, as they reveal a fear of being rejected by your loved ones in waking life or uncertainty about the affection of someone about whom you care deeply in waking life. *See also* RELATIONSHIPS; SEX.

PUZZLES, MYSTERIES AND DIFFICULTIES

According to Jung, dreams are the small hidden door to the deepest and most mysterious part of your nature; they act as a teacher and guide on the road toward understanding and wholeness.

Most dream analysts agree that one of the most helpful aspects of dream interpretation is that it helps present to you in symbolic language the challenges you are facing in waking life so that you can understand them and yourself better. These challenges can often be represented by symbols that are easy to understand, but in some cases these symbols appear to have no clear-cut explanation.

This chapter explores those symbols that seem to have no obvious associations and suggests ways for you to interpret them. Bear in mind, however, that in some instances the nature of your problem in waking life might not be at all evident to you. It may simply be that you have lost your sense of purpose but, because you have been so busy with your routines, you have not consciously realized that something is amiss. Your unconscious mind, however, will have picked up on this; a dream that depicts you wandering in a maze, for

example, may be an attempt to make you consciously aware of your lack of direction so that you can do something about it. *See also* SURREALISM AND FANTASY; MIND, BODY, SPIRIT.

Dream Mysteries

DIFFICULTY/PROBLEM

Dreams in which you are **struggling to climb an unknown mountain or cliff, fighting your way through snow and ice, wading through a bog, or lost and wandering alone in a forest or jungle** apply to a number of difficulties you may be encountering in your waking life. In most instances, such dreams only occur when you have tried to solve a problem and all your options seem to have been exhausted. Such a dream may be reflecting your real-life difficulties and the emotional or mental struggles you are facing. If you are prone to such dreams, you might want to try asking your dreaming mind to show you a way off the mountain or out of the jungle, forest or bog just before you go to sleep. Your dream may respond by offering you another dream scenario that may contain symbolic clues to help you solve your waking problem.

Any problem, obstacle or irritation you face in dreamland, such as being **unable to find a pen when you need one, light bulbs suddenly going out, being unable to pick something up, trying and failing to start a car or put up a deckchair or assemble a pushchair** can suggest a problem in waking life that you are finding difficult to resolve. Your dreaming mind has thousands upon thousands of symbolic disguises to draw upon, so whenever things don't go smoothly in dreamland, the chances are this indicates situations in waking life that you are struggling to resolve.

Knot

If you dreamed of a **knot or tying a knot** and are aware of the practice of tying a knot so you don't forget to do something, your dream may have been reminding you to carry out some important task in your waking life. Alternatively, tying the knot is a symbol of marriage or entering into a relationship. If you find yourself unable to **untangle a dream knot in a string, cable, cord, elastic or shoelace**, was your unconscious telling you that you are tying yourself in knots or that you are responsible for the current muddle in your waking life? If

you dreamed of **knots that you find impossible to untie, such as the string on a parcel or entwined fishing nets**, this may have represented a knotty or complicated problem that is holding you back in waking life. Your dream may tell you whether or not these problems will defeat you or whether you will solve them. If you lose your patience in your dream, the dream may in fact be urging you to have more patience. **Mystery packages, parcels and containers that you cannot open** in your dreams may also highlight aspects of your personality that you are denying; the appearance of the dream package may give you a clue about its nature. For example, if it was **gift-wrapped**, this may suggest a gift or talent you have repressed. A dream **treasure chest that you cannot open** may also suggest potential emotional riches lying just within. *See also* LETTERS AND COMMUNICATION.

Lock and key

Keys are clear symbols of freedom and opportunity in dreamland. They are also symbols of home ownership and trust, as you only give the keys to your home to people you trust. Bear in mind, though, that **jailers** also carry keys, so they can also be symbols of restriction and confinement. If your unconscious highlighted a key in your dream, it could have been drawing your attention to any of these symbolic associations or reflecting your waking hopes and fears.

Keys might also represent an explanation or solution to a dilemma that has been worrying you. This is especially the case if your dream **key fitted and a lock opened**, as locks are symbolic of obstacles to success

Labyrinth and maze

A **labyrinth** is a complex system of paths and tunnels in which it is easy to get lost. On one level, the appearance of a labyrinth in your dream suggests the need to explore the hidden side of your nature; the twists, turns, trials and tribulations of the labyrinth are a powerful symbol of the life journey towards the center of your existence. Within the labyrinth you can meet and overcome challenges and obstacles in life that prevent you from moving forward. From a psychological point of view, we must all take the heroic journey through the labyrinth of experience and come to terms with our fears and anxieties before confronting our shadow. Any dream image that has **underground passages** suggests a labyrinth. Some believe it represents an exploration of the feminine principle.

Jung saw the dark, enclosed labyrinth as a symbol of the tortuous depths of the unconscious and a dream of entering it as a voyage of self-discovery or an attempt to locate a deeply buried emotion. The void at the center of the labyrinth may suggest despair but it can also symbolize serenity and calm. A labyrinth is an archetype with which you can have direct experience. It is a metaphor for your life's journey. As in the Greek myth of Theseus who entered King Minos' labyrinth in Crete to slay the Minotaur, your descent into the unconscious, hidden aspects of your nature may involve confronting impulses that threaten your personal security and well-being.

Mazes are often confused with labyrinths but they are quite different. Labyrinths tend to symbolize the quest for knowledge and freedom, whereas mazes mirror the general confusion that may be fogging your sense of purpose in waking life. A maze is first of all open to the light, whereas a labyrinth is in the dark; furthermore, a maze has numerous entry points whereas a labyrinth only has one. A maze is like a puzzle to be solved, possessing twists, turns and blind alleys. It is a task that requires logical, sequential, analytical activity to find the correct path into the maze and out. A labyrinth, on the other hand, involves intuition and creativity. With a labyrinth there is only one choice to be made. The choice is to enter or not to enter. With **mazes** there are many choices to be made, with many entrances and exits. Dead ends and cul-de-sacs present riddles to be solved. Mazes challenge the choice-making part of yourself.

In dreams, a maze can therefore reflect the difficulty in finding a direction to follow in life. No one can predict what is right or wrong, so you may have to rely on your instincts. If, in your dream, you have a **map, chart or password to help you navigate your maze**, this may reassure you that you are on the right path. Mazes can also often portray a confusion of ideas and feelings, the difficulty in finding your way through the mass of apparently irrational emotions and images arising from within, or the variety of opinions and seemingly authoritative sources of information with which the modern world bombards you. You may dream of a **maze of corridors**, for example, during periods in which your life seems particularly complicated and you are faced with choices and decisions. In this sense, the maze represents an attempt to find your way through conscious thoughts, opinions and doubts, to an opinion or mindset that is yours alone.

If you enlisted the aid of a **ladder to help you get out of your maze**, your dreaming mind may have been suggesting that you take a more logical, rational overview of your situation. If you **found a way out of your maze**, this suggests that you will find a way to break free; but if you found yourself **ending up in the same place whatever path you took**, this could be reflecting your sense in waking life of going round in circles, covering the same ground or not being able to make a breakthrough. Bear in mind that **tunnels and paths** in dreams represent transitions, and **entrances** represent new directions; perhaps you have been so overwhelmed with emotion and confusion that you have not seen the opportunities already being presented to you.

and self-knowledge. Where the lock was located in your dream may be significant. If it was on a **door**, this is a symbol of transition or opportunity, but if it was on a **cupboard, box or safe**, this can represent your true nature and hidden inner qualities that are latent or repressed. If, however, the **key, code or password did not match the lock in your dream**, this could be a suggestion that you need to look elsewhere if you want to unlock or release the insight that will help you find a solution. According to Freud, keys are phallic symbols and the lock can signify the vagina, so if you dreamed of a **key being inserted into a lock**, the dream may have had an erotic significance. On the door of whose house was the lock that was being unlocked?

Puzzle

If you dream of **trying but failing to complete a puzzle or crossword**, this suggests an intellectual approach to problems in your waking life. Such dreams may be urging you to allow emotion to play a greater part in your decision making. On the other hand, if you **complete the puzzle or crossword and are satisfied with the result**, your dreaming mind may be suggesting that you should use an intellectual rather than an emotional approach to solving your problems. Dreaming of being **unable to find a word in a Thesaurus or dictionary** may be suggesting that you should listen to your instincts or your emotions. If you **find the word you are looking for**, however, this may suggest that you should adopt a more objective approach.

The Element Encyclopedia of 20,000 Dreams

If you are **puzzled by a mathematical equation or can't understand someone who is speaking another language** in your dream, this suggests an inability to understand a certain person or situation in your waking life. How you reacted in your dream may help you find a new approach to the situation. If a **code that is hard to understand or decipher** appears in your dream and you are the one who found it, this suggests some problem or person or aspect of your personality that is puzzling you. If you **awoke from a dream with a riddle running through your mind**, are you feeling confounded by someone or something in your waking life? Your dream may have contained clues to both the meaning of your dream and a real-life riddle, but if it continued to mystify you perhaps you need to use an intuitive, rather than an intellectual, approach to solving problems in your waking life.

In Greek mythology, the Sphinx posed the famous question to Oedipus: 'what goes on four feet, two feet and then three, but the more feet it goes on the weaker it will be?' Oedipus replied 'man'; it is man who crawls as a baby, walks as a man and then uses a cane in old age. Oedipus' answer shows the importance of using your gut instinct or intuition rather than a rational, logical approach to seemingly impossible questions. The same applies for any dream situation which leaves you flummoxed. Your dreaming mind may be urging you to use the powers of your intuition and to channel your instincts into that place where the answer lies.

SECRET

If you are **sharing or keeping a secret to yourself** in your dream, this means there is something about your private thoughts and feelings of which others need to be aware. Are you hiding something from both yourself and others? Are you too secretive? If **you are actually keeping a secret in real life and you dream of sharing it with a friend** and immediately feel as if a burden has been lifted from your shoulders, your unconscious may be encouraging you to be more open during your waking hours. Or did you dream of **betraying someone's confidence** in your dream and discover that this leads to unhappy or terrible consequences? If you did, your dreaming mind may be urging you to keep an important secret to yourself because there may be terrible repercussions if you revealed what you know.

Symbols of secrets and deception in dreams may be offering you a warning. If you were **cheating or someone cheated at your expense** in your dream, this was certainly a warning. For example, if you **cheated in a race, in a game or in a relationship** in your dream, are you willingly involved in some kind of deception in waking life? If you are, your dream is urging you to mend your ways; on the other hand, the dream may also be suggesting that someone is cheating on you. Any hint of **counterfeit goods, fakes or forgery** in your dream also suggests that you are not being true to yourself or honest with others in waking life. If the **fake is an antique** of some kind, this may be referring to a deceit that happened in the past. If you are **caught cheating or deceiving somebody** in your dream, perhaps you are in danger of being

Dream mysteries

For Jung, life was a great mystery, something about which we know and understand very little. He never hesitated to say, 'I don't know,' and always admitted when he had come to the end of his understanding. Since dreams reflect life, it is hardly surprising that dreams are just as intriguing, challenging and ultimately mysterious as life itself and some times just as difficult to understand.

If you have looked through this encyclopedia and are still having problems understanding what your dream meant, it might help before you go to sleep to ask your dreaming mind to make a confusing situation clearer for you or to present you with images or symbols that you can understand. When a dream seems important but you find it impossible to understand, ask yourself just before you go to sleep to be sent another which will give you further insight. If you can relate the dream to a particular incident, problem or situation in your waking life but cannot understand the message, think about the incident before making your request. Some dreams reflect the worry associated with problems, showing that you are wasting your energy and could be putting it to better use. Even insoluble problems can be helped by a change of attitude – and that is how dreams can help.

Put your request as a direct command to your dreaming mind. In your thoughts, just before you go to sleep, state to yourself quite clearly what you want to know, and tell yourself that in the morning you will remember all that you have dreamed. To show you are sincere, you might want to put a notebook and pen by your bedside in readiness to write down the first thing that comes into your mind when you wake up – your dream. Sometimes it can take a few requests, depending on the link between your conscious and unconscious mind, but eventually your efforts will achieve results.

found out in waking life. Cheating and faking in dreams may also suggest feelings of inadequacy in waking life.

If you were **performing a trick** in your dream, try to remember if your audience was impressed or not, as this dream may suggest that you are trying to manipulate people in waking life. If you were **plotting or scheming or are a part of a group of people plotting** in your dream, your unconscious is telling you that you are not being completely open and honest in your dealings with everyone in real life. Dreams of **hiding** or dreams in which you **lock up your possessions or hide them away in a safe, strong box, under the floorboards in the attic** may also represent some form of deception or fear that you are not facing

The Element Encyclopedia of 20,000 Dreams

up to. *See also* Surreal impossibility entry in SURREALISM AND FANTASY.

Spy

If **spies** feature in your dream or you actually **become a spy**, this can reveal a disturbing ambivalence, or lack of trust and love, towards someone or something in your waking life. Alternatively, spies may be an analogy for whatever worries you or gets you down. The image may also refer to loss of privacy or feeling as if you are being observed or watched. If **computer spyware** features in your dream, this suggests that you may be concerned about your privacy or that you are retrieving personal information about someone else's private affairs.

Unknown person and place

Is the person or place in your dream someone you know in waking life? Is the setting of your dream familiar? If the **person or place is familiar**, this may refer to your unconscious thoughts or perceptions about that particular person or place. **Unknown people or places** in your dreams, however, generally represent aspects of your character that you have not acknowledged or have neglected. How these mystery strangers look and behave will give you important clues to the nature of the problem area. The settings and features of a mystery landscape will also reflect your feelings about yourself and your life. *See also*; PEOPLE; PLACES.

RELATIONSHIPS

Most dreams depict human relationships in one way or another, but some can highlight intimate relationships with a lover or partner.

Dreams with romantic themes are attempts to answer your questions about relationships and the nature of love. As your dreaming mind searches for answers, it will review your past and present relationships, and try out other people or even celebrities as lovers or partners in order to give you a glimpse of how different your life could be. Such dreams are significant because they can reveal things about your relationship of which you may be unaware in waking life. Because of this, they can be extremely enlightening. Some dream analysts will interpret dreams about relationships as examples of wish-fulfillment or as opportunities to get intimate with people you cannot be close to in waking life. Although this may be true in some cases – we all share the universal longing to be loved – it may not apply to all such dreams. The dreaming mind can use relationship symbols for many different associations.

This chapter focuses on dreams with a romantic theme. For dreams that concern relationships with family members, friends, celebrities and other people, *see* FAMILY; FAMOUS PEOPLE; GATHERINGS; PEOPLE;

POSITIVE EMOTIONS. For dreams with an explicit sexual nature or content, *see* SEX.

Relationship Dreams

ADULTERY

Dreams in which **you or your partner have an affair** with someone else may reflect your feelings about adultery and betrayal but may also suggest that you are feeling insecure or lonely in your current relationship. Perhaps you suspect that your partner is cheating on you in real life; your unconscious may be showing you the worst-case scenario in an attempt to prepare you for the possibility of betrayal. Alternatively, if you are the one having an affair, this may simply be a way of once again experiencing the intoxicating high of falling in love, and sharing passion and sexual pleasure. Your dreaming mind may be highlighting your need for more intimacy and togetherness in your current relationship. Your feelings in the dream will give you an important clue. If you feel exhilarated, this suggests that you need to spice up your sex life with your partner, but if you felt guilty it may be warning you of the consequences of having an affair in waking life. You should also ask yourself if you have been faithful to your partner in thought and deed, as unkind thoughts and words might be seen as betrayals by other names. Another interpretation suggests that such dreams indicate that you are being unfaithful, not to another person, but to an idea or principle in waking life; perhaps you have stolen someone else's idea?

Bigamy dreams in which **you or your partner have more than one lover** can suggest a desire for more variety in your sex life but they can also suggest that you are trying to cope with too many ideas and activities at once. Wife-swapping dreams in which **married couples swap partners for sexual gratification** may reflect a longing for another partner or a desire to spice up your sex life. If the dream involves a couple you know, think about whether you are attracted to either partner or whether there is something about their relationship or their lifestyle that you admire or envy.

COURTSHIP

Jung identified the archetypal male and female aspects of the psyche and called them the 'anima' and 'animus'. These form a part of what he termed the 'collective unconscious' and play an important role in both forming your view of the opposite sex during sleep and in how you choose your partner in waking life. For example, a woman dreaming of her **idealized version of a man** is reflecting the masculine part of her psyche, the animus. The anima is the embodiment of the feminine parts of a man's psyche. If you dream that **you have a sweetheart**, this may represent your perfect match, prompted by the animus in women or the anima in men.

A dream in which **you are in love** is generally a sign of reciprocated affection or the desire for it. If the object of your affection is your partner already, this is a positive sign for the relationship but only if your partner looks contented; if he or she looks ill at ease, the signs are less positive. If you are in a relationship and you dream of **falling in love with someone else**, this could be a sign that you are attracted to that person in waking life. If this isn't the case, try to figure out what qualities that person represents and how you can incorporate them into your current relationship. If you dream of having **rivals for the affection of your sweetheart**, this could be a sign of jealousy or indecision on your part.

If you dream of your **current boyfriend or girlfriend**, then this is a symbol of your emotional attachment to him or her. If you dream of an **ex-lover**, this does not mean that you are still in love with them; your dream is simply revisiting feelings or hopes connected with them. Your ex-lover becomes a symbol for all the hopes for love that may not currently be satisfied. In dreams, lovers may be your waking partner or your ideal wish-fulfillment partner; whoever they are, they may be compensating for a waking situation that is unsatisfactory. If you are single and dream about a **future husband or wife**, this should not be interpreted literally; such a dream may be expressing some other hope for the future. For dreams about husbands or wives, *see* FAMILY.

Influential relationship theories

The Oedipus complex is one of Freud's best-known and most influential theories in the realm of dream interpretation. The term refers to a group of largely unconscious ideas and feelings that focus on the desire to possess the parent of the opposite sex and eliminate that of the same sex. The complex is named after the mythical Oedipus, who killed his father and then married his mother without knowing they were his parents. When Oedipus discovered the truth, he felt full of remorse and even though he was not personally responsible for the crimes, he gouged out his own eyes and wandered blind and exiled.

Although the term is now applied to both men and women, at first it only referred to the male version of the complex. In women, the Electra complex was said to exist. In the myth of Electra, she masterminded the murder of her mother to avenge her father's death. According to Freud, the Oedipus and Electra complexes are universal phenomena, being responsible for much unconscious guilt and for dreams that focus on the **death of a parent or lover**.

Jung saw the world of dreams and relationships quite differently. He rejected Freud's heavy emphasis on sexuality and the Oedipus and Electra complexes as a key to interpretation. For Jung, dreams were not just a way of helping us to understand conflicts and anxieties, but also a way to encourage the creative unfolding and development of a person's whole potential. Jung developed a theory called the 'soul image', in relation to the human need to create a sense of wholeness. The soul image tends to be an archetypal image. The symbols that represent the soul image often appear in dreams that involve **intimacy with the opposite sex**, but they can also be represented in countless other ways. For example, the **sea** is feminine in dreams as it is associated with waters of the womb and the **earth** is also feminine. Symbols of masculinity can appear in dreams as **bulls or lions** or any other phallic symbol, such as a **tall building**. Jung felt that dreams can be used to discover and explore soul images to help us become a fuller and more balanced person.

DIVORCE/SEPARATION

Dreams that involve **divorce or separation from your partner** in some way may be expression of anger towards your current partner. Such dreams may also represent some kind of emotional breakdown or lack of communication in the relationship. If you have a dream in which your **partner demands a divorce**, you may be feeling

The Element Encyclopedia of 20,000 Dreams

concerned about the robustness of your marriage. On the other hand, your unconscious may be traumatizing you with such a dream to remind you of how lucky you are to have such a wife or husband, thereby warning you not to take them for granted.

If it is you who is **asking for the divorce** in your dream, ask yourself if you are longing to escape from your marriage. If you do have dreams which feature divorce, they can be extremely unsettling, especially if you are in a committed relationship in waking life; it is important to bear in mind, however, that your unconscious may have used your partner as a symbol for something else to which you are wedded, such as a job, an ideal or an opinion. If so, your dreaming mind may have been urging you to leave your job, change your mind or open your mind to new possibilities. A dream of **saying farewell to your lover or partner** is similar in many ways to dreams about death, as it does not mean you are going to leave someone, it means you are saying goodbye to something they represent.

GAY RELATIONSHIP

Many psychologists believe that each one of us has at least some element of homosexuality within us and dreams in which you experience **homosexual or lesbian urges** may suggest a desire for paternal or maternal love, conflict or anxiety about your gender, or feelings of sexual inadequacy. The dream may also be urging you to explore the masculine or feminine side of your nature.

INAPPROPRIATE PAIRING

At whatever stage of life you are, if there is a deep imbalance or lack of harmony in your current relationship, you may find that your dreams take on a warning quality, even becoming haunted and strange. **Plants, trees, animals and fish** in particular tend to appear as symbols of the life or vitality of the relationship; if you are having relationships problems, you may dream of **trying to rescue an injured animal or watering dying plants**. Another common dream is **entrusting your beloved pet or fish to your partner's care**, only to return and find it neglected, dying or even dead. These may all be symbols of those of your emotional needs that are being starved or denied, and of relationships that are struggling to survive.

Other dreams that signal emotional imbalance in intimate relationships are dreams of **houses on fire, bombs that are about to explode or images of starvation, loneliness, torture or neglect**. These images are warning you that your relationship is out of balance, dangerously fragile or in need of rescuing in your waking life. An **inappropriate meeting or pairing of two objects** in your dream, for example a **kangaroo and a light bulb**, might suggest that you are somewhat concerned about an unsuitable partner; this might either be your own partner, or that of someone close to you – say a son or a daughter. **Repeatedly getting the wrong person on the phone, seeing an email error message or simply being unable to communicate** may also indicate a disturbing inability to communicate with someone in your life who is important to you. If you are having **problems with your cellphone,** this might be seen by Freudians as a symbol of sexual dysfunction or anxiety. Another potent symbol of a relationship coming to an end is the image of **gold dust or precious jewels running through your fingers** in a dream. The image is even more eloquent if you are running with **two cupped hands full of water in an attempt to quench your own or someone else's thirst and the dream water falls through your hands**.

A real-life need to resolve relationship problems may be symbolized by dreams about repairing something, perhaps **fixing a car or attaching things together with glue, sellotape or bluetac**. If you experience blocked communication in your relationship or suffer from an inability to get through to someone close to you, you may have dreams in which **people are staring at one another in your dream but no one is saying**. Such a dream may also suggest that now is an excellent time to deepen your relationship, as the silent figures await your signal for a new and exciting phase of your relationship to begin.

MARRIAGE/ENGAGEMENT

Dreams about **proposals** may simply be wish-fulfillment, especially if the person to whom you are getting married is someone you are attracted to in waking life. If you are already married and dream that **someone else, a person you know or a stranger proposed to you**, you need to think about what your dream suitor could represent to you, as this will hold the key to the interpretation. The dream suitor may represent a commitment that you may be being asked to make in real life, for example a new job offer. Your dream reaction to both

the proposal and to the **engagement ring** will give you an indication as to how you feel about committing yourself to this person or project.

Like dreams about proposals, dreams about **weddings and marriage** may be simple wish-fulfillment. If you have such a dream and are about to get married, pay attention to how you feel. Are you beaming with joy or filled with panic? If you are feeling anxious, your unconscious may have been urging you to acknowledge your qualms and either come to terms with them or call off the wedding. If the **church altar** features in your dream marriage, bear in mind that this is a symbol of sacrifice too; if you are **wearing white**, this is a symbol of purity and innocence. Are you in danger of sacrificing yourself to someone who isn't good for you? If a **wedding dress or cake** appears in your dream, this may refer to your feelings and hopes about relationships and wedding. If the **wedding dress is given by your mother**, it refers to qualities and strengths associated with your mother that are relevant to your relationship. Listen to the uncertainties your unconscious is expressing and try to resolve them before the wedding day.

If you have **no intention of getting married in real life and you are getting married in your dream to someone you know**, this could suggest that you harbor unconscious romantic feelings towards them. Alternatively, your dream may be sending you such a dream to highlight another form of joining together, such as a marriage of ideas or a merging of plans and projects. Another interpretation suggests that your dreaming mind has conjured up a marriage scenario to indicate the need to bring together two opposing aspects of your personality – Jungians would suggest the masculine and feminine qualities we all possess – to create a harmonious whole. Could your bride have been your anima if you are a man and your bridegroom your animus if you are a woman?

Similarly, **marrying a stranger** in your dream may suggest the possibility of uniting two different but complementary aspects of your personality – your intuition and your intelligence for example. Such a partnership may empower you to take a new direction in your life and any children of this marriage may suggest the outcome or result of this new potential. If you dreamed of **being at someone else's wedding**, your unconscious may also have been highlighting two different aspects of your personality. On the other hand, if you **know one of the partners getting married** in your dream, perhaps you are worried about losing a close relationship with them.

If you were the **best man or bridesmaid** in your dream, pay attention to your feelings; if you felt jealous, this could suggest your fear of loneliness in waking life as in 'always a bridesmaid and never a bride'. Finally, if you have been married for many years and dream of **marrying again**, this may suggest that your feelings for your partner are as vibrant as ever. It may also suggest that your mutual commitment is showing signs of strain and needs special care and attention to revive it. In some cultures, to dream of a **wedding** signifies a death in the family or change in the family's circumstances. To dream about a **honeymoon** may reflect a period of happiness in your waking life.

RELATIONSHIP SYMBOLS

Animals, reptiles, birds and insects often represent aspects of relationships in dreams. Birds in particular can take on a specific meaning. For example a **bird or prey, or a thieving magpie** might suggest adultery or the threat of it, whilst the **sweet singing of the dove or nightingale** suggests harmony or the need for reconciliation between loved ones. **Feathers**, aside from their phallic form as quills, often represent warmth, affection and tenderness. To dream of a **spider's web** might suggest insecurity about your relationships in general or the need to remove yourself from a current relationship that you are entangled in. The dream may also be warning you against becoming entrapped in an obsessive or destructive relationship.

In dreams, **hotels, inns or guesthouses** are symbols of the short-lived nature of some relationships, although hotels can also suggest that your relationship may be heading towards a new level of intimacy. Pay particular attention to the **view from your hotel room**. Is it beautiful and bright, or dark and gloomy? A **harmonious serene landscape bathed in gentle light** is always a comforting image and may suggest nostalgia for a lost friend or lover.

Fire gives both heat and light, and is the symbol of strong emotions such as love and anger and self knowledge. In dreams, the appearance of **flames or fire** may therefore be suggesting some kind of resolution or compromise with your partner. Bear in mind, though, that flames flicker and can be extinguished, so you need to act quickly before they go out.

Relationship dreams at different stages of your life

Dreams about relationships are extremely common. This is because the health and survival of your relationships is a primary goal for your unconscious; in your dreams it constantly reviews your relationship options, mulls things over and tries to identify what went wrong and how to do things better. It may also give you a glimpse of how different things might be if you married someone else, had an affair or got divorced.

Although the following dreams can occur at any stage of your life, you may find that the focus of your relationship dreams shifts during your lifespan. In your teenage years, dream scenarios in which you are **suddenly thrown together with someone to whom you are attracted** are very common. The goal of the dream is to help you determine if someone is or is not interested in you in waking life. By the mid-twenties, however, relationship dreams move beyond initial attraction and begin to explore who is or is not right for us. This is the time when **strangers, celebrities and friends** tend to appear as dream lovers and partners. You may find the images shocking but it is important to bear in mind that the images are unlikely to represent the real person and more likely to represent qualities that you are evaluating.

During your thirties and forties, romantic dreams focus on explanations for why relationships may have disappointed in the past and offer dreams that can show you what to go after or avoid in the future. Dreams in which your **current partner or lover is unfaithful** are extremely common at this time; it is as if your dreaming mind is urging you to pay attention to your relationship, and secure or safeguard what you have.

During your fifties and sixties, dreams shift their focus onto things you have learned to value in your life. **Past and present partners** become shorthand symbols for the quality or experience you had with them. For example, your **first lover** represents passion and excitement or the **partner who was unfaithful** represents someone who cannot be trusted. Although you may dream of people from your past, your dreaming mind is using them as symbols to refer to your current relationships. From your seventies onwards, dreams are more likely to zoom in on the **very nature of love itself** to help you gain a deeper understanding of love and affairs of the heart.

RELIGION

If you have a dream that features religious or spiritual imagery, it is essential to take your own beliefs into consideration.

If a figure or image of your own personal faith appears in your dream, the most likely interpretation is that your dreaming mind is reminding you of the importance your faith plays in your life; it may also be urging you to make decisions in accordance with your beliefs. If, however, you dream of an aspect of a belief system that is not yours, the meaning is less obvious; the key to its interpretation lies in what the figure or image means to you in waking life. For example, if you associate Christ with humility and self-sacrifice, your dreaming mind may be suggesting that you need to make some kind of personal sacrifice.

Dreams that feature a strong religious factor do not only occur to those who practice a faith. Indeed Jung said that many of his patients who had such dreams had lost their faith and their dreams were referring to their sense of guilt and loss. When an individual neglects the spiritual in waking life, dreams may try to compensate with images that highlight the existence of an inner truth.

It is impossible to include here all the symbols of all religions, but many of the symbols mentioned in this chapter can be applied to other faiths. *See also* MIND, BODY, SPIRIT; SURREALISM AND FANTASY; SYMBOLS.

BIBLICAL FIGURE

According to Jung, the figures of **Adam and Eve** play a positive role in the unconscious mind as they are symbols of the 'self affirming ego'. Together they are seen as the source of all intellectual independence. **Eating the forbidden fruit** is also considered a powerful image of self discovery and fulfillment. **Cain and Abel** are archetypal figures of sibling rivalry and human strife, and according to Freud, the **murder of Abel by his jealous brother Cain** symbolizes the rivalry among brothers and sisters for their parental love. The dream may also suggest that childhood anxieties or animosities have persisted into adult life.

The Biblical patriarch **Abraham** who breaks with idolatry to seek enlightenment is a symbol of the importance of exploring the unfamiliar to find wisdom and self-knowledge. **Jacob** is another Old Testament figure who stands for higher aspirations. **Moses**, on the other hand, is the bringer of law who dies before entering the Promised Land to which he leads his people from captivity in Egypt. In dreams, he may symbolize moral integrity on the path to spiritual enlightenment or the holy figure that can lead us out of difficulty. Dreams that feature images of **Samson and Delilah** suggest castration anxiety or warn against the destructive power of an overheated libido as Delilah cut Samson's hair that was the secret of his strength. If any **Biblical figure** features in your dream, it might be worth your while to re-read or rediscover their story or character to see how it applies to your current situation in waking life.

GOD/GODDESS

You may have a dream in which the image of a **god**, such as the **warrior lord Mars** or a **goddess** such as **Aphrodite, the goddess of love**, appears. The characteristics of gods and goddesses that populate the world's religions are in many ways similar; this is because they are archetypal figures that embody universal human emotions and characteristics, such as love, hate, anger, justice, jealousy or other potent energies. This should be borne in mind when you try to interpret your dream. If you **become a deity** in your dream, the message is even more potent and perhaps you do feel god like in waking life or are aware that you are being given the opportunity to reach your fullest potential; bear in mind though that such a dream also warns against the dangers of egotism or overreaching yourself in some way.

If a **woman dreams of mythical gods**, it may help her to understand those aspects of her own personality that are generally considered to be more masculine. If a **man dreams of mythical gods**, he is linking with his own sense of masculinity. The powerful need that exists within us all for approval and love can often be recognized in the mythical gods. For example, **Adonis** represents health and self-love, **Apollo** represents sunny optimism and **Chiron** healing. **Jehovah** in the guise of a vengeful God alerts you to the negative side of power. **Mars** as the god of war suggests the drive to succeed and win, whilst **Zeus** is the father figure in both its positive and negative form.

If a **woman dreams of mythical goddesses**, this will connect her to the archetypal images of femininity and sisterhood with other women. If a **man dreams of mythical goddesses**, this signifies all that a man fears about female power. There are goddess figures that are perceived as destructive such as **Kali, Bast and Lilith** but also beneficial ones such as **Athena**, the goddess of wisdom and strategy or **Aphrodite**, the goddess of love and beauty. **Artemis** is the goddess of the moon and female intuition and independence. **Demeter** is the maternal archetype and **Hera** represents the woman whose goal in life is marriage. **Hestia** is a symbol of loneliness and patience, whilst **Persephone**, Queen of the Underworld, expresses the need of some women to please others and be needed by them; her behavior must turn from passive and submissive into an ability to take responsibility for own life.

You may dream of **Hindu deities** such as **Brahma**, who is the source of the cosmos, **Vishnu** its protector and **Shiva**, who is both the destroyer and protector of life. Together with the **Devil**,

Major religions and dream interpretation

Buddhism and dreams

The principle aim of **Buddhism** is to achieve liberation from the things that bind consciousness to what Buddhists see as the illusory concepts of the self and the world. This principle or goal is called liberation or Nirvana, and it is sometimes associated with the obliteration of a sense of self or ego. This is not the death of the self but an untangling of the self from the illusions that emotions and thoughts create. Dreams are therefore thought to depict the illusions of the everyday experience of life in that they express a person's fears, hopes and opinions.

Christianity and dreams

According to traditional **Christianity**, the purpose of dreams is to improve communication with God; this can be shown by the constant references in the Bible to communication through the medium of dreams between man and God, man and the angels, and between man and his higher self. The moral standards of the dreamer may be reflected in the clarity and degree of quality of their dreams.

Hinduism and dreams

Hindu dream interpretation puts great importance on individual dream images, and relates them to gods and demons. This belief that dream symbols may be universal as well as individual is similar to the more modern ideas put forward by Carl Jung in his theory of the 'collective unconscious'.

Islam and dreams

Dreams, according to Muslim scholars, are of three types. The first of these are sound dreams that are indicative of glad tidings. These can include premonitions of the future. A second type of dream is said to be evil and the result of Satanic whisperings or inspirations. A third type of dream can be termed as 'idle dreams', and they are the result of eating unpalatable foods, the over-exercise of one's imaginations, or experiences in life which might also be reflected in one's dreams.

Judaism and dreams

Dreams have long been considered a legitimate form of divine revelation in **Jewish** mysticism and throughout Jewish history – from Hagar, Joseph and King Solomon to Sigmund Freud and beyond – Jews have honored their dreams and searched for their deeper meanings. Judaism takes dreams very seriously. In the Bible, we read of the dreams of the great people of Israel: Abraham, Jacob, Joseph and many of the prophets. Judaism is of the opinion that all prophecy, except for the prophecy of Moses, was transmitted to the prophets when they were in a dreamlike, almost catatonic, trance. The Talmud places heavy emphasis on the interpretation of the dream as the key to its fulfillment. If a seemingly bad or frightening dream is interpreted positively, no ill effects from that dream will ever actually occur.

Other traditions and dreams

Oriental traditions concerning dreams are comparative and philosophical; the dreamer's state of mind is thought to be of more importance than the predictive power of the dreams themselves. Ancient **Chinese philosophy** holds that the soul is separated from the body whilst dreaming and that several levels of consciousness exist; the dreamer's horoscope, time of year, and the individual's physical condition are all taken into consideration when interpreting dreams.

their appearance in a dream expresses confusion but also great creativity and liberation. If other figures from ancient myth and legend feature in your dream, refer to the ARCHETYPES and SURREALISM AND FANTASY. You may also like to do your own research on dream images inspired by ancient myths, gods and goddesses to see if you can discover their role in your dream and how their universal archetypal energy relates to you.

PROPHETS

If you are deeply committed to your faith, a dream encounter with a **prophet or a figure of great spiritual significance** such as **Muhammad** to a Muslim, **Gautama Siddhartha** to a Buddhist or **Christ** or the **Virgin Mary** to a Christian, is likely to affect you deeply. Your dreaming mind may conjure up such a profoundly important image to give you strength at a time in your life when you need to make a decision about your future. On the other hand, such a dream may also suggest that you have something on your conscience. Whatever the case, your dreaming mind is urging you to follow the example of the spiritual role model as it will help you make the right decision. If you dream of a **prophet or leading religious figure of a faith you do not share**, do not dismiss the image as false because all religious figures are united by the same universal truths of love, peace and integrity. Prophets and in some cases **priests** in dreams can also suggest some kind of conflict between your past and your present.

Jesus Christ is a symbol of both the divine and the human; in dreams, he depicts powerful influences acting upon your personality and your life. The image of **Christ on the cross** is a symbol of life, death and salvation, the perfect man or state to which you can aspire; if you have such a dream it tends to occur at a crisis point in your life or perhaps when something good in you is being crucified. Christ appearing on the cross also suggests redemption through suffering; you do not need to be crucified physically to suffer. Jesus, like the compassionate, meditating Buddha, is also a symbol of peace, humility and service to others.

The figure of the **Buddha** appearing in your dreams reminds you of the power of suffering and renunciation. If you dream of **being a Buddhist**, you need to look at the difference between Western and Eastern spirituality. In fact, any dream in which you **convert to or see images related to a religion, be it Judaism, Christianity, Islam or branches or sects of religions such as Scientology, Kabala or the Moonies** suggests a need to open your mind to new possibilities and to explore new outlooks and approaches to life.

Saint/Angel/Perfect being

Dreams that feature **saints, angels, icons, bodhisattvas, immortals, avatars or any other perfect being** that possesses a high level of spiritual development that lifts them above the imperfect human race all embody higher religious aspirations and positive qualities to which you can aspire. The same applies to symbols of transcendence and illumination that can appear in your dreams, such as **halos, auras of light and angelic wings**. Bear in mind that, depending on the other details of your dream, saints can also indicate martyrdom and extreme self-sacrifice, so you need to consider whether or not you are being exploited by someone in waking life.

Saints and angels are also traditionally considered to be divine messengers between the Supreme Being and humanity, so if you dream of them, what message are they trying to impart to you? Do you need to adopt a more moral stance in your waking life? Perhaps there is a moral issue you should not ignore; or is your unconscious telling you that you have righteousness on your side? Your dream may be urging you to develop your spirituality. If the meaning of your dream still remains unclear, try to meditate on it for a while since you may find that it leads you to new insights.

Angels are associated with dead children, so may play a comforting role at times of bereavement. In spiritual terms, angels also symbolize pure beings and freedom from earthly matters. **Dark angels** are said to be those who have not totally rejected the ego and earthly passions, and if images of them appear in your dream, you may be being warned about some kind of spiritual transgression. If you dream of the **Virgin Mary**, this may be a symbol of the feminine ideal; the Virgin mother of Christ represents purity, compassion and motherly love.

Spiritual authority

Priests, rabbis, popes, cardinals, priestesses, lamas, gurus, yogis, Jedi knights, monks, mullahs, nuns and curates are all symbols of spiritual authority in dreams and in some cases they represent your own spiritual wisdom. The key to interpreting their appearance in a dream is the message or feeling they convey to you. If you were uneasy because the message was an unwelcome reminder of a duty you have neglected, your dreaming mind may be urging you to take positive action that will transform your spiritual well-being. Such figures may also stand for parental disapproval or advice; perhaps you are yearning for some moral certainties and direction in your waking life. According to ancient dream-lore, any dream concerning a **priest** is a fortunate one. In particular, it means the end of a quarrel.

Symbols of faith

Candles and chalices are common religious symbols. The candle's flame suggests divine enlightenment, so if candles appeared in your dream this may indicate your hope of seeing the light in some way in your waking life. Chalices carry the water of life or, in the case of the Holy Grail, the blood of Christ; they are typically images of healing and renewal in dreams. If a chalice does appear in your dream, pay attention to its appearance, as it is also a symbol of your destiny and reflects how you see yourself. Is the **chalice encrusted with gold and jewels, or is it simply a humble cup**?

If your dream contained a message delivered from a **pulpit or altar**, this suggests that the dream comes from the highest authority or the highest part of your inner wisdom. Dreams that feature other well-known symbols of faith, such as the **cross or a crucifix**, serve as reminders of your faith if you are religious. If you are not religious, they may be an indication of the need for some kind of faith or spirituality in your life. If **crucifixion** figures in your dream, this may be a reflection of some area of your life in which you feel you are being crucified or making a huge sacrifice. It may also represent your need to sacrifice yourself through passion and pain. To dream of the **Resurrection** is a good sign, as it is a powerful symbol of hope and renewal.

An **eagle soaring to the heavens** is a common dream symbol of religious aspiration; if the **eagle is falling to earth** this may be a warning against mortal pride. **Incense** is a form of prayer through perfume and smoke, and if you are aware of its presence in your dream, it suggests a need to raise your consciousness or improve yourself or your environment in some way. To dream of a **third eye** – whether it is on your own or someone else's forehead, is a sign of the developed awareness and intuition that comes from spiritual development; it may represent the third eye of the Buddha and suggests unity and balance. If you dream of the **Tree of Life**, symbol of the divine union of heaven and earth in the Kabala, it suggests that you have developed the ability to live life successfully on both a spiritual and a material level. Dreams of **fish** may be related to Christianity or may symbolize the depths of the unconscious.

Supreme Being

Each one of us will have a different belief about the existence of a supreme God or being. For some it may be the one God of Judeo-Christian or Islamic tradition, for others it may be a universal and eternal life force of goodness or a state of enlightenment; others may deny its existence altogether. However you perceive or understand the nature of the **Supreme Being**, the important thing when it comes to interpreting dream in which it appears is your understanding of its almighty power, and your feelings of humility and insignificance or anger and disbelief in relation to it. You are most likely to have such dreams at times in your life when you feel that your life is out of control; your dreaming mind may send you this image as a way of urging you to seek guidance from your intuition. Alternatively, your dreaming mind may conjure this image because someone important in your life – a boss or a teacher – is 'playing God', and your fear and reverence for this person may be misplaced.

Central to the Jungian interpretation of dreams is the **being of light**, an archetypal image or universal spiritual principle. The image may appear bathed in light of the **seven-branched menorah candelabrum** of Judaism or simply wearing a **halo of light**; however it appears, such a light expresses divine energy and illumination.

Heaven and Hell

Devil

Dreaming of a **devil or any other personification of evil such as an imp or a demon** does not mean that you are heading for eternal damnation. In most cases, such images are simply a warning that you may be succumbing to temptation or heading down a path that will lead to unhappiness. Your conscience may be making a timely appearance, asking you whether there is some wrong you need to right in real life. The devil may also refer to your shadow or to repressed sexual drives that need your attention. Alternatively, devil dreams may be warning about a danger that lurks outside you rather than within. Is there someone in your waking life who does not have your best interests at heart? Finally, if spirituality is neglected in your waking life, it may reappear in its negative or terrifying forms, such as the **devil, demons or the vengeful gods of the Hindu faith**.

Heaven

Dreams of **being in heaven or other states of bliss and perfection such as Nirvana or Samadhi** reveal either your current state of mind or – as with all wish-fulfillment dreams – your hopes for the future. Are you feeling peaceful and content at the moment? Or is your waking life so difficult that your dreaming mind is sending you escapist images? Bear in mind that dreams about heaven, just like dreams

Rituals and religious ceremonies

Each of the symbols that appear in a religious dream should be taken into account as each will contribute in some way to its meaning. Their significance is likely to accord with your religious faith but whether you are religious or not, the interpretation tends to be similar. If you were **reading, hearing, singing or chanting from a religious book, manuscript, sacred scripture or text such as the Bible or Koran**, your dreaming mind is highlighting your desire to know the truth or the answer to a question that is on your mind. You may feel the need for some kind of guidance and your dreaming mind is urging you to pay attention to the problem or issue on your mind before it gets any worse. Dreams about **praying** also reflect a feeling of helplessness and the need for guidance in waking life.

If you **attended a religious ceremony or rite or were part of a congregation** in your dream, your feelings about this are crucial. If you felt **uplifted and comforted**, this suggests that you feel at peace with your moral code; but if your **attitude was one of rebellion or anger**, your dreaming mind may be urging you to assert your individuality, as you are currently being stifled by the restrictions of your belief system. Alternatively, if you are **not allowed to participate in your dream ritual**, you may be harboring feelings of guilt because you have broken some important rules. As ceremonies are used to attain deeper awareness and to establish a new

order, another interpretation suggests that dream ceremonies and rituals refer to major life changes or new attitudes in your waking life that are having a profound effect on you. **Religious processions and carnivals** in dreams reflect a need to stimulate your imagination and perhaps increase your faith.

A dream of **visiting a religious place** may be commenting on the lack of spirituality in your life; this is especially so if the **church, mosque, chapel, temple, cathedral or religious site** was peaceful and calming, as it suggests that you need to seek out a place where you can feel secure and reflect on your waking life. If you dreamed of a **crypt or religious burial ground**, this may be suggesting that your spiritual self is buried. If the **religious site or building was in ruins**, you need to consider which aspect of your spiritual life is crumbling away. If you heard **church bells or religious music** in your dream, this suggests a desire to expand your spirit.

A dream that features **baptism or an initiation of some kind** suggests spiritual renewal or a new life for the dreamer. If you were **baptized and given a new name**, this indicates a new start; the significance of that name will be important. If you attended the **baptism of a baby**, this may represent an idea or project you are working on and for which you need approval. If you were **blessed** in your dream, this suggests approval of some kind of action or attitude in your waking life. **Blasphemy,** on the other hand, reflects irreverence or insults of some kind in your waking life. If you dream of taking **Holy Communion,** because in real life this is a form of blessing for forgiveness and renewal, in dreams it represents sacred sharing. If **bread and wine** appears in your dream, these refer to the basic needs in your life. As always, your feelings in the dream are important. Did you feel comforted or anxious? If you dream of a **crusade,** this suggests that you need to fight for or against something or someone in your waking life. *See also* GATHERINGS.

about hell, are more likely to relate to your waking life on earth and are not predictive of the afterlife, although for many people who believe in life after death such dreams can be extremely comforting.

Heaven can appear in your dreams in the traditional forms depicted in religious art with **God surrounded by choirs of angels** or as a **beautiful idealized landscape**. If you witness yourself in such a setting, it could symbolize your quest for spiritual truth. On the other hand, standing before your God may also conjure images of the Last Judgment, so perhaps you are feeling unworthy of entering a spiritual plane or feeling judged in some way in waking life. *See also* Near-death experiences entry in STAGES OF LIFE.

HELL

Dreams of being **tormented in hell** can reveal either your current state of mind or your fears for the future. Is life particularly hellish at present? Are you wracked with guilt about something you have done or are thinking of doing? Hell in dreams is also an image of negative illusions or self-created misery perhaps arising out of pain from past traumas or a situation that made you deeply unhappy. Hell therefore represents the projection of your inner state onto the world; if you feel miserable, the world will seem miserable too. In other words you create your own heaven or hell.

Images of hell in dreams also indicate that you may be punishing yourself in some way but they do offer some hope, as once you have passed through this period of inner turmoil you can emerge a new and better person. It is important to bear in mind that dreams about hell relate to your waking life on earth and are not predictive of the afterlife; for people who believe in an afterlife, however, such dreams can be extremely frightening. On the psychological plane, hell is also a symbol of the unconscious and such a dream may suggest that you are confronting the darker side of your personality.

REPTILES, FISH AND AMPHIBIANS

According to Jung, fish represent the deepest levels of the unconscious mind.

He suggested that this was due to their cold-blooded nature and their early evolution on earth. Dreams that feature creatures of the sea are therefore indicators of deep-rooted instincts, fears and anxieties that have not been fully uncovered in waking life. Jungians think that fish symbolize a spiritual quest or seeking, whilst other dream interpreters claim that fish symbolize abundance and fertility. Fish are sometimes also recognized as a symbol for Christ and Christianity. Given all these possible interpretations, it is worth focusing on the condition and appearance of the fish and other sea life in your dreams so that you can discover the personal meaning they hold for you.

There are a number of possible interpretations for dreams that feature reptiles and amphibians but in general they suggest danger, energy and the powers of healing and transcendence. If you are scrupulous in remembering the kind of behavior displayed by the creature in your dream, it should help you identify which feeling or emotion is applicable to your current situation. As with all dream interpretations,

when it comes to underwater dreams that feature fish, reptiles and amphibians, it is also important to consider whether your unconscious is using word-play to get its message across.

Creatures of the Deep

CRUSTACEAN/CRAB/LOBSTER/SHRIMP

Crabs mainly inhabit the sea and therefore have traditionally been associated with aspects of your unconscious. They may symbolize the ability to cultivate homely energy in various circumstances, as crab power is the energy of making a home, however far away from home you may be. Crabs also represent the energy of the psyche that rejects change and finds it hard to let go; the side of us that hangs back instead of taking a chance. If you are **bitten**

or pinched by a crab in your dream, it is possible that some part of your current situation is resistant to change; this might be because of yourself, or because of another. The **armored body of the crab** suggests the need to protect yourself against something or someone, and the **pincer-like claws** show a willingness to attack or tackle whatever obstacles lie in their path. If a crab appears in your dream, could it be a reflection of a crabby or bad-tempered aspect of your personality; an aspect that resists the attempts of others to penetrate the rough outer shell you have developed in waking life to protect your soft emotional center?

If your dreaming mind saw a **crab or lobster without its shell**, this is a symbol of your feelings of emotional vulnerability. If the **crab scuttled sideways** in your dream, this may mirror a tendency to be evasive when others try to get too close to you or it may also reflect your inability to think logically or in a straight line. Additionally, with their habit of **burrowing under the sand**, the crab may represent anything that is sapping your energy. Bear in mind, too, that the crab is the symbol for someone born under the astrological sign of Cancer, so your dream crab may be referring to them. If a **shrimp** appears in your dream, this may represent rivalry or resentment towards someone, as 'shrimp' is often a disparaging nickname. But when coupled with the mother image of the sea, the shrimp may represent the reawakening of dormant sibling or childhood rivalries.

DOLPHIN/PORPOISE

Dolphins are actually mammals but many people think of them as being fish. They have incredibly positive associations in both the real and the dream world. They are intelligent, friendly creatures that are reputed to steer sailors to safety when their ships are in trouble. They were also once believed to guide the spirits of the dead to the afterlife, which is why they are a symbol for Christ. So if a dolphin appears in your dream or you are **swimming with dolphins**, it may indicate fun, friendship and a sense of optimism. They may also symbolize your sense of connection with others; when dreams of dolphins happen during low points in waking life, dreamers tend to report feeling more positive the next day. Because dolphins are often thought of as spiritually advanced beings, full of love, awareness, inner harmony and healing energy, if **playful dolphins** appear in your dreams, perhaps you need to adopt a non-resistant stance to life and learn to go with the flow. If, however, the dream **dolphin is injured or in danger** in your dream or the **dolphin is attacked by a shark**, this implies that some important connection is being threatened in waking life. **Two dolphins facing in opposite directions** in your dream can represent the duality of your nature, suggesting that you may need to accept that you are not one dimensional and that negative aspects of your character contribute to your wholeness as a human being.

FISH

Water is the element in which **fish** live, so there may be a strong emotional factor in a dream about fish; fish can also represent unconscious insights, as the unconscious is often represented by the sea, the fish being ideas flitting through it. According to Jung, fish are symbols used in the dream to mimic impulses that suddenly dart out of the unconscious and which have a frightening or redeeming effect in waking life. In the realm of sleep, fish are considered harbingers of inspiration and creativity, so a **fish or schools of fish glimpsed beneath the surface** often represent unconscious material or truths hidden within yourself. To dream of a **fish's eye** symbolizes a watchful and diligent nature, but to see a **dead fish** signifies a worry about the way you interact with others. Is your lack of emotional warmth turning you into a cold fish? If you dreamed of a **fish leaping out of the ocean** before returning to the waves or **fish caught in the net and brought to the surface**, this may indicate the brief emergence of intuition. If the **fish are dirty, injured or ugly**, this doesn't mean that you are too; it just means the phase you're currently in may be painful and tough. This is a time for patience and gentleness with yourself.

If **fish are swimming just below the surface**, they may represent the wisdom you have not yet brought to consciousness in waking life, whilst **dead fish** in your dream may suggest you have failed to express your basic urges or emotions. If, in your dream, the **fish are in an aquarium**, this may refer to aspects of your personality that are prevented from expressing themselves, or constricting emotional conditions in general. The dream may also refer to aspects of yourself that need to be nourished emotionally; a **goldfish bowl** may simply suggest boredom or a lack of privacy or confidentiality. If you dream of a **fish that needs your care**, it is likely that you are a creative, sensitive person who has become trapped in a lifestyle that inhibits self-expression. According to Freud, fish

are a phallic symbol because of their elongated shape, and, because females spawn hundreds of eggs, he also associated them with fertility.

The symbol of Pisces in the Zodiac is a fish, and dream fish may perhaps be reminding you of a person you know born under that sign. The fish is also one of the oldest symbols of Christianity, so a dream of a **fish, fishing or eating fish** may also reflect your desire for spiritual nourishment. Fish may also appear in your dream as messengers telling you that something does not feel right, that something 'smells fishy'; alternatively, they may be telling you that you are feeling misplaced or you don't belong, like a 'fish out of water'. A **fish on a hook** may suggest accepting something completely, without hesitation or question; but be attentive to what being a 'wet fish' means. *See also* PETS.

FISHING/FISHERMAN

If you were **fishing** in your dream, you may be looking for insight into a particular problem in waking life. The dream may also suggest that deep emotions are being brought to the surface. Consider what you were fishing for in your dream; was it compliments, attention or the truth in a difficult or 'fishy' situation? Did you **catch your dream fish** in your dream? If you did, it may indicate that you will find that an answer to a long-standing question suddenly pops into your mind. Alternatively, if your catch **gasped for breath as it flapped around on the ground**, do you feel like a fish out of water in waking life? If it **wriggled frantically**, could your dream have been drawing your attention to a 'slippery fish' or elusive

Fish species

Individual fish species impart their own meanings to dreamers. Pay particular attention to the color of the fish as this will add to the interpretation; for example, a **purple fish** connotes spirituality. When interpreting the meaning of specific fish in your dreams it is also important to bear in mind cultural associations with certain types of fish that may imbue them with extra meaning. For example, if you are familiar with Japanese lore you may equate **carp** with courage, love or good luck; the dream carp could, however, be pointing to your tendency to carp on or nag at someone in waking life.

While for Freudians, all fish are phallic symbols, the dream image of **cod** may suggest a yearning for a homely situation, as cod is basic food for lunch or supper. Because of its legendary instinct to find distant spawning grounds, to dream of **salmon swimming up a river** suggests that home and family are always paramount in your mind, no matter how far you travel. Dream salmon can also suggest single-minded persistence and wisdom. In folklore, **solitary trout** were sometimes regarded as guardians of the pool and to dream of these fish offers encouragement that you will rise to the top of your chosen profession.

An **eel** in a dream may symbolize a slippery acquaintance – someone who makes you feel uncomfortable, because they are not to be trusted. According to Freudians, the **eel** represents temptation and sexual desires. Dreaming of **numerous eels writhing in the water** therefore symbolizes a longing for sexual orgasm. If you managed to **catch an eel** in the dream, this may be a sign of good fortune. Your good luck may, of course, be tempered if you cannot hold your dream eel in your hands and it slips away from you. If the **eel is wriggling**, it is a warning that someone of the opposite sex may be trying to impress you, but may have less than honorable intentions.

Jellyfish may suggest feelings arising from the unconscious that are painful, as well as a sense of helplessness or spinelessness. If jellyfish appear in your dream, you may feel that you're unsupported at an emotional level. On the other hand, it could imply a sense of drifting aimlessly, lacking backbone and being spineless in some way. A **starfish** carries the same symbolism as a star, but represents your physical expression or manifestation of your level of connection to your Universal Source.

If **sea bass** appear in your dream, they may refer to spiritual talents and the generous sharing of them. A **pike** also refers to spiritual nourishment, whereas a **trout** denotes a satisfaction with your spiritual development. To dream of **catfish** can denote a catty, pretentious or arrogant attitude towards your spirituality, whilst **clownfish** suggest foolish factors connected to your spiritual development.

Because of its association with the term 'ray of light', a **manta ray** in your dream may suggest moments of inspiration or intuition. A **sea anemone** may represent spiritual diversity, **sea urchins** suggest spiritual immaturity, whilst **sea horses** relate to spiritual beliefs that are more grounded in fantasy than reality.

■ *Idioms: big fish; big fish in a small pond; cold fish; fish for compliments; fish out of water; queer fish; something smells fishy.*

person in your real life? If the **fish was cold to the touch**, could this perhaps refer to someone in your life who is emotionally cold, perhaps even you?

On the other hand, dreams about fishing – particularly ones in which a **freshwater fisherman or angler** appears – could simply indicate the need for rest and relaxation. If a fisherman does appear in your dream or **you are the fisherman**, pay attention to the actions that are performed, as they will help you interpret the dream. Often a fisherman will represent a person, such as a provider, or a concept, such as bravery. This latter is especially the case if he is a **deep-sea fisherman**. A **fishing line** refers to a length or measure of spiritual inquiry, a **fishing rod** signifies a life aspect that can assist you in your spiritual search and a **fishing trip** symbolizes a desire to gain further information regarding a particular issue. Consider also if you are trying to catch something like a job or a partner in waking life. If you visit a **fish market** in your dreams, try to recall the species of fish, the amount you bought and their condition, as a fish market may refer to your own personal spiritual belief system. Finally, because of its Christian association, a fisherman may suggest a priest or someone with priest-like qualities in your dreams.

FROG/TOAD

Although **frogs and toads** may appear similar to each other, their symbolism in dreams is very different. Toads, with their warty appearance and squat body, are often characterized as creatures of evil or loathing, so if one appeared in your dream, is there someone or something in your waking life that you loathe? Bear in mind, though, that the toad's association with witchcraft and the sinister side of life is not the whole story. Toads were once associated with wisdom and the creature was thought to possess a precious jewel within its head that enabled it to see the pure and sacred in all things. To dream of a toad may therefore imply that you must look for the true worth within a person or object, and become insensitive to flattery.

Dream frogs are likely to have positive associations with transformation and fertility. This is because a frog undergoes dramatic changes in form, starting life as a tadpole and then changing into a frog. If

Fish miscellany

Bait

If you **see fish bait or are fish bait** in your dream, this can suggest feeling exposed or vulnerable. Other explanations are that you are setting, or being caught up in, a trap or an enticement that could carry dire consequences. It may also mean that you or someone else are being persecuted or teased.

Fin

Any type of **fin** in your dream signifies a factor in your life that is a motivational or directional force.

Gill

In dreams, **gills** may suggest highly developed spirituality; the intake of spiritual aspects is as natural and effortless as breathing.

Hook

Dreams that feature a **hook** may indicate that you are feeling caught or held, possibly against your will; this may be by a person, a lifestyle, or a substance, as suggested by the phrase to be 'hooked on' drugs. They may, however, be more positive, suggesting perhaps a hope to be hooked up with someone who accepts you hook, line and sinker. Consider also whether a dream of a hook might not be referring to secret sexual gratification, as in a prostitute or hooker.

Net

If a **net or nets** appear in your dream, possible interpretations include: you are securing something; you are feeling trapped or caught up in a situation against your will; you are losing out or losing something, as suggested by the phrase 'falling through the net'. Dreams of nets can also refer to the Internet; if you are dealing with money matters, nets could be meaning the bottom line or the net figure, with all expenses, financial or otherwise, taken into account.

Weighing

If you dream of **weighing your fish**, it may indicate the need to strike a balance, make a decision or weigh up the pros and cons of a situation. It may also refer to spiritual caution or, if related to **measuring scales**, indicate concerns about your weight or something that is progressive or graduated. Be attentive to the other meanings of the word 'scale', such as fish scale, small scale and scale the mountain.

frogs appear in your dream, they may therefore be suggesting a whole new stage in your life. **Frogs that lead or guide** you in your dream (**especially ones that can talk**) reflect a side of you that is very basic and trustworthy, i.e.; this is the side of your intuition and the dream could be urging you to follow your instincts on a particular matter. Frogs also produce masses of eggs so to dream of a frog may indicate a desire to transform your waking life by having children, or by taking care of a project or person. In some amusing dream scenarios frogs can also represent men who did not turn out to be princes. This kind of dream isn't trying to make you feel worse but urging you to give the search a rest and focus on enjoying other things for a while. A **tadpole** in your dream may suggest a transformation of some kind in your waking life, but can also suggest dangerous obstacles ahead.

MOLLUSK/OCTOPUS/ SHELLFISH/SNAIL

If a shelled mollusk, such as a **scallop** or **cowry**, caught your eye in your dream, this may suggest female sexuality. Dream **shellfish** – in the same manner as the crustaceans – represent the defensive shell you may use in waking life to avoid hurt or emotional involvement. If you came across an **oyster** in your dream, was the shell open or closed? If the **oyster shell** was shut, it may be hinting that your unconscious contains a pearl of wisdom. Oysters are also traditionally thought to be aphrodisiacs, so is it time to reinvigorate your love life? If the **oyster shell was empty**, could your unconscious have been indicating events that have passed you by, or do you think the

world is no longer your oyster? If a **mussel** features in your dream, this may suggest that you are afraid to reveal your soft, pulpy and vulnerable interior and are in a state of hiding. Another interpretation is that you are worried about your state of dependence, having attached yourself to someone or something because you believe that you cannot make it on your own. Consider also the homonym for mussel. Should a **clam or clams** appear in your dream are you closing up, withdrawing, withholding, avoiding, being reticent or clamming up in some way in waking life? Perhaps you are keeping a secret. Alternatively, it could be that something in your life feels sticky or uncomfortably close, as in clammy. On the other hand it may also imply happiness, euphoria, and that you are as happy as a clam.

If a freshwater or land-based **snail** featured in your dream, do you wish to creep into your shell or, as snails move slowly, is a project taking longer than you thought in waking life? Other interpretations for snail include: lacking in vitality or enthusiasm, needing to slow down or speed up, being ready to protect or defend yourself, and feeling at home wherever you go. If **slugs** feature in your dream, this can suggest any of the following: that you are lacking in energy or vitality, functioning below par, being unenthusiastic or making slow but steady progress. They could also suggest a devious, unmannered or deceitful person, a slug or slime ball, that you are feeling vulnerable, or that you or someone else is being spineless and is acting in a cowardly manner.

Octopuses have numerous tentacles that operate independently, so could your unconscious have been commenting on your multitasking ability? As a sea creature, the octopus carries the energy of emotion and the many ways to hold or connect. In their positive form, these creatures reflect emotional depth and the ability to direct your energy in many directions without losing your center. A dream octopus may therefore suggest successful business deals or any other project involving much multitasking. It may also be associated with a person or situation that has many ways of holding or affecting you, such as a mother or a debt. If a **squid squirted a cloud of black ink in your face** in your dream, could this be indicating that emotional conflicts are being obscured rather than confronted?

Seal/Otter/Penguin

As the **seal** can emerge from the water entirely and live on land, it is sometimes used to represent the emergence from the womb and the losses and gains associated with life. This is particularly so if you dream of a **young or baby seal**. In dream interpretation it therefore is associated with the emergence of instincts and intuition into your waking life. The **otter** indicates the recognition of inner spiritual joy, whilst the **penguin** suggests strong determination.

Shark

The **shark** has a universal significance as a deadly predator, so if you dreamed of swimming happily at the beach but then were terrified to see a **shark's fin circling around you**, your unconscious may be alerting you to someone who is potentially dangerous in your waking world, perhaps even a loan shark who is offering you money at high interest rates. In their positive aspect, sharks reflect power, instinct, intelligence and the ability to survive. In their negative aspect, sharks typically represent hidden fears that may have an intense impact on you. They are also terrifying symbols of death, destruction and the killer instinct. In many cases, the shark represents the fears you may have about what it may mean to strike out on your own. If you are **sailing over shark-infested waters** in your dream, some things in your life may be compromising your individuality, or you may be experiencing conflicts that are pulling and pushing you in opposite directions.

Whale

In dream lore, **whales** still carry much of their ancient folk memory. The biblical story of Jonah – reborn spiritually from the belly of a whale – may be echoed in dream symbolism which sees the creature as the womb of nature, wherein the dreamer may undergo spiritual transformation. In dreams the whale is a symbol of power and hope. It offers assurance that a huge force within you is available from which to draw strength, healing and wisdom. The whale is also the symbol of the **mother** archetype – probably on account of its enormous belly – so if a whale figures in your dream is your unconscious longing to return to feelings of warmth and security associated with childhood? On the other hand if the **whale is menacing or tries to swallow you up** in your dream is there a mother figure in your life who is overpowering and dominating or has some problem, habit or misunderstanding taken on huge proportions in your life? Or do you simply long for more thrills and stimulation in your life according to the pun having a 'whale of a time'. And does your dream of whales have any connection with wailing or reflect your concern over ecological issues as whales are an endangered species?

Reptiles

ALLIGATOR/CROCODILE

Floating half submerged by the river bank, the **crocodile** swims in the murky waters of the unconscious, projecting an image of danger with its jaws and an image of hypocrisy with its tears. If **crocodiles appear and the atmosphere is pleasant** in your dream, then they may be a symbol of being comfortable in your own skin. Your unconscious may be reminding you of the importance of timing and focusing your energy so you are ready to seize the moment when it comes. On the other hand, crocodiles also represent the hazards that may lie beneath the surface of a seemingly harmless situation, so the crocodile may be alerting you to a potential problem and urging you to trust your instincts. When it comes to hunting prey, crocodiles and alligators are masters of disguise, so if they feature in your dream, ask yourself what aspect of yourself you are disguising in real life. Consider also if someone you know is shedding crocodile tears. If an **alligator** appears in your dream, it may represent problems that have appeared suddenly as if from nowhere and knocked your sense of balance. If you're **battling an alligator** in

your dream, it means you are dealing with an intense situation that has upset your world.

LIZARD/CHAMELEON

Lizards can often resemble snakes, so much of their symbolism in dreams will be similar. But if you watched a **chameleon's skin slowly change color or blend into the background** in your dream, ask yourself whether your unconscious was questioning the wisdom of camouflaging your true feelings; on the other hand, perhaps it was highlighting your fickleness.

SNAKE

Snakes are archetypal symbols that have both negative and positive associations, being on one hand thought evil predators and on the other hand agents of healing and transformation. Dreams that feature snakes in them will also arouse different reactions depending on your associations with snakes in waking life. If you are like most people and snakes arouse fear and loathing in you then if your dream focuses on a snake it may well turn into a nightmare. Snakes can often represent intimidating situations in waking life.

The most common dream is of a **pit of snakes or piles of snakes lying on the floor around you**; this may represent the many worries that are threatening you, or the poisonous words and innuendo of people around you. If, however, you admire snakes or keep them as pets, your dream is unlikely to have been sinister. Dreams that feature **snakes poised to strike their victims with venom or suffocate them with their coils** may be warning you about

The Element Encyclopedia of 20,000 Dreams

Underwater scene

A journey into the unconscious may be symbolized by an **underwater** dream. The underwater descent is a journey of discovery into your unknown parts and is a sign that you are ready to explore your own intuitive and instinctive aspects. The symbolism may also be a representation of the womb, the underwater scene symbolizing regression and the hope of rebirth. Perhaps you are feeling helpless, unable to care for yourself and long to return to a stage where you are dependent and free of responsibilities. To dream that you are underwater may also indicate that you are feeling overcome with emotions and are in need of greater control in your life, or that you may be in over your head regarding some situation.

How the water behaves in your dream is also significant. **Rising water** indicates rising emotions. **Turbulent, choppy waters** symbolize being overwhelmed emotionally. Being **caught in a swift moving current** suggests being 'swept up' in one's emotions. **Cloudy water** suggests lack of emotional clarity or a fear of emotional contamination. **Swimming or bathing peacefully in water** symbolizes a comfortable immersion in your emotions. The ability to **breathe underwater and interact with creatures of the sea** indicates that you have access to your unconscious feelings and awareness. **Seeing a diver or becoming a diver** suggests that you are delving into your unconscious, or trying to 'get to the bottom' of a current situation or problem. Not surprisingly, Freudians believe that underwater diving may have sexual connotations and represents intercourse.

In addition to fish and sea creatures, what you observe in your underwater dream may be significant. If you see a **sea chest**, this indicates what you carry with you on your spiritual quest, or in everyday terms, your spiritual baggage. The **sea floor** refers to your spiritual foundations. Is it ablaze with color and life, or barely inhabited? **Sea foam** stands for spiritual confusion or a stirring of your beliefs, **seafood** for spiritual knowledge and nourishment. Recall the condition and type of food. **Sea level** pertains to spiritual truths, whilst **sea legs** suggest spiritual comfort or feeling at home with your spirituality. **Sea monsters** suggest spiritual danger and an **earthquake at sea** warns that your beliefs might be shaken. **Sea salt** stands for strong spiritual beliefs, **seashells** for spiritual gifts and talents. Recall the quality and quantity of the shells. **Sea slugs** warn of spiritual laziness or entrapment, **sea snails** denote a slow and steady progress with your spiritual development, **sea sponges** stand for spiritual over absorption and **sea spray** represents spiritual gifts or insights. Finally, coral symbolizes your spiritual attributes, **coral fish** stand for spiritual protectiveness and guarding your beliefs from outside influences and a **coral reef** represents the difficulties of maintaining a spiritual balance in the physical world.

an emotionally cold person who is suffocating you in waking life. Is there a viper in your midst or a snake in the grass, someone who appears friendly but who is about to stab you in the back? Your dream may also have been influenced by Christian symbolism of the serpent in the Garden of Eden; the snake may have represented someone who is trying to tempt you to deviate from your moral code of conduct.

The snake's positive associations date back to ancient Greece and Rome; the Greek god Hermes (the Roman Mercury), for example, bore two entwining snakes around his neck to symbolize the harmonization of two conflicting forces. If the **snake doesn't try to attack or harm** you in your dream, it may therefore be referring to physical or emotional healing that has begun in your waking life. If the **snake sheds its skin** in your dream, this may indicate your desire to cast off the past. According to Freud, the snake is a phallic symbol so it could also denote repressed sexual urges or fears of masculine energy that are creating power issues in your relationships. Besides being an obvious phallic symbol, for Jungians the snake embodies the dark incomprehensible and mysterious aspects of the self that must be contained. In addition, in the Indian mystical tradition, the *kundalini* snake is a symbol of latent energy, instinct and sexuality, so your dream may also have represented your spiritual or intellectual awakening.

Pythons in dreams embody the power to dominate a situation by having a potent grasp on it. If, in your dream, the **python is not a menacing but a benevolent presence**, it is likely to be a reminder of your power to cope with a challenge by wrapping yourself around it. Pythons can also represent people or situations who are trying to put the squeeze on you in waking life. For example, a jealous lover who watches your every move or a financial commitment that limits your freedom to spend.

TURTLE/TORTOISE

Sea turtles and tortoises suggest a cautious spiritual search or path, so dreams involving them underline the importance of patience and fortitude in waking life; remember the story of *The Tortoise and the Hare*, in which slow and steady progress won the race. In this sense, turtles certainly symbolize the benefits of determined, calculated and well-thought-out actions as opposed to hastiness. Being a fertile egg-layer that can live for many centuries, the turtle's symbolism relates both to wisdom and fertility, so if you dreamed of **watching a turtle on its back frantically trying to right itself**, could your dream have reflected your waking sense that your real-life circumstances have turned upside down? Turtles also represent the ability to protect yourself and take life at your own pace. Since they enjoy both air and water, turtles represent the ability to think clearly and feel deeply at the same time. If your dream **turtle is wounded or has been kept in a container**, this may suggest issues with your body image, and may also indicate that you do not feel safe and secure in your body.

The Element Encyclopedia of 20,000 Dreams

SCHOOL
AND WORK

Dreams that focus on school and the workplace reflect your anxiety about how well you are being perceived or how well you are performing in waking life.

If you are still at school, or if you have a job and your dream referred to your actual workplace, then your dreaming mind was probably referring to your everyday concerns. If you have left school, or the school or workplace in your dreams is unfamiliar to you, your dreaming mind may have been suggesting a past feeling or experience that has relevance for your current situation. Such dreams could also indicate a sense of restriction and your resentment that you can't spend your time doing what you want. They could also be commenting on your social interaction with your peers and authority figures, since relating to others is an essential part of school and work.

Jung regarded dreams as teachers and guides on the road towards wholeness; from his perspective, dreams that feature schools and teachers were especially significant because schools are places of learning and maturing into a healthy adult. Jobs are closely linked to self-esteem in waking life, so the type of job that features in your dream – and the reward or lack of reward associated with it – can be significant indicators of your feelings of self-worth and of the success or failure of your approach to life's challenges.

Education

COLLEGE/UNIVERSITY

Whether or not you attended university or college, in dreams they often symbolize the hunger for knowledge. A dream about **graduating** suggests a sense of independence and success, and the beginning of a new phase in your life; it can, however, also indicate how you feel about your progress. Are you the one receiving the honors or are you watching from the back row?

EDUCATIONAL PARAPHERNALIA

The **blackboard** sets information out in black and white, so in dreams it can represent unambiguous insights or the need to make your mark on the world. Because **chalk** can be rubbed out it is a warning against having rigid opinions that do not allow the possibility of change. According to Freud, **holding a piece of chalk** suggests masturbation whilst **breaking a piece of chalk** suggests a fear of castration. A **school desk** is a symbol of your most private self. If your **initials are carved on the desk**, this also expresses your desire to make your mark on the world. Freudians would argue that **opening a desk and searching inside** is a symbol of sexual intercourse.

Many of us associate ink with our schooldays and if **ink is spilled over a sheet of paper** in your dream, this may suggest feelings of guilt. The shade of ink will be significant: black ink will symbolize evil thoughts or deeds, whilst red will symbolize impulsive acts. Dreaming of **notebooks or schoolbooks** can suggest a great deal; are the **notebooks neat,** suggesting an ordered mind or are they **messy,** suggesting confusion? If there are **doodles alongside the scribbles**, this suggests a creative personality that thrives in chaos. If, in your dream, your **schoolbag is filled with pens, papers, books and apples**, this suggests the happiness gained from happy experience but if the **schoolbag is heavy and cumbersome**, you may be feeling weighed down by the past. Pay attention to the quality and condition of the school bag as it could reveal a lot about your current approach to life. If the **school bell rings suggesting that a lesson is over**, this may indicate the end of a difficult phase in your life but if the **bell comes at the end of a playtime**, it could signify regret that a happy period in your life is coming to an end.

EXAMINATION OR TEST

A dream of **taking an exam or being singled out by a teacher** usually highlights waking anxiety about facing a difficult challenge in your real life. Perhaps you are trying to live up to impossibly high standards or are worried about some test of self-value, such as a new job or a new relationship. A common dream involves **turning up naked to an examination**, which may point to a fear of social humiliation. A feeling of powerlessness to control your life may be suggested by a dream in which you **arrive late for an examination or hand in a blank paper at the end of the exam**. If you find your **name on a list of those who have not passed a school exam**, you may feel that you have failed in some way in waking life or that someone is marking you down.

LESSONS AND LEARNING

Dreams that focus on **lessons and the business of learning** are concerned with the acquisition of knowledge. If a **lesson is being taught by a school teacher, college lecturer or university tutor**, your dream is turning the spotlight on the acquisition of knowledge or learning. The subject matter of the lesson will be of great significance here, as the implication may be that you can find fulfillment by stimulating your mind and exploring your creativity in this particular subject. On the other hand, the lesson may also be alerting you to the need to address a specific area of your life. For example, if you dreamed of **learning a foreign language**, your dreaming mind may not be encouraging you to learn a new language but to open your mind and try to understand the point of view of others.

Dreams of **classrooms** often indicate your relationship to authority. If you are **trying to avoid your teacher's eye** in your dream, you may be trying to avoid responsibility, whereas **eagerly raising a hand** suggests a desire for attention or to prove yourself. Your dreaming mind may also be urging you to think about what you really learned at school. If you dreamed of being **punished in class**, such dreams may point to masochistic sexual pleasure but are more likely to suggest feelings of guilt about not meeting your responsibilities.

School

You may have had a dream in which you were a **child again and you felt lost and lonely at school**. Perhaps it was your **first day in a new school**? Your unconscious often draws on past experiences to reflect current feelings, so perhaps you have recently started a new job or moved to a new area. Or are you just feeling insecure and uncertain about yourself? If your **school dream was positive**, you may just be feeling nostalgic about an exciting time in your life. If your **school dream was negative**, however, and you hated school, then your dream may be suggesting that you have not resolved your feelings about this life experience. You need to reassess your school days from an adult perspective.

If the **school was ruined or dilapidated** in your dream, this can represent the collapse of youthful illusions; your dreaming mind is urging you not to dwell on the past but to move on. Another interpretation of dreams about **being back at school** is that you are feeling suffocated by rules, regulations and restrictions in your waking life that are preventing you from leading the life you want to live. It can sometimes refer to feelings of rejection, aloneness and stress on leaving your mother for the first time. Your dreaming mind may also be urging you to seek out knowledge or learn new skills in waking life. **Specific places or rooms in the school** represent attitudes learned at school. For example, the **library** is a place of knowledge and stored information; the **gymnasium** is associated with physical health and a place where you take risks. **School clothes** suggest the social image you developed at school and **school friends**, those of your attitudes that you developed at school.

In general, dream of **high school or secondary school** are not so much about the lessons you learned there, but about social concerns or the desire to fit in at all costs. Whether you **couldn't find a classroom or were unprepared for an exam**, the primary concern of such dreams centers around your own abilities and what others think of you. Dreams set in high school reflect your insecurities and social fears. If you dream of the **school playground**, this represents the importance of relaxation or recreation to balance the time you spend working. **Not wanting to join in with school games** suggests an inability to switch off from work, whilst **reluctance to leave the playground** suggests a lack of discipline. If you dream of **bullying and are identifying with the victim**, you may be expressing old memories of school

People at work

A dream in which the main focus seems to be **someone else's job or occupation** isn't urging you to change career. It is most likely using the symbol of a certain profession to comment on your own behavior, attitudes and actions. Roles often play an important part in your self-image and identity. Without a well-defined social role or identity, many of us feel uncertain in waking life. It is a sign of maturity to cast off this need for a role of some kind and appreciate that we can be many things. *See also* ARCHE-TYPES; PEOPLE.

Accountant/Bookkeeper

To dream of being an **accountant or bookkeeper** highlights the importance of objective and analytical skills; is your unconscious urging you to adopt a more unemotional and logical approach to a problem or is it a warning to manage your finances better?

Actor/Artist

An **actor or actress** is a representation of your desire for happiness. If you favor a certain celebrity and you find yourself dreaming of them, it may refer to a physical or character trait that you wish to possess. If **you are an actor or actress**, it may refer to the hard work that you have been putting into your job. Pay attention to the role you are playing; it may be a sign. Dreams of **artists, photographers and cameramen** may be suggesting that there is an artist or photographer within you that is crying out for expression. Take note of what you were drawing, painting, photographing or filming, as it could have special significance. A dream **conductor or musician** suggests an urge to control your creativity or to shape the destiny of others. Music is also often associated with spirituality, so a conductor may suggest spiritual aspirations. *See also* ARTS AND CRAFTS.

Analyst

If you dream of an **analyst, psychologist, therapist or psychiatrist**, this may be a symbol of self-assessment that has the power to transform your life; it might also suggest important insights or fears concerning your emotional well-being.

Baker/Cook/Butcher/Bartender

If you dream of **bakers**, this has associations with creative ability and sexual intercourse, as loaves are images of male sexuality and the oven of female sexuality. Baking may suggest the birth of a child. If your dream featured a **cook**, who were you cooking for in your dream? Cooks are also thought to be bad tempered, so is this referring to you or someone you know? If a **butcher with his hands covered in blood** appears in your dreams, this suggests the sacrifices you have made in your life. Blood is also associated with female sexuality and may suggest a fear of it; the dream may also have links to feelings of aggression. The meaning of dreams about **bartenders** will depend upon your relationship with alcohol in waking life. Is it a symbol of loneliness or of sociability?

Barber/Hairdresser/Beautician

For men, a visit to the **barber** may be a classic Freudian symbol of castration anxiety. Going to a dream **hairdresser**, however, suggests improvements to your image. If **you were the hairdresser** you have more power over others than you realize. Dreaming of being **pampered by a beautician** may suggest a need for relaxation or that you need to improve your image and self-confidence.

Builder/Carpenter/Architect/Engineer

A **builder** is a father figure in dreams; this is because he is a typically male figure working on the house, which represents the self. He can be a reminder of the important influence of your father in your life. Dreams of **carpenters and architects** represent that side of yourself that is creative but practical at the same time. **Engineers** fix things for us in waking life and in your dream they may represent a friend or advisor who is helping you manage destructive emotions. The engineer is also a symbol of the desire to impose order over emotional chaos in waking life.

Bus driver

Dreams of **bus drivers or fare collectors** symbolize the part of yourself that is concerned with paying your way or how you give authority in a group situation.

Captain/Admiral/Soldier/Sailor

Because he represents an authority figure in your waking life, dreams of **captains** may represent an aspect of your personality that is steering you (the ship or airplane) in the right direction. It is important to decide if your dream **captain or admiral** was decisive and in command, or weak and indecisive. A symbol of the Jungian archetypal hero, the **soldier** is a symbol of the desire to succeed in life. Freudians may see this symbol as an expression of sexual desire. **Sailors**, by contrast, express the more adventurous aspects of your personality. They live and work at sea, a Jungian symbol of the unconscious, so the dream may suggest a desire to explore your inner self.

Chemist/Scientist

If you dream of a **chemist**, this may be a reference to alchemy, which Jung related to the dreamer's spiritual transformation. Dreams of **scientists** might be posing you the question as to whether you need to adopt a strictly reasoned and objective approach to a challenge in your waking life.

Dentist

Toothache often stimulates dreams of **dentists**. According to Jung, **women's dreams about dentists** are associated with giving birth, whilst to Freud, **men's dreams of tooth extraction** relate to a fear of castration.

Detective/Policeman

If a **detective** appears in your dream, this may be a sign that you may be attempting to solve an issue or are worrying about something that needs to be cleared up. If a **detective is following you** within a dream, it may be a sign that other people want to know more about you. A dream about a **police officer or army officer** may suggest the importance of following correct procedure or correct behavior. Perhaps an aspect of your behavior in waking life is upsetting others? **Policemen** can also represent the father figure, whilst a **policewoman** can bring to mind a dominant female in your life. A **fireman** relates to how you deal with your emotions or outbursts of energy.

Farmer/Shepherd/Gardener/Miner

Farmers represent all that is material, practical, down to earth and instinctive. If you dream of a farm or a farmer, are you focusing on the rewarding side of farming, symbolized by the harvest, or the tough side, such as the slaughtering of animals? Try to decide how your dream applies to your waking life. Are you struggling to survive harsh and difficult times, or reaping the benefits of your hard work? If the person on the farm is specifically a **shepherd**, this represents being in touch with your instincts. A **gardener** in your dream is generally a positive symbol that reflects on your aspirations for the future. Dreams of **planting seeds** suggest the planting of new ideas, and **picking fruit** the rewards of experience. If you dream of **miners**, this suggests a desire to explore the unconscious to discover precious insights.

Fisherman

Since water is symbolic of your emotions, a dream featuring a **fisherman** suggests your own search for emotional satisfaction. Did you catch a fish or throw it back? If the fish got away, are you being too emotionally reticent in waking life?

Lawyer/Solicitor/Barrister/Judge

Dream **lawyers, solicitors or barristers** are a symbol of the supportive friend or relative in times of stress, but may also indicate that you are becoming too dependent or losing your sense of right and wrong. In Jungian terms a **judge** can represent the archetype of the wise old man. Perhaps you should appreciate your own wisdom and powers of judgment more, or perhaps you feel persecuted by arbitrary forces in waking life?

Medical professions

Dreams of **members of the medical professions – such as doctors, nurses, surgeons** – may suggest that you need to take better care of yourself in waking life; **nurses**, in particular, often indicate that you are in need of healing, nurturing and affection. The **doctor or physician** in dreams is also a classic parent figure.

Missionary

If a **missionary** figures in your dream, try to work out if the advice they gave was inspirational or misguided, as the missionary figure could be referring to you or someone who is advising you in waking life.

Official/Bureaucrat/Secretary

In dreams, an **official or bureaucrat** may express lack of emotion or emotional coldness that you feel exists in the world around you. **Secretaries** in dreams may be representing a protective mother figure, but can also suggest in both male and female dreamers the desire for sexual domination.

Pirate

If a **pirate** features in your dream, he may be echoing a sense of someone else having taken something or someone that is important to you; he might also be a symbol of a person or dilemma that may be compromising the emotional aspect of your life, or a violation of your creative decisions or integrity may be occurring within your waking life. Sometimes a pirate is a symbol for freedom and breaking the rules. You may have to consider taking a risk or engaging in some sort of adventure when this character appears to you in a dream.

Plumber

The job of a **plumber** can be dirty and unpleasant and in dreams there is often a link between water and the emotions; so have you been experiencing a lot of negative emotion lately? If you **cleared a blocked drain** in your dream, this may refer to blocked emotions. Seeing **yourself in the role of the plumber** may suggest a process of self-examination.

Salesperson

Salespersons appearing in your dream would suggest that you are trying to sell an idea, project or yourself in waking life. If you **buy something from a salesperson** in your dream, are you trying to buy love and affection or are you giving away too much in waking life?

Shopkeeper

A **shopkeeper** in your dreams may relate to how you supply your own needs or who supplies your needs to you, or help show you how you can gain essential support from other people.

Sportsperson

Sportspersons or athletes in dreams are symbols of personal achievement or your potential to achieve your goals in life.

Tailor

Should a **tailor** crop up in your dream, he might be suggestive of your ability to create a project from scratch or a change to your public image.

Waiter/Maid/Cleaner

If you hated being cast in the serving role of a **waiter, maid or cleaner** in your dream, is someone exploiting you or are you taking unfair advantage of someone? Or are your duties in life overwhelming?

experiences that were upsetting. Alternatively, the bully might represent a domineering figure in your current life or aspects of your own character that are domineering.

Teacher

If you dream of a **teacher, tutor or lecturer you know or don't know but who treats you kindly and with respect**, it may mean that you are in need of guidance, advice or knowledge. Sometimes the subject with which the teacher in your dream is associated may be a clue as to why they have entered your slumber. Teachers are authority figures that have power over children so your dreaming mind may also have summoned a teacher into your dream to represent your boss or even yourself, if you are in charge of others. If you dreamed of a **teacher who was an overbearing bully**, is this referring to aspects of yourself or someone you know?

Work and Employment Settings

Occupation

There is often a good reason why your unconscious highlights a particular job or activity in your dream. The message may be easy to understand – for example, dreaming of an **artist** may encourage you to explore your artistic talent – but if an explanation is hard to arrive at, ask yourself which qualities you associate with that particular profession. For instance, discipline is a quality that immediately springs to mind when a soldier is mentioned, so if you dream of a **soldier**, ask yourself whether this is a quality you need to bring into your life or whether you are sufficiently disciplined for this to be an unlikely interpretation? The different people in your dream represent different abilities, weaknesses or interests you yourself have. Even if you know the person, the dream still suggests that person's quality or skills in yourself. The only difference might be that your personal associations with the specific doctor or teacher you know who appears in your dream will also play a part.

Office

If you work in an **office**, the chances are that this will feature every now and again in your dreams. Sometimes your dreams will be connected with your work, but in general such dreams represent another aspect of your waking life, aside from work; this may be a particular problem, your emotions or your attitude to life and authority. If you **feel crowded in by computers, typewriters and people**, this may indicate a crowd of problems whereas an **office that is suddenly closed or deserted** may reflect an emotional emptiness in your life.

If you were **stocktaking** in your dream, you may be taking stock of your present situation; if **goods are being carried out** you may feel as if your inner resources are being depleted. If you had a dream in which you were **storing away documents in a filing cabinet**, this may have been urging you to store away memories that are no longer relevant to your waking life. Alternatively, could your unconscious have been urging you to restore order to a waking life littered with chores and obligations? For office items such as computers, *see* MEDIA AND TECHNOLOGY; for pay and pensions, *see* MONEY AND SHOPPING; for factory and warehouse, *see* BUILDINGS.

WORKPLACE

Schools, colleges, universities and the workplace have much in common. They are all centers of learning, anxiety and ambition, and places where people interact and learn from each other. This is why the unconscious may use them as interchangeable dream metaphors. Your **boss** may appear in your dream as a **teacher**, or **colleagues** may appear in the guise of **school friends or classmates**. So if a dream places you in a workplace, remember to look for any links with school scenarios.

If your dream featured your **actual workplace and colleagues you work with everyday**, it may have been highlighting your preoccupation with your job. It may also have been trying to draw your attention to a specific aspect of your job. You spend much of your time at work, so work is of considerable importance emotionally. If you are comfortable at work, dreams of the workplace and the people with whom you work may become symbols of reassurance and reward; but if you are not comfortable at work, they can become symbols of frustration. If you had a dream in which you were **performing mindless repetitive tasks on an assembly line**, perhaps you feel as if you are being treated like a mindless automaton in waking life or that others are making relentless demands on you. Or do you feel that you are losing your sense of identity in your job or that people in your life are taking you for granted?

SENSES

Dreams can seem incredibly real when you are having them; as if you really are interacting with your environment and the people within it.

Although your five senses of taste, smell, touch, hearing and seeing are not conscious when you are dreaming, you may find yourself waking with lingering memories of sensual interaction that seemed so real at the time of dreaming. For example, you may recall seeing a beautiful sunset in your dream or hearing a conversation. Or perhaps you remember the smell of burning wood, the touch of a lover's hand or the taste of a fine wine. You may wake up with a feeling of relief or regret that the terrible or exciting events in your dream simply weren't real; and a part of you may need convincing that the events in the dream did not actually take place.

According to Jung, dreams are important messages from your unconscious to your conscious mind and nowhere is this more true than when the clarity, vividness and realism of your dreams are so incredible that you have no idea you are dreaming. Although some people are aware of when they are dreaming, many of us aren't; if you regularly find your dreams both convincing and compelling, many dream analysts believe that your dreaming mind is creating

an atmosphere of intense realism to shock you into action or a change of perspective. See also BODY; PLACES; SOUNDS.

The Five Senses

HEARING

If your dream homed in on an **ear**, maybe yours or someone else's, your unconscious may have been urging you to keep your ears open or to stay informed about what is going on around you. Alternatively, you may be being urged to pay more attention to what people are telling you; perhaps you have closed your ears to the truth, have been ignoring opinions or turning a deaf ear to someone in waking life. Another interpretation suggests that you are intrigued by gossip. *See also* SOUNDS.

SIGHT

Dreams are an overwhelmingly visual experience and Freud generally treated dream images as signs. Signs are images that point to something else. Freud believed the unconscious was purposely hiding the meaning of the images from our conscious minds. He believed that dreams contained a secret, hidden key and that once this key was slipped into the lock keeping a dream's meaning from you, almost everything could be seen to have a connection with sex, death, taboo and incest. Jung, on the other hand, treated dream images as symbols intent on bringing healing to the psyche. Images, when treated as symbols, are images which have meaning in and of themselves. He believed the unconscious was purposely trying to speak to us, in order to bring forth a sense of wholeness and added meaning to our lives. For Jung, our nightly dreams were not trying to hide anything from us but trying to communicate with us.

Many dream analysts today regard the images we 'see' in dreams as a symbolic reflection of aspects of the dreamer's life, in particular their attitudes and responses. By taking time to consider what it is that you are 'seeing' in your dream and the impressions involved, you can 'see' or become aware of what the dream is getting you to look at regarding yourself or your life. The 'view' you have in a dream, the environment you see, reflects how you see your life and yourself at the time of the dream. It shows how limited or wide your 'vision' is. **Being looked at** in a dream suggests seeing yourself from their point of view or from a point of view that is not your own.

■ *Idioms: from the look of things; look after; look at; look before you leap; look down on; look forward to; look into; look over; look small; look the other way; look up to; don't like the look of; looking for a fight; as I see it; do you see what I mean; I'll see; I'll see about that; see eye to eye; see red; get out of my sight; lose sight of; out of sight, out of mind; second sight; at first sight.*

If you have a dream in which you are **searching for something**, this typically indicates an attempt to find something in waking life; perhaps a past way of life, a person from the past, an answer to a problem or a sense of identity; it may also indicate a feeling of having lost something valuable, such as your youth, energy or motivation. If you are **searching for someone** in your dream, you may be conscious of your loneliness and if you are searching for something but do not know what it is, this could represent an unfulfilled need or a spiritual hunger. If a **searchlight** appears, this indicates concentration and focused attention. It can also indicate insight into an important matter in your waking life.

Said to be the windows on the soul, the eyes are instruments of unconscious communication as well as vision. If you found yourself **gazing into someone's eyes** in your dream, your unconscious may have been mirroring your sense of seeing eye to eye with someone in your waking life. But if you find you **cannot meet someone's eye** in your dream, you may be feeling guilty about something you have said or done. If the **color of someone's eyes** caught your own eye in your dream, pay attention to the symbolism by referring

Blind people and dreams

People who are blind do dream. The dreams of people who have been blind from a very early age (called 'congenital blindness') tend to be different to those who are blind now but who had sight before. Those who are congenitally blind often have dreams that include more instances of sounds. Both groups experience dreams as imaginatively rich as those of sighted people.

Dreams are a universal feature of the human mind. Carl Jung even believed that visions in our dreams offer glimpses into universal archetypes, instinctive primordial images derived from a collective unconscious built into the very structure of the human brain. You might think, then, that even blind people could tap into this instinctive pool of primordial images and see them in their dreams.

There have been studies into whether or not congenitally blind people dream in visual images, but the findings have been mixed – some studies conclude that congenitally blind people do not dream in visual images, whilst other reports conclude that may do. The general consensus is that although people who are blind certainly do dream, their dreams are believed to be visual only to the extent that they can see, or could see before their blindness, in their waking life. People who are blind from birth are believed to have dreams that are primarily auditory, with their other intact senses participating to about the same degree that they do in a sighted person's dreams. Such people are not thought to dream in visual images. People who are legally blind but are able to see blurs of movement, light and color would have a visual dimension to their dreams matching what they see when they are awake.

to the chapter on COLORS; if you noticed a **squint** in your dream, could the message have been that you are looking at things in a cockeyed way? If your **eyes were shut or you noticed you were blind** in your dream, your unconscious may have been alerting you to your tendency to close or shut your eyes to the truth in waking life. And if you found yourself **wearing spectacles or contact lenses** in your dream, do you need to focus on something or someone more closely in waking life, or do you wish that others would respect your intelligence more? *See also* Eye entry in BODY.

Perception of color is an intensely personal experience. We only have to look at our clothes and interior decoration to see how color plays a part in our lives, whether through understatement or overstatement. Color is also a form of communication and mood; for example, red means stop and black is often associated with loss in

The Element Encyclopedia of 20,000 Dreams

Western society. Think about how you would describe a color to someone who is blind. What feelings and thoughts arise when you think of red, blue or yellow, for example? If a **color particularly stands out** in your dream 'view' (you are wearing, for example, a color you never usually wear) take a look at the relevant entry in COLORS for some clues to its meaning; as with all things in dreams, look for the associations that make sense to you. *See also* the Do you dream in color? entry in COLORS.

SMELL

At times you may experience the sense of **smell** in your dreams. If there is a strong smell in your sleeping environment, you may perceive it and incorporate it into your dream. Otherwise, the smell in your dreams is triggered by a memory. You may be associating your dream experience with a pleasant or unpleasant odor. For example, if you are dreaming about your mother, you may **smell the aroma of a food she once cooked**. The smell may trigger emotions and reflect the general quality of the experience. If the **smell is repulsive** in your dream, ask yourself what is rotten or corrupted in your life; alternatively, is your unconscious telling you that it has sniffed out danger or 'smelt a rat'?

Smells can remind you of a particular person or situation; they can also suggest good or bad feelings. For example, a **pleasant smell** could depict happy times or memories, whereas a **bad smell** could hold memories of trauma or difficulty. Smells can also act as a warning in a dream, as intuitive information is often recognized by a particular smell. You may have a good or bad reaction to the smell depending on

your associations with it. Dreams involving the sense of smell may also be explainable by the large number of idioms regarding smell: on the right scent, throw someone off the scent, smell a rat, smells fishy, stinks to high heaven, what you did stinks and so on.

The appearance of **your nose or the nose of someone you** know in your dream may be significant. If the **nose suddenly grows long**, could you be telling lie after lie in the real world? If it **transforms into a broken one**, are you about to fall out with someone in the real world? If your **nose was blocked**, is there something about your waking circumstances that is getting up your nose? *See also* Nose entry in BODY. When you dream of **smelling perfume** you are often being reminded of particular memories. Smells in dreams can be evocative and you may need to recapture or re-examine a certain emotion associated with that perfume.

TASTE

In dreams, the sensation of **taste** suggests your likes, dislikes, desires and standards. If something is **not to your taste** in your dreams, this suggests that it does not conform to your ideals. To have a **bad taste in your mouth** suggests that something in your life is not nourishing or satisfying you. If you recognize that your **surroundings are in good taste**, this suggests that you appreciate beauty in life. In waking life, we often know what we do and do not like but in dreams this can sometimes be distorted for the purpose of highlighting the need for change. For example, if you find yourself **liking someone or something you normally dislike**, this suggests that you

Aromatherapy

Aromatherapy is an ancient healing art that is currently enjoying a new-found popularity. Essential oils are used to stimulate healing through the senses. They are highly concentrated and some can be dangerous if overused or if placed directly on the skin, so be sure to follow directions on the package if you decide to experiment with them.

Lavender is one of the few essential oils that can be applied directly to the skin. It is frequently used in lotions and face creams since it is said to diminish wrinkles and bring a healthy glow to the skin over time. The effects of essential oils appear to be cumulative. Lavender is known as a comforting, relaxing scent and is frequently recommended by aromatherapists and other holistic practitioners because of its calming influence. The scent of lavender can balance body and mind, and help induce sleep. When you are getting enough rest, you're more likely to get more out of your dreams because you're in good health. There are several ways you can use lavender to help you achieve restful sleep and dreaming. It can be placed in a diffuser, or on a cotton ball or piece of fabric tucked inside your pillowcase. You can make a room and pillow spray from water, witch hazel and lavender essential oil. The mixture should be kept in a dark glass bottle since sunlight can diminish the effects of essential oils. Simply spray a mist in the air around the bed or spray directly onto the pillows and sheets. You may want to test the fabric first to ensure that it doesn't stain.

There are hundreds of aromatherapy oils with which you may want to experiment but make sure you follow safety guidelines or consult with an aromatherapist first. The following essential oils are all thought to reduce stress and encourage restful sleep and dreaming: lavender, vetiver, rosemary and chamomile. For essential oils thought to encourage lucid dreaming, you may want to try the following: clove – improves dream recall; mugwort – increases visualization; anise – repels nightmares; clary sage – promotes intuitive awareness.

need to study the qualities of this person, object or place to see what it can teach you. Bear in mind that the words used to describe taste are also often used to describe feelings, for example bitter, sweet, sour.

■ *Idioms: bad taste; taste blood, have a taste for; leave a nasty taste; acquire taste.*

Did you sit down to a lavish meal in your dreams and find that you had **lost your**

The Element Encyclopedia of 20,000 Dreams

appetite or could not taste anything? If so, then perhaps you have lost your appetite for something you once loved or relished. On the other hand, if you found yourself **endlessly chewing**, then perhaps you need to chew over some facts before you make an important decision in real life? In dreams being aware that you are **swallowing** something suggests either that you are holding back your emotions or that you need to take in something important in real life. *See also* Mouth and Teeth entries in BODY.

TOUCH

In dreams, **touch** suggests making contact in some way or the need to reach out to someone or something. Your dream may be drawing your attention to your need for other people and their need for you. The transference of power and responsibility can also be signified by the act of touching in dreams, so perhaps you are about to take on new responsibilities in real life. In general though, being aware of **touching or being touched** in dreams suggests intimacy, contact or a linking up with something. You may also have touched feelings or drives that are shocking you into action.

If, in your dream, you are **surrounded by people or things but do not feel touched or held**, this suggests emotional inhibition and an inability to reach out or express your need for others. If you are **actively avoiding being touched** in your dream, this suggests hidden anger or aggression towards someone in your life. Touching is also a means of communicating feelings or intentions to others and it may have the same meaning in your dream.

If something is **hard to the touch** in your dreams, this suggests lack of feeling or response, or emotional difficulties in real life. If, by contrast, something is **soft to the touch**, this suggests a desire for comfort and love or the ability to self-comfort. It may recall memories of a soft toy you had as a child, or a non-threatening emotional relationship that can be controlled by you.

■ *Idioms: keep in touch; lose touch; get in touch; out of touch; touch and go; touched up; touched upon; common touch; Midas touch; soft touch.*

The Sixth Sense

Your dreaming mind can easily transcend the laws of everyday life and thought. Your dreams can bridge the gap between space and time and many people believe that they have had psychic experiences in their dreams. You may or may not recognize some of the following psychic dreams in your own dream life.

GLIMPSE OF THE FUTURE

You may notice that a day or so after your dream an element of it occurs in your waking life. Is this an example of your dreams coming true? Some dream experts believe this is impossible but others believe that your dreaming mind can borrow imagery from your future. If you do notice glimpses of your future in your dream be sure to consider the symbolic relevance of what was glimpsed. Don't get carried away and start crediting yourself with being able to foretell the future just make a careful and accurate record of your dreams and include what many believe is a perfectly normal and natural part of the dreaming process into your dream interpretation.

PRECOGNITIVE DREAM

There are many types of **precognitive dream** that allow you to visit potential futures, giving choices and decisions a run through to learn about the possible consequences. If you are prone to having dreams that are more than just glimpses of the future but include entire stories or sequences of events that later happen in waking life, you may find that as well as examining possible causes of action that lie ahead, they may also zero in on important junctures or decisions in life long before they arrive. Experts disagree over whether or not this is possible, but it is possible that your life previews are set up by your dreaming mind to alert you to, and help you recognize, the importance of your actions and decisions at these significant points in our life. If you have a dream that you believe may contain a **precognitive warning of a future accident or disaster**, remember that it is only highlighting a possibility not a fact; if the time comes when it is fulfilled, you have the upper hand as your sense of familiarity with the situation will help you avoid or minimize harm or hurt. *See also* Precognitive dream entry in DISASTERS.

SHARED DREAM

Sometimes people discover – usually accidentally – that they have **experienced a virtually identical dream**, perhaps at the same time. In this variety of psychic dream,

two or more people seem to experience the same events and have similar images. As an example, two people might both report having dreamt of mending the same component on a car, having the same conversation or visiting the same place. Shared dreams may be much more common than we imagine, because the discussion of dreams is usually fairly limited because of the fast pace of modern life. The theoretical implications are fascinating. Are they caused by the dreams using a common symbol representing a similar thought concerning something that happened in the day? Is there telepathic communication between the dreamers? Or can a part of your consciousness actually enter someone else's mind? These questions need to be explored. Such anomalies often act as clues that lead to great new truths.

TELEPATHY IN DREAMS

You may experience dreams in which you **pick up emotions or experience the same situations as others**. For example, you dream of a loved one being rushed to hospital only to find in the morning that this is in fact the case and your father has had a stroke. In most cases, telepathic dreams occur between people who are close to each other; for example between family members, married couples or close friends. These dreams will be generally be for and about you; but if you really do not think this is the case, keep your mind open to the possibility that you may have been picking up sensations or feelings from loved ones. If you are an empathic or sensitive person and know you are prone to such dreams, you can easily recognize them to avoid confusion.

The Element Encyclopedia of 20,000 Dreams

Lucid dreaming

A **lucid dream** is simply one in which you realize that you are dreaming. In one form or another, lucid dreaming has been practiced with great seriousness in certain religious and philosophical traditions. Tibetan Buddhism, in particular, has an ancient discipline of meditative techniques designed to encourage not just lucid dreaming, but a continuously unbroken state of consciousness whilst both sleeping and awake.

Lucid dreaming can be incredibly exciting and rewarding. If you are aware that you're dreaming, you can do things that are impossible in waking life, such as flying, becoming invisible, or traveling to distant times or places. But on a more practical note, interacting with dream characters in a lucid state can help you interpret the meanings of your dreams. Lucid dreams can also help you find creative solutions to problems, work through difficult emotional issues, and promote physical and mental healing. Many people believe lucid dreaming is a path to, or at least a necessary step towards, a form of enlightenment.

A researcher named Hervey de Saint-Denys introduced the notion of lucid dreaming to the Western world in his 1867 book *Dreams and How to Guide Them*. But the term lucid dream itself was coined by Frederik Willems Van Eeden in his 1913 paper 'A Study of Dreams'. The best-known modern figure in lucid dreaming is Stephen LaBerge, a professor at Stanford University. For nearly three decades, LaBerge has been studying lucid dreaming in a laboratory setting, and he proved that subjects can be taught to dream lucidly, using a technique he calls Mnemonic Induction of Lucid Dreams (MILD).

To use this technique, you form a habit in waking life of asking yourself, 'Am I dreaming or awake?' every time you encounter some common stimulus. Sooner or later, you'll encounter the same thing in a dream, and if you ask the question while dreaming, you'll probably figure out that you're really asleep. Other methods include exercises performed right before going to sleep to focus one's attention on having lucid dreams, meditating on certain symbols or sounds, and listening to specially designed audio recordings whilst falling asleep.

With lucid dreaming it may be possible to intentionally access the creativity of the dream state to help solve problems in your waking life. Before bed, decide on a problem you would like to solve. Frame your problem in the form of a question. For example, 'What is the topic of my next book?' or 'How can I become less shy?' If you have an illness, you might consider the problem, 'How can I regain my health?' Once you have selected a problem question, write it down and memorize it; keep going over it in your mind before you go sleep. Visualize yourself looking for the answer in your dreams and then, if you fall asleep and become aware that you are dreaming, explore your dream world with your question in mind. Look for any clues that might suggest an answer. This includes seeking out advice from other characters or experts in your dreams.

Regardless of the details of one's approach, anyone who tries to practice lucid dreaming will end up wondering, on increasingly regular occasions, 'Is this real? Could I be dreaming?' This is what so many people find fascinating about the notion of lucid dreams: if dream reality is as convincing as waking reality, how do we really know that waking reality is not itself a kind of dream and dreams a kind of reality?

UNBORN CHILDREN

Dreams in which you **meet someone who is yet to be born** and they talk about their future life or birth and in time this comes to pass are one of the most stunning types of psychic dreams. They suggest that your dreaming mind may be able to communicate across the boundaries of time and space. Skeptics often dismiss such dreams as flights of fancy, but in dream interpretation, as in all disciplines, it is important to keep an open mind.

The Element Encyclopedia of 20,000 Dreams

Sex

Freud believed that all dreams were wish-fulfillment dreams about sexual activity.

According to Freud, virtually every dream topic – from the phallic symbolism of a clenched fist or a tall building to the feminine associations of a cave or a rosebud unfolding – represented the release of sexual tension. Although Freud's classic work built a solid basis for dream analysis, Jung rejected Freud's idea of the libido being exclusively sexual and argued that Freud saw sexual symbolism in too wide a range of phenomena. According to Jung, sexual dreams were more likely to represent the search for perfect balance between the masculine and feminine principles within oneself. They served as pointers towards psychological growth and wholeness

Today most dream analysts regard dreams as emotional safety valves. The energy behind the sexual drive is enormously important and can express itself in many different ways apart from genital sex, for example caring for others. If this energy is blocked, however, it can lead to poor emotional health, and feelings of loneliness and low self-esteem. Your dreams show you in detail just how you are dealing with this important area of your life, and what is preventing you from feeling satisfied and healthy. If you pay attention to your dreams, they will reveal your intimate and individual needs, thereby considerably enriching your waking life. *See also* ANIMALS; BODY; RELATIONSHIPS.

Sexual Encounters

BIRTH CONTROL

The appearance of **contraceptive pills, coils, condoms or other methods of birth control** in your dream suggests your thoughts and feelings about preventing pregnancy. It may also express worries about sexual contacts. Another interpretation suggests that it indicates feelings or attitudes regarding responsibility and is connected with sexual decisions and feelings.

FEMALE SEXUAL PARTNER

In a **woman's dream, female lovers** are symbols of what you deeply crave, need, hope for or avoid. In a **man's dream, female lovers** are about your relationship with the feminine aspects of your personality, and a **satisfying sexual experience in your dreams with a woman you know or don't know** suggests harmonious union between the masculine and feminine aspects of your personality. **Sex with more than one woman** suggests an element of wish-fulfillment but it may also point to conflicting desires within the male dreamer. The younger the woman in the dream, the more vulnerable are your emotions.

FLIRTING/FLATTERY

In dreams, **flirting** could suggest ostentatious behavior in waking life that could have disastrous consequences, or it could suggest the need for diversion in waking life. **Flattery** is an equally ambiguous symbol suggesting wisdom if you see through the flattery, and gullibility if you do not.

GAY SEX

If you are **heterosexual and had a dream in which you were having sex with a person of the same sex**, this may suggest that you are sexually attracted to members of your own sex but have repressed this inclination. If this is the case, your dream may have been fulfilling your unconscious fantasies and was encouraging you to be honest with yourself. Many psychologists believe that we are all bisexual at a deep level; a dream like this may have given you the opportunity to explore in a safe environment an experience that your conscious mind finds objectionable due to social conditioning. If, however, you are convinced you are not gay or lesbian, your dream may simply have highlighted the intimate nature of your friendships with people of the same sex or your desire to meet someone similar to yourself. Your unconscious may also have been highlighting the fact that if you are in a relationship, you sometimes you feel closer to your friends than you do to your partner. If you are **homophobic** in waking life or in your dream, your unconscious may have been urging you to be more open-minded.

If you are **gay and dream of making love to a person of the same sex**, this will have much the same interpretation as dreams concerning heterosexual sex and partnerships. If you are **gay and have dreams of heterosexual sex**, your unconscious may be highlighting unconscious attractions or emphasizing the closeness of your emotional bonds with friends of the opposite sex.

GENDER ROLE

Within each one of us there is masculine and feminine potential, and when there is conflict between the two, this can sometimes show itself in dreams of **bisexuality or transvestism**. Dreaming of a person who is both masculine and feminine either suggests bisexuality or the perfect balance in one person of the masculine and feminine qualities. If you have a gender-shifting dream in which you believe that you are a **member of the opposite sex**, this generally is a dream about changes in perspective

The Element Encyclopedia of 20,000 Dreams

Some common questions about sexual dreams

If I make love to someone I know in my dream, does that mean he or she is interested in me? In most cases such dreams have more to do with your own feelings rather than hidden passions coming from other people. Remember your dreaming mind uses sexual imagery to give you a taste of how things might be different and teach you about love and passion.

Why do I dream of being intimate with people to whom I'm not attracted? There are several reasons for this. If you honestly don't find the person attractive in waking life, they may represent a quality or characteristic that is closely linked to a quality you are exploring or discovering within yourself. If the partner is particularly unsavory, your dreaming mind may be encouraging you to say no to things that are not right for you.

Are dreams of my partner's infidelity a warning sign? In some cases, yes, but in the majority of cases such dramas are metaphors for some kind of emotional abandonment or neglect; perhaps your loved one is showing more attention to the children – or to their job or hobbies – than to you.

Do repeated dreams of my first love mean I have not got over him or her? Your first love tends to be a symbol of romantic love in dreams but when they appear in your dreams, it is likely that your dreaming mind is using them as an emblem of love to help you work through your current relationship issues. In most cases, your dreaming mind is focused on current issues.

What do dreams of being back with my ex mean? Dreaming about your ex does not mean you want to be with them. Unless you are convinced that your latest ex is the 'one', your dreaming mind is using them as an actor to represent your love interest. In most cases, such dreams suggest that you are going over old issues or relationship patterns, and that your dreaming mind is using such images to help you heal and move on to a more positive future. When any relationship breaks down, your dreaming mind will delve into memories, fears and hopes to help you unravel mysteries and gain understanding about what makes real love work. Your inner mind is constantly sorting through what works and what doesn't work in a relationship, and it will refer back to past relationships to compare strengths and weaknesses and try to make sense of things.

If I have a perfect dream romance, does this mean the perfect partner will appear in my life? In you are single and you have a perfect romantic and sexual dream, this could be wish-fulfillment but it could also be your dreaming mind's way of reminding you that love and passion are still out there and you should open yourself up to the possibility of romance.

or exploring different aspects of yourself. Don't judge yourself too harshly if you have such a dream, as these are more often markers of psychological maturity and development than an indication that something is amiss.

INTERCOURSE

Your longing for sexual adventure that isn't expressed in waking life may attempt to express itself in your dreams. If you **have sex with other people** in your dream, this doesn't mean you are dissatisfied with your partner; we all have secret longings and it is healthy to express them as you sleep. If you had a dream in which you were **having sex and you are a teenager or young adult**, this is perfectly normal. Adolescents frequently dream of sex, partly because the onset of puberty causes sex hormones to flood the body awakening sexual curiosity. Such dreams are caused by these natural physiological stimuli, combined with feelings of anxiety or excitement about what making love is like. Sexual frustration is another reason why you may have erotic dreams. The sexual drive is extremely powerful and if you are not in a sexual relationship or have not had sex for a long time with your partner, your unconscious may find release in your dreams.

Similarly, if you are having unsatisfying or boring sex in real life, you may have a dream in which you have **passionate and exciting sex**, giving you an insight into your true sexual yearnings. If you have low self-esteem, your unconscious may also try to boost your sense of self-worth by depicting you **making love to a sexy stranger**. If you dreamed of **making love to someone you know in waking life**, you may be unconsciously or consciously attracted to that person or your unconscious may again be boosting your self-esteem by conjuring up such images. This is particularly the case if your **dream lover is a celebrity** or a person countless people have a crush on in waking life.

If none of the above applies to you, dreams in which you are making love to someone you know or don't know could, according to a Jungian interpretation, depict your union with the anima or feminine aspects of your character if you are a man, or the animus or masculine traits within you if you are a woman. Your dream may have symbolized the complete integration of your masculine and feminine qualities or a longing for a part of yourself that has been lost. The other character in your dream – the sexual partner – represents the closest you can get to that part and helps you understand what your deepest needs are. Another interpretation suggests that dreams in which sex is the theme are referring to your creative powers, although not necessarily fertility, and the use you could be making of them in waking life.

Because semen is a symbol of masculinity and of physical and sexual maturity, dreams of **ejaculation or emission** can suggest the nature of your attitude to sex and the conflicts which arise in you. If you dream of **seducing someone or being seduced yourself**, this suggests that you make compromises too easily in both business and love, and you should not commit yourself so cheaply. To dream of **undressing in front of your dream partner** suggests confidence, but to be **shy or reticent to reveal yourself naked** suggests body-image concerns. Having **sex fully dressed** in a dream suggests feelings of guilt; to dream of being **naked or your genitals being exposed in public** suggests feelings of sexual insecurity. It can also suggest indiscretion in your waking life, whilst **deformed genitals** warn against over-indulgence. *See also* BODY.

KISSING

This can indicate a mark of respect or a desire to arouse someone; and that someone might be yourself. According to Jung, the image of **kissing** in dreams is likely to be rooted in memories of sucking at the mother's breast. If your sexual needs are repressed or denied, this may manifest in dreams about masturbation in an attempt to release sexual energy and comfort yourself.

MALE SEXUAL PARTNER

In a **man's dream, a male lover** is a symbol of what you deeply crave, need, fear, hope for or avoid. In a **woman's dream, a satisfying sexual experience with a man** you know or don't know can suggest a harmonious union with the masculine aspects of your character, and your power to be competitive and challenging in the world; an **unsatisfactory sexual experience with a man** would suggest the opposite. **Sex with more than one man** would represent different aspects of yourself. **Sex with an ape or wildman** would suggest sexual urges at odds with your present circumstances.

VIRGINITY, LOSS OF

If you dreamed of **losing your virginity** and you are a virgin in real life, your dream may have mirrored your fear or anticipation of the event. If, however, you are no longer a virgin and have a dream like this, your unconscious could be referring to a loss or innocence or sense of disillusionment in your waking life. Perhaps a friend wasn't as kind or thoughtful as you thought they would be or someone let you down.

Sexual dreams and symbols

The interruption

In this dream, you are **making love and somebody, perhaps your boss or your friend or someone you don't know, interrupts you** and speaks to you as if you are not in the middle of sex and you have a conversation. This kind of dream suggests that there are outside forces intruding on your relationship and spoiling moments of passion or intimacy. These forces could be anything from financial worries to pressures at work or the demands of young children. Such a dream could also suggest sexual inhibitions or insecurities.

Nowhere to make love

In this dream, **you and your lover undertake a fruitless search for privacy and are constantly frustrated**. This isn't so much a dream about sex but about the difficult forces or obstacles in your life which are preventing you from feeling intimate with someone close to you. Such dreams may occur after a relationship breaks up or when communication has broken down between yourself and your partner.

Public lovemaking

In this dream you find yourself **making love in a very public place**; such a dream suggests that you feel your private life has been made public in some way or that people are speculating about your private life.

Vanishing partner

You are **making passionate love when your partner just vanishes**; such a dream suggests passion that is frustrated in some way. A variation is the dream of **making love to a stranger with no face**, but in this case the emphasis is on your desire to experiment sexually.

Female sexual symbols

Flowers, lilies, figs and ripening fruits all have female sexual symbolism. The **red rose** is a traditional symbol of romantic love and passion, suggesting to Freudians the female sexual organs. A **rose with thorns in a man's dream** suggests an ambivalent attitude towards female sexuality. **Velvet** is a soft and sensual fabric, and is associated with pubic hair by Freudians. Other dream analysts link **velvet and moss** in dreams with a desire for comfort and peace. **Purses**, according to Freud, are symbols of female genitalia or the womb; when the purse opens, this suggests sexual availability and when it is snapped shut, this suggests withholding.

Male sexual symbols

Weapons are often seen as phallic symbols and a **stabbing, penetrating knife** can represent violent male sexuality. **Guns** are another image of aggressive male sexuality with the added orgasmic symbolism of firing a bullet. **Wielding a gun or a knife** in a man's dream can, however, indicate doubts about virility.

A **cigar or cigarette** can symbolize a penis; even Freud admitted that his passion for cigar smoking was a substitute for masturbation, although he did once joke that a cigar is sometimes just a cigar. **Cars** can represent the penis – especially if the car has a powerful, thrusting motor. A **weathercock in a woman's dream** is thought to be an especially powerful sexual symbol. **Darts, fingers, snakes, guns, hammers, screwdrivers, horns, icicles, javelins, spheres, engines, lorries and poles** are all phallic symbols, as are **spires and towers standing tall**.

Quills and pens are obvious Freudian symbols, especially if they are **dipped in ink**. Jungians suggest that the quill can represent the archetype of the animus, the male aspect of the female psyche. **Cell phones** can be interpreted as phallic dream symbols as they often take the place of a loved one and can evoke sexual yearning or stand for the act of masturbation. The image may also represent frustrating attempts at sexual intimacy.

Drinking from a cup, glass or horn can represent oral sex with a woman. **Socks** or other items of clothing which fit the body part snugly are often interpreted as symbols of female genitalia; such items may stand for the act of intercourse if they are being put on or off. **Gloves and shoes** are other common images of this type. Shoes can also suggest authority and sexual domination.

Other symbols of intercourse and sex

Flying dreams were declared by Freud to be one of the classic examples of sexually inspired dreams. Other symbols associated with sexual intercourse according to Freud include **hammering and chopping, sliding down a banister or slide, a train entering a tunnel, a lighted candle and riding a bicycle or horse**.

Horses, especially stallions, may be a symbol of sexuality and **mounting a horse** represents intercourse. **Spectacular explosions** are associated with orgasm. In the form of **fireworks** this suggests exhilaration but **destructive explosions** can express the desire to dominate. **Water gushing from a tap, champagne spraying white foam or cascading waterfalls** are also orgasmic symbols.

Dream analysts have noticed an association in women's dreams between dreams of a **plane crash** and rape or fear of it. Freudians would interpret a **man's dream of a plane crash** as fear of impotence. **Churches with a steeple and an arched portal** combine male and female symbolism and such an image may express conflict between sexual expression and moral responsibility.

Dreams in which you **become invisible** may simply indicate that you feel unnoticed by those around you, but they may also suggest an element of sexual voyeurism.

Disturbing Sexual Dreams

ABANDONED

If you dreamed of being lured into bed by a person with sexual magnetism only to be **rejected or criticized after the sexual act**, your unconscious may have been warning you to steer clear of the **archetypal huntress or siren** if you are a man, or the **archetypal wastrel** if you are a woman.

ANIMAL

Enjoying **sex with an animal**, such as being caressed by a bear, is the way that your dreams describe your basic sexual urges at their most basic and uncomplicated level. It doesn't mean you are weird. In such dreams, you are simply dispensing with social conventions and experiencing lust.

ASSAULT

If you have been the victim of sexual assault and dream of being **sexually assaulted**, your dream may have recreated the attack as a sign that you have not yet come to terms with it. If this is the case, it might help to seek counseling to deal with the pain, guilt, anger and fear. If this is not the case, try to identify your dream attacker. Is it someone in your life who has a powerful or domineering influence over you, or someone with whom you are having a dispute? If the attacker is either of these, your unconscious may be depicting your

sense of having no choice but to submit or go along with things. You may have a strong fear of being humiliated if you lose the struggle. Alternatively, you may have detected that this person is a threat or danger to you.

CASTRATION

In a **man's dream, castration** suggests loss of masculinity and sexual power, or anxiety about satisfying a partner sexually. In a **woman's dream, castration** may also express fears that someone wants to disempower you in some way; but it could also reveal hidden aggression against a man in your waking life. Bear in mind that there are many possible symbols for castration such as **cutting off a necktie or destroying a tall building**.

DISTRESSING, VIOLENT AND GRAPHIC IMAGES

In the 1800s, sexual dreams were considered to be a great source of worry to the men and women who had them because, at the time, sexual dreams were thought to cause mental and physical illness. It is, however, over-simplistic to describe all sexual dreams as a form of frustration or wish-fulfillment. The desire to have sex is a healthy human urge and your dreams allow you to give free reign to this urge as well as to indulge in all kinds of erotic experiments in which no emotional or physical harm is inflicted upon any one. If you do wake up from a dream in which you have had **sex with someone inappropriate or that contains graphic, disturbing or violent imagery**, there is most likely to be a non-sexual interpretation. However, if you do find the dream distressing and it repeatedly recurs, be sure to seek professional counseling. Unless your erotic dreams are seriously disturbing (when psychiatric help should be sought), there is no reason why you should not enjoy them like any other fantasy.

DOMINATION

Dreams in which **one partner dominates the other** often have sexual overtones. If you are in the **role of dominator**, this may mask sexual insecurity; if you are in the **role of the submissive**, this may mask incestuous desire for a parent. On the other hand, such dreams may stem from the strong desire to gain the upper hand in a relationship. **Whips** often symbolize a desire for, or fear of, domination in dreams. A similar interpretation can be attributed to accompanying sadomasochistic equipment such as **silver chains, leather clothing and straps, and black boots and heels**. Fetishes are a fixation on an external object without which there would be no sex act, and in dreams they can highlight fear, immaturity and a lack of libido

INAPPROPRIATE PARTNER

If you are in a committed relationship and dreamt of **sleeping with someone else's husband or wife or someone who is sexually off limits**, such as a cousin or your doctor, remember that the message from your unconscious may not have been that you desire that person, although this is a possible interpretation, but that you would like to have a closer emotional connection to them. If you wake from such a dream with feelings of remorse, perhaps you have been unfaithful or less than honest with your partner in other ways. It is also worth bearing in mind when trying to interpret dreams that depict you making love to someone who plays a major, but definitely non-sexual, part in your life that your unconscious may simply be reflecting your waking preoccupation with them at the same time that you are becoming sexually aroused. So if you dreamt of **making love to your unattractive boss**, it may simply have been a coincidence that they stepped into the lover role in your dreams.

INCEST

This is one of society's great taboos and if you had a dream in which you **slept with your brother, sister, mother, father or any close relative**, you may awake feeling utterly violated and repulsed. When your unconscious creates such images in your dreams, it is not attempting to highlight any form of sexual attraction but is showing your preoccupation with that person in some other way. Perhaps you are extraordinarily close to your brother or sister and your unconscious is trying to shock you into independence. Another interpretation suggests that you are involved with someone who has qualities similar to your relative. Alternatively, you may be picking up on something unwholesome or unhealthy about a current relationship.

Masochism/Sadism

The desire to **hurt yourself through sex** in dreams is a symbol of guilt or the desire to feel extreme emotion. Perhaps you are not allowing yourself to feel deeply in waking life? In dreams, any form of **sadism** would suggest a counterbalance to the dreamer's conscious way of being in the world. For example, a timid person may have dreams of sadistic sex as an escape mechanism; similarly, a domineering person may have the dream to show an unconscious need to be controlled. The explicit eroticism of sado-masochistic acts could also suggest a battle of wills or extreme sexual tension.

Orgy

The Victorians suggested that dreams of **orgies** suggested fear of catching syphilis in men and a woman's concern about being labeled frigid. Modern dream analysts, however suggest that orgies serve as a safety valve to temper propriety and moderation in waking life.

Pornography

If you find yourself enjoying **pornographic photographs or films** in your dream, this suggests that a small part of you is not as repelled by pornography as you like to think it is. Such a dream may be urging you to relax more about your attitude towards different types of sexual behavior and to be more open-minded.

Prostitute

If you are a man and dreamed of **visiting a prostitute or wandering in a red light district** and your sex life is unsatisfactory in the real world, it may be that you are considering relieving your frustration in the same way. If you are a **woman dreaming of working for a pimp or as a prostitute or visiting the red light district**, your unconscious may be craving an element of danger or you might desire to have power over men. If the dream left you feeling violated and disgusted, this suggests that in real life your partner may just be using you for sex or taking advantage of you in some other way. Alternatively, do you feel that you have prostituted yourself in some way in waking life?

Rape

Dreams of **rape or of being raped** can suggest that you are feeling overwhelmed in some way by events in your life or that other people are dominating you. Images of rape appearing in dreams can also be associated with the violation of personal space. In rare instances, such a dream can express emotions that have been rejected or lingering pain from past experiences returning to haunt the dreamer.

Sexual inadequacy

Dreams in which you feel **inadequate, impotent or embarrassed during sex** are in no way predictive and most dream analysts suggest that they are a way for your unconscious mind to vent its frustrations and anxieties. To imagine **voyeurs watching or spying on you during love-making** suggests unease with your sexual performance.

Venereal disease

To dream of catching **venereal disease** – or any other form of sexually transmitted disease (STD) – suggests feelings of some kind of contamination; these may not necessarily be sexual but could also be emotional.

SHAPES

It is very common for shapes and patterns of all sorts to appear in your dreams.

You may not realize how often shapes and patterns appear in your dreams but if you were reading a book you were holding a rectangle; if you paid someone a coin, you were using a circle and so on. Whether they are dots, spirals, circles, crescents, stars, triangles, squares or crosses, shapes and patterns are just as much an everyday part of your dream world as they are a part of the real world, although when they feature in dreams their significance can be heightened. This is because shapes and patterns are considered to be amongst the most ancient and powerful of archetypal symbols, and, according to Jung, they can reflect the very structure of your mind.

From the very beginnings of humankind when our ancestors first recognized that the moon often became a crescent and that the sun was a circle, the human mind has been conditioned to read meaning into shapes and patterns. In much the same way as absent-minded doodling can reveal information about your unconscious mind, many modern dream analysts believe that shapes and patterns in dreams are a visual presentation of your psycholog-

ical state or inner world. Bear in mind that the number of sides the shape has, as well as its color, will be important to any interpretation. *See also* COLORS; NUMBERS; SYMBOLS.

Shapes

CIRCLE

According to Jungian theory, the **circle** is the perfect expression of infinity, continuity and connection; the circle represents the ideal self, within which the psyche's various opposing elements have achieved perfect balance. It has no beginning and no end, with no turns or corners in between. This perfect geometric shape symbolizes the center and perfection of the self in all its wholeness. It is a concept inherent in the Eastern yin-yang symbol, in which the white active masculine yang principle is united in symmetrical equality with the black yin force of passiveness and femininity.

If you find yourself in the **middle of a circle** in your dream, it can represent your self or your spirit. Alternatively, the middle may also indicate conflict between opposites or the feeling of being involved, protected or in the middle of something. For Freud, the circle represented the vagina; for Jung, it was an archetypal symbol of the whole psyche, as opposed to the body, which was symbolized by the square. When someone has made the transition through all aspects of life and has returned to their beginning, we say that they have come 'full circle'. Family groups are referred to as the 'family circle', whilst social groups are sometimes called a 'circle of friends' or a 'community circle'. When the apparent solution to a problem in a series of events creates a new problem and increases the difficulty of solving the original problem, it may be called a 'vicious circle' or 'vicious cycle'.

To determine the meaning of your **dream circle, round, sphere or ball**, look at the symbols and events connected with it, as there is a wealth of often conflicting possible interpretations to consider. For example, if you are **traveling round in a circle**, you may be progressing toward wholeness or running around uselessly chasing your tail! If the **circle is smooth**, it suggests harmony and centeredness; but if it is **irregular**, it may suggest the dull round of routine. Jewelry is given in many cultures to express emotion and **rings, bracelets and necklaces** are usually circular. In many societies, marriage and lifelong commitment are symbolized by exchanging rings. Did someone you desire give you a ring in your dream? Perhaps there's a

chance for the relationship, or maybe it is just wishful thinking. If you dream of a **broken necklace or bracelet**, you may fear that a relationship will break and come to an abrupt end; you may, however, feel that it is time for a connection to come to a conclusion.

Circles also contain and restrict. For instance, a new pupil is outside the group until she settles in and is accepted at her new school; dog collars allow an animal to be restrained. In some pagan traditions, a circle of intent is cast to contain positive energy and protect against negative energy. Was your dream circle keeping something out or keeping you in? You may feel a need for protection, or you may feel trapped by a relationship or situation. **Knots** begin with circles and usually contain several. Perhaps something is knotted up? As well as suggesting the potential for unity, wholeness and perfection, circles also represent eternity or the cycle of life because they have no beginning or end, as well as security and protection because they enclose. The fact that the **sun** is circular means that if it appears in your dream, it may be signaling masculine, active energy or even the life force itself. Don't forget, though, that circles also possess feminine connotations due to their resemblance to eggs.

With so many possible interpretations, it can often be difficult to decide what a dream circle may have been suggesting but considering the context of your dream, along with your waking circumstances, should help you with the interpretation. Bear in mind that it is always worth considering whether the appearance of circles was telling you to work on harmonizing conflicting elements of your inner self in order to achieve contentment and serenity. For example, if you dreamed of **dropping a round plate and it smashed**, your dream may have been portraying your rebellious nature and your need to exercise greater self control.

In dreams, **round balls** tend to represent the interaction between two people, as in 'throwing the ball' or 'the ball is in your court'. They may also be a symbol of your need to get someone's attention. **Ball games** suggest challenge and competition in the game of life, but may also be associated with aggression or sex, as in a man's balls. As the **center of a circle** is the point from which everything starts, if you dreamed of a **target enclosed in a circle**, was your unconscious telling you to aim for psychic wholeness? A **circle with a dot in the center** can signify balance and centeredness. It can also represent woman. A **sphere** shares much of the symbolism of a circle, and indicates perfection and completion of all possibilities; it can, however, also evoke a spherical object such as a breast or testicle, and therefore have a sexual association.

CRESCENT

Due to its association with the moon, the **crescent** in dreams indicates femininity, and non-rational, intuitive power and creativity. It can also represent the beginning or the ending of something in your life. If the **crescent is C-shaped**, it may suggest that something in your life is waning or disappearing; but if the **circle is a reversed C**, then waxing and growth may have been implied, perhaps even the conception of a baby. If you are a Muslim, the crescent is a symbol of Islam, whilst if

you are a Christian, it is a symbol of the Virgin Mary. In both instances, a crescent appearing in your dream may have been focusing on your faith.

CROSS

Until around AD 33, the **cross** was a symbol of punishment, as well as being a simple symbol of connection. Since that time, the cross has become a powerful symbol of religion, but it also indicates the challenges and tribulations that you face in life. The most obvious connection the majority of us make is with the cross on which Jesus died. If you are religious and focus on the pain and suffering of Jesus, the cross could mean that you feel there are great burdens in your life that are almost too much to bear. You are being crucified – tortured – for the things in which you believe. The pain is unwarranted but you bear it all the same, and are seeking for a way to handle your problems. Yes, there may be troubles, but if you approach them with a joyful spirit and optimism, you will find a path through them. Your dreaming mind is telling you that you have the spiritual strength within you to overcome any hurdle.

If you are not religious, the cross could stand for a power in your life over which you have no control or that is trying to influence you. It could mean that you have a certain path you wish to take, but that forces are preventing you from taking that path. The cross may also represent something in your life that is wrong or forbidden, or something you need to cross off a list. If the **cross is upright as in +**, this suggests correctness and self-assertion; but if the **cross is in the shape of an x**, it represents reaching out and wholeness.

The Element Encyclopedia of 20,000 Dreams

Mandala

From a Sanskrit word meaning 'magic circle or disc', a **mandala** is a circular visual representation that is used as a focus point for the practice of meditation. When creating a mandala, the artist attempts to coordinate their personal circle with the universal circle, reflecting how their life fits into the larger whole. Although the mandala form is often associated with Tibetan monk artists, who use them as an aid to meditation and visualization, and Navaho Indians, who create them out of multicolored sand as a formal geometrical expression of sacred vibrations, mandalas transcend culture and religion, time and place. When a person concentrates on a mandala they are attempting to approach a higher plane of consciousness and, according to Jung, they are the ultimate symbols for uniting our inner and outer selves, being an archetypal expression of the soul. Jung found that the integrative properties of the mandala possessed considerable benefits in psychotherapy; by drawing mandalas, patients could impose order upon their inner confusion.

A mandala is typically a circle enclosing a square with a symbol in the center representing the whole of life. In dreams, it can appear in many ways: as a **square garden with a round pond, a square with a circle in the middle, a painting with a circle** and so on. It can often appear in dreams without you realizing what it represents and it is only when drawn afterwards that it is recognized as a mandala. This suggests that it is a true expression of your individuality. It can also appear as an **eight-pointed star** that represents both your aspirations and your burdens, and indicates what you have achieved with your life and what you have learned from your experience, both good and bad. The mandala may often appear in dreams when your waking life feels confusing or difficult; your dreaming mind conjures it as a symbol of the journey from chaos to order.

OTHER SHAPES

Similar to the compass needle, a **diamond** shape in your dream suggests choices and directions in your life; you are at a crossroads and you either have more or fewer options than you thought you had available. In dreams, an **oblong** shape suggests a specific area of your experience in life, whilst an **oval** is symbolic of the womb and feminine life. It is also associated with the halo that denotes a spiritual figure in religious iconography. The **rectangle** may represent the Golden Mean, a geometric figure of ideal proportions that symbolizes the perfect union between earth and heaven.

SQUARE

Squares are very stable and well ordered, and they indicate things that are down to earth, the physical reality and the materialization of ideas and plans. Leonardo da Vinci's depiction of a man in a circle in a square represents the complete balance of the various aspects of human nature. Squares also suggest the four directions on a compass. It could be that you seek stability and order in your life, and aren't quite sure how to achieve these. Look at how the square is used in your dream for a hint as to which direction to take. Squares represent the material world with its stability but also its limits and restrictions. Squares are dreamt about most often by those trying to bring order into their lives.

If you dreamed of a square – be it a **square room, a city square, a television screen, a book or a paving stone** – the reference may be to your own stable, dependable personality. On the other hand, are you trying to find a solution to a problem that vexes you? Squares can also represent feelings of restriction or the boring, tedious, day-to-day grind of life, so in dreams they could be reflecting stagnation, inhibition, and your need for freedom and excitement. If you dreamed of a **cube**, this is a symbol of wisdom, truth and perfection as it gives depth and stability to a square. The cube may also stand for a house, and is therefore a symbol of the self. If **you or another person are within a cube** in your dream, this represents you. If the cube is in the form of a **die**, it suggests life's uncertainties.

STAR

The **star** is a symbol of success or aspiration in modern life. The star is a shape that is widely used to represent a variety of tangible and intangible things. Stars are used to decorate birthday presents and are seen on balloons and cards congratulating us for success: 'You're A Star!' The star is used as a symbol to represent law enforcement agencies, and is used on lapels to represent high military rank, as in a four star general. Most religions look above to the Divine and stars seem to be sprinkled along the path to higher consciousness.

A **five-pointed star** that is written or drawn is called a pentagram, whilst the same star enclosed by a circle is called a pentacle. This symbol has been used in many religions for centuries, such as Judaism and Christianity, as well as in pagan and Wiccan belief. In pagan religions and in alchemy, the **five points of the star** represent the four elements and the Divine: earth, air, fire, water and spirit. The suit of **pentacles in Tarot** represents prosperity and abundance. If you dream of **drawing a star**, you may be mapping out your success. A **five-pointed star or pentagram** suggests harmony between mind, body and spirit. In magical tradition it is a symbol of protection and, when depicted pointing upwards, it represents goodness; when it is pointing downwards, however, it represents evil.

A **six-pointed star or Star of David** represents the reconciliation of opposites into a harmonious whole. Sometimes called the Seal of Solomon (a defensive symbol in Kabalistic magical belief) and sometimes the Creator's star (because its six points can be equated to the six days in which God created the world according to Judeo-Christian tradition), the hexagram is better known as the Star of David, the national emblem of Israel. It is a geometric figure which symbolizes the union and development of physical, social and spiritual elements of your life.

TRIANGLE

For many, the **triangle** represents the three parts of the Holy Trinity – the Father, the Son, and the Holy Spirit; it can also represent the number three and its various manifestations in father, mother and child, or body, mind and spirit. If you are religious, the triangle could be telling you to pay more attention to your religious teachings. It can also mean feeling independent or being able to stand on your own two feet. If the **triangle is facing upwards**, this suggests that it would be better to channel your energies into your conscious objectives but if it is **pointing downwards**, you should turn inwards and explore your unconscious mind.

On the other hand, the triangle was a symbol used in Third Reich to mark out those who were 'different' and 'bad'. If you are **seeing a triangle in a negative manner** in your dream, it could be that you are feeling singled out, feeling like people are harassing you for no good reason and that you are frustrated and frightened by this. For Freudians, the triangle is an image of sexuality, male pointing upwards and female pointing downwards. If your dream incorporated a **triangular figure or shape**, it may also have denoted three people who are closely linked to you in the waking world; perhaps your children and your partner, or perhaps a love triangle.

According to Freud, a **pyramid** is a symbol of an erect phallus. Others suggest that this powerful image represents spiritual aspirations. Alternatively if you dreamed that you **found yourself in an Egyptian setting awed by the sight of the Great Pyramids**, perhaps your unconscious is urging you to travel and see the great wonders of the world or to explore your own inner world. The **square base of the pyramid** can denote your unconscious foundations and the **apex of the pyramid** your aspirations. The pyramid can also represent a mountain you need to ascend in order to achieve your highest ambition, which may be spiritual enlightenment. There is a well-known game – square, circle or triangle? – in which you draw a square, circle or a triangle and ask someone to elaborate each of these shapes into a drawing. Whatever your playing partner makes of the square is supposed to relate to their outlook on the world, the circle to their inner being and the triangle to their sex life. See if any of this makes sense if squares, circles or triangles appear in your dreams.

Patterns

DOTS

If **dots** appeared in your dream or you **took extra care to dot the i's in your dream handwriting**, your dreaming mind may have been urging you to pay more attention to detail. But if you dreamed of **ending your letter with a period or full stop**, then perhaps there is something in your

Dream doodles

In both real and dream life, **doodles** are expressions of your unconscious mind. Doodles, like dreams, involve a form of picture language, and it is the interpretation of these pictures that reveal their meanings. If you **see yourself doodling or see a doodle** in your dreams, there are several factors to be taken into account besides the doodle itself. The **size and position of the doodle** on the page have a significance that contributes to the overall meaning of the doodle.

For example, if you were to **draw a very large doodle in the center of the page**, then this would indicate how important you would like your role in life to be. However, if you **doodle in the margin or corners of a page**, you would be revealed as a quiet individual. The intensity of the ink or pencil marks can also indicate the mood of the person, **lighter strokes** indicating a good day, but **dark, heavy strokes** sometimes signaling depression. The symbolism of specific doodles in your dream will have much the same interpretation as the dream symbol itself if it wasn't being doodled, but the interpretation would typically be personal and referring to your feelings and your creative expression, rather than to the feelings or situation of someone else. *See also* Drawing entry in ARTS AND CRAFTS and Writing entry in LETTERS AND COMMUNICATION.

---

waking life that is coming to an end. Dots also shared the same symbolism as eggs or seeds, which represent growth or the potential for growth and development; your dream may have been highlighting something that is beginning rather than ending in your life.

LINE

A **line** is a symbol of movement but also of division or a dividing force, such as a boundary, as expressed in the phrase, 'drawing a line in the sand'. If someone is **drawing a line** in your dream, it indicates their decisiveness or their extent of their boundaries. As your geometry teacher probably told you many times, a straight line is the shortest distance between two points. It is the straight path, the road to take to reach your goal. If you are dreaming about a **straight line**, it means you want to find an efficient way to reach your goals rather than meandering and wasting years and years before attaining your dream.

If the **line is tangled or knotted**, this suggests indecision and confusion in your life, whilst if the **line zigzags**, this suggests change and movement. Whereas a straight line represents the straight and most immediate path to a goal, a **wavy line** is one that meanders around, taking in the sights

The Element Encyclopedia of 20,000 Dreams

and taking its time. The person taking the straight path only cares about the goal and getting there, but the person taking the wavy line, the curvy path in life, is exploring all the options. They are enjoying each day for what it brings, enjoying the side trips, relishing the changing of the seasons and the turning of the days. Yes, they might not reach their goal as quickly but for the person taking the wavy line, the journey and living every day to the full is the goal.

SPIRAL

Patterns such as those printed on cloth or displayed in mosaics represent the order or chaos of your inner thoughts and feelings; the patterns, habits and beliefs by which you choose to live. Dream **spirals** indicate the things you repeat over and over again in your life so that they become habits. They can also represent intuition, or the movement towards greater awareness and insight in your real life. The idea is that everything is in constant motion. In waking life, spirals appear as **whirlpools or spinning wheels**, all centers of energy and activity; your dreaming mind may use these images to reflect your own energy in waking life.

Water is also a symbol of the unconscious so if you dreamed of a **whirlpool**, could this reflect your feeling of going round and round in circles in waking life and getting nowhere? Or could a **spinning wheel** have reminded you of your simmering anger? Evocative of staircases and snakes, the spiral is also a symbol of sexual intercourse or movement either towards higher aspirations, if it is **rotating clockwise and upwards**, or basic instincts, if it is **rotating anticlockwise and downwards**. If the **spiral is moving toward the center**, this suggests approaching your center indirectly. If the **spiral is inert and stylized**, like those that appear on **seashells or the winding paths of a labyrinth or maze**, this suggests a concentration of inward energy; your unconscious may be urging you to gain a deeper level of self-awareness.

SWASTIKA

The **clockwise swastika or hooked cross** portrays all that is good and pure in humankind. In Eastern symbolism, it represents the movement of the sun. Moving **anticlockwise**, it suggests the opposite; all that is sinister and wrong with humanity; although Hitler and many top Nazis such as Himmler had an interest in the occult, it is not known if the choice of the swastika was deliberate or not. If this shape or pattern appears in your dream you may immediately associate it with Hitler, fascism or extreme right-wing views and your unconscious may be urging you to steer clear of someone with those kinds of beliefs. Bear in mind, however, that the ancient association of the swastika is far more positive and your unconscious may have been drawing on that. Swastika is a Sanskrit word that means well-being and to Hindus, Buddhists and Jains it is a symbol of good fortune.

SICKNESS AND HEALTH

Unless you are actually ill or sick, dreams in which your general health and well-being are highlighted may be commenting not just on your physical state, but on your psychological or emotional condition as well.

Such dreams can pinpoint areas of potential conflict and help you achieve a more balanced approach. If any part of the body is injured or painful in a dream, this may be well worth following up, since illness has been diagnosed in this way before. Bear in mind that dreams usually use body parts and illnesses as symbols for other areas of your life. So try to make a link between your dream ailment and your waking life.

Sigmund Freud pioneered the use of dreams in psychological healing and most dream analysts today agree that in dreams, painful memories and feelings can surface disguised as physical illnesses or weaknesses. Sometimes such dreams foretell real illness if you don't take better care of yourself, but most of the time they represent the way you approach life. Perhaps you feel you can't cope with a situation, and illness is the easy way out. Dreams of this sort suggest that you are in conflict with some aspect of your personality and therefore not putting yourself in touch with a force that can give you health in both body and mind. Part of you isn't well and needs to be cared for.

You need to heal these inner troubles and find psychological harmony.

Body Fluids, Functions and Internal Organs

BLOOD

Blood is an important symbol, not only of life itself, but also of the soul, of physical strength and rejuvenation. Whether you were cut or seriously injured, dreams in which you are **losing blood or suffer a hemorrhage** may therefore refer to loss of moral or physical strength; they may simply indicate a need for more emotional nourishment. Dreaming of **drinking blood or receiving a blood transfusion** may refer to the opposite: gaining strength and vitality. If a **person you know gives you**

blood in your dream, your unconscious may have signaled that they have the potential to revitalize you. If a **woman dreams of blood**, it may be associated with the onset of a period, the blood depicting whatever feelings she may have about menstruation. Blood is also a symbol of passion, love, anger and even violence.

Blood on the ground or blood stains on clothes in a dream suggest great injury or emotional pain to someone, perhaps to you or someone you know. If you dream of **blood in a sexual context**, this may refer to loss of virginity, fertility or menstruation.

■ *Idioms: after one's blood; blood brother; blood on one's hands; blood relative; blood sucker; blue blood; draw blood; blood is thicker than water; blood boil; blood run cold; out of blood; taste blood; young blood; bleed someone dry; one's heart bleeds; cold or hot blooded; blood money; blue blood.*

BONE/PELVIS/SKELETON/ SKULL/SPINE

In dreams, a **human bone** represents strength, the structure and support within yourself, and the need to be aware of your basic instincts. If you are **burying a bone**, perhaps you are hiding something about yourself or saving something for the future. If you are **digging up bones**, you are remembering something from the past. **Broken bones** may reveal your insecurities, depending on which limb is broken. For example, a **thick plaster cast around a broken leg** in a dream can suggest reluctance to face up to problems that are hindering your progress.

Dreams that feature the **spine, back or backbone** are all symbols of your moral power and your strength and ability to stand up for yourself; but if you dream about the **pelvis**, it refers to your sexual functioning as a whole, including your reproductive success. The pelvis also links in with the way you merge with someone else in a relationship, or if you can allow that merging to happen. Some dreams show the **pelvis connected with snakes or lizards**; this is a symbol of powerful instinctual drives and urges that can flow up your spine and expand your consciousness.

If you saw a **skeleton** in your dream, especially if it was **in a cupboard**, are you concerned that certain things in your life you are trying to hide may come out into the open? The symbol could also refer to feelings or talents you have cut off or killed in real life. If you see a **complete skeleton**, you may need to reconsider the full structure of your life. The **skull and crossbones** are a symbol of danger but since the **skull** is a representation of the head, it can also symbolize intellectual ability. To be **conscious of your skull** is to appreciate your intellectual skills. To **see a skull where there should be a head** represents a part of the person that has died. To dream that you are **talking to a skull** is to recognize the need to be talking to people with whom you may have lost contact. When a **skull is talking to you**, a part of you that has been rejected or denied is coming back to life. As symbols of death, if you were frightened by **skeletons, skulls and bones** in your dream, this could point to your fear of dying or of a loved one's demise.

Breathing

A dream in which you have **asthma or problems breathing** may refer to problems in your waking life. In women, it may indicate difficulties with your animus or the male part of your personality; in men, it may relate to your sense of manhood. Alternatively, it may indicate a need for more space, air or freedom. Dreaming of **respiratory ailments or breathing problems** can also suggest general anxiety about work, relationships or a difficult situation. **Heavy breathing, panting, perspiration or sweat** in dreams is a symbol of some kind of fear, but also of excitement. If you dreamed that you needed an **oxygen mask**, your dream might be suggesting that you need to get some fresh air into your life, not just in the form of outdoor activity, but in the form of ideas and energy.

■ *Idioms: in a cold sweat; no sweat; sweat off one's brow; old sweat; sweat it out.*

Internal Organ

If your dream features images of an **appendix**, either your own or someone else's, this indicates something within yourself that may have become a problem; it may also suggest an internal problem to do with appendix itself. If you are **having your appendix out** in your dream, this represents inner pain or problems that urgently need to be attended to in waking life.

If you dream of your **brain**, are you concerned about your poor memory? In dreams, brains indicate your intellect, insight and creativity but they can also suggest what you really think. You may dream of **something happening to your brain**; something may tear at it, shoot it or it may be impaled. Things that invade or harm your brain in dreams typically represent current factors in your life that are coloring your perspective or outlook. On the other hand, if you dream of having **brain surgery or of prying a foreign object out of your brain**, this may reflect a change in your way of thinking.

In dreams, the **heart** generally indicates emotion, pity, sympathy and likes and dislikes; not just romantic love but your way of loving all things. It can also reflect problems with not having followed your heart or a change of heart. **Being stabbed, shot or in any way injured in the heart** may depict emotional hurt; it could also be a warning of a physical heart problem, reflecting an anxiety about, for example, your high blood pressure.

Unless you are a heavy drinker and your dream is urging you to take better care of your **liver**, in dreams this organ represents the liver as in someone who 'does the living'. The dream is reminding you that you are not a machine and life should be lived to the full if you are to find true fulfillment. In dreams, **lungs** might relate to tension or feelings of being suffocated in a relationship or situation; they may also be to do with smoking and your desire to give up.

Dreams of the ovaries and uterus (for women) and **testes** (for men) represent not just sexuality, but a sense of validity or adequacy in the real world. Such dreams may also represent fears or feelings about having children or the ability to express your creativity. But if you were to dream of the **rectum** – a place often seen by children as the origin of babies – it may indicate the place from which things begin, your deeply personal self, your need for privacy and your resentment of intrusion.

MENSTRUATION

Dreams that feature images of **menstruation** indicate the very mystery of life itself; the acceptance of the life processes in yourself if you are menstruating in your dream, and non-acceptance if you are not. Such dreams can also represent the desire to have children. If **irregular periods, PMS or problems with menstruation** appear in your dream, these may refer to emotional problems needing your attention, or issues concerning sexual selfishness on your part. In his book *Our Dreaming Mind*, dream expert Robert Van de Castle describes research he did on the subject of menstruation and dreams with the help of nursing students in Miami, Florida. He found that dreams changed according to the different phases of a woman's menstrual cycle. Before ovulation, more male characters appeared in the dream and the women found them more appealing, with women characters pushed to the background. After ovulation, the dreams tended to be more hostile towards men, depicting them as less attractive. If you are a **man dreaming of menstruation**, it may refer to your receptive, nurturing nature, or the aspect of yourself that is creative.

Research has shown that in the week or so leading up to menstruation, women who suffer from PMS spend an increased length of time in dreamland, the dreams they report being extremely vivid and colorful. The conclusion drawn by researchers is that one of the functions of the dreaming mind is to help dreamers deal with difficult states of emotion and anxiety. Dreams that focus on the **menopause** are likely to indicate change, the end of one phase and the beginning of another.

TOILET DREAM

According to Freud, **toilet dreams** are associated with what he called the anal phase of a child's psychological development. In Freud's opinion, if parents didn't handle their children's toilet training well it might mean that these children feel shame about these natural functions and become 'anally retentive' in their adult life. The **act of excretion** in a dream can therefore suggest expression and creativity that might have previously been repressed before; to dream of **constipation** may stand for frustration and pent-up rage. Jungians regard toilet dreams on the one hand as indicating a need for self-expression, on the other as anxiety about our public image. **Using the toilet** in a dream may simply show your desire to rid yourself of something that contributes nothing to your well-being in waking life. Bear in mind, too, that your dreaming mind may simply be calling your attention to your actual physical need to use the toilet while you sleep. Your unconscious dream recognizes your need and uses your dream to wake you up. On the other hand, if you are **happily or defiantly going to the toilet in front of a large audience**, this may suggest anger at your lack of popularity or approval from others. *See also* Toilet and Elimination Dreams in BODY.

Health

DETOXING

If you dream of **trying to give up smoking or going on a detox**, it may be the case that your dreams will be commenting on your progress or lack of it. Dreams in which **you have a cigarette and enjoy it, or indulge in a naughty-but-nice cream cake** may be escapist. On the other hand, if you **stubbed out your cigarette or refused the cake** in your dream, you are making good progress. Bear in mind, too, that the cigarette is often seen as a phallic symbol and it could be so in your dream; similarly, there might be another meaning to that dream detox – it may be about unhealthy attitudes, habits and emotions that are poisoning your system and not food.

DIET/KEEPING FIT

A dream about **dieting** may be referring to some kind of restriction upon you in waking life. In your dream, you may be **carefully measuring out food and drink portions, or longing for forbidden fruit**. In waking life, have you been measuring out your time or restricting how much emotion you show? Are you holding back your feelings in some way? Similarly, if you **overindulged or broke your diet in some way** in your dream, are your emotions out of control? **Vitamin pills and dietary supplements** in your dream may be referring to your health. Does your health need

a boost in some way? Are you lacking variety? If you **can't decide which vitamin pill to take** in your dream, then perhaps this represents the variety of possible ways in which you can reinvent yourself in real life.

If you were **exercising or lifting weights in a gym** in your dream, this may be referring to your body image. How easy or difficult you found the exercise may be commenting on your psychological and physical ability to complete a project in waking life.

GETTING WEAKER/GETTING STRONGER

Are you weak in your dreams or so strong you can manage any physical feat required of you? If you are **feeling weak**, a medical check-up might be required, but it could also suggest that you feel somehow less than perfect in waking life and unable to accomplish what is required of you. Dreams in which you **simply can't keep up with the action or are outrun by the bogey man** are experienced more frequently as you age, and may well be your dreaming mind's way of helping you adjust to the natural aging process. If your dreams often feature **themes of illness or loss of strength** and you are concerned by these, see your doctor by all means; the chances are, however, that you feel unable to meet some internal or external commands in waking life. In your dreams, your unmet goals and high standards are making you ill. But dreams in which you have boundless energy and physical power seem to be telling you that you are capable of far more than you realize. In some cases, as with people who are seriously ill or disabled,

Healing dreams

There is a long tradition of dreams being a resource for physical and psychological healing. The ancient Greek god Aesculapius was believed to come to people in their sleep to offer healing through their dreams. The sick and wounded would travel from far away places to sleep in the temple of Aesculapius to let the healer enter their dreams and heal them. The Greek philosopher Aristotle believed that premonitory dreams of sickness could be caused by the dreamer's unconscious recognition of the symptoms. He postulated that dreams may be premonitions of an illness coming from within the body, where some 'unconscious' mind recognized early symptoms that had not yet come to the attention of the 'waking self'. The Iroquois Amerindians used a social form of dream therapy and one of the earliest recorded instances of such healing is the famous story in the Old Testament, when Joseph revealed the meaning of dreams to Pharaoh.

Sigmund Freud pioneered the use of dreams in therapy, bringing them to widespread attention, but many other approaches have been developed since then. The common feature for people who use dreams as therapeutic tools for physical and emotional healing is that dreams can empower them; they feel in touch with a powerful inner process that they believe is working actively for their own good.

Since time immemorial, people have created special places in which to sleep and dream. The dreaming chamber on the island of Malta is one example, but ancient dream temples can be found all over the world. These places were meant to 'incubate' wise, deep dreams that would bring guidance and healing to the dreamer. Most of us do not have a dream temple located conveniently nearby; but the idea of receiving valuable, healing dreams is an appealing one, so here are four simple steps for creating a dream temple anywhere you like.

1. Find or create a special place for dreaming.

For those of us fortunate enough to have more than enough rooms in our living space, the answer is simple: make one of those rooms – perhaps a guest room that is rarely used – into a dream place. Furnish it sparklingly, but make sure that the bed is comfortable. For the majority of us who don't have a room to spare, we need to be a little bit more creative. Clear some space in a room in which you are comfortable and designate it as your dream place. All the time, keep in mind that you are preparing your sleeping space to facilitate your dreaming.

2. Prepare yourself.

You are going to be welcoming dreams in a way that you don't ordinarily do, so treat the experience as special from the outset. You might want to take a long bath. Make yourself comfortable. Eat lightly, if at all, for dinner. It's probably best if you don't consume alcohol or smoke the day before your dream incubation. As you go through your activities, keep in mind that you are preparing yourself to welcome dreams.

3. Focus on dreaming.
Throughout your day, you are simply preparing yourself to be more receptive to dreams. Focus on dreaming. If you have a particular issue in your life, you might tell yourself to ask for guidance in your dream.

4. Sweet dreams.
This is not a one-shot exploration. Try it for a few days or even for a week – or for as long as you like.

dreams of extraordinary energy and good health are compensatory or wish-fulfillment dreams.

If, in your dream, **you are weak because you have lost weight**, this can suggest concern about body image but it can also indicate possessive, demanding behavior from the people in your life. Conversely, **gaining weight and strength** may show an excessive need for their approval and a childish need for instant gratification. Finally, if **other people are watching either your feats of strength or growing weakness** in your dream, this suggests that you are preoccupied with themes of competition. Who or what are you trying to compete with, surpass or vanquish?

HYGIENE

If **hygiene is an issue in your dream or you feel dirty** in some way, your dream may be commenting on an unpleasant past experience whose influence you can't quite shake off. Do you feel emotionally unclean in some way? Is it time to make a fresh start? **Washing and bathing** in dreams may stand for a need to rid yourself of something you regard as harmful, whilst **relaxed bathing in a warm bath** may suggest a wish to return to the comfort of the mother's womb. For Jungians, a **shower** has suggestions of an act or renewal, whereas a dream that focuses on **washing hair** may refer to a desire to rid yourself of someone, echoing the song, 'I'm gonna wash that man right out of my hair.' **Rubbing and cleaning your body with a towel** can be a dream symbol of masturbation and sexual frustration. Dreams in which you appear **naked or nude while washing or cleaning yourself** can suggest anxieties about being found out in some way in waking life. For Freudians, it suggests frustration at not being able to express yourself creatively.

The Element Encyclopedia of 20,000 Dreams

Sickness

ABSCESS/ACHE/PAIN

Dream **abscesses** may indicate a site of physical illness that is not yet obvious when awake, but it is more likely that they represent swollen and painful emotions that are repressed and may be causing psychological infection. **Aches** in dreams indicate places where there may be blocked energy relevant to that part of the body. For example, we tend to refer to nagging problems in waking life as headaches and, since the head represents an authority figure, a dream **headache** may suggest an unresolved issue with an authority figure in your life. **Throat aches** may suggest an inability to express yourself verbally, whilst dreams of **injury or strangulation to the throat** almost always relate to current pressures in your life. Such dreams do not always urge you to speak your mind but they do remind you to be aware of those dynamics around you that are affecting you, as well as urging you to be honest with yourself about how you feel about what is going on. **Chest aches** indicate withheld emotions and **back aches** blocked anger.

The **sensation of pain** in a dream may be a warning against taking unnecessary risks or an attempt by your dreaming mind to urge you to take a more positive approach to life. Dreams in which you are **fatigued or racked with aches and pains** may signify that in waking life you are worrying needlessly over problems that really aren't that important. Take a more relaxed approach. Sometimes, however, your dreaming mind will inflict a pain dream almost as an act of revenge over some supposed fault or misbehavior in waking life. For example, if you are on a diet and have slipped recently, your unconscious may punish you in dreams that have the sensation of pain. Perhaps one of the most horrifying pain scenarios in a dream is to be **impaled**. Whether this is caused by a slip from a high spot onto railings or a vampire stake through the heart, such a dream refers to the pain of unwanted intrusion or enemies in real life.

BACTERIA/GERMS/VIRUS

In dreams, the presence of **bacteria, germs and viruses** suggest hidden attacks that can weaken or destroy your sense of well-being. They might suggest anxieties about your health or simply reflect a sense of inadequacy in waking life. The word 'germ' can also be used in its positive sense as the beginning stages of something, the point at which great growth can occur. If you dream of **bacteriological warfare**, it suggests the undermining of your personal or social well-being. Any form of **infection or virus** in a dream might be symbolic of ideas or thoughts that cause irritability or anxiety in waking life, or might be indicating that you are taking in negative attitudes from others to the detriment of yourself. Such dreams may also be a warning about your physical health and the need to boost your immunity.

BLIND/DEAF/DUMB

One of the things most of us fear is losing control of our faculties. Dreams in which **you are blind or you see blind people** may represent your refusal to see the truth or face reality. Perhaps you are unable to see any other point of view but your own, and it is time to open your eyes. The blindness may relate to an object you seek but are unable to find because of your blindness; this object is generally your hopes and goals in life, and becoming blind indicates that you have lost sight of your ambitions and are unclear about how to regain your focus. For Freud, loss of sight indicated a man's fears of being castrated. In the Greek myth that inspired Freud's theory of the Oedipus complex, Oedipus unwittingly killed his father to marry his mother. Once aware of what he had done, he blinded himself, an act Freud saw as a symbol of self-castration. Another interpretation suggests that blindness is a mystical dream symbol that represents inner vision, wisdom and self-knowledge. To imagine that you are **deaf or dumb** in a dream, or unable to make contact with people, may symbolize irresponsibility, laziness or an inability to get your point across

Blister/Boil/Bruise/Burn/ Rash/Scar

If you dream you have a **blister**, consider what irritant in your real life may have caused it. If you **burned yourself**, have you got too close to the flames emotionally? Dreams in which **you are burned alive or someone else is torched** suggest the need for some kind of drastic change in your life. **Rashes, sores and eczema** are all unpleasant ailments that are not serious but uncomfortable as well as embarrassing. So if these conditions appear in a dream, what are you feeling 'sore,' uncomfortable or embarrassed about? Although it may seem

a big deal to you, your dream is telling you that you have no need to feel anxious as the situation is not as serious as you might think. The skin is a symbol of how you present yourself in public, so **rashes** are recognized as one of the most clearly psychosomatic disorders. In dreams, therefore, a **skin rash** can express lack of confidence in your ability to face the world. A dream **bruise** may reflect some emotional hurt or emerging health problem, whilst **scars** can carry their figurative sense of hurtful memories and suggest an awareness that emotional healing takes time.

For Jewish or Christian dreamers, **boils** may express feelings of guilt for how they have behaved towards someone in their waking life; this is because in the Bible, boils were the sixth of the ten plagues visited by God on the Egyptians to force Pharaoh to free the Israelites. **Rough skin** suggests a rough exterior, whilst **burnt skin** might indicate hurt in a relationship with the outside world or people. If you are **shedding skin** like a snake, you are changing your way of life and leaving old attitudes behind. **Spots and blemishes** represent your sense of not being good enough in some way, and a feeling that other people see you as unattractive or see failings in you; they can also indicate shyness and the difficulties you experience being in the company of others.

Breast, buttock and genital injuries

Dreams about breasts are likely to be sexual. **Swollen breasts** may be connected with the desire to have children, although you need to consider who or what the baby you'd like to have represents. A dream of being **kicked or hit on the buttocks** is a clear symbol of some kind of disapproval in waking life – perhaps self-disapproval. Dreams in which you are **beaten or whipped** may have a straightforward sexual meaning, but they could also refer to an overambitious friend or colleague. If **you are the person doing the beating**, is the dream referring to your ambition? If a man dreams of **injury to his genitals**, it may be highlighting his fear of impotence; for a woman, such dreams may highlight her anxiety about reproduction or sexuality. A dream of **castration** can be terrifying for a man as it alludes to his whole sense of power and virility.

COLD/CANCER/STROKE

If you dream you have a **cold**, the most logical explanation is that you are literally feeling cold because you have kicked off your bedclothes. On the other hand, you may be feeling run down and your dreaming mind is urging you to give your immune system a boost with plenty of rest, good food and gentle exercise to prevent you succumbing to a cold. If you are having a **stroke** in your dream, is there an area of your life in which you feel unable to take action and about which you are feeling particularly frustrated? If you dream that you have **cancer or some other life-threatening disease**, it is unlikely that you actually have the disease in question. However, if you are concerned and feel run down, it might be worth seeing your doctor. It is more likely that the cancer in your dream is referring to a person or a problem that is eating away at you and lowering your resistance in real life. Try to work out who or what it may be. On the

Castration

Can there be a more horrific dream for a man than the dream of being **castrated?** A **woman dreaming of castrating a man** is also expressing powerful emotions, perhaps a harsh desire to subdue a man in waking life or the masculine aspect of her personality. Bear in mind that in dreams there are many possible symbols for the penis; for example, dreams of **cutting a necktie off, or losing an arm-wrestling competition or demolishing a tall building** all suggest the loss of the penis. When interpreting such dreams, your own feelings are important. For example, were you scared, confident, or unconcerned? You also need to find out who the person or thing attacking you was. Sometimes the dream may indicate a fear of impotence, or the fear that someone wants to emasculate you in some way. The attack may also not be on your physical manhood but on other areas of your life, such as your ability to do a job, provide for your family or pay the bills.

other hand, you may know someone who is born under the **Zodiac sign of Cancer**, and the dream could be referring in some way to them.

Deformity / Dismemberment / Paralysis

A dream in which you find yourself **deformed** in some way is most likely a self-critical dream; its interpretation will depend upon what body part or body parts are disfigured. If you find yourself deformed in your dream, in what way do you feel disabled or frightening to others in waking life? Or have you been crippled by an emotional situation and been unable to do anything about it? Has someone in waking life hurt you? A dream of **someone else's deformity** may be symbolic of a deformed part of yourself, but it might also be showing you some distasteful part of another person's personality of which you were previously unaware. A person with a deformity in your dream may represent the trickster archetype mocking your own pretensions, although for Freud it represented a fear of male impotence, and for Jung it was a symbol of the devouring mother. A **limp** can be a warning from the unconscious of those dangers of pride and ambition that bring humiliation rather than success upon the dreamer. If you are using **crutches** in your dream, are you relying on crutches, such as alcohol, nicotine or controlled drugs, in waking life?

Very often dreams of **paralysis and numbness** may be induced by the dreamer's arm or leg going to sleep as the result of a trapped nerve. If this is not the case, dreams of being **unable to move** (as if rooted to the spot) may be equating paralysis with frigidity; in waking life, the dreamer might suffer from fears of sexual intimacy. Your dream may also be referring to an area of your life in which things have stagnated or not progressed as they should have. This will usually be an emotional paralysis or a feeling of helplessness in a particular situation in your life. For example, you may be caught between a spouse and a lover, or between two possible courses of action. **Dismemberment** of your body in a dream suggests feelings of powerlessness in waking life. Is some situation tearing you apart or do you need to take your feelings apart?

Disease

Some people believe that dreams can sometimes spot illness before your waking self is aware of its symptoms, so if a **dream of disease** persists or you can't shake the memory of it, get your health checked by a doctor. On the other hand, the dream may be focusing on anxieties and inner conflicts with which you need to deal so that you can move forward with your life and find emotional harmony. Dreams that feature disease as a theme may refer to some discomfort or uncertainty in your waking life. Perhaps someone in particular is making life difficult for you?

If you have **leprosy** in a dream, do you feel like a social outcast? If **another person is unwell** in your dream and you recognize them, you may either harbor negative feelings towards that particular person or fear for their emotional health. Memories of childhood illnesses, such as **chicken pox or measles**, may express a simple longing for the unconditional love of a parent. For Jungians, dreams of **fainting** may be prompted by a sudden insight into the essential nature of a personal ambition, whilst for Freud these are wish-fulfillment dreams relating to orgasm.

According to ancient predictive dream-lore, your interpretation of dreams concerning your health should reverse the state of health pictured in the dream. Dreams of **poor health**, therefore, predict a period of good health, whilst **dreams of disease** suggest a period of good health.

FACIAL INJURY/FACIAL DEFORMITY

A dream of a face is likely to be about the image you present to the world, so a **swollen face** may refer to self-importance and a **blemished face** to a character weakness or defect. A dream of **injuries to your eyes or ears** may simply refer to being unable to see or hear – or unwilling to see or hear – what is going on around you, rather than to any disease. A dream of being **struck on the mouth or slapped across the face** suggests an inability to get your point across, whilst dreams of **injuries to your nose** suggest difficulties getting to know other people intimately in your life.

Hair is an important sexual symbol for both men and women, so dreams of being **forcibly shaven** might be a symbol of castration or a sign of subjugation. **Baldness** in the dreams of both sexes suggests anxiety, not about going bald, but about a lack of intellect, either your own or someone else's. Dreams in which your **teeth fall out** are very common and almost always associated with self-image or fear at having spoken out of turn (*See also* Tooth entry in BODY).

FITS/MADNESS

If you have dreams that involve **uncontrollable trembling, fits or fever**, such dream can be alarming but in general suggest that you are worrying more than you need to about trifling affairs or matters of little consequence, whilst the important things slip by unnoticed. You should try to relax and cultivate more interests. On the other hand, are you in a fever of excitement about something or someone? To dream that you are **insane or mad, and unable to perform everyday tasks** reflects an unjustified humiliation from the past or an embarrassing moment from the present that is unsettling you. Being mad or irrational in a dream, or **meeting a mad person** may also indicate that you are facing urges or emotions that feel threatening or that you cannot control properly. If you are **confronted by a mad man or woman**, this can indicate a part of yourself that you have not integrated successfully.

If **you are that mad person**, then are you feeling threatened by the irrational parts of your personality or do you sense that you don't fit in with your social group? Occasionally, you may experience a **trembling or wave sensation** when you awake, especially when you are aroused quickly from deep sleep; although disconcerting, this is usually the result of temporary confusion between the sleeping and waking worlds that should pass without need for concern. If, however, this occurs on a regular basis and you feel faint and dizzy when you get up, it might be wise to have a check-up with your doctor to rule out problems with your blood pressure.

HAND AND FOOT INJURY

Hands can symbolize the whole pattern of your life and a dream of an **injured or disabled hand** may refer to some inability to perform a task in waking life, a task which may or may not be physical. Dreams about your **feet** tend to refer to your general progress, so dreaming of **lameness**, for example, may signify an inability to move forward.

INDIGESTION/NAUSEA/SICKNESS

In dreams, **indigestion** suggests an idea or attitude that does not agree with you or which you are finding hard to stomach in waking life; it may be something you have taken in, or upon, yourself that you did not realize was toxic when you welcomed it. We are ruled by our emotions and the stomach – being a nerve center which reacts to negative stimuli – is often the first to register changes in our emotional state. The dream may also point to actual indigestion. Alternatively, could your stomach have been protesting in your dream because it is literally crying out for nourishment, either literally or because you are feeling starved of love?

If your **intestines** were the source of discomfort in your dream, could your unconscious have been focusing your attention on them to ask if you have the guts to do something that you have been dreading? If you felt **nauseous or sick** in your dream, your dreaming mind might have been trying to pinpoint a bad or negative feeling in waking life with which you need to deal; if you were **physically sick** in your dream, this suggests you were getting rid of it. Perhaps you are sick of a job, a relationship or a situation in waking life. A dream of a **stomach ache** may refer to your having to stomach someone or something, and feeling unable to do so. Try to discover who or what is upsetting you.

WOUND

Any kind of **deep flesh wound inflicted on your body by a knife** in your dream may express a fear of sexual aggression. In general, dreams that feature wounds or being wounded are giving voice to the parts of your personality that are being neglected.

Medical Intervention

ANESTHETIC/INJECTION

If you dream that you are **having an anesthetic or are being put to sleep for an operation**, this suggests that you may be trying to escape reality in some way in waking life or attempting to deaden some emotional pain. There may be something in life you don't want to face or simply want to forget about for a while. The answer may be simple as taking a much-needed vacation. To be **having an injection** in your dream indicates the need to inject more enthusiasm into your life. If the idea of **inoculation or vaccination** is present as well, you may want to protect yourself from intrusive emotions or unwanted urges. Injections imply healing and protection, so this dream may be trying to show you how to become emotionally fit. Bear in mind that the **syringe** is also a phallic symbol, so your dream may have sexual connotations. Although much disliked and feared, the syringe is generally a benign symbol in dreams that work for your benefit. It emphasizes the message that in life, sometimes a little hardship and pain is needed for the greater good.

CARER

You may dream of **carers or being a carer yourself**. Perhaps you are ill in your dream and **no carer answers your cries for help**? Or conversely, are there **too many carers** surrounding your bed? Does the carer give you the right kind of medicine or TLC? And who is the carer: a stranger, or someone you know and love? If you have dreams of carers or caring, such dreams may simply be reflecting your anxiety about becoming old and vulnerable. As we live longer, it is natural that issues of caring should show up more frequently in our dreams. If you are a carer yourself, you may have dreams in which **you are a terrible carer, and unwilling or unable to tend to your patient's or loved one's needs**. If this is the case, don't take it literally; your dreams are simply letting you know what the repressed part of you feels and suggesting to you that it might be a good idea to find some outlet in waking life to let off steam.

DOCTOR/DENTIST/NURSE

Many people feel anxious about **visiting a doctor or a dentist**, so when these symbols emerge in your dreams they may be urging you to overcome your fears and bravely face what is coming to you. As is the case with many dreams that feature health and sickness, they may be signaling the onset of illness so it might be worth your while to have a dental or medical check-up. As archetypal authority figures, if **dentists,** **doctors, surgeons and nurses offer you advice** in your dreams, it might be wise to listen to it. Seeing yourself **working as a hospital nurse or doctor** is perhaps an expression of a desire to take charge of an area of your life in which you feel you do not have much control. To see a **nurse or doctor leaving your house** suggests good health, but to see yourself **being cared for by a doctor or nurse** suggests that you are feeling vulnerable and in need of support. If an **alternative practitioner or quack doctor** appears in your dream, this may suggest that you are employing desperate measures in waking life and are in danger of becoming an obsessive.

EXAMINATION/DIAGNOSIS

Examination and diagnosis in dreams, if favorable, indicates that you feel secure and satisfied in waking life. If you are **diagnosing illness** in a dream, this points to insecurity and an over-sensitive approach to life. If you dream that you are **diagnosed with a fatal illness or have a fatal illness**, it might be worthwhile seeing your doctor for a check-up as illness has been diagnosed in this way before; typically, however, such dreams represent any condition or situation that you feel is taking you away from the life you were meant to live. There is a big difference between existing and leading a life that is worth living, and your dreaming mind may be urging you to find ways to live your life to the full, before it is too late.

HOSPITAL

A dream of **lying ill in a hospital bed** may simply be promoted by fear of getting ill but it could also indicate your desire to hand control of some aspect of your life to someone else. Being **hospitalized** in a dream may indicate that you feel under intolerable pressure in real life and need to unburden your load. If you are **lying in a ward that has endless lines of beds**, perhaps you feel abandoned in some way, or perhaps you are at a time of turmoil such as divorce, bereavement or job loss. If you are **healthy and dream of getting better**, this indicates well-being, but if you are **ill and dream that you are ill**, it may suggest a delay in recovery. Rather than simply expecting to get better without any effort on your part, you should pay greater attention to your mental attitude, fitness levels and diet to boost the recovery process.

MEDICAL INSTRUMENT

Medical instruments in a dream about disease and diagnosis, such as a **scalpel or a stethoscope**, act as a warning not to take unnecessary risks with your health. A **thermometer** reveals a strong sense of personal responsibility and discipline. A **laboratory microscope** can reveal the tiniest of organisms that, if harmful, can result in poor health; in dreams, the symbolism begs the question: are you in danger of looking at things in too fine a detail and missing the bigger picture? If you dream of **scanners and X-ray machines**, could your dream be telling you to look at the heart of the matter or get to the bare bones of a situation so you can see the truth?

MEDICINE

Medicine administered to you by a doctor may point to a reliance on others to sort out your problems for you, rather than finding your own solutions. If the medicine comes in the shape of a **pill**, are you finding something hard to swallow in waking life? Generally though dreams where you are given a dose of medicine, especially if it tastes bitter, are good and suggest a positive turn of events. Paradoxically to **administer tablets to someone** else suggests that you are the cause of distress or pain to that person.

OPERATION/TRANSPLANT

If you are undergoing a dream **operation or surgery**, this may signal your willingness to cut out old prejudices or attitudes that have hindered your psychological growth. The symbolism of an operation also implies taking stock of your life to date. Have you achieved what you hoped? Are you happy? The dream is telling you to get out and live your life, and not waste another second with excuses or regret. The **transplantation of a limb or body part** in a dream may symbolize a new arrangement in your life. It is especially common for people in new relationships to dream of having a new pair of legs or hands, or a new heart or head. This sounds gruesome but it is your dreaming mind's way of helping you adjust to a new way of life. Unless you are actually in need of, or awaiting, organ transplant surgery, if you dream of getting a new body part, you can be sure that you are going through a significant change in your life.

SOUNDS

A dream is the subjective experience of mental images, thoughts and sensations, as well as those sounds, voices or words heard during sleep.

According to Freud, there is no original speech or sound in dreams; sounds are derived from what is actually spoken or heard in waking life. Jungians, however, think that the sensation of hearing in dreams is a symbolic representation of an issue troubling you in your life. This is because sounds in dreams have a similar impact on us as they do in waking life. They carry information and can give rise to pleasure, fear, anger and so on, depending on the sound. Therefore if a sound features clearly in your dream, the important thing is first of all to define your feeling reaction to that sound. Ask yourself if the sound is a warning or whether it carries information? Is it a positive sign or does it make you feel anxious? Sounds can sometimes have great power in dreams and if they cause something to happen, they suggest a use of positive will, a positive and confident expression of your desires that encourages results. Bear in mind, too, that sometimes your dream incorporates sounds such as an alarm clock or the traffic outside your bedroom, weaving them into the dream's symbolism. *See also* BODY; LETTERS AND COMMUNICATION; SENSES.

Noises

ANIMAL

The **animal** sound will reflect the symbolism of the animal with which it is associated. For example, the **crow of a cock** is an awakening, alerting us to new challenges; the **bark of a dog** suggests a loyal companion, the **hiss of snake**, sexuality and so on. Bear in mind that animals are thought to express the more primitive side of your nature and the raw urges related to sex and aggression – things that polite society often tries to curb. *See also* ANIMALS; BIRDS.

BELL/ALARM

You may have had a dream in which a **ringing telephone** urged you to pick up the receiver. If this was the case, who was calling and what did they have to say to you? In both dreams and waking life, telephones are symbols of communication telling you that someone wants to communicate something to you, so perhaps your unconscious is trying to tell you something. If you **picked up the telephone and heard nothing but abuse**, this signals guilt about some issue in your waking life. If the phone rang in your dreams and you **picked it up but no one was there**, could your dreaming mind have been urging you to remember something or someone, as in 'ringing a bell'? Hearing a **doorbell** in your dream indicates something new coming into your life; this can be negative or positive, depending on the dream. It could also suggest the desire to hear from someone or make contact with them.

The **ringing of an alarm clock** in a dream indicates the need to get up and do something; it may also be a reminder of something or someone you have neglected. The **ringing of a school bell, or the timer on a cooker, kettle or any kitchen appliance** in a dream may also be prompting you to move forward with an idea or gain a new experience in the world. In real life, loud alarms – such as **sirens, or fire, burglar, smoke or car alarms** – warn us of impending threat and danger, and they do the same in dreamland. Perhaps your unconscious has noticed that your front door is not properly closed or that your car is vulnerable to theft. Alternatively, your unconscious may have been warning you about an overheated situation in your waking life, such as

loss of control, invasion of privacy or an impending crisis.

Other sounds that are clear symbols of warning in your dreams include **whistles blown by teachers, police officers or referees, the growling of angry dogs or the horns on cars, ships or trains**. Such sounds may also indicate that you are defying authority figures in some way; there may have been an allusion to whistle-blowing, drawing your attention to a transgression of some kind, either your own or someone you know? Alternatively, the growling of a dog could have suggested that you or someone you know are about to unleash their anger on the world in some way. **Air-raid sirens** are associated with the fear and pain of World War II and in dreams may express fear of the unknown or longing for old comradeship.

CHURCH BELL

If you have a dream of hearing **church bells**, it is important to take into account any religious associations you may have; if you are a Christian, the sound of bells suggests a call to worship or celebration, whilst **tolling bells** denotes a funeral and sadness. If you are not a Christian, the sound of bells underlines feelings of happiness or sadness that are present right now in your waking life.

ECHO

If you heard **echoes** in your dream or **repeated words**, can you recognize the voice and can you recall the words? If the **voice belongs to a figure from the past, dead or alive**, the echo may be trying to remind or warn you of something about

Musical sounds

Music/Musical instrument

Hearing **music** in your dreams generally has positive connotations. Music is a healing balm to the soul, and as you are listening to it in your dream, you may be connected to the wonderful, creative spirit or flow of life, suggesting a degree of inner harmony and emotional expression. Music in waking life is one of the most powerful and expressive mediums available and through music it is possible to convey feelings that are impossible to put into words. It is much the same in your dreams, where a **beautiful melody** can express your sense of feeling sweet, peaceful and harmonious, whereas a **clash of harsh notes** may reflect emotional discord or feeling out of tune with the people in your life.

The type of music that features in your dreams may have significance, especially if it was music you do not usually listen to in waking life. For example, if you love **classical music but dreamt of a pop song**, your unconscious may have retrieved the song from your memory because it portrays perfectly how you are feeling at present. If you **dreamed of classical music but are a modern music fan**, this may be a reference to old-fashioned tastes and values with which you feel in tune. The dream may also be urging you to listen a little more to the advice of older people. If you dreamed of **choosing a song on a juke box**, the song you chose may express how you are currently feeling.

Dream drum rolls may be urging you to pay attention to someone or keep in step and conform to others in waking life. According to Freud, a martial or rhythmical drum beat could suggest intercourse but another interpretation suggests that it could symbolize the voice of your unconscious or unspoken feelings that arise from the depths of your inner self.

If you were **listening passively to music** in your dream, this may be referring to your emotional reaction to a waking situation, but if you were **actively making music, humming along or tapping the rhythm**, this may be about your emotional involvement with someone or something. Dreams about **music** may also be urging you to explore your perhaps neglected potential for personal creativity, of which music is a common symbol.

If you were **playing an instrument**, the choice of instrument will also be significant. If you were **playing drums**, are you trying to drum up support for something or someone, or did the dream suggest that something needs to be drummed into your head? If you **clashed a pair of cymbals**, this might suggest a clash of conflicting opinions, whilst **blowing a trumpet** may suggest bragging or your feelings of triumph. The black and white symbolism of **piano keys** could indicate the need to see things clearly, in black and white, or to harmonize extreme opinions. Don't forget the sexual symbolism of musical instruments too. Freudians would, for example, regard a **flute** as a phallic symbol and the curved bodies of **violins or guitars** as a feminine symbol. Finally, dreams of **playing instruments** may simply be encouraging you to nurture a real-life talent for music. *See also* ARTS AND CRAFTS.

Song/Singing

To hear **singing** in a dream is a symbol of self-expression or of the desire to be more creative and feeling. To **be singing** is to express your joy and love of life. If you are **singing alone**, you are being urged to become independent and if you are **singing in a choir or with a group of people**, you are being urged to interact more socially. If you are a singer in waking life, your dream will be expressing your waking preoccupation with music. Singing is also an act of worship and an important part of many belief systems.

A **football anthem**, for example, will suggest camaraderie and encouragement, whilst if the type you are doing is more akin to **chanting** suggests that you may be in touch with a higher vibration or your inner wisdom, especially if the chanting is a **mantra**. Dreaming of **singing the blues** could reflect your real-life sense of melancholy. If the **lyrics** of the song are clear, pay attention to them and see how they apply to your waking circumstances. *See also* ARTS AND CRAFTS.

which you may have forgotten. If the **voice was yours and you are repeating the words of someone else**, your dreaming mind may be urging you not to imitate or parrot someone else. Consider if your dream was evoking memories from the past or whether it suggests that you are stuck in a routine from which you need to break free in order to express your creativity.

GUNFIRE

Guns are associated with violence, death and war, and to hear a gun in your dream may suggest your unconscious wish for someone to be taken out of your way as they are blocking your progress. A **single shot**, such as the shot fired by a starter pistol at the beginning of a race, may suggest the pressure you feel if you are under a harsh deadline for completing a project.

KNOCKING

If you are **knocking on a door** in your dream, this suggests a desire to make contact with or hear from someone. It can also indicate the need for love and care, or to be the focus of someone's undivided attention in waking life. Alternatively, you may have been knocking on wood in a superstitious attempt to ward off misfortune. Another interpretation suggests that your attention is being called to whom or what was knocking, perhaps some aspect of yourself that needs to be allowed in.

Mantra

A **mantra** is a sound that corresponds to a name or an aspect of God and is believed to be a creative vibration that can help the speaker become closer to themselves and the Universe. Spiritually, sound produced over and over again induces a change in consciousness and awareness.

Name

In dreams, you often hear the **sound of your name**; this suggests the opening up of possibilities for greater wisdom. **Hearing someone call your name** may also suggest that you are currently in the spotlight in your waking life. If you are **called by a name you do not know or recognize**, then this may be an aspect of your personality you are trying to repress.

Silence

If you **hear nothing in your dream or are conscious of silence**, this suggests uneasiness, unspoken feelings or being unable to voice your feelings. It can also suggest expectancy or waiting for something to happen. If **someone is silent when you expect them to speak** in the dream, this suggests that you are unsure about what part of yourself to present in waking life or how to react in some situations. When you are silent you can't explain your feelings or opinions, so the image could also suggest inhibition caused by your own insecurity. A spiritual interpretation would suggest that temporary silence and withdrawal from the bustle of daily life may be needed right now.

The Human Voice

Crying/Screaming/Laughing

If you or someone else was **crying, screaming or laughing** in your dream, this may be a confirmation of how they are feeling in waking life. Similarly, if you **woke up laughing, screaming or crying** after your dream, could these vocalized emotions be expressing the happiness, excitement and sadness you are experiencing in waking life? Or were you crying for help or screaming in terror? Have you been repressing powerful emotions in waking life and did venting them in dreamland give you a sense of release?

Dreams of **crying** may function as a release for the sorrow or grief that has been holding you back consciously or unconsciously in waking life. Alternatively, such dreams may be an intuitive awareness of something ending or someone leaving in your waking life; or are your tears crocodile tears? Dreams of **laughing** suggest a release of tension or an attempt to put yourself and others at ease. Depending on your feelings during the dream and on waking, the laugh may however be a sign that you are hiding the truth or taking things too lightly, as sometimes laughter can hide sadness and the truth. Bear in mind that laughter can also be a sign of contempt, and if someone laughs in your face, your unconscious may have used the archetype of the Trickster in an attempt to make you rethink something or reconsider your values. When the laughter becomes the kind of **cackling** associated in folklore with wicked witches and mischief-making, this may represent your inner voice questioning and ridiculing your pretensions.

■ *Idioms: don't make me laugh; laugh it off; laughing stock; hollow laugh; laugh on the other side of your face.*

CONVERSATION

If you hear a **conversation** in your dream, either your own or someone else's, you need to consider your dreaming reaction to what is being said and what it may have signified for you in the waking world. You may have had a conversation in your dream and felt uncertain about what it meant. Bear in mind that in the symbolic language of dreams, the words used often communicate a truth of which you may be unconsciously aware but are disregarding. This is why a dream voice can be the voice of your conscience, especially if it was nagging you.

FOREIGN LANGUAGE

If you had a dream in which you **could not understand what people were saying to you**, this suggests that you are feeling excluded from your social circle or family, and that everyone seems to be speaking the same language apart from you. Alternatively, your unconscious may be urging you to learn a new language or broaden your horizons in some way. If, in your dream, you were **talking to others but they could not understand you**, does your dream mirror your real-life inability to communicate with others or your feelings that you are not being listened to?

SWEARING/SHOUTING

Swearing or using bad language in your dream suggests hidden anger or fear. Both Jung and Fritz Perls believed that each dream character and object is an aspect of yourself. They believed our character is multifaceted and strives towards wholeness, so if your dream contained foul language, you might consider that the raunchy vocalizations are trying to get your attention. Maybe you are too timid in waking life and need to listen more to the parts of yourself that are forceful, pushy or lewd? If you find that **someone is shouting at you** in your dream, this may be a warning, urging you to slow down and think things through; it may also, however, be a greeting or applause for your achievements. If you hear **cheering** in your dreams, this often indicates happy or triumphant feelings, although it could also be wish-fulfillment.

TALKING

In dreams, **talking** suggests what you feel and think, as well as standing up for what you believe in; it may also suggest attempts at justification or the correcting of an opinion. If you have **difficulty in talking** in your dream, this suggests repressed anger, difficult feelings or an absence of social contact in waking life.

■ *Idioms: on speaking terms; nothing to speak of; speak as one finds; speak for yourself; speak out; speaks volumes; speak your mind.*

Unexpected utterance

Sometimes you may hear the most **unexpected or even ridiculous things** in your dreams, whether they are said by people, animals or even objects. If you simply **can't understand what someone is saying to you**, look first of all at whether what they are saying is being cloaked in metaphor. Bear in mind, too, that an unexpected utterance by a dream character may be giving rise to something you are not ready to hear; sometimes we put our unconscious fears into someone else's mouth, or the utterances represent old issues or negative voices you have not yet banished.

Freudian slips are everyday occurrences in which we express strange or unacceptable thoughts or urges. For a split second, the censoring aspect of your self is put on hold and what is really on your mind pops out in a seemingly bizarre and unexpected way. These slips happen in every day speech as well as in dreams, so if **verbal mistakes or slips** appear in your dream – such as 'I thought you were dead instead of retired' – they will tell you something about your unconscious wishes. It is possible to have a dream in which you say the most unexpected and embarrassing but secretly true thing to a dream character.

Voice

The **voice** is the tool we use to express ourselves, so when you hear voices in your dreams the unconscious aim is to draw your attention to the information being given. From a psychological point of view, when you repress certain parts of your personality they can surface in dreams as disembodied voices; dream voices could therefore be drawing your attention to aspects of yourself that you are neglecting or denying in your concern with everyday distractions. If the voice was that of **God or an angel**, this may also be an expression of your intuition or unconscious wisdom that is not yet integrated into yourself. **Recognizable voices** may remind you friends or family who have been neglected. If you hear a **call or cry as if from a great distance**, your unconscious may be suggesting that someone you know is in distress. It could also indicate that you should not be so proud and seek support from others when you need it. If the voices in your dream come out with nothing but **babble or gibberish**, this suggests barely controlled rage that needs to be confronted and dealt with if it is not to erupt and create chaos in your waking life.

Whisper

If, in your dream, **your voice or the voice of someone else is very quiet**, this could suggest that you or they are having difficulty getting their point of view across. If you heard a **whispered conversation or whispers**, do you fear that others may be gossiping about you or keeping a secret from you? Or if you **saw someone else whispering in another person's ear**, do you feel excluded in some way from their closeness in waking life? If you **overheard but were not a part of a conversation**, does this emphasize your sense of being excluded? **Whistle, sound** of: A signal to take action or an affirmation of life as in the old superstition of whistling as you pass a grave.

SPACE AND SCIENCE

O uter space represents the ultimate in mystery, challenge and unexplored potential in dreams as much as in waking life.

This general interpretation is reinforced by the well-known expression 'to reach for the stars' – or to strive to achieve your ambition – and if your dream focused on one particular star or plant, your dreaming mind may have been attempting to bring your aspirations to your attention. The sun, the moon and the stars are traditionally thought to influence a person's destiny and, according to Western astrology, the Zodiac sign under which you were born, derived from the position of the stars and planets at the time of your birth, is thought to influence your character and the direction of your life.

Jung associated different archetypes with specific planets and believed that birth charts would generate archetypal images telling him something about the subject of the chart. He frequently looked at the birth charts of his patients with the assumption that the symbols in the charts made suggestions to him from the collective unconscious about that person's psyche. Whether you believe in the principles of astrology or not, your unconscious may have tapped into these ancient associations, which is why it is always worth considering

them when interpreting your dreams. *See also* MIND, BODY, SPIRIT.

Space, The Final Frontier

COMET

Comets indicate pleasures that are short lived, although according to ancient dreamlore they suggest shattered hopes and wrecked affection; the **longer the comet's tail**, the longer will be the misery. But if you felt happy when you glimpsed the dream comet, could it have mirrored short-lived success in the world or an elusive flash of insight?

EARTH

To see **earth in space** in your dream suggests that you may be feeling emotionally insecure or lost in some sense. Dreams of **leaving the earth** may indicate a fear of death. Alternatively dreams of the Earth may have implied that you need to be more realistic and come down to earth. It may also have mirrored your belief that a current situation in your life is wonderful or 'out of this world'.

MOON

The **moon** symbolizes the mysteries and creativity of the feminine, and in dream-lore it represents the emotional aspect of the self. Its constant changing shape and wandering across the sky establishes the moon as a symbol of the cyclical nature of life. Because of its connection to the tides, the moon also indicates the tides of feeling or mysterious dark desires that are over-powering you. The **full moon** is a symbol of hope when times are difficult; a **waxing crescent moon** may symbolize gestation or new ideas; a **waning crescent moon**, ambivalence or a life force that is weaken-ing; the **black or invisible moon**, death; and the **new moon**, rebirth. A **dream journey to the moon** could suggest a search for inner wisdom or a longing to experience the flowering of your imagina-tion or, if you are a female, a desire to conceive a baby. If you **failed to reach the moon**, could the message have been that you are attempting the impossible?

PLANETS

In general, the **planets** represent areas of change and progression in your life or emerging personal qualities. All over the world, the planets and Zodiacal constella-tions have inspired myths and superstitions, along with the belief that their positions and movements influence the course of human life. If you have a scientific mindset, you may find this concept difficult to accept; but even if this is the case, you may still be influenced by age-old associations. This is why dreams that feature the planets or the constellations or drew a particular planet to your conscious attention should never be dismissed; your dreaming mind may have been using the language of astrology to send you a message. Each of the planets is named after a Roman god or goddess, and is thought to share the attributes of its name-sake. *See also* MIND, BODY, SPIRIT.

SOLAR AND LUNAR ECLIPSE

Solar and lunar eclipses can send a warning in dreams. If you watched the day become darker and colder as the sun seemed to disappear behind the moon, the message may be that the rational powers of your conscious mind are being over-whelmed by emotions (typically negative ones), or vice versa if it was a lunar eclipse. Another explanation suggests that in a **man's dream a solar eclipse** suggests a dominant woman in his life and in a **woman's dream a lunar eclipse** suggests an overbearing male figure. Is there someone in your life eclipsing your person-ality or putting you in the shade?

SPACE

Space is a powerful symbol of thinking outside the box or going beyond limiting concepts or boundaries. If you are **travel-ing in space or become an astronaut** in your dream, this suggests an expanded awareness of there being more out there than merely your own personal experience.

Specific planets and their associations

In Western astrology, every planet is believed to impart some of its characteristics to people born under the Zodiac sign that it governs, so if you dreamed of a **particular planet or one of its signs**, your dreaming mind may be suggesting that you can improve your chance of success by developing some of the sign's qualities within yourself. On the other hand, such dreams can on occasion represent someone in your life who is currently influencing you in a positive or a negative way.

Jung felt that we could learn a lot about the human psyche through astrology, not only because the stars and planets are an external reflection of our inner selves, but also because the inherently symbolic nature of astrology allows us to consciously correlate symbols with unconscious knowledge. He associated different archetypes with specific planets, and frequently looked at the birth charts of his patients, believing that the symbols in the charts made suggestions to him from the collective unconscious about that person's psyche. The following summary of specific planets and their astrological as well as some of their universal archetypal associations will help you make sense of dreams in which planets feature.

Jupiter

Guide and guru. **Jupiter** (father of the gods) is the ultimate authority archetype and father figure. The Jupiter archetype is associated with the Greek mythic figure of Zeus, the king of the Olympian gods; it is related also to Fortuna and Providence. Jupiter is therefore related to your vocation and the way in which you can be successful. The largest planet in the solar system, Jupiter also represents the principles of growth and expansion.

Mars

Action and initiative. **Mars** is the first planet outside the orbit of the Earth and is associated with action, assertion, aggression or initiative. The Mars archetype is associated with the Greek mythic figure of Ares, the god of war, and it tells you how you can control your anger and get things going. Mars is embodied by the warrior or hero archetype.

Mercury

The mind and communication. Mercury is the light in the ever-changing consciousness within us that moves from idea to idea. The Mercury archetype is associated with the Greek mythic figure of Hermes, the messenger of the gods. Mercury has always represented thoughts, ideas and mental processes in general, but it can also represent the trickster archetype. Mercury governs not only ideas but communications, such as those by phone, letter, spoken or email.

Neptune

Ideals and imagination. **Neptune** is the archetype of the transcendent, of ideal reality, of imagination and the spiritual. Neptune, the god of the sea, dissolves boundaries and barriers, enabling us to connect with the Universe. Neptune relates to inspiration, imagination, compassion, ideals and communion. The darker side of Neptune is about confusion, illusion and diffusion. In general, Neptune shares the symbolism of water, suggestive of the hidden highs and lows of the unconscious.

Pluto

Transformation. **Pluto**, Roman god of the underworld, is the planet of profound change, of starting deep within and moving toward the surface. Pluto is the archetype of primordial energy, the universal life force which impels all evolution and transformation. It is about spiritual, intellectual or emotional death and rebirth, the transformation that comes from letting go of that which is unessential so that you can get to the core of things

Saturn

Responsibilities. **Saturn** shows you your boundaries and limits, and where and how we need to take responsibility in life. It represents wisdom but also suggests gloom and pessimism. It is associated with the Greek mythic figure of Kronos, the stern father of the gods, and the wise old man and hermit archetypes.

Uranus

Breakthroughs and revolution. The planet **Uranus**, sky deity of the Romans, was discovered between the American and French revolutions and it symbolizes our capacity to go beyond limits. It is about inventiveness, originality and independence but also unpredictability. The Prometheus archetype associated with the planet Uranus correlates with that stage in the archetypal birth process in which one is suddenly liberated from the constrictions of the birth canal and experiences sudden freedom, awakening, new life, new identity and a radical expansion of horizons: Prometheus Unbound.

Venus

Planet of love. Venus describes how you love and what you want to be loved for. It's a key to relationships, pleasure, art and beauty. The Venus **archetype is** associated with the Greek mythic figure of **Aphrodite,** the Roman Venus, the goddess of love and beauty. It bestows femininity and an appreciation of beauty but can also represent the archetype of the **lover, siren or huntress.**

Alternatively, such images may suggest that you are feeling out of touch with reality or other people, or that you feel ill at ease with yourself. If your dreams take you through the **boundless infinity of space** it can be both unnerving and exhilarating, and such a vision may suggest changes in circumstances that have the potential to offer independence and freedom. If you dream of traveling by **spaceship or shuttle**, this suggests your intuition or a means of exploring your inner resources.

SPACE IN BUILDING OR LANDSCAPE

This represents your potential or those opportunities that are available to you. To be 'spaced out' is to widen your personal boundaries through the use of stimuli, some of which may be illicit. **Space** is also a representation of your cosmic center or place that is, was and ever will be. This idea can widen your present view of the world.

STAR

The **planets, stars and constellations** have been considered good-luck omens since the earliest times. Dreaming of them represents your wish to guide your own fortune, hence 'wishing upon a star'. In general, they suggest exciting new opportunities as long as you possess the necessary self-belief. To view the **twinkling of a star on a dark night** portrays a birth, either physical or symbolic, whilst to imagine a **five-pointed star** was once thought to be a sign of great wisdom. Dream stars can also represent intuition and insight. The **Pole star** aids navigators and may act as a symbolic guide to the

unconscious. A **shooting star or meteorite** can suggest a flash of inspiration, or a memory of someone in the past or someone dead, as many cultures believe that human spirits manifest themselves as stars. On the other hand, you might want to consider whether your dream star symbolized your ambitions, hopes and dreams in some way. **Nebulas** are the birthplace of stars, so if you saw one through a **telescope**, are you celebrating a birth or some kind of new beginning or breakthrough in the waking world?

SUN

The **sun** is at the center of the solar system, and is a source of creation, light and insight. Its predominance as illuminator and life giver is reflected in dream-lore in which it is regarded as a good omen. The sun suggests creative energy and penetrating insight or intelligence. It is also a symbol of inner power and fiery, masculine energy. From the sun comes light, that which draws us into life. The sun represents your identity or self, and relates to your will, consciousness, creativity, and father and authority figures in general. It reflects how you can shine in your life.

If **sunlight** features in your dream, this suggests positive feelings. If you are **sunbathing**, this suggests that you are allowing positive energies to enhance your life. The daily solar cycle is paralleled by the stages of human life with **dawn or sunrise** being a symbol of realization, as in 'it dawned on me'; the **rising sun** represents increasing vitality; the **midday sun**, your life's work or the height of your energy; and **sunset**, old age or the latent period prior to a new birth. An **eclipse of** the sun suggests negative emotions clouding your judgment. If **clouds obscure the sun**, this foretells of unexpected obstacles placed in your path. A **dream journey to the sun** could suggest a search for intellectual enlightenment but it may also symbolize your desire to be infused with optimism and energy in waking life. If you were **badly scorched by the sun**, your dreaming mind may have been warning you that you are in danger of intellectual burnout.

UFO/Alien

Dreams of **UFOs** suggest personal growth. As the awareness of the infinity of possible person choices can be an overwhelming experience, your dreaming mind may express it as alien contact, UFO or an experience of extremely bright light. Such a dream also suggests that a new area of experience, or a new way of experiencing yourself, is emerging. A UFO dream may often come before significant life changes; you should consider what changes are occurring in the way you relate to people and events.

If an **alien** appears in your dream, this suggests feelings of being an outsider in a group or society. It may also represent something new and not previously experienced. In some cases, the alien may symbolize a meeting with an aspect of yourself that has great potential. A dream about **alien abduction** is generally considered to be nightmare; if the alien is benign, however, you may respond like an overawed child to an idolized parent in your dream.

Science and Math

Atom/Molecule

Dreams **of atoms or molecules** refer to the importance of small aspects of your life, and to the need to pay attention to details or the little things that are being overlooked. An **atom bomb** in your dream may be a symbol of the end of one way of life and the beginning of another. It may also represent fear of the irrational forces of life and feeling at the mercy of external and uncontrollable forces, or a lack of compassion and a disregard for life.

Biology

The **study of biology** in your dream suggests an interest in all aspects of your world. It also indicates a high regard for life. Dreams of **bionic men or women** suggests that you have a talent for innovation or visualizing future advances.

Chemistry

The **study of chemistry** in your dream suggests an interest in the way that substances may or may not connect or interrelate with each other. **Chemicals** symbolize compound aspects, often negative, whilst a dream of **chemical warfare** suggest that the way you go about conflict resolution has negative consequences. If you dream of **radioactive compounds**, this may reflect the effect of other people's thoughts or feelings upon yourself, or indicate the extent of your influence on the lives of other people.

ENERGY

References to your energy levels may occur in dreams. An **electricity or gas failure, power cut or light bulb going out** typically suggests that your energy levels are low; your dream may be advising you to get more rest or to pay attention to your life style. On the other hand, a dream about a **gas fire, cooker, stove or light that is burning well** would suggest great energy reserves. Bear in mind, too, that symbols of **fire and heat** are also often associated with sexuality; furthermore, a dream of a **car running out of petrol** might suggest low libido or sexual energy. The **blowing of a fuse** in a dream is a warning that you are close to losing your patience with someone or something in waking life, or that you are not using your energy wisely. Your dreaming mind may also be suggesting that you should take more exercise.

MATH

Dreams that feature **calculation, measurement or mathematics of any kind** are often related to some kind of calculation you need to make in waking life. Perhaps you need to take an objective look at a certain situation or problem to find a rational and unemotional way around it. A dream of an **accountant working on account books or counting figures** suggests a problem in your waking life that needs a coolly calculated and unemotional solution. The accountant may represent yourself but it may also represent someone who is trying to help you keep your feet on

the ground. If you are trying to **add up a sum in your dream or an equation but are having problems doing so**, this indicates a slight error in your thinking or a slip or mistake that is undermining your efforts.

MEASUREMENT

Dreaming of **measurements that involve a calculation of flow, temperature, length or weight** relates to your attempts to control and make sense of your emotions. For example, dreams of a **barometer or thermometer** (instruments that measure the weather and body temperature, two constantly fluctuating variables) can often relate to your mood; if the measurements were high, have your emotions taken over? Have you lost your cool? The dream is warning you that difficult times may lie ahead and is urging you to keep your temper or think clearly to avoid problems. Dreams of **gas or water meters** may have similar meanings. Are you allowing your emotions to flow too freely in waking life? Dreams that involve **rulers, compasses or other measuring instruments** reflect a desire to put a situation or your emotions into perspective; if you keep a cool head, there is no reason why you should not achieve success. If a **radar screen** appears in your dream, this may refer to your intuition or sense of other people's feelings.

SCIENCE

In general, **science or scientists** in your dream represent your analytical mind and may stand for your attempt to weigh and measure life, to discover its usefulness and, if practical science is highlighted, let you

The science of dreams

We typically spend more than two hours each night dreaming but there is much that scientists do not know about how or why we dream. Freud, who greatly influenced the field of psychology, believed dreaming to be a 'safety valve' for unconscious desires, but it was not until the 1950s that scientists were able to study sleep and dreaming and come to some of their own conclusions.

In 1953, Eugene Aserinsky of the University of Chicago noticed that the eyes of sleeping babies moved beneath their eyelids at certain regular intervals. This led to the discovery of REM (rapid eye movement) sleep periods, which occur at roughly sixty to ninety minute intervals throughout the night, and contain the dreams that are the most vivid and most often remembered. Since then, EEG recordings that monitor brain activity during sleep have been used to map the various stages of sleep. Scientists soon realized that the strange, illogical experiences we call dreams almost always occur during REM sleep. Whilst most mammals and birds show signs of REM sleep, reptiles and other cold-blooded animals do not. REM sleep begins with signals from an area at the base of the brain called the pons. These signals travel to a brain region called the thalamus, which relays them to the cerebral cortex – the outer layer of the brain that is responsible for learning, thinking and organizing information. The pons also sends signals that shut off neurons in the spinal cord, causing temporary paralysis of the limb muscles. If something interferes with this paralysis, people will begin to physically 'act out' their dreams – a rare, dangerous problem called REM sleep behavior disorder.

REM sleep stimulates the brain regions used in learning. This may be important for normal brain development during infancy, which would explain why infants spend much more time in REM sleep than adults. Like deep sleep, REM sleep is associated with an increased production of proteins. One study found that REM sleep affects the learning of certain mental skills. People taught a skill and then deprived of non-REM sleep could recall what they had learned after sleeping, whilst people deprived of REM sleep could not.

Some scientists believe dreams are the cortex's attempt to find meaning in the random signals that it receives during REM sleep. The cortex is the part of the brain that interprets and organizes information from the environment during consciousness. It may be that, given random signals from the pons during REM sleep, the cortex tries to interpret these signals as well, creating a 'story' out of fragmented brain activity.

know how to apply what you have learned; science may, however, symbolize an intellectual and unfeeling attitude. If you are **attending a science fair** in your dream, this suggests innovative thinking and possibilities. A **scientific experiment** in your dream signifies the need to consider your options and decide whether or not you want to move ahead with a particular plan. It may be suggesting that you need to adopt a reasoned and impartial approach to a challenge in your waking life. If you find yourself **busy inventing something in a laboratory** in your dream, this suggests intellectual exploration and creativity.

TELESCOPE/MAGNIFYING GLASS

Using a **telescope** in your dream suggests the need to take a closer look at something. Your dreaming mind may be urging you to look at things from both a short- and a long-term view, as this may help you navigate through life's sometimes choppy waters. In spiritual terms, a telescope can signify the art of clairvoyance – the ability to see the future from the perspective of the present. A **magnifying glass** may appear in your dream when something needs to be brought to your attention. You need to examine yourself minutely and become aware of the consequence of your actions.

SPIRITS AND GHOSTS

Even the most prosaic and materialistic of us have dreams that include supernatural creatures or incidents.

Ghosts, witches, out-of-body experiences, UFOs, haunted houses and a whole plethora of spirits, creatures and unexplained phenomena exist in the world of the supernatural. When these images appear in your dreams, they can be unsettling, especially when psychics claim that they are connected with the supernatural. Even though there is no evidence to suggest this is the case, the mysterious and often bizarre nature of dreams has led many to interpret dreams as supernatural gifts or messages, as predictions of the future or as messages from the past. Modern oneiromancy, the prediction of the future through the interpretation of dreams, is a tradition that has its roots in pagan and ancient Greek and Roman thought, as well as in the Jewish and Christian religions.

Freudians and Jungians, together with most other dream analysts, reject the supernatural origin of dreams. Their view is that dreams bubble up from the unconscious mind and are metaphors for events or emotions occurring in our waking lives. Theologians, however, continue to admit the possibility that dreams may be supernatural or divine in origin. Whether or not you believe dreams have a supernatural origin, if you are experiencing such dreams, your unconscious might be urging you to be more open-minded towards unexplained phenomena; alternatively, they might be suggesting a need for radical change in your life or attitude. *See also* MIND, BODY, SPIRIT; NIGHTMARES; SURREALISM AND FANTASY.

Haunting Dreams

GHOST

If **ghosts** appear in your dreams, they often symbolize unfinished business, just as ghosts – or the unsettled dead – are supposed to have unfinished business on earth, not having found their place in the afterlife. Because of a ghost's ephemeral nature, being only partially visible to some and invisible to others, they can also represent uncertainty or a lack of clarity in your thinking. Another interpretation is that seeing ghosts in dreams is a way of facing your own mortality; for this reason they can be quite disturbing, but because they may offer evidence of life after death, they could be seen as offering some comfort. You can also look at a ghost as a shadow of yourself, your own dark nature personified; the side of yourself that you'd rather not face up to.

If you want to understand the significance of dreaming about ghosts, you need to look at how they behaved in your dream. Whilst most ghosts are invisible and silent, some **ghosts are noisy and throw things around**; these could represent your lack of control regarding things that are happening around you in waking life. Ghosts may interact with you in dreams, but often they will not do it directly. You may feel comforted by their appearance in your dream; you may feel stressed or afraid. They may be strangers, friends, relatives or famous people that have died – your relationship to them or how you feel about them will affect what they mean in your dream – for instance the ghost may be a nagging relative who is still very much alive, but casts a shadow over your life and is always trying to push you one way or another.

At times, ghosts represent those things that are unattainable or fleeting. If, however, the **ghost feels solid**, you may be touching aspects of your own mind or awareness that exist beyond your own preconceived ideas and beliefs. **Ghosts of living people** in your dream have nothing to do with the possibility of their death in the near future; such dreams suggest, rather, a sense of their thoughts or presence haunting you. Or perhaps you are haunted by desire for them or have unexpressed feelings about them. Alternatively, and particularly if you **shrank from the ghost in your dream**, could the specter have represented someone whom you once wronged, a ghost from the past that is still haunting your conscience despite your conscious efforts to push it to the back of your mind?

GHOST OF SOMEONE WHO HAS DIED

Some believe that the ghosts in their dreams are real representations of the dead. This is an unlikely explanation of such dreams. More likely, to dream of the **ghost of someone who is departed** represents a part of you that is unclear and that you do not understand. Ghosts can also be all that you have left of loved ones who are no longer alive, so they can offer you comfort by appearing in your dreams, representing a welcome opportunity to speak once again to that special person and to come to terms with the fact that they are gone. To dream of the ghost of someone who has died might also represent something that you wanted that is no longer in your reach. This dream is telling you to move on. Another explanation is that your unconscious was pointing out an uncomfortable truth that your conscious mind is working hard to repress, just as the ghost of his father appeared to Shakespeare's Hamlet to tell him something that he may already have known – that his father was murdered by Hamlet's new stepfather.

To dream of **touching a ghost and having it disappear** indicates that you are trying to confront and come to terms with painful memories. **Demonic ghost images**

with no face or dark shadows ('dementors', if you are a Harry Potter fan) may represent your negative tendencies, unpleasant parts of personality or your 'shadow'. Old superstition-based dream interpretations say that dreaming of **friendly ghosts** is a lucky omen, and that you should be receiving unexpected good luck. On the other hand, if you were **very frightened by the ghost** in your dream, then others will try to impose their will on you and you must be vigilant in order to stand up to it.

HALLOWE'EN

If **Hallowe'en** figures in your dream in some way, this illustrates personal revelations or dramatic insights into yourself or someone else. Hallowe'en – also known as All Hallow's Eve – is the night when witches, ghosts and spirits are believed to walk the earth and reveal themselves; so is there something in waking life you need to reveal or come to terms with? Observed annually on the night of 31 October and originally a pagan festival of the dead, Hallowe'en is celebrated today as a night of fancy dress, trick or treating, and superstitious fun and games. Wiccans and pagans, however, observe All Hallow's Eve (also known as Sanhain) as one of their most important sacred days. For them it is a time to honor the dead, communicate with spirits and observe rituals. It is also thought to be a particularly good time to make a fresh start and commence new projects. So if Hallowe'en images float into your dream, perhaps your dream is urging you to do just that.

HALLUCINATION/ HALLUCINOGEN

Hallucinations can occur quite naturally without the use of psychotropic drugs such as peyote or LSD. We all have the innate ability to suffer from hallucinations and, according to Freud, one of the definitions of a dream is precisely its hallucinogenic quality. Whilst asleep, we can create full sensory, vocal and emotional experiences in our dreams that most of us believe are real at the time. A waking hallucination is merely an experience of a dream occurring with our eyes open. The voices heard and images seen, although appearing outside of us, are no more exterior than the images in our dreams.

The hypnagogic state is that state between being awake and falling asleep during which the mind is most receptive to ideas, images, sounds, feelings, impressions and intuition. It also the time when people are most likely to see ghostlike figures. (It should not be confused with the hypnopompic state, which is a transition state of semi-consciousness between sleeping and waking.) Some dream experts believe that the sketchy imagery typical of these states can be helpful to the individual in terms of self-understanding. Images are often presented through the individual's own set of symbols and once interpreted symbols can provide answers to problems and even alert one to future events. Some believe that taking the time to record these images, feelings and sounds can be just as helpful as recording dream imagery.

Incubus/Succubus

If you **woke up from your dream sweating with fear and had the feeling that some force was crushing your chest, causing you to struggle to breathe**, this may represent two different things, depending on your sex. If you are a woman, you may have suffered an **incubus** attack; if you are a man, you may have suffered a **succubus** attack. In the past, when sexual pleasure was considered sinful, women who had erotic dreams were said to have been visited by the incubus, or male demon, whilst a sexually voracious succubus, or female demon, was said to visit a sleeping man. These evil spirits were thought to pin down and paralyze their sleeping victims in order to have sex with them. The words 'incubus' and 'succubus' are still used today to describe the sensation of having a weight press down on your chest, accompanied by a feeling of dread and being unable to move while you are sleeping. They are no longer applied to dreams about sex, which are of course natural and normal.

Incubi (plural of 'incubus', meaning 'one who lies upon' in Latin) were thought to be particularly fond of seducing nuns and other women committed to the celibate life. Sexual repression is thought to be the most likely explanation but the cause of this phenomenon remains unclear. Dream experts have ruled out demons and malevolent spirits as the cause, suggesting instead that they may have been caused by temporary breathing difficulties combined with sleep paralysis, a condition that occurs in the state just before dropping off to sleep or just before fully awakening from sleep. The condition is characterized by being unable to move or speak. It is often associated with a feeling that there is some sort of menacing presence, a feeling which often arouses fear but is accompanied by an inability to cry out. The paralysis, which experts are unable to explain fully, typically lasts a few seconds but leaves a lasting impression on the dreamer.

Out-of-body experience

When a person feels that they have stepped out of, or been separated from, their physical body and have the ability to travel to another location on earth or even to non-worldly realms, they are said to have had an **out-of-body experience** (OBE). An OBE can occur when a person is awake, or before, during and after sleep. It can also occur during times of stress, illness, trauma and fear, as well as being able to be induced by hypnosis and meditation. Also known as astral projection or travel, such experiences are believed to occur during sleep, as well as during times of great physical or emotional trauma. So if you had a dream in which you **left your physical body, perhaps even watched your body for a while as you floated on the ceiling, and then flew up the stars and the moon or to a location miles away**, you may not have been dreaming; you may have been traveling out of your body.

This isn't as crazy as it sounds. Descriptions of OBEs, or of the separation of the consciousness from the body, have been recorded since ancient times. The ancient Egyptians believed in a life force, called 'ka', which was independent of the body. Plato believed the soul could leave the body and travel, whilst both Socrates and Pliny gave many descriptions of experiences that closely resemble OBEs. The

The Element Encyclopedia of 20,000 Dreams

Journeys out of the body

Some of the earliest research into **OBEs** was conducted by Frenchman Yarm Louis Forham (1884–1917), who believed that everyone was capable of astral travel in a variety of guises, recording his observations in *Practical Astral Travel*. Forham claimed to have made astral visits to a woman he later married and to have experienced astral sex. Between 1902 and 1938, Englishman Oliver Fox took research into OBEs one step further when he claimed to have succeeded in inducing OBEs with lucid dreaming (see INTRODUCTION). He published his discoveries in 1920 in the journal *English Occult Review* and later in a book, *Astral Projection*. A fellow Englishman and OBE investigator, J. H. M. Whiteman claimed to have had thousands of OBEs, sometimes in the form of a woman or a child, between 1931 and 1953, which he described in *The Mystical Life*.

Robert A. Monroe (1915–1995), former television executive of Westchester County, New York, attracted widespread interest in OBEs from both the public and the scientific community when he published his account of OBEs in *Journeys out of the Body* (1971). His interest in OBEs had been triggered in 1958 when he began having spontaneous OBEs in his sleep. In his book, he described the experience as follows:

'In 1958, without any apparent cause, I began to float out of my physical body. It was not voluntary; I was not attempting any mental feats. It was not during sleep, so I couldn't dismiss it as simply a dream. I had full, conscious awareness of what was happening, which of course only made it worse. I assumed it was some sort of hallucination caused by something dangerous – a brain tumor, or impending mental illness. Or imminent death. It occurred usually when I would lie down or relax for rest or preparatory to sleep – not every time but several times weekly. I would float up a few feet above my body before I became aware of what was happening. Terrified, I would struggle through the air and back into my physical body. Try as I might, I could not prevent it from recurring.'

In his books, Monroe sets out an astonishing range of experience, some of which was unpleasant and involved meeting entities or thought forms that attacked him. He also described an overwhelmingly powerful energy: meeting the astral forms of other humans and sexual experiences on the astral level. He outlines his belief that there were various levels of existence in the OBE state. Locale I is earth, the here and now. Locale II is the infinite astral plane where everyone goes to sleep and dreams, and where countless entities exist. Locale III transcends space and time and is a parallel universe. In his writings, Monroe described a technique for triggering out-of-body states and here is a brief description of it:

1. First lie down in a darkened room in a relaxing position.
2. Loosen your clothing and remove all jewelry.
3. Enter a very relaxed state and consciously tell yourself that you will remember everything that happens to you.
4. Begin breathing through your half-open mouth.
5. Concentrate on an object.
6. When other images start to enter your mind, just passively watch them.
7. Try to clear your mind and observe your field of vision through your closed eyes.
8. Do nothing more for a while.
9. Simply look through your closed eyelids at the blackness in front of you.
10. After a while, you may notice light patterns.
11. When these cease, you will enter a state of such relaxation that you lose all awareness of the body.
12. You are almost in the state where your only source of stimulation will be your own thoughts.
13. It is in this relaxed and refreshed condition that out-of-body journeys are triggered.
14. To leave your body, think of yourself getting lighter and of how nice it would be to float upwards.
15. With sufficient practice, Monroe claims that a wide variety of experiences can occur.

If Monroe's theories are correct, the implications for dream interpretation would be enormous. Even though surveys suggest that one quarter of the population believes they have had an OBE, recent research on OBEs has been inconclusive. This may be because OBEs vary from individual to individual. Laboratory tests have been equally inconclusive, even with individuals who claim to be able to project out of body at will. Tests with animals have been a little more promising, with kittens showing a change in behavior during out-of-body efforts to comfort them; skeptics, however, argue that this was achieved through telepathy or clairvoyance. Although OBE's cannot be disproved, to date there has been no solid evidence that anyone has actually left their body during sleep or while dreaming.

ancient Chinese thought that an OBE could be achieved through meditation, whilst tribal shamans, firm believers in body doubles, claim to be able to project themselves out of their bodies.

Common to most OBE experiences is the existence of a second body, described as a ghostly double of the physical body. It is usually invisible to the eyes of others, although it may be sensed or witnessed as an apparition. In some cases, a silvery cord connecting the astral to the physical body is reported and it is said that if this cord is severed from the body, death will occur. In this astral form, OBE travellers report floating around the earth or to an astral plane, claiming that they travel as fast as the speed of thought, feeling neither pain nor anxiety. Individuals claim that they leave their body through their head or simply rise up and float away. Re-entry occurs by simply re-entering the head or melting into the body. It is worth pointing out that even those who describe the experience as something fantastic that occurs during sleep are very specific in describing the experience as one which was clearly *not* a dream; and many stress a sense of feeling more awake than they felt when they were normally awake. Despite the documented records of those who claim to have had an OBE, scientific evidence for the phenomenon remains inconclusive, prompting skeptics to argue that OBEs are nothing more than vividly fantastic dreams or altered states of consciousness.

SPIRIT

Spirits are commonplace in the religions and folklores of the world, coming in a multitude of shapes and forms, such as fairies, elves, demons and angels. The term is often used to describe all non-physical entities, including ghosts, but a spirit is not strictly speaking the same as a ghost, even though the distinction between the two is sometimes vague. In some cultures, they are also thought to personify characteristics and forces of nature, which are then worshipped by proxy. They are believed to exist in an invisible realm, but can be seen by clairvoyant seers. They are also thought to intervene at times in the affairs of humanity, for better or for worse.

In dreams, spirits represents feelings or intuition about the dead or death, and their appearance can help you come to terms with these. Whether you think they are actual spirits or not will depend on your own belief system. Typically, spirits in dreams are a comforting presence to help you through various times of transition. Are they aspects of your unconscious or of the dream world? In the end, the answer is in fact immaterial, since their function is to help you progress.

SPIRIT GUIDE

Spiritualists, shamans and mediums often claim that **spirit guides** visit them in their dreams. The spirit guides often appear in the forms of animals, but may take on other forms: the form of loved ones already passed on, past teachers or elders, or important figures in the relevant mythology. According to Jungians, archetypal figures, such as the wise old man or the priestess that appear in dreams and offer guidance, are not guides from the spirit world but from the depths of your unconscious. Either way, they perform the same function as spirit guides. So if **supernatural or archetypal figures** appear in your dreams, are you in need of some sort of guidance? Could you use any of the advice they offer effectively in your waking life?

SUPERNATURAL DREAMS

There is a long tradition in almost every religion of dreams with **messages from a supernatural power**. Many people are inclined to accept that dreams containing religious symbols, such as the **Cross, Star or Crescent Moon,** or leaders of their faith, such as **Christ, Buddha, Muhammed or Moses,** appear as direct instructions from that power. If you have been brought up in a particular faith, it is most likely that such dreams are instructing you to act in accordance with the moral standards of that faith. They may also be urging you to regard some waking problem in the light of your religious beliefs. A dream of a religious symbol may therefore be suggesting that a part of your life needs moral, as well as practical, attention. A dream featuring a **religious leader** tends to occur when there is an important moral decision to be made in your waking life. *See also* RELIGION.

UFO/ALIEN

According to Jungians our current interest in **UFOs** (unidentified flying objects) suggests a need for wholeness. In *A Modern Myth of Things in the Sky* (1958), Jung showed that his theories about archetypes explained much of this phenomenon. In his patients, Jung discovered that the mandala emerged from the unconscious as a sign of the urge towards a new wholeness. The round shape of most UFOs was significant because circles are mandalas. UFOs reported in waking and dreaming life were therefore fantasies projected by the modern psyche's need for meaning and striving for wholeness. Jung claimed that UFOs were an archetype that could herald a great shift in human history, since they were an indication that something important was changing in the universal consciousness. Others suggest that UFOs represent an aspect of yourself that you are afraid to believe in.

Aliens in dreams tend to suggest that something unknown or frightening in waking life needs to be faced. Assuming you were not abducted during the night, dreaming of aliens may also indicate dealing with something unfamiliar in yourself. Are you behaving in ways that are alien to you, for example? Aliens are something humans have never encountered, so the dream is urging you to prepare for the unexpected. Sometimes in dreams, aliens suggest evil forces, but more often than not they suggest that you feel different or set apart in some way from others. Perhaps you have started a new job and feel the odd one out.

VAMPIRE/BAT/WEREWOLF

The most obvious image of a **vampire** is of a creature that is dead and sucks the blood of the living, rising from the grave at night to do so – then sleeping all day in a most inhuman-like fashion. Your blood is your life force, it carries with it everything you need to survive; if your blood drains away, you become weak and die. Vampires are therefore the parasites of the supernatural realm; they share a world with ghouls (creatures that prey on the dead), and the succubi and incubi that take on human form to have sex with sleeping people. In the past, when the Catholic Church was a little more superstitious, they blamed a person's apparently sudden sexual awareness on these sexual interlopers of the night. Vampires are often repelled by simple, natural things like daylight; they are also turned away by religious symbols in mythology.

Dreaming of these parasitic creatures can signify a number of things: that a part

Dreams don't come true, do they?

You may have dreams that appear to predict the future. Whilst many of these dreams can be easily explained, there are a few that seem impossible to explain and which might therefore be genuinely supernatural. During some periods of its history, the Christian Church regarded dreams as a way in which God showed his chosen people the future: St Augustine, for example, 'saw' his conversion in a dream ten years before it took place. The Bible itself is packed with predictive dreams and, as late as the sixteenth century, bishops would take careful note of their dreams to predict events.

Although there is some evidence that dreams may be able to reveal the future or events, they are perhaps best explained by anticipating what is likely to happen. For example, many dreams predicted the assassination of President John F. Kennedy. However, it must be remembered that President Kennedy was one of the world's most well-known men and presidents are always vulnerable to assassination. Such dreams, as Jung put it, 'are not more prophetic than a medical diagnosis or weather forecast. They are merely an anticipatory combination of possibilities which may coincide with the actual behavior of things but need not necessarily agree on every detail.' Dreams of personal disaster are usually a common cause for concern; for example, a plane crash or car crash. However, such dreams are typically born out of apprehension.

Even though there is no scientific evidence that dreams can reveal the future, some dreams do seem to be genuine predictions. Just before his title fight in 1947, Sugar Ray Robinson dreamt he was in the ring with Jimmy Doyle. 'I hit him a few good punches and he was on his back, his bland eyes staring up at me. Doyle never moved and the crowd was shouting, "He's dead! He's dead!"' Robinson was so upset by the dream he asked Adkins, his trainer and promoter, to call off the fight. Adkins told him: 'Dreams don't come true. If they did, I'd be a millionaire.' In the eighth round, Doyle went down from a hook to the jaw. He never got up and was dead the next day.

If you are interested in this aspect of dreaming – whether you yourself have had predictive dreams or simply want to study the subject – it is vital to keep a detailed diary of your dreams. If you do have a dream that seems to predict a serious event or important event, such as an explosion or a tornado, make a note, have it dated and witnessed, seal it in an envelope and send it to a reputable institution such as your bank with instructions to date it on arrival. *See also* Precognitive dreams entry in DISASTERS.

of your existence is having the life sucked out of it, that you need to take a closer look at the more tiresome aspects of your life and dispel the worries connected with them or that you need to employ some kind of self-protection or preservation. It may be that your partner is holding you back, or that your mother is trying to control every aspect of your life so that your energy is being drained away. It is also possible, but rare, that you are the one behaving in a parasitic manner and are subconsciously quite disturbed by it. Alternatively, to dream of seeing a vampire may indicate that you are feeling seductive, powerful and very sensual.

Werewolves and bats, like vampires, come out at night to suck people's blood; just as vampires go through a metamorphosis to become bats, so too werewolves undergo a transformation from human beings during the full moon. It is thought that these creatures in your dream mean that there is something going on in your life that is awkward and difficult to deal with. To dream of a werewolf may also suggest that some part of your life is not what it seems. Both vampires and werewolves have been regarded as symbols of dark forces since medieval times. Both drain their victims of their vital essence. To imagine one or other of these creatures in your dream should be taken as a warning to distance yourself from someone in waking life who doesn't have your best interests at heart. It could also refer to some activity or habit that is having a negative effect on you. Bear in mind that while werewolves are believed to have a particular preference for young women (suggesting dangerous sexual predators), vampires, their fanged fellow fiends of the night, are opportunistic

killers who take their sustenance from any kind of human blood, be it a man's, woman's or child's. So if you had a dream in which **someone you know came too close for comfort before baring a set of needle sharp fangs**, your dream may be alerting you to someone who is feeding off your energy, or else sponging off your fiancé and thriving at your expense.

VISITATION DREAM

Perhaps you, or someone you know, have had a dream where you or they are absolutely convinced of a **visit by a departed loved one or religious figure** in your sleep. The reason for believing such a visit actually occurred may be a deep and emotional understanding about the purpose of the visit. 'My mother wants me to know she is doing fine,' or 'my friend wanted me to know she did love me, even though she found it hard to show it.' Perhaps you had a dream in which **someone you know visited you to say goodbye**; later you learn that they have in fact died. Was their spirit saying goodbye, or were you worried about their poor health and the dream realized those fears? If you dreamed that a **spirit comforts you when you are ill** is this really a spirit or a form of self comfort? Or did you dream of someone who died of a disfiguring disease and in your dream they appear young and whole and beautiful again. Is this their spirit visiting you or your dreaming mind's way of helping you move beyond what his pain and suffering did to your friend physically? It's impossible to be able to prove that dream visits from those who have passed on do or do not occur. To a great extent it does not really matter. What

Dreams and the grieving process

Dreams that focus on the early stages of mourning after the loss of a loved one are often dreams in which the **dead person is still alive and well, and continuing to participate in your life**. You may, for example, dream of having breakfast with them or taking a walk in the park, just the same as you did when they were alive. The reason for this is that your dreaming mind has not yet accepted the person's absence from your life. This is a natural and healthy type of dream to have in the first phase of mourning as it allows your dreaming mind to escape the pain of reality. Some dream analysts describe such dreams not as denial, but as a catalogue of all the memories the survivor has of that person.

You may well find that feelings of hostility or anger feature in these dreams because, along with deep feelings of sadness, there are also feelings of fury that the person you cared about has left you. You may have dreams that express how guilty you feel; for example, you may dream that you are once again **tending your sick relative but your attention is focused elsewhere and you can't make them feel comfortable**; similarly, you may dream that **you become sick yourself or try to prevent the death happening**.

At some point, however, your dreams will begin to reflect the grief and awareness that your loved one has died. Perhaps you dream **you are at a restaurant and suddenly realize you need to eat alone because your partner isn't delayed**. Such dreams are often characterized by deep sadness and tears, and it is quite normal to feel depressed after having one of these. You may find yourself revisiting earlier stages of your grief again at this time, and it is very common for **dead people to come into dreams to let us know it is time to stop mourning**. Even if your spiritual beliefs lead you to believe that the person who has died is still with you, you still need to go through the grieving and healing process, acknowledging all the good and bad feelings you had about this person and what their death means to you. Dreams can help you with this process and experts believe it typically takes around two years to fully pass through all the stages of grief.

But what if you are still having **vivid and emotional dreams of a departed loved one ten years after their death**? It's possible that you are still holding onto feelings of love and anger. Perhaps you are stuck with your grief or are simply unable to process it. For example, you may dream that a **loved one keeps turning up and shouting at you**. If you have always been taught that showing emotion is a sign of weakness, then such a harmful and narrow stereotype is interfering with the natural processes of grief. Your dreaming mind will therefore highlight the issues that are stopping you completing the grieving process and moving forward with your life. If you find yourself unable to resolve 'unfinished business' and move beyond feeling stuck in the grief process, consulting a therapist could be helpful.

Bear in mind that that for which you mourn may not be solely your family, friends and pets. You grieve for what you have lost and your dreams may express your sense of loss concerning important objects, such as a home; important relationships, such as the end of a marriage; important projects, such as losing a job you loved; important dreams for the future, such as the loss of a baby due to a failed IVF attempt or miscarriage; and important feelings, such as the loss of trust if you have been the victim of a violent crime. Make note of whom or what you are mourning and try to ascertain which stage of grief you are in. Do your dreams reflect this and do they give you a suggestion for how far you might begin to accept the loss?

matters is how you feel about the dream. What messages do you feel they were bringing you, and are those messages helping you heal your grief if the person who appeared in your dreams has recently died or if the person died years ago resolve issues you may have had with them in your life so you can move forward with your life?

WITCHCRAFT/MAGIC

A dream in which **someone casts a spell on you or uses magic, voodoo or witchcraft either to help or hinder you** may refer to someone in your waking life who is seeking to influence you, or people or events around you. The dream may also be commenting on the validity or success of your reactions. The success or failure of the spell will be important; if it is successful, the witch or wizard may be offering you valuable advice and you should pay attention. Whenever magic features in a dream, it suggests that you are using your energy to accomplish something but are not controlling that energy and using it effectively. It does, however, indicate that you are capable of controlling a situation that you are in and making things happen. Psychologically, when magic appears in a dream, it links in with your deepest powers. These can be powers of self-control or sexuality, or power over your surroundings.

If your dream **features the occult and you have little or no knowledge of the subject**, this usually suggests a need to come to terms with your hidden fears. If you think of the occult in the negative sense, as in Satanism or black magic, the dream may have a negative significance or link in with the egotistical side of your nature. But if you think of the occult in more positive terms, as in Wicca and shamanism, the dream may have a positive spin or link in with the giving, nature-loving side of your character. If you do possess occult knowledge, your dreaming mind may be urging you to apply that awareness and sense of the mystery and wonder of life to your everyday situation.

The rule for both should always be, 'do no harm or harm no one'. Finally, due to its complex and mysterious nature in dreams, the occult may be alerting you to your hidden potential. *See also* MIND, BODY, SPIRIT.

Zombie/Ghoul

A **zombie** is a dead person that has been brought back to life through supernatural means, usually through a voodoo ritual. To dream that **you are a zombie** indicates that you are feeling dead inside, perhaps stifled by your responsibilities or the lack of variety in your waking life. Perhaps you feel out of touch with the rest of the people around you. A **ghoul** is someone who takes bodies from graves and sells them for dissection. It is also thought to be a creature that feeds on human bodies. Dreaming of a ghoul suggests that your negative ways are hindering your growth. Some dream interpreters think that dreaming of ghouls may indicate new beginnings and a desire to change your life so you can begin afresh.

Witch/sorcerer/wizard

In dreams, the appearance of a **witch, sorcerer or wizard** suggests the presence of a powerful archetype. In most dreams, witches represent destructive forces and repression. They may also suggest moodiness, dislike of wisdom, vindictiveness or jealousy. Some interpreters believe that witches reflect difficulties in relationship with our mother and, if the dreamer is a woman, she may become the 'witch' in relation to someone else. Since the early days of Christianity, witches have had a bad press; their association with the devil meant that dreams of witches have been linked with misfortune. Their original role, however, was as divine priestesses and bringers of wisdom and healing. You will need to consider your personal associations with witches and notice the feelings the dream triggers to fully interpret its meaning.

Magicians, wizards and sorcerers in dreams suggest magical abilities you possess but are not using to their fullest extent. If the **magician is using black magic**, this suggests negative or selfish ways in which you might use your power of wisdom. To dream of **magic that turns out to be a trick produced by a conjurer, hypnotist or magician** should be regarded as a warning that all is not as it seems in waking life. Try to find out who is deceiving you; the identity of the conjurer may give you a clue. If **you are the conjurer**, the dream may reflect some unease or anxiety about a current plan or negotiation in your waking life that rests on your skill and personality rather than on facts and common sense.

STAGES OF LIFE

In his 1930 essay 'Stages of Life', Jung postulated four stages of life – childhood, youth, middle age and old age – based on his own clinical observations.

He viewed youth as a period of expanding consciousness, middle age as a period of questioning long-held convictions, and old age as a period of increased introspection and preoccupation with self-evaluation. According to Jung, dreams are important tools of self-discovery for you, whatever your age or life stage. This is because in every stage of your life you will face many challenges: emotional, intellectual, spiritual and physical. These challenges can trigger fascinating dreams, some of which can help you to meet those challenges and pass on to the next phase of your development.

Jung believed that what prevents people from becoming independent, fulfilled and ultimately happy is their refusal to open themselves to change or to new and unfamiliar experiences that potentially threaten their sense of self. His approach to finding balance in every stage of life was through the analysis of dreams and a process he called 'individuation'. Dreams are a powerful tool for self-discovery and individuation is a self-analysis, a self-discovery, a way of analysing your own reactions and responses at every life stage so you can discover what truths lie underneath your conscious and egocentric personality.

In this chapter you will explore dreams that are believed to be typical of distinct life stages; some dream analysts refer to them as 'developmental dreams'. This is because they seem particularly to reflect the typical stresses, questions and issues you may face at specific times in your life. This makes sense as you would expect the dreams you had when you were fifteen to reflect the concerns of your life as a teenager, just as you would expect the dreams you have now to have evolved into a mirror of your current situation and age group. Bear in mind, however, that how the stresses and challenges of your current life stage is represented in the dream world depends upon your personal circumstances, your sleep patterns and your ability to remember your dreams. Bear in mind, too, that it is possible to have any one of these dreams even if you don't fit the life-stage profile that coincides with it.

Dreams of death will also be explored in this chapter, as death is the final stage or change that comes to us all. Although dreams of death may explore your feelings about death or represent potential you may have missed or not expressed in general, dream analysts believe that such dreams represent the ending of one phase so a new one can begin. They reveal forthcoming finalities such as the end of a relationship or career and should not be interpreted literally. Because in the past we were terrified at the idea of death, it also represents upheaval, calamity and the sense that things will never be the same again. It was something that could only be endured but never be understood. Today, as our attitudes towards death have changed, death in a dream represents a challenge that cannot be avoided and which must be confronted if progress is to be made in waking life. The message is that some approach or attitude to life needs to be changed or adjusted; if you can find the courage to make that adjustment successfully, there can be a fresh start or a new beginning

For dreams concerning childhood, *see* BIRTH AND CHILDHOOD. *See also* LOSS AND FRUSTRATION; NIGHTMARES; SPIRITS AND GHOSTS.

Growing Up Dreams

ADOLESCENCE

Technically the teenage years or **adolescence** extends from about the age of twelve to eighteen, or twenty-one at the latest. As you grow older, you may find that your dreams look back to your teenage years with feelings of wistfulness. You may not want to go through the torments of adolescence again but you may like to unite your maturity and experience with your youthful energy and enthusiasm. Whereas **dreams of childhood** tend to be nostalgic, **dreams that feature teenagers** tend to be about wish-fulfillment. If you are no longer a teenager, a dream in which you **become a teenager again and hang out with your friends at a disco** suggests that you are coping with life at present and not taking it too seriously. On the other hand, your dreaming mind may be urging you to chill out more. If you revisit your teenage years in your dream or dream of teenagers, your dreaming mind may be urging you to recover some of your creativity, energy and sense of freedom. If the **young man or woman in the dream was acting in an immature way**, as adolescents are prone to do, could your dream be warning you that your present behavior is stupid, immature and unproductive? If your dream featured images of **school, examinations or college**, the implication may be that you need to broaden your mind or take up new challenges. Alternatively, if school was a place of unhappy memories for you, it could be urging you to have a more positive, upbeat approach to life.

TYPICAL TEENAGE DREAMS

Although the following dreams can be experienced at any life stage, they are believed to be amongst the most common for teenage dreamers. If you dream of **burying a dead body**, you may be aware that you have killed someone, although you may not remember why or how. Your concern in the dream is to bury the body

Teenagers and dreaming

By the time a boy or girl reaches puberty, their sleep patterns and dreaming closely match those of an adult. Just like an adult, they spend about twenty-five per cent of the time in REM sleep and are biologically and intellectually able to dream the most fascinating dreams. There is a great deal going on in the life of a teenager; there are many challenges, self-doubts and new responsibilities. Just as a teenager's body is undergoing huge physical changes, a teenager's emotional world is also changing, the developmental task at this age being to form a solid identity.

All this is exciting and stimulating but most teenagers feel anxious and vulnerable too. Not surprisingly nightmares increase during adolescence, but often parents are not aware of them because teenagers do not talk about them. Adolescence is a time of introspection and self-assessment, so although your teenage child may be unwilling to discuss their dreams, they might enjoy keeping a dream journal that records significant dreams and explores possible meanings.

before someone makes a terrifying discovery and exposes you. Despite the horror of what you have done, the main issue in your dream is not the fact that you have killed someone but your desire to cover your tracks and avoid discovery. The dream is all about your need for acceptance and to rid yourself of things that are undesirable in your life. The person you have murdered represents what you would like to get rid of; that is why there is no remorse in the dream and the panic in the dream indicates your fear that people will recognize your anxiety. The teenage years are all about deciding what is or is not acceptable or desirable in your life so, not surprisingly, this dream is most common at that particular time. The things you want to bury can include parental expectation, childish hobbies or activities and so on.

During your teenage years you are very likely to dream of meeting a celebrity and becoming their close friend. This kind of dream focuses on the importance of feeling accepted and admired within your peer group. It is not uncommon for a teenager to dream about the **death or funeral of one or both parents**. Such dreams are not predictive, being simple reflections of the death of the past and the beginning of a new parent–child relationship.

YOUNG ADULTHOOD

Whether you left home at sixteen, eighteen or thirty-five, there will have been a point in your life when you struck out on your own. Your dreams during that period would have reflected your urge for independence and sense of adventure, mingled with the fear and uncertainty about your ability to cope on your own. In your early

The Element Encyclopedia of 20,000 Dreams

twenties, your dreams may therefore center on **battles** of some kind. They may also focus on your **ability to perform well at school or work**. The characters in your dream are likely to be less well focused than your own, suggesting that your adult identity is yet to emerge.

Dreams at this time may also be marked by separation anxiety. This is because most twenty-somethings do not yet have a strong sense of identity; their dreams will therefore reflect a wish to become a child again, go home or avoid growing up in some way. For example, you may dream of your grown-up self being back in your childhood bed, with your mother reading you a fairy story. Such dreams may be viewed as an attempt by your dreaming mind to fulfill parental functions yourself; in other words learning to take care of yourself in a responsible caring way.

One's twenties are also the decade in which we try on possible relationships and careers to see if we can find the perfect fit; not surprisingly, your dreams during this life stage may reflect your concerns and anxieties, often containing scenes and situations that are frantic and frustrating. Your focus may be on split-second mistakes, such as **taking wrong turns in a vehicle, being unable to find your keys, going to the wrong examination room** and so on.

By the time we reach our early thirties, we tend to be more realistic about what we can do in life and what constitutes a perfect partner; your dreams will reflect a sense of resignation but may also start to contain elements of frustration. Conflicts between what you hoped for and reality may be played out in your dreams. Many of us decide to have children in our twenties and thirties; this decision can stimulate some interesting dreams. If you are not in your twenties or early thirties, a dream about this stage in life may reflect a longing for excitement and adventure, whether you are a teenager or a pensioner.

One very common dream during our thirties is that of **missing a plane or train**. In this dream, you have packed your bags, rushed to check in but there is trouble with your ticket, seating, ID or passport. Eventually you manage to break free and run for the gate but the flight, boat or train leaves without you. This kind of dream is very common for people who are juggling responsibilities and trying to advance their careers; the plane in the dream represents your ability to move to the next stage in your career. The frustration and disappointment in the dream reflects an internal experience rather than a situation in waking life. If you have this dream, your dreaming mind is telling you that running faster, working harder or taking on more responsibilities is not always a solution.

Many young mothers have nightmares in which they **go off to do some errands and completely forget their child or children in a restaurant, office or shop**. Such a dream may be a warning that you have taken on too much. It could also be urging you to focus more on the important things in life (your children) and less on the details (your errands). If you have this dream, try and see if you can adjust your routine so that you do not neglect what is most precious to you. *See also* BIRTH AND CHILDHOOD; RELATIONSHIPS; SCHOOL AND WORK.

MIDDLE YEARS

The thirties and early forties tend to be the ones when concern about finances peak and this typically translates into working harder and longer. It can feel as if personal goals have been pushed aside, especially if you have children, and this can trigger dreams that tell you you're feeling out of control. These often take the form of dreams of **cars spinning out of control or natural disasters**. These are also the years in which proving ourselves at work or making a mark on the world comes to the fore, and this can translate into dreams of competition and aggression.

Unfortunately, during this time we tend to recall fewer dreams as we feel that we simply haven't got time to remember them or think about them. By the time we are in our forties, however, many of us begin to catch our breath and start to reflect on our lives so far. Often in the middle of our lives there is a feeling that some kind of change is essential. For example, we may explore our creative potential, go back to school, change career or partner, take up an exciting new sport, downsize and so on. If you are in your forties, your dreams may well reflect this craving for change with their **themes of adventure, romance and daring**, but if this craving isn't acknowledged, themes of conflict and aggression may feature strongly in your dreams.

The need to look back at your early promise may also prompt dreams of school, old friends or the search for a lost car. During the middle years you may also find yourself with the new-found responsibility of caring for parents with failing health. Not surprisingly dreams experienced if this is the case often involved **themes of escape** – part of you wishes to be free from this enormous responsibility. In waking life, you may take your duties seriously but this cannot stop your dreaming mind booking your parents – or parents-in-law – on a plane to nowhere or on an endless cruise. If you aren't in this stage of life, a dream about **fast forwarding or returning to your thirties and forties** will most likely reflect your growing sense of responsibility and longing to make your mark on the world.

One of the most common dreams in midlife is that of the **lost car**. You park the car and return to find it's gone. You wander anxiously around the area but cover the same ground with no results. In short, this is a dream about feeling lost because you have followed the rules rather than your instinct or intuition. If you have this dream, the indication is that some part of your waking life is unfulfilling and you feel as if you have lost something precious; you are not only upset when you recognize you have lost it but your life comes to a complete standstill. Another common dream at this time is that of a **forgotten baby or child**; in this dream, you are going about your routine as normal but hear a child or baby crying. You search for a while then discover a baby or child in the cupboard and suddenly realize that they have been in there, not for hours, but for days. You are filled with feelings of shock and regret. The baby in the dream indicates the part of yourself that was initiated and then abandoned; for example, a college education that was postponed for marriage. In other words, the child is something you began but set aside. Such dreams emerge to remind you that it is not too late to exploit your hidden potential or rediscover an idea or passion from the past.

The Element Encyclopedia of 20,000 Dreams

Aging and dreaming

As you age, your sleep patterns change; so too will the time you spend dreaming and the subjects of your dreams. By their mid-forties, many people begin to go to bed a bit earlier than they used to and sleep becomes more fragmented due to naturally occurring biological changes. However, contrary to popular opinion, the need for sleep doesn't decrease with age; the pattern of sleep may change but the need for it does not. Brain waves both in sleep and whilst awake change as you get older. The older you are, the more time you spend in the first two stages of sleep and the less time you spend in stages three and four. This means less REM sleep, and less REM sleep means that not only is your sleep less restorative but you have less time in which to dream. Because deep sleep decreases with age, it might be tempting to turn to over-the-counter sleep medications, but they can have undesired side effects. If you are having serious problems sleeping, consult your doctor; but if you are simply more wakeful and restless in the night, the DIY perfect sleep and dreaming remedies on page xxiv of the Introduction should help you sleep and dream better.

OLD AGE AND MATURITY

As we move towards maturity, we find that we are freer to explore parts of ourselves that may have been put on hold because of family or work responsibilities. During this stage of their life, men often explore more feminine or softer modes of being – or their anima – in their dreams. This usually occurs in their fifties or sixties, when they can relax more after having attained a level of mastery at work and children may have left the nest.

Women also feel freer to explore the world in bold new ways in this stage of their life. They often feel confident and full of energy; dreams in which the animus expresses itself or in which they find hidden rooms and valuables are not uncommon. Although the menopause marks the beginning of the second part of life rather dramatically for women, men are also subjected to reminders that time is chasing them and these may show up in dreams of being **chased by a tiger or escaping a fire**. Dreams of **losing teeth or body parts** at this stage of life may reflect a concern with aging and the loss of their youthful self. Additionally, dreams with **themes of impotence or loss of fertility** signal a loss of sexual power.

Dreams of **loved ones who have passed away** may also occur, both as an expression of grief and also as a way to help us accept our own mortality. Dreams about **getting sick or ill** may also reflect the typical concerns of this stage. Alongside dreams of loss and adjustment, however, dreams at this stage of life also reflect hope and renewal; for example, dreams in which you **discover hidden treasure.** You may dream of a **well drying up in your garden, but**

Recurring dreams

Recurring dreams often coincide with phases in your life and are particularly common when in transition from one life stage to another, or when you are forced to deal with a new and unknown situation. As such, they can be seen as signposts on your journey through life, providing signals about where you are heading and how you are feeling. By looking at the themes that feature in recurring dreams, you can then identify which part of your life is being indicated. Although some recurring dreams are associated with stress and trauma, when these dreams occur they offer a unique opportunity to understand what motivates you from the very deepest level. Some of the most common recurring dream themes that can occur at any life stage are as follows:

Barrier

These are dreams which express the theme of something blocking your progress through life. Dreams of **locked or forbidden rooms** fall into this category, as do **bridges that are impossible to cross**. If you often have dreams in which barriers prevent you from progressing or escaping, your dreaming mind is urging you to dissolve limiting factors in your life and in your mind. This doesn't mean all of your problems are down to negative thinking; but if you can think of problems as challenges and rejection as setbacks, your chances of success are far greater.

Hidden treasure

In dreams of **hidden treasure**, something ordinary becomes something magical; sometimes treasure or something valuable is discovered in the most unlikely place. Such a dream involves the discovery of how you fit into the world and what special gift you have to offer; this process of discovery will not be answered immediately but will run the course of your life. Often the dream will be hinting that the way you don't fit into the world will be your greatest strength. In other words, stop trying to change your essential nature and look closely at the things you take for granted.

Life and death struggle

The struggle for survival in dreamland is reflected in symbols such as **quicksand, dangerous animals, wildfire, war and enemies**; these all suggest the need to find a kind of security that cannot be taken away from you. If you are prone to life-and-death struggles in your dreams, your dreaming mind is telling you that there is only one way to find the security that cannot be lost: you need to place value on things that are not material, as everything else is at risk. The things that cannot be lost reside in your heart and your spirit. This doesn't mean you should stop focusing on the material in life; it simply means that you need to find peace and content-

ment by being more flexible and tolerant in waking life.

Recurring character

You may dream of a **particular person
who appears repeatedly** in your
dreams. This may be someone you are
related to or close to, but it could also be
someone you barely know or even
someone who is no longer alive. When a
recurring character appears in your
dream it is often because they are associated with a particular feeling or set of
experiences, and even if you no longer
keep in touch with that person, they can
still appear in your dream when you are
affected by types of feelings you had
when you knew them. In other words,
recurring characters are often pictures
of patterns that are operating in your
present-day life. Sometimes recurring
characters can also represent qualities
you possess but are not using, or qualities you admire but do not feel you have.
In general, when it comes to recurring
characters, if this person is someone you
feel positive about they represent qualities you can and should apply to your
current life. Those people you associate
with painful memories tend to represent
feelings and patterns that are affecting
you in your current experiences.

Recurring object

If a **specific object or objects appears
and reappears** in your dream, it tends
to point out a valuable perspective or
new approach towards a problem. Try
to take note of the function of the object,
what purpose it serves and in what kind
of situation you would be likely to find it,
as it can show how your response to a
situation can be improved. For example,
a **set of embroidery needles** may
suggest you should pay more attention
to detail, whereas a **hammer** would
suggest you might profit from a direct,
hard-hitting approach.

Recurring symbol

Symbols in dreams generally occur
because they illustrate a quality or function, or because of the association you
may have with them. So if particular
symbols, such as a **jungle setting,
theme park or castle** appear in your
dream, this is because these particular
images express something significant
about the way you feel or because they
offer you a key to understanding a
particular challenge. If a particular
landscape or setting of a dream reoc-
curs, it tends to illustrate the way something affects you or how it makes you
feel.

Rejection

In this kind of dream **trusted friends or
allies end up betraying you or
murdering you**. If you are prone to this
kind of dream, the chances are you are
extremely loyal, kind, helpful and
unselfish in waking life and your dreaming mind is urging you to say 'no more'
in an attempt to try and put your own
needs first for once.

then discover a casket of treasure at the bottom of the well, which suggests the uncovering of hidden resources and new opportunities. If you aren't in this stage of life and dream of it, your dream is most likely reflecting your hunger for the wisdom, calmness and maturity that only age and experience can bring.

Typical dreams of later life

Dreams in later life can be extremely tense and memorable; two of the most common are dreams of losing your purse or wallet and dreams of getting lost. The former dream reflects frustration and anxiety, and the experience of change as loss and threat. The latter is about trying to find your way through a situation that seems unfamiliar. In this second dream you typically find yourself in a strange neighborhood and, if you do stop to ask for directions, people give you the wrong ones. This dream represents a situation that is unfamiliar; the advice of others is not only unhelpful, it can actually make matters more confusing. The dream is reminding you that the more closely you follow your instincts or intuition, the easier it will be to find your way home or have self-knowledge.

The Final Stage

Dead person/Corpse

To dream of a dead person or corpse usually represents some aspect of your life that has died. It can refer to the death of

feelings in connection with someone, to the depression that follows big changes in your life or to the feeling that you are going nowhere. Alternatively, the dead person may be a part of yourself that you want to leave behind or it could be a warning that you are taking too much from life and not putting enough back. If you dreamed of the death of a loved one who is seriously ill or advanced in years, your unconscious may have been preparing you for their future departure from your life. By exposing you in the dream to emotions that will overwhelm you, your shock may be lessened and thus easier to bear.

Dreams such as this one may also be urging you to tell loved ones how much they mean to you before it is too late. If, in your dream, you felt no emotion at all when a loved one died, the interpretation is likely to be different, as it represents something in your life that is coming to an end or that should end. An alternative explanation is that you fear the death of your relationship, particularly if your partner has withdrawn emotionally from you in the waking world. A dream in which you became a widow or widower or suffer bereavement can indicate feelings of loneliness in waking life. If you are in a relationship, such a dream may suggest that there is a lack of understanding or a communication breakdown between you and your partner. For dreams of a dead person *see* GHOSTS.

Death

Death is the final change we all must face and also the most mysterious and frightening, so it is small wonder that anxieties concerning it are pushed to the back of your

Near-death experience

A **near-death experience** (NDE) is a phenomenon reported by people who have been declared clinically dead by medical experts, or passed close to death through accident or illness, but are later revived. They report an altered state of consciousness in which they feel they are traveling through a tunnel towards a warm and bright light or they are floating above their body watching medical efforts to revive them. Intriguingly, near-death reports from different cultures around the world are generally consistent and in many instances are identical to the features of the post-mortem state that is described in the *Tibetan Book of the Dead*. There is also a marked similarity between NDEs and reports of the inner journeys of shamanism, astral travel and out-of-body experiences.

The term 'near-death experience' was coined by American doctor Raymond Moody in the 1970s to describe the phenomenon outlined above. Prior to publication of Moody's book, *Life After Life* in 1975, NDEs were not openly talked about; once the book came out, more and more people began to talk about them. By 1982 a Gallup poll suggested that as many as eight million Americans had had some kind of NDE. Moody and a number of other NDE researchers, such as Kenneth Ring, a psychologist and founding member of the International Association of Near Death Studies at the University of Connecticut, were able to identify a number of traits common to all NDEs, even though the experience was always unique to each individual. They concluded that in a NDE, people typically experience one or more of the following phenomena in this sequence: a sense of leaving the material world behind or an out-of-body experience in which they feel they are floating above their bodies looking down; cessation of pain, a feeling of great calm and peace; traveling down a dark tunnel towards a light at its end; meeting spirit beings, many of whom are dead friends and relatives; meeting a spirit guide who takes them through their life story and puts their life into perspective without any negative judgment; and, finally, an abrupt and sometimes reluctant return to life.

The great majority of NDEs are described as being positive and uplifting; around three per cent are described as negative or frightening. Almost anyone can have the experience and it is not limited to those who have religious beliefs, although many people who have experienced a NDE do become more religious or develop a spiritual belief system afterwards. Almost all say they lose their fear of death, this being replaced by a strong belief in an afterlife. Many discover a meaning and purpose to their lives that they may have previously lacked. In some cases, the NDE leaves a person with heightened intuitive or psychic powers.

Even though millions of people claim to have had an NDE, it is impossible for researchers to prove scientifically that the experience is genuine. Evidence is therefore based entirely on anecdotal reports. According to skeptics, the NDE is a dream or hallucination caused by, amongst other things, a lack of oxygen, the release of the body's natural pain killers called endorphins and increased levels of carbon dioxide as the brain dies. NDEs were reportedly reproduced by Ronald Siegel, a researcher at the University of California, Los Angeles School of Medicine, when LSD and other drugs were administered. NDE supporters stress, however, that drug-induced hallucinations and NDEs are totally different things. Such explanations also do not take into account the fact that many people brought back to life can give accurate accounts of their resuscitations, of medical procedures carried out on them or report conversations they overheard at the time they were allegedly dead. This suggests that some part of consciousness can separate from the body at death. There is no doubt that the near-death experiences are supported by impressive documentation and, for believers in them, these reports constitute a very powerful argument for the existence of an afterlife.

conscious mind during waking hours. You cannot banish them completely though and when your unconscious forces you to experience dreams of death and dying, it does so for a purpose. For example, if you know someone who is ill or mature in years, your unconscious may be preparing you for the actual event. If you dream of a **deceased loved one**, this may be to comfort or enlighten you. Dreams of **your own death, or the death or execution of loved ones** are extremely frightening but also extremely common. Such dreams rarely signify death. **Sad or traumatic losses** in dreams typically signify change, a fresh start and new beginnings. A dream in which **you attended your own funeral or the funeral of someone else, or walked through a cemetery or crematorium** does not mean that you or someone you know will die soon; your dreaming mind is simply preparing you for change.

So if you have dreams about death, try to think about which change or changes in waking life might have triggered them. Death signifies the end of one phase but also rebirth and the beginning of another; these types of dream typically occur at major turning points in your life, such as leaving home or getting married. Another interpretation suggests that these dreams are exploring your feelings about death and dying, or else they mirror waking feelings of oppression and depression. Try not to be frightened when you have dreams of death, for, as Jung put it, 'when it is a dream of death, the dream speaks another language'.

DEATH SENTENCE

A dream in which **you received a death sentence or were being led to your execution or are requesting euthanasia** is a rather dramatic way of symbolizing the need to change a certain aspect of your life as soon as possible. If you dreamed that **you were waiting for your execution, perhaps even standing on a platform with a blindfold on**, this suggests feelings of guilt in waking life or the refusal to acknowledge some feeling or action. Your dreaming mind is urging you to make amends, or express or even confess to something before it is too late. Also ask yourself whether you feel you are dead meat or a dead man walking in waking life, whether you are in danger of losing your head or are waiting for the axe to fall. If, however, **you were the executioner** in the dream, who or what do you need to put to death or put an end to in waking life? If the person you needed to kill was unknown to you, is there an unpleasant task or duty that you must execute in waking life?

If you dreamed of **someone being sacrificed**, perhaps even yourself, the message may be that the well-being of your family, loved ones or community needs to take precedence right now over your own hopes and desires. If the impending martyrdom upset or angered you in your dream, your waking mind was probably mirroring your feelings of resentment in waking life at having to make a sacrifice. Try to see who was wielding the sacrifice in your dream. If it is someone you know, are they making demands on you and are these demands reasonable?

FUNERAL

If you are part of a **funeral party led by an undertaker towards a grave**, your unconscious may be suggesting the possibility of great change in your life. Bear in mind, too, that ill is rarely spoken of the dead at funerals, so perhaps you are in need of a confidence boost in waking life or perhaps you want your friends and family to appreciate you more. If the **funeral is your own**, try to identify who the mourners were and what they said about you. In the realm of the unconscious, funerals are susceptible to much the same interpretation as dreams about death, so ask yourself whether you are worried about your health or whether there is something in your life or personality you need to lay to rest. The dream funeral may even have represented the end of a relationship or particular phase in your life.

An **undertaker** in a dream may represent an authority figure or someone in waking life who undertakes a difficult but necessary task for those who cannot do it themselves. Are you the undertaker carrying a burden of responsibility or, if someone else is the undertaker, are you trying to pass the burden to them? If **you see a coffin or are about to be buried** in your dream, it is likely that the change is already occurring. As well as being symbols of death, thereby denoting the end of a certain stage in life, dream **coffins** also represent loneliness, isolation and a sense of hopelessness. By featuring a coffin in a dream or depicting you in it, your dreaming mind may be suggesting that you feel unable to rise above the problems that are trying to bury you or box you in. If your dreaming mind conjured up images of a **burial**, what life phase or feeling is about to be dead and buried for you in waking life? Dream **cremations** send the same message, although the symbol of **fire and ashes** does hint at potential and perhaps immediate rebirth.

Tombstone/Grave

If the **name of someone you know appears on a dream tombstone**, ask yourself which characteristics you associate with that person and whether or not you should eradicate or change (kill) these characteristics in yourself. If your attitude was sad in the dream, perhaps you need to reconsider your attitude towards that person and what they represent to you. For example, ask yourself if you need to be more polite, kind or unselfish if these are the qualities you associate with the person. If the vision was of **your own grave**, this suggests problems you need to dig your way out of; if a **grave is neglected**, this is a reminder from your subconscious not to take your health or the good things in your life for granted. If the **tombstone was of someone you knew or loved who has died**, you may also simply be experiencing a sense of nostalgia for those happy days when you could pay them a real-life visit. If, however, the person is not dead, this could be a warning that your relationship is in danger of dying unless you concentrate on keeping it alive in real life.

If a **vault** appears in your dream, this suggests a more tentative approach to change; in older cemeteries it is possible to peer into family vaults to see the coffins, so perhaps you are aware of the need for change but are not yet able to make a clean break with the past. If you had to **visit a mortuary** in your dream, is this a sign that you do not want to let go of the past? Do lingering feelings of guilt or regret remain? Or has the past caught up with you? If you dream of **your own coat of arms and can see it on a tomb or monument**, this reflects a desire to rise above a perceived station and to be accepted by those you incorrectly assume to be your superiors. A common nightmare is to dream of being **buried alive**. This may be a symbol of guilt or it may suggest a need to move away from a bad influence that is threatening to overwhelm you. *See also* NIGHTMARES.

Violent death

If you **watch a murder**, this refers to aspects of yourself that have been denied expression. If you are **running from a murder** in your dream, it depicts something you feel threatened by in waking life. If **you are the murderer**, this may express intense emotional hurt towards someone, typically parents; the murder itself will be a symbol of the killing of the emotional bond or a warning that you are on an emotional 'knife's edge'. Dreams in which you kill someone may also point towards an internal conflict, especially if you harbor no ill will towards your dream victim in real life, or indeed if they were a stranger or an animal. If **someone provoked you into killing them** in your dream, this may tell you what it is about yourself that you need to kill off. **Animals** symbolize aspects of your instinctual nature in dreams, so if you **killed a cat, dog or any other animal** in your dream, ask yourself what that animal represents within you. If **someone is trying to kill you** in your dream, your unconscious may be alerting you not to a physical threat but to a real emotional or professional threat that someone poses to you. If you were unable to identify the dream killer, your unconscious may have been suggesting to you that you are being victimized in waking life by a person, a group or an organization.

Dreams in which you are **choking or strangled** suggest conflict or indecision, as when you choke on your words. They can also suggest repressed emotions, or emotions or memories struggling to be recognized. Because it is associated with the element of water, **drowning** indicates a sense of being overwhelmed by difficult emotions or problems. If the symbol of the **guillotine** appears in your dream, you may be afraid of losing self-control or of losing contact with a part of yourself or someone you value. The guillotine also represents severance of some kind, so what is it that you need to cut out of your life? If someone is **poisoned** in your dream, this refers to attitudes, thoughts and behavior patterns that are not good for you. If **you commit suicide** in dreams, it may depict a sense of hopelessness; perhaps you have been working too hard lately and haven't been taking care of your health. Or do you feel a desire to retreat from life's problems or suffer from feelings of failure? It may also be a sign of repressed anger concerning relationships or business. If **someone else is committing suicide** in your dream, this could be a sign that you want them out of your life.

YOUR OWN DEATH

Dreams in which **you appear dead or are dying** are unlikely to presage your actual death. If you were **struck down by a disease** in your dream, then your unconscious may have been amplifying fears about your health in waking life. Alternatively, dreams which feature your death could also symbolize your desire to escape the burdens and responsibilities of waking life. Another explanation suggests that your dreaming mind has used your death as a symbol for something that has run its course in your waking life, encouraging you to start afresh with someone new or to make a change. Freud believed that everyone has two contending basic drives; eros – the drive towards pleasure and life – and thanatos – the drive towards death. If the dead person in your dreams was yourself, you might want to consider what is being expressed in your dream. Perhaps you fear dying and the dream is reminding you of your own mortality. Or are you trying to liberate yourself from something? Do you want to free yourself of emotional burdens and open yourself up to new possibilities?

SURREALISM AND FANTASY

When your dreaming mind conjures up fantasy images, you are being powerfully influenced by unconscious forces.

According to Freud, fantasies develop in childhood in response to sexual desire and aggressive impulses. Jung also claimed that fantasy developed very early in life as a safety net to help the child deal with real conflicts in the family, conflicts that may be too difficult or painful to deal with directly. Jung observed that childhood fantasies include many mythological themes that may be inherent in everyone. He believed that fairy tales and myths do not differ fundamentally from dreams and speak in the same symbolic language. The archetypal images stir something in the unconscious part of yourself; they are dramatic symbolic projections of your identity.

In dreams, fantasy is unrestricted and moral judgment is suspended. Dreams can therefore reveal your most secret desires and the fantasies you experience in your dreams say a lot about you, often helping you tackle problems you might normally repress or deny. If you can understand what your dream is highlighting, you can gain important insight into yourself. Fantasy dreams highlight problems, offer solutions, show what aspects of yourself may be limit-ing your progress and help you discover new approaches. In other words, fantasy dreams, like all dreams, can help you change and progress. *See also* MIND, BODY, SPIRIT; NIGHTMARES; SPIRITS AND GHOSTS.

Fantasia

ANGEL/VIRGIN

At first glance, it would seem that the **angel and the virgin** represent the Christian faith, but both actually predate it. The virgin was known as Isis to the Egyptians, Myrrha to the Greeks and Juno to the Romans. In each incarnation she may be seen standing on the crescent moon with stars circling her head. The virgin, in whatever guise she reaches your dreams, is considered a symbol of good fortune. Pay attention to what she is holding in her hands. If she carries a **ray of sunlight**, this represents spiritual progress. If she carries a **chalice of dew**, this may be seen as encouragement to reform your ways, and if she is playing a **lyre**, this suggests a period of calmness and introspection.

Angels are another form of celestial messenger sent to guard over us. To imagine one appearing is, as with the virgin, a symbol of spiritual protection and inspiration. If **angels give you advice** in a dream, what they tell you should always be taken very seriously. Nowadays, with a greater acceptance of the appearance of angelic figures, they are once again accepted as messengers of enlightenment. If you are religious, visions of an angel in your dream may be taken as validation of belief, but if you are not religious, you can take solace in the thought that you have a spiritual protector watching over you. Another interpretation suggests that dreaming of an angel suggests you are searching for this unconditional love and support in waking life, and the dream is urging you to find these qualities within yourself. *See also* Goddess entry in RELIGION.

Damnation

Your dreaming mind may at times employ sinister symbolism to address what it perceives to be the darker side of human nature. It has a wealth of material to call upon from both religion and mythology. There may be **imps from hell** to drag you into a fiery torment, **demons of plague and pestilence, Beelzebub the 'Lord of the Flies', Asmodeus the demon of anger and lust**, and a host of other **demons, fiends and evil spirits in the form of toads, serpents, hobgoblins and elves**. Each represents darker aspects of your own nature, perhaps a fear of the unknown that

is not expressed in waking life, perhaps your frustrated desires and loss of control. Dreams of the **devil** himself (or modern representations of evil such as **Darth Vader** from *Star Wars* or **Lord Voldemort** from the Harry Potter books) may be seen as a representation of your dark, unconscious and baser urges. For Jungians, such a figure would be the ultimate shadow archetype. Devil dreams tend to occur when people are breaking with tradition in some way. They may also be related to evil or negative influences within yourself, possibly linking to a recent or impending decision or action of yours in waking life. *See also* Devil entry in RELIGION.

Monsters may present, in hideous form, untamed impulses that fill you with disgust and loathing. By giving these impulses a monstrous rather than a human form, you can evade personal responsibility for them. Many dreamers report feelings of a great weight on their chest and a sense of great evil. Sometimes the dreamer sees a figure who is sexually rapacious. These figures are known as **incubi and succubi** and they are demons in the form of imps. They were often included in paintings in the medieval period and symbolize the uncontrolled world of dreams and desire. If you are able to **kill your dream demon or evil spirit**, this may help you resolve your innermost fears in waking life. *See also* NIGHTMARES; SPIRITS AND GHOSTS.

Fabulous and fabled settings

On occasion your dream may select a **fabulous and fabled place** to add weight to its message. For example, if you dream of **visiting the legendary place of Atlantis** or the sacred realm of Avalon, this suggests a yearning for spiritual fulfillment in waking life. To dream of the **pyramids** is neither uncommon nor surprising, given that their symbolism goes to the core of humanity's search for understanding of its place within the universe. A dream featuring the **Great Pyramid of Khufu** suggests the ability to overcome obstacles, because its geometry symbolizes an ancient mystery. **Mazes** may also appear in dreams; their meaning is dependent on whether or not you found your way or got lost. The classic symbolism of **Theseus** (you the dreamer) in the **labyrinth** (the entanglements of your real life) guided by the **spiritual thread** (your intuition) to slay the **Minotaur** (your debased animalistic side) may filter into your dream. If you find your **way out of the maze**, this suggests the end of a mystery or the resolution of a dilemma in waking life. *See also* BUILDINGS.

FAIRY TALES

Fairy tales are full of rich psychological symbolism that expresses our innermost fears and dreams. Beginning with the fathers of the field, Sigmund Freud and Carl Jung, numerous psychoanalysts have turned to fairy tales in an effort to understand the human mind. Just as many fairy tales hinge upon a revelation of the truth about those who have been somehow disguised, so too fairy tales cut to the essence of adult identity. Freud suspected that dreams and fairy tales stemmed from the same place, and the relaxation of inhibition that occurs in the dream state is also true of many storytellers. So fairy tales might prove, as with dreams, to be windows opening into the unconscious. (Indeed,

many fairy tales include dream-states as important plot points.) For Freud, fairy tales are rife with wish-fulfillment fantasies and complicated sexual undercurrents.

As far as Jung was concerned, the 'collective unconscious' that lies at the core of his work, and which he believed is shared by all human beings, is revealed through archetypes, forms and symbols found in ample quantity in fairy tales. Jungian therapists study fairy tales to help analyze the dreams of their patients. Jung's disciples have gone on to interpret fairy tales as lives in miniature, suggesting, for example, that each character within a tale may represent an aspect of human personality.

More recently, perhaps the best-known – and certainly the most widely-quoted – psychologist to incorporate fairy tales into their practice is Bruno Bettelheim, who published *Uses of Enchantment: The Meaning and Importance of Fairy Tales* in 1976. Bettelheim argued that fairy tales are an important tool for children learning to navigate reality and survive in a world ruled by adults. The family conflicts and moral education of the protagonists (conveniently often children themselves) could provide models of coping. Others have disputed aspects of this interpretation. The German cultural critic and philosopher Walter Benjamin notes that the morality of fairy tales is rather complicated, with the heroes and heroines often known to lie, cheat, steal and torture villains. But there remains something empowering and psychologically insightful in these stories that, as fairy tale scholar Maria Tatar writes, demonstrate the 'triumph of small and weak over tall and powerful'.

To sum up: one of the most useful functions of the fairy tale is to use fantasy to

The Element Encyclopedia of 20,000 Dreams

help address the problems of growing up. During the course of the fairy tale, the hero or heroine is taken on a journey to greater self-awareness and psychological wholeness. In a child's life there may be many conflicts and the fairy tale helps the child express the hostility these situations may cause. Many psychologists recommend fairy tales as beneficial to children, believing they help children assimilate problems such as violence, sexuality, growing up and learning to deal with family conflict. In many ways, fantasy dreams share the same functions as fairy tales; not only do they provide a healthy outlet for socially unacceptable behavior, they can also empower the dreamer and teach hidden lessons.

FICTIONAL CHARACTER

In dreams, **fictional characters** that do not exist in everyday life may appear. For example, you may dream of sharing a birthday party with a twin sister you don't have in waking life; perhaps a character from your favorite TV show, movie or novel appears in your dreams. All your dreams are connected in some way with your life, so just because these people don't exist in real life doesn't mean they are less meaningful in dreamland or have any less resemblance to your waking life. In general, fictional characters exaggerate the qualities found in someone close to you so you can better understand the dynamics of the relationship or situation; one might say that the characters are often one dimensional so that their message is more easily understood. For example, **Darth Vader** from the *Star Wars* movies may represent, or highlight, a mean streak that your boss is displaying. And fictional characters can also reflect an aspect of yourself that has relevance to your waking life. If this is the case, they usually do so to let you know the source of your current problem or to remind you of qualities you didn't know you had. For example, dreaming about **Scarlet O'Hara** from *Gone with the Wind* may remind you that you are tougher and more resilient than you think you are.

MAGIC AND SORCERY

In past centuries, because of their supposed malignant influence, **witches** were often made a scapegoat for the calamities that affected society. It is little surprise, therefore, that in dreams they are regarded as harbingers of evil. To dream that you **fall under the influence of a witch** may suggest that you are surrendering to your baser instincts in waking life to your own personal detriment. **Wizards** have a less negative connotation in dreams and are usually concerned with ritualistic magic, control over natural forces and raising the consciousness of the divine. The wisdom of the wizard is born of age and experience, so if a wizard appears in your dreams, this is symbolic of a desire to reach a higher plane of consciousness. On the other hand, an occult male figure in your dream may represent an **alchemist**. Alchemists believe that a human is a microcosm of the universe and all things in the universe exist within humanity. The alchemist dedicates his life both to the search for the elixir of life and to the transmutation of base metal into gold. Because of these associations, his presence in a dream is considered empowering. *See also* SPIRITS AND GHOSTS.

Fairy tales and symbolism

The symbolism in fairy tales speaks to adults as well as children, and deals with childlessness, sexual maturation, remarriage, jealousy across the generations, sibling rivalry, incest, murderous rage, inheritance issues and other timeless problems. If you find yourself **transported to the scene of a well-known fairy tale**, the following tips may help with the interpretation. First of all, consider what common fairy tale motif your dream scene is depicting. For example, it could be:

Courtship tale

A strong theme in many fairy tales is the idea that love and goodness triumph. In the animal bridegroom tale, the **girl protagonist marries some kind of beast, who is transformed by love in the course of the story into a (usually handsome) prince**. In your waking life, do you feel you deserve the reward of love and security for your efforts? Do you believe love can conquer all? Or is your dream urging you to reconcile your masculine and feminine attitudes in waking life?

Good and bad choice

Most fairy tales involve a moment when the protagonist is faced with a choice. These include: **helpless people or creatures to be kind or beastly to; opportunities to tell the truth or lie, or cheat or be honest; a choice to stand up for your principles or betray the innocent and submit to tyranny**. If someone's inside and outside are at odds, typically by the end of the tale the two are reconciled (as in the Beast's transformation in 'Beauty and the Beast'). Notice the elemental justice of this fairy tale motif and see whether you can relate any of its themes to your waking life.

Magical gift

A mirror that allows one to see one's heart's desire (or one's loved ones); a table that sets itself with food and dishes; a stick that beats one's enemies; a goose that lays golden eggs; a pouch that replenishes itself with gold. Consider the symbolism of these motifs. To what gift or hidden quality is your dream referring?

Magical Helper

These would include: **an old crone, a talking frog, a fairy godmother, a swan to convey one across a river, a bird that carries one in his claws**. Also, and not always in a helping role, one might encounter magical creatures such as **witches, ogres, fairies, mermaids, unicorns, trolls, gnomes and dragons**. Consider the symbolism of any helpers, or non-helpers, that appear in your dream; they represent psychological energy or strength that you either possess or need to find. What qualities do they represent, and how will they help or hinder you?

The 'Rule of Three'

Many fairy tales, as well as many dreams, seem to obey what might be called the 'rule of three'. They may contain **three characters** ('Goldilocks and the Three Bears', 'The Three Little Pigs', 'The Three Billy Goats Gruff'); **three wishes; three tasks that a prince (or princess) must do to win his (or her) true love; three times for a request or saying to be repeated** ('I'll huff, and I'll puff …'). If you find yourself in a story in which three is significant, *see* NUMBERS.

Trial or test to win one's love

Going 'east of the sun and west of the moon' and bringing back a treasure; learning the answer to a riddle; spinning straw into gold (and guessing Rumpelstiltskin's name); breaking through the 100-year-old forest to find the sleeping princess. Can you relate such tests to your waking life? What trials and tribulations do you need to overcome?

Remember that these stories have been told and retold for centuries because they have resonated with their hearers and expressed something important to their audiences. So if scenes from a specific fairy tale appear in your dream, consider the symbolism of the fairy tale motif, and see how the story and the lessons it teaches apply to your waking life.

If a specific character appears in your dream out of context from his, her or its fairy tale, for example **Cinderella** wandering the streets of New York on her own, **Sleeping Beauty** buying a house or **Puss in Boots** accompanying you on a train journey, consider what aspect of yourself or your life the character represents. So if you find yourself having lunch with **Rapunzel** in your dreams, think about the symbolism of her hair, which was cut off to punish the girl for her indiscretion. Is there something you feel guilty about in waking life or should feel guilty about? Or do you feel imprisoned in an ivory tower and long for freedom of expression?

Finally, don't forget that, above all, fairy tales encourage you to believe in possibilities and the hidden 'magic' that can be discovered in the most unexpected places.

Magical Creatures

Centaur

Part horse, part human, the **centaur** combines human intelligence and warmth with the characteristics of the horse. In dreams, it may appear as a caution against hasty activity or behavior. It may also represent the fusion of the horse's strength and stamina with a human's intellect and skills; the result is a successful union between the conscious and the unconscious minds, something for which your dream may be urging you to aim, particularly if the **centaur was holding a bow and arrow**. The centaur is also the symbol of the Zodiac sign of Sagittarius, so could your dream have been referring to someone you know who was born under that sign?

Dragon

Fierce and fire-breathing, the **dragon** is a potent animal of dream-lore that is neither good nor evil, male nor female, light nor dark, but a symbol of the primal energy that upholds the world. The dragon embodies the union of opposites and the four elemental energies: of fire in its breath, air as it uses its wings, water because of its serpent scales, and earth as it dwells in caverns. In Chinese belief, the dragon is one of the creatures of the Chinese Zodiac, the Year of the Dragon being said to bestow energy, enthusiasm and charisma.

By contrast, Christianity brands the dragon as the embodiment of Satan, an evil creature who must be slain by the saintly hero; Jungian theory, meanwhile, suggests that the dragon may be a form taken by the terrible mother archetype who must be rendered powerless before freedom can be attained (we echo this personification in waking life when we call a fierce woman 'a dragon'). So if you share the Chinese view of the dragon, your unconscious may have been trying to instill optimism by summoning it into your dream. If you are influenced by the Western view of dragons, your mind may have been trying to alert you to a hostile person or presence in your life.

Dragons were also said to be guardians of treasure, so your unconscious could have highlighted a desire to undergo a dynamic process of inner renewal. The **fire-breathing dragon** in your dream may be a symbol of great inner strength and vision that the dreamer can draw upon to overcome doubt. It also may be urging you to come to terms with and confront your own passions and chaotic beliefs; the only way to do this may be through your dreams.

Fairy

Fairy is a collective term for many different beings, often tiny, beautiful, delicate and possessing magical powers. Many fairies have a human form, but some have animal or human/animal shapes. **Elves, goblins, gnomes, dwarves and trolls** are the most representative of Faerie races among the many different cultures of Europe. Some cultures believe that fairies – also called 'fae' or 'fey' – are real beings who can direct the powers of nature. As 'devas', they help plants grow and thrive when called upon for their help. Some also believe that fairies can play tricks on humans and blame them when shiny, pretty items such as jewelry are lost. If one appeases the fairies by leaving treats or trinkets in the garden, they may be less mischievous.

Other cultures believe that fairies are both male and female and the image of butterfly innocence and sweetness may in fact be a deceptive one, as fairies were traditionally malevolent towards humans. In dreams, these old beliefs may linger and fairies may be regarded as untrustworthy beings that foreshadow trouble. Fairies in dreams may be of either sex but are typically female. For Freudians, they can represent incest fantasies with a female relative. In the symbolism of dreams, fairies can also hint at your own latent powers or potential, so if your eyes were captured by a **vision of a host of ethereal fairies dancing in the moonlight**, was your unconscious encouraging you to discover your own inner magic potential? In the dream world, fairies can also represent hopes and desires. Maybe you've been going through a bad time, and have been wishing that your fairy godmother would appear and make it all go away with her magic wand.

If a **woman dreams of fairies**, it can symbolize the nurturing, maternal and feminine side of herself. **Fairies in men's dreams** might represent the anima, the female aspect of the personality or, in line with its colloquial sense, repressed homosexual urges. When we accept and integrate both our masculine and feminine traits, we can achieve emotional balance. What was the role of the fairy in your dream? Were your wishes granted or did you fly away to some faraway land? If **you were the fairy in your dream**, what kind of power did you have? How did you use it? You may need to get in touch with the magical side of your personality and believe that you really do have the power within you to make your dreams come true.

Giant/Ogre

An encounter with a **giant or ogre** in your dream suggests an uphill struggle in waking life. The giant or ogre may also be a symbol of insecurity or feeling small, perhaps reminding you of your childhood when adults seemed huge. Maybe you had a dream in which you were **running as fast as you could from an ogre**, a hideous giant-like being who seemed intent on devouring you. If you had a nightmare like this, it could represent your father or some other figure of masculine authority, such as a demanding teacher. On the other hand, a dream giant may represent spiritual or physical power. A **giant among men** in your dream may be a guide who comes to give you spiritual insight.

Not all giants are ogres, and maybe you dreamed of being **rescued from the ogre's clutches by a gentle giant**, perhaps another influential figure in your life who you respect for their moral courage. Any **towering presence** in your dreams tends to represent either something that poses a problem to you, or someone whose power makes you feel protected, or small and helpless.

Leprechaun/Goblin

In Irish mythology, a **leprechaun** is a type of male elf said to inhabit the island of Ireland. They are a class of 'faerie folk' associated in Irish mythology and folklore, as with all faeries, with the Tuatha Dé Danann and other quasi-historical races said to have inhabited Ireland before the arrival of the Celts. They usually take the form of an old man and enjoy partaking in mischief. Their trade is that of a cobbler or shoemaker and they are often described as being seen working on a single shoe. They are said to be very rich, having many treasure crocks buried during war-time. If anyone keeps his eye fixed upon them, they cannot escape, but the moment the eye is withdrawn they vanish. To **see a leprechaun** in your dream, suggests that you will reap the benefits and rewards of your hard work through perseverance and dedication. Alternatively, you may need reminding of the importance of keeping your focus on the task in hand. To dream that **you are a leprechaun** refers to the mischievous aspect of your personality.

In folklore, a **goblin** is a small grotesque creature that likes to cause trouble for humans. Some dream interpreters suggest that dreaming of a goblin suggests an awareness that you haven't been as helpful as you could be, the dream goblin representing a secret desire to change the way you act.

Mermaid/Merman/Siren

The sea temptress combines beauty with vanity and lures sailors to their doom. If you are a man and you dream of **mermaids and sirens**, this may represent the image of a woman who you feel you could love, but who may also reject and destroy you. To dream that you follow her siren song suggests shallow will-power, or being easily misled by lust and base passion. So potent is this myth that the word siren is today used to describe a heartless, treacherous but irresistibly seductive woman. Alternatively, the mermaid may represent your anima, the feminine part of your personality, who, by leading you out to sea, is encouraging you to explore the depths of your own emotions. Traditionally, the mermaid or merman belongs to the sea as well as the land and this symbolizes an ability to be deeply emotional and deeply practical at the same time.

In a woman's dream, the mermaid is thought to represent a love rival. Finally, mermaids and mermen are feminine and masculine images of the link between your conscious self and darker forces you may not understand. Many stories tell of the difficulties of mating with a creature from the sea, showing how difficult it can be to unite the two sides of our nature.

Ouroborus

The **Ouroborus** is a mythical snake from ancient Egypt that swallows its tail, dreams may also indicate that some situation in your waking life is fundamentally unworkable. If **your body or face is distorted** in your dream, it suggests you suffer from low self-esteem or have a body image issues, but if **other people are distorted**, is there someone in waking life that you distrust? **Sex reversal** dreams may suggest wish-fulfillment or simple curiosity, as well as the need to explore your anima or animus. **A painting or a sculpture coming to life** in a dream may be inviting you to become less inhibited. Is it time to become more animated and show the creative side of your personality? **One object transforming into another** can mean a wish to make changes in waking life; the two objects involved may suggest what direction that change will take. For example, a **pen turning into a book** may point to a desire to stop gathering information and to get to grips with the task in hand.

Talking animals may signal a need to draw on the instinctive side of your nature for inspiration and encouragement, whereas **animals transforming into humans** suggests the opposite: a desire to transcend instincts of which you may feel ashamed. If, however, a **person transforms into an animal**, this may suggest a desire to explore the deeper levels of your unconscious. If you, or someone else, in your dream transform from a **person into a plant or tree**, this may suggest a need to withdraw from the world for a while. On the other hand, it could warn against being rooted to the spot, or being unwilling to make changes. The transformation of a **plant into a person** suggests some form of awakening, as when inertia finally gives way to action.

Myth and Legend

One amazing aspect of dreaming is that it can introduce you to ancient mythological figures of whom you thought you knew nothing. Jung put this well when he said that 'The great ones of the past have not died, as we think; they have merely changed their names.' Our dreams may also relate to modern legends, such as those from the *Star Wars* or *Superman* films or from the Harry Potter books. Our distant ancestors lived with the dangers and uncertainties of an existence that drove them to seek comfort in beliefs that reached far beyond the bounds of reason. They lived in a world where the magical and mythological was accepted without question. Despite the efforts of established religion and science to impose their own belief systems, these ancient beliefs in gods, spirits and superheroes continue to haunt, fascinate and enchant us with the mysterious images that seep into our sleeping world.

The myths of the ancient Greeks and Romans survive because the human characteristics they represent are universal: love, lust, anger, fear, greed and so on. Such human characteristics are the basic stuff of the stories the ancients dreamed up, and, according to Jungians, these myths lie deep in our unconscious. The personalities of myth may only be recognized by those who study them but, by recognizing their characteristics and studying them, you can learn a lot about yourself. Any character that appears prominently in your dream will be worth measuring against the mythological figure it closely resembles. The following are some of the most well-known myths and legends, but the list is by no means comprehensive.

ACHILLES

Achilles, like others before and after him, is the archetypal hero with a fatal flaw. In his case, this flaw is his uncontrollable rage that has its physical counterpart in his heel, the one vulnerable part of his body. In dreams, powerful figures with a debilitating weakness – such as the corrupt business-man, the crooked policeman or the boss with weakness for alcohol – may warn us against complacency and a false sense of security.

APHRODITE/VENUS

The ancient goddess of love symbolizes a loving sexuality that encourages you to be at ease with your body and your sexuality. Her appearance in your dream generally signals that your love life is healthy and fruitful. Ancillary romantic gods include **Eros**, the god of sexual desire and his Roman form, **Cupid**; they indicate the playful part of desire and the effects of being pierced by love's arrow. For men, the appearance of an **unknown but beautiful woman** in a dream may call for a sensual explanation directed not at a particular woman, but at women in general and what you are looking for in a mate.

ARTEMIS/DIANA

Artemis is the virgin huntress who is proud and wild, mirroring the beasts she hunts. For men, **images of powerful women** in dreams may represent the dominating, devouring mother archetype. In women, such images may denote a wish to be more assertive.

DIONYSUS/BACCHUS

If figures such as **Dionysus or Bacchus** appear in your dream, particularly if accompanied by hordes of drunken revelers, they suggest the need to take risks in your life, if you have the courage to do so. If the ancient god of wine does appear in your dream and is encouraging you to indulge in some way, your dreaming mind may be urging you to explore your full potential.

HERAKLES/HERCULES

The ancient hero **Herakles** represents the strengths and weaknesses of brute force. Depending on your circumstances in waking life, Herakles – or another aggressive archetype, Ares or Mars, the ancient gods of war – may be represented in dreams by any figure that is attacking you or someone else. If this is the case it may suggest a need to be more forceful and take action in waking life. Alternatively it may also indicate the need for a quieter, more thoughtful approach.

Hermes/Mercury

Hermes was the messenger of the gods, and any dream in which someone delivers a message to you is one that you should not ignore. Think about the message but also the nature of the messenger. Hermes was also a trickster, as well as being impulsive and self-centred, so should the messenger in your dream be trusted? There may be an indication that some person bringing news or gossip in waking life is not wholly reliable.

Hero/Heroine

The **hero or heroine** is the person who has elected to undertake their own journey of exploration. They are able to consider options and decide the next move. They will overcome challenges, solve problems and, more often than not, rescue someone who is in distress. The focal point of myth, legend and fairy tale is, in most cases, the psychological growth of the hero and heroine; modern fantasies express many of the same themes as their more ancient precursors. Whether heroes and heroines appear in modern or ancient garb, they represent the same impulses within the dreamer, such as an expression of bravery, ambition or adventure.

For example, *Star Wars* grips its audience not just because of its ground-breaking special effects, but because it also speaks to our unconscious mind. The themes in the film exhibit many of the same structures possessed by myths and fairy tales. Extraordinary things happen to ordinary people and tragedy is the catalyst which sets the story in motion. For example, in *Star Wars*, the turning point for the young

Luke Skywalker is the devastation of his family home. This may reflect the circumstances of your waking life. For many people, psychological growth begins with a tragedy or change in circumstances. Allies join the hero, Luke, just as they do in classic myth, and in Jungian psychology this represents psychological energy and the wisdom of the unconscious. The fantasy adventure goes on to express a classic hero myth, giving Luke greater self-realization and psychological wholeness.

So if a hero figure appears in your dreams whether in the guise of **Luke Skywalker**, **Superman**, **Spiderman**, **Batman**, **James Bond**, **Robin Hood or Lara Croft**, they often symbolize your search or desire for psychological wholeness. These figures – if you can properly understand their appearance and intention – are all assisting in the process of individuation, helping you to find yourself.

The Holy Grail legend

Said to be the cup from which Jesus drank at the Last Supper and which caught his blood at the Crucifixion, the **Holy Grail** is a symbol of spiritual perfection. Of all the **knights of King Arthur's Round Table**, only **Sir Galahad** is pure enough to look into it. **Sir Lancelot** is unable to, because he is bound by earthly desire for Arthur's queen **Guinevere**, the temptress. Alternatively, the Holy Grail in dreams may refer to the theory popularized by Dan Brown in *The Da Vinci Code* that the Grail is not a cup but a feminine principle or archetype embodied by Mary Magdalene, who allegedly married Christ. Typically, however, to dream of the Holy Grail represents something miraculous that allows you to move forward and reach your full potential. It can also relate to the cup of happiness and to see it in your dream suggests some form of positive change about to occur in your waking life, or to the satisfaction achieved by the overcoming of challenges and obstacles.

HYBRID BEING

The bodies of mythological **hybrid beings** were thought to be composed of two or more animal species. If a creature that is a mixture of two or more animals appears in your dreams, work out what each of its component characteristics means to you in isolation – and then in combination with the other animals; this may help you identify the nature of your beast. There are many combinations of beasts which are possible archetypes, giving you virtually limitless potential for your creative abilities within your dream. Such dreams show the freedom of the unconscious mind from conventional principles; given the freedom to create, however, your mind can produce both fantastic and grotesque creations. Both of these remind you to be aware of your powers and whether you can control them.

ICARUS

Jung pointed out that one of the dangers for the person embarking on a journey to psychological wholeness is that they can fall victim to what the Greeks call 'hubris'. This describes the fate of a person whose head has become swollen with powers that are not his personally. The myth of **Icarus**, who flew too high, causing the sun to melt his waxen wings so that he fell to his death

in the sea below, is a classic example of pride before a fall.

JASON AND THE GOLDEN FLEECE

Jason's voyage to find the Golden Fleece can be interpreted by Jungians in the following way. Jason, the archetypal hero, must slay the dragon guarding the fleece; the dragon represents those dark impulses of his that he has to overcome if he is to attain the spiritual purity symbolized by the fleece. Unfortunately, Jason only defeats the dragon with a magic sleeping potion, leaving his dormant impulses undefeated.

MAIDEN IN DISTRESS

The **imprisonment of a maiden by a wicked guardian figure** represents the repression of unconscious insights. In dreams, any **rescue by a hero or knight** symbolizes a strong mind motivated by a quest for truth, represented in this instance by the maiden.

MEDUSA

One of the three Gorgons in Greek myth, **Medusa's gaze** turns people to stone. In dreams, Medusa – or figures like her who terrify you with a glance – may represent a distorted image of yourself or an inability to deal with your own destructive impulses.

KING MIDAS

Everything **King Midas** touches turns to gold. Initially this seems to be a blessing, as he accumulates golden objects of great worth; eventually, however, the gift turns into a curse; he touches food and it turns

The Element Encyclopedia of 20,000 Dreams

into an inedible metal, and he touches his daughter, who turns into a golden statue. In a dream, Midas, or a **banker counting coins**, warns against the dangers of materialism; but he may also indicate that when it comes to seeking spiritual truth, there can be no compromise.

MINOTAUR

If you dreamt of the man-eating, subterranean-dwelling **Minotaur**, the coupling of a human body with a bull's head may point to a man in your life who is governed by instincts and who is easily enraged. It could also indicate a dangerous instinct hidden deep within yourself. Your dreaming mind could also have summoned the bull-man into your dreams to draw your attention to your own bullheadedness in waking life, and to your stubborn or even stupid approach to a situation.

NARCISSUS

Narcissus was the handsome man in Greek myth who fell in love with his own reflection in a pool. When he tried to grasp the image, he fell in and was drowned, only to be turned into a flower. Dreams in which concern with appearance take center stage, such as a **catwalk show**, or dreams in which **you are constantly changing your outfit or checking your appearance in a mirror**, may be a stark warning against the danger of vanity and the preoccupation with appearance.

PEGASUS

In dreams, the sky or air tend to be the province of freedom and spiritual or intellectual transcendence, so if you have a dream in which you **mount a winged horse like Pegasus** in order, perhaps, to escape a indomitable pursuer, your unconscious may have been urging you to use your intellect to soar above the mundane problems of your waking life.

POSEIDON/NEPTUNE

Poseidon was the explosive and unpredictable god of the seas. If he or other creatures of the sea appears in dreams, his stormy nature may point to great changes – or the need for you to make great changes – in your waking life.

THE SUPERHERO

From **Herakles to Superman and Spiderman**, the legendary **superhero** with magical, superhuman powers can come in many guises but his purpose is clear: he must defeat evil, and defend truth and justice. There is, however, always a price to pay or a sacrifice to make for his superhuman powers. For example, **Superman** must resist the advances of reporter Lois Lane, to whom Clark Kent would easily succumb. If the image of a superhero or heroine appears in your dream, it is not only reminding you that your powers might be far greater than you think; it is also suggesting that there may be sacrifices you need to make along the way.

Zeus/Jupiter

The supreme deity in the Greco-Roman pantheon is the father archetype at its most uncompromising, ruthless and dominant. The powerful presence of any authority figure in your dream may evoke anxiety about the father figure, or other figures of authority in your life. As Jung pointed out, 'here is the archetypal leader, the voice of collective authority, the Lord, king or tyrant, but also protector, the figure whose word is law.' It is important to bear in mind that sometimes Zeus got it wrong and was ridiculed by his subjects.

SYMBOLS

D ream symbols are the images that are featured in a dream.

Teeth falling out, a house being burnt, a winter storm, a foreign country, your sister, a child, a stranger, a painting, a werewolf, a church and a ballet are some of the limitless number of images or symbols you can find in dreams. Most dream symbols are not to be taken literally, but rather metaphorically. A metaphor is where the meaning of one thing is transferred to another thing – a 'happy ship', for example, might mean a good-humored family or workforce. In most cases, to fully understand the message in the dream you should interpret your dream symbols as metaphorical rather than literal references to your thoughts and feelings. For instance, a burning house might contain references both to yourself (the house) and to your passion, anger, desire or bodily fever (the fire).

Symbols and pictures predate language. They point to the emotions and instincts, many of which are hidden or repressed; these are stored in the unconscious mind, where they reside until some stimulus brings them to consciousness. Jung tells us that dreams speak in the language of symbols and these symbols can have more than one meaning. This has to do with the personal and collective unconscious. The former refers to the dreamer's ego life, where those things that have been repressed or rejected from consciousness reside. The collective unconscious, which is rich in symbol and metaphor, is older than the individual and indeed older than consciousness itself. It consists of 'the whole spiritual heritage' of mankind's evolution born anew in the brain structure of every individual. The representation of a symbol in the personal unconscious points to the anxieties of everyday life, whereas the collective unconscious addresses the deeper sense of who we are. This is the true self that is often disguised in the ego-life, a spiritual and creative being that inhabits our psyche. Jung tells us we cannot be fully whole until we recognize these 'collective' aspects and make them a part of our everyday lives.

Dream dictionaries fill shelves in bookstores and each one will tell you what the symbols in your dreams say about you. The trouble is that most of them contradict each other; in many instances they can also contradict you. The language of dreams is above all personal and symbols cannot have fixed meanings. However, this does not mean that a dream encyclopedia such as the one you are reading now has no useful role to play; quite the contrary. If used correctly, it can be incredibly helpful. It can spark your imagination and can give you inspiration to help you to interpret your dream.

Although there is often confusion and difficulty surrounding symbols, not helped by the fact that many sources of information come from ancient texts, distant cultures and far-off periods of history, kernels of truth often reside in what might be called a clichéd reading of any particular symbol; this is because we all share common needs and therefore share common experiences giving rise to common dream symbols. Bear in mind, however, that one interpretation can never have a universal application and the specific meaning will differ from person to person. As stressed throughout this encyclopedia, the only way to get a satisfactory interpretation for your dream symbols is to consider your personal associations in conjunction with the universal symbolic meanings. *See also* ARCHETYPES; COLORS; SHAPES.

The Most Common Dream Symbols

This section explores some of the most common dream symbols and the chances are you are likely to have had at least one of the dreams below. Dreams that you are falling or naked in a public place, or losing your teeth or flying are all dreams shared by a great many people. One of the great mysteries about dreams is that people of diverse backgrounds and cultures with varying experiences and of different ages can share these dream themes. The human mind has the ability to generate and conjure up a myriad of images, yet we can still share such similar themes in our dreams. Perhaps we are not so different after all?

These so-called universal dreams transcend all generations and cultures. Whilst not all experts agree on the same list and frequency, these symbols are perhaps the most commonly reported in dream psychology, and you will find them listed below in alphabetical order. Their interpretations are meant as starting points but don't forget that their exact meaning will vary depending upon your personal associations. Although people tend to have more negative dreams than positive ones, bear in mind that most dream themes have both negative and positive sides. *See also* EVERY-DAY THINGS for the ten most common dreams.

ANIMAL/REPTILE/INSECT

Animals in dreams are generally associated with behavioral patterns or your natural instincts, the beast within. Being bitten or attacked by an animal may suggest feeling hunted, vulnerable or doubting your own strength. **Cats, dogs and horses** are the most common dream images. **Snakes** are the most common dream reptile. They can be symbols of trouble or male sexuality but they can also represent the afterlife or the potential for transcending a difficult situation. **Birds** are a universal symbol of spirituality. **Spiders** are the most common dream creepy-crawly, and they can have a wide range of meanings ranging from being industrious or helpful, to provoking irrational or hidden fears and phobias.

Baby

A **baby** is the result of the uniting of a male and female. In the language of the unconscious, this represents the cooperative use of the aggressive and receptive principles to create something new. In other words, a baby is a universal symbol of new beginnings.

Chased/Attacked

The origin of dreams of being **chased or attacked** probably dates back to an era when humans fought off beasts or other tribal members to survive. The 'monsters' of today are more likely to be emotional beasts, such as fear, anxiety, anger, hatred and envy, or the pressures put upon us by the fast pace of life. In these dream scenarios you are often being pursued by some attacker who wants to hurt or possibly kill you. Chase dreams may represent your way of coping with fears, stresses or various difficult situations in your waking life. Instead of confronting the situation, you are running away and avoiding it. Ask yourself who is the one chasing you, as that may give you some understanding and insight into the source of your fears.

Cheating

To dream that you are **cheating on your spouse or partner** suggests feelings of guilt and self-betrayal. You may have compromised your beliefs or integrity in some way. Alternatively, your dreaming mind may be conjuring up various scenarios to give you an idea of how different things might be or encouraging you to develop an aspect of yourself represented by the dream lover. To dream that your **spouse or partner is cheating on you** indicates your fears of being abandoned. You may suffer from a lack of attention in the relationship. Alternatively, you may feel that you are not measuring up to the expectations of others. To dream that you are **cheating at a game** suggests that you are not being honest with yourself.

Clothes

In dreams, **clothes** tend to represent the image you are presenting to others or the identity you have assumed at the time. Many cultures describe the three-fold nature of the self as: the person we show to others, the person we believe ourselves to be and the person we truly are. Clothes signify what we allow others to see.

Contemporary images

You are unlikely to have dreams about **riding a horse** instead of using a car. Today our dreams are filled with **cars, televisions, plastic surgery, airplane crashes** and the most common contemporary images include: **shopping centers, computers, car parks, factories, hospitals, broken glass, and condoms**. Such images work with the same logic and consistency as all symbols and they also have both universal and individual meanings. *See also* EVERYDAY THINGS.

Death

Death in a dream is frightening to most dreamers because they lack an understanding of the nature of physical life and death. For the philosopher, the physical life is known as a temporary existence for the soul. In the universal language of mind, death signifies a change from one state of being to another. One myth about dreaming is that if you **die** in your dream, you die in life. This is not true, of course, but dream deaths do occur. They involve **deaths of famous people, your parents or children, a lover and even yourself**. It is generally accepted that when you dream about an **accidental death** of any person, that person's death symbolizes something in you that is no longer functioning.

Examination/Test

An **examination or test** in a dream symbolizes a time for reflection and evaluation. The **subject of the exam or test** will give further insight into the theme for reflection. For example, a **medical exam** will indicate the need to identify attitudes producing wholeness or disease. You have probably dreamed of **arriving for a test and found the exam has already started or you search fruitlessly for the examination room**. Such dreams tend to occur when you are feeling anxious or challenged in waking life. You may, however, dream of a **great test or another fine performance**. This may occur when you feel you are doing well in waking life. Not limited to exams, the dreamer may envision doing precise spins on the ice or scoring a sensational goal. Sometimes people master certain activities after they have successfully performed them in their dream.

Falling/Drowning

There is an old wives' tale that says if you dream you are **falling and you hit the bottom**, you will die. This is not true. Falling is one of the most common nightmares amongst people of all ages, and may be a reflection of feeling insecure, helpless or of having no support or solid grounding. Dreaming about **drowning** is less common and often occurs when you feel overwhelmed. Both scenarios involve life-or-death situations and can be traced back to prehistoric origins; dreams of falling reflect a time when our ancestors took risks when climbing trees. Falling dreams of modern life often take place from **high buildings, elevators and rooftops**. Likewise, dreams of drowning relate to our inborn need to breathe for survival. People often awake to 'escape' the danger in the dream.

Flying/Swimming/Dancing

Have you had that feeling of **zooming through the air, feeling free and unhindered**? Flying is one of the most popular dreams because such images can inspire the dreamer, lifting them to spiritual heights or filling them with creative notions. Pleasurable **swimming** may mean exploring your unconscious depths, whilst dreams of **dancing** may be a metaphor for creativity, joy and freedom.

Food

Physically, **food** nourishes the body. Mentally, knowledge nourishes the mind, thus the old adage of 'food for thought'. In the universal language of mind, food represents an experience of a type of energy to be taken in. The **preparation of food** represents the formulation and creation of something important, and the **consumption of food** represents the taking in of knowledge.

GAMES

Dreams that feature **games** represent the perspective on life held by the dreamer. Individual games such as **solitaire** indicate the dreamer's tendency for self-amusement, in which excelling or enjoyment is a significant motive. Interactive games, like **chess**, indicate the dreamer's tendency towards challenge, in which competition with another is a significant motive. In either case, the dream is highlighting your mental dexterity.

GUN/KNIFE

Guns are associated with power, aggression and, in some cases, masculine energy and sexuality. If the **gun is a weapon you carry** in the dream, it may be a symbol of your personal power but if **someone is threatening you with a gun**, it may suggest their power over you. If you are **having trouble finding or using a gun** in your dream, this may represent your indecision and confusion. **Knives** represent emotional experiences that are hurtful

HAIR/HAND

How **hair** appears in a dream gives the dreamer insight into the way they are thinking and the type of alterations that can be made to enhance their thinking. For instance, if **hair is being cut**, this will symbolize the dreamer's current tendency

to reorganize thoughts. Hair is also a symbol of strength and virility. When **hands stand out** in a dream, they will usually indicate the dreamer's need to give attention to the intentions behind the actions.

HOUSE

Your inner being, inner sanctum or your physical body, **houses** in dreams often serve to guide you to a specific period or feeling within your life. If your dream house is a **home from the past, or a specific room within the home**, the dominant memory or feeling from that time or place will provide further interpretational clues. The most common room in the house to appear in dreams is the **bathroom**; this represents purification or refreshment. A **messy bathroom** may suggest an area of your life that requires attention or cleansing.

KILLING

Dreams of **killing** indicate the changes occurring within you, since death in a dream always represents change. The type of change is signified by who or what is killed in the dream. For instance, the dreamer **killing a tiger** represents changing a habit.

LATE

You **rush to catch a departing bus, train, airplane or ship but just do not get there in time**. These dreams leave you engulfed in an overwhelming feeling of frustration and such dreams may reflect feelings that you are not keeping up with the pace of life. Alternatively, such a dream may be urging you to reorganize your busy schedule.

LOST/TRAPPED

In these extremely common dreams, you **are lost and feeling desperate. You may be buried alive or locked in a cage. Or you dream of not being able to move; you are powerless to scream or breathe.** Such dreams may occur when you feel confusion or conflict about how to act in waking life. The images are influenced by biological roots and experiences. **Feeling trapped or unable to move** also mirrors what occurs to the large muscles of the body during normal REM sleep, when they are paralyzed to prevent the body from acting out dreams. Such dreams could reflect frustrations in waking life, such as feeling trapped in a relationship or a dead-end job. The flip side to such dreams is a dream of **discovering new spaces; you may open a door in your home to find a new room or find something new in the neighborhood.** These dreams occur usually when you feel that an aspect of your life is opening up.

MACHINE MALFUNCTION

These dreams are moderately common, being more frequent in women. They occur when you feel anxious about making an emotional connection or when you feel you are losing touch with someone. **Elevators** often appear in dreams suffering from some kind of bizarre malfunction. **You push a button and go sideways or fly hurtling upward through the roof or the elevator crashes** and so on. As with all symbols of movement, elevators tend to reflect your progress with a current situation or problem in waking life; if the elevator malfunctions, you are not getting what you

bargained for or may be contributing unwittingly to a pattern that is no longer in your best interests. The flip side to such dreams is a dream in which **smooth operation** is the order of the day. This type of dream usually occurs when you feel there is an improvement in an emotional connection.

MARRIAGE

Marriage is the union of a male and female or two people deeply in love. In the universal language of mind, marriage represents the commitment between the conscious and subconscious minds. Dreams of marriage indicate the initiation of a new awareness for the dreamer.

MONEY

A symbol of communication and the exchange of values, **how the money is being used** in the dream will indicate what is being valued. For instance, if **money is being used to buy a house**, this will symbolize the value the dreamer places upon their own mind; if **money is being invested for future use**, it will indicate the permanent wealth derived from experience and understanding.

MOUNTAIN

A well-known symbol of challenges or obstacles in the dreamer's life, **mountains** signify something that has to be met and understood. It can only be ascended if you use your mind and your abilities to move forward, so if you are unaware and unenlightened concerning your own capacities, the mountain will constitute a formidable obstacle to overcome.

The Element Encyclopedia of 20,000 Dreams

NAKED

When **someone appears naked** in a dream, this will represent an aspect of the self that is being expressed openly or ideas manifest in their true form without alteration or limitation. Nakedness is a common dream scenario that occurs at all ages, even when we are very young. The dreams involve feelings of exposure and vulnerability, and often include an element of embarrassment or shame. Appearing **partially nude** is more common than being **totally naked**. Meanings vary depending on whether the nakedness occurs at school, at work, or on an open street; they will also depend on what part of the body is exposed.

Wearing the wrong clothing has various meanings too. A **bride being inappropriately dressed for her upcoming wedding**, for example, could suggest second thoughts she has about the union. If you dream of being **dapper or wearing a special outfit**, however, this may suggest you feel good about your body or your life.

NATURAL OR MAN-MADE DISASTERS

You are often confronted in dreams by overwhelming **floods, tidal waves, earthquakes, volcanic eruptions, tornadoes, hurricanes, bombings or chemical warfare**. These dreams may depict personal problems raging out of control and can be amongst the most frightening of dreams.

NATURAL BEAUTY

Dreams of **vibrant flowers, verdant hillsides or uplifting music** can leave you feeling refreshed and rejuvenated. Color is intensified, with **bright yellow green** being the one most often mentioned by dreamers. This may illustrate new growth. Dreams of natural beauty can inspire and invigorate.

PEOPLE

In most cases, **people** in your dreams represent aspects of yourself, such as ways of thinking and expressing yourself. An easy way to recognize aspects of the self is to acknowledge the roles you play in life: the devoted spouse, loving parent, reliable employee or the good friend. Aspects reflect characteristics within you: the comic, the shy one, the ambitious one, the generous one. Whatever quality you attach to that person in your dream, is the quality of self being addressed in the dream message?

RADIO

A symbol of receiving mind-to-mind communication, the **radio** symbolizes the means to receive thoughts from another, whereas a **broadcasting station** symbolizes the means to project or send thoughts.

ROAD

In the universal language of mind, a **road** represents the direction of your life which can be determined by the goals and ideals you make your own.

SCHOOL

In the language of mind, a **school** signifies the dreamer's awareness of their personal growth or of the lessons that need to be learned.

Sexual arousal

Sexual images in dreams symbolize the unification of the conscious and subconscious minds for the purpose of creation. In a dream, the man and woman represent the conscious and subconscious minds. Intercourse symbolizes the unified effort for the purpose of creation. Research has documented that both men and women experience sexual arousal during REM sleep; dreams of sex might supply the desired missing elements in an unsatisfying marriage or emotional life, or heighten the sense of anticipation during an intense love affair.

Spirits

You feel you are being **haunted or berated by someone who has died**. There may be feelings of terror, guilt, resentment or abandonment. These dreams may occur when you feel guilty or responsible for a death, or anxious about a situation. Although they are quite rare, these can be among the most uncomfortable dreams we can ever have. The flip side to such dreams is a dream in which we are **being guided by the dead or a spirit or angel**. These usually occur during times of active grief, which can last years. **Visits from a deceased loved one** may give you the feeling that they are OK, or inspire you to change your life. In either case, there may be a feeling of hope and comfort. A **spirit guide** is one more knowledgeable than the self; dream interaction with such a teacher indicates a desire and need for communication and rapport with the deepest part of your mind and being.

Teeth falling out or crumbling

This dream might have a physical origin in people gritting or grinding their teeth during sleep. Freud suggested that dreams of **teeth falling out** are related to fears of castration, but women have this dream as often as men, suggesting that tooth troubles in dreams are related to hidden anger, with a dreamer acting out the clenching of teeth. Other dream analysts believe the dream reflects anxiety about appearance and how others perceive you. Teeth can also represent a means of assimilating knowledge so it can be used. Teeth are the first instruments of the digestive system, so in dreams they represent the acquisition of knowledge. **Losing teeth** is a common symbol in a dream, indicating a change in the way the dreamer assimilates what is learned.

Vehicles

All **vehicles** symbolize a means for experience or the progress you are making in life. The **use of the vehicle** will give indications as to the type of experience being related in the dream message. For instance, an **ambulance** will indicate a need for healing in the giving and receiving of experience, whilst a **police car** will signify the need for discipline in life. **Vehicle malfunctions** are a fairly common nightmare amongst all people and all ages, whether or not the dreamers actually drive. Sometimes you might have **problems with an aircraft you are flying**; such a dream typically takes place when you feel that events in waking life are out of control. When your **time in a car or another vehicle is delightful**, this

Your dream dictionary

You may find that certain symbols keep cropping up in your dreams. Maybe your **mother always appears carrying a first-aid kit** or you are always aware of **clocks** in your dreams. **Repeated elements** in your dreams are likely to be personal symbols intended to convey certain meanings that go beyond their universal meanings. A **clock**, for example is a universal symbol of time, but it may also suggest to you that your time is running out or that you need to keep things in order. As always, the context of your dream will help you determine its meaning. It might help to create your own personal dream journal or dictionary to help you identify reoccurring personal dream images and their meanings. Here are some guidelines:

For one week write down as many images as you can recall for your dream. Try to use single words for each image; for example, dog, cup, spoon and so on.

Do this as you first wake up when the images are still fresh in your mind. Then write down beside each symbol any associations that occur. If a symbol crops up on more than one occasion, make a special mark by it and note whether the context was different. At the end of the week, organize your list alphabetically and see which images appear most often. You might want to repeat this for another week afterwards to add to your personal dream dictionary.

Bear in mind that dream images change as you do and may require additional meanings. You are also more likely to have dreams at turning points in your life, such as leaving school, finding a new job or getting married. If you find yourself inundated with symbols and messages, try to concentrate on only one or two dreams, or on those dreams that you recognize as being important by their power and the feelings with which they leave you.

represents freedom or moving in the direction of your choice.

WATER

Water is essential to life. In the universal language of mind, water symbolizes the emotions, and the everyday situations and circumstances that arise bringing opportunities for enrichment.

WEATHER

The **weather conditions** in a dream tend to reflect the emotional climate or the forces with which you are currently contending. **Tornado** dreams are particularly common in the United States, and tend to represent some kind of emotional storm or someone in the dreamer's life who is prone to emotional outbursts.

TIME

Your dreams may sometimes remind you that every day is precious and you need to make the most of the time that remains for you.

The passage of time is one of those basic conditions of life that we all take for granted. Yet, as Jung observed, whilst the true home of the psyche is outside of both time and space, the annals of sleep are full of anxiety dreams in which time exerts a relentless pressure. Meanwhile, symbols of time such as the clock, calendar, day and night, light and darkness, and the seasons have a special significance in dream interpretation because they can all parallel the stages of human life.

A mundane interpretation of dreams featuring symbols of time may be that your dreaming mind is prompting you to remember to do something or to wake up in time. In some cases, your dreams may place you not in the present but in the past, or you may visualize a scenario set far in the future. If you dreamed of a past occurrence, this may indicate nostalgia or be an attempt to remind you of an unresolved emotional problem. If you dream of being fast-forwarded into the future, your dream may have been warning you of a course that your life may take if you carry out a particular action. *See also* NATURE AND THE SEASONS; NUMBERS.

The Passage of Time

CONSCIOUS OF TIME

It is hard to know how the **passage of time** is expressed in dreams, as you are not in real time when you dream, since situations or adventures that appear to take a long period of time can be dreamed of in moments. Any dream in which you are aware of the passage of time indicates a progress report on your life, in that the 24-hour cycle of day and night has a parallel with both physical and spiritual birth and development. **Dawn** signifies birth and beginnings; the **morning** signifies childhood and potential; **midday**, middle age and maturity; the **afternoon**, late middle age and relaxation; and the **evening**, old age, with the dead of night suggesting death. A dream in which you suddenly realize it is afternoon could therefore suggest that you need to relax or that time has passed by so quickly and you haven't achieved all that you hoped you would achieve by late middle age.

Arriving **too early or too late** in your dream for an appointment may be significant in your waking life; if you were too early, you should ask yourself if you are worrying too much and overplanning some aspect of your life. If you were too late, you should consider whether you are worried in waking life about missing the boat or being the last person to be informed about something important.

PHOTOGRAPH/PICTURE

Photographs are a record of your past and mark the passage of time so if **photographs of your life** appear in your dream, this may represent memories, nostalgia; or perhaps your dreaming mind is pointing to a specific period in your life to remind you of lessons learned then but since forgotten. If the **photographs are not familiar** to you, your dream may have been signifying an aspect of yourself or your sense of direction in waking life. Was the **photo clear or out of focus**? This may signify how certain or uncertain you are of your attitudes. If you were **taking the photograph**, this suggests that you feel in control of your daily life. If you were **studying a negative or are in a photographic darkroom**, this suggests negativity in your daily life but you may also simply be waiting to see what will develop. If the **photos come to life**, this suggests the living influence of past experience and your continuing involvement in what the picture depicts. **Talking photos** suggests that you need to remember or take notice of someone or something in your waking life.

TIME OF DAY

If a dream is **specifically set during daylight or night-time**, take into account your waking associations with early morning and night-time. If you are a night owl, a night-time dream will have a far more positive interpretation than if you were an early bird. You may also associate daytime with routine and work and night-time with relaxation and freedom. Dreams that take place in **bright daylight** also suggest your conscious waking life and feelings of optimism and clarity, and dreams of night-time can indicate the unconscious as well as negativity and ignorance. **Twilight** in dreams can suggest a period of uncertainty and possible ambivalence as far as your direction in life is concerned. It may also suggest the afterlife.

Just as the 24-hour day is symbolically linked to the human life cycle, so too are the seasons: **spring** symbolizes birth and childhood and new beginnings; **summer**, adulthood; **autumn**, middle age; and **winter**, aging and death. The seasons can also signify your state of mind with **spring** representing optimism; **summer**, confidence, **autumn**, relaxation and reward; and **winter**, retreat. When several **days, weeks, months, years or even longer pass** in your dream, your unconscious is reflecting changes in your life or suggesting that your focus has currently been on things that are not relevant. Along with the **second and minute hands on a clock**, these dream images suggest slow and careful progression – or the need for it – in your waking life. Dreams of **specific hours of the day** may refer to your age, to a regular event in life or to a saying; for example **12 noon** is middle age, or may refer to something that happens at that time of day, **11 o'clock** may be the eleventh hour and so on. **Noon** may also be associated with lunch and nourishment, **midnight** with mystery and **6 o'clock** with finishing work. *See also* NUMBERS.

The Past and the Future

AGING

You may have a dream in which **you or someone close to you appears to age rapidly, sometimes becoming an elderly person or even a skeleton**. Such dreams can be frightening, reflecting your anxieties and fears about aging; but some people find such dreams comforting, as they can indicate that the aging process is not necessarily a negative experience. Whilst on the subject of time and aging, did you know that by the time you reach seventy, you will have spent nearly six years of your life dreaming and will have slept for twenty years? *See also* STAGES OF LIFE.

HISTORICAL PEOPLE AND EVENTS

Some people have dreams in which they appear at a **particular past event of national or world historical importance, such as Waterloo, World War II or walking on the moon**. They may also come **face to face with a famous historical figure, such as Queen Victoria or Abraham Lincoln**. These dreams are often a reflection of your interest in a particular time period or particular character in history, but they may also have a deeper significance. For example, if you find yourself in the middle of a **World War**, perhaps this relates to personal conflict in your life; a **historical figure** may be a symbol of someone close to you.

THE PAST

A dream that **plunges you back into your childhood or an earlier stage of your life** may indicate nostalgia for happier times or regret for the lost years. Alternatively, your dream may be urging you to recapture the high spirits and optimism of your youth, or be reminding you of an important lesson that you learned at that time but seem to have now forgotten. If your dream sent you back to a **period of your life that was unhappy**, the purpose may have been to help you re-examine and resolve your emotional baggage.

THE FUTURE

Dreams of the future could indicate wish-fulfillment if a scenario you have been daydreaming about played itself out in your dreams. If your dream of the future involves a **disaster, tragedy or accident**, this may be anxiety related but it could also be possible that your unconscious has signaled that you need to take extra care to protect your health and safety. If you dreamed of **visiting a clairvoyant**, are you eager to know the outcome of a situation in the real world? *See also* Precognitive dreams entries in ACCIDENTS, ACTION AND ADVENTURES and DISASTERS.

The Element Encyclopedia of 20,000 Dreams

Reincarnation

Throughout his life, Jung admitted his strong fascination with the theory of reincarnation but never declared himself for or against the idea. We simply don't know whether he believed in past lives, nor can we say whether dreams reflect images from past lives. There are certain dreams set in a **past time or place unfamiliar to you** that you may find extremely hard to explain away as being merely symbolism, metaphor or allegory. There are those who do believe the dream state can be a gateway to past lives and that dreams featuring events before you were born are snapshots of past lives. It is said that these kinds of dreams, also known as karmic dreams, are incredibly real and intense. There's a certain 'grand dream' feeling that often accompanies them. Even as the dream is taking place, you may be feeling a sense of awe and wonder. You awaken knowing that this dream is very special and that it relates to something about your distant past. There's an inescapable feeling that the dream is about a past life.

In most cases, it is impossible to prove beyond doubt that a dream relates to a past life experience, as your dream is unlikely to give you the facts needed to prove them with public records of births, marriages and deaths. In the end, it simply comes down to a gut feeling, an unshakable belief that comes from deep within you. Whether you believe in reincarnation or not, what is important here is what you take from the dream as a lesson for your current life. If the goal of reincarnation is to improve karma – the Buddhist principle of cosmic reward or punishment for the things you have done or left undone in past lives – then this dream offers you an opportunity for personal growth.

TIME TRAVEL

If you were **traveling in time to the past** in your dreams, try to remember if you travelled to a time within your life span or to an era before you were born. **Traveling into your own past** can be linked to a desire to connect with a situation in your childhood or youth that remains unresolved. Traveling into an **era before you are born** could suggest the possibility of reincarnation, but also an association between that period in time and your life at the moment. It might be worth getting the history books out to do some studies to see if any connections or lessons emerge. **Traveling into the future** can indicate impatience but also optimism and anticipation. If the **future scenario was depressing**, this represents your fears and anxieties concerning your personal or the world's future. From a mystical point of view, sometimes in dreams past, present and future become one and the idea of time vanishes; only when this happens can the individual fully concentrate on the present.

Symbols of Time

Calendar

A common dream symbol, **calendars** may be referring to your past or your future. If a **date is highlighted in a calendar** in your dream, consider first of all whether or not the date has any significance to you; if it does, it is simply reflecting your interest or anticipation. If the date has no significance for you, it might be worthwhile checking your calendar to see if you have forgotten something. If this also is not the case, then **calendars and dates** in dreams may be drawing your attention to the speed of time, and therefore are urging you to focus on achieving your goals before it is too late. If you come across an **old calendar** in your dream, this suggests nostalgia for the past, whilst **pages torn from calendar** represent the passing of the years. When you write in a **diary** you are recording your experiences and making a record of your past. If you dream of finding a **diary**, your dreaming mind may be urging you to make the most of every day.

Special days

If your dream **calendar or diary highlighted an important day, anniversary, birthday or holiday,** your dreaming mind may simply be reflecting your anticipation or your dread of the occasion. Your mood in the dream will help you decide on the significance of the message.

If the **date of your birthday is highlighted** your dreaming mind may be reminding you again that your days are numbered. Alternatively it could be reflecting your desire to be noticed or made to feel special or your discomfort with being in the spotlight. If an **anniversary** is highlighted in your dream and your mood is positive, your unconscious may have been congratulating you on your past successes or reflecting pride and pleasure at having achieved a personal milestone. If the mood is negative, the opposite would apply. Special days like **New Year, Christmas, Easter, Mother's Day, Valentine's Day or bank holidays** can communicate several meanings and it is important to take your waking associations with that day into account.

SUNDIAL

The **ancient appearance and archaic workings of a sundial** in your dream may suggest that an aspect of your life is unrealistic, out of date or no longer needed. Is there something in your life that needs modernizing? Alternatively, a sundial may suggest a simpler and purer way of life without the interference of modern gadgets, so the dream could be suggesting your yearning for a life with less technology and bustle.

WATCH/CLOCK

If a **timepiece** appeared in your dream, it is important to remember how you felt during and after the dream as it will suggest the way in which you allocate time in your life. Were the **hands moving slowly or quickly**? Was the timepiece telling you to speed up or slow down? The **type of clock or watch** is also important. Was it **old-fashioned or modern?** Dreams of clocks or watches can also suggest that you rely too heavily on clock time instead of enjoying and experiencing life as it happens. If your dreaming mind zoomed in on a watch or clock, this could also be a reminder to make the most of your time and not to waste it.

If you **keep checking a clock or a watch** in your dream, this suggests anxiety and worry about some future event. If you don't feel this to be the case, your unconscious may have conjured this panic-stricken theme to urge you to prepare better for a future event or opportunity that may soon present itself in waking life. For example, have you done enough study to pass your driving theory test?

Alternatively, your dream may have indicated frustration and regret at your inability in the past to make the most of an opportunity when it was presented to you.

If you dreamed that a **watch or clock slowed down**, this could reflect your feeling that events are moving slowly in your waking life or that time is dragging. Alternatively, the symbol of a watch may indicate your ticking heart, so if the clock stops or slows down, this may suggest either an emotional standstill or problems with your cardiovascular system. According to ancient dream-lore and superstition, when a **clock stops**, somebody will die but your dream will almost certainly have a different meaning. In the symbolic language of dreams, clocks and watches reflect your emotional state and a **stopped clock or a clock that is broken** may indicate emotional blockages or standstills, and a **clock whose hands race out of control** may indicate feelings run amok.

If you dreamed of a **stopwatch**, this highlights your sense of feeling pressured or working against the clock. If you are a **woman dreaming of ticking clocks**, such a dream may indicate your biological clock. Dreams that focus on timepieces may also have been measuring the passage of your lifespan and the ticking clock could simply be a reminder that the seconds of your life are ticking away and there is still much for you to do. **Watching the clock** in your dreams suggests that you need to make time work for you. A **clock tower** combines this with a phallic form to offer an image of courage and determination. Evoking great occasions, the **chimes of a clock tower** may relate to a momentous personal or national event, such as a marriage or a coronation.

Time

TRAVEL

Making a journey within a dream can be a direct replay of a real journey, but in most cases the journey is a symbol of the dreamer's travels through their inner world.

According to Freud, dreams of a pleasant journey suggest steady progress in psycho-analysis; but the imagined motion of the journey also represents a wish for sexual intercourse. For Jungians, dreams of journeys act as a message telling you that it is time to take note of new possibilities and reach out for new challenges that can help you towards our spiritual destination. In some cases, dream journeys reflect how easy or difficult you are finding your life. Many modern dream analysts might see in such dreams a desire for change in some aspect of your life, a desire to 'move on'.

When trying to understand the meaning of your dream, it is important to take note of your mode of transport, whether you are walking or in a vehicle, the pace at which you are moving, the direction you are taking, any obstacles in your path, the weather, any luggage you were carrying and the person or people with whom you were traveling. All these details, along with your emotional reaction to the dream, will give you a good understanding of the progress you are making in waking life. *See*

also ACCIDENTS, ACTION AND ADVENTURE; FOREIGN COUNTRIES.

Journeys

DEPARTURE

Dreams of **beginning or setting out on a journey** suggest that you are beginning a quest for meaning, whilst **dream arrivals** often hint that you have achieved your goal or are envisaging yourself doing so. If passports appear in your dream, they are often a symbol of opportunity or of the need to escape present frustrations; your dreaming mind is urging you to go ahead with a project in waking life. If **check-in staff refused your passport or you do not make it across the border,** do you feel that your ambitions are being frustrated by an authority figure or do you need to update an important part of your life before you can move on?

DIRECTION

According to Jung **traveling towards the west and following the setting sun** may suggest the approach of old age or even death, whereas **journeying east** suggests rejuvenation. The direction in your dream will send a clear message about your sense of purpose in life. If the **path is straight**, then you are following a direct and unproblematic route to your objective. If it is **twisted**, then your course is slow and frustrating; if you were **going round in circles**, you feel as if you are going nowhere. If you are going **backwards**, you may feel as if your position has worsened or that you are backing off from a commitment.

If you **encounter a road block**, your dreaming mind may have placed it in your path to represent the obstacle that is stopping you from moving forward in life. If you **turn off the beaten track**, this suggests you are being sidetracked or diverted from your waking goal. If you **turn a corner**, this suggests progress. Were you **going uphill in your dream or downhill**? The former suggests forces that are working against you; the latter, forces that are working for you in waking life. If you **got lost** in your dream, this is a metaphor for losing your sense of purpose in life. If you consulted a **map, compass or atlas** in your dream, this indicates options open to you. If the **compass needle suggested heading north**, your dreaming mind may be urging you to take an intellectual route but the reference may also be to winter and old age. If the **compass pointed you south**, your unconscious may be urging you to take a more relaxed approach; if the direction was **east**, this suggests spiritual renewal, whilst **west** suggests the need to conserve your energy. Finally, bear in mind that a **right-hand or upward direction** suggests a rational approach, whilst a **left-hand or downward direction** suggests an intuitive approach. In all such instances, try to link the circumstance of your dream with your situation in real life.

LUGGAGE

Packed bags are associated with death and endings, whilst being **unwilling to let go of your baggage or luggage** suggests a desire to ward off aging and death. **Baggage left on a platform** suggests a willingness to begin a new phase or stage in your life. Although **suitcases** can denote travel in some dreams, an alternative explanation is that they represent emotional baggage you carry around in your head and that is why it is important to consider the luggage or lack of it in your dream.

PATH

The **path** is a classic symbol of the direction your life is taking. A **rocky path** suggests obstacles in your way. When a path suddenly **inclines uphill**, Freudians would interpret the climb as a desire for sex. If you are **traveling alone**, this suggests independence or loneliness. If you are traveling in a group, pay attention to the people accompanying you. Are they helping or hindering your progress? **Traveling companions** suggest your involvement with others in life or the feelings and attitudes that influence you and give you direction. If the **path was wide, open and straight, the sun was shining, you had a clear view ahead and were walking with confidence**, this suggests optimism, independence, well-being and a sense of direction in life.

If, however, the dream **path is foggy, hazy or you are walking in darkness**, the message is that you have lost your focus. The same would apply if you are **struggling to push your way through foliage or other obstacles, such as rocks, holes and other pitfalls**. If you **overcame the obstacles**, the message is that you will find a way of doing so in waking life; if you gave up, this suggests that you feel defeated. If you felt **frustrated that you could not move as fast along the path as you would have liked**, this also suggests obstacles inflicted on you by others or by yourself.

If you are **following a trail of footsteps** in your dream, perhaps this reflects your sense to follow someone else's example in waking life. An **open road** suggests a desire for freedom, whereas a **narrow road** suggests constraints. Dreaming of a **highway** can express your desire to fast-track to success in life. A **fork or bend in the road** can indicate indecision.

Transition point

If your dream journey reflects your progress in waking life, **transition points such as bus stops, airports, taxi queues, stations, ports and harbors** often represent transitional points in your life. So too do **tunnels, crossroads and bridges**. Such images suggest that you are about to leave one stage of your life behind and are getting ready to take a new direction. Pay attention to your feelings in these dreams, as they will mirror your desire to move on with your life. Dreams of **crossroads** are a potent symbol of the need to make choices and changes in your waking life. Remember that whenever you make a choice you also reject something, so pay attention to the path on which you decide to travel in your dream and the surprises it might have in store. **Signposts** have a similar interpretation and if the sign bore words, can you make any connections with your waking situation? Did you follow the directions or decide to take a different route in your dream? If you followed a different route, your unconscious is urging you to depart from the route you are following in your waking life. **Bridges** are points of transition that link the past with a potential future, so if you dreamed of **wandering across a bridge**, could you see what was waiting for you on the other side?

Modes of Transport

Aircraft

In dreams, **aircraft** represent a desire for new experiences and excitement. According to Freudians, aircraft are phallic symbols associated with new sexual experiences. Because air symbolizes spiritual aspiration, if your dream featured an **aircraft or an air journey**, could your unconscious have been encouraging you to explore your spirituality or rise above the limitations of daily life? Do you feel you are on a fast track to success or do you really need a holiday?

In dreams, as in life, **airports** can be busy, noisy and crowded places, and they can suggest a phase in your life you are trying to leave behind or a transitional phase. If you are **looking in vain for a familiar face at an**

airport in your dream, this suggests there may be aspects of your old way of life or thinking that you are unwilling to leave behind. If you dreamed of being in the **middle of a flight**, your unconscious may have been commenting on your current progress in life. Are you flying high or being buffeted by turbulence? Or is everything up in the air or beset by uncertainty? Dreams of being **hijacked or attacked in a plane** can suggest anxieties about flying, but they can also represent a fear of rape in women. A dream of a **plane crash** can suggest you have set your sights too high; perhaps you are expecting too much and have doubts about your ability to reach your goals? *See also* ACCIDENTS, ACTION AND ADVENTURES.

BICYCLE/MOTORBIKE

According to Freud, **riding a bicycle** is a symbol of sexual intercourse. Both **bicycles and motorbikes** symbolize the need for balance in life and the need to reconcile the often opposing demands of the conscious and unconscious. The **speed of the bike** will be significant, as it suggests how strong your desire for independence is. For Jungians, dreaming of a motorcycle suggests determination and a person in control of their destiny. A dream of **riding a bicycle** may therefore mirror your sense of powering your own progress in the world.

BUS

According to Jung, **riding on any form of public transport** suggests that you are being too conformist in your waking life. If you have a dream of being on a **bus**, your dreaming mind may be urging you to become more independent. A **double-**

In the air

Dreams of **hot-air balloons** indicate a desire to rise above mundane or worldly responsibilities. They can also represent a new sense of direction and purpose, symbolized by the fire lifting the balloon into the air; a note of caution must be sounded, however, as the fire needs to be attended to if it is to stay alight and keep everyone lifted. Flying in a **hang-glider** shares some of the exhilaration of flying unaided. According to Freudians, if the hang-glider is launched from a cliff or mountain it suggests the sexual act.

If you find yourself **flying in a bed, car, chair or any other kind of inappropriate vehicle**, this suggests a desire for the type of adventure that is not too radical a break from the familiar. If you are **flying in a bicycle**, this may recall the image of Spielberg's famous film *ET*, and express a desire to find refuge, security or to go home. If you are **flying a kite**, this suggests a sense of freedom that is enjoyed with both feet firmly on the ground. The kite may also represent an ambitious and risky project that is clouded by uncertainties.

decker bus symbolizes the many levels of a problem and the need to consider things from a different angle.

CAR

Dream **cars** can symbolize the image or persona you are trying to project to others; this can be sleek and powerful, or practical and powerful. Whenever a car appears in your dream, the first thing to do is to consider your personal associations with that car. If you do not envisage yourself owning this particular car, ask yourself why your dreaming mind selected it. What does it say about you? The answer should tell you a lot about your character, your self-image and your driving force or ambition. Dream cars can also represent yourself and your ability to control your life.

Are you a **good driver** in your dream? If you are, this suggests you are in control of your life. If you **drive badly**, however, your unconscious may be warning you that you are making too many mistakes and heading for an emotional crash. If a **back-seat driver** appears in your dream, could this represent someone who is trying to influence your life? Is **someone else driving the car**? Do you feel that this person is controlling your life or influencing you? Your dream may be expressing your dependence and lack of control. Pay attention to **the people you are driving** as this might suggest your feelings of responsibility towards them. If **you are not driving**, are you happy to be driven by someone else?

If a dream car symbolizes your persona, then the **steering wheel** represents your conscious mind, and the **engine and gas** your unconscious, or your inner power and energy. If your dream **journey was smooth**, this suggests stamina and energy, or to Freudians, progress in psychoanalysis. A **bumpy road** suggests anxieties

arising from the unconscious. If you **broke down or ran out of petrol**, this suggests that you are on the verge of depleting your physical, financial or emotional resources. If you have a dream in which you are **speeding or get a speeding fine**, this suggests your pace of life is way too fast or that you are living life in the fast lane. Are you in danger of losing control? Your dreaming mind may be urging you to slow down – particularly if **brakes** feature in the dream.

If any other part of your dream car was featured, you can draw a parallel with your waking life. For example, if a **tire was punctured**, do you feel deflated? If the **pedals were not working properly**, do you need more energy to make further progress in waking life? If **car wheels** appear in your dream, this is a call to action. For Jung, the wheel is a potent symbol of the life force and creativity energy, whilst for Buddhists and Hindus a wheel indicates universal truth. Dreams of **seatbelts** suggest a sense of safety and caution, whilst whether you have your **headlights switched on and off** may symbolize whether your awareness is on or off. **Car mirrors** are clear symbols of looking at the past and seeing the effect of past events on your possible plans for the future.

If you are **taking a taxi** in your dream, this suggests that you are willing to take a back-seat in life and let others do the driving, rather than relying on your own efforts. If **you are driving the taxi or car**, this suggests a willingness to guide others. Dreams of **drunk driving or driving without a license** suggest that you are not fully in control of your life. They may also reflect feelings of inadequacy, or even an unwillingness to conform to social stan-

The Element Encyclopedia of 20,000 Dreams

dards. If **you are overtaken** in your dream car, this suggests feelings of being left behind, whilst if **you are overtaking**, you may feel that you are getting ahead in life. If you are **reversing your car**, you may suffer from a sense of not getting anywhere, whilst if you dream of **running over someone**, are you killing an aspect of yourself? If you end up finding yourself **having to be towed**, this suggests anxieties about the dependent or needy part of yourself. **Traffic** in dreams generally means the opinions and concerns of other people, but if you are **stuck in a dream traffic jam**, this reflects your frustrations in life.

HORSE

For Freud, **riding a horse** is a symbol of sexuality. The **gallop** suggests passionate intercourse, and the **trot**, gentle enjoyment. Another interpretation suggests that **horse riding** suggests a desire for a slower pace of life, whilst **galloping or horse racing** suggests a competitive streak. **Falling or being thrown from a horse** suggests that you are worried about taking on too many responsibilities and finding it hard to cope. If the **horses pulling a carriage are out of control** in your dream, this suggests loss of control in your waking life but if the **carriage is plodding along**, it suggests an old-fashioned approach to life and reluctance to look forward to the new. If you dreamed of **riding a horse, or being pulled by one in a carriage or other horse-drawn vehicle**, try to decide what the horse symbolizes to you and then note if it was doing your bidding. This will help you see if your unconscious is going along with, or rebelling against, you. *See also* ANIMALS.

Traveling and water

In Greek mythology, **river crossings** are often associated with death or a journey into the unconscious and they may have this same association in your dreams. It takes great physical effort to **row a boat or canoe**, and your dream may be emphasizing how demanding your journey of personal growth is. For Freudians, a rowing boat or canoe is a phallic symbol, and the **act of rowing or paddling a canoe** indicates masturbation. A dream of a **barge or towpath** suggests heavy emotional burdens slowing your progress in life, whilst if you are **swimming** in your dream, this is often interpreted as representing a desire for sex or a wish to return to the safe waters of the womb. According to Jung, **swimming towards land** suggests a desire for rebirth or renewal, but **swimming against the tide** suggests personal struggles.

SEA VOYAGE

According to Jung, a **voyage at sea** suggests an exploration of the unconscious. Freudians might see the sea as a symbol of the mother or the womb and therefore might regard a sea voyage as an incest wish. Freudians would certainly regard a ship as a phallic symbol, with a **ship being tossed about in turbulent seas** representing passionate love-making, and a **sinking ship** suggesting doomed love. If you do dream of traveling in a boat, pay close attention to the **conditions of travel** as they will reveal much about your waking situation. Are the waters calm or is a storm building?

If the **boat is drifting aimlessly on the water**, you may feel that you are lacking direction, whilst if the **boat capsizes**, this suggests imminent danger or obstacles ahead. If you are **enjoying a tranquil boat ride that is slowly but surely heading in the right direction**, this could imply a sense of anticipated success with a particular project in real life. A **ferry** is an archetypal vessel associated with transition from one stage of consciousness to another, and the **ferryman** is the archetypal wise old man. If you dream of **docks**, this is a symbol of the safe ground you leave behind as you begin your voyage of discovery.

Train

As with trams and buses and other forms of public transport, dreams about **trains** suggest that you are no longer controlling your life and have become too dependent on someone or something else, such as your parents, your partner or a job. According to Freudians, trains with their huffing and pumping are phallic symbols, and a **train entering a tunnel** is a symbol of sexual intercourse. A **broken-down or cancelled train** may actually be a positive sign in dreamland, as it suggests that you are considering making your own way under your own steam. To dream of **missing a train or passing a destination** may also suggest missed opportunities. If the **train is stuck on a platform**, this may suggest a problem that needs ironing out before any

further progress can be made in waking life. If the **train makes an emergency stop**, this warns against moving too fast and if the **train stops at a crossing**, this suggests the need for patience.

Vehicle

As well as indicating the manner in which you are progressing towards your goals or what is driving you forward in waking life, dream **vehicles** tell us whether we are in control of our lives or being driven by something or someone else. So if any vehicle appears in your dream, pay attention to the **identity of the driver** and try to make a connection to your waking life.

If you dream of a truck, much of the symbolism associated with cars also applies, but since trucks are often associated with business and work your dream may have hinted at the progress you are making in your working life. If you dreamed of a **rubbish truck**, your unconscious may have been urging you to get rid of emotional pressures that are dragging you down. A dream of a **taxi** suggests a quick and direct means to your goal, but bear in mind that there is a price to pay for the trip. Are you prepared to pay it?

Walking

Walking is a classic symbol of your thought processes or progress in life; the **surrounding landscape** will give you a clue as to the meaning of the dream. If you shake **dust away from your shoes as you are walking**, this suggests that you are breaking successfully from the past. Dust is a symbol of the earth and if you are **gathering dust on your clothes, shoes or in your hands as you**

The Element Encyclopedia of 20,000 Dreams

Common traveling dreams

Traveling dreams can be incredibly insightful because they show you what is keeping you from getting what you want in life. Always take note of the mode of transportation used and whether the vehicle is designed for one person or many, as these will say something about the approach you are using to handle a certain situation.

Perhaps the most common of all traveling dream is the one in which you **miss your plane, boat or train**. No matter how frustrating this dream is, it is actually trying to help you get what you want. Look closely at what you should have done in the dream to make your connection; if there is clearly something you could have done differently to ensure you were on time, your dream is encouraging a shift of emphasis, understanding or action in waking life.

Another common dream is taking the **wrong bus, train or plane**. This dream is particularly common to people who have problems making decisions in life because they are worried about what other people think. Your dreaming mind is urging you to correct this tendency by focusing on what you think is right. Yet another common dream involves being **on board a boat, ship or plane and the person in charge becomes unable to pilot or steer. You are suddenly called upon to steer**. This dream suggests that you are about to be thrust into a position of authority and that others are relying on you. For dreams of crashes or disasters whilst traveling, *see also* DISASTERS.

Dreams of **traveling to a safe harbor or haven** highlight the need for comfort and security in waking life. Remember that the trials, frustrations and challenges that you face in the dream symbolize real-life impediments and emotions that are slowing you down or helping you along your way. When interpreting traveling dreams, always consider the reactions and solutions that the dream calls upon you to make to improve your dream journey. The necessary ingredient to encourage your progress is often a symbolic representation for the action or position in waking life that will be most beneficial to you.

walk, you may be thinking about the approaching of old age. A dream limp may suggest your movement is being crippled or restricted in some way in waking life.

Always consider how you were moving in a dream and try to make the connection to your attitude in waking life at present. Are you walking purposely in your dream and do you know where you are heading? If you can answer positively to both of these questions, this suggests a sense of direction and purpose in life. The opposite is true if you are lost. If you were skipping or dancing, you are feeling carefree but if you are dragging your feet, this may suggest reluctance. Tripping or stumbling suggests making a mistake; jumping, taking a short cut; crawling, humiliation or extreme hardship. And if you could not move at all, your dreaming mind may be reflecting your sense of being at a complete standstill in your waking life as a result of your indecision. Running in a dream suggests impatience to reach a destination. It can also indicate a desire to please others or to run away from them. *See also* ACCIDENTS, ACTION AND ADVENTURES.

TREES

Linking the earth with the heavens, the tree is an archetypal symbol that can represent cosmic unity; in dreams, however, it generally refers to your spiritual and emotional growth.

The tree's roots draw on the depths of the unconscious, the trunk is the solid body and the branches reach to the enlightenment of heaven. According to Jung the tree is 'a symbol of the self … depicted in the process of growth'. If this interpretation is used, dreams about trees can be seen to be symbolic of the basic structure of your inner life, telling you a great deal about yourself and your personal growth. Because each element of the tree's structure also denotes aspects of you, your life, your past, your present and even your future, when one appears in your dreams it is best to work with the image fairly extensively. The shape of the tree and the condition of its roots, trunk, branches, leaves and fruit all send important messages, as does the landscape in which the tree is growing. And if you dreamed of a particular species of tree, understanding its symbolic associations will further aid your interpretation and your self-knowledge. *See also* FLOWERS; NATURE AND THE SEASONS; VEGETABLES AND FRUIT.

Tree Anatomy

APPEARANCE OF TREE

If you dreamed of a **well-shaped tree** that is pleasing to the eye, this would suggest a personality that is ordered; a **large, messy tree** would suggest a chaotic personality. The **seasonal appearance of the tree** in your dream will be significant because the stages of a person's life are reflected in the effects of the seasons on a deciduous tree. If your dream tree was **covered in spring blossoms and tiny leaf buds**, the association is with spring, and the vigor and energy of youth. If the tree was **covered in deep green foliage**, this suggests summer or the prime of life; if its **leaves were starting to fall**, this suggests autumn and middle age; and if the **tree looked bare**, this suggests winter and old age, or concerns about getting older.

According to Freudians, **acorns** are a phallic symbol and **nuts** symbols of the female genitals, so **seeds and nuts on the tree** can suggest new beginnings. **Seedlings and saplings** are generally associated with young children, **flourishing and mature trees** suggest maturity and **ancient trees**, old age. A **dead or withered tree** could be a symbol of a lost loved one; it not only reminds us that all living things die, but also that the cycle of rebirth and new beginnings never ends. If your dreaming mind featured a **tree with a crown or apex** (or you dreamed of **climbing a tree and struggling to reach the top**), this suggests a desire for spiritual growth. Alternatively, it could suggest ambition in your professional life or the desire for safety or refuge, as when you climb a tree to escape. If you dreamed of a **falling tree**, this represents a sense of threat to your identity.

Tall trees are a symbol of aspiration and reaching up to the sky, whilst a **short tree** is a symbol of low aspirations or selling yourself short. A **tree that is fallen or cut down** may symbolize obstacles in your path, and a **tree struck by lightning or in flames** may represent a situation that is about to erupt. It can also symbolize electrified energy or being 'on fire' for a goal or desire. *See also* Forest entry in PLACES.

■ *Idioms: family tree; top of the tree; barking up the wrong tree; tree of life; Tree of Knowledge; dead wood; can't see the wood for the trees.*

Branch

Branches symbolize the various directions you have taken in your life. Branches could also represent your children, or the birth of new ideas that may one day flourish and bear fruit. A **tree with wide branches** could suggest a warm, open personality, whereas a **small, close-leaved tree** would suggest an uptight personality. The **noise of the wind rushing through the branches** was considered by ancient people to be the voice of nature; in dreams it signifies truth telling or the need for it. You should look for clues in your dream as to what truth your unconscious wants you to hear or tell.

Flowering tree

People have worshipped trees for centuries and profound symbolism is associated with them. The dream image of a **mature flowering tree** can evoke the Tree of Knowledge and the Tree of Life at the heart of Eden or the cross on which Jesus was sacrificed, which is also called a tree and is a symbol of redemption. These Judeo-Christian images have their counterparts in other cultures and myths, with divine trees that sustain knowledge, spiritual growth and divinity, perhaps the best known being the mighty ash Yggdrasil of the Norsemen. And in Islamic belief a tree symbolizes a spiritually mature person. A tree can also represent time; the root, the past; the trunk, the present and the branches, the future. Perhaps your dream says something about your hopes for the future.

According to ancient dream-lore, **climbing a tree** is said to be lucky. If you dream of a **fruit-bearing tree**, take a look at which type of fruit is present and its meaning for you. If you noticed the species of tree, what is that species associated with for you? Did you dream of the mighty, strong oak, dainty cherry tree or somber, dark conifers? Did you dream of a single tree or a forest? If you find yourself **lost in a forest**, perhaps you 'can't see the forest for the trees' or have lost sight of your goals. **Walking through a forest** may symbolize a need to get back in touch with your inner self and your instinctual nature.

Leaf

Fresh new leaves signify new ideas, new interests or the part of you that is still vulnerable because it is new. **Withered and dying leaves** suggest waning enthusiasm and **falling leaves** suggest things that have happened in the past. If the tree in your dream does not shed its leaves and is an **evergreen**, this denotes an energetic and healthy approach to life. You can also be blown like a leaf, suggesting changing moods or opinions, or separation. **Birds in the branches** may also represent your thoughts.

The Tree of Life

Spiritually and in dreams, the tree is a symbol of the **Tree of Life**; an ancient idea common to many cultures and mythologies. Often regarded as an all-nourishing, all-giving Mother, many myths speak of the Tree of Life or **World Tree** as involved in the creation of the universe.

Britain was once covered by mighty oak, lime and pine forests, and reverence for trees is a major feature within Celtic religion, reflecting a link between the upper and lower worlds. Druids had their teaching center in the midst of oak groves, and the words for wood and wisdom are similar (Welsh *gwydd* and *gwyddon*). The Celtic Tree of Life is one of the most popular and enduring motifs of Celtic art, found both on Northumbrian and Celtic crosses and on illuminated manuscripts. It is also portrayed variously as the Golden Bough, vine, or mistletoe. The ancient Celts envisioned the cosmos in the form of a great tree, whose roots were deep in the earth and whose branches stretched to the heavens.

The Celtic Tree of Life is therefore a symbol of balance between these worlds; the unification of above and below; a symbol of balance and harmony. Its branches and roots form a map of the cosmos wherein all things are interwoven and connected; it dwells in three worlds – a link between heaven, earth and the underworld. In dreams the appearance of the Tree of Life or any kind of tree can therefore be a powerful symbol of harmony, success, integration and fulfillment. These can be achieved in waking life when there is a union between the material and the spiritual, and the feminine and masculine aspects of your personality.

Root

The **roots** of a tree represent your unconscious mind, as well as your childhood and your past, the 'roots' from which you have grown. If the **roots in your dream appear strong**, this suggests that the past is still heavily influencing your present. It could also suggest that your past was stable and supportive. If, on the other hand, the **tree in your dream was a young one**, the message may be that you are in the process of putting down your roots or establishing yourself in the waking world. A dream in which the **roots are in the sky** suggests wisdom and insight. **Spreading roots** would indicate an ability to relate well to others, whereas **deep roots** would suggest a more self-contained attitude. An **uprooted tree** symbolizes a feeling of being uprooted in waking or spiritual life. Are you losing your hold on the ground? Roots symbolize home, family and stability. Are any of these things changing in your waking or spiritual life?

Trunk/Bark

A symbol of family tradition, the tree **trunk** can also represent your individuality and your conscious mind, whilst the **bark** symbolizes the image or persona you present to others. If the **bark on the tree was strong and tight**, then your approach to life is straightforward and direct but if it was **peeling**, then perhaps you are feeling vulnerable or are worried that others can see right through you. A **rough trunk** suggests a rough and ready personality, whereas a **smoother trunk** would indicate more sophistication. **Tree sap** can be associated with blood so if it appears in your dream, perhaps with **insects feeding on the oozing sap**, it could be that your energy levels are currently low and you are feeling worn down by petty irritations. You can tell the age of a tree by counting the rings on the felled stump; in a dream, these **rings** may represent your past experiences and the wisdom you have gained in your life.

Species of Tree

Specific trees may be significant to you, so try and identify the feelings and associations a specific tree evokes if one appears in your dream. For example, does the **magnolia** that graced your childhood garden conjure up a happy childhood memory or is it the tree you carved your initials on with the name of your first sweetheart? If your dream tree reminded you of nothing in particular, it may be that you are unconsciously aware of its traditional, mythical or religious symbolism and this may have relevance to your waking situation. Specific trees carry with them ancient associations and although it is unlikely that these association have much relevance in modern urban life, they can and do still carry weight in your dreams. If you believe a tree in your dream was significant but you have no idea why, the following guidelines might help you; if your species of tree is not listed here, it may be worthwhile researching its traditional meaning.

Plants and trees

Ivy: In dreams, **ivy** can suggest determination and persistence to overcome problems. It can also suggest an unwanted presence in your life because despite its attractive appearance, ivy is hard to get rid of in a garden.

Mistletoe: Firmly associated with kissing at Christmas, **mistletoe was** once believed to have great healing powers and symbolized wisdom. Today the dream is likely to have sexual overtones and may signify your attraction to someone in waking life.

ASH

A symbol of optimism, creativity and generosity, according to ancient dream-lore to dream of an ash tree is considered extremely fortunate. The wood of the ash makes handles for all sorts of sports and DIY equipment; perhaps you feel that you might have handled a situation badly. Or perhaps you were simply dreaming of the mythical Norse tree Yggdrasil, which was an ash.

BAY

In mythology, a **bay tree** was thought to protect against witchcraft and it still carries the association of protection against something unwanted. Victors were crowned with **laurel of bay leaves** in ancient Rome, so if this tree was the focus of your dream could it reflect your longing for professional achievements in the real world, or was your unconscious warning you to keep someone or something at bay?

BIRCH

Birch is a symbol of honesty, virtue and honor, perhaps because of its tall, straight trunk, pure white bark and translucent catkins. The birch tree is also known as the tree of rebirth, spring and fertility. People were once 'birched' to drive out evil spirits, whilst twigs were given to newly weds to ensure fertility. These twigs are still used today for invigoration in Scandinavian saunas and spas. Birch therefore may suggest dispelling negative energies and influences, or the need for an honest fresh start.

ELM

Associated with old age, the **elm** also represents the need for caution, responsibility and endurance. Elm was almost wiped out by Dutch elm disease in Britain at the end of the twentieth century; is there something beautiful in your life that is also vulnerable?

OAK

A symbol of majesty, justice and protection, **oak trees**, along with **ash, beech, birch, rowan and hawthorn**, were regarded as sacred by early Europeans. The mighty oak, however, was the most potent symbol of masculine strength and its acorns suggest incredible potential. According to

Conifers and evergreens

As symbols of eternal life, **conifers and evergreens** suggest a vigorous, healthy approach to life but they can also express a warning to be cautious and conserve your energy.

Cedar: If your dream featured a cedar, could this be a reference to Lebanon (just as a maple might be a reference to Canada)? Perhaps you associate it with the precious furniture of the Middle East, or is it a reference to the Bible, in which it was often mentioned?

Cypress: Common in graveyards, the cypress or false cypress is a symbol of the inevitability of death, but also conjures up the hope of rebirth and new beginnings.

Fir/Spruce: Strongly associated with Christmas, the fir or spruce is linked to the birth of Jesus. The image in a dream may express strong positive or negative feelings about family occasions.

Holly: Traditionally associated with Christmas, holly is a dream symbol of family festivity and joy, mingled with pain.

Leylandii: If you dream of this fast-growing conifer, is someone trying to erect a boundary between you and them in waking life? Or perhaps you are undecided about something and are 'hedging your bets'?

Pine: If you dream of pine trees, are you pining for someone or something in waking life? A pine cone, depending on the context of your dream, may also symbolize masculine virility or feminine fecundity.

Freudians, the oak is a potent symbol of male sexuality or a father who is strong and comforting.

OLIVE

The **olive**'s association with peace is derived from the Old Testament, so in dreams it may have been advising you to make peace with someone or something in waking life. If you are Jewish, a dream of an olive tree may symbolize your desire for a prosperous, fertile future.

PALM

A powerful symbol of luxury and exotic abundance, **palm trees** grow with their roots near water and their trunks in the sun, so they also represent a union of masculine and feminine forces. Perhaps your unconscious was referring to the **palm on your hand**; perhaps you should perhaps extend this hand to someone with whom you have been feuding during your waking hours. **Coconuts** are filled with milk, so they can be a symbol of lust or lack of

Ancient Celtic tree correspondences at a glance

Alder: Completeness, spirituality

Apple: Symbol of living life to the full, focusing mind and heart together positively

Ash: Prosperity, protection, healing

Aspen: Intuitive knowledge, understanding

Beech: Inspires us to let go of old patterns, to see more of the good that is in the world. Also a symbol of narrow-mindedness and sorrow.

Birch: Protection, purification

Blackthorn: Cleansing and renewal, leading to a sudden, spontaneous flowing of the spirit

Cherry: Success, productivity

Dogwood: Clarity, vision

Elder: Exorcism, prosperity, banishing, healing

Elm: Mystery, encourages renewed faith in the value of our life's work

Fir: Ancient wisdom, regeneration

Hawthorn: Fertility, prosperity

Hazel: Manifestation, protection, fertility

Holly: Protection

Maple: Luck, strength, family

Oak: Strength

Pear: Hope, generosity, inner growth

Pine: Ancient wisdom, eternal life

Poplar: Vision, peace

Rowan: Healing, empowerment

Willow: Love, healing, protection, fertility

---

inhibition, maternal feelings or infantile refreshment.

PLANE

The **London plane** is often the only reminder of nature in urban areas and in dreams it may serve the same purpose: to encourage you to keep in touch with natural feelings and to get away from what is artificial.

WILLOW

Often associated with motherhood, the **willow** is also thought to symbolize emotional difficulties. This is particularly true if it is a **weeping willow**. Or perhaps you are a keen cricket player and the tree has appeared in your dream because you are anticipating a match.

VEGETABLES AND FRUIT

Vegetables and fruit are a vital source of nourishment in the real world, and in dreamland their reference is usually to feeding the emotions rather than nourishing the body.

In general, fertility and readiness are associated with ripe and succulent fruit. To see fruit in your dream may therefore signify a period of growth, abundance, sweet reward and financial gain. However, if you dream of fruit that is past its ripeness, it is said to represent a missed opportunity or a loss of fertility. You are thought to be concerned with nourishment, fullness or abundance if you dream of vegetables; or feel you are lacking these things if the vegetables are spoiled or of poor quality. According to Freud, dreams that feature vegetables and fruits may be of a sexual nature, depending on the shape of the vegetable and your feelings in the dream. For Jungians, vegetables are symbols of personal growth indicating the need for spiritual nourishment.

Interpreting the symbolism of fruits and vegetables in your dream depends on how you feel about them in daily life; whether you like them for their taste and nutritional value, or find them dull and boring. You may be projecting a need to feed your body or soul, or reflecting on a dull and not very satisfying part of life.

The number, shape, color, taste and type of vegetable or fruit and the overall content and feeling of your dream also need be considered. *See also* FOOD AND DRINK.

Vegetables Directory

Vegetables, like fruits, provide nourishment and nutrients but unlike fruits they are seldom regarded as delicious or sweet treats. This is why in dreamland they symbolize experiences that are good for us, providing basic emotional nourishment. But vegetables are not always good news; because we often refer to people who are slow, lazy, sluggish or inactive as 'vegetables' or 'cabbages' or 'couch potatoes', a dream image of vegetables may be referring to your own inability to think, function or get active in waking life.

In dreams, vegetables can symbolize the most basic human emotions. There may also be an allusion to your diet; in waking life you may not be getting enough fiber, cereals and vegetables. Bear in mind, too, that your own personal associations and preferences concerning specific vegetables will influence your interpretation; for example, if you were forced to eat spinach as a child, you may associate it with punishment. If, however, you have taken personal associations into consideration and they still can't help you interpret your dream, it may be that your unconscious was drawing from a wider source of symbolism.

For example, if you dreamed of a long, rigid vegetable such as a leek, carrot or cucumber, this could be a phallic symbol referring to intimacy issues in waking life. Also consider the words associated with vegetables such as 'cool as a cucumber', 'mushrooming', 'dangling a carrot', 'peas in a pod' and 'hot potato'. Because many vegetables grow in the soil, they also have numerous associations with death and rebirth, often being considered as a powerful symbol of spiritual growth. In the broadest sense, vegetables are a connection to your family and community, and represent the goodness you can take from earth. Vegetables force you down to the depths of your unconscious.

Eating vegetables signifies the taking in of fundamental spiritual nourishment, and in this sense, cooking vegetables can be seen as an alchemical process. If the vegetables in your dream are overcooked, this could suggest that you are concentrating too long and too hard on a particular problem, or 'overcooking' a relationship by allowing it to become claustrophobic. On the other hand, cooked or prepared vegeta-bles could refer to ideas which are developing or simply offering themselves to you, ready for growth and nurture. Growing vegetables indicates fertility and renewal. Rotting vegetables are a symbol of death and endings but they are also the precursor to renewal and growth. Seeing rows of neatly planted vegetables in a dream could mean the loss of freewill or the imposition of too rigid a sense of order in your life. Wild vegetables, by the same token, symbolize disorganization. Frozen vegeta-bles show a state of suspended emotional animation, whilst processed vegetables have had some, or all, of their nutrients removed and suggest the dominance of style over substance in waking life.

The color of the vegetable will also be significant. A common dream image pres-ents a variety of vegetables in great abun-dance for the dreamer to feast on suggesting a desire to enjoy the goodness of nature. However, such dreams may also reflect concerns about your lack of money or abundance. As with fruits, don't forget that the color, shape, number and condition of the vegetables in your dream will all be significant. *See also* COLORS; NUMBERS; SHAPES.

If a vegetable, or group of vegetables, featured strongly in your dream and you'd like to know more about the symbolism of vegetables, it might be worth doing some research on the historical, cultural, reli-gious and medicinal significance of specific vegetables to enrich your interpretation. The list on pages 646–48 of specific vegeta-bles and their meanings in dreams is by no means comprehensive.

Artichoke/Asparagus/Aubergine

In dreams, **artichokes** may warn against concealing the truth or giving – or being given – incomplete accounts of the truth. In dream-lore, **asparagus** is regarded as a symbol of lust and desire on account of its phallic shape. Asparagus can also suggest prosperity, vitality, youth and abundance. If the image of an **aubergine** appears in your dream pay attention to its purple color, but remember that it is also called the egg-plant, which may give rise to a quite different interpretation.

Bean/Beetroot/Broccoli

A **bean or beans** in your dream may suggest abundance, wealth and prosperity. Many idioms contain the word 'beans', so it might be worth considering whether the following possess any relevance for your dream: are you full of energy and vitality, or 'full of beans'; have you disclosed something confidential, or 'spilled the beans'; is there something in your life that doesn't amount to much, or a 'hill of beans'; are you a 'bean counter', always keeping the score; or are you about to have a party or celebration, sometimes called a 'bean feast'?

To dream of **beetroot** may be on account of its red color, which could suggest the need for an injection of passion or enthusiasm into your life. It could also symbolize embarrassment, or being 'as red as a beetroot'. In dreams, **broccoli** signifies talents and the productive use of them. On the other hand, it could also be referring to your diet: are you eating enough vegetables?

Cabbage/Carrot/Cauliflower/Celery/Cucumber

In some parts of Europe, **cabbages** are connected to conception or childbirth, because children are told that babies are found in a cabbage patch. On the other hand, cabbage may also refer to tough and difficult aspects of your waking life. To see a **carrot** in your dream signifies abundance. It may also symbolize a lure – as in the pun 'dangle a carrot' – or can be interpreted as a phallic symbol. In dreams, **cauliflower** could denote someone who displays little intelligence, as suggested by the phrase 'having cauliflower between your ears'. It could also suggest something that becomes distorted or misshapen as a result of repeated blows, such as cauliflower ears. **Celery** in dreams denotes problems and issues that need to be faced up to and dealt with, whilst the size of **cucumbers** in dreams may offer a surprising insight into the extent of your appetite for sex or for life.

Kale/Leek/Mushroom/Onion

In dreams, **kale** represents a personal need of some kind; only you will know what that need is. Pay attention to the color and condition of the kale, as they will help you with the interpretation. To dream of **leeks** represents a positive force, or the need for a positive force against an aspect of negativity in some area of your life. Often mentioned in Chinese literature and legend, many species of **mushroom** have hallucinogenic properties. They can take you away from mundane existence so if they appear in a dream, could they suggest

Harvest time

Dreams of vegetables may also feature scenes of the **garden or field** in which the produce was harvested. In such cases, the imagery suggests the importance of following a natural cycle within a project, career or relationship. Your dream is urging you to be conscious of choosing the right time to plant, tend or harvest. In some cases, dreams about vegetables can indicate hard toil without reward, but if the dream involves **planting or tending vegetables** this is a sign of inner strength that will bring rich reward. If, however, you dream of **cutting the heads off plants**, you may have been duped or imposed upon in some way in waking life.

To dream about a **harvest** suggests you are going to reap the rewards of something you have done previously.

For example, you may have worked hard and are now in a position in which finance is not your main concern. Dream harvests can therefore indicate looking back to the past to reap the rewards of the future, but they can also mean looking towards to the future in order to use the wisdom and experience you have gained. The other circumstances in your dream will dictate the interpretation. Much, of course, depends on the quality and quantity of the harvest, but a **rich harvest** indicates abundance, fruitfulness and fertility. If you are **taking part in a harvest or are attending a harvest festival**, this suggests a celebration of your life energy; enjoy it. A **poor harvest**, on the other hand, may suggest disappointment and disillusionment.

your need for time out or for more excitement and drama in your life? They may be also be a symbol of longevity or even of immortality. In dreams, onions typically suggest sorrow or something to cry about, no doubt because of the vegetable's tendency to make the eyes water. According to ancient dream-lore, to see a quantity of onions represents the amount of envy and spite the dreamer will meet in their life. In dreams, onions can also suggest different layers of your personality, representing both the inner and the outer self, as well as the many layers in between.

PARSLEY/PARSNIP/PEAS/ PEPPERS/POTATO

In dreams, **parsley** represents unrecognized but nourishing benefits in your life. Are you taking some things for granted, such as your health or the love of your family? If **parsnips** appear in your dreams they may signify neglected opportunities in waking life, whilst the appearance of **peas** could indicate difficult decisions that need to be made. **Shucking peas** is thought to portend recovery from illness, **dried peas** are symbolic of tenacity and strength of purpose, but to dream that you **eat peas** suggests some form of deception. When **peppers** appear in dreams pay attention to their color; are they **red or green**, as this will influence the interpretation? Peppers typify the need for a response of some kind in waking life and to dream about pepper or peppers indicates that you need to put a little more spice and variety in your life. Alternatively, there may be something that is bothering or irritating you, and your dream may be trying to point to the source.

In dreams, a **potato** could suggest an essential or basic element in your life; it could also suggest being inactive or a 'couch potato', as well as a delicate or awkward situation or a 'hot potato'. If you see **mashed potatoes** in a dream, you may have to make decisions involving financial cutbacks. **Potato skin** relates to the most potent aspects of an issue; the place from which the greatest number of benefits will be derived. **Yams or sweet potatoes** are symbols of pleasant memories.

Radish/Salad/Spinach/Squash

If **radishes** appear in your dreams, it may mean that you are caught up in an emotionally volatile situation. In dreams, **salad** can sometimes refer to the lack of essential nutrients offered in such foods —you may be being short-changed over something; it can also refer to lack of experience, as in 'green'. But if you are **eating a salad** in your dream, this may refer to the experiences that can trigger personal growth. Similar to cabbage is the delicious salad filler, **lettuce**. When you see **lettuce growing** in your dream, it may mean that you are in for a blissful or pleasurable

moment in the future. If you are **eating lettuce** in your dream, negative thinking may be hindering your progress in waking life. If **spinach** appears in your dream it could be referring to the need to include extra iron in your diet. On the other hand, it could also refer to the need for you to have more strength in waking life. **Squash** in dreams may suggest that you are distorting or pulverizing something, suppressing something, or even humiliating somebody.

Tomatoes/Turnip/Watercress

A **tomato** should more strictly be termed a fruit, but most people assume it is a vegetable. In dreams, it may suggest recovery, good health and renewed strength. **Turnips**, by contrast, may suggest a reversal, a changed attitude or decision. **Watercress** is a symbol of spiritual nourishment.

Fruit Directory

When you see fruit in a dream, it usually refers to readiness, financial gain and sexuality, as well as suggesting that you are going through a time of personal growth. The type and condition of the fruit that appears in your dream will influence its meaning. Ripe fruit, for example, is associated with lush and rewarding experiences, rich with promise for the future (because fruits are full of seeds). If you see fruit that is green, or not yet ripened, it may refer to a certain hastiness that you may be displaying in waking life, as well as failed attempts to achieve a goal. More hard work for a longer period of time is suggested. If rotting or bitter fruit is seen in a dream, it may suggest that you are missing out on a wealth of opportunities that are available to you. You are essentially hindering your growth and the amount of pleasure you could experience. A fruit pip may represent something that is capable of major growth. A pip sound may symbolize detection or communication. It could also suggest defeating somebody by a small margin, pipping them at the post.

Fruits have connotations other than just reward in dreams and when interpreting a dream that highlighted a particular fruit, it is important to take into account its shape, texture, and freshness as your unconscious may have selected it to reflect your sexuality. A dream of fruit can often have sexual connotations because the food is sweet, juicy and delicious. In ancient times, fruits were considered symbols of feminine fertility because of their seeds. As a result of the influence of Freud certain fruits – especially the banana – are considered phallic symbols. The banana is associated with masculine virility on account of its shape, so a ripe banana may indicate a man who is at his sexual peak. Soft and curvaceous fruits like melons, apples and peaches have been compared to female breasts or the child-bearing womb, so if you are a man taking a bite out of a juicy melon, could this mirror your desire to become more intimate with a woman? If you were a woman eating a shriveled apple in your dream, could this echo a regret for the loss of youth? Numerous cultures have also associated round, seed-packed fruits with the fruitfulness of the womb, so if you are a

woman hoping to conceive in waking life, dreaming of eating a pomegranate could reflect your wishes. Fruit is also thought to symbolize immortality and it is easy to see why; its seeds signify the beginnings of life, leading to ripe fruit from which seed again springs, making the cycle begin all over again.

HARVESTING FRUIT

If you are **picking ripe succulent fruit from a tree** in your dream, this may confirm a sense of satisfaction in waking life that you can at last enjoy the sweet taste and rewards of success. An abundance of health, goodness and the fruits of your labor are also indicated if an **orchard** appears in your dream. And if you dreamed of **feeding and watering a young fruit tree**, your unconscious may have focused on your nurturing nature. On the other hand, if your **fruit crop was damaged, stunted or blighted**, your unconscious may be mirroring your real sense of regret that you are unable to enjoy success or the fruits of your labor. Your unconscious may also have been warning you to take steps to safeguard your health, your family, your relationships or your business before the damage becomes irreversible.

Dreaming of a **fruit bowl overflowing with freshly picked fruit** may reflect your own sense of being blessed in waking life. Dream fruit in a bowl indicates the culmination of actions that have been taken in the past. You have been able to harvest the past and make a new beginning for yourself. **Peeling fruit** in dreams introduces elements of bitterness and separation, but it can also suggest necessary action that need to be taken to further your development in waking life. If you are dreaming of **buying or selling fruit**, it may be that you are participating in a business that is plentiful, but will not reap much profit.

APPLE

In Judeo-Christian belief, the **apple** denotes sin and temptation because of the expulsion of Adam and Eve from the Garden of Eden after the serpent tempted Eve to eat the apple growing on the Tree of Knowledge. Greek mythology associated the apple with sexual attraction. So if you are married and **tempted to bite or steal an apple** in your dream, this could represent the attraction of a forbidden affair. Their association with the Tree of Knowledge means that apples may also indicate the self-knowledge and insight gained from experience. On the other hand, they may also symbolize a desire to return to lost innocence.

To see **apples growing** in a tree in your dream symbolizes wisdom and that well-earned rewards will be gained in the future. Consider also the common phrase, 'an apple a day keeps the doctor away'; this may imply that you need to take better care of your health. To see **green apples** represents developing love or love that has yet to blossom. To see **a rotten or half-eaten apple in your dream** denotes that what you are striving and aiming for may not only be unfulfilling; it may even be harmful to you. A popular image of the comforts of home and childhood, **apple pie** probably reflects a desire to return to the security of childhood. Old rivalries and resentments may be expressed if you appear to be served a **smaller slice of pie** than the others present in your dreams.

APRICOT

In dreams, **apricots** suggest a healing force from within or a pleasant outlook on life. If, however, you see **rotten or sour apricots** in your dream, this suggests that your apparently rosy future may be filled with bitterness and sorrow.

BANANA

A dreamtime **banana** is usually interpreted as a symbol of an erect penis, but it may also be reminding you of an area of your life you may have been denying or suggesting that you are too easily shocked. Dreams of **peeling a banana** may have a considerable erotic charge. A **banana skin lying in your path** on the ground in your dream may represent your misgivings about taking a particular course of action.

BERRY

There are many **berries** that can appear within a dream, but they all possess significantly different meanings. **Raspberries** suggest that a dangerous but entertaining relationship may be on the horizon. If you are **eating raspberries** in a dream, it may be a reference to some sort of distress that you will feel because of unkind words that may be floating around about you. **Blueberries** in a dream refer to the dreamer's youth, as well as to a desire to return to youthful ways. Blueberries are also a symbol of eternity and an optimistic future. If you are **gathering gooseberries** in a dream, you will experience happiness in the future. To dream of **mulberries** represents an illness that may prevent you from achieving the goals that you have set for

The Element Encyclopedia of 20,000 Dreams

yourself. If you are **eating mulberries** in a dream, you may be experiencing bitter disappointments in life. The delicious **strawberry** is a symbol of both temptation and sensuality.

CHERRY/DATE/PLUM

Many slang expressions incorporate fruits within them, so if you **ate or plucked a cherry** from a dream tree, this may refer to your tendency to cherry-pick only the best in life. It may also have been a reference to someone's virginity or naivety. The **cherry** is synonymous with desire due no doubt to its resemblance to seductive human lips. In dream-lore to taste cherries bodes for good or ill depending on whether the taste is sweet or sour. Similarly, if you dreamed of **eating a date**, could it have represented a dream date? If a **plum** features in your dream, this could be a symbol of a highly paid or plum position you have been offered, or hope to be offered. *See also* SENSES.

EXOTIC FRUIT/DRIED FRUIT

Dreams of exotic fruit may be urging you to be more adventurous in your waking life. On the other hand, the larger and more exotic your dream appetite, the more interesting and robust your sexual hunger. **Papaya** connotes a need to calm emotions or anxiety. **Dried fruit** in your dreams, such as **raisins,** suggests pleasant memories or emotional nourishment from an unexpected source in waking life. They can, however, also suggest missed opportunities, negative thinking or bad timing.

FIG

Figs are often seen as a female sexual symbol because of their appearance when split open to be eaten. In some societies, by contrast, they symbolize the testicles. In dreams, figs are therefore symbols of fecundity and libido, but if you dreamed of **refusing a fig or disliking their taste**, could this have unconsciously expressed your feeling of not 'giving a fig' about someone or something in waking life?

GRAPE/GRAPEFRUIT

Grapes are a symbol of sexual pleasure, being a fruit that is meant to be shared with a lover or placed in another's mouth. Grapes therefore express sexuality in all its erotic joy. If the **grapes are sour** in your dreams, this can suggest disgust or displeasure. Given its origin from grapes, **wine** is a dream symbol of the free spirit – the sense of intoxication can allow the dream to rise above the mundane. To see **grapevines** in your dream is a symbol of opulence, wealth and decadence. To see or eat grapes in your dream, represents sexuality but they can also represent wealth and prosperity. To dream that you are **picking and gathering grapes** may signify profit and the realization of your desires. To see or eat a **grapefruit** in your dream represents a sense of well-being and a refreshed state of mind and body. If you dream of a **grapefruit tree** in your dream, it is symbolic of your talents, belief system and good deeds. It may also represent the fruits of your labor.

Lemon/Lime

Lemons can be extremely sour, so if you were **sucking a lemon** in your dream, this could mirror your acid tongue in waking life or the acerbic behavior of someone you know. Lemons generally denote inferiority within a dream, so if you see **shriveled lemons** in a dream, you may experience separation or divorce with a loved one. **Eating or sucking on a lemon** within a dream symbolizes the need to be cleansed or go through a period of healing. When you dream of a **lime**, it is a symbol that hard times may be in the future, but after these are endured you will experience periods of great prosperity.

Melon/Mango

From the verses of ancient poets to modern jokes, **melons** have often been compared to women's breasts, and so if melons appear in your dream, are you curious about anything other than fruit? **Mangos** are symbols of fertility and lust, although the mango may simply be a pun on 'man go', in reference to a relationship in which you should let go and move on.

Orange/Peach

Symbols of health and prosperity, **oranges** in dreams recall the sunny times in your life. To see **orange trees** in your dream signifies health and prosperity. In dreams, **peaches** indicate pleasure and joy — as suggested by the idiom 'life is peachy' — but they can also indicate lust and sensuality, as well as a tendency to be easily bruised. They may also suggest bisexuality, with the leaf being a phallic symbol and the fruit being the vulva. The poets of Arabia compared the peach's dimpled appearance to a pair of young, pert buttocks. In Chinese and Japanese tradition, the peach is a symbol of immortality, so perhaps you are feeling invincible at the moment?

Pear/Pineapple/Pomegranate/Prune

In China, the **pear** is regarded as a symbol of longevity, and in the West, the **pineapple** is an emblem of fertility, quality and self-confidence behind a prickly exterior. If **pomegranates** appear in your dream, they signify fertility, good health and longevity, as well as the allure of sex. To see **prunes** in your dream symbolizes an emotional or creative blockage. They may also represent aging, as suggested by the saying 'as wrinkled as a prune'.

Watermelon

To see a **watermelon** in your dream represents emotions of love, desire, lust and fiery passion. Pregnant women, or women on the verge of their menstrual cycle, often dream of fruit such as watermelons. Watermelons may also suggest spiritual nourishment in dreams and **watermelon seeds** point to the seeds of spirituality ready to sprout within you.

Nuts and seeds

Although less juicy then fruits, **nuts** are equally nutritious and satisfying, sharing fruit's general symbolism of reward, fertility and well-being. And because their edible parts are encased in hard shells, they also denote wisdom and insight that may be hidden or yet to be discovered. To dream that you are **gathering nuts** could suggest success in business and in love. You may also be trying to get to the core of a matter or situation. To dream that you are **eating nuts** signifies prosperity and attainment of your desires, but if you dreamed of **exerting enormous force to crack open a nut**, your unconscious may have been referring to someone in your waking life who is a tough nut, presenting a hard face to the world whilst possessing a tender interior. Alternatively, it may signify some project in your life that is proving to be a tough nut to crack. Bear in mind also that your unconscious may have been making a reference to testicles or 'nuts', or was reflecting the current craziness of your waking life. Consider also the association with health, as in a 'health nut', or feeling passionate or nuts about something.

Your dreaming mind may also home in on a particular nut and if it does there may be a sexual connotation. **Almonds**, for example, resemble female genitalia and because the almond is a symbol of the Virgin Mary, they may also denote virginity or innocence. Bear in mind, too, the phrase 'almond eyed', which indicates a perceptive individual. Although most nuts symbolize masculine sexuality, the **walnut** does so more than others, suggesting fertility in particular. To see or eat **filbert nuts** in your dream signifies peace, harmony and profitable business ventures. **Nutmeg** indicates a basic natural ability or talent you may be unaware that you have. A **nutcracker** will exemplify a need for solutions or resolution, whilst a **nutshell** relates to the shells you use in waking life to protect yourself. A nutshell may also indicate a need to consolidate your beliefs into a basic, simple formula. To see a **nut tree** in your dream signifies happiness and rewarding experiences in waking life.

Dreams of **seeds or kernels** pertain to your inner talents and abilities. Other interpretations include: the beginning of something or the completion of a phase or cycle, mission accomplished, fertility and going to seed. They may also be a homonym for 'cede', or surrendering. **Sunflower seeds** suggest the emergence of spiritual joy, **pumpkin seeds** stand for opportunities to express yourself in waking life, **hemp seeds** refer to a strong or powerful factor in your life and **flax seeds** signify a way of life that offers multiple benefits.

WEATHER

The weather in your dream often symbolizes your mood or state of mind.

According to ancient dream-lore, dreaming of fine weather foretells happy events and dreaming of bad weather indicates future misfortune. Although dreams in which weather features strongly may be presenting you with a forecast of sunny or stormy times ahead, modern dream analysts tend to follow the Jungian interpretation; this suggests that weather dreams often reflect the emotional climate in your waking life. Whether your dream featured sunshine, snow, rain or a gentle breeze, it is likely that the symbolism of the weather mirrored your current emotions or thought processes in waking life. Another interpretation focuses on the changeability and fickleness of weather, suggesting that your unconscious is forecasting your own change of mood in the real world.

The message of your dream is often highlighted if you felt extremes of temperature or if the weather was uncharacteristic in some way, such as snow falling in summer. Stormy skies may show arguments and anger, sunshine may show happiness and optimism, and snow may indicate that your emotions are frozen. Dreams of earthquakes, avalanches and other natural disasters suggest emotions that are so powerful and uncontrolled that they can have disastrous effects when unleashed on your waking world. *See also* DISASTERS; NATURE AND THE SEASONS.

Sun and Snow

FROST

Frost is formed when water is deposited as ice crystals on the ground and, since water is symbolically linked to the emotions, a dream which features frost suggests emotions that are cold, frozen or icy. This may apply to you or someone you know who is behaving coldly or frostily towards you.

SNOW

A dream that features **snow** has a similar interpretation to dreams that feature frost, only this time the message is highlighted ever more. Snow in dreams could reflect your emotional isolation or a cold interaction with someone close to you in waking life. Alternatively, the dream could be suggesting that you have shut down your emotions as a self-defense mechanism to protect you from getting hurt. If, however, the **snow was thawing** in your dream or you were **playing in the snow or throwing snowballs**, this indicates that the icy mood is slowly warming and melting. Alternatively, do you feel snowed under with responsibilities in waking life?

Snow is also a symbol of purity, but if a **white blanket of snow** is covering everything in your dream this could suggest that the rich complexities of life are being covered up. Dreams in which **ice** appears are symbolic of emotional rigidity or indifference to the feelings of others. The image may have been conjured up to warn you against narrow-mindedness and to urge you to open your mind to new possibilities.

SUNSHINE

Dreams in which you are **enjoying the sunshine** reflect your sense of joy, energy and optimism in waking life. You feel warm towards yourself and towards others. If, however, your waking life does not match this sense of optimism, your dreaming mind may have sent you this dream as a form of encouragement. If you are **scorched or burned by the sun** in your dream, it may be that you have overexposed yourself to something or someone that is not good for you.

TEMPERATURE

If you are **very hot or very cold** in your dream, you first of all need to consider whether your bedroom is too hot or too cold and your unconscious has simply incorporated your physical reaction in your dreams. If this is not the case, the dream may be pointing to your frame of mind. **Extreme heat** could indicate unpleasant or difficult circumstances, or a person you consider hot or sexy. Feeling hot can also warn you of impending danger, as in 'finding yourself in a hot spot' or of burning passions, such as lust or anger. Your unconscious may be warning you to remove yourself from a source of potential danger.

If the atmosphere is **humid** in your dream this indicates that you feel as if your waking situation is oppressive. If, however you are aware of feeling pleasantly **warm**, this is a positive sign indicating that you are feeling content in your waking life; if you are **shivering with the cold**, the opposite is true. In waking life you may feel emotionally cold or perhaps someone is being cold to you. Alternatively, do you feel as if you have to act ruthlessly, as in 'cold-bloodedly', or is it fear that is making your blood run cold? If you feel **uncharacteristically hot** when it is cold outside, this suggests your warmth and optimism is overcoming the coldness and hostility in which you find yourself; but if you feel **cold when it is warm outside**, this suggests you are cutting yourself off from emotional interaction in some way.

Clouds and Rain

CLOUD

Gathering or black clouds in your dream may suggest real-life feelings of apprehension. Alternatively, you may feel as if you are living under a cloud because somebody is about to accuse you of something. If the **clouds shifted and sunshine broke through** in your dream, this is a positive sign suggesting a ray of hope that your gloomy mood will soon lift. **Gray clouds** denote despondence, but **white clouds** symbolize contentment.

FOG/MIST

Fog and mist are dreamland symbols of confusion, or of an inability to make progress and see the way ahead. They also suggest lack of clarity and that emotions are clouding your judgment and making you feel uncertain. If the **fog lifts** in your dream, this is a positive sign. If you sense that the **light is about to break through**, this suggests a state of expectation rather than confusion.

RAIN

If you are caught in a **rain shower or storm** in your dream, the key to the interpretation will be your reaction. Did you feel miserable or elated? If the former, it is possible that an outpouring of emotion – your own or that of someone you know – is raining down on you in real life. The dream might also signify emotional release or the desire to feel love again. Rain does often have positive liberating associations in dreams, but if the descending water takes the form of **hail**, the message is negative as it may suggest that you are about to become the victim of stinging verbal abuse. Hail has similar associations to rain, but is much colder and harsher. A mere **spot of drizzle or a brief shower** would suggest a situation that is less serious.

In the Bible, the **flood** is a symbol of preparation for a new way of life or a fresh start. This meaning fits well with both Freud's association between water and the womb, and Jung's symbolism of the flood or deluge as both deadly and life giving. As a mother image, a **flood submerging you or a house** could suggest an intense relationship with your mother or another dominant female figure in your life; it may also suggest that you are feeling overwhelmed by life's pressures.

SKY

In dreams, the **sky** often represents the mind or your thoughts. It can also suggest your potential. **Floating or flying in the sky** can indicate that you are trying to avoid the mundane or are exploring your potential. If the **sky is dark**, it can suggest a mood of gloom; but if the **sky is bright**, it suggests joy. The **daytime sky** represents infinity and a **star-studded sky** is a symbol of the unconscious.

Jung saw the **night sky** as the most suitable place onto which people could project their unconscious desires. The symbolism of the constellations and Zodiac signs are archetypal expressions of the inner world of the unconscious. The image of a **blue sky**

The Element Encyclopedia of 20,000 Dreams

in your dreams may suggest spiritual aspirations but it is also a symbol of contentment. Most dream traditions suggest that to dream of a blue sky brings good luck, whilst cloudy skies are a harbinger of misfortune. Some claim that to dream of a **red sky** foretells a terrible disaster that will befall the nation. *See also* SPACE AND SCIENCE.

WEATHER SUPERSTITION

In the past, when people lived and worked on the land, the weather was very important and people watched for patterns to help them predict the future weather. They then made up rhymes to help them to remember these patterns. Some of these sayings do contain a grain of truth. Others, particularly those that try to predict the weather for the following season from a single event, are unlikely to contain much truth. It is possible that your unconscious may draw on these ancient sayings not to predict the weather, but to predict your changing emotions or state of mind. So if an image of a **red sky in the morning** appears in your dream, could this be a warning, not of a storm, but of possible emotional conflict?

Here is a list of some of the most well-known sayings. If images that are reminiscent of them appear in your dreams – for example, **cows standing in a line or crickets chirping** – as well as referring to the specific symbols involved, it is always worth looking for possible interpretations concerning your mood or state of mind using the weather-related entries in this chapter as your guide:

Weather summary

As we have seen in this chapter, a dream about the **weather** is usually symbolic of your emotional state. For example, **sunny skies and clear weather** may indicate smooth sailing, and an easy and clear road ahead. Other possible interpretations for weather-related dreams include: enduring something, 'weathering it'; poor health, 'being under the weather'; putting a great deal of effort into something, 'making heavy weather'; exposing yourself to 'prevailing conditions or circumstances'; undergoing changes within. It may also be a homonym for whether, indicating doubt or choice.

To dream that you are **reading or listening to the weather report** foretells a change of address or some other important change in your life. To see a **weather vane** in your dream indicates unpredictability and versatility. You may feel that you are going around in circles. The dream may also be a pun on being vain or doing something in vain.

Red sky at night, shepherd's delight; red sky in the morning, shepherd's warning

Rain before seven, fine by eleven

A sun shiny shower, won't last half an hour

If cows are standing in a field it will be fine, but if they are lying down it is going to rain

Clear moon, frost soon

When squirrels lay in a big store of nuts, look for a hard winter

When bees stay close to the hive, rain is close by

Rain, rain go away, come again another day

Haloes around the moon or sun mean that rain will surely come

When forest murmurs and mountain roars, close the windows and shut the doors

Moss dry, sunny sky; moss wet, rain you'll get

When smoke descends, good weather ends

A cow's tail to the west is weather coming at its best; a cow's tail to the east is weather coming at its least

Flies will swarm before a storm

If crows fly low, winds going to blow

If crows fly high, winds going to die

When sea birds fly to land, there truly is a storm at hand

The sharper the blast, the sooner it's past

Rain is on the way if people with curly hair find their hair curlier and people with straight hair find their hair straighter

Rain is on the way when old people with joint or muscle problems such as rheumatism or arthritis have stiffness and discomfort

You can tell the temperature by counting a cricket's chirps

You can tell it will rain if: cats clean themselves more and meow more; pigs wallow about and squeal; cows huddle together as if seeking comfort from each other; horses 'switch and twitch' and sometimes bolt; insects fly low and bite more; birds chirp more loudly; dandelions close their blossoms tightly; morning glory 'tucks in' its blooms as if ready for a long nap; clover folds up its leaves; leaves on many trees roll up or show their undersides

Winds and Storms

BREEZE

If you dreamed of stepping outside in your dream and feeling a **fresh and gentle breeze**, this has symbolic associations with the life force or spirit that is trying to breathe new energy into your waking life. Alternatively, your dream may have been urging you to have a brighter and breezier attitude to your waking life by blowing away the cobwebs and pulling yourself together.

GALE/HURRICANE

In both the real world and in dreamland, **gales and high winds** suggest potential disaster. Your dreaming mind may be warning you that someone's pent-up emotion is about to burst out of control;

that person could be you. Or has a situation reached a crisis point? A **tornado or hurricane** is an even stronger image of feeling powerless against violent and chaotic emotions. The image of a **hurricane or tornado flattening houses or hurtling cars in the air** may suggest the frailty of the material world or reflect your own feelings of insecurity.

A dream **whirlwind** has a different message, as it suggests confusion or a romance that may be about to completely change your life. An argument with a loved one may turn into a dream storm or hurricane, but your dream may contain clues for avoiding the worst of the storm. For example, the sun may have shone through, you may have found shelter or a gentle breeze may have lifted your spirits.

If you **lost your struggle** against the wind, this indicates that you feel as if you are being forced to go along with others. If you **enjoyed being carried along by gusts of wind**, this may suggest a longing for adventure, unpredictability and freedom from responsibility.

STORM/THUNDER/LIGHTNING

Storms suggest emotional eruptions but, because storms often blow out over the course of a dream, they also suggest that your emotional crisis will eventually calm down. A dream storm may also represent a brainstorm or the unleashing of creativity, especially if **bolts of lightning** figured. The flashes of lightning could represent flashes of insight but they could also be associated with anger issuing from an authority figure (bolts of lightning were associated with the wrath of the gods, according to ancient peoples). An **object or**

Rainbow

If a **rainbow** appears in your dream, this is without doubt a message of hope from your unconscious. For Jungians, the rainbow is a symbol of redemption and personal growth. The rainbow represents the enlightened mind that is a bridge between heaven and earth, and this dream image can fill you with optimism about the possibilities ahead. The rainbow is also celebrated in many religions and cultures; you may be unconsciously or consciously aware of some of its associations. For example, in Chinese, African and Norse belief, the rainbow links the earth with the divine. In ancient Greece it was said to represent Hermes, the messenger of the gods. Buddhists and Hindus regard the rainbow as a symbol of transcendence and according to Celtic religion, a pot of gold lies at its foot. The Judeo-Christian tradition tells that God placed a rainbow in the sky as a symbol of deliverance and as His covenant with humankind. So if a rainbow appears in your dream, did it suggest spiritual or material gain, reconciliation, peace or inspiration? Or did it simply indicate that one day your dreams will come true.

person appearing in a dream that features thunder may therefore represent someone you are planning to oppose in waking life or may suggest an aspect of yourself with which you feel uncomfortable. If the latter is the case, the thunder may be the voice of your own conscience or an authority figure such as a parent or teacher or boss at work. Try to work out what the thunder was saying; it is a strong image and the advice may be equally impressive.

Finally, were you **personally involved during the storm or did you fear for the safety of someone else**? If you were worried about someone else, it may be that you fear the consequences of your actions on other people. And if your **house or any other building was under threat from the storm**, you should consider the dream from the point of view of that which was under threat.

THE DREAM DIRECTORY

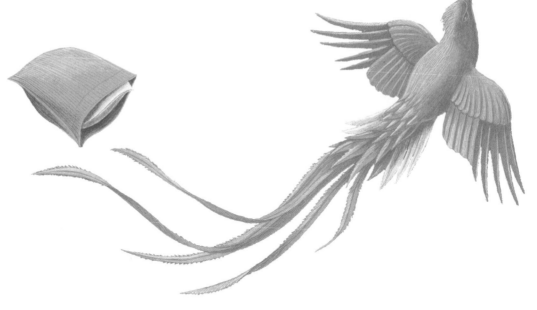

auras 485
auspicious dreams 296
Austen, Jane 238
Australia 280
Austria 277
authority figures 20, 428,
    430–1
  burying 332–4
  killing 138
autumn 400, 623, 637
avalanches 79, 135, 180,
    393, 406
Avalon 598
avenger archetype 50
axes 140

babies 46, 96–7, 615
  dead/malformed 95
  forgotten 586
  shipwreck rescue 6
  unborn 93
baby animals 29, 441, 497
baby birds 82, 85
baby sitters 98
backgammon 326
backs 111–12
  ache 545
backyards 300
bacteria 407, 545
bacteriological warfare
    545
bad deeds 74–8
bad feelings 79
badgers 32–3
badges 25
baggage 332, 629
Bahamas 277
bailiffs 404
bakers 504
baking 259–60, 262, 264
balconies 122, 300
baldness 116, 407, 549
ball games 532
ballet 65, 456
ballet shoes 149
ballroom dancing 65
balls 532
bamboo 298
bananas 650
Bangkok 280
Bangladesh 277
bangles 153
bankers 611
banknotes 387
bankruptcy 350–1, 388
banks 129, 385–6
banquets 262
baptisms 97–9, 488
Barbados 277
barbecues 204
barbed wire 79

barbers 505
Barcelona 280
barges 633
bark (trees) 640
barns 129
barometers 566
barracks, confined in 123
barriers 588 see also
    obstacles
barristers 506
bars 124–5, 261
bartenders 505
baseball 325
basements 300, 303
basketball 324–5
baskets 212, 298
Bast 482
bathing 13, 200, 544
  fully clothed 147
  in milk 272
  in sea 334
bathrooms 109, 300, 617
  secret 310
bats 33, 578
battlefields 139–42
battles 585
bay trees 641
bayonets 141
bazaars 390
beaches 332–4, 456, 462
    see also seaside; sand
beacons 205
beans 266, 646
beards 116, 407
bears 33
beasts 33
beaten (hit) 417, 547
beauticians 505
beauty parlors 129
beavers 33
beds 210
  spiders in 320
bed and breakfasts 124
bed wetting 79
bedrooms 301
  monsters in 310
  secret 310
beef 266
bees 314
Beethoven 238
beetles 314
beetroot 646
beggars 389, 407, 428–9
  archetype 50
behind (someone) 79
beige 159
Belgium 275, 277–8
Bell, Alexander 240
bells 465, 554
  church 488, 554
  school 502, 554

belly 110–11
belts 149
bereavement 351, 590
Berlin Wall 280–1
Bermuda Triangle 278
berries 650–1
best man 479
betrayal 402–3, 471
betrothals 466
betting 330 see also
    gambling
biblical figures 481–2
bicycles/cycling 13,
    14–15, 631
  accidents 4, 181
Big Ben 128
big cats 35
bigamy 404, 475
bikinis 155
billiards 326
biology 565
bionic men/women 565
birches 641
birds 81–2, 298, 407, 434,
    479, 614–15
  A to Z 84–91
  caged 83, 435
  color 82, 161, 167
  eggs 82
  flocks 84
  flying 23, 84
  large 84
  nests 82
  pet 83, 434–6
  in trees 639
  wounded or dead 84
birdsong 82–3, 88, 479
birth 92, 94–6, 132, 298,
    407
birth control 519 see also
    contraceptives
birth stones 177
birthday cakes 264
birthdays 131, 626
biscuits/cookies 262, 264
bisexuality 520–2
biting 79
  apples 650
  food 260
bitten 79
  by animals 30, 436, 438
  by crabs 490–1
  by leeches 318
black 159–60, 407
  birds 82
  cats 34–6, 79, 436–7
  coffins 159
  dogs 37, 438
  feathers 83
  funerals 160
  horses 439

black magic 581
black widows 320
black and white dreams
    160, 331
blackbirds 84
blackboards 502
blackmail 75, 76, 404
blasphemy 489
bleeding
  nose 118
  penis 115
  vagina 115
blessed 488–9
blindness 407, 512,
    545–6
blisters 436
blood 407, 504–5, 538–9
  on hands 116–17
  from wounds 78
  see also bleeding
blood transfusions 538
blossom 248, 455
blue 161, 164
  sky 198, 298, 656–7
blue jays 84
bluebells 250
blueberries 650
blushing 113, 407
board games 325–6
boarding houses 124, 129
boars 34, 42, 79
boats 199, 633, 634
  drifting 134
  missing 635
body/bodies 106
  anesthetized 107
  cold 107
  dead 107
  headless/faceless 117
  covered in leeches 318
  diseased 107
  distorted 607
  dismembered 107–8
  injured 108
  left/right side 110, 218
  marks on 108
  murdered 108
  worms crawling on 321
body fluids, functions and
    organs 538–41
body image scenarios
    107–10
body parts
  A to Z 110–19
  animals 30
  confusion in family
    221–2
  loss 353
  transplants 552
bogs 467
boils 546

celebrations 131, 287
  inappropriate emotions
    352
celebrities 236, 237
  as lovers/partners 480,
    522
  rescue by 295
celery 646
cellars 300
cellphones *see* mobile
    phones
cemeteries 592
centaurs 602, 606
centipedes 316
chains/chained 79, 87,
    355–6
  eagles 87
chairs 210, 211
chakras 369–70
chalices 486, 597
chalk 502
chameleons 36, 498
champagne 288
change scenarios 131–4
chanting 556
charity workers 431
chased 8, 216, 258, 356,
    358, 403, 412, 615
  by animals 30, 35, 358,
    587
  falling when escaping
    137
  by gang/yobs 289
chasing *see* pursuit
chasms 180–1, 194, 448
  crossing 450–1
cheating 19, 49–50, 74,
    324, 325, 471–2, 615
  see also infidelity
checks 212, 386, 387
cheeks 114
cheering 558
cheese 264
cheesecake 264
chemical warfare 565,
    619
chemistry 565–6
chemists 505
cherries 651
chess 325, 327, 617
chest (body) 112
  aches 545
  cold 107
  hairs on 116
chewing 118, 260, 515
chewing gum 214–15
chickadees 85
chicken (meat) 266–7
chicken pox 548
chickens 85
chiffon 156

child 46, 92–3, 100
  in adult clothes 145
  alone 352
  archetypes 50–1, 100,
    146
  feeding milk to 272
  forgotten 586
  naked 146
  shipwreck rescue 181
  violence towards 139
child of nature archetype
    50
childhood homes 301
childhood revisited
    scenarios 104–5, 624
  see also school/s
children 101, 407
  forgetting 585
  unborn 518
  see also daughters; sons
children's dreams 101–2,
    441
Chile 278
chimes 128, 465, 627
chimneys 128, 310
China 279
Chinese Zodiac symbols
    370–2
Chiron 482
chocolate 23, 264
choking 155, 181, 272,
    595
Christmas 287, 399, 626
chrysanthemums 250
church bells 488, 554
church congregations
    290, 488
churches 446, 488, 525
  lilies in 252
Churchill, Winston 239
cigarettes/cigars 219, 525
Cinderella 601
cinders 308
cinema 331
circles 45, 530–1
circuses 63, 70
citadels 121–2
cities 122, 447
clairvoyants 624
clams 496
clarinets 66
classrooms 447–8, 503
claws 30
clay 71–3, 394
cleaners 129, 507
cleaning 13, 306
Cleopatra 239
cliffs 194, 396, 414
climbing 12, 16–18
  hills 12, 17
  ladders 17

mountains 12, 17, 194,
    296, 369, 393, 448,
    467
  stairs 12, 17
  over stiles 448
  to top of fences 303
  trees 638
  over walls 17
Clinton, Bill 236–7
cloaks 150
clock towers 627
clocks 407, 621, 623, 627
  alarm 554
  racing against 18
  ticking 128, 627
closets 210–11
clothes 144, 363, 615
  A to Z 149–57
  attacked by moths 318
  color 160, 161, 163, 165,
    167
  dressing in other
    people's 144–5
  inappropriate 45, 148,
    217, 358–9, 619
  ironing 174
  problems 148
  recovering lost 353
  school 503
  shopping for 391
  storing 211
  tight 148, 355
  torn 45, 148
  washing 147
clothing scenarios 144–8
clouds 196, 198, 565, 656
clover 250
clown fish 493
clowns 63, 407
  archetype 51, 63
clubs 289
coastguards 406
coats 150
coats of arms 25
cockatoos 435
cockroaches 316
cocks *see* roosters
coconuts 642–3
codes 343, 344–5, 471
coffee 272
coffins 593
  in living room 307
coins 212, 386, 387
  counting 611
colanders 308
cold 275, 407, 461, 655
  body 107
  fish 494
cold-blooded animals 36
colds 547
colleagues 20, 509

behaving out of
    character 289
  in burning buildings
    182
  in love with 464
college/s 501, 509, 583
Colombia 279
color/s 158–9, 407,
    512–13
  birds 82
  directory 159–70
  eyes 112–13, 511–12
  underwear 155
coloring books 162
Columbus, Christopher
    240
comets 560
communes/communities
    289–90
communication 335–48
  blocked/breakdown
    355, 477, 478
compasses 629
compassion 295
compensatory dreams 462
composite animals 36
composite characters 429
composite scenes 449
computer games 362
computer spyware 473
computers and
    peripherals 215,
    361–2, 407, 615
  malfunction 215, 359
  see also emails; Internet
concentration camps
    445–6
concerts 68
condoms 215, 519, 615
conductors 504
conferences 288–9
confession 404
confinement 355–6, 407
conflict scenarios 131,
    134–43
  family 221
Confucius 240
confusion 402–3
  family body parts 221–2
congregations 290, 488
conifers 642
conjurers 368, 581
conservatories 453
constipation 408, 541
containers 207–8, 406
  unable to open 468
contemporary images 615
continents 280
contraceptives/family
    planning 94, 228, 519
  see also condoms

The Element Encyclopedia of 20,000 *Dreams*

fancy dress 154
fans 152
fantasia 596–607
farewells 132, 351–2, 403, 477
    to lovers/partners 477
farmers 506
farms/farmyards 124, 452
farting in public 7
fashion 151
fathers 59, 230–1, 344, 430
    archetype 53, 295, 430
    transforming into some-one else 226–8
fawning 22
faxes/fax machines 336, 363
fear 134–5, 403
fears, common 407–9
feasts 262
feathers 83, 479
February 397
feces 109–10, 208–9
feeding-bottles 98
feet 114
    cold 107
    heavy/stuck 137, 356
    injuries 550
    losing 353
feminine principle 59
fences 303, 304, 448
fencing 323
Feng Shui 372
Fermi, Enrico 241
ferrets 38
    pet 438
ferries 634
ferrymen 634
fertility 132
festivals 287
fetishes 527
fictional characters 599
fields 163, 393, 450, 647
fights/fighting 76, 133, 137, 406
    with alligators 498
    with pets 442
    pub brawls 125, 261
    roosters 90
    with siblings 225
figs 524, 651
filberts 653
filing 508–9
finches 435
finding
    jewelry 152, 153
    money 386, 387, 389
    treasure 21
fines 404

finger-nails 115
fingers 114, 525
fins 495
fire/s 7, 182–3, 408, 479, 566
    element 203–6
    lighting 204–5
    tending 205–6
fire-fighting 183
firehouses 129
firemen 204, 506
fireplaces 203
fireworks 204, 525
firing squads 77, 404
firs/spruces 642
first love 521
fish 408, 477, 486, 491–2
    eating 265, 492
    miscellany 495
    species 493–4
    weighing 495
fish bait 495
fish bowls 438, 492
fish eggs 265
fish markets 455, 494
fish sandwiches 269
fishermen 494, 506
fishing 22, 333, 395, 492–3, 494
fists, orange 163
fits 549
five 422
flags 274
flames 166, 206, 479, 638
flamingos 87
flats 126
flattery 520
flax seeds 653
fleas 317
Fleming, Alexander 241
flies 317
flirting 520
floating (in sky) 10, 461, 656
floating (in water) 199, 200
flocks of birds 84, 87
floods/flooding 183, 406, 408, 619, 656
    bathrooms 300
floors 176, 303
flower arranging 248
flower gardens 454
flowering trees 455, 638–9
flowers 245–6, 408, 524
    artificial 248
    in bloom 245
    colors 163, 165, 167
    cut 248
    garden 245–6

giving and receiving 25–6, 247–8
    individual meanings 250–8
    parts 249
    wild 248
    withered or dead 25, 247, 248–9
flutes 66, 556
flying 9–11, 197, 217, 408, 461, 525, 615, 656
    children's dreams 103
    hot-air balloons 196–7, 631
    in inappropriate vehicles 631
    see also aircraft
flying birds 23, 84, 91, 435
fog 656
food 208, 259, 408, 615–16
    A to Z 262–71
    colors 167
    gifts of 296
    seeking/becoming 262
    shopping for 391
food poisoning 260
food scenarios 259–62
football 324–5
forbidden desires 138
forbidden fruit 481, 542
Ford, Henry 241
foreheads 114
foreign cities 280–1
foreign countries 273–85
foreign languages 275, 471, 558
    learning 503
foreigners 47, 275, 433
forensic teams 75
forests 194, 393, 414, 452
forgeries 75, 471
forges 204
forget-me-nots 251
forgiveness 404
forks 208
fortresses 121–2
fortune tellers 330, 372, 406–10, 429
fostered 223
fostering 97
foundations (house) 304
fountains 202, 453–4
four 421–2
four-leaved clover 251, 373
fowl 87
foxes 38
foxgloves 251–2
fractions 421
France 275, 282

fraud 75
freezers 461
Freud, Sigmund 239–40
Friday the thirteenth 78
friends 287–8, 429
    act/speak out-of-character 343, 429
    applauding speeches 345
    anxious feelings with 405
    in burning buildings 182
    death 132
    as lovers/partners 464–5, 480
    performing a play 70
    rejection by 589
frogs 38, 494–5
frost 654
frozen food 265
fruit 163, 260, 261, 265–6, 644
    directory 648–53
    harvesting 506, 649–50
    peeling 649–50
fruit-bearing trees 455, 638
fruit bowls 649
frustrating tasks 357–8
frustration 349–50, 403–4, 355–60
funeral parlors 129
funerals 592, 593–4
    inappropriate emotions 352
    parents 222–3, 584
fur 156
furnaces 204
furniture 210–11
    rearranging 211
fuses, blown 359, 566
future 624
    travel to 625–6
    glimpsing 515–16, 577
    see also precognitive dreams

gagged 355
gales 658–9
Galilei, Galileo 241
gall 79
gambler archetype 53
gambling 327
game animals 39
games scenarios 325–30, 617
Gandhi, Mahatma 243
gangs 289
garages 303
garbage 208–9

The Element Encyclopedia of 20,000 *Dreams*

falling from 40, 439, 633
reined/harnessed 356
riding 13, 525, 633
horseshoes 373, 441
hosepipes 202
hospitals 124, 215, 408,
551–2, 615
hostage 11
hostility 405–6
hot/heat 275, 408, 461,
566, 655
hot-air balloons 196–7,
631
hotels 124, 479
house alarms 136
household items 209
houses 125, 126, 299,
305–7, 408, 617
A to Z 299–312
damage to 216–17
dark/cold/empty 126,
351
disasters in 185
fires/burning 182, 203,
477
flooding 183, 656
leaving/moving
125,126, 304, 307
new 126, 132, 307
in ruins 133
threatened by storms
660
see also home
housework 306
hovering 10
human voice 557–9
hummingbirds 87
hunger 183
hunted 412, 415
hunting 333
falcons 87
rabbits 42, 443
turkeys 91
hurdles 19, 448
hurricanes 184, 408, 619,
659
husbands 232
future 475
hybrid beings 610
hydra 605
hyenas 40
hygiene 544
hypnotists 368, 581

ibises 88
Icarus 601
ice/icebergs 80, 199, 467,
655
ice cream 266
Iceland 282
illness see sickness

immobility 80 see also
paralysis
impaled 545
impossible tasks 357–8
impotence 529, 587
imps 487, 597
incense 486
incest 222, 527
incongruous emotions 352
incubi 572, 597
India 282–3
indigestion 550
Indonesia 283
infernos 204
infidelity
dreamer 4, 138, 404–5,
471, 522, 527
partner 521, 615
influential people 240–1
injections 408, 550–1
injuries 78, 108, 216, 353
arms 111
buttocks 546–7
facial 549
fingers 115
genitals 547
hands/feet 116, 549–50
neck 118
stomach 110
see also wounds
injured
animals 29, 436, 477
babies 96
boys 101
dolphins 491
fish 492
pet birds 435
see also wounded
ink 497, 502
ink blots 348
in-laws 233
inns 125, 479
insects 313, 317–18, 408,
479, 615, 640
A to Z 313–21
swarms 315
insecurity 406–10
internal organs 540–1
Internet 362, 390
interpreters 343
interviews 341, 359
intruders 403
invasions 142
inventor archetype 49
investment/s 212, 386,
388, 618
invisibility 107, 134, 525
iPods 363–4
Iraq 283
irises 252
iron 174

Israel 283
Istanbul 281
Italy 275, 283
Ivan the Terrible 243
ivory towers 130
ivy 641

jackals 41
jackets 150
Jacob 481–2
jade 172, 176
jaguars 35
jailers 431, 468
jails see prisons
jam 268
January 397
Japan 283
Jason and the Golden
Fleece 610
jaws 118
jaybirds 88
jealousy 410
Jehovah 482
jelly beans/rolls 268
jellyfish 493
Jesus Christ 243, 484, 576
on the cross 484, 532
jewels/jewelry 21,
152–4, 178, 212, 478,
531
gifts of 153, 178, 212
losing 410
jokes 461
Jordan 283
journeys 628–30
joy 463
judges 404, 431, 448, 506
archetype 54
juggling 63
Julius Caesar 239
July 398
jumping/leaping 12, 18,
65, 311, 408, 636
June 398
Jung, Carl 239
jungles 454 see also
rainforests
Jupiter 562
juries 431, 448–9

kale 646
Kali 482
kangaroos 41
keeping fit 323, 542
Kennedy, John F. 239
Kenya 283
ketchup 269
kettles 308
keyholes 302
keys 302, 468–70
losing 352–3

kidnap 11, 76
killing 138, 412–14, 617
animals 30, 41, 138, 594,
617
authority figures 138
demons/evil spirits 597
eagles 87
insects 314, 315, 321
larks 88
parents 224
sons 230
see also murder
kilts 156
kindergarten 98–9
kindness 295
kingfishers 88
kings 47, 240, 430–1
archetype 55
kissing 114, 523
kitchens 306, 307, 308
kite flying 197, 631
kittens 437, 465
knees 117
knights 293, 298
archetype 55
knitting 14, 71
knives (cutlery) 208
knives (weapons) 140,
414, 524–5, 550, 617
knocking 556
knots 209, 468, 531

laboratories 454, 568
laboratory animals 28
labor/delivery 95
labyrinths 133, 354, 469,
537, 598
ladders 17, 209, 470
walking under 78–9
ladybirds 314
lagoons 202
lakes 197, 202, 296, 395
lamb (meat) 267
lambs 41, 42
lameness 550 see also
limps/limping
lances 140
landlords/landladies 430
landscapes 449–50, 634
alone in 352
recurring 589
rocky 175
transformation 133
landslides 135
language 341–3 see also
foreign languages;
words
larks 88
late 101, 217, 341, 359,
406, 502, 617, 623
laughter 461–2, 557–8

messages 344
　secret 344–5
　supernatural 575–6
metals 171, 172–4
Mexico 283
mice 41, 408
Michelangelo 241
microscopes 552
mid-life dreams 480, 586
Midas 610–11
　archetype 55
midday 622
midges 317
midnight 623
milk 272
minerals 174
miners 506
mines/minefields
　(explosives)141, 445
mines/mining
　(underground) 142,
　174, 193, 458
Minotaur 598, 611
minus numbers 426
mirror images 432
mirrors 151, 209, 408
　faces in 114, 134
miscarriages 94
misers 388–9
　archetype 55
missionaries 507
mist 656
mistletoe 641
mists 80
moats 122
mobile (cell) phones 218,
　345, 363, 525
　problems 477–8
　see also texting
mockingbirds 88
models (catwalk) 151
modems 362
molasses 264–5
molecules 565
moles 41
money 21, 212, 327, 385,
　386–7, 408, 618
　finding 386, 387, 389
　losing 352
monkeys 32
　Chinese Zodiac 371
monks 485
　archetype 56
Monroe, Marilyn 236
monsters 47, 358, 405,
　415, 597
　archetype 56
　children's dreams 103,
　104
　sea 499
months of the year 397–9

moon 561 see also crescent
　moon
moonlight 450
moorland 448
moose 38
morning 622
mortgages 387
mortuaries 594
Moscow 281
Moses 241, 482, 576
mosquitoes 317
Mother Teresa 238, 243
mothers 47, 59, 232–4,
　478
　archetype 56, 59, 234,
　294, 295, 430, 497,
　608
　death 222–3
　transforming into some-
　one else 226
moths 318
motorbikes 13, 631
mountains 194, 393–4,
　448, 450, 618
　climbing 12, 17, 194,
　296, 369, 393, 448,
　467
　falling down/off 194,
　393, 448
mousetraps 41
mouth 118
　struck on 549
　washed out with soap
　212
movers and shakers 242
Mozart 238
mud 193–4, 394
muffins 264
Muhammad 241, 484, 576
mulberries 650–1
murder 138, 402, 412–14,
　594–5
murdered bodies 108
murderers 47, 415
museums 64, 127
mushrooms 646–7
music 64, 555
music making 555
music players 363–4
musical instruments 6, 68,
　555–6
　types 66–7
musicians 504
mussels 496
mustard 269, 270, 395
mustard seeds 269
mutiny 136
mysteries 467–73
mystical arts 369–84
mystical creatures 606
mystical dreams 297–8

myth and legend 409,
　607–12

nails 213
nakedness 45, 145–6, 217,
　358–9, 502, 523, 544,
　619
names 70, 346–7
　family 228
　hearing own 557
naming ceremonies 97–9
nannies 98
nappies 98
narcissi 251
Narcissus 611
natural beauty 619
natural disasters 135,
　180–90, 217, 406, 586,
　619
natural features 392–6
natural ground 394
nausea 550
navels 110–11
nebulae 564
necklaces 153, 531
necks 118
needles 72, 213, 589
needlework 71
negative emotions
　401–10
negative symbols 79–80
neglect of animals 30, 477
neighbors 304
Neptune 563
Nero 239
nests 82, 265
　doves 86
　eagles 87
　hornets 317
　solitary eggs 388
　wasps 321
netball 324–5
Netherlands 283
nets 356, 495
networker archetype 56
New Age 374
New York 281, 287
New Zealand 284
news 333, 365
newspapers 365
Newton, Isaac 241
nickel 174
night sky 24, 198, 656
night terrors 416
nightdresses 157
nightingales 88, 479
nightmares 411–18
　precognitive 187
nightwear 157
nine 424
nipples 112

noises 409, 553–7
　animal 31, 553
noon 623
nooses 80
North America 280
North Korea 279
North Pole 280
Norway 284
noses 118, 513
　injuries 549
　red 166
nostalgia 352
notebooks/schoolbooks
　502
notices 344
November 399
nuclear bombs 141
nuclear war 186–7
numbers 419–20
　directory 420–6
nuns 431, 485
　archetype 56
nurseries 98–9
nurses 215, 431, 506, 551
nutcrackers 653
nutmeg 653
nuts 638, 653
nuts and bolts 213
nutshells 653
nylon 156

O'Hara, Scarlett 599
oaks 641–2
oases 451
oatmeal 267
obelisks 73, 128
obscenity 80
obstacles 630
occupation 508
oceans 199–200
October 399
octopuses 496–7
offices 215, 508–9
officials 507
ogres 604–5, 606
oil (cooking) 267
old people 409, 432
　aged faces 113
　violence towards 139
older people's dreams 480,
　587–90
older women 433
olive groves 455
olive trees 642
omelets 265
one 420
onions 647
opal 172, 176
opera 68, 465
operations 215, 552
orange 163

orange trees 652
oranges 652
orchards 455, 649
orchestras 68, 290
orchids 253
organs 67
orgies 528
Oriental women 433
orphans/orphaned 223
    archetype 51
ostriches 88
otters 41, 497
Ouroboros 604–5
out-of-body experiences
    572–5
ovals 533
ovaries 540
ovens 308
overalls 149
overdressed 147, 358
overspending 136
owls 88–9
oxen 41
oxygen masks 540
oysters 261, 267, 496

pacifiers 98
packages see parcels
pain/s 136, 409, 545
    animals 28
painting (decorating) 68,
    306
painting (pictures) 24, 62,
    68
paintings
    coming to life 607
    looking at 68
pajamas 157
palaces 121
palm trees 642–3
palmistry 374
panic 405
    shop closing time 391
pansies 253
panthers 35
pantomimes 69, 70
papaya 651
paper 215
parachutes 10, 196
parakeets 89, 435
paralysis 356, 357, 415,
    548, 618, 636
paranoia 403
parasites 80
parcels/packages 344
    unable to open 468
parents 20, 223–5
    abandoned by 99
    conflict with 221
    death/funerals 222–3,
        224, 585

killing 138
Paris 281
parks 455
parrots 89, 435
parsley 270, 395, 647
parsnips 647
parties 288, 455–6
partings see farewells
partners
    death 222–3
    infidelity 521
    inappropriate 527
    leaving/being left by
        410
    losing 354
    negative dreams 222
    see also husbands; wives
partridges 89
passages/passageways
    122, 304, 309
    underground 469
past 624
    addresses 98–9
    echoes from 554–6
    houses/homes 125, 133,
        301, 617
    people from 432
    recurring scenes 449
    reincarnation 625
    travel to 615–16
    see also childhood
        revisited scenarios
pasta 267
paths 163, 175, 445, 470,
    629–30
patios 309
patterns 535–7
Paul, St 241
pawnbrokers 388
payments 212, 387
peace 463
peaches 652
peacocks 89
pearls 178, 652
peas 266, 647–8
Pegasus 611
pelicans 89
pelvis 111, 539
pencils 64, 70, 348
pendulums 374
penguins 89, 497
penises 115
    washing 202
pens 70, 348, 525
pensions 389
pentagrams 368, 534
penthouses 128
people 427–33, 619
    from the past 432
    recurring characters
        589

at work 504–7
    see also familiar people;
        historical figures;
        influential people;
        religious figures;
        strangers
pepper 267, 268–9
peppers 648
perfect beings 485
perfect romance 521
perfume 116, 513
Persephone 482
persona 45
personal achievements
    22–6
personal stereos 363–4
pet shows 441–2
petals 249
pets 434, 441–2
    A to Z 434–43
    birds 83, 434–6
    losing 410
    neglect by partners
        477
pheasants 89
Philippines 284
phobias, common 407–9
phoenixes 89, 605
phones see telephones;
    mobile phones
photographers/
    cameramen 504
photographs 68–9, 623
piano keys 555
pianos 67
Picasso 238
pickles 268
picnics 455
pictures 69
    coloring in 162
    see also paintings;
        photographs
pies 264, 267
pigeons 89
pigs 42
    Chinese Zodiac 371
pike 493
pills/tablets 552
pilots 431
pineapples 652
pines 642
pink 163–5
pins 72, 213
pioneer archetype 56–7
pipes (musical) 66
pirates 507
pistols 141
pits 195, 356, 458
pizza 267
places 444
    A to Z 444–59

childhood 104
    familiar 449, 473
    religious 488
    unknown 449, 473
plains 448
plane trees 643
planes see aircraft
planets 24, 561
    specific 562–3
planting seeds 71, 192,
    506
plants 394, 477
    transforming into
        people 607
plastic fabrics 156
platinum 174
Plato 241
playgrounds 105, 503
playing 461
    boys 101
    musical instruments 66,
        67, 556
    with dogs 437
plays 69, 70, 456
plotting 472
plows 213
plumage 82
plumbers 507
plums 651
Pluto 563
poet archetype 57
poets/poetry 64
poison 138, 186, 595
    food poisoning 260
poker 326, 330
Pol Pot 239
Poland 275, 284
police cars 620
police uniform 147
policemen 431, 506
policewomen 506
political rallies 290, 456
pollen 249
pollution 185–6, 209
polyester 156
pomegranates 652
ponds 395
pool (game) 326
pools 47, 197, 202, 453
popcorn 265
Pope, the 239
poppies 253
porches 309
porcupines 39–40
pornography 528
porpoises 491
ports 630
Portugal 284
Poseidon/Neptune 611
position 457–8
positive activities 296–8

positive emotions 460–6
positive signs 296–8
post offices 456
postcards 344
postmen 344
post-traumatic stress
    nightmares 416–17
potatoes 268, 648
pots and pans 308
pottery 71–2
poverty 80, 183, 350–1
power cuts 566
prairies 448
praying 488
praying mantises 80, 319
precognitive dreams 5,
    187, 188–90, 516
pregnancy 93–4
preserves 268
presidents 238, 430–1
pretzels 268
pride 463–4
priestesses 47, 57, 368
priests 47, 404, 485
    archetype 57
    see also high priests
princes 59, 240
    archetype 57
princesses 47, 59, 240
prison officers 431 see also
    jailers
prisons/jails 11, 125, 431,
    451
    breaking free 8–9, 136
    exploring 123
    sentenced to 404
prizes 24–6, 386
problems 467–8
processing plants 215
professional authorities
    431
prophets 484–5
proposals 479
prostitutes 47, 219, 528
    archetype 57
prunes 652
psychiatrists 406–10, 504
psychologists 406–10, 504
public houses 124–5, 261
puddles 202, 208
pulpits 486
pumpkin seeds 653
punishment 75, 416
puppets 331, 332
puppies 437
purple 49, 165
purses 151–2, 212, 524
    empty 351
    losing 354, 590
    recovering lost 353
pursuit 12

of foxes 38
pus 80, 112
    from nipples 112
pushing/pushed 13
Puss in Boots 601
puzzles 470–1
    Chinese 279
pyramids 121, 298, 535,
    598
pythons 500

quagmires 456
quails 89
quarries 456
queens 47, 240, 430–1
    archetype 57–8
quicksand 356, 414–15,
    451
quills 525, 585

rabbit holes 443
rabbit's foot 373
rabbits 39, 42
    pet 442–3
races/racing 15, 18, 19,
    356, 357, 471
    horse 440
radar screens 566
radioactive compounds
    565–6
radios 365–6, 619
radishes 648
rafts 134
railroad stations 129
rain 201, 450, 656
rainbows 298, 450, 659
raincoats 150
rainforests 452
raisins 264, 651
rams 42
rape 74, 77, 402, 528 see
    also sexual assault
rapids 202
Rapunzel 601
rashes 546
raspberries 650
rats 42
    Chinese Zodiac 370
    pet 42, 442
rattles 98
ravens 90
ravines 396
razors 213
reading 333
rebel archetype 58
rebellion/rebelling 136,
    402, 430, 488
receptions 289
recognition 21
recorders 66
records (music) 363

rectangles 533
rectum 540–1
recurring dreams 588–9
    about parents 224–5
recurring symbols 621
recurring landscapes 449
recurring nightmares
    417–18
red 165–6
    roses 166, 253–4, 524
    sky 198
    underwear 155
redundancy 354
referees 431
refrigerators 461
regattas 324
regiments 142, 290
reincarnation 625
reindeer 36–7
rejection 410, 589
relationships 474–80
    new 132
    symbols 479
    see also infidelity; love;
    marriage
relay races 19
release 462–3
religion 481–9
religious books 63, 488
religious buildings 127–8,
    446, 488
religious ceremonies
    488–9
religious figures 186, 578
religious leaders 576
religious places 488
rent 305, 387
reptiles 36, 409, 479,
    498–500, 614
rescued 9, 293–5, 610
rescuing 4–5, 9, 181
    animals/plants 28, 477
reservoirs 201, 456
restaurants 129, 261
    festive gatherings 288
    refused table 359
Resurrection 486
reunions 290, 432
rice 268
riddles 471
riding
    bicycles/motorbikes 13,
    14–15, 631
    elephants 38
    horses 13, 633
rifles 141
right see left and right
rings 153, 531
    engagement 478

set with ruby 176–7
ringworm 321
rituals 488–9
rivers 201, 394
    crossing 450–1, 633
road blocks 629
roadrunners 90
roads 619, 630
    crossing 450
robbing banks 386
robins 90
robots 362
rocking horses 332
rocks 171, 174–5
Romania 284
Rome 281
roofs 309, 414
rooms, white 167 see also
    particular rooms
roosters/cocks 85, 90
    Chinese Zodiac 371
    crowing 553
roots 640
ropes 8, 355
roses 250, 253–4, 270
    red 166, 253–4, 524
rowing teams 325
Rowling, J. K. 238
royalty 240 see also kings;
    princes; princesses;
    queens
rubbish trucks 634
rubies 176–7
rugby 324–5
rugs 210
ruins 121, 133, 447, 488
running 14–15, 18–19,
    636
    from attack 135
    after departing train
    359
    from horses/cavalry
    440
    from a murder 594
    horses 440
    races 19, 323, 324
    on a treadmill 322
    up stairs 310
Russia 275, 284
rye 267

sacred books 63, 488
sacrificed 593
sadism 80, 528
sadness 410
safes 386, 470, 472
sailing 395
    over shark-infested
    water 497
sailors 505
saints 485

The Element Encyclopedia of 20,000 Dreams

tests *see* examinations;
  medical tests; driving
  tests
texting 336, 362
Thanksgiving 287
theatres 70
therapists 406–10, 504
thermometers 552, 566
Theseus 598
thief archetype 60
theft 75, 414
thighs 117
thimbles 73
third eye 113, 486
thirst 272
thistles 394
thorns 248, 249, 254, 524
thread 73
threatened 405
  by animals 30, 403
  by guns 617
  by hospitals 124
  by someone in black 160
  by storms 660
threatening 405
  boys or girls 100
three 421
  'Rule of Three' 601
throat 118
  aches 545
throwing 14
thumbs 115
thunder 136, 184–5, 408,
  659–60
tiaras 25, 153
ticks 319
tidal waves 414, 619
ties (neckties) 155
  cutting off 547
tigers 35
  chased by 587
  Chinese Zodiac 370
  killing 617
  pet 442
tightrope walking 63
time 622–4
  conscious of 622–3
  symbols 626–7
time of day 133, 623–4
time travel 625–6
tin 174
tipsy 464
toads 43, 494–5, 597
toes 114
toilet themes 108–9, 311,
  541
Tokyo 281
tomatoes 648
tombstones 409, 594
tongue 118, 261
tools 213

top of the world 17
torches/flashlights 212
tornadoes 184, 408, 619,
  621, 659
torpedoes 142
Torquemada, Tomas de
  243
tortoises 442, 500
torture 80, 477
touch 515
touching 298, 466
towering structures 128
towers 128–30, 525
towns 122, 456–7
toxic waste 186
toxins 219
toys 100, 105, 331–2
  losing 410
  sinister 103
trading 390
traffic/jams 360, 633
trains 409, 634
  crashes 6, 181–2
  late for/missing 134,
    217, 356, 359, 585,
    617, 634, 635
  taking wrong 635
traitors 80
tramps 47, 429
transformation 133–4
  family 222, 226–8
  surreal 607
transition points 630
transitions 134
transplants 552
transport, modes of 630–6
transvestism 144–5,
  154–5, 520–2
trapped 137, 216, 356, 618
  in cupboard 211
  in jungle 454
  in washing machine 13
trapping 137
travel 628–36
treasure 21
  digging for 389
  finding 587–90
  hidden 588
treasure chests 11, 468
Tree of Life 486, 639
trees 477, 637
  anatomy 637–40
  appearance 637–8
  climbing 638
  fallen 133
  flowering 638–9
  species 640–3
  white 167
trenches 445
trespassing 80
trials (for love) 601

triangles 535
tribal peoples 396
tribes 289
tricks 472
tried (in court) 448
triple digits 426
tripping 7–8, 636
triumph 21
trophies 24–6
trousers 151
trout 493
trumpets 67, 555
trunks (trees) 640
trying hard 21
tsunamis 183
tube/subway 458
tulips 258
tunnels 97, 137, 193, 356,
  458–9, 470, 630, 634
turbans 152
Turkey 284
turkeys 90–1
turnips 648
turquoise (gemstone) 172,
  177
turtle-doves 86
turtles 500
Tutankhamen 239
tutors 502, 508
twilight 623
twins 432
two 420–1
typewriters 70, 348

UFOs 565, 576
ugliness 108, 409
umbilical cords 95–6
umbrellas 155
umpires 431
unborn children 93, 518
uncles 229, 430
underdressed 146, 358
underground 193, 458–9
  passages 469
  see also cellars; mines
undertakers 593
underwater 196, 499
  breathing 102, 499, 540
  surreal scenes 200
  swimming 14
  see also divers; diving
underwear 155–6
  black 160
  washing 147
undressing 147
unemployment 80, 354
unexpected utterances
  559
unfamiliar countries 275
unicorns 43, 374, 605
uniform/s 147, 311, 431

United Kingdom 284–5
United States 275, 285
university/ies 501, 509
unknown people *see*
  strangers
uphill struggles 17–18
uplifting feelings 463–4
Uranus 563
urination 109
urine 109
uterus 540

vacuum cleaning 306
vaginas 115
  washing 202
vagrants 428
Valentine's Day 397, 626
valleys 396
vampires 80, 415, 576–8
Van Gogh, Vincent 238
vases 161, 248
vaults 127–8, 385, 594
vegetables 163, 271, 644
  directory 644–8
  growing 192
vegetable gardens 453,
  647
vehicles 620–1, 634
  out-of-control 216
veils 132, 152
velvet 524
venereal disease 529
ventriloquists 70
Venus 563
verbal abuse 405 *see also*
  shouting
verbal communication 345
  see also talking
vermin 43
victim 77–8
  archetype 60
  bullying 100
  self-imposed violence
    139
  see also attacked;
    murder; rape
Victoria, Queen 624
village fetes 287
village stores 390
villages 122, 307, 447
vinegar 269
vines/vineyards 455, 651
violence 76–8, 138–9, 418
  sexual 526–7
violent death 594–5
violins 67, 556
Virgin Mary 484, 485
virginity, loss of 353, 523
virgins 596–7
viruses 545
Vishnu 482–4